Origins of Legislative Sovereignty and the Legislative State

Volume Six
(Book I)

By A. London Fell

Origins of Legislative Sovereignty and the Legislative State

Volume One	*Corasius and the Renaissance Systematization of Roman Law*
Volume Two	*Classical, Medieval, and Renaissance Foundations Of Corasius' Systematic Methodology*
Volume Three	*Bodin's Humanistic Legal System and Rejection of "Medieval Political Theology"*
Volume Four	*Medieval or Renaissance Origins? Historiographical Debates and Deconstructions*
Volume Five	*Modern Origins, Developments, and Perspectives against the Background of "Machiavellism"* *Book I: Pre-Modern "Machiavellism"* *Book II: Modern Major ""Isms" (17th–18th Centuries)* *Book III: Modern Major "Isms" (19th–20th Centuries)*
Volume Six	*American Tradition and Innovation with Contemporary Import and Foreground* *Book I: Foundations (to Early 19th Century)* *Book II: Superstructures (since Mid-19th Century)**
Volume Seven	*World Perspectives and Emergent Systems for the New Order in the New Age**
Volume Eight	*Reflections on Systems Old and New (with Bibliography and Index)**

**Forthcoming*

Origins of Legislative Sovereignty and the Legislative State

Volume Six

American Tradition and Innovation with Contemporary Import and Foreground

Book I: Foundations (to Early 19th Century)

A. London Fell

PRAEGER

Westport, Connecticut
London

Library of Congress Cataloging-in-Publication Data

(Revised for vol. 6, 1)
Fell, A. London

Origins of legislative sovereignty and the legislative state.

Vol. 5–has imprint: Westport: Praeger.
Includes bibliographical references and indexes.
Contents: —v. 2. Classical, Medieval, and Renaissance foundations of Corasius' systematic methodology —v. 4. Medieval or Renaissance origins? Historiographical Debates and Deconstructions.
1. Legislation—History. 2. Law—History and criticism. 3. Political science—History. 4. Coras, Jean de, 1513–1572. I. Title.
K284.F44 1983 340´.09 81.22332

ISBN 0-899-46140-9 (v. 1)
ISBN 0-899-46141-7 (v. 2)
ISBN 0-899-46142-5 (v. 3)
ISBN 0-275-93974-X (v. 4)
ISBN 0-275-93975-8 (v. 5, 1)
ISBN 0-275-95689-X (v. 5, 2)
ISBN 0-275-96753-0 (v. 5, 3)
ISBN 0-275-93976-6 (v. 6, 1)

British Library Cataloging in Publication Data is available.

Library of Congress Catalog Card Number: 81-22332
ISBN 0-275-93976-6

First published in 2004

Praeger Publishers, 88 Post Road West,
Westport, CT 06881
An imprint of Greenwood Publishing Group, Inc.

Printed in the United States of America

10 9 8 7 6 5 4 2 1

Acknowledgements include Princeton University Press, Julian Boyd (ed.), *Papers of Thomas Jefferson*; Columbia University Press, James Young, *The Washington Community*; and University of Virginia Press, Donald Kennon (ed.), *A Republic for the Ages*.

To Helpers Known and Unknown

(See Preface, page ix)

Preface

This first book of the sixth volume of *Origins of Legislative Sovereignty and the Legislative State* centers on the Revolutionary and Constitutional Eras in early American history, while also carrying the story ahead into the early 19th century. Subsequent studies will take up the same basic themes in American thought and events from the mid-19th century to the present period. Accordingly, this book deals with the American "foundations" of issues important for this series. Ensuing studies will examine the "superstructures." (This nomenclature finds historical expression below in a statement on page 171 by James Madison where he says: "[T]he existing [Confederation] constitution is founded on principles which are fallacious. . . . [W]e must consequently change this first foundation, and . . . the superstructure resting upon it. . . .") The subtitle of this sixth volume, *American Tradition and Innovation with Contemporary Import and Foreground*, goes to the wide mixtures of old and new ideas found in American thought as examined here from the perspectives of this series. Of central interest for the book at hand will be how the American founders adapted and utilized European thought in their political and legal ideas on sovereignty, state, and legislation.

The wide range of European thought represented in our preceding books, from antiquity through the 18th century and into the early 19th century, finds expression in writings composed by, as well as books owned by, the American founders looked at here. Their indebtedness should come as no surprise to those familiar with the vast private libraries of such luminaries as Thomas Jefferson and John Adams. Jefferson's collection alone reveals, in historical legal thought, an amazing array of works in the same traditions of Roman civil law dealt with in our initial volumes on Corasius. Such works include the great *Lexicon I[J]uridicum*, which on the main title page singles out Corasius and several other "illustrious" jurists (Cujas, Doneau, Duaren, etc.) because of their particularly noteworthy contributions to the *Lexicon*. Writings by John Adams pertaining to Bodin and Machiavelli (along even with Ficino) yield many points of comparison with our books on those and related figures, who are represented in the libraries of Jefferson as well as Adams. Our prior book on the seventeenth and eighteenth centuries charted the development of European thought on subjects like those studied here. Writers such as Hobbes and Locke, Harrington and Sidney, Rousseau and Montesquieu, Domat and Voltaire, along with myriad others, were likewise represented in the libraries and writings of Jefferson, Adams, and their fellow founders. For the early 19th century, writers like Bentham and Comte, examined in our most recent book, are also represented in their libraries.

Because of the seismic impact of European thought (and classical traditions) on America's foremost founders, it comes as no surprise that some of the most basic documents in the emergent new Republic were significantly influenced by European writers. The influence of Locke and others, for instance, on the Declaration of Independence has long been widely recognized, as has the influence of Montesquieu on the U.S. Constitution. The present book will show that Bodinian traditions on legislative sovereignty decisively influenced Jefferson's Declaration of Independence; they did so not only indirectly through such writers as Locke and Hobbes but also through Jefferson's direct reading of Bodin's *Republic*, as evidenced in his own well-marked copy of it. Similarly, the strong Bodinian elements of legislative sovereignty that infused Montesquieu's political thought, which impacted the separation of powers in the U.S. Constitution, was also central for James Madison as the chief architect of that all-important document. But these hints are just the beginning of a vast and complicated story.

The leading founders featured here either did, or should have, become President. Quite differently, the focus throughout this series has been on European intellectual authorities, who for the most part, had comparatively little active participation in politics at high governmental levels. The focus here on leading early founders at or near the summit of American government may seem surprising. Yet it is surely a testimony to their consummate intellectual merits and achievements that such men emerged at the beginning of the American nation to give it shape and guide it forth. Would that it had ever thus been so. Ensuing studies will adopt a corresponding perspective on later American developments.

The author is most grateful to a large number—perhaps several dozen—of others cited in the notes below. Their information on in response to my queries on particular points in the different segments of this book proved most helpful.

When the apostle Paul passed by the many statues or images erected by the Athenians to their various supportive deities, he took special note of the altar inscribed to the "unknown" god, whom he proceeded to glorify on Mars Hill (*Acts* 17:23). In our own ways, I suppose we all have our unknown unseen helpers, and I am deeply grateful for mine, more generally, as in the present dedication.

Contents

Origins of Legislative Sovereignty and the Legislative State

Volume Six
(Book I)

Chapter I

Introduction

1. FOUNDERS AND FOUNDATIONS

Because of the huge existing historiography on the American Revolutionary and Constitutional Eras, it might be thought that there is little opportunity left for exploring major untrodden areas, even from perspectives of this series. Nothing could be further from the truth. A wide array of basic documents can still yield broad fresh views on concepts of sovereignty and state central to the Founding Era in American history. Through the vantage point of this series on the European intellectual heritage from the 16th through 18th centuries (and even earlier), many new conclusions can be drawn from some of the most important writings of that period as well as others less studied by historians. To go no further than the Declaration of Independence and the U.S. Constitution, along with a plethora of related documents and sources, vast vistas still remain to be opened up on them. But the present story begins—not ends—there. It traverses, thematically, writings by leading American founders and a host of lesser figures, proceeding on to important library collections and to the new Capital city and Capitol building in Washington.

By far the longest chapter of this book is the second one, which is on Thomas Jefferson—the most prolific writer and most prodigious book-collector among the leading American founders. The methodology there is—as Jefferson aptly described the organization of his library catalogue—sometimes chronological, sometimes topical, sometimes a combination of the two. After beginning with an overview of Jefferson's early thought and career, we turn first to his basic writings concerning the constitution and laws of his native Virginia. These materials formed a crucial backdrop to the genesis and evolution of his Declaration of Independence. Later on—before, during, and after his rise to President—Jefferson's writings on fundamental topics such as the U.S. Constitution and Kentucky Resolutions provided further materials on issues of present interest. His remarkable private correspondences over long periods of time with John Adams and James Madison on constitutional, cultural and bibliographical matters will also be revealing. The final section, on Jefferson's library, will yield additional contexts of his ideas. The main focus throughout the chapter will be on Jefferson's legislative concepts of sovereignty and state as seen aganst a broad background of European sources, including Bodin's *Republic.*

Bodinian ideas of legislative sovereignty and the legislative state, transmitted by a range of European writers, also influenced John Adams, as detailed in the third chapter. In his contributions to the Massachusetts state constitution and the U.S. Constitution, Adams' legislative standpoints on sovereignty and state were broadly imbued with European traditions of thought adapted by him to the American situation of his day. Particularly noteworthy are Adams' uses of history in connection with the Florentine state and Machiavelli as well as the French civil wars and Bodin. Adams' letters to Jefferson and others are filled with significant references to European writings, especially those included in his large private library.

On James Madison in the fourth chapter, there is further ample testimony of the wide influence of European concepts of legislation, sovereignty and state. Madison's formative constitutional outlines prior to the Convention in Philadelphia in 1787 were put forth in his letters to Jefferson, Randolph, and Washington. These outlines helped to shape his thinking as chief architect of the U.S. Constitution and its often forgotten legislative foundations of sovereignty and state, and as official note-taker at the Convention. Madison's post-Convention essays also display a rich adaptation of European traditions on such topics.

Alexander Hamilton, too, in our fifth chapter, along with George Washington at its end, viewed sovereignty and state in Bodinian fashion, including on legislation. Hamilton's *Federalist* essays and National Bank furnish two principal areas for examination. His library, too, will be of interest.

Parts One and Two thus deal with the most prominent American founders during the Revolutionary and Constitutional Eras, their stories continuing on into the early 19th century. Part One features Jefferson and Adams, men of the earlier generation who were directly involved at Philadelphia in 1776 in the framing of the Declaration of Independence. Part Two centers on Madison and Hamilton, younger men who were involved at Philadelphia and New York in 1787–1788 in the forging and acceptance of the U.S. Constitution. Their story and ours go further ahead in time.

Part Three looks at further legislative and related foundations in the Revolutionary and Constitutional Eras (together comprising the Founding Era). Chapter VI deals with a wide variety of lesser figures during those periods. The chronological sequence of writings from the Revolutionary Era ranges from 1763 to 1783, that is, up to the final treaty at War's end. The Early Constitutional Era in the same chapter concerns the period of the Constitutional Convention and its immediate aftermath in 1787–1788. The ensuing selection of post-Convention writings extends from 1794 to 1804, this being a more suitable rubric than the potential misnomer "Post-Constitutional Era." In any case, the adoption of the Bill of Rights in 1791 gives a logical *terminus ad quem* to what, in a larger sense, could be called the original "Constitution-Making Era." Of course, the Constitutional Era more broadly was not confined to the years 1787–1788, but overlapped with the post-Convention Era and extended with the whole Founding Era to around 1800.

Finally, in Chapter VII the topic of Congress and its residence in the Capitol building and Capital city is investigated for outward symbols of sovereignty. Views on legislative sovereignty held by Jefferson and the engineer-architect L'Enfant were reflected in early designs and construction of Congress' new home on Capitol Hill in Washington, where it moved to in 1800. This symbolism of legislative sovereignty was guided along by Jefferson especially after he became President in 1800 but also during the preceding decade; and it bears a striking correspondence to Jefferson's emphasis on legislative sovereignty in his Declaration of Independence and Virginia constitution. In these and other cases, European intellectual traditions cast a wide influence. In closing, other aspects of Congress in its Continental, Confederate, and early Federal stages will be considered, as will the Supreme Court.

2. LIBRARIES AND LEARNING

It has long been recognized that the Founding Fathers of America were generally men of considerable learning, deeply read in European as well as American writers. Of the first four Presidents, it has been said, three were bookish "eggheads." Jefferson, Adams, and

Madison could be called that, as could their close associate Hamilton, who was arguably the most important founder not to become President. Those four worthies had all received good educations at leading colleges, were well versed in European classics of cultural, political, and legal thought, and possessed formidable book collections. Even George Washington—who was largely self-taught and prone to practical subjects in his reading—amassed a sizable well-rounded library and sought good classical educations for his stepchildren. His cultivated self-image as Rousseau's lawgiver was reinforced through his copy of the *Social Contract*, a work deeply imbued with Bodinian ideas of legislative sovereignty, and also through his close association with Hamilton, himself a reader of Rousseau.

Each of the four chapters comprising Parts One and Two ends with a section on private library holdings that helped to shape their owners' thoughts on subjects treated in the earlier parts of those chapters. Previous historical accounts have not taken a comprehensive detailed approach of the present kind to the founders' libraries, not the least with regard to the topics at hand. This close look at certain books available to the founders will extend to those in Congress' original library resources located nearby in Philadelphia during the periods of the Declaration of Independence in 1776 and the U.S. Constitution in 1787. The study will also extend in passing to the books available to key founders at the colleges where they had once studied.

Most strikingly, Jefferson's vast unrivalled collection will furnish a rich mine of valuable materials on subjects of present interest. A special case in point is his well-marked copy of Bodin's *Republic*. He probably already possessed it during the period when he composed the Declaration of Independence, his draft of which contains some bracket marks of the kind also found in his copy of Sidney's *Discourses*—an English radical republican treatise in the age of Locke and an outstanding example of Bodinian legislative sovereignty (as we earlier saw). The issue of legislative sovereignty has a wider deep significance not yet fathomed by American historians of the Founding Era (comprising here the whole Revolutionary and Constitutional Eras).

Second in size and interest to Jefferson's private library is that of Adams, who also possessed Bodin's *Republic*. The libraries of Madison and Hamilton are more problematic yet likewise of value here. The libraries of Washington and Jay will also be consulted.

3. STRUGGLES FOR SOVEREIGNTY

At many different levels in early American political and constitutional thought, a cardinal issue was the struggle for sovereignty. This issue lay behind the forming of the two most foundational American documents—the Declaration of Independence and the U.S. Constitution—along with a multitude of related writings. Other variegated materials, included below, will also bear out this point. Struggles for sovereignty occurred between America and Britain, the national or federal government and the state governments, the bigger states and the smaller states, the three branches of the federal government, Federalists and Democratic-Republicans, Federalists and Anti-Federalists, and so forth. These struggles for sovereignty typically turned ultimately on issues of legislation.

Although historians such as Bernard Bailyn have occasionally paid attention to concepts of sovereignty in the Revolutionary Era influenced by European thinkers like Locke, Sidney, and even Bodin, their inquiries have been relatively restricted. The same holds even truer for historiography on the Constitutional Era. The full range of documents assembled here requires, for the first time, comprehensive detailed analyses of legislative concepts in sovereignty and state from European Bodinian standpoints spanning the 16th through 18th centuries and drawing upon much older traditions.

What explains this great previous neglect? Academic compartmentalization may have been a factor in inhibiting a broad-ranging detailed study of the European roots of sovereignty and state in early American thought. This is not to minimize the value of studies on the immediate European background of, for example, isolated themes in the Declaration of Independence, the U.S. Constitution, and the Bill of Rights. The frequent tendency of general historians to restrict themselves to limited periods, often in keeping with their departmental curricula, may have disinclined them to explore broader themes over longer periods of time. Sweeping overviews conducted by some are another matter. In addition, the constraints imposed by contemporary publishing may well have dissuaded historians from venturing forth into an in-depth series of studies spanning much of European and American history and showing fuller relationships between the two on select topics. Other factors no doubt include the changing cycles and dynamics of historiographical fashion. In recent decades, subjects of sovereignty and state have not received the attention they once did. Political history still tends to be eclipsed by social history, and with it legal (and legislative) history has also experienced some decline. There, perhaps, lies the real crux of the dilemma.

4. THE CENTRALITY OF LEGISLATION

Among the vast myriad topics explored by historians of Jefferson, whose "universal" interests have given rise to so many books on him, why has his extensive legislative thought never before been given a full-scale direct treatment like the present? That neglect is surprising in view of how centrally the subject of legislation permeates his writings on issues of sovereignty and state. Is it because most historians are not now, and never have been, much interested as a whole in the topic of legislation in itself, even when looking at subjects of sovereignty and state? A case in point may be found in the classic older study by Bernard Bailyn already alluded to on "the ideological origins of the American Revolution." In it (as cited below), he included a lengthy section expressly devoted to and entitled "Sovereignty"— with initial discussion of Bodin's seminal idea of sovereignty but without recognition of its central legislative component (much less the influence thereof in American thought). And that study was done in the 1960s when strong interest in political history still prevailed. Thus the neglect of this important theme in Jefferson historiography is symptomatic of its much wider neglect by American historians of the Founding Era (and later eras).

Throughout the present series, a more pervasive oversight of legislative sovereignty and the legislative state among historians of political-legal-constitutional thought has frequently been observed. This oversight has extended to Bodin experts themselves as well as to specialists in 17th-century English thinkers like Locke and Sidney, who were deeply imbued with Bodinian concepts and who greatly influenced early American viewpoints. Innumerable other instances could be cited, all pointing to a fundamental relative disinterest in legislation by general historians and constitutional historians alike, though often for different reasons. Without this central component, however, sovereignty and state cannot be precisely grasped, for their parameters will remain too loose.

Accurate historical perspectives, stretching across many centuries, on correct defining essentials of sovereignty and state can enable long lines of writers and writings to fall naturally into place amid the changing complexity of materials and with often surprising results. Who would have originally thought, for example, that the fortuitous find several decades ago of a long-forgotten French jurist of the 16th century could hold a crucial key for unlocking neglected areas of Bodin's legislative thought in multiple ways with wide future import? Yet there can be little doubt of the long-range impact of legislative principles enunciated long ago by Corasius and Bodin, which entered into the mainstreams of political-legal thought even in early America. Granted, the documents here examined from the Revolutionary and Constitutional Eras require first and foremost the vantage points of their own contemporary American setting in order to be understood properly. Even so, the broader perspectives of history can enable vast fresh vistas to be opened up onto fundamental principles of sovereignty and state that are present, for example, in Jefferson's Declaration of Independence, Madison's Convention *Notes*, and the new Capital city of Washington. Jefferson's influential concept in the Declaration of Independence and Virginia constitution that each state has the inherent sovereign right of legislative self-government, regardless of outside questions of its jurisdictional right to legislate, strikingly parallels Corasius' comparable principle of legislative self-determination as given classic shape in Bodin's *Republic* of 1576, exactly 200 years before Jefferson's Declaration of 1776.

PART ONE

American Founding Fathers, Jefferson and Adams: Profiles in Legislation

Chapter II

Jefferson in Legislative Profile

As a foremost writer among the leading Founding Fathers, Thomas Jefferson presents one of the clearest cases of their enormous debt to traditions of European thought on politics, law, culture, and other matters. Even when helping to construct the new paradigms for the new American nation-state, Jefferson's writings exhibit the continuing influence of European intellectual traditions in the arenas central to the present series. He affords a striking illustration of the importance of legislation, sovereignty, and the state in the thought of the American Founders. Jefferson's special contributions make him a unique, though by no means solitary, representative of the ways in which the Founders stood, in their own right, alongside their noted predecessors and contemporaries in the European intellectual background. His mixtures of tradition and innovation, theory and practice, were vital to the emergent American models pertinent to this series. However, only a relatively small germane portion of Jefferson's vast thought can be treated here.

Although the approach below is largely new, it goes to the heart of Jefferson's political and legal thought on sovereignty, the state, and related topics. Indeed, some of his most basic writings and documents have never before been subjected to this kind of intensive analysis along legislative lines of sovereignty and state. Such works include his proposed Virginia constitutions, his revisions and systematizations of Virginia laws, his Declaration of Independence, and his writings relating to the U.S. Constitution. These and related other subjects will be taken up below. Jefferson's letters to James Madison and John Adams will shed further light, as will various books in his library, which include his marked copy of Jean Bodin's *Republic.*

Because of the great interplay between Jefferson's thought and activities as a thinker and statesman, it wil be useful at the outset to recall some fundamental points of his chronology. Born in 1743 in Virginia, Jefferson graduated from the College of William and Mary in 1762. In 1767, he was admitted to the bar and began practicing law in his native state, becoming elected to the Virginia House of Burgesses in 1769. He was elected delegate in 1775 to the First Continental Congress in Philadelphia. As a delegate to the Second Continental Congress in 1776, he wrote the Declaration of Independence. While a member of the Virginia House of Delegates in 1776–1779, he supported proposals on land reform, religious freedom, and many other matters. From 1779 to 1781, Jefferson was governor of Virginia. In 1783–1784, he was a Virginia delegate to the national Confederation Congress, helping to establish the country's coinage system. As American ambassador to France from 1785 to 1789, he was out of the country during the events surrounding the creation and adoption of the new U.S. Constitution in 1787–1788; yet he kept in close correspondence with its architect, James Madison, and others involved with the formation of the new federal government. Other pivotal dates are: 1790–1793, when he was Secretary of State under President George Washington; 1796–1800, as Vice President under President John Adams; 1800–1808, as U.S. President, followed by his retirement to his Monticello home; 1819, his founding of the University of Virginia; and 1826, his death on the fiftieth anniversary of the signing of the Declaration of Independence.

The accounts to follow center on close examinations of select texts composed by Jefferson. Although typically a masterful, penetrating stylist, his finished and unfinished (draft) writings often convey idiosyncrasies of expression peculiar either to his era or to him. These include matters of punctuation, capitalization, spelling, syntax, grammar, possessives (it's for its), and occasional circumlocution or verbosity to the point of being stilted or even opague. (The intended or unintended ambiguities of Jefferson's language, for instance, in his lists of charges against the British king and parliament, as found in his preambles to his Virginia constitution and in his Declaration of Independence, have long puzzled historians; yet his legislative focus there will help us to clarify his long obscured meaning.) However, for sake of exactitude, the texts chosen for analysis in our text and notes have not been altered or modernized in any way, other than to clarify them through explanations or brackets. The same applies to excerpts from other Founders encountered in ensuing chapters.

1. JEFFERSON IN AUTOBIOGRAPHICAL OVERVIEW

Bodinian Echoes

An important overview of Jefferson's early legislative history up to 1790, when he became Secretary of State, was afforded by Jefferson himself in his broad and detailed Autobiography,[1] begun in 1820 at age 77. A wide variety of other subjects are indeed included. By then, certain details had become somewhat impressionistic in his mind through the passage of time, though his accounts are generally detailed and accurate. It has not heretofore been duly recognized how central is his inclusion of his legislative involvements and observations. Indeed, his emphasis on legislative topics in his Autobiography serves here as a preliminary indication of their larger crucial place at the core of his thought on sovereignty, the state, and other subjects of interest to this series.[2]

After initial short accounts of his early background and education, steeped in classical languages and learning, Jefferson turns briefly in his Autobiography to his earliest legislative involvements. "In 1769, [I] became a member of the [Virginia] legislature by the choice of the county in which I live, and so continued until it was closed by the Revolution."[3] In short order, he proceeds at greater length to the initial breaks from Great Britain in the Second Continental "*Congress, . . . June 7, 1776*": "The delegates from Virginia moved . . . that the Congress should declare[:] that these United colonies are, and of a right ought to be, free and independent states, that . . . all political connection . . . [with] the state of Great Britain is, and ought to be, totally dissolved; . . . and [that] a Confederation be formed to bind the colonies more closely together."[4]

Those words of 1776 were incorporated into Jefferson's original Declaration of Independence by the whole Continental Congress, with the exception of the last phrase about a Confederation. Similar other phrases emphasizing that the "colonies" were "states" were employed in another place of his original draft, as Jefferson's own composite presentation of the original and altered portions indicates. More generally, Jefferson depicted the conflicts between the British and American states, leading to America's bid for independence, as having been caused by Britain's legislative fiats for America, which the final official Declaration of Independence enumerated and which certain deleted passages of his original draft had further emphasized. In his Autobiography, Jefferson then turned to the Articles of Confederation drawn up and adopted shortly thereafter to govern the American states, with a Congress to pass laws in limited measure and to bind them loosely together.

Beginning to come into view here is the Bodinian background to Jefferson's perspective on legislative sovereignty and the legislative state. This feature of his thought was alluded to in our earlier volumes when looking ahead to him.[5] Bodinian themes will come increasingly to the fore in this chapter on Jefferson.

Classical Models for New Systems in Virginia

Jefferson went on in his Autobiography to trace the development of government and laws in his home state of Virginia. Here he tied more closely together legislation and the state. He also elaborated on the need for new or revised legal systems, partly within contexts of classical models. In the Virginia legislature at Williamsburg, Jefferson played a central role not only as a law-maker but also as a law-systematizer, as the passages given below will indicate. They form a key part of his wider discussions about his roles in Virginia as a legislator and systematizer prior to becoming governor there.

As Jefferson readily acknowledged, "our Revised Code" of legislation, as he aptly called it,[6] was a collaborative effort by him and his several fellow committeemen selected for this purpose; yet he was intent in his Autobiography to focus largely upon his own guiding involvements and principal accomplishments in this enterprise during the later 1770s. Jefferson perceived early on the need for a completely revised Virginia code of legislation. His recourse not only to republicanism but to "reason," in opposition to arbitrary despotic decrees, seem an echo of wider European thought on the codification of law in that Age of Reason.

> In giving this account of the laws of which I was myself the mover and draughtsman, I, by no means, mean to claim to myself the merit of obtaining their passage. I had many occasional, and strenuous coadjutors in debate, and one, most steadfast, able and zealous; who was himself a host. This was George Mason, a man of the first order of wisdom. . . .
>
> So far we were proceeding in the details of reformation only; selecting points of legislation, prominent in character and principle, urgent, and indicative of the strength of the general pulse of reformation. When I left Congress, in '76, it was in the persuasion that our whole code must be reviewed, adapted to our

> republican form of government; and, now that we had no negatives of Councils, Governors, and Kings to restrain us from doing right, it should be corrected, in all its parts, with a single eye to reason, and the good of those for whose government it was framed. Early, therefore, in the session of '76, to which I returned, I moved and presented a bill for the revision of the laws, which was passed on the 24th of October; and on the 5th of November, Mr. Pendleton, Mr. Wythe, George Mason, Thomas L. Lee, and myself, were appointed a committee to execute the work.[7]

Not included in the above excerpts is Jefferson's lengthy praise of James Madison. Madison's admirable "classical language" and frame of mind facilitated and infused his guiding role in framing the U.S. Constitution, although he was not in the immediate picture here.

In the long passage of his Autobiography that then ensues on the codifiers' overall methodology, Jefferson makes it plain that his side won out in the question of whether to scrap the old system of Virginia laws and write a completely new one, or to systematize a revised set of existing laws into a thoroughly new code. But by arguing against the former positions as requiring the single hand of a Justinian, Bracton, or Blackstone, Jefferson was by no means rejecting their validity as legal systematizers *per se* in general, but only as sole creators. In fact, Jefferson's continuing discussion of the systematic principles he and his colleagues adopted would seem a worthy successor to those of Justinian, although in reworking Virginia's legal system Jefferson sought to advance republican rather than monarchical principles.[8]

Here, Jefferson's deep reading and grasp of classical sources, including on law and methodology, would have come into play. He was surely well aware that the Roman emperor Justinian, in his famed *Digest, Code,* and *Institutes* in the sixth century A.D., oversaw a committee headed by Tribonian in order to revise and systematize older and existing law into new forms relevant to their own era. That is, Justinian was not a sole creator himself, and he did not do away with older law and create wholly new law—as Jefferson (or his allies) intimated perhaps for rhetorical purposes and with allusions to the monarchical bent of those historical codifiers of law and legislation. Jefferson's periodic uses of the words "distribute" and "distribution" (as exemplified in the citations immediately above and below) will recall to mind Renaissance legal systematizers like Bodin and Corasius. To be sure, books in the Roman law tradition are found in abundance in Jefferson's library.

More elaborate systematic methods are also reported in Jefferson's Autobiography for a thoroughgoing resystematization of law and legislation in Virginia. These methods were even more a worthy indirect successor to earlier traditions in Europe on reducing a huge mass of disorganized legal-legislative materials into a coherent single simplified system.[9]

When Jefferson then turns in his Autobiography to criminal law, he displays his ready knowledge of Roman law and English law, as well as the law of his own land.[10] He also demonstrates an acute awareness of the 18th-century writer Beccaria, whose discussions on the subject of crimes and punishments were also treated earlier in this series.[11]

Jefferson's further disquisition in his Autobiography on the procedures and methods he adopted in his own efforts to revise and codify Virginia law and legislation give ample testimony to his great expertise and knowledge on the subject. The enormous tasks of revising and reconciling English common law, British statutes going back to Magna Carta, and Virginia laws eventually came to fruition. Years after Jefferson left the Virginia legislature for the governor's office, that body enacted the project into law. His varied related work on certain separate laws concerning religious freedom, slavery, and inherited wealth was likewise detailed, extensive, and consistent with his democratic values and dislike of privilege.[12]

The American Congress

Jefferson's subsequent participation in the American Confederation Congress in the early 1780s and his involvements with the emerging French National Assembly in the later 1780s brought wider national and international scope to his own early legislative history. Before then, in the mid- to later 1770s, he had been primarily concerned with state legislative affairs in his native Virginia, although he also had considerable activities at Philadelphia in the First and Second Continental Congresses. Throughout all these periods in Jefferson's autobiographical account of his early public life, the legislative undercurrents remained strong. His record appropriately ends with the sentence "I arrived at New York . . . [in early 1790] where [the Federal] Congress was in session."[13] He had returned from France to Virginia in late 1789 and was taking up his post as Secretary of State.

Jefferson recounted, with typical vivid expressiveness, his period in the inchoate Confederation Congress, to which he had been appointed by the Virginia legislature. His account begins with his arrival in Trenton, where it was then meeting before moving on to Annapolis. In his Autobiography, Jefferson described the slow, frustrating workings of its legislative machinery at different points during this period.

> Congress had now become a very small body, and the members very remiss in their attendance on its duties, inasmuch, that a majority of the States, necessary by the Confederation to constitute a House even for minor business, did not assemble [in timely fashion]. ... [The congressional] body was little numerous, but very contentious. Day after day was wasted on the most unimportant questions. ... [Some members were] afflicted with the rage of debate ... [and] heard with impatience any logic ... not his own ...[14]

Jefferson also outlined his ideas for "dividing" the Confederation's Congress into distinct and coherent "executive and legislative" branches. He sought to provide a stronger central executive to deal with various kinds of important matters. The kind of pluralistic executive body that eventually came into being in the Confederation disappointed Jefferson because of its tendencies to schism and indecisiveness.[15]

Jefferson expertly pointed out at length in his Autobiogaphy the main problems of the Articles of Confederation, which impeded the work of its Congress, as well as the solutions later provided by the new U.S. Constitution, written in 1787 while he was in France. First and foremost, Jefferson tacitly stressed that the Confederation's Congress was typically rendered ineffective as a national legislature by the more strongly exercised and conflicting powers of the state legislatures, which appointed representatives to the Congress. This tacit legislative accent by Jefferson must itself be accentuated here. Secondly yet significantly, Jefferson pointed out the difficulties caused by the lack of separation between the limited legislative, executive, and judicial functions. After the new U.S. Constitution was devised in order to compensate for these drawbacks, Jefferson pressed its chief architect, Madison, along with its principal signer, Washington, to have individual freedoms and rights incorporated. Jefferson also supplied, from France, a significant voice, if not an actual vote, in the Convention's various strategies for adopting the new U.S. Constitution without yet resolving its defects, which were dealt with in subsequent amendments. He did not want to risk, at that point, losing the basic accomplishments already achieved if the Convention waited until later to adopt or redo it. Jefferson expressed considerable satisfaction, despite his various reservations, with the basic form of the new U.S. government as a solution to the defects of the old government of the Confederation.[16]

The foregoing suggests that Jefferson had a significant influence on his close friend Madison in the genesis of the new federal structure. (It had already been taking shape in Madison's mind in the months leading up to the 1787 Convention as indicated in his papers of that time revealing his reading and thinking.) The fact that the new U.S. Constitution was not merely a revision of the old Articles of Confederation, and that it began in Article I with the Congress as the federal legislature, by far the longest article of all, was due in some measure not only to the highly independent mind of Madison but also to the ongoing influence upon him of Jefferson. The need for a strong central national legislature over and above the state legislatures, while providing for them, was a pressing need for both Jefferson and Madison. True, an effective independent executive branch was also necessary; yet the new presidency was not then the powerful office it later became, and it occupied a much shorter Article II in the new Constitution.

In addition, Jefferson urged in his Autobiography that legislatures at both the state and federal levels should have more control over the judicial arm of governments than was proving to be the case in the decades after the new U.S. Constitution was adopted. Judges must not become too independent and unresponsive, he warned. Yet he voiced approval that they were not dominated, as earlier in England, by monarchical or executive authorities.[17]

The French Assembly

In his Autobiography, Jefferson's descriptions of his ambassadorship to France centered around his vivid accounts of the tumultuous events of 1788–1789. As that early stage of the French Revolution burst forth, he became embroiled in the effort to find new governmental structures to meet the urgent problems of a nation in upheaval. By the time he left France in September of 1789, Jefferson had been a close witness to the great events of the summer of 1789. They included the Oath of the Tennis Court in which the revolutionaries vowed to form a new constitution, the storming of the old royal prison known as the Bastille, the proclamation of the *Declaration of the Rights of Man*, and the final downfall of the old system of Estates-General. The Third Estate, or majority of the people, had had only a limited voice in relation to the First and Second Estates, or the clergy and aristocracy. As the monarchy of Louis XVI was declining and the power of the new Nationl Assembly of the people arose to replace the old Third Estate, Jefferson tried not to take sides in the swirling debates over the actions to be taken and the governmental forms to be adopted. Nevertheless, his Autobiography is full of his own reports, observations, and proposals. He was fascinated by the downfall of the old order and the emergence of the new. Written from the vantage point of his later years, Jefferson's account looked back with the knowledge of how the French

Revolution had, to his mind, eventually gone astray. He bemoaned the ensuing Napoleonic Empire, with which he himself later had difficult dealings as U.S. President. Jefferson's numerous discussions of the background and rise of the French National Assembly reveal his continuing great interests in issues of legislation, sovereignty, and the state.

It was natural that Jefferson became drawn into the initial revolutionary struggles in France for new forms of freedom, independence, and democracy. His legendary role in writing the U.S. Declaration of Independence over a decade earlier was well known in France. As American ambassador, who had had recent input in the formation of the U.S. Constitution while in France, Jefferson was ideally positioned to be sought out and of service in the quest for new constitutional forms in France. He points out, in his Autobiography, the unique influence of the American Revolution in France, although "the remote causes" of French problems "go a little [further] back." "Celebrated writers of France and England had already sketched good principles on the subject of government; yet the American Revolution seems first to have awakened the thinking part of the French nation in general, from the sleep of despotism in which they were sunk."[18]

The evolution, or devolution, of the French Third Estate into the French National Assembly, culminating in the summer of 1789, was well noted in Jefferson's autobiographical discussions of events coming to a head at that time. "The object of the Patriots was, to establish representative and republican government. The majority of the States General were with them, but the majority of the populace of the towns were with the Prince of Orange. . . . The States, therefore, exceeding their rights of sovereignty, deprived him of his powers."[19] After "[t]he States General were opened on the 5th of May, '89," the nobles "had not yet learned to suspect their inconsistence with reason and right. They were willing to submit to equality of taxation, but not to descend from their rank and prerogatives to be incorporated in session with the Tiers État."[20] Jefferson had close personal interest and involvement in the developing debates.[21]

Following the Oath of the Tennis Court later in June, 1789, Jefferson came into close touch with the Assembly members. His expression of his own ideas did not prove successful, for he favored relative moderation. Yet Jefferson showed an ongoing comprehensive grasp of the governmental forms that were being debated and coming into existence, including the legislative components.[22] He also bemoaned the opportunities lost by the National Assembly to avoid future bloodshed by compromising with the king, who "was now become a passive machine in the hands of the National Assembly."[23]

Jefferson increasingly elaborated in his Autobiography on the emerging intricacies of the constitutional crisis, with his usual interest in legislative matters. Following the Assembly's demolition of aristocratic titles and privileges in August, 1789, much time was spent putting all this into legislation. Then, after the principles of the *Declaration of Rights* were rapidly agreed upon, the harder protracted work of forging a new French constitution was seriously undertaken. The Assembly sought Jefferson's assistance and participation, but he felt bound to excuse himself since he was U.S. ambassador to the French Court and the king was still chief magistrate of France. Nevertheless, he closely reported on the contentious Assembly debates that followed its preliminary agreement on a tripartite division of executive, legislative, and judicial powers. A number of prominent Assembly members, headed by the famed Marquis de Lafayette, arranged in due course to convene at Jefferson's Paris residence in order to debate their constitutional ideas before him. The meeting lasted for six hours, with Jefferson as "a silent witness." The debates centered on the nature of the proposed legislature and its relation to the king as executive. Jefferson found the debates worthy of certain ancient ones cited in classical literature. He saw this as an historic occasion, for the members present finally came to important agreement on the main organizational issues for the new French constitution.[24]

As Jefferson then ended his detailed autobiographical accounts of the early stage of the French Revolution, he notably remarked on its special significance for both America and Europe, especially with regard to the rights of man.[25] He might have added that his unique involvement in the events and debates unfolding in France intensified the influence upon him of European intellectual traditions.

2. JEFFERSON'S CONSTITUTION AND LAWS OF VIRGINIA

Jefferson's early writings on his home state of Virginia included many crucial considerations of legislation, sovereignty, and the state. His ideas on these and related subjects went through complicated stages of development during his early formative years in the 1770s and 1780s. A limited intensive examination within the broader parameters of this series will again shed new light on Jefferson, just as he does on them.

Historians have long analyzed and debated the complex relationships between Jefferson's three successive drafts of preambles and plans for a Virginia constitution, drawn up prior to June 13, 1776, as well as their relationship not only to the official constitution adopted by the Virginia Convention on June 29, 1776, but also to Jefferson's evolving drafts for the Declaration of Independence adopted on July 4, 1776. The wider connections between all these basic documents and a wide variety of others by Jefferson and by his contemporaries and predecessors have added to this huge complexity. A fresh look at select texts and issues of present interest will yield some new points of view not yet adequately seen in the voluminous historiography on Jefferson.

Just as Jefferson's preambles to his proposed Virginia constitution of 1776 form vital links to his Declaration of Independence, his constitutional plan itself had important links to the U.S. Constitution framed in 1787 by his close friend Madison. Jefferson's Virginia constitution, together with the version officially adopted, also supplied partial prototypes for ensuing other state constitutions, including the Massachusetts constitution drawn up in 1779 by his good friend John Adams, who had been on the committee with Jefferson to write the Declaration of Independence. Taken together, Jefferson's Virginia preambles and constitution plans of 1776 serve to point up central fixtures of his political-legal thought and to provide a backdrop to his other writings also examined below. His subsequent efforts not only to revise and rewrite the official Virginia constitution finally adopted in 1776, but also to revise the laws of Virginia, will raise manifold further points of interest. In essence, Jefferson's labors for the state of Virginia in constitution-making and legislative systematizing will furnish a kind of microcosm for his related national endeavors.

Creating the Preamble: First Draft

The long preamble to the first draft of Jefferson's proposed Virginia constitution of 1776 was revised to serve as a basis for the preamble to his third draft, the form in which his preamble was adopted in the official Virginia constitution approved by the Virginia Convention. In turn, his preamble to the Virginia constitution of 1776 was further revised by him as a basis for the preamble to his original version of the Declaration of Independence.

What makes this evolution of Jefferson's draft preambles so significant here is that their lengthy lists of charges against the British king and parliament are largely framed in terms of legislative sovereignty. These draft Virginia preambles, prior to the final Declaration of Independence, were not prefaced by more general statements of philosophical-political principles, whereas the final Declaration of Independence was. Hence it is a striking feature of these draft Virginia preambles that they begin abruptly with a listing of charges that in their first parts center on issues of legislation and legislative sovereignty. Historians have not yet duly appreciated the overwhelming initial legislative format of these draft preambles. Although, at the same time, some historians have not overlooked the obvious legislative contours of these opening charges against the British king and parliament, they have typically divided up such lists in different ways according to other issues and criteria. Historians have largely overlooked, or insufficiently stressed, the preambles' overriding legislative orientation *per se*, especially in matters of European thought treated in the present series.[26]

The first draft of Jefferson's preamble to his proposed Virginia constitution[27] begins with an extremely long sentence of compounded clauses in which he first briefly rejects King George III's pursuit of a "detestable & insupportable tyranny by . . ." This is followed by an extensive series of "by" clauses listing separate charges and abuses. This list of particular grievances (cited immediately below) comprises nearly the first third of the first draft of Jefferson's preamble to the Virginia constitution. All items—except for two toward the end that concern the military and war—revolve directly and explicitly around issues of legislation and legislative power in the struggles between America and Britain over sovereignty. It is noteworthy that the celebrated issue of taxation (without representation) does not appear in this list until the last "by" clause, where it is included along with numerous other items under broader legislative contexts. Thus the legislative factor predominates throughout the relevant passages (given in the corresponding note below).[28]

Much has been written by historians about the background and sources for such lists of grievances, which appear in different and varying forms in certain other early writings by Jefferson and in a range of other works and documents of the same period, as often shaped by changing events and circumstances. Clearly, Jefferson had been thinking long and hard about such matters and had read widely concerning them. The immediate issues and exigencies of his day were obviously pressing and formative for him. Yet Jefferson was also typically attuned to broader philosophical and historical ideas of deep import for him in gaining a proper fix on the situations at hand.

Jefferson's unusually well-developed lists of grievances in their entirety in his Virginia preamble's first (and third) draft version can be shown to bear striking relationships to the charges against King James II in the English Declaration (Bill) of Rights of 1689. That document also featured legislative issues of sovereignty (as seen in our earlier studies, with an eye ahead there to the Declaration of Independence[29]). The English Declaration furnished obvious partial precedents for

Jefferson's Virginia preambles, notably in its special legislative forms in its first two charges against James II. Even so, Jefferson's mostly different lists of charges against George III were much more extensively geared toward legislative matters.[30]

The English Declaration of Rights passed by Parliament in 1689 (also known as the Act of 1689) was followed a year later by John Locke's famed discourses on government, which also featured legislative factors of sovereignty in addition to theories of contract and just revolution. Jefferson was well familiar with Locke's ideas, which would be directly echoed in his Declaration of Independence. On some levels, there were apparent incongruities between Locke's and Jefferson's approaches to the structure of government in relation to legislative sovereignty, which remain to be resolved.

It would also be instructive to compare this early Virginia constitution's preamble with preambles to other state constituions in order to determine the extent to which their charges against the British king and parliament, in justifying their own independent statehoods, were oriented to legislative issues. The same applies to local resolutions advancing the cause of independence in the American colonies. In other connections, some historians have indeed searched through such documents for similarities with, or precedents for, Jefferson's lists of grievances in his Virginia preambles.

Yet one stimulating recent study has argued in detail that the initial items in Jefferson's lists of charges (precisely the ones we present in a new legislative light) are not only too vague or generalized to be understood fully or clearly in their own right. They also do not clearly correspond, it is further maintained, to actual events and circumstances to which they allude; and, moreover, their approach differs considerably from other state and local lists of grievances justifying revolutionary independence from England.[31]

Finally, the striking last part of Jefferson's lengthy preamble in his first draft plan for the Virginia constitution of 1776 declares (as cited below)[32] that the British king and parliament have, through their acts of legislation, represented a tyranny needing to be overthrown. The particular slant given by Jefferson is a partial echo of Locke and the English Declaration of Rights. The legal as well as political justification for declaring Virginia's revolutionary independence lies for Jefferson in Britain's violation of the so-called contract between the British authorities and the new colony, dating back to the age of Queen Elizabeth I. That compact's convoluted series of statements is far more verbose and dificult than can be conveyed in the highlighted portion given below. The text seems suitably matched by Jefferson's own somewhat stilted use of it, as he grapples haltingly with the emerging exigencies and their solutions both in actuality and in theory. His final concluding statement, seeming to call for the actual overthrow of the king himself, stretches further the comparison with the English struggles over sovereignty and legitimacy in the later seventeenth century in order to lend further credence and legality to Virginia's case for independence and statehood. Nonetheless, by couching his language in this fashion, Jefferson could more convincingly justify for his compatriots the legitimizing comparison with the English precedent a century earlier.

Revising the Preamble: Later Drafts

Whereas there was no preamble listing the charges against the king in Jefferson's second draft of 1776 for a Virginia constitution,[33] a short preliminary statement there makes a more cogent case for the actual overthrow of kingly powers than appeared in the final part of his preamble to the first draft. It reads in part: "Be it therefore enacted by the authority of the people that . . . [King] George . . . is hereby . . . deposed from the kingly office (*& powers within this colony*) . . . [and] divested of all . . . rights & powers, & that the sd. office shall henceforth cease & be never more erected within this (*government*) colony." This sharpened language concerning legislative enactment in this document—in keeping with that concerning revolution and independence more broadly—is reinforced by the [1] opening and [2] closing lines before and after it: [1] "A bill for new modelling the form of government and for establishing the Fundamental principles of our future Constitution" and [2] "[B]e it further enacted by the authority aforesaid that . . . the following fundamental laws and principles of government shall henceforth be established." Clearly here, Virginia's independent statehood, in the proposed constitution that Jefferson then presents in his second draft version, is to be created by and founded upon the legislative enactments and powers of the sovereign people of the independent state of Virginia. The fuller legislative impact of the initial list of charges in his first draft preamble is not really lost here in the second one. For just below the prefatory statement's opening line quoted above appears a similar kind of introductory "by" clause ("Whereas George [space] king of Great Britain [etc.]"), followed by several blank lines prior to the "Be it therefore enacted" statement cited above. The blank lines, denoted by empty spaces left for them, seem to indicate Jefferson's intended inclusion of his first draft's "by" clauses omitted for abbreviation's sake in this revised second draft. Nonetheless, there are typically thorny problems of textual transmission that cannot be fathomed here.[34]

In Jefferson's third draft of a preamble to his proposed plan of 1776 for a Virginia constitution,[35] the same kind of "Whereas George . . ." clause that opened his first and second draft preambles again appears; it is followed by the same extensive "by" clauses, almost verbatim, that appeared in his first but not his second draft. The changes in the third draft's corresponding list of charges in the preamble are slight.[36] There are two notable differences, however, between Jefferson's first and third draft preambles in what follows next. Whereas his first draft preamble went on at length with the diffusive "compact" arguments and passed over the specific language of legislative enactment for promulgating the document itself, his third draft preamble, considerably shorter than the first, omits the extended "compact" arguments of his first draft and, in place thereof, adopts the specific and extended language of legislative enactment found at the end of his second draft. As in Jefferson's second draft, then, there are two concluding substantial statements of legislative enactment. The first statement disestablishes the British king: "Be it therefore enacted by the authority of the people that . . . George . . . hereby is deposed from the kingly office within this government [etc.]." The second statement authorizes the new Virginia constitution: "And be it further enacted by the authority aforesaid that the following fundamental laws and principles of government shall henceforth be established." The second and third drafts' versions of these two statements are the same, except that the second is a little tighter and smoother in style.

The weighty import of the changed third draft of Jefferson's preamble to the Virginia constitution is thus his even heavier stress on legislative matters. Clearly, he was finding his way toward a solid legal basis for legitimizing Virginia's independence and new constitution. Putting aside the onerous and unwieldy "compact" ideas set forth in his first draft, with its forced Lockean allusions to the overthrow of kingly power in England, Jefferson found in the specific and immediate language of legislative enactment a more satisfactory solution in his quest for legal justification. The legislative "by" clauses in his first draft's list of charges against the king were kept and made even more effective by the elimination of other matters in various passages that in the first draft had ended the lists of charges—that is, just before the final presentation of the long "compact" discussion, which Jefferson no doubt now found too convoluted to be effective. He retained such expressions as "public liberty," in keeping with his ideas of popular sovereignty, while not entirely eliminating echoes of his continued beliefs about contract theory more generally. But the emerging legislative basis for sovereignty and the state is here most striking. Jefferson's renewed blending of tradition and innovation, practicality and theory, resulted in a preamble with ever more distinctiveness. This quality is not lost by the partial outside precedents for his preamble, or by the shape given to it by the press of events, or by Jefferson's interactions with others who were involved in drawing up a new constitution for Virginia.

Despite Jefferson's dissatisfaction with aspects of the official Virginia constitution finally adopted in 1776,[37] and despite his subsequent proposals for revising it, the preamble of that new official constitution was based almost verbatim on Jefferson's third draft (leaving aside here the issue of his influence on the constitution's main body).[38] The Virginia constitution, adopted "in a General Convention" on June 29, 1776, begins in its preamble with the familiar "Whereas George the Third . . ." clause and then gives the lengthy "by" clauses centering at length in their first part on legislative matters. The "compact" arguments concerning Sir Walter Raleigh etc. were omitted, as were the two concluding paragraph statements of legislative enactment as given at the end of Jefferson's second and third drafts. The official preamble simply ends matter-of-factly by proclaiming: "We, therefore, the Delegates and Representatives of the good People of Virginia, . . . and in compliance with a Recommendation of the General Congress, do ordain and declare the future Form of Government of Virginia to be as followeth . . ." Thus even the official Virginia constitution passed by the Virginia legislature (which would be named differently than in the colonial past) did not involve or incorporate the specific developed language of legislative enactment that Jefferson had devised for it; he had done so partly in order to give a more impressive or official form of legitimacy to his "bill" (as he called it at the very outset of his second and third drafts) proposing a plan for a new constitution. In a sense, therefore, this discrepancy serves to accentuate all the more Jefferson's own accent on legislative factors when adding such enactment statements, in addition to his legislative "by" clauses in the list of charges against the king and his parliament, which were retained in the preamble to the official Virginia constitution.

Demystifying the Preambles (with Bodin and Corasius)

Notwithstanding the enormous cumulative contributions of many noted scholars in recent decades, a veil of uncertainty and even mystery still partially surrounds Jefferson's meanings, contexts, and sources in his successive preambles of 1776 to his three drafts of a plan for the Virginia constitution. The enigma is all the more intensified by virtue of the close relationships between those preambles and the ensuing Declaration of Independence. Because of the unique perspectives brought to this subject by the present series, the remaining veil can now be largely lifted, although further treatment of the Declaration itself awaits us below. The resulting revelations, already coming into view above, carry some surprises. Further levels of complexity are involved, yet the foregoing discussions now permit some revealing conclusions. The demystifications of the charges in the Virginia draft preambles (as in the Declaration of Independence) can be viewed, in a sense, as Jefferson's own, arrived at through his own preamble statements as presented above and now explicated in their wider import. The mystifications, needing to be cleared away for historians, were not intended as such by Jefferson himself and can be dealt with from Jefferson's own preamble statements stressing the legislative factors, to which historians have not yet assigned the full weight that he did.

It is likely that Jefferson's special emphasis on the "tyranny" of King George III, in order to justify American revolution and independence, was partly based on arguments against King James II in the British Declaration (Bill) of Rights (1689) and in Locke's *Two Treatises of Government* (1690), which advanced ideas of parliamentary legislative sovereignty. Thus the uniqueness of Jefferson's unusually long lists of charges against the king was due, especially in their crucial opening particulars, at least as much to their focus on legislation as on tyranny. True, the unusual length of his lists of charges against George III (in comparison with other previous lists made by others) served to reinforce his own portrayal of the king as a tyrant needing to be overthrown, as one expert has recently rightly stressed.[39] Yet Jefferson's argument was also heavily couched in terms of legislative sovereignty, under the influence of Locke, the English Declaration of Rights, and related Bodinian and other traditions of thought adapted to his own purposes.

It becomes clear, then, that Jefferson, in his draft preambles to his proposed plans for a Virginia constitution, framed the issues, in Lockean terms, not only around the right or duty to rebel against a tyrant, who had violated an original "contract" with the people. Jefferson also affirmed the independent sovereignty of an American state founded on its own legal right to legislate for its own affair, in accordance with Lockean-Bodinin traditions of thought adapted to the situation at hand. Here Jefferson the lawyer and political thinker merged in a powerful way with Jefferson the practical statesman to promote the legality of the case for revolution as well as for independence. He decisively underscored, as we shall further see, the legislative issues in the struggle for sovereignty fought between Britain and the American colonists. He elevated the legislative struggles between the two sides to a more generalized or universal level that partly transformed and obscured his references to situations then current. Those historians[40] who have admirably tried, but with incomplete success, to fathom what specific actual occurrences Jefferson may have been alluding to in his opening lists of (legislative) charges against the king can arrive at a fuller picture through the present (legislative) perspectives on his theory.

It would be instructive in these matters to regard Jefferson's Virginian preambles and constitution plans of 1776 as two sets of documents for two sets of circumstances. His draft preambles, foreshadowing his Declaration of Independence, were geared to the issue of sovereign legislative independence and statehood. His draft constitution plans, anticipating in part the later U.S. Constitution framed by his friend Madison, divided government into separate legislative, executive, and judicial branches. The more unitary legislative sovereignty of his 1776 preambles served a different purpose than did the separated sovereign powers involving legislation in his corresponding constitution plans of 1776. Looked at in this light, the two sets of approaches are inherently reconcilable in their legislative vantage points, as his constitution plans themselves will further reveal.

Meantime, this dichotomy points up another seeming contradiction, which is likewise resolvable. In Locke's idea of parliamentary legislative sovereignty, the executive and judicial powers were largely subordinated or subsumed under it. Jefferson proposed that all three functions or powers should be duly separated. But the fuller implications of a national federal system of divided powers for traditional ideas of sovereignty, as adapted in the American Revolution by Jefferson and others, still lay ahead in the next decade. In the documents at hand, Jefferson was intent on developing not only a full plan for the Virginia constitution—indeed the only one of its kind drawn up and submitted to the Virginia Convention. He also saw the need for a detailed corresponding preamble that would set forth the wider principles upon which the independent state of Virginia (and, by extension, of other colonies) could be based. The differing dimensions of the Revolutionary era of the 1770s and the Constitutional era of the 1780s seem already to be coming into view. Yet a unifying link will be the ultimate sovereignty of the people, as variously undergirded by the English Declaration of Rights, Locke, Jefferson, the Declaration of Independence, and the U.S. Constitution.

In the final analysis, the idea of legislative sovereignty and self-determination was strikingly affirmed in Jefferson's draft preambles of mid-1776, incorporated into the Virginia constitution enacted into law shortly thereafter. Those documents clearly and elaborately indicated that the colony of Virginia was henceforth to be an independent state founded on its right to make laws for its own affairs, including on the celebrated matter of taxation. They also strongly indicated that the

British king and parliament had no jurisdictional right to suspend, abrogate, or disallow the laws passed by the Virginia legislature, much less to legislate for Virginia from England without Virginia's consent (by then a moot point because of the state's new independence). Virginia's legislative power, as a state unto itself, to pass laws for its own affairs on all matters "necessary for the public good" was not dependent on any "foreign jurisdiction," as Jefferson declared in his preambles, especially since the British government often refused to legislate properly, or even at all, on many matters of pressing concern to the colonists. Jefferson's two concluding "enactment" paragraphs in the second and third draft preambles reinforced these positions.

Although he could not have known it, beyond his reading of Bodin's *Republic* (a marked copy of which he possessed), Jefferson was here strongly echoing a cardinal theme first articulated and underscored in the early modern period by Bodin's immediate predecessor, Corasius. It was Corasius who first decisively avowed that the power to make law is not a question of jurisdiction but can be exercised inherently by any legally recognized state or body for its own affairs.[41]

The importance of the foregoing legislative issues infusing Jefferson's successive preambles to his proposed Virginia constitution has required the present lengthy treatment of them. Because of their great impact on Jefferson's Declaration of Independence, written very shortly thereafter, his Virginia preambles occupy a crucial stage in the genesis of what has often been called the most important document in American history. Their influence on it has long been recognized, yet the overwhelming legislative thrust of those preambles has heretofore been neglected by historians. To be sure, some experts have included legislative issues in their discussions of the preambles, but in very different contexts,[42] while other historians have focused on legislative matters but in entirely different areas.[43] One prominent scholar recognized several decades ago that traditional Bodinian concepts of sovereignty, especially in their English carry-overs, entered as central issues into "the ideological origins of the American Revolution."[44] Still, the legislative factor *per se* has generally been overshadowed by other issues in historiography on sovereignty and state, as has been seen repeatedly throughout this series.

A fuller reconsideration of Jefferson's Virginia preambles of mid-1776 will be afforded in the next section on his Declaration of Independence and on several other early writings by him that also contributed to its genesis. Before turning to his ideas on the national level, we must continue here with his works on the state of Virginia. For they provide a kind of microcosm for his views on legislative sovereignty and the legislative state at the national level.

Creating the Constitution

Like his first draft of a preamble to his plan for a Virginia constitution in mid-1776, Jefferson's adjoining first draft of his proposed plan for the constitution itself was rough yet well-developed.[45] At the very outset, he sets forth in clear, succinct fashion what he believes the overarching guiding principle should be: "Legislative[,] Executive & Judicial Powers shall be for ever separate." The constitution's three sections or articles that follow (marked in Roman numerals) take up each of those three powers in turn, with further explicit and implied understanding of the separation of powers. Jefferson sought to ensure that no one branch of government would dominate the other two. He did not want the legislature, for instance, to dominate or absorb the executive and judicial powers, as he later found to be the tendency in the official Virginia constitution issued shortly thereafter. Yet by placing the legislative power first in his plan and the executive and judicial powers after it, Jefferson, like others, gave an inherent priority of authority to the lawmaking power. That is, the executive and judicial powers centered respectively around the administering and adjudicating of the laws made by the legislature, although this relationship was not yet as clear-cut as it became a decade later in the much different U.S. Constitution. A corresponding apparent paradox would remain, however, in the U.S. Constitution framed by his close friend Madison, who provided a similar tripartite separation of powers in the first three articles of that national document. In the final analysis, the priority of law and legislation in relation to all three branches in Jefferson's proposed Virginia constitution, not unlike that in the later U.S. Constitution, can be squared not only with the idea of legislative sovereignty in his corresponding preamble, discussed above, but also with his concept of the separation of powers.

The three branches of government in Jefferson's first rough draft of a Virginia constitution were to operate separately yet in conjunction with each other. "Legislative [power] shall be exercised," as stated at the start of section I, "by two separate houses." The General Assembly or House of Representatives will be elected annually throughout "the whole colony," according to certain qualifications and procedures, and have a two-thirds quorum (a point of later dispute for Jefferson). The members of the Senate will be appointed by the House and serve for life. "[T]hese houses shall each have power to originate[,] amend & negative [*sic*], except that money bills shall originate with representatives." The British model of the House of Commons and House of Lords had here a partial general influence. "Executive powers," according to section II, "shall be exercised by an [Administrator]," chosen annually "but not . . . invested with powers" until a year later by the House. The Administrator "shall possess the powers formerly held by the king"; but he is "bound by acts of legislature," has "no negative on bills," and cannot dissolve the House, declare war or peace, or engage in a host of other activities all granted instead to the legislature. Under this section are also included provisions for lieutenant administrator, privy council, judges of general courts, Supreme Court, sheriffs, treasurer, and so forth. "The Judicial powers," as section III begins, "shall be exercised 1st by . . . county or borough courts . . . or other Jurisdictions inferior to these as . . . established by Legislature." Secondly and thirdly are matters handled by other such courts and bodies "as the laws have already given" or "future laws shall direct to them." Other cases are included in different fashion with reference to what the acts of the legislature shall direct. Toward the end a kind of Bill of Rights is given. It is built into the constitution itself (as Jefferson initially preferred for the U.S. Constitution) and is not separated from it. Freedom of religious belief is guaranteed, but "seditious behavior" is authorized to be punished "according to the laws already made or henceforth to be made." No standing armies except in times of war was another provision, along with no payments to officers "but by act of legislature." The final lines of the document accentuate the sovereign power of the legislature as the supreme authority behind the establishment of the constitution itself and of the laws themselves. Hence: "None of these fundamental constitutions to be (*alter*) repealed but by unanimous consent of both legislative houses. The laws heretofore in force in this colony shall be still in force save only so far as they may be changed by the foregoing fundamental laws by future acts of the legislature." Thus although Jefferson would later criticize the official Virginia constitution of 1776 for granting too much power to the legislature on such matters as the quorum and exclusivity, he clearly assigned great powers and priorities to it, particularly in relation to the concept of legislative authority more generally.

The second rough yet developed draft[46] of Jefferson's plan of mid-1776 for the new Virginia constitution omitted an actual preamble; it began abruptly with two paragraphs formally authorizing the enactment of his "bill" into law, as discussed above. Although not numbered or even spaced apart, the same tripartite division of the constitution appears as in the first draft. At the outset, Jefferson reaffirms the separation of powers, while adding a clear qualifying clause: "The Legislative, Executive, & Judicial offices shall be kept for ever separate, & no person exercising the one shall be capable of appointment to the others or to either of them." Again the legislature is divided into two houses, each needing a two-thirds quorum for conducting business. "The . . . executive powers," moreover, "shall be exercised (*by*) . . . the

. . . Administrator . . . (*who*) shall be . . . annually appointed by the . . . [H]ouse of [R]epresentatives. . . . [T]he same [H]ouse & at the same time [also appoints] a Deputy Administrator . . ." Judicial powers are exercised in the first, second, and third levels by county courts, a General Court as well as High Court of Chancery, and a court of appeals. The jurisdictions of all three are partly defined in various ways by the legislature; each must have a quorum of two-thirds of the members present in order to proceed to business. A sprawling series of rights and liberties follows toward the end of the document, beginning with restrictions against slavery. "No person hereafter coming into this country shall be held in slavery under any pretext whatsoever." With this statement, one manuscript of the document ended; but, in any case, the provision could have caused obvious problems for members of the Virginia Convention, to which the proposed constitution was being submitted.

Jefferson's second draft of his proposed Virginia constitution ends somewhat differently from the first draft. Near the close, are the same two qualifications or conditions regarding any future alteration or repeal that appeared at the end of the first draft. The two statements again serve to underscore the legislature's ultimate authority in the matter. The first is, however, much longer in this case. It begins as follows: "None of these fundamental laws & principles of government shall be repealed . . . or altered but by the personal consent of the [assembled] people . . . meet[ing] in their respective counties . . . by an act of Legislature to be passed for every special occasion . . ." If Jefferson's accent on the need in such cases for large-scale direct democratic approval by the people at large proved too onerous and decentralized for many members of the Virginia Convention, he still assigned prior or ultimate power to the legislative authority in contexts of representative democracy. And yet, Jefferson closes on the need for the constitution's ratification by the people at large (which was not truly done when the official Virginia constitution was finally enacted): "It is proposed that the above bill, after correction by the Convention, shall be referred by them to the people to be assembled in their respective counties: and that the suffrages of two thirds of the counties shall be requisite to establish it." Yet despite Jefferson's various provisions designed to ensure popular democracy from the local level up, however inefficient that might prove, his proclivities toward the British model of a representative legislature, which appoints the chief administrator and has considerable jurisdiction over the judiciary, tended to place ultimate sovereignty in the legislative authority. Notwithstanding his idea of the separation of powers designed to avoid the concentration of power (and privilege) in the hands of the few, Jefferson would later complain that the official Virginia constitution tended to do just that.

The third draft[47] of Jefferson's proposed Virginia constitution is divided into four numbered sections and, in many respects, represents the most finished form among the three versions he prepared. The substantive changes in the main body are minimal. Yet the fourth section—following the first three, entitled "Legislative," "Executive," and "Judiciary"—is likewise given its own distinguishing title, "Rights Private and Public." Once again, the House and Senate both have the power to originate and amend bills of legislation, while only the House can do so for bills levying money (another apparent safeguard against privilege), although the assent of both bodies is required for passage of a law. Again, moreover, it is the House that appoints the Administrator for a one-year term, after which he cannot be reappointed until after three years. Although the Administrator again has "the powers formerly held by the king," he is again "bound by acts of legislature" and by many other related limits. His executive powers as an "administrator" (a somewhat bland or passive job description) seem designed to wipe away the vestiges of power and privilege held by the colonial governors. However, by attributing the main authority of government to the legislature, Jefferson was presented with new needs for other kinds of safeguards. For the judicial sphere, as well, the provisions remain the same in Jefferson's third draft, including various names for courts evocative of British models. The final section is considerably tighter and smoother than before in its presentation of a kind of Bill of Rights, yet again contains much the same provisions including a restriction against slavery.

Because the main focus of this chapter is on Jefferson and his ideas, there is little need or space here for an analysis of how his plans of 1776 for a Virginia constitution related to the constitution finally enacted. Although his preamble was indeed almost fully taken over by the Convention, his proposed constitution had only a partial and limited direct influence on the substantive contents of the official version, which he came to criticize so ardently on various grounds. In addition to Jefferson's three drafts composed prior to June 13, 1776, which were the only full-length preliminary plans drawn up for submission to the Virginia Convention, there were, in particular, two shorter alternate plans of government drawn up by George Mason, for whom Jefferson had high personal regard, as already indicated.[48] Mason's first plan of June 8–10, 1776, was revised by the committee of the House, which then "they have ordered to be printed for the perusal of its members," the revised plan dating from June 22. The draft reported by the committee on June 24 contained "amendments thereto offered in Convention." The constitution of Virginia in the form enacted by the Convention dates from June 29. A brief consideration below[49] of these stages in the genesis of the constitution must suffice for present purposes.

What remains distinctive about Jefferson's proposals for a Virginia constitution is, in essence, their strong provisions for democratic participation, especially in connection with the central role of the legislature. The people's representatives in both houses must originate and repeal laws, while the people at large in all the counties of the state must meet to approve the repeal of special important measures through an act of the legislature. The two-thirds quorum obtains in many different areas of the legislative process, including in the ratification of the constitution itself by the people in all the counties. Measures must not be passed by reducing the size of the quorum or by avoiding the people's participation; otherwise, power could become concentrated in fewer hands. Meanwhile, the three branches of government must be well separated in terms of appointment to them. The Administrator's limited, short-term role is precisely what his title suggests, rather than a more powerful position reminiscent of colonial governors. The concluding Bill of Rights—with restrictions against slavery and with guarantees of religious freedom—is further distinctive of Jefferson's outlook. Clearly, his strong blend of direct and indirect democracy was too decentralized and inefficient for many of his colleagues. But Jefferson was not deterred.

Revising the Constitution

After the official Virginia constitution was passed in 1776, Jefferson became a member of the Virginia House of Delegates for three years, from 1776 to 1779, amd then served as governor of Virginia from 1779 to 1781. After he retired as governor (having been briefly investigated by the legislature for his official conduct during the enemy advances on Virginia and Monticello), Jefferson wrote, in 1781, his *Notes on the State of Virginia.*[50] In it he made many pointed criticisms of current governmental affairs, especially on the part of the Virginia legislature through defects in the state's official constitution. A masterful broad survey of the state, ranging from its boundaries, rivers, and seaports to its commerce, finances, and state papers, this full-length book was the only one Jefferson ever wrote. Two of the twenty-three chapters (or "Queries") are devoted to the state's official constitution and its laws. Taken together, they offer a unique composite picture of his views on subjects of legislation and as such have been surprisingly neglected by historians. More generally, Jefferson was responding in part to the crisis of 1781 when British troops invaded Virginia; some of his compatriots sought to misuse the constitution of 1776 to promote a kind of dictatorship by exploiting its defects, which Jefferson sought to remedy.

Chapter (Query) XIII of Jefferson's *Notes on the State of Virginia* is entitled "Constitution." It gives a substantial critique of defects in the officially adopted constitution of Virginia, chiefly as regards the legislature. After tracing at length Virginia's changing government under British rule from the late-16th to late-18th centuries, with attention to legislative matters, Jefferson gives a brief outline of the independent Virginia constitution adopted in 1776. "This constitution," he declares, "was formed when we were new and unexperienced in the science of government. It was the first [!] too which was formed in the whole United States. No wonder then that time and trial have discovered very capital defects in it." Six main defects are then explored at increasing length, with particular regard to legislative topics. The first defect is that "[t]he majority of men in the state, who pay and fight for its support, are unrepresented in the legislature." The second defect is that "[a]mong those who share the representation, the shares are very unequal." The third defect is: "The senate is, by its constitution, too homogeneous with the house of delegates. Being chosen by the same electors, at the same time, and out of the same subjects, the choice falls of course on men of the same description. The purpose of establishing different houses of legislation is to introduce the influence of different interests or different principles. Thus in Great-Britain it is said that their constitution relies on the house of commons for honesty, and the lords for wisdom . . ."

However much Jefferson recognized the inherent centrality of legislative standpoints in the relationships between the three branches of government, as set forth in his own proposals for a Virginia constitution, he did not want the legislature to absorb or overwhelm the executive and judicial branches. He remained committed to a strong separation of the three powers. The fourth defect in the official Virginia constitution of 1776, as pointed out in Chapter or Query XIII of his *Notes*, concerns the dangers of letting the same people who control the legislature also command the executive and judicial branches.

> All the powers of government, legislative, executive, and judiciary, result to the legislative body. The concentrating these in the same hands is precisely the definition of despotic government. It will be no alleviation that these powers will be exercised by a plurality of hands, and not by a single one. 173 despots would surely be as oppressive as one. Let those who doubt it turn their eyes on the republic of Venice. As little will it avail us that they are chosen by ourselves. An *elective despotism* was not the government we fought for; but one which should not only be founded on free principles, but in which the

> powers of government should be so divided and balanced among several bodies of magistracy, as that no one could transcend their legal limits, without being effectually checked and restrained by the others. For this reason that convention, which passed the ordinance of government, laid its foundation on this basis, that the legislative, executive and judiciary department should be separate and distinct, so that no person should exercise the powers of more than one of them at the same time. But no barrier was provided between these several powers. The judiciary and executive members were left dependant on the legislative, for their subsistence in office, and some of them for their continuance in it. If therefore the legislature assumes executive and judiciary powers, no opposition is likely to be made; nor, if made, can it be effectual; because in that case they may put their proceedings into the form of an act of assembly, which will render them obligatory on the other branches. They have accordingly, in many instances, decided rights which should have been left to judiciary controversy. . . . And this is done with no ill intention. The views of the present members are perfectly upright. . . . And this will probably be the case for some time to come. But it will not be a very long time. Mankind soon learn to make interested uses of every right and power which they possess, or may assume. . . . The time to guard against corruption and tyranny, is before they shall have gotten hold on us. . . .[51]

In his fifth point about the defects in the official Virginia constitution of 1776, Jefferson launches in *Notes* XIII into a lengthy analysis of the alterability of that document. Leaving aside here his extended historical consideration of the early conventions themselves, in the movement toward independence from Great Britain, there are pertinent passages comparing the work of the conventions to that of ordinary legislatures. Jefferson aims to show that the official constitution itself is indeed alterable as legislation (upon which, therefore, the entire constitution of the state is founded, in another dimension of the legislative state).

> [T]he ordinary legislature may alter the constitution itself. On the discontinuance of assemblies, it became necessary to substitute in their place some other body, competent to the ordinary business of government, and to the calling forth the powers of the state for the maintenance of our opposition to Great-Britain. Conventions were therefore introduced . . . on the plan of the former house of Burgesses, to whose places they

> succeeded. . . . But they received in their creation no powers but what were given to every legislature before and since. They could not therefore pass an act transcendant to the powers of other legislatures. If the present assembly pass any act, and declare it shall be irrevocable by subsequent assemblies, the declaration is merely void, and the act repealable, as other acts are. So far, and no farther authorized, they organized the government by the ordinance entitled a Constitution or Form of government. It pretends to no higher authority than the other ordinances of the same session; it does not say, that it shall be perpetual; that it shall be unalterable by other legislatures; that it shall be transcendant above the powers of those, who they knew would have equal power with themselves. Not only the silence of the instrument is a proof they thought it would be alterable, but their own practice also: for this very convention, meeting as a House of Delegates in General Assembly with the new Senate in the autumn of that year, passed acts of assembly in contradiction to their ordinance of government; and every assembly from that time to this has done the same. I am safe therefore in the position, that the constitution itself is alterable by the ordinary legislature.[52]

Under his fifth point in *Notes* XIII about the Virginia constitution's defects, Jefferson gives three main refutations of objections "by some persons" to his views. First, he answers that their concept of special powers vested in the Virginia conventions for purposes of achieving independence is unfounded. In short, the regular assemblies have just as much power as do the conventions to model or remodel the government. Secondly, Jefferson presents an elaborate and learned account of the various significations of the word "constitution" in relation to legislation. In the passages to follow, many of the words in italics and quotations originally appeared in Latin, further reflecting his deep knowledge of classical Roman terms and texts. Indeed, his terminological approach to the language of legislation is remarkably consistent with that of Renaissance juristic writers like Corasius in connection with the promulgation, forms, forces and abrogation of legislation, as based in part on Roman models supplied by writers like Livy. Even more apparent here is Jefferson's deep knowledge of the history of English law (as is also seen in the following text's continuation in the note below). He cites English statutes under King Henry VIII and writings of the English jurist Edward Coke (1552–1634) in order to show the great influence of the civil law traditions upon English law in the issue at hand. What in this case joins laws, statutes, constitutions, and the like under the frame of legislation and legislative power is the continuing possibility of changing them when necessary, whether through new promulgation, amendment, or abrogation. A constitution issued in the form of legislation by a (properly empowered) legislative body is not thereafter unalterable scripture.

> They [opponents] urge that if the convention had meant that this instrument should be alterable, as their other ordinances were, they would have called it an ordinance: but they have called it a *constitution*, which *by force of the term* [originally in Latin] means "act above the power of the ordinary legislature." I answer, that *constitutio, constitutum, statutum, lex,* are convertible terms. "A *constitution* is called that which is made by the ruler. An *ordinance*, that which is rewritten by emperors or ordained. A *statute* is called the same as law [originally in Latin]." *Constitution* and *statute* were originally terms of the civil law, and from thence introduced by Ecclesiastics into the English law. Thus in the statute 25. Hen. 8. c. 19. §1 [King Henry VIII, in 1534–35] "*Constitutions* and *ordinances*" are used as synonimous. The term *constitution* has many other significations in physics and in politics; but in Jurisprudence, whenever it is applied to any act of the legislature, it invariably means a statute, law, or ordinance, which is the present case. No inference then of a different meaning can be drawn from the adoption of this title: on the contrary, we might conclude, that, by their affixing to it a term synonimous with ordinance, or statute, they meant it to be an ordinance or statute. But of what consequence is their meaning, where their power is denied? If they meant to do more than they had power to do, did this give them power?[53]

The sixth main defect in the official Virginia constitution of 1776, as more recently utilized under duress of enemy invasions of Virginia in 1781, revolves in Jefferson's *Notes* XIII around the Virginia legislature's reduction of its own quorum for passing laws to a majority of less than the whole body. The defect could lead, he believes, to the same kinds of heavy-handed measures perpetrated by British parliaments and early Virginia assemblies that fixed and reduced their own quorum of members needed for conducting business. Such action is against the principles of common law and common right as well as natural law. Nor does the dangerous situation at hand in 1781 justify the House of Delegates in voting to change the quorum's size, thereby setting a dangerous precedent that could lead ultimately to a despotism of the many, the few, or the one. In fact, Jefferson notes, a proposal was made in the House of Delegates in 1776 to create a temporary dictator to assume all powers—legislature, executive, judicial, etc.—in order to deal with the crisis of that period. The same proposition was again being made during the crisis of 1781 when Jefferson wrote these passages, and it almost passed in the Virginia legislature. No such power, he argues, can be derived from either "our ancient laws" or "our new constitution." The latter provides for a republican government and commonwealth, upon which is founded "the whole system of our laws" as well as "the exercise of all powers undefined by the laws." None of this can ever be suspended by the legislature, much less without consulting the people. So-called necessities do not justify abandoning the present form of government. Indeed, no other American state, he points out, has taken that path. Transfering power to other hands would constitute treason against the people and could result in a dictator who would later destroy the very people who gave him power. Some of his well-intentioned colleagues and friends, laments Jefferson, have succumbed to unreasoned fear of present dangers. They have been seduced by the fatal form of supposed republican government in ancient Rome that was adopted in times of crisis but led to aristocratic and dictatorial controls. Jefferson's extended discussion of the later Roman Republic holds potential parallels for Virginia and America if a temporary dictator were created and later enabled to become permanent, thereby destroying "public liberty."[54]

Jefferson closes his treatment in *Notes* XIII of the sixth defect in the official Virginia constitution of 1776 by citing the dangers of an oppressive, all-powerful legislature. He calls for a new convention to amend the constitution's defects. He seeks to reestablish the constitution, the state, and all three branches of government on a firmer foundation of laws. His statement on the separation of powers is tied to his further belief in the supremacy of the legislation and constitution of the state of Virginia, which are indeed the foundation of the state and the sovereign powers.

> Searching for the foundation of this proposition, I can find none which may pretend a colour of right or reason, but the defect before developed, that there being no barrier between the legislative, executive, and judiciary departments, the legislature may seize the whole: that having seized it, and possessing a right to fix their own quorum, they may reduce that quorum to one, whom they may call a chairman, speaker, dictator, or by any other name they please.—Our situation is indeed perilous, and I hope my countrymen will be sensible of it, and will apply,

> at a proper season, the proper remedy; which is a convention to fix the constitution, to amend its defects, to bind up the several branches of government by certain laws, which when they transgress their acts shall become nullities; to render unnecessary an appeal to the people, or in other words a rebellion, on every infraction of their rights, on the peril that their acquiescence shall be construed into an intention to surrender those rights.[55]

Rewriting the Constitution

As just seen, Jefferson ended his *Notes* XIII (1781) with a call for a new convention, in order "to fix the constitution, to amend its defects, to bind up the several branches of government by certain laws." Subsequently, he drafted in 1783 a wholly rewritten constitution for Virginia that was more of a new creation than merely a revision of the older one. Included as an appendix in his *Notes on the State of Virginia*,[56] it was intended for submission to the new convention that was expected to be called in the summer of 1783 by the Assembly of Virginia for the purpose of establishing a constitution. As Jefferson stated at the outset: "The following Draught of a Fundamental Constitution for the Commonwealth of Virginia was then prepared, with a Design of being proposed in such Convention, had it taken place." Noteworthy here is the even greater extent to which legislation and legislative power became for Jefferson the foundation of both sovereignty and the state in Virginia. The manner in which he placed renewed emphasis on the separation of legislative, executive, and judicial powers reinforces this point.

The formal preliminary statement in Jefferson's new proposed Virginia constitution in 1783 is addressed to the citizens of that state or commonwealth; it underscores the rights of Virginia and the other former American colonies of Great Britain to exist as "free, sovereign, and independent States." The "Sovereign Dispenser," God, has enabled this earthly sovereignty to come about and to continue through acknowledgement by Great Britain at the end of the American Revolution. The sovereignty of Virginia, like that of the other American states, has continued under the Articles of Confederation, through which they constitute the United States. It was, as here stated, "the legislature of the commonwealth of Virginia" that promulgated that state's constitution of 1776, under the duress of war. This was a temporary legislative measure designed to prevent anarchy at that point in time. The Virginia constitution of 1776 can and must now be changed and rewritten by subsequent legislatures for the changed new circumstances, as expedience requires. A new constitutional convention, of delegates chosen by the people, has been urged by the legislature, as here reported, in order to prepare a new constitution. The form of government in Jefferson's new proposed constitution, to be established by the delegates, would firmly separate the legislative, executive, and judicial powers, so that persons of one department could not serve in another. The legislature would be a General Assembly divided into a House of Delegates and Senate, both of which must approve a bill before it can become a law.[57]

The second article of Jefferson's new proposed Virginia constitution, which he drafted in 1783, deals with the executive authority in such a way as to reinforce the priority of the legislative power. The governor is to be chosen by both houses of the legislature for a five-year term—during which he is barred from holding other state offices and after which he is ineligible to be governor again. The executive has "those powers only, which are necessary to execute the laws" in connection with the administration of the government. Only by the legislature's approval, and that only occasionally, can the executive engage in any other activities, such as creating courts and a variety of others expressly listed; for these lie outside his ordinary powers. A range of other kinds of powers—from declaring war and contracting alliances to coining money and regulating weights—are left to the Confederation's Congress. All other powers that lie outside the Confederate's sphere and that are exercised by the governor are strictly "under the regulation of such laws as the legislature may . . . pass."[58]

Suffice it to say, that if Jean Bodin could have probed such strong explicit statements and their ramifications, he would surely have concluded that legislative sovereignty was an ultimate guiding principle. Nevertheless, under Jefferson's proposed new Virginia constitution, the legislature must not be allowed to acquire the heavy-handed authority he felt it exerted in the years following the passage of the official version of the Virginia constitution in 1776, as he makes plain in a section on "limits of power."[59]

Jefferson's typical great interest in the legislative process is manifest in the fourth and final article in his proposed new Virginia constitution of 1783, following the first three articles on the legislative, executive, and judicial branches of government. Here he gives special attention to the intricate series of stages through which all bills must pass before they can become laws. By subjecting the passage of bills to this arduous journey through various departments of the government and its legislature, Jefferson seemed intent on preventing its undue acquisition of power. The initial parts of Article IV, which is entitled "Council of Revision," thus deal with the "revision" of bills as they pass though the difficult yet democratic stages on their way to final enactment (if they survive this process).[60]

The ensuing parts of Article IV take up in turn matters pertaining to the national Confederation and its congress (under the Articles of Confederation), to which Virginia delegates are sent. "The Confederation is made a part of this constitution, subject to such future alterations as shall be agreed to by the legislature of this state, and by all the other confederating states." The three short sections that follow on habeas corpus, the military, and printing-presses are all that Jefferson includes here by way of the kind of bill of rights that he appended to his previously proposed constitutions in 1776. "The benefits of this writ of Habeas Corpus shall be extended, by the legislature, to every person within this state . . ." The military is subject to the civil power, and the press cannot be subjected to restraints other than liability to prosecution for making false statements. The final longer section is entitled "Convention" and deals in particular with the convention that Jefferson thought (or hoped) would meet soon to rewrite the existing Virginia constitution of 1776. "The [new] constitution being authorized only to amend those laws which constituted the form of government, no general dissolution of the whole system of laws can be supposed to have taken their place: but all laws in force at the meeting of this convention, and not inconsistent with this constitution, remain in full force, subject to alterations by the ordinary legislature."[61] Once again, the legislative state and legislative sovereignty are acutely affirmed by Jefferson.

In the end, the efforts of both Jefferson and Madison to reform the prevailing official Virginia constitution of 1776 proved fruitless, perhaps due in part to Patrick Henry's hostility. It was not until 1830, after Jefferson's death, that it was finally replaced. Thus Jefferson retained his objections of 1781 to the 1776 constitution as stated in Query XIII of his *Notes on the State of Virginia.*

Yet Jefferson's proposed constitution drafted in mid-1783 (which appeared as an appendix in the privately printed edition of his *Notes* in 1785) remained another testament to his early, consummate abilities as a constitution-maker in the crucial years prior to the U.S. constitution of 1787. That was the same year, 1787, in which Jefferson's proposed new Virginia constitution appeared as Appendix 2 in the first regular edition of his *Notes*. There soon followed in the next year, 1788, the extensive "Observations" on Jefferson's proposed constitution for Virginia (in the 1787 *Notes*) by his close friend Madison, the architect a year earlier of the U.S. Constitution. Madison, who had received from Jefferson back in mid-1783 a draft copy, included here extended observations on "[t]he power of the [Virginia] Legislature" and on "republican patriots and lawgivers" more generally. These interconnections render Jefferson's legislative orientations as a constitution-maker all the more instructive for a fuller appraisal of Madison's work on the U.S. federal Constitution, to which Madison also made a number of references in his "Observations."[62]

Revising the Laws

Jefferson's great interest in the laws of the state of Virginia is reflected in Query XIV, entitled "Laws," in his *Notes on the State of Virginia.* His efforts to revise and codify the Virginia laws, as described there and in his "Autobiography," marked a special contribution on his part, even if, as in the case of his plans for a Virginia constitution, they did not bring the kind of acceptance he had envisioned. A recent editor of Jefferson's *Notes* has underscored the uniqueness of Jefferson's efforts, going back to his student days in Williamsburg, to find, preserve, restore, collect, and publish the scattered and neglected historical records and texts of Virginia's laws. "In his preoccupation with such materials, Jefferson is a notable and isolated figure among eighteenth century Virginia book collectors. . . . [These attempts] constitute probably his greatest contribution as a book collector." As for Jefferson's related endeavors toward a codification: "Jefferson's continued efforts to remodel the legal structure of Virginia in accordance with 'truly republican' principles culminated in the 'Report of the Committee of the [three] Revisors' . . . submitted to the Virginia Assembly on June 18, 1779. . . . [It] . . . aimed at 'reforming the entire structure of law so as to strip it of all vestiges of its earlier monarchical aspects and to bring it into conformity with republican principles.'" The report was not considered or adopted as a whole by the legislature, but over fifty of its separate 126 proposed bills later became, by 1786, enacted into law.[63]

Following a discussion of the early history of Virginia laws under English rule, from the 1600s to his own day,[64] Jefferson in *Notes* XIV gives a synopsis of the plan that he and two others (Edmund Pendleton and George Wythe) submitted to the legislature for revising and codifying the laws of Virginia. To this he added highlights of the numerous individual bills that were offered in the plan. These included controversial measures on slavery and other notable provisions on religious freedom and on education.

> Many of the laws which were in force during the monarchy being relative merely to that form of government, or inculcating principles inconsistent with republicanism, the first assembly which met after the establishment of the commonwealth appointed a committee to revise the whole code, to reduce it

> into proper form and volume, and report it to the assembly. This work has been executed by three gentlemen [Jefferson and two others], and reported; but probably will not be taken up till a restoration of peace shall leave to the legislature leisure to go through such a work.
>
> The plan of the revisal was this. The common law of England, by which is meant, that part of the English law which was anterior to the date of the oldest statues extant, is made the basis of the work. It was thought dangerous to attempt to reduce it to a text: it was therefore left to be collected from the usual monuments of it. Necessary alterations in that, and so much of the whole body of the British statutes, and of acts of assembly, as were thought proper to be retained, were digested into 126 new acts, in which simplicity of stile [*sic*] was aimed at, as far as was safe. The following are the most remarkable alterations proposed:
>
> To change the rules of descent, so as that the lands of any person dying intestate shall be divisible equally among all his children. . . .
>
> To make slaves distributable among the next of kin. . . .
>
> To have all public expenses . . . supplied by assessments on the citizens, in proportion to their property.
>
> To hire undertakers for keeping the public roads in repair. . . .
>
> To define with precision the rules whereby aliens should become citizens. . . .
>
> To establish religious freedom on the broadest bottom.
>
> To emancipate all slaves born after passing the act. . . .
>
> The revised code further proposes to proportion crimes and punishments. . . .
>
> Another object of the revisal is, to diffuse knowledge more generally through the mass of the people.
>
> [Etc.][65]

Jefferson's prodigious labors as a Virginia legislator on the enormous project known as "The Revisal of the [Virginia] Laws" has remained a lasting monument to his abiding interests in the whole subject of legislation. Jefferson's bill explaining the complex project[66] was submitted to the Virginia legislature in October of 1776 and was passed the following month, with Jefferson and four others appointed as a committee for this purpose. The committee's plan of January 1777 further reveals the ambitious scope of this legislative project.[67] The 126 bills reported by the committee of revisors in June 1779 encompassed a vast array of subjects.[68] Perhaps the most celebrated bill was for establishing religious freedom, a distinctive Jeffersonian hallmark; drafted by Jefferson in 1777, it was eventually adopted by the Virginia General Assembly in 1786.[69] The immense complexity of this project to revise the laws of Virginia—which Jefferson outlined in his Autobiography and to which he devoted three years as its guiding force—has been well described by Julian Boyd. In his lengthy editorial note to his typically masterful presentation of "The Revisal of the Laws," Boyd indicates the relationship between the failed efforts by Jefferson to win passage of his proposed Virginia constitution in mid-1776 to his ensuing labors for a revision and systematization of Virginia laws.[70] Also included in Boyd's magisterial edition of Jefferson's *Papers* are multitudinous other writings by Jefferson pertaining to his interests and activities as Virginia legislator during the years 1776 to 1779.[71]

"[T]he labors of this republican Solon"

Secondary works at times (differently than here) dealing with Jefferson's prodigious efforts for Virginia in constitution-making and legislative systematizing have on occasion cast him in the light of legendary ancient lawgivers like Solon and Lycurgus. On the American national scene, for which his Virginia state endeavors in these affairs furnished a kind of microcosm, such comparisons might be even more apropos. In any case, a concluding historiographical comment will help to draw together some germane points.

In a short general chapter on "The Way of a Legislator: Freeing the Land, 1776–1779," in his multi-volume work on Jefferson and his era, Dumas Malone aptly observed: "The years during which Jefferson was a legislator in his own Commonwealth comprised his most creative period as a statesman during the American Revolution, and there was no part of his entire career that he afterwards looked back upon with greater satisfaction [as in his later Autobiography]."[72] Malone's appreciation of the singular regard Jefferson himself had for his period as a legislator (from Oct. 1776 to June 1779) in the Virginia House of Delegates is followed by another telling chapter on Jefferson as "Architect of Laws: Slavery and Crime." Preceding chapters are also devoted to Jefferson's early years as a Virginia lawyer and member of the Virginia House of Burgesses (the predecessor of the House of Delegates), in addition to Jefferson's efforts in 1776 to frame a new Virginia constitution as well as a new set of principles for American independence.

In a chapter on Jefferson as "Virginia Reformer" in his book on *Jefferson and the New Nation*, Merrill D. Peterson has discussed Jefferson's quest, in the drive for revolutionary independence, to gain acceptance for his proposed new Virginia constitution and then for a new system or code of laws for that state. He quotes from Jefferson's Autobiography on how the Revisal of Laws "brought [together] so much of the Common Laws as it was thought necessary to alter, all the British statutes from Magna Carta to the present day, and all the laws of Virginia from the establishment of our legislature ... which we thought should be retained [within 126 bills] ..." Peterson then goes on to state: "[T]he major corpus [of the bills in the Revisal of Laws] was not taken up by the [Virginia] assembly until 1785, when to Jefferson's undying gratitude, 'by the unwearied exertions of Mr. Madison, in opposition to endless quibbles [etc.] ..., most of the bills were passed by the legislature with little alteration.' He [Jefferson] was justifiably proud of his Revision of the Laws, even though the original aim of a revised code miscarried. The *Report* was never acted on as a unit; and the revisal became, to employ Madison's figure, 'a mine of legislative wealth,' rather than a single great monument of legislation. And a mine . . . not only for Virginia but for many new American states over several decades." Moreover: "The revisal, ample and compendious as it was, did not exhaust the labors of this republican Solon [!]. In the day-to-day affairs of state, Jefferson ... drafted reports and bills on every variety of subject. As Julian P. Boyd has observed, 'He was in himself a veritable legislative drafting bureau.' " Jefferson's bills dealt with such subjects as lands, crime and punishment, religion, education, and slavery; the revisers' bill on slavery, finally enacted in 1785, was mostly a "digest" of older laws and contained no provision for emancipation. "Jefferson's name is omnipresent in the legislative history of Virginia during these formative years of statehood ... [, even though] he attempted too much too soon" and became "[d]isappointed by mindless and selfish opposition to reform."[73]

It is true that numerous other books on Jefferson have included germane general discussion of his legislative interests and activities in connection with the Virginia constitution and with legal reform in that state. However, there has been relative neglect of his legislative thought *per se* as a foundation for the concepts of sovereignty and state in the writings featured here. Other secondary works have studied Jefferson as a lawyer, a constitutionalist, a man of statecraft and government, a nationalist and republican, and so forth, whether through his Virginia writings or more broadly. Jefferson's views on legislative issues have sometimes entered into wider books on such topics as the Declaration of Independence. Many other kinds of legislative angles can sometimes be found in secondary literature on Jefferson. Yet the central legislative core of his writings has not before been subjected to intensive analyses in line with this series on sovereignty and state. Much the same verdict can be rendered when we turn from Jefferson's Virginia constitutions and his Virginia Revisal of Laws to his more national ideas centered around the Declaration of Independence and the U.S. Constitution. Even Jefferson's collaborations with Adams and Madison in these areas have not yet been adequately examined from the perspective of legislation. Indeed, "the Jefferson image in the American mind," whether in a popular or scholarly sense, has generally been focused on issues of democracy, freedom, and equality at the expense of his legislative thought that was often pivotal for those and related issues.[74]

3. JEFFERSON'S DECLARATIONS OF AMERICAN SOVEREIGNTY

From Jefferson's concerns with the state of Virginia, we turn to his wider views on the emerging nation-state of America. From his proposals for a new Virginia constitution and system of legislation, we turn to his Declaration of Independence and his ideas relating to the U.S. Constitution. Those Virginia writings formed an important background to these national writings. By thus dwelling on the fundamental writings of Jefferson during his formative period, we can arrive at a basic understanding of the origins of legislative sovereignty and the legislative state in the thought of the most celebrated writer among the American founding fathers during the genesis of the new country.

Summary View

Perhaps the most extensive and explanatory of Jefferson's writings in the immediate background to his Declaration of Independence of 1776 was his *Summary View*, composed two years earlier in 1774 prior to his call for American revolutionary independence from the British empire. As Julian Boyd has succinctly characterized it: "This draft of resolutions to be presented to the Virginia Convention of Aug. 1774, and intended by TJ to serve as instructions for the guidance of the Virginia delegates to the first Continental Congress in preparing an address to the King [George III], is best known to the world as *A Summary View of the Rights of British America*—the title given this paper by TJ's friends, who printed it without his knowledge when he, because of illness, could not attend the Convention."[75] Hence the title in Boyd's edition is "Draft Instructions to the Virginia Delegates in the Continental Congress" (July, 1774).[76]

Jefferson begins his *Summary View* by directly and closely linking the colonists' grievances in the First Continental Congress to the central issue of legislative sovereignty: "Resolved that ... an ... address be presented to his majesty . . . as chief magistrate of the British empire . . . [concerning the Americans'] complaints which are excited by many . . . usurpations . . . by the legislature of one part of the empire upon those rights which god and the laws have given equally . . . to all." There follow extended historical discussions by Jefferson concerning the earlier history of laws in England, going back to the Saxon "system of laws which has so long been the glory and protection of that country [England, which, by contrast, never tried to reduce the Saxon system to dependent status]." Regarding Britain's American colonies in the 17th century, there is reference here in various ways to "sovereignty of . . . state." Britain later rejected provisions on free trade that had been authorized for Virginia by its House of Burgesses in agreement with Britain, which in contradistinction continued to have its own authority to conduct "free trade . . . according to the laws of that Commonwealth." On into the 18th century, there has been a series of unjust "acts of British parliament" prohibiting or restricting all sorts of American economic activity. But "experience confirms the propriety of those political principles which exempt us from the jurisdiction of the British parliament. The true ground on which we declare these acts void is that the British parliament has no right to exercise authority over us." Driving these points home, Jefferson succinctly sets forth the principle (first articulated by Corasius and Bodin in the 16th century) that each state has, or should have, the inherent power to legislate for its own affairs, independently of any supposed foreign or outside jurisdictions over it. This principle of legislative self-determination applies here to the American "states" (not "colonies"), individually and collectively, as well as to Britain itself. Although not yet advocating a complete revolutionary independence from Britain, Jefferson's arguments for American legislative sovereignty already seem to anticipate precisely that, if only as the logical conclusion to his argument here.

> One free and independent legislature hereby takes upon itself to suspend the powers of another, free and independent as itself, thus exhibiting a phaenomenon, unknown in nature, the creator creature of its own power. . . . [H]is majesty's subjects here can [not] be persuaded to believe that they hold their political existence at the will of a British parliament. . . . Can any one reason be assigned why 100,000 electors in . . . Great Britain should give law to four millions in the states of America, every individual of whom is equal to every individual of them in virtue [etc.] . . .? [Certain strictures against Boston by the British parliament aim at] setting a precedent for investing his majesty with legislative power. . . . [T]hese are the acts of power

> assumed by a body of men foreign to our constitutions, and unacknowledged by our laws; against which we do . . . protest. And we . . . intreat his majesty, as yet the only mediatory power between the several states of the British empire, to recommend to his Parliament . . . the total revocation of these acts, which . . . may yet . . . cause . . . further discontents . . . among us.[77]

Jefferson then proceeds in his *Summary View* to denounce the British government's "executive" attempts to annul the legislation and legislative powers of the Americans. "[W]e next . . . consider the conduct of his majesty, as holding the executive powers of the laws of these [American] states. . . . By the constitution of Great Britain as well as [the colonial constitutions] of the several American states, his majesty possesses the power of refusing to pass into a law any bill which has already passed the other two branches of legislature." Here Jefferson is speaking as much in terms of Britain as of America, for which he is not yet seeking revolutionary independence. Nonetheless: "It is now therefore the great office of his majesty to resume the exercise of his negative power, and to prevent the passage of laws by any one legislature of the empire which might bear injuriously on the rights and interests of another. Yet this will not excuse the wanton exercise of this power which we have seen his majesty practice on the laws of the American legislatures. For the most trifling reasons, . . . his majesty has rejected laws of the most salutary tendency."[78] Here, as elsewhere, in his *Summary View*, Jefferson is careful to suggest to the British authorities that Americans still seek to work, as states (if not as colonies), within the British empire, while leaving strong hints to the contrary if Americans' legislative concerns are not met.

Continuing this litany of legislative woes in his *Summary View*, Jefferson protests the "still more oppressive" way in which "his majesty [still a gesture of deference] . . . has laid his [American colonial] governors under such restrictions that they can pass no law of any moment unless it have such suspending clause: so that, however immediate may be the call for legislative interposition, the law cannot be executed till it has twice crossed the Atlantic, by which time the evil may have spent it's [*sic*] whole force." Even worse is "a late instruction to his majesty's governor of the colony of Virginia, by which he is forbidden to assent to any law for the division of a county, unless the new county will consent to have no representation in assembly . . ." By trying to take away "the glorious right of representation," the British king would have Virginians—and all Americans—"submit themselves [as] the absolute slaves of his sovereign will" and "confine the legislative body." In this light, Jefferson points out that the British "constitution" founded at the time of the Glorious Revolution in 1688 did not allow the monarch arbitrarily to suspend or dissolve parliament if it passed measures obnoxious to him, although such is precisely what has more lately been attempted in Britain as a parallel to what has been attempted by the crown in relation to the American colonies and their legislatures.[79]

Then follows in *Summary View* a remarkably clear statement on legislative sovereignty, in line with Bodinian tradition on each state's rightful innate ability to legislate for its own affairs. It not only anticipates the final independence declared two years later in 1776, but also establishes the fuller foundation for legislative sovereignty in Jefferson's Declaration of Independence, a much shorter and less elaborate document than his *Summary View* of 1774. The excerpt to follow also suggests the wider extent to which Jefferson was also influenced in his Declaration of Independence by Locke's ideas on a range of topics: representation, dissolution of governments, natural rights rooted in the original state of nature, sovereignty of the people, rightful revolution against unjust rulers, and, again via the Bodinian tradition, legislative sovereignty. King George III and the British parliament could have little doubt as to Jefferson's veiled threats of further action. At issue, here as elsewhere in *Summary View*, is the independent legislative sovereignty of the American states, with anticipation of a more national legislative statehood able to meet their common threat.

> But your majesty or your Governors have carried this power beyond every limit known or provided for by the laws. After dissolving one house of representatives, they have refused to call another, so that for a great length of time the legislature provided by the laws has been out of existence. From the nature of things, every society must at all times possess within itself the sovereign powers of legislation. The feelings of human nature revolt against the supposition of a state so situated as that it may not in any emergency provide against dangers which perhaps threaten immediate ruin. While these bodies are in existence to whom the people have delegated the powers of legislation, they alone possess and may exercise those powers. But when they are dissolved by the lopping off of one or more of their branches, the power reverts to the people, who may use it to unlimited extent, either assembling together in person, sending deputies [as in a new legislature], or in any other way they may think proper. We forbear to trace consequences further; the dangers are conspicuous with which this practice is replete.[80]

As for the presence of British troops in America, the territorial integrity and autonomy of the American states, individually and collectively, are based on the laws of the land. "From the nature and purpose of civil instruction, all the lands within the limits which any particular society has circumscribed around itself, are assumed by that society, and subject to their allotment only. This may be done by themselves assembled collectively, or by their legislature to which they may have delegated sovereign authority . . ." However, "his majesty has . . . sent forth among us . . . armed forces, not made up of the people here, nor raised by the authority of our laws. . . . But his majesty has no right to land a single armed man on our shores; and those whom he sends are liable to our laws . . ." The same kind of reasoning applies to Britain herself: "[In] Great Britain, . . . liberties would not be safe if armed men of another country . . . might be brought into the realm . . . without the consent of their legislature. He [the king] therefore applied to parliament who [*sic*] passed an act to that purpose. . . ." The same logic extends again to America: "In like manner is his majesty restrained in every part of the empire. He possesses indeed the executive power of the laws in every state; but they are the laws of the particular state which he is to administer within that state, and not those of any one within the limits of another. Every state must judge for itself the number of armed men which they may safely trust among them . . ."[81]

The alternately condemnatory and conciliatory outlook on the British crown and parliament in Jefferson's *Summary View* reaches a climax in its final passages. The harsh use and context of the word "criminal" is striking: "To render these proceedings still more criminal against our laws, instead of subjecting the military to the civil power, his majesty has expressly made the civil subordinate to the military." With bluntness, Jefferson asserts that he need not "flatter" the king with false obsequious praise. For "kings are the servants, not the proprietors of the people," and "[t]he whole art of government consists in the art of being honest." Yet Jefferson appeals to the king's better nature, urging him to see the light, to open his heart and mind to liberal views, and not to be a blot on British history by denying "the rights of human nature." "Let no act be passed by any one legislature which may infringe on the rights and liberties of another. This is the important post in which fortune has placed you, holding the balance of a great, if a well poised empire." This singular, permeating issue of legislative sovereignty in *Summary View* includes here a related remark on taxation: "Still less let it be proposed that our properties within our own territories shall be taxed or regulated by any power on earth but our own." The final exhortation to the king "to procure redress of these our great grievances" is full of respect as well as warning. "It is neither our wish nor our interest to separate from her [Great Britain]." However, the strong statements on the rightful innate legislative sovereignty of the American states in Jefferson's *Summary View* provided a strong partial basis for his declaration of America's new legislative independence and sovereignty as a nation-state two years later in 1776.[82]

Declaration of Causes

"The Declaration of the Causes and Necessity for Taking Up Arms was one of several addresses issued by Congress [in Philadelphia] in the summer of 1775 with the object of justifying to the American people and to the world the necessity for armed resistance."[83] As Julian Boyd further explains in his lengthy editorial note, the authorship of the Declaration of Causes is a complicated issue that has long been debated. In addressing it, Boyd presents three preliminary drafts: "Jefferson's Composition Draft," "Jefferson's Fair Copy for the Committee," and "John Dickinson's Composition Draft," together with "The Declaration as Adopted by Congress [July, 1775]." For purposes here, Jefferson's "Fair Copy" sheds further good light on the developing central ideas of legislative sovereignty closely associated with Jefferson and other founders in the immediate background to the Declaration of Independence of 1776. Although considerably shorter and less expansive than his *Summary View*, Jefferson's "Fair Copy" of the Declaration of Causes contains many illuminating details and ideas.[84]

Roughly the first half of Jefferson's "Fair Copy" of the Declaration of Causes, following the several preliminary lines furnishing a kind of working title,[85] consists mostly of a strong series of legislative complaints against the British government. It begins as follows: "The large strides of late taken by the *legislature of Great Britain* towards establishing over these colonies their absolute rule, and the hardiness of the present attempt to effect by force of arms what by law or right they could never effect, *render* it necessary for us also to change the ground of opposition, and to close with their last appeal from reason to arms." The document goes on to point out, again in line with Bodinian tradition on each state's rightful inherent ability to legislate for its own affairs, that, historically, the American colonists "established civil societies with various forms of constitution(s) (*but possessing all what is inherent in all, the full and perfect powers of legislation*). . . . [T]hey arranged themselves by charters of compact under . . . the same common king, who thus completed their powers of full and perfect legislation and became the link of union between the several parts of the empire." In more recent times, however, "it pleased our sovereign to make a change. . . . [He] assumed a power of unlimited legislation over the

Colonies of America. . . . [T]he spirit of the new legislation . . . leaves no room to doubt the consequence of acquiescence under it."

Various examples are then given. "[S]everal acts of parliament passed" recently have "undertaken to give and grant our money without our consent." Moreover, "they have declared that American subjects charged with certain offences" shall be taken to England "to be tried before the very persons against whose pretended sovereignty the offence is supposed to be committed; they have attempted fundamentally to alter the form of government in one of [the] Colonies, a form . . . secured by charters on the part of the crown and confirmed by acts of its own legislature." In addition, "by one act they have suspended the powers of the American legislature; & by another have declared they may legislate for us themselves in all cases whatsoever."

In short, the British government has sought "to erect a despotism of unlimited extent." How, then, "shall a British parliament encounter the rude assault?" In roughly the second half of the document, the "cruel aggression" of British troops against Boston, Lexington, and Concord is briefly recounted, along with other related matters. But the guiding framework of the document as a whole is thus clearly legislative in scope.

The same distinctive and forceful focus on legislative issues in Jefferson's "Fair Copy" of the Declaration of Causes is also present in his somewhat longer "Composition Draft," but not in Dickinson's "Composition Draft" or in the Declaration as adopted by Congress. Jefferson's "Composition Draft," for example, begins, like his "Fair Copy," with a strong statement on the British legislature's recent strides toward absolute rule over the American colonies. Then follows much the same material found in the "Fair Copy," again with significant echoes of Jefferson's lengthier *Summary View*. In counterdistinction, both Dickinson's "Composition Draft" (twice the length of Jefferson's "Fair Copy") and Congress' final text (similar in length to "Composition Draft") omit any such opening legislative focus and instead possess a more philosophical and religious quality. The rather rambling beginning part of Dickinson's "Composition Draft" is filled with frequent multiple references to such items as "Divine Author of Existence," "contemplating the works of Creation," God's "Goodness & Wisdom," "Reverence for our great Creator," "Principles of Humanity," "Dictates of Common Sense," "Welfare of Mankind," etc. To be sure, there do follow a variety of statements relating to the abuses of the British legislature or parliament toward the American colonies, in violation of those higher matters and without due reverence for them. Yet such legislative statements tend to be further overshadowed by other more general considerations. The same holds true for Congress' final text, yet it has more specifics on the pressing struggles at hand, together with more clarity of presentation. Whereas these two documents appeal more to higher principles and to the better natures of king and parliament, the two Jefferson texts largely omit that idealism, along with the deference found in his *Summary View*; they now adopt a more compelling, even pungent, case for outright action against the government and troops of Britain. It may be that Congress' adoption of Dickinson's idealism in the Declaration of Causes in 1775 influenced Jefferson's much different idealistic preamble for Congress a year later in his Declaration of Independence, which in its main body drew upon Jefferson's previous writings pointing up the legislative characteristics of sovereignty and state. It may also have seemed ironic to Jefferson not only that many of the passages deleted from his draft Declaration of Independence by his fellow committeemen dealt with higher general principles, but also that Dickinson was the only one at the Congress in Philadelphia not to sign the Declaration of Independence, as Jefferson sharply noted when introducing the version included in his Autobiography.[86]

Declaration of Independence

The vast secondary literature on the American Declaration of Independence has inspected it from seemingly every angle. Yet new valuable insights continue to be gained into this endlessly fascinating foundational document. The great weight of legislative and other evidence presented above, within broader parameters of the present series, affords a fresh appraisal of the Declaration of Independence as a declaration of the sovereign national legislative independence of the united American legislative state(s). In this connection, it is again surprising that little adequate attention has heretofore been drawn to legislative sovereignty and the legislative state in the above other early writings by Jefferson, which have long been deemed most crucial in the immediate background to his Declaration of Independence and which serve to show its fuller legislative scope.

In a nutshell, the central part of Jefferson's self-styled "original Rough draught" of the Declaration of Independence (along with his ensuing version as amended by the Committee of Five and by Congress and later included in his Autobiography) revolved around his lengthy lists of charges aagainst the British crown that were contained in what has been called his initial "composition draft." The latter draft had presented a slightly modified *numerical* listing of the charges contained in Jefferson's preamble to the Virginia constitution. He drew as well from his *Summary View* and Declaration of Causes. Jefferson then expanded and reworked his listing of legislative and other charges that had appeared in his Virginia preamble. This central portion of his "original" draft Declaration of Independence remained intact in Congress' adopted version. Yet much of Jefferson's draft discussions on related other matters such as tyranny, slavery, and colonial history were either deleted or altered by the Committee and by Congress. Jefferson included the amended version—with the deletions, rewordings, and additions—in what Boyd has called his "Notes of Proceedings in the Continental Congress," which Jefferson later incorporated into his Autobiography.[87]

The Declaration of Independence was indeed above all—from Jefferson's "original draft" to the version adopted by Congress—a declaration of sovereign national independent statehood and self-determination. When introducing the amended text of his Declaration of Independence in his "Notes" and Autobiography, Jefferson made one such statement pertaining to independent statehood: "The delegates from Virginia moved [in early June, 1776] . . . that the Congress should declare that these United colonies are, and of right ought to be, free and independent states [!], that they are absolved from all allegiance to the British crown, and that all political connection between them and the state of Great Britain is, and ought to be, totally dissolved . . ."[88] These central points also appeared in Jefferson's "original draft" and in Congress' adopted Declaration. Jefferson's "original draft" wording was: ". . . and finally we do assert and declare these colonies to be free and independent states." Congress' adopted version, also referring to "free and independent states," was essentially the same. Left unchanged from Jefferson's draft to Congress' final version was: ". . . and that as free and independent states, they have full power [sovereignty] to levy war, conclude peace, contract alliances, establish commerce, and to do all other acts and things which independent states may of right do." One recalls that in *Republic* I, 10 and elsewhere, Bodin had presented a strikingly similar list (likewise beginning with war and peace) of the marks of sovereign power in a state, including taxation. Bodin had grouped all such marks under the highest, most all-encompassing power, namely, legislative sovereignty. The enduring Bodinian tradition in this regard embraced republican as well as monarchical governments.

In this light, the Declaration's list of charges against the British king and his parliament was ultimately a statement on the illegitimate and despotic legislative powers and acts of the British government, in contradistinction to the rightful sovereign legislative authority of the American states. Whereas Jefferson at various points directly named the British "parliament" as the obvious source of British legislative acts against Americans, Jefferson's colleagues deleted such explicit references, so as not to dignify parliament's "pretended" powers both to make laws for Americans and to abrogate Americans' own laws. The following excerpts (with our brackets) of charges in Jefferson's version are the same wording as in Congress' final version and highlight, as Jefferson's enduring paradigm, the underlying comprehensive theme of legislation running throughout. This theme encompasses topics (not unlike those included by Bodin under legislation's sway) of taxation, representation, population, judicial powers, jurisdiction, courts, trials, warfare, constitutions, crime, trade, and so forth, even "in all cases whatsoever." Moreover, judicial and jurisdictional matters are ultimately here (as in Bodin) included under the sovereignty of legislation.

> He [the king, George III] has refused his assent to laws the most wholesome and necessary for the public good.
>
> He has forbidden his governors to pass laws of immediate and pressing importance, unless suspended in their operation till his assent should be obtained . . . [, which] he has utterly neglected to [give]. . . .
>
> He has refused to pass other laws for the accommodation of large districts of people, unless those people would relinquish the right of representation in the legislature. . . .
>
> He has called together legislative bodies at places unusual . . . and distant . . . for the sole purpose of fatiguing them into compliance with his measures.
>
> He has dissolved representative houses [of legislature] repeatedly. . . .
>
> He has refused for a long time after such dissolutions to cause others to be elected, whereby the legislative powers . . . have returned to the people at large . . ., the state remaining . . . exposed to . . . dangers of invasion . . . and convulsions. . . .
>
> He has endeavored to prevent the population of these states[,] . . . obstructing the laws for naturalization of foreigners, refusing to pass others to encourage their migrations hither. . . .
>
> He has . . . refus[ed] . . . his assent to laws for establishing judiciary powers. . . .
>
> He has kept among us in times of peace standing armies . . . without the consent of our legislatures. . . .
>
> He has . . . subject[ed] us to a jurisdiction foreign to our constitutions and unacknowledged by our laws, giving his assent to their acts of pretended legislation[:] for quartering . . . troops among us; for protecting them . . . from punishment for any murders . . . [in] these states; for cutting off our trade . . .; for imposing taxes on us without our consent; for depriving us . . . of trial by jury; for transporting us beyond seas . . . for [trial] . . .; for abolishing the free system of English laws in a neigh-

> boring province . . .; for taking away our charters, abolishing our most valuable laws, and altering fundamentally the forms of our governments; for suspending our own legislatures, and declaring themselves invested with power to legislate for us in all cases whatsoever.[89]

As here set forth, the inherent independent power of a state to make "laws . . . necessary for the public good" in conducting its own affairs was an idea harking back to Corasius, Bodin, and their contextual uses of maxims and terms of Roman law. These had included: "The welfare (safety) of the people is the supreme law," "Necessity knows no law," and the state (*res-publica*) is a "public thing" founded on legislated "public law" (*lex publica*). Likewise cited toward the beginning of the Declaration is "their [Americans'] safety and happiness" and "their future security." Traditional concepts of necessity or reason of state are here influential in the Declaration along with notions of popular sovereignty.

In the preceding lengthy charges against the king—constituting the main part of the Declaration of Independence in both Jefferson's draft and in Congress' adopted version—all clearly revolve around legislative factors of sovereignty and state. This orientating feature obtains both in the rightful powers and acts of the American states and in the wrongful ones of the British government. The various other charges against the king that follow, in the same kind of "He has" constructions, are largely subsidiary to, or derivative from, the primary charges just presented.

True, there has long remained some uncertainty and controversy as to exactly what conditions or situations the Declaration was referring to in many of the initial legislative charges as given above.[90] However, the document's overwhelming broader concentration on legislative factors of sovereignty and state is the crucial point to consider here. That is to say, the exact meaning and contexts of the Declaration's initial (and ensuing) legislative charges have long puzzled many scholars, who have often regarded them as not clearly or closely related to the immediate historical situation, even at times supposing them to be rhetorical. To be sure, many valuable clues and parallels have been found by historians in such areas as: Jefferson's similar lists in his own previous writings, state and local declarations from that period, events and records of those times in America and Britain, the English Declaration (Bill) of Rights against King James II, and writings by Locke and others. Those leads can be helpful and have long been pursued by historians in their search for clarification.[91] Nonetheless, the enduring Bodinian tradition of legislation sovereignty and the legislative state opened up for

Jefferson a crucial dimension not yet duly noticed by students of his distinctive constructs in the Declaration of Independence. Without full consideration of that document's place in the broader history of legislative thought going back to Bodin, answers to these conundrums will be incomplete, as in so many other cases where legislative factors have been neglected.

Also not to be overlooked are various other statements toward the end of the Declaration of Independence that further deal with the legislation and sovereignty of the American states. By congressional proclamation, these states are now officially declared to be the independent "United States of America."[92]

Bodinian Dimensions

As already noted, a classic study of the American revolution's "ideological origins," by Bernard Bailyn, has included a significant section entitled "Sovereignty."[93] In it he made prominent references at the outset to Jean Bodin's ideas on sovereignty, explaining that they entered British thought during the mid-17th-century civil wars and the 1688 revolution. Professor Bailyn succinctly summarized the English tradition of Bodinian sovereignty—which enormously influenced Locke (as well as Hobbes)—in terms of the ultimate, undivided absolute power either in monarchical or in parliamentary democratic government. The surprising aspect of Bailyn's short but well-developed discussion of sovereignty in the American setting is that he, not unlike many other scholars, almost wholly omits what for Bodin as well as for Locke was the cornerstone of sovereignty, namely, legislative power.

Indeed, in the vast realms of English and French thought on sovereignty in the 17th and 18th centuries, as studied in our earlier book, legislation was generally the first and most all-embracing mark of sovereignty. Locke theorized about the English parliament in terms of legislative sovereignty, as had Bodin about the French monarchy, although Bodin applied his doctrine to both forms of government (and others as well). Even in his 18th-century doctrine of the separation of powers, Montesquieu in France assigned special weight and priority to the legislative power in relation to the executive and judicial powers. Without this central element of *legislative* sovereignty, the Bodinian tradition cannot be fully apprehended when studying English or American thought in the period under present discussion.

Among the many excellent recent contributions to studies on the Declaration of Independence, there have been occasional partial forays into legislative issues, especially in one notable recent case,[94] although much more remains to be done. Meantime, a recent isolated book on "the authority to legislate," in the "constitutional history of the American Revolution," astonishingly omits any consideration either of the Declaration of Independence or of Bodin and later Bodinian tradition, despite many useful inclusions of Locke, Blackstone, and other English theorists of parliamentary supremacy (with related inclusion of the U.S. Constitution and Bill of Rights).[95]

There are wider implications behind how Jefferson founded his Declaration of Independence upon his previous writings pertaining to legislative sovereignty, as well as upon his adaptations from Locke and others concerning universal "self-evident" "truths." Clearly, Jefferson sought in that Declaration to set forth much more than a long list of specific grievances against the British government. He sought justification within a broader Bodinian conceptual framework of the rightful legislative sovereignty of all independent states to legislate for their own affairs, aside from questions of their jurisdictional right to do so, as with the legislative self-determination of the American states in relation to the British king and parliament. Sometimes the most obvious general points can be the ones most generally overlooked, not the least when it comes to historians' frequent indisposition toward the topic of legislation. This is not to say that in his legislative lists Jefferson was primarily intent on constructing a new political theory, in the manner of Locke or Bodin, for American independence. Rather, as both a statesman and a philosopher, he sought to balance and blend the immediate facts and issues of contemporary events with more universal or generalized principles in legislative sovereignty and other matters. Certainly he was doing just that in his prefatory statements—partly influenced by Locke, Paine, and others—on all men being created equal and having natural rights to life, liberty, and pursuit of happiness.[96]

The American and British sources alluded to above, including Locke, will present to historians theoretical Bodinian prototypes for Jefferson's thinking on legislation and sovereignty only when they adequately account for the legislative dimensions of the Bodinian tradition itself (of which Jefferson was well aware, especially through his marked copy of Bodin's *Republic*). Even then, exact parallels or precedents may still prove elusive. As with many previous European thinkers on legislative sovereignty, Jefferson was shaping his own ideas to the needs of the moment as well as the future. Could anything less be expected from someone so deeply learned and eminently practical as that unique philosopher-statesman?

Jefferson's lengthy lists of legislative and other grievances against the British government in the Declaration of Independence can be studied not only in connection with traditional Bodinian lists of the marks of (legislative) sovereignty, as variously represented in numerous 17th-century English writers culminating with Locke and Sidney; they can also be considered in regard to ideas of revolution against tyranny associated with Locke and Sidney. Among Jefferson's colleagues who thought he had not proved his case in the Declaration of Independence against George III as being an actual tyrant or despot was John Adams. Like some since then, Adams may have missed the theoretical point toward which Jefferson was reaching when he spoke in the Declaration of the duty as well as right to rebel. ("But when" a ruler "reduce[s]" a free people "under absolute despotism, it is their right, it is their duty to throw off such government . . .") Derived mainly from Locke, this idea of the duty of carrying out a revolution against a tyrant became for Jefferson a compelling device that also helped to shape his somewhat generalized initial legislative charges against the king. With his abiding interests in law and legislation, Jefferson well understood that the ultimate test of legitimacy and illegitimacy, legality and illegality, in affairs of state and sovereignty lay precisely in law and legislation. To prove the king a tyrant, in order to justify revolution, was therefore to disprove his supposed legal-legislative right to sovereignty over the American states. That right not only would cease to exist now and in the future, but had already ceased to exist in the past, as the Declaration explicitly indicated, when the British rulers became tyrants over the Americans. Here Locke's ideas on revolution diverged greatly from Bodinian traditions on legislative sovereignty in a state. But in Jefferson's hands the two elements came together to provide further theoretical as well as practical linchpins for arguments justifying American revolutionary independence from Britain.

By omitting Jefferson's original draft references to the British parliament as the perpetrator of legislative abuses against Americans, and instead ascribing those abuses primarily to the king, the Declaration of Independence as adopted by Congress was bound to cause some uncertainties in its lists of legislative charges. From some royalist sympathizers in that period to various recent historians, Jefferson has at times been accused of confusion, error, or ignorance as to who was in charge in Britain and doing what to whom in America. In fairness to Jefferson, however, it should be reemphasized that explicit references to the British parliament's involvement in legislative matters vis-à-vis the Americans were indeed included in his draft Declaration, as in his previous writings examined above; these references were deleted or altered by his colleagues in their own effort not to give Parliament legitimacy or to offend possible "friends" among the British people and their representatives in Parliament. That prevaricating notion of British friendship was called "pusillanimous" by Jefferson when introducing the Declaration's version included in his Autobiography.[97] There, in his extended discussions of Congress' work in drawing up the Declaration, he also made extensive explicit references to Parliament's involvement in legislative and other matters.

Historians' neglect of *legislative* sovereignty in Jefferson's draft Declaration of Independence as well as in Congress' final official version may, again, be due in part to their disinterest in the topic of legislation more generally, even when discussing sovereignty and state. Time and time again throughout our series, we have encountered important political-legal theorists of sovereignty and state whose integral thought on legislation has previously been unduly neglected, but without consideration of which their ideas cannot be properly or fully grasped. Although historians have long noted the contributions of Locke and other Europeans to ideas of revolutionary independence held by Jefferson and other American founders, the blindspot often encountered among historians toward legislation *per se* is particularly noticeable in their studies on the Declaration of Independence. Even when forced to account, if only in passing, for the dominance of the *legislative* factor in the initial leading and lengthy listing of charges against the king, experts often seem intent to move on to other, seemingly more interesting, subjects, seldom appreciating how extensively legislative matters permeate the lengthy lists of charges beyond the initial items. By considerably expanding his orienting legislative lists of charges in the Declaration of Independence, beyond what they had been in his preamble to the Virginia constitution, Jefferson came to see, in his drive for independence rather than reconciliation, the fuller importance of America's self-determining claims to legislative sovereignty and legislative statehood.

Thus in the intellectual background to Jefferson's Declaration of Independence, Bodinian traditions of legislative sovereignty and the legislative state, especially as expressed in 17th-century English thought culminating with Locke, Sidney, and the English Declaration of Rights, conmingled with Jefferson's other earlier writings pertaining to those twin topics. Just as the ideas of Locke and the English Declaration of Rights on sovereignty and statehood cannot be fully understood without a full investigation of Bodinian *legislative* traditions on those twin topics in previous English and other writers, so, too, Jefferson's ideas on sovereignty and statehood in contexts of Locke's theories cannot be adequately grasped without due consideration of the same Bodinian *legislative* traditions. Similarly, just as Jefferson's Declaration of Independence upholding American sovereignty and statehood cannot be fully fathomed without grasping his debt to Bodinian *legislative* traditions, through his wide reading of Locke and many other English and French writers including Bodin himself, so, too, Jefferson's *legislative* ideas in that Declaration must be properly viewed against the background of his own previous writings dealing with sovereignty and statehood in legislative perspective. Even the legislative currents running throughout Jefferson's later Autobiography—in which he included his Declaration of Independence as amended by Congress and included in his "Notes"—serve to underscore his related legislative preoccupations in that Declaration.

4. JEFFERSON AND NEW NATIONAL SYSTEMS OF STATE

Parliamentary Models

While serving as Virginia delegate to the Confederation Congress in late 1783 and early 1784, Jefferson wrote a short but substantive "Resolution on the Privileges and Immunities of Congress." In it he wrote "[t]hat as the United States in Congress assembled represent the sovereignty of the whole Union, their body collectively and their President individually should on all occasions have precedence of all other bodies and persons."[98] During that period, Jefferson proposed a separate committee to provide an ongoing visible head of the sovereign Confederation Congress when its members were on vacation, after the Revolution was over. This proposal led to the extensive documents of the "Report on the Powers of the Committee of the States."[99] Of Jefferson's "legislative experience" during that six-month term, "he distinguished himself serving 'on practically every committee of consequence,' and drafting, as has been estimated, no fewer than thirty-one papers." The years following showed "his continuing interest in the study of parliamentary law," as reflected in his book purchases during his diplomatic years in France.[100]

Compiled by Jefferson between the late 1760s and earlier 1800s, the materials in his "Parliamentary Pocket-Book" revealed his longtime great interest in parliamentary legislative procedures and processes. "Jefferson's service in the House of Burgesses and his attendance at the Continental Congress gave him his first opportunity to observe the day-to-day workings of parliamentary law in a legislative assembly." So, too, did his ensuing years as a member of the Virginia legislature and of the Confederation Congress, as well as president of the U.S. senate while Vice President under John Adams in the later 1790s.[101]

Jefferson's continued interest in the central importance of parliamentary legislative procedure was further revealed in his *Manual of Parliamentary Practice: for the Use of the Senate of the United States*, published in 1801 and 1812. In it he sought "to collect and digest" the legislative rules of the British parliament into "a system of rules" to act as "the model" for "a code of rules" for the U.S. Senate and, by extension, the House of Representatives. The British parliament had provided the key "prototype" for the American state legislatures, including the Virginia House of Burgesses, and its "example" helped Americans "to build law." Jefferson sought to collate and compare the relevant British and American rules of legislative process with the hope that his efforts would be carried on by others in the future. His first three sections on "The Importance of Rules," "Legislature," and "Privilege" {recalling his earlier "Privileges . . . of Congress") are typical in their admixtures of parliamentary and senatorial rules along with their quotations from and references to the U.S. Constitution. Jefferson was particularly approving of the ways in which the British adherence to parliamentary rules and protocol enabled the minority to check the majority in legislative affairs and thereby to control "the wantonness of power."[102]

Thus Jefferson's interests in British parliamentary models of legislative rules of procedure continued and developed from his years in the Virginia legislature before and after Independence to his periods in Congress during the early Revolution and to his years as president of the Senate, culminating with the publication of his *Manual* in the early 1800s. Moreover, British models of legislative sovereignty, derived from Locke and others, would continue to occupy Jefferson's attention after the formation of the new national government established by the U.S. Constitution, with its separations between the legislative, executive, and judicial powers. His continuity of interest in Parliament and Locke would also become visible in other areas, including religion, within the changing American scenes following Independence.[103]

The U.S. Constitution

Jefferson's ideas on the new national government established by the U.S. Constitution occupy a vast, well-studied documentary and bibliographical field.[104] Yet some basic points about his legislative views on the subject have not yet been adequately comprehended. Aside from his extensive correspondence with Madison and Adams, which will be examined later, there are innumerable other sources of information, which show the consistency as well as changes in his thinking.

On the adoption of the new U.S. Constitution, composed in mid-1787, Jefferson expressed early on mixed and changing thoughts. In a letter from Paris in late 1787, he wrote: "As to the new constitution, I find myself nearly a neutral. There is a great mass of good in it, in a very desirable form, but there is also, to me, a bitter pill or two."[105] In early

1788, he wrote in another letter from Paris that the constitution should not be ratified until "a declaration of rights" was added.[106] Another letter from Paris in early 1789 declared: "The Constitution . . . is unquestionably the wisest ever yet presented . . .," being made possible by "assembling the wise men of the State."[107]

The ultimate source of sovereignty to Jefferson was the people of a state or nation, expressed in their self-government (or self-determination). This principle runs consistently throughout his career. It can be found, for instance, in his Declaration of Independence, as well as in the U.S. Constitution ("We the people . . .") framed by his close friend Madison and in many of his letters. "I consider," said Jefferson, "the people who constitute a society or nation as the source of all authority in that nation" (1793).[108] Moreover, "love of order and obedience to the laws [!] . . . characterize the citizens of the United States. . . . [T]he elective function . . . will . . . dissipate all [effort] . . . to subvert a Constitution . . . resting on the will of the people. The will of the people is the only legitimate foundation of any government . . ." (1801).[109] In addition: "We surely cannot deny to any nation the right whereon our own government is founded, that every one may govern itself according to whatever form it pleases and change these forms [and the laws] at its own will. . . . The will of the nation is the only thing essential to be regarded [1793]."[110]

Self-government is a broad topic in Jefferson's writings. It rests on traditions of natural rights, on traditions of popular sovereignty, and on traditions of each state's inherent right to legislate for its own affairs—as all joined together in Jefferson's own distinctive blend. The sovereignty of the popular will as expressed in laws and a constitution is a basis for self-government in America and other states or nations. The centrality, continuity, and changeability of sovereign legislation in the American state(s) before and after the promulgation of the U.S. Constitution was further enunciated by Jefferson in a letter to George Washington (1792):

> I consider the source of authority with us to be the nation. Their will, declared through its proper organ, is valid till revoked by their will declared through its proper organ again also. Between 1776 and 1789, the proper organ for pronouncing their will, whether legislative or executive, was a Congress formed in a particular manner. Since 1789 it is a Congress formed in a different manner, for laws, and a President elected in a particular way, for making appointments and doing other executive acts. The laws and appointments of the ancient Congress were as valid and permanent in their nature as the

> laws of the new Congress or appointments of the new Executive, these laws and appointments in both cases deriving equally their source from the will of the nation; and when a question arises whether any particular law or appointment is still in force, we are to examine not whether it was pronounced by the ancient or present organ but whether it has been at any time revoked by the authority of the nation, expressed by the organ competent at the time.[111]

Under a constitutional system in which there was a division of powers into legislative, executive, and judicial branches, sovereignty naturally encompassed all three functions together. At the same time, however, the laws of a state or nation bind all three powers together in such a way as to give priority to the making of laws, which are then executed and interpreted through organs set up for those purposes. Because the laws continue on even when the organs for it change, they represent the supreme will of the people. Once again, the power to make law for its own affairs is an innate independent right of each legally constituted and recognized body or state; it rests on the will of its people and is not a question of their jurisdictional right to do so in relation to other outside powers or entities (as, in different ways, Corasius and Bodin had long ago first set forth).[112] In a Virginia issue over sending representatives to Congress, Jefferson emphasized (1797) that "the legislature, ... [in] that wise and cautious distribution of powers made by the Constitution between the three branches, ... [is] that branch which most immediately depends on the people themselves and is responsible to them at short periods."[113] Here, too, legislative sovereignty and self-government are intertwined.

In Jefferson's thinking on the independence of each state or nation to decide on its own constitution and laws, the natural right of self-government combined with the inherent legal-legislative right of self-determination, as already suggested above. On these bases, laws as well as constitutions can be changed in order to reflect the changing will of peoples and generations within a given state such as America. Jefferson was typically more a believer in the changeability of the U.S. Constitution, especially through continual amendments, than in its fixity. Self-government extended, for him, to each house of Congress, within the framework of Article I of the U.S. Constitution. Yet the ability of legislatures at the national or state level to alter and amend the constitution was given considerable thought by Jefferson. State constitutions formed by state legislatures during the Revolution—when, as Jefferson noted in the case of Virginia, the individual states were (mini) nations—often required subsequent alterations by the state legislatures.

Nevertheless, great care must be taken in such matters, in contradistinction to the ease with which Parliament can change the so-called British "constitution." Resistance to changing a constitution can be as dangerous as excessive change. In America, a constitution is, according to Jefferson's use of a traditional term in Roman law, the *lex legum* at the national and state levels.[114]

The Federal-State System

Jefferson's idea of self-government by the people was greatly opposed to the Federalist party's concept of a strongly centralized and consolidated federal government, which he believed would absorb and devastate the state governments. This result would subvert the U.S. Constitution, circumvent the national will, and even lead to a corrupt monarchy.[115] Jefferson hoped that a main benefit of the new U.S. Constitution would be to limit the orbit and power of the General Government at the federal level to "foreign" affairs and inter-state matters, leaving to the individual states independence in managing their own domestic affairs.[116] Under the U.S. Constitution, there should ideally be a gradation of republics, "standing each on the basis of law [!]." At the top is national government or "republic of the Union," concerned only with national defense and foreign as well as federal relations. Then come the individual states, counties, wards, and ultimately private owners and citizens—all together ensuring the greatest measure of participation by the people.[117]

Jefferson's opinions concerning the new U.S. Constitution changed considerably during its early years. In a letter of 1786, a year before the U.S. Constitution was written while he was in France, he had averred that the Confederation's Congress had too much power (not too little). For it held both the legislative and executive powers (which were, in fact, vague and limited). The proper model for it should have been the separation between those two powers, along with the separated judiciary, as found in the state constitutions.[118] In August 1787, while the Constitutional Convention in Philadelphia was nearing its conclusion, Jefferson highly praised the Confederation's constitution because of the great independence it allotted to the states in their own internal affairs, notwithstanding that constitution's imperfections particularly in matters of commerce between the states.[119] Over a month later, at the conclusion of the Constitutional Convention, Jefferson seemed wistful yet resigned at the prospect of the diminution of individual "State sovereignties" under the overarching "federal sovereignty." Yet the new arrangement seemed to satisfy his former desires for a federal government with a tripartite division of powers similar to that found (somewhat differently) in the states, just as he hoped the federal government's role would still be limited to foreign and inter-state affairs.[120] By the beginning of 1789, Jefferson displayed enormous satisfaction with the early success and strength of the new U.S. constitutional government, no longer so dependent on the state legislatures. Still in France, he now realized that new necessities while he was away had brought the states together in common constitutional ways he had not foreseen. This turn of events demonstrated to him once again the wisdom of letting the people decide for themselves on matters.[121]

However, Jefferson did not give up his underlying belief in the continued need for strong effective state legislatures and governments in relation to federal authorities. In a letter written two years before his death, Jefferson seemed to revisit with renewed conviction his earlier views under the Confederation. In outlining his avowedly "radical" interpretation of the constitutional relationships between the federal and state governments, Jefferson assigned sweeping authority to the states. He calls for a dramatic reduction of the federal government's role in the face of vastly greater state authority in "foreign" as well as in "domestic" affairs. Indeed, his proposal for a new "foreign branch" or "distinct government," under the jurisdictional authority of the states themselves, would seem to leave little or no real role for the federal government, which would have no power over the domestic doings of the states.[122]

If, then, it might seem that by 1824 Jefferson had become a more provincial Virginian than formerly, it also seems clear that he had never truly embraced the "federal" system as Webster defines that word—namely, "formed by a compact between political units that surrender their sovereignty to a central authority but retain limited residuary powers of government." Nor had he gotten over the Federalist party's applications of that term in the later 1790s and early 1800s. Jefferson's ongoing relationships with two special friends in this matter are too complicated to treat here—that is, with Madison, a writer of *The Federalist*, and Adams, the Federalist president under whom Jefferson served as Vice President. Both figures played a part in the unfolding struggles over certain controversial Federalist laws in the later 1790s that were opposed by Jefferson in his noted Kentucky Resolutions, which Madison was for and Adams against.

Federalist Laws and the Kentucky Resolutions

In 1798 the Kentucky Resolutions[123] were drafted secretly by Jefferson and were passed with minor changes by the Kentucky legislature, similarly to the Virginia Resolutions of that year drafted by Madison and passed by the Virginia legislature. Both documents, with certain differences, were prepared and issued in response to the Alien (Enemies/Friends) and Sedition Acts enacted previously that year by Congress (respectively giving to the President broad wartime powers over aliens and giving to the government wide latitude over its critics, a clear threat to the Bill of Rights). Both documents were drafted behind the scenes, without public acknowledgement of their authorship until many years later. At the time, Jefferson was serving as Vice President, under the Federalist presidency of John Adams, and thus as president of the U.S. Senate. Jefferson's Kentucky Resolutions, somewhat more radical than Madison's Virginia Resolutions, pressed the republican case that the repressive Federalist Acts were an unconstitutional invasion of states' rights and violation of individual rights. In arguing that the U.S. Constitution was a compact made between sovereign states, which retained the right to declare congressional acts unconstitutional, the condemnatory resolutions by Jefferson and Madison were as much ideological and political in their scope as they were legal or constitutional. In any case, they provide a celebrated instance of the struggle for legislative sovereignty in the early history of the new American republic.

These circumstances also shed further light on Jefferson's great interest as president of the U.S. Senate in adherence to parliamentary procedures as a way to give the minority a check against the majority in the legislative process. This was a purpose of his above-cited *Manual of Parliamentary Practice: for the Use of the Senate of the United States*, published in 1801 and 1812. In it he sought safeguards against "the wantonness of power."[124] Yet the legislative orbit and scope of Jefferson's Kentucky Resolutions have received insufficient attention by historians in present matters of sovereignty and state.

The first of Jefferson's Kentucky Resolutions declared as follows: "1. *Resolved*, That the several states composing the United States of America are not united on the principle of unlimited submission to their general government, but by a compact under . . . the Constitution . . . they constituted a general government for special purposes, . . . reserving, each State to itself, the residuary . . . right to . . . self-government . . ." The crux here was that "whensoever the general government assumes undelegated powers, its acts are unauthoritative, void, and of no force . . ." In other words, "the government created by the compact was not made the exclusive or final judge of the extent of the powers delegated to itself, since that would have made its discretion, and not the Constitution, the measure of its powers . . ."

According to Jefferson's second Kentucky resolution, "the Constitution of the United States, having delegated to Congress a power to punish treason, [and various other specified crimes] . . . and no other crimes whatsoever, . . . the power to . . . punish such other crimes is reserved . . . solely and exclusively to the respective States, each within its own territory" [and also, it would seem, within its own inherent sovereign right to legislate for its own affairs, as Jefferson above argued in other American contexts after the manner of Bodin and his followers]." This line of reasoning is continued in the third resolution, where Jefferson cites the tenth amendment to the U.S. Constitution, which declares: "The powers not delegated to the United States by the Constitution, nor prohibited by it to the States, are reserved to the States respectively, or to the people." On this ground the act passed by Congress, stipulating punishment for certain crimes, "does abridge the freedom of the press" and "is not law but is altogether void and of no force." The setting here, then, is largely the Sedition Act of 1798.

On the Alien Act of 1798 Jefferson in the fourth Kentucky resolution applies the same constitutional arguments with even more forceful ramifications for concepts of sovereignty and statehood. "4. *Resolved*, That alien friends are under the jurisdiction [!] and protection of the laws of the State within which they are: that no power over them has been delegated to the United States, nor prohibited to the individual States distinct from their power over citizens. And it being true as a general principle and one of the amendments to the Constitution [quoting again the tenth amendment to the U.S. Constitution] . . .[,] the act of the Congress . . . which assumes powers over alien friends not delegated by the Constitution is not law but is altogether void and of no force." In addition, Jefferson's sixth resolution declares "That the imprisonment of a person under the protection of the laws of this commonwealth on the failure to obey the simple order of the President to depart out of the United States, as is undertaken by said act . . ., is contrary to the Constitution . . ."

In short, according to Jefferson's seventh Kentucky resolution, the Federalist-controlled Congress has usurped and extended an arbitrary and unconstitutional legislative sovereignty over the individual states. "7. *Resolved*, That the construction applied by the General Government . . . to those parts of the Constitution . . . which delegate to Congress a power 'to lay and collect taxes [etc.], . . .' and 'to make all laws . . . necessary . . . for carrying into execution the powers vested by the Constitution in the government of the United States . . .,' goes to the destruction of all limits prescribed to their power by the Constitution . . ." Indeed, "words meant by the instrument to be subsidiary only to the execution of limited powers ought not to be so construed as themselves to give unlimited powers, nor . . . to be taken as to destroy the whole residue of that instrument . . ." In these ways, according to Jefferson's eighth resolution, "the inhabitants of these States being by this precedent, reduced, as outlaws to the absolute dominion of one man, and the barrier of the Constitution thus swept away from us all, no rampart now remains against the passions and the powers of a majority in Congress to protect from a like exportation or other more grievous punishment the minority of the same body . . ."

More fervent personal denunciations of the repressive Federalist legislation later appeared in two letters by President Jefferson to Abigail Adams in 1804.[125] His renewed stress on the "nullity" of such legislation set a further remote precedent for the later arguments by some Southern legislatures, on the grounds of sovereign states' rights, for the nullification or avoidance of federal legislation on various issues prior to the Civil War. In general, Jefferson's extensive letters over many decades to Abigail's husband, John Adams, provide a window into Jefferson's thought and sources. To those letters we now turn, then to his letters to Madison.

5. JEFFERSON'S LETTERS TO ADAMS AND MADISON

Jefferson's letters to John Adams and James Madison offer telling insights not only into Jefferson's thinking on law and politics but also into the sources of influence and inspiration operating upon him concerning it. Jefferson's sources and his library have long presented vast fields for inquiry by historians. Aside from his references to historical and contemporary sources within his formal works and writings, there appear extensive references to them in his informal letters, especially to his closest longtime friends and associates with whom he was engaged over a long course of time in intellectual discourse. Perhaps the most renowned exchanges of this kind were with Adams and Madison. Yet the huge corpus of Jefferson's papers and works, along with the enormous secondary literature on them, abundantly reveal the great richness and range of his reading, knowledge, and learning with regard to European as well as American intellectual traditions. His personal library—which was the largest private one in America and which became the nucleus of the Library of Congress—yields a wealth of materials across a broad spectrum of disciplines. Many books in his collection relate closely to topics and writings included in our present and previous studies.

Letters to Adams: Constitutional

The first of three areas of present interest in Jefferson's letters to John Adams[126] centers on the months before, during, and after the Constitutional Convention of mid-1787, which neither of them attended.

Their exchanges while on different diplomatic missions in Europe throughout that period dealt at points with (1) constitutional issues of the Confederation and its states, on which Adams had just written a timely booklet, and with (2) the federal Constitution newly issued by the Philadelphia Convention. True, their correspondence during this period was not as extensive as that between Jefferson and Madison, to whom Jefferson was sending large numbers of books from Paris that would prove useful to Madison in framing the Constitution; it was, nevertheless, greatly revealing of their thinking.

The letters of 1787 between Jefferson in Paris and Adams in London concerning Adams' *Defense of the Constitutions of the United States* provide preliminary glimpses into their deep interest in historical as well as current issues of constitutional government. In February, Jefferson wrote to thank Adams for sending a copy of his *Defense* and predicted for it great influence. Jefferson did take exception to Adams' brief comment in it that the Confederation's Congress was essentially a diplomatic assembly. Jefferson countered that it is (or should be) a legislative as well as executive body, from which the judiciary is separated. These three components comprise the separate parts of "the whole sovereignty of our states," which is the constitutional "law of the land," superior to individual state legislatures and their laws.[127] In March, Adams wrote back to Jefferson that the comment in the booklet was not meant as a firm opinion but as a topic for consideration. Adams asked Jefferson to correct it if and when Jefferson secured a French translation of the booklet.[128] (Jefferson well perceived the necessary legislative authority of the Confederation's Congress in relation to the individual state legislatures that it took priority over, just as he did in his draft of a bill in 1777 to give the Articles of Confederation the force of law.[129]) In mid-September, a day before the Constitutional Convention adjourned in Philadelphia, Adams sent Jefferson a copy of the new second volume of his series and asked if he should write a third volume on confederations.[130] Shortly thereafter, at the end of September, Jefferson wrote to thank Adams for his latest booklet and to encourage him to write a third volume on confederations, which would compare them throughout history and in the present. Jefferson lauded the American Confederation still in effect and the American state constitutions; he declared the former to be better than all other confederations and the latter to be superior to the English constitution. The chief virtue of the American forms of government was their proper distributions of powers into executive, judicial, and legislative branches, with the legislature divided into two branches. And yet here, a week and a half after the new federal Constitution was completed but not yet ratified, Jefferson also bemoaned the failure of his fellow countrymen to appreciate adequately their benefits under the existing forms of government, the excellence of which he hoped would be shown by Adams' comparative-historical approach.[131]

Here it may be asked how Jefferson, together with Adams, could still favor the existing forms of American government so soon after the new federal Constitution had been issued. After all, Jefferson's close friend Madison was the chief architect of the new federal Constitution. Jefferson had been in extensive correspondence with Madison concerning it and had also been supportive in sending Madison shipments of books from Paris. Moreover, in their diplomatic missions in Europe for the Confederation's Congress, Jefferson and Adams had both sought ways to strengthen its hand in Europe, especially in commercial affairs.[132] Also, Jefferson and Adams had shared their differing concerns over Shays' Rebellion in Massachusetts and over the government's difficulty in handling it, which became a crucial factor in convening the Convention in order to adopt a stronger central federal authority.[133] In addition, Jefferson's prediction of success for Adams' *Defense*, published in London in early 1787, was proved correct when it gained good circulation in the United States toward the outset of the Convention. One delegate to the Convention reported that because of the great impression made by the booklet, "there is little doubt of our adopting a vigorous and compounded federal legislature."[134]

By the end of August 1787, less than three weeks before the Convention adjourned, Jefferson still had no concrete news about the outcome to report to Adams. Jefferson expressed his continued grave disapproval of the imposed silence and secrecy surrounding this "assembly of demigods" presided over (without Jefferson and Adams being present) by Gen. Washington. Yet Jefferson still held out high hopes for the end result.[135]

In mid-November 1787, Jefferson expressed great disappointment to Adams over the new federal Constitution. He feared that the new Congress' authority would be too weak in conducting domestic and foreign affairs. The President, he felt, could become a monarch if not limited to one term. A declaration of individual rights would also be needed. At this early point, Jefferson still preferred the old Confederation system, which he felt the Convention should instead have improved upon in a few short articles, in place of the lengthy new Constitution.[136] In early December, Adams wrote back that he feared the potential aristocracy of the Senate under the new federal Constitution, more than he feared the potential monarchy of the presidency, for which he favored continued reelection.[137] The future political divide between the two men was already germinating. Yet after Adams was elected Vice President under Washington, Jefferson wrote in May 1789 to congratulate him with "cordial homage."[138]

In their own different ways, however, the two men seemed to agree in 1787 on the crucial need for a more effective federal legislative body. Jefferson feared that the new Congress would not be effective enough as a legislature. Adams wanted a much more potent legislature than the old Congress of the Confederation had been. This had perhaps been the real intent and meaning behind Adams' above comment in his *Defense* with which Jefferson disagreed when affirming that the Confederation's Congress was indeed a legislative body. Speaking to this very point was the above-quoted delegate's statement that the *Defense* was a timely tool for the Convention in fashioning a strong effective federal legislature. In time, both men came to agree also, from their own different vantage points, that the new U.S. Constitution was truly excellent—Jefferson hailing it as "the wisest ever yet presented to men" (1789)[139] and Adams praising it as "conformable to such a system of government as I had ever most esteemed" (1797).[140]

The extent to which Adams' *Defense* and its sequel were a source of information and influence for Jefferson (as well as for Madison) cannot be measured here. Adams' rich comparisons between historical and contemporary forms of government clearly made a decisive impression on Jefferson and others. In their intellectual exchanges after retirement from public life, the two former Presidents would later reflect on their reading about such subjects in broad historical parameters. It is clear that Adams' *Defense* had a significant impact on the move for a new balanced federal government—with a stronger legislative Congress than was present under the old Confederation—when the Constitutional Convention met in Philadelphia in mid-1787.

Letters to Adams: Cultural

The second area of present interest in Jefferson's letters to Adams, along with Adams' replies, centers on the years from 1812 to 1815. The two friends discussed a wide range of cultural subjects. Their extended exchanges between Monticello and Quincy culminated with the sale of Jefferson's library to form the nucleus of the Library of Congress.

In January, 1812, Jefferson wrote to Adams that he had given up politics and newspapers for Tacitus, Thucydides, and other intellectual authorities.[141] In February, Adams wrote back that he admired Jefferson's intellectual pursuits, high above mundane current history and events. Adams deferentally belittled his own understanding and appreciation of such classic writers—which he had spent much time reading—as Plato, Aristotle, Harrington, Sidney, and Hobbes, along with many others. His frequent past readings of Thucydides and Tacitus have left him, he reported, with the uneasy feeling of reading about his own past life and times. The future of the Union, Adams added, worried him as much as had Independence.[142]

In mid-1813, Adams called into question Jefferson's toleration for full expressions of differing religious as well as political views. Adams feared the perils of unchecked excesses of such freedoms.[143] Shortly thereafter, however, Jefferson wrote to Adams that Epicurean tranquillity of mind and ease of body were now for him the highest good, above and outside history's inevitable factional disputes when men have been permitted free expression. As in Greece and Rome, so too in the U.S. during the struggles for independence and for the new Constitution, such internal disputes could become, he acknowledged, bitter and violent. He depicted Adams and himself as having been united against fellow countrymen opposed to immediate Independence and Union. From those struggles Jefferson now sought solace in the contemplation of higher things.[144]

In mid-1814, an exchange of letters between Jefferson and Adams over the merits and demerits of certain ancient and modern writers again pointed up their extensive reading while in retirement, as well as their strong intellectual preferences. Expressing great dissatisfaction and frustration with Plato's *Republic*, Jefferson berated Cicero, whom he otherwise admired, for being taken in by Plato's vague abstractions and sophistries. Admiring "the Roman good sense" and Cicero's writings more generally, Jefferson also favorably acknowledged Plato's style as well as Demosthenes' logic. Yet early Christianity and modern fashion remained, for him, too accepting of Plato's philosophy.[145]

Adams soon replied with lengthy like-minded criticisms of Plato's *Republic, Laws*, and other writings. Adams considered Plato's ideas of communal property, and the like, to be antithetical to republican government and human happiness. Plato's later disciples, from early Christians to Rousseau and Paine, have been misguided in succumbing to the lure of mystery and paradox, which are so prevalent in Plato; so too, in other respects were Hume, Gibbon, Voltaire, Turgot, Helvétius, Diderot, Condorcet, and dozens of other writers. Cicero can, nevertheless, be partly excused for readily accepting Plato, since Plato held a prominent place in educational ideas during Cicero's period. Responding to Jefferson's queries about appropriate subjects for educational curricula, Adams ventured some modest limited thoughts. After noting that he has looked into Locke, Rousseau, and others on education, Adams proceeds to divide the disciplines into various groupings. For instance, he would, of course, include history and chronology, despite their limitations, while to abstract metaphysics and theology he would give little attention.[146]

Adams' fuller thoughts in that letter were of further interest to Jefferson in light of his own attempts at dividing the branches of knowledge into various categories in his catalogue of books in his vast private library. He was soon, in 1815, to sell his books to the U.S. as the nucleus of the second Library of Congress (after the burning of the Capitol by the British in 1814). Adams congratulated Jefferson on this mark of distinction, noting the lesser size of his own library and a few of its books.[147] Jefferson responded that although he had ceded his library to Congress he could not "live without books," despite his lessened practical need for them. With Adams' indirect assistance, Jefferson was not only preparing a catalogue of his library but was hopeful of "reprocuring" part of it (his subsequent new acquisitions becoming extensive).[148]

A third area of present note in the Jefferson-Adams correspondence revolved around their exchange of thoughts, between Monticello and Quincy in 1819, on the subject of "good government." Their use of classical contexts enabled them to put into broader perspective the current governmental crisis over the admission of Missouri into the Union as a slave state. Their wide historical knowledge was further evidenced.

Calling the crisis over Missouri a greater one than was ever faced during the war for independence, Jefferson sought solace and lessons from Roman history, about which he discoursed at length, posing various questions to Adams. In particular, Jefferson reflected on Cicero's voluminous letters and their portrayals of Caesar and the Roman people. Jefferson concluded that even if Caesar had been as virtuous as Cicero, or if men like Cicero had been given the chance as leaders, little could have been done to achieve good government in Rome. The fault lay with the corruption and vices of the people throughout Roman history. Cicero, Cato, and Brutus had no real positive enlightened idea of government, while the people had no real understanding of liberty. Later, the emperors had the will and power to improve government but did not do so, again largely because of the degeneration of the people, without whose good control good government is always difficult. Only good education could have taught the Roman people virtue over vice, right over wrong. Praising Adams' great knowledge of history and of the science of government, Jefferson asked Adams for thoughts on how such virtuous great men as that triad could have achieved good and free government for so unenlightened a people.[149]

On these issues, Adams answered Jefferson obliquely yet agreeably. Has there ever been a people in history, he asked Jefferson, who have gone from corruption to virtue and freedom, or who have prevented their riches and luxuries from leading to vice and folly? While less anxious about the Missouri crisis than Jefferson, Adams nonetheless feared for the future of the Union through the actions of men, similar to Hamilton or Burr, who might divide it asunder.[150]

Letters to Madison: Constitutional

It was in his correspondence with James Madison, even more than with John Adams, that Jefferson worked out much of his changing constitutional ideas in the later 1780s. This was perhaps natural in that Madison, as architect of the U.S. Constitution in mid-1787, became an obvious central contact in America for the renowned author of the Declaration of Independence while he was away in France during that critical period in U.S. constitutional developments. Jefferson (b. 1743) showed great respect for the somewhat older Adams (b. 1735), his close colleague (along with the much older Franklin) on the committee that had prepared that Declaration. Yet Jefferson was closer in friendship and outlook to his younger protégé and fellow Virginian, Madison (b. 1751). If, however, Jefferson's dialogues with Adams in their letters produced points of sharp disagreement, as over Shays' Rebellion prior to the Constitutional Convention, those with Madison produced even stronger ones, at first not only over the secrecy surrounding that Convention but over the new Constitution itself. The transformations in Jefferson's thinking from initial partial disappointment over the Constitution to more enthusiastic acceptance of it were partly worked out in his evolving correspondence with Madison, as also with Adams.

In December of 1786, Jefferson wrote to Madison that at the federal level the executive functions of the Confederation Congress should be transferred from it to special committees during its sessions and recesses in order that Congress could become more fully and fundamentally focused on legislative matters. This redistribution of functions or powers would have to be imposed upon Congress, Jefferson believed, because Congress would not have the self-discipline necessary to divest itself of its executive capacities, notwithstanding the judiciary being already separated from these other two federal branches. Jefferson also noted his long-standing proposal for a stronger, more distinct and independent legislatively-oriented Congress, a proposal going back to his earlier years while serving in Congress. Here seems to be the real import of an above-noted exchange with Adams—in which Adams thought that the Confederation Congress had become more a diplomatic than legislative body, whereas Jefferson replied that in principle it was (or should be) distinctly legislative.[151] Jefferson reemphasized his same proposal for Congress in another letter to Madison (probably meant to influence him) in late June, 1787, after the Constitutional Convention was under way but before any real information was available outside about its proceedings. In again urging that the executive be separated from the legislative function, Jefferson felt that even a reorganization would have to be imposed on Congress by a federal act. In addition, he complained to Madison about the plan he was then hearing about to give to the Congress a legislative "negative" over the acts of the state legislatures insofar as they related to the Confederation (which was the case much of the time). He proposed instead a kind of judicial review.[152]

In late December, 1787, three months after the Constitutional Convention adjourned, Jefferson wrote a lengthy letter to Madison on the proposed new federal Constitution, after it reached him in France and the Convention's secrecy was finally lifted. To Jefferson's liking was the federal government being independent of the state legislatures and divided into three branches. The national legislature's powers of taxation were well assigned, he felt, to the House of Representatives, elected directly by the people, so as to avoid taxation without full representation (a Revolutionary battle cry). Curiously, however, Jefferson also thought that direct election to the House was in some ways an "evil" that could bode "ill" for the federal legislature in having properly "qualified" people to legislate for the nation in foreign and other matters. He approved of certain methods of direct voting in other respects and also the methods for proportioning the small and large states in the two houses of Congress. He also approved of the Executive's veto power over the Legislature, but wished the same for the Judiciary. First among Jefferson's list of disapprovals was the omission of a Bill of Rights, which should guarantee basic freedoms for individuals under a just government; these freedoms were enumerated by Jefferson in remarkably similar ways to the Bill of Rights later adopted. Secondly, Jefferson warned against a potentially unlimited succession of presidential terms. That could lead to a kind of monarchy, a subject on which Jefferson cites ancient and modern history. Thirdly, Jefferson was not in favor of making officeholders in the three federal branches take an oath to uphold the new U.S. Constitution, which would require ongoing change and improvement (as a work in progress). While allowing that Madison had no doubt taken all considerations and contingencies into account, Jefferson freely expressed his distrust of powerful government, which even in France, England, or Turkey (as cited by Montesquieu) was unable to put down insurrections like Shay's Rebellion. Pledging his ready acceptance of the new Constitution if the people approved it, he reaffirmed his cardinal principle of majority rule. Jefferson nonetheless believed that the American nation would be best preserved if it endured as a virtuous and free agrarian society, uncorrupted by excessive urbanism and enriched by wise and good education for common people. Ever interested in legislative matters, Jefferson added a P.S. in which he proposed a legislative mechanism for Congress in the new Constitution so as to counteract the "immense evil" posed by "instability in our laws."[153]

As already seen in his correspondence with Adams in the months before, during, and after the Constitutional Convention of mid-1787 in Philadelphia, Jefferson's constitutional ideas were undergoing a profound evolution during this period; this evolution was even more evident and elaborate in his exchanges with Madison. Clearly, Jefferson was somewhat miffed by Madison's explicitly expressed inability to break for him the secrecy imposed on the Convention's proceedings. As noted, he told Adams it was an "assembly of demigods." Yet Jefferson was less frank and more understanding on this business in his letters to Madison. As also noted, Jefferson soon came to praise, as did Adams, the merits of the new U.S. Constitution. By early February, 1788, Jefferson expressed to Madison his considerable pleasure in hearing about its growing acceptance by the states. While hoping for its ultimate passage, he also hoped that a few states would hold off their support in order to force the adoption of a Bill of Rights.[154]

Letters to Madison: Bibliographical

While in Paris in the mid- to later 1780s, Jefferson purchased large numbers of books not only for his own library but also for Madison's. During this period, leading up to (and beyond) the Constitutional Convention of mid-1787 in Philadelphia, the developing constitutional thoughts of both men were reflected in their correspondence about books. Jefferson's letters to Madison contained various detailed accounts of the elaborate arrangements and conditions for his purchases for Madison. Included in Jefferson's letters were titles, inventories, costs, payments, and shipping transactions. Jefferson's lists of books purchased for, and available for purchase for, Madison give some indications of the intellectual interests and wide reading not only of Madison but also of Jefferson, during that critical period in the formation of early American constitutionalism.

Some of the titles and descriptions of books listed for Madison by Jefferson at that point were broadly comparative, others widely historical, and some of narrower focus. Among the books of more contemporary scope were various encyclopedias, including some by the famed Diderot. Various kinds of constitutional, legal, and administrative works were well represented, together with dictionaries of civil and other law. Some works pertained to legislation, as in the case of *Principes de leg-*

islation universelle. Others were more culturally oriented, as with Pascal's letters and Voltaire's memoirs. A variety of "universal histories" were included, some dealing with ancient history. Natural history was also represented. Most books were in French, as to be expected in that Jefferson found then in Parisian stores and stalls. Many works were multi-volume. In addition to Jefferson's listings of books purchased for Madison were accounts of books available for purchase if Madison should be interested. Among Jefferson's descriptive general remarks to Madison were that he was interested in certain books for their "utility" and was finding Greek and Roman authors in shorter supply in France than elsewhere because they were little read there then and hence seldom reprinted.[155]

The titles and inventories of books given in Jefferson's letters to Madison in the mid- to later 1780s can also be seen from other angles. For instance, Jefferson's (as well as Madison's) *historical* interests in books, during this (and other) periods of their correspondence, can be better determined in ways other than through Jefferson's letters to him, which were nevertheless important in the intellectual background to the new U.S. Constitution. Moreover, just as Jefferson is seen by some as having written the Declaration of Independence without having had real historical precedents for it, but rather writing it ad hoc for pressing current needs, others might view Madison as intent on framing a new U.S. Constitution geared to new American needs, without resorting to historical frameworks that may have proved controlling upon him. In any case, a specific look at what Madison was reading in the period leading up to and beyond the Convention will indeed reveal much about his significant intellectual interests that influenced his general thinking as chief architect of the new U.S. Constitution. A general look at library books possessed by both Jefferson and Madison can reveal the magnitude of their deep historical as well as contemporary interests across a range of subjects.

As for Jefferson's response to allegations that he drew from other writers in his Declaration of Independence, he staunchly declared in a later letter to Madison from Monticello in 1823 that he had consulted no books or pamphlets when drafting it. He left to the judgment of history whether, as claimed by some, his ideas therein were particularly evocative of Locke's *Two Treatises of Government* (1690) and James Otis' *The Rights of the British Colonies Asserted and Proved* (1764). Jefferson denied having even seen Otis' work. He did not deny or affirm here a prior reading of Locke's treatise, stating only that he had not consulted it or any other work when actually writing the Declaration. Jefferson declined to judge the extent to which it or other sources had influenced him at that point. Nor would he judge whether, as also charged, his Declaration's ideas were mere commonplace rehashes of concepts already current for some time in the colonies and in Congress. Again expressly leaving for others to decide, he would only answer that his object had not been to write a wholly novel document but rather to respond to the gravity of the immediate situation. Jefferson also absolved his old friend Adams for any slips of tongue or failures of memory in his old age when thinking back to 1776 in a letter that Jefferson's opponents, Pickering and Lee, seized upon in maligning Jefferson's Declaration of Independence.[156] Madison soon wrote back from his nearby Montpelier home that Jefferson's letter to him was completely accurate in these and other fuller details about the drafting of the Declaration of Independence.[157]

However much Jefferson had put to rest the recent charges of his critics, the debate will continue to endure as to what sources of influence and inspiration lay behind his Declaration of Independence, aside from its extensive uses of his own lists of grievances against the king in his preamble to the Virginia constitution. The varied sources of influence and inspiration operating upon Jefferson's political and legal writings more broadly have long posed much larger problems and debates for historians. It has, for instance, long been accepted by many historians, and correctly so, despite their neglect of legislative sovereignty, that writers like Locke and Sidney had considerable general influence on Jefferson. Yet scholars just as often agree, again correctly, with Jefferson's own opinion that his Declaration of Independence was both an original response to the events at hand and a new restatement of existing ideas (including those of Locke and many others) on a wide range of issues.

It is noteworthy that in their subsequent correspondence in 1824–1825, Jefferson and Madison exchanged extensive ideas for books to be included in the library and curriculum of the new University of Virginia, which opened in 1825, the year before Jefferson's death. Jefferson's special interest and role in the University was accentuated in his inscription for his tombstone at Monticello. Its lines credited him as "Author of the Declaration of American Independence/[and] of the Statute of Virginia's [*sic*] for religious freedom/and Father of the University of Virginia."[158] Aside from his Declaration of legislative independence and sovereignty for the American nation-state and his legislative statute for religious freedom as a foundation for the state of Virginia, Jefferson's inclusion of his role in establishing Virginia's university reflected his commitment to a good education for the people as another foundation of state and society. The Jefferson-Madison letters dealt not just with library books and courses of study, across a range of subjects from theology to law, but also with recruitment of professors, details of finances, and many other points.

In one of his replies to Jefferson regarding the choice of standard books for students of law, Madison began by affirming the importance of Locke and Sidney (both strong on legislative sovereignty). Those two authorities would, he agreed, be particularly suited for inculcating respect for liberty and free government in relation to the political systems of America and other nations. However, although good guides for promoting freedom, the two are lacking as good guardians for defending it. Next in Madison's descriptive enumeration of curricular choices were, with their pros and cons, the Declaration of Independence and *The Federalist*, of which Madison was one of the authors. The Declaration, Madison said, laid the foundation not only for independence but also for the Union, while *The Federalist* remains the best guide to the new U.S. Constitution, which he largely framed. Among his other inclusions were George Washington's incoming and outgoing speeches as President, containing good principles for students of politics. In addition, responding to Jefferson's request, Madison drew up an extended listing of books for students of theology; it comprised a kind of encyclopedic catalogue of authorities spanning a large spectrum of religious history, from Christian antiquity to modern times. In these and other ways, Jefferson's efforts to prepare catalogues for the new University's library again underscore not only his commitment to education but also his grasp of a broad array of traditional authorities and sources.[159]

6. JEFFERSON'S LIBRARY

Collections and Catalogues

Of immense complexity is the subject of Thomas Jefferson's vast private library—or libraries he compiled at different stages of his life and career. On this subject many modern studies have been conducted and various catalogues produced.[160] Before proceeding into new depths, we must first bring succinctly together salient disparate details in the overall chronology of Jefferson's book collections.

Jefferson's personal book collections fall into three main chronological stages. The first stage began in 1757 when he inherited his father's Shadwell library (well supplied with law books), which he expanded upon through purchases at Williamsburg and through importations of books. When Shadwell burned in 1770, most of the library of perhaps 400 volumes was destroyed.

The second main stage extended from roughly 1770 to 1815. During the earlier part of that long period, Jefferson purchased, inherited, and acquired collections from various individuals that totalled over 2,600 volumes by the time of his handwritten catalogue of 1783, which he began earlier and continued to update pior to his reorganized "fair copy" catalogue of 1812. During the years 1784–1789, he bought books in Europe while on diplomatic service in France, subsequently inheriting the collection of his former law teacher, George Wythe, in 1806. In 1815 Jefferson sold his Great Library to Congress in order to replace Congress' smaller library, which was destroyed in 1814 when the British burned the Capitol building. By then, he had amassed a remarkable collection of about 6,700 volumes, by far the largest private library in America.

The third stage of Jefferson's book collecting lasted from 1815 to his death in 1826. Although he had willed its approximately 1,600 volumes (or about 1,000 titles) to the University of Virginia, this third personal library was sold by the executors of his estate at auction in Washington, D.C., in 1829, due to his estate's poor financial situation. Finally, in addition to his "retirement" Monticello library, there was a small collection of about 70 volumes at his retreat in another Virginia county.

When the Library of Congress burned in 1851, nearly two-thirds of the original Jefferson volumes, then interspersed in its wider collection, were destroyed. Fortunately, two volumes (and others) of particular note in the discussions below survived. Of the approximately 6,700 individual volumes sold to the Library of Congress in 1815, nearly 2,500 volumes remain there today. A fair number of his books not sold to Congress can still be found in other locations, such as at the University of Virginia (including there his copies of legal-political writings by Jean Domat, William Blackstone, Jeremy Bentham, and Auguste Comte).

An apt statement on Jefferson's reasons for selling his Great Library to Congress in 1815 is given below from the Introduction to an excellent edition of a handwritten catalogue that was prepared for Jefferson in 1823 by his grandson-in-law (N. Trist) and that was commissioned and emended by Jefferson. (It restored the original order and classifications of books in Jefferson's lost manuscript catalogue—or 1812 "fair copy" that he submitted in 1814 to Congress. The Librarian in 1815 devised a differently arranged printed catalogue for the Library of Congress (and naturally far different from the printed 1812 catalogue of Congress' collection prior to the fire of 1814). Our bracketed additions below will further help to drive home the point that it was not primarily Jefferson's need for money (though a factor) that impelled him to sell his library to Congress. Paramount was Jefferson's great desire for the best and widest knowledge to be made available for congressional legislators in the interests of the young Republic.

> [Jefferson's Great Library] encompass[ed] virtually the whole of recorded knowledge. . . . At some point Jefferson decided that this splendid library should not remain private property, thinking at first that he might donate it to a university. [In 1805 he had stated his intention of bequeathing his library to the University of Virginia.] But when [in the War of 1812–] the congressional library in Washington was burned . . . in [late August,] 1814, the former president promptly [within weeks] offered his own. Though he was then in serious financial straits, Jefferson's primary purpose was to assure that the nation's legislators [!] had access to the best sources of information and ideas, for he said that he would accept whatever price and terms of payment Congress thought appropriate as long as the entire collection was purchased.
>
> When Jefferson offered his library to Congress in September 1814, he sent along his handwritten catalog for the inspection of the congressional library comnmittee. . . . [T]his catalog [a "fair copy" of his updated 1783– catalogue] arrange[d] the books in subject categories . . . [as] part of an overall [encyclopedic] classification scheme . . . adapted from . . . Francis Bacon . . .[161]

It remains possible, of course, that Jefferson's "fair copy" catalogue of 1812, drawn up well prior to the Capitol fire of 1814, was partly intended as preliminary to an offer of sale to the Library of Congress. His other related catalogues were put together for certain reasons or purposes. His so-called "1783" catalogue was begun well earlier (during the mid-1770s according to some experts); yet it became chiefly designed as an inventory of books he either owned (as indicated in the margin with check marks) or wanted to obtain, in advance of his mission to France soon to begin in 1784, although he continued for a few decades to update this catalogue (with additions, erasures, etc.). The catalogue that Jefferson sent to Congress in late 1814 was the 1812 "fair copy" (now lost) of the updated "1783" catalogue and was obviously an integral part of the sale to Congress. The 1823 catalogue was related to the intended eventual transfer of Jefferson's "retirement" library to the University of Virginia, in connection with which he sought to reestablish his earlier classifications. Even if, however, it could be shown that Jefferson's aim in the 1812 "fair copy" catalogue was in part to offer his library for sale to Congress, prior to the 1814 fire, knowledge rather than money would still be the crux. That is, as in the eventual 1815 sale to Congress, he would have been thinking primarily of the great benefit of knowledge his books (which he was generous in loaning to others) would bring to Congress, rather than the financial benefit a sale might bring to him. (The eventual sale price, though substantial, was not that great to solve his financial needs, and with some of the proceeds he started buying more books, eventually dying in considerable debt.)

All in all, Jefferson's vast book collections, unrivalled in the young Republic, encompassed virtually the entire range of subjects for those times, as his and subsequent catalogues of his books abundantly reveal. His well-known avid reading habits and the encyclopedic knowledge displayed in his writings and correspondence are further testimony to an exceptionally learned mind, all the more remarkable for a leading public figure so continually immersed for so long in everyday affairs. Indeed, the books, subjects, and traditions represented in Jefferson's collections and catalogues—as in his own vast body of writings—connect at many points with this author's historical series.

The fuller details of Jefferson's encyclopedic collections and catalogues of books yield further valuable information for this study, including on methodology, jurisprudence, and politics as seen from his historical and contemporary vantage points.[162] To his three manuscript catlogues of 1783–, 1812, and 1823 can be added a fourth, that of 1789, which is discussed below.[163]

Political and Legal Books

The hand catalogue (recently "rediscovered") that Jefferson commissioned in 1823, in order to reconstruct the order and classifications in his lost library catalogue or "fair copy" of 1812, has been rightly labelled, by its recent co-editors, "A Catalogue with the Entries in His Own Order" as well as "Thomas Jefferson's [own] Catalogue."[164] Jefferson's catalogue order in Chapter (or category) 24, "Politics," is a typical combination of topical and chronological listing of works by author and title. Cited at the outset are the main divisions to be followed, in turn: "General Theories of Government," "Special Governments, Ancient" and "Special Governments, Modern." Further subdivisions to be followed in turn are: "France" ("Monarchical–Revolutionary–Imperial–her Colonies"), "England" ("Constitutional–Parliament–Dependancies"), the "United States" (". . ."), and "Political Oeconomy" (". . ."). This "chapter" on politics is especially long in proportion to the other "chapters" in the catalogue.

The listings under "General Theories" at or near the beginning of this 1823 chapter on politics are especially interesting for present purposes. They typify his self-styled approach in that catalogue as sometimes chronological, sometimes topical, and sometimes a combination of the two. First come ancient works. These comprise the first seven entries and are, in order, as follows: "Platonis republica," "Spews' Republic of Plato," "Les Politiques di Aristotle," "Aristotle's Treatise on Government," "Xenophontis Hiero, sive de Regno," and "Xenophontis Oeconomica, Agesilaus, Hieron, Lacedemoniorum et Atheniensium Politic. Gr." The very next item listed after these ancient works is "Hobbes de Cive." Immediately after Hobbes in entry eight come Machiavelli in entries nine through twelve (in turn, the *Prince* along with *Discourses, Letters*, and *Works*) and then Bodin in entry thirteen (the *Republic* in French). Then follow in entries fourteen through nineteen: More (*Utopia* in Latin and English), Harrington (*Oceana*), Hooker (*Ecclesiastical Polity*), Filmer (*Observations Concerning Government*), and Sidney (*Discourses Concerning Government*). Among the many ensuing items of interest, also listed toward the beginning of this same lengthy chapter on politics, are, in turn: an edition of "political classics" (by Sidney, Rousseau, and More), the "Works" of Montesquieu in French, Wilhams' lectures on Montesquieu's political principles, Priestley's *Principles of Government*, the *Principes de la Législation Universelle*, the *Della Necessità di Reformare la Legislazione dal Antonio*, Godwin's *Political Justice*, Beccaria's *Crimes and Punishments*, Voltaire on Beccaria, Bentham's *Panopticon or Penitentiary, Xenophontis Lacedaemonorum Republica*, and so forth, including numerous other works relating to legislation.

In Jefferson's earlier rough, updated so-called "1783" catalogue,[165] there were some striking differences (and a few anomalies) in the placement and order of the same corresponding entries at or near the beginning of Chapter 24 on "Politics," under "general theory." Here, the first four entries of the 1823 catalogue were absent. Instead, the first three "1783" entries were works by Xenophon, centering on his same above-cited works in the 1823 catalogue but here in somewhat different arrangement. The fourth "1783" entry was "Aristotle's Treatise on government," which would occupy the above-cited fifth position in the later 1823 catalogue. Immediately after these ancient works in the "1783" catalogue appeared Bodin's *Republic* ("Bodin de la Republique") in a most prominent position, as entry five, at the very head of Jefferson's extremely long listing of other modern works, which included the same corresponding 1823 items as cited above though in somewhat different sequence. To the right of the entry for Bodin's *Republic*, in somewhat smaller size, Jefferson later inserted Priestley's *Principles of Government*, which appears further down in the above-cited entry in the 1823 catalogue. The next "1783" entry was Goodwin, who is much lower down in the 1823 listing. About a dozen-and-a-half entries below Goodwin appeared Machiavelli's "Princeps," much further down the list and less prominently positioned than in the ninth through twelfth positions allotted to him in the 1823 catalogue, where the *Prince* appeared just before Bodin's *Republic*. Eight entries lower appeared "Filmer's observations on government," followed immediately, in turn, by "Locke on government" and "Sidney on government." Below that appeared, in turn, "Hooker's ecclesiastical polity," "Harrington's Oceana," "More's Utopia," and "Political classics" (Sidney, Rousseau, More).

In this "1783" catalogue listing, therefore, Bodin appeared not just chronologically before such 17th-century theorists as Filmer, Locke, and Sidney, but also well prior to Machiavelli before them and Hooker after them, both being of the 16th century. In other words, Jefferson's prominent positioning of Bodin in the "1783" catalogue shows his especially high estimation of Bodin's importance. This was not just a matter of chronology, which was much more irregular and mixed here than in the later 1823 catalogue, especially when one looks at all the other works (of lesser present interest) that are interspersed with the ones we have considered here.

That the orders of the listings in the "1783" catalogue were not just chronological, but also topical, arranged according to Jefferson's own particular viewpoints on their relevance to his own interests and purposes, is further shown by his ensuing placement after More's *Utopia* of Plato's *Republic* and Aristotle's *Politics*. This placement in Jefferson's "1783" catalogue wholly differed from the kind of stricter chronological order later followed in his 1823 catalogue, where Plato and Aristotle are grouped together at the outset of Chapter 24 on politics. Granted, More and Plato evidently held a close association in Jefferson's mind, but in his "1783" listings, Jefferson did not yet have the interest in Plato's speculative ideas that he later partially expressed in his more reflective retirement years; Jefferson was more inclined to place Plato lower down in the "1783" listing rather than prominently at the very beginning as in the 1823 catalogue, albeit Jefferson's entries in this section fell under his category of "political theory." After Plato and Aristotle in the "1783" catalogue come Beccaria on crimes and punishments, Voltaire on Beccaria, Machiavelli's "Works," and Williams's "Lectures on Montesquieu" together with a commentary on Montesquieu's *Spirit of the Laws*. Here, too, the placement of Machiavelli just before Montesquieu was out of chronology but perhaps, like Plato and More, represented a juxtaposition of certiain topical affinities in Jefferson's mind.

All these further matters of sequence tend to underscore, once again, Jefferson's prominent placement of Bodin's *Republic* at the very outset of his extremely long, sometimes irregular, listing in his "1783" catalogue of modern books on political theory, immediately following a bare partial listing of just a few ancient books by Xenophon and Aristotle. Jefferson was motivated at least as much by his obvious estimate of the special importance of Bodin's *Republic* as by its chronological place, as he saw it, at the onset of modern political theory. The other main 16th-century contenders for that spot—Machiavelli, More, and Hooker—were placed much further down in the list and were mixed in out of chronological sequence with later political theorists of the 17th and 18th centuries. Even the importance of Locke and Sidney for Jefferson, as often rightly cited by historians, takes on a different dimension through this perspective, especially considering their great debts to Bodinian traditions of legislative sovereignty in their political and legal theories, as seen in our earlier studies.

Jefferson's placement of Bodin's *Republic* near the very beginning of his "1783" catalogue's chapter on politics and political theory not only showed the high importance and priority it held for him. It also demonstrated Jefferson's early possession of that work in the mid-1770s, when he began the catalogue (in early entries of that and other chapters) and when he was writing his foundational documents of American independence, which were reflective of Bodinian legislative concepts of sovereignty and state.

A variety of further details are needed at this point. It is well established that Jefferson intended to use his "1783" catalogue as a guide, once he got to Paris in 1784, for books he already had and those he wanted to obtain. On thc front cover (see illustration), he cited the date ("1783, Mar. 6"), the number of books included at that point in his collection ("2040 vols."), and his system of check marks to the left of books he already possessed ("✓ this mark denotes the books I have. those unmarked I mean to procure."). In the "chapter" or section on politics, beginning with political theory, Jefferson placed check marks (Diagram 6) to the left of all the initial books cited above, including Bodin's *Republic*. Such marks are lacking especially for many later entries in the chapter on politics, some of which bear dates of materials up to about 1810. These parameters are typical of other chapters as well—Millicent Sowerby calling this the 1783–1814 catalogue, although Douglas Wilson has criticized her attempt to use the so-called "1783" catalogue as a basis for restoring the order and classifications in Jefferson's lost "fair copy" catalogue of 1814 sent to Congress in 1814.[166] Profesor Wilson's firm position that the "1783" catalogue was begun in the mid-1770s seems entirely correct when one considers: the huge number of books Jefferson already owned by 1783, his lifelong habits of keeping inventories of his possessions (as well as his expenses), and, above all, his system of check marks. It would appear that early on, well prior to 1783, Jefferson started listing here, in the example of the section on political theory, books he already had, not yet anticipating a mission to France and the opportunities there for book purchases. He later added in 1783 check marks (Diagram 6) alongside his current books so as to distinguish them from the unmarked items he wanted to obtain in Europe. Other kinds of margin marks were made at different points (Diagram 3, 4, 5). The (untitled) so-called "1783" catalogue is thus a misnomer because of the many entries made in it before and after that date, which Jefferson placed on the front page beneath his explanation of checked and unchecked entries. Jefferson recorded the date corresponding to the point in time at which he added the check marks to (many) entries that had already appeared in the catalogue (though he continued to add to it) to serve as more exact reminders of what he had and did not have (and when). Hence, it is almost certain that Jefferson already possessed his copy of Bodin's *Republic* by the mid-1770s at the time when he was composing the basic documents of the American Revolution, with their abundant indications of the influence of Bodinian doctrines of legislative sovereignty and the legislative state. (See Diagram 1–9 below, page 96.)

A fitting companion to Jefferson's vast collection of books on politics was his huge collection of law books. Although the latter are classified separately, an impressive array of books on law and legislation also appear under the category of politics in Chapter 24. The fuller range and classifications of Jefferson's law books were cited above, including those grouped around foreign law under jurisprudence. In Jefferson's later 1823 catalogue, Chapter 23, "Jurisprudence. Foreign Law," begins with an extensive sequence of titles in Roman (and Greek) law, followed by later works in the civil law tradition. The first eighteen entries are as follows: "Justinian's Institutes, Lat. Eng." (two editions), "Justiniani Institutiones," "Theophil, Antecessonis Institutiones, Gr. Lat.," "Codex Justinianus," "Corpus Juris Civilis, Gothofredi" (two editions, the second being of 1598), "Jus Graeco-Romanum," "Ulpiani Fragmenta," "Fontes quatuor juris Civilis," "Vinnii Partitiones Juris Civilis," "Gravione origines Juris Civilis," "Gravina, Esparit des Loix Romanes," "Schomberg's History of the Roman Law," "Les Loix des Grecs et Romains," "Taylor's Elements of Civil Law," "Zouchaei Questiones Juris Civilis," and "Zouchaei Elementa Iuris prudentiae." Other ensuing entries include "Calvini Lexicon Juridicum," "Domat's Civil Law," "Code Civil des François.1804," and "Code Napoleon Civic." Many of these works were all noted in our previous studies. As in his (catalogue's) long chapter on politics, Jefferson in this much shorter chapter (one of several chapters on law or jurisprudence), albeit still under "foreign law," has added entries on the laws of numerous American states with some dates as recent as 1807–1810.

Under "foreign law" in Chapter 23 of Jefferson's earlier catalogue of "1783" (or, according to Sowerby, of 1783–1814), the above entries on Roman law were checked off in order to show his possession of them. They largely followed rather than preceded the entries concerned with various American states other than Virginia (though some other such American entries do follow at chapter's end). Those states were still deemed "foreign" by Jefferson when he organized the catalogue long prior to the new national system established in 1787–88 under the new U.S. federal constitution. The sequence of the entries under "foreign law" in the "1783" catalogue proceeds roughly from American states (one entry being dated 1786) to Roman or civil law and briefly again to American states (one entry being dated 1788). This sequence is somewhat jumbled due to changes and is far less clear than the sequence for political theory at or near the beginning of the ensuing Chapter 24 on politics (although its later entries are often in unclear sequence due to additions, etc.).

In any case, it is thus an interesting feature of the "1783" catalogue that its entries on Roman (and Greek) law, as well as on the civil law tradition, appear toward the end of Chapter 23 on "foreign law," that is, on the page just before the entries on Xenophon, Aristotle, Bodin, and so forth at the beginning of the ensuing Chapter 24 on "politics." This close proximity of Justinian's *Corpus Iuris* on the page prior to one including Bodin's *Republic* will represent for us below an apropros juxtaposition, which fits in with the transition from classical law books near the end of the chapter on "foreign law" to the classical political books listed at the outset of the next chapter on "politics."

Also of current note is Jefferson's handwritten late-1789 catalogue[167] of his huge acquisitions in Europe during his five Paris years. Justinian's *Corpus Iuris Civilis* (1598) is significantly included. Bodin's *Republic* is conspicuously absent and was therefore not a later added entry in the "1783" catalogue but was in it from the start, as has already been demonstrated.

Markings in Bodin's *Republic*

The library catalogues examined above clearly indicate that Jefferson almost certainly possessed his copy of an early edition (Paris, 1580) of Bodin's *Republic* by the mid-1770s, during the period when he composed the Declaration of Independence and other foundational writings of the American Revolution. Our evidence for this early dating has included the prominent place of Bodin's *Republic* near the very beginning of the initial pre-1783 part of the chapter on politics in Jefferson's so-called "1783" catalogue. Also significant has been the Bodinian framework of Jefferson's Declaration of Independence and his other related documents. In more general ways, Douglas L. Wilson[168] has dated the initial inception of the "1783" catalogue to the mid-1770s, although without reference to Bodin and other key writers cited above from the beginning of Jefferson's chapter on politics. The inclusion of Bodin's *Republic* among that chapter's initial entries, dating back (like those in many other chapters) to the mid-1770s, shows that Jefferson obviously had the book in his library by that early period. Other evidence relates to markings in these and other works. (See Diagram of Markings with columns 1–9, below page 96.)

Another authority, J. P. Mayer[169] (a British researcher like E. Millicent Sowerby), has presented brief but compelling evidence that Jefferson not only possessed Bodin's *Republic* in the mid-1770s but marked numerous passages in it with brackets (Diagram 8) that resemble those made (Diagram 9) in portions of Jefferson's own draft of the Declaration of Independence (and the changes by the Committee and Congress). Mayer did not treat the kinds of issues and materials studied here, including Jefferson's collections and catalogues of books. Nevertheless, his rough typescript article, included in his edition of Bodin studies in the 1970s, presents a wide range of promising clues as to who made the "many hundreds" of markings he alludes to in Jefferson's copy of Bodin's *Republic*. They were made, Mayer argues, by Jefferson himself. The present writer's somewhat more extended examinations of Jefferson's copy of Bodin's *Republic* in the Library of Congress, in conjunction there with many other books in the Jefferson Collection, has yielded many further results.

As Sowerby (almost ignored by Mayer) had accurately indicated,[170] Jefferson "inscribed" his fine initials in Bodin's *Republic* at the I and T (T.J.) "signatures" (the alphabetically sequenced sections or gatherings of pages that printers put together to make up a book). Jefferson often, but not always, did this in his books as a mark of his ownership. Evidently referring to the writing made inside the cover, while ignoring the "many hundreds" of markings alongside or within the text, Sowerby gave a misleading impression by cursorily alluding to "some other writing not by him [Jefferson]." While noting the presence of "the Library of Congress 1815 bookplate," Sowerby did not offer clues as to the earlier provenance of Jefferson's ownership based either on his own early catalogue or on other outside evidence. Yet it now becomes reasonably certain that the markings, though not the writings inside the cover, are by Jefferson and that they date from the mid-1770s, as Mayer impressionistically suggested but without appreciating the fuller evidence and fuller import.

Inside the front cover of Jefferson's copy of Bodin's *Republic* is written a date (1749, or possibly 1719), a number (279), and some short lines of writing in different hands—none of which appears to be by Jefferson though the lowest writing is at least a possibility. The date and number may well relate to previous owners of the book and to its sale, although the date and number are not necessarily related as entries. To draw inferences from this data (ignored by Mayer) would be speculative. There seems no real evidence to link this handwriting or ink inside the cover to the markings within the book, even though it cannot be ruled out as a partial possibility. At the same time, the difference in texture between Jefferson's "signature" inscriptions and the vertical lines of short vertical dash marks in many margins opposite select passages of Bodin's text may reflect different time frames and writing conditions in Jefferson's handlings of the book (which he did not procure when in France but possibly obtained through earlier importations of books).

Scattered frequently throughout the crucial first book of Bodin's *Republic* on sovereignty, in the copy owned early on by Jefferson, are little vertical dashes in the left or right margins, each placed next or near to a line of text that the reader thought of particular note (Diagram 2). Their numbers and positions vary, but they are typically a half dozen or so in number and form a short broken vertical line that marks off passages in the text. These marks, left undiscussed by Mayer, have been carefully, neatly, and unobtrusively placed (like the "signature" initials?), in lieu of underlinings, so as not to mar or clutter the book and its text; yet these dashes are thick enough to be readily noticeable when one is looking for them as a guide. A heavy preponderance of such marks is found in the central "sovereignty" chapters (VIII–X) of Book I, where Bodin sets forth the definitions and characteristics of sovereignty in the legislative contexts for which he has long been so famous. Indeed, the very opening lines of Chapter VIII lay out a central definition and context of sovereignty, and these lines bear next to them in the left margin precisely such marks in a short broken vertical line of neatly sequenced short vertical dashes (Diagram 2). Whoever placed such marks here and elsewhere in that crucial chapter and book was a close and consistent reader of *Republic* I. Far fewer of these kinds of marks appear elsewhere in Jefferson's copy of Bodin's *Republic*. While the texture of these marks does not seem to match the quality of Jefferson's initials in the "signature" inscriptions, it also does not seem to match that in the jottings by various hands inside the front cover. All of which is no proof against these short marginal dashes having been made by Jefferson. His ink and markings in other works often varied from one time and circumstance to another. He could well have marked Bodin's text at a slightly later point than when he initially inscribed it as sign of his ownership. Nor was it uncustomary of book owners in his day for him to initial proof of ownership in an unnoticeable and somewhat hidden manner, while then highlighting certain passages of the text with more readily visible markings. On the other hand, the unobtrusive careful placement of the vertical lines of short dashes in the margins of *Republic* I does bear a similarity in other ways to that of Jefferson's well-known inscriptions of his initials in many of his books.

Because Jefferson almost certainly owned his copy of Bodin's *Republic* in the mid-1770s, at the time when he was composing his basic Revolutionary documents centered on the country's rightful independent legislative sovereignty, it makes perfect sense that his attention would have been drawn to the central parts of *Republic* I on that very subject, adapting them to his own purposes. This line of inquiry becomes all the more convincing in light of Mayer's brief but conclusive demonstration of the close correlations between the bracket marks (Diagram 8) placed within the text in ensuing books of the *Republic* and those (Diagram 9) in Jefferson's own draft of the Declaration of Independence (and the changes by the Committee and Congress). In both cases, the brackets were made in order to mark off or highlight select passages. It is well known that Jefferson was long an avid reader and user of the books in his library, as Mayer has correctly acknowledged. Mayer incorrectly said, however, that Jefferson often marked or wrote in his books when reading them. If the extensive vertical markings found in many margins of Book I in Jefferson's copy of Bodin's *Republic* were indeed made by Jefferson, as can be further established, it would clearly indicate that Jefferson was not only a close reader of Bodin but found the *Republic* to be of special significance and utility for his own several declarations of America's independent sovereignty in the mid-1770s (and beyond). However, Mayer is typically interested in broad questions of constitutionalism and just government rather than in *legislative* sovereignty more specifically, and thus he misses the larger import of his findings for Jefferson's Bodinian ideas, which Mayer completely overlooks. The many provocative additional points raised in Mayer's article—in ways that relate closely yet indirectly to the present study of Jefferson in the Bodinian tradition of legislative sovereignty—are treated in greater detail below (together with materials from Jefferson's 1771 library list and his commonplace book).[171]

Markings in Other Works

Various other works either owned or composed by Jefferson can be used afresh, largely for the first time, in analyzing his marginal markings in the first book of his copy of Bodin's *Republic*. None of these other works were considered by Mayer in his brief visit to Special Collections in the Library of Congress. There, first of all, is one of the few books with extensive marginal writings well known to be in Jefferson's hand, namely, his copy of a 1767 edition of a book of Latin poetry by the Roman poet Horace.[172] Two blank front cover pages contain extensive handwriting by Jefferson in very fine print and in schematic layout. His handwriting in the same style appears extensively throughout the margins of roughly the first half of this book of over 200 pages, but there are none of these markings in the second half. There may be a parallel here with the markings in Bodin's *Republic*, where the first book has extensive marginal marks of a kind not found in the ensuing books of the *Republic*.

More persuasive outside evidence appears in Jefferson's copy of the 1598 edition by Gothofredus of Justinian's *Corpus Iuris Civilis* in two volumes. As discussed above, this work was listed under the subject of foreign law in Chapter 23 of Jefferson's book catalogues of "1783" and 1789. Having been procured by him during his Paris years and therefore listed in his 1789 Paris catalogue, this edition of the *Corpus Iuris* was then added by him to the updated "1783" catalogues, which he also kept with him in France. Jefferson's acquisition and inspection of the 1598 *Corpus Iuris* during his later Paris years may help to explain the changed style (for whatever reason) of his marginal markings in it, in relation to those he made in the previous decade in his copy of Bodin's *Republic*. Not duly noted in the Sowerby catalogue's brief entry for the 1598 *Corpus Iuris*[173] are the occasional solid vertical lines placed (in pencil) in the margins opposite select passages of Justinian's *Code* (Diagram 1) in the second volume (Justinian's *Institutes* and *Digest* being in the first volume). In view of his own great interest in codification and legislation in Virginia, and more broadly, it is entirely likely that Jefferson took particular note of Justinian's code of legislation as well as the new legislation contained respectively in the *Code* and *Novels* in this easy-to-use small-sized edition. (Jefferson's copy of the large-size two-volume *Corpus Iuris* of 1726—which he also obtained in Paris during the same period and which is listed in his catalogues—lacks such markings.) There is clearly a parallel between these solid vertical lines in some margins of Jefferson's copy of Justinian's *Code* and the vertical lines of short vertical dashes comparably placed in the margins of Jefferson's copy of Bodin's *Republic*.

Even more compelling evidence for Jefferson as the source for the single vertically-spaced lines of short vertical dash marks placed next to select passages in many pages of Book I in Jefferson's copy of Bodin's *Republic* can be found on many pages of his early updated "1783" catalogue. In particular, Chapters 23 and 24 on foreign law and politics contain, like other chapters, similar types of broken lines, short and long (often in pencil), in a variety of vertical and horizontal positions (Diagrams 3, 7). On the whole, these lines possess a precisely-placed quality similar to that found in the left or right margins of Jefferson's copy of *Republic* I. This holds strikingly true for the frequent small slanted short dash marks (corresponding in angle to the bottom portion of his check marks) that frequently appear (next to or in place of his check marks) in vertical lines (Diagrams 4, 6) opposite the entries in ways that are comparable to the vertical lines of vertical dashes (Diagram 2) in the margins of his copy of *Republic* I. But this is not all. On a number of pages in Jefferson's "1783" catalogue, there appear in the left margins short or long solid vertical lines, sometimes curved slightly inward at top and bottom (Diagram 5), next to various entries as if to designate a group. These vertical solid marginal lines can be compared with those in Jefferson's copy of Justinian's *Code* in the 1598 edition of the *Corpus Iuris*. The page of the "1783" catalogue on which Bodin's *Republic* appears offers partial examples of the configurations just mentioned. Jefferson's diagrams at the beginning of his "1783" catalogue provide some further kinds of examples. As to be expected, the consistency of the markings in thickness and shape varies in the updated "1783" catalogue, for they and the entries next to them were made over a long period of time. These kinds of differences in markings can help to explain those between Jefferson's "signature" inscriptions and his vertical marginal dashes in *Republic* I.

Among the various other pertinent Jefferson books examined by the present writer for corroborative evidence on margin marks were works by Sidney, Rousseau, More, Hobbes, Montesquieu, and Machiavelli. Of these, an English translation of Machiavelli's *Prince* proved of particular interest in a notable English translation (1762), made during Jefferson's younger days, of Machiavelli's works in two volumes (each "inscribed" by Jefferson)[174]; in addition to some handwriting, there are some vertical margin marks in a solid line (in pencil) that can be compared to those (also in pencil) in Jefferson's 1598 edition of Justinian's *Corpus Iuris* in two volumes (Diagram 1). Furthermore, there are various promising marks, writing, and underlining in the margins of More's *Utopia* (in English), which is included along with Rousseau's *Social Contract* (also in English) and Sidney's *Discourses Concerning Government* in an even more recent (1794–1795) three-volume *Political*

Classics (devoted primarily to Sidney and his works), owned but not initialled by Jefferson (the other two books lacking such marginalia).[175] A separate edition of Sidney's *Discourses on Government* owned and inscribed by Jefferson, although evidently without marginal markings in the form of vertical dashes, bears a rich relationship to Jefferson and his interests; it dates back at least to 1771 in his possession, as Sowerby has ably indicated through outside evidence (and as Mayer has shown in connection with its bracket marks within the text similar to those in the draft Declaration of Independence).[176] Jefferson's copies of Hobbes' *De Cive* (ordered and received by Jefferson in 1788 while in France) and Montesquieu's *Spirit of the Laws* bear no marginal markings to be cited here.[177] It is interesting to note that whereas Jefferson praised Sidney's *Discourses* as a rich repository of basic republican principles including on natural rights, his attitude toward Montesquieu's *Spirit* was mixed and guarded.[178] In general, Sowerby's *Catalogue* provides useful information on other related matters that could be utilized in more exhaustive inspections of book markings in the Jefferson collections (although such undertakings might quickly reach the point of diminishing relevant returns).[179]

It may be that the evidence presented above for Jefferson as the source for the short vertical lines of dash marks in many margins of *Republic* I is not yet completely conclusive, however persuasive it may be. Nevertheless, as reported above, the bracket marks placed elsewhere in the *Republic* (Diagram 8) definitely are close in kind to those in Jefferson's draft Declaration of Independence (Diagram 9) as Mayer has briefly but conclusively demonstrated. Therefore, the likelihood that the marginal lines of dashes in *Republic* I were made by Jefferson is greatly enhanced. Perhaps an exhaustive search through all of Jefferson's books would produce additional positive results in the form of comparable provable markings in Jefferson's hand. Yet the short vertical line of horizontal as well as slanted dash marks in the margins to the left of many entries on numerous pages of his "1783" catalogue (Diagram 3, 4) may well come close enough to positive final proof, as on the pages (133–134) citing the *Corpus Iuris* and the *Republic* (some other pages containing even better examples). Sufficient proof may likewise be found in the many horizontal lines of short horizontal dash marks in the "1783" catalogue (Diagram 7). Even if, however, the vertical marginal lines of short dashes in *Republic* I could someday be conclusively proved (though highly unlikely) to be not by Jefferson, but rather by a previous reader of this copy of Bodin's huge classic work, their placement alongside crucial passages relating to sovereignty, the state, and legislation would have caught Jefferson's eye and guided him to important points on those subjects (in addition to many other passages he found).

Either way, the influence of Bodin's *Republic* on ideas of legislative sovereignty in Jefferson's Declaration of Independence and related documents was clearly significant. Whether by him or someone else, the extensive and precise markings made in his copy of Bodin's *Republic* are evidence of a close and careful reading of the work, especially in the crucial first book centered on legislative sovereignty to which Jefferson's attention was certainly drawn. Jefferson's debt to and knowledge of the Bodinian tradition on legislative sovereignty was reinforced through his reading of a wide variety of celebrated political writers, like Locke and Sidney, indebted to that tradition. Still to be discussed is the related great interest in Bodin's *Republic* shared by John Adams, Jefferson's fellow committeeman in preparing the Declaration of Independence.

Diagram of Markings (1–9)

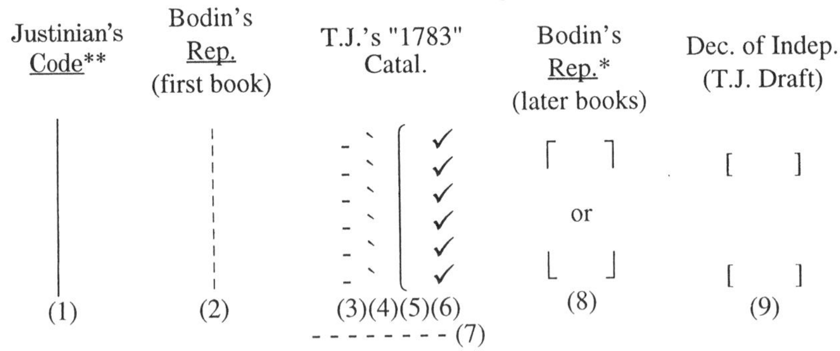

*T.J.'s copy of Sidney's *Discourses* has similar markings.
**T.J.'s copy of Machiavelli's *Prince* (English) has similar markings.
(The nine different columns in this single composite diagram are referred to separately in our text as Diagram 1, 2, 3, etc. and correspond to illustrations in Appendix below, as also cited in our table of contents.)

Conclusion: Bodinian Tradition and Legislative Sovereignty

Many of the books on politics and law in Thomas Jefferson's library help to explain his abiding concerns with matters of legislative sovereignty. This is particularly true for books of the 17th and 18th centuries in his immediate background. These included a wide array of important works by Hobbes, Locke, Harrington, Sidney, Filmer, Domat, Rousseau,

Montesquieu, Beccaria, Blackstone, Bentham, and others. In our previous studies on that period, such works and writers revealed some common patterns relating to legislative sovereignty. Above all, in those and other cases, the legislative character of sovereignty and state provided a continuum or common denominator amid a wide spectrum of divergent ideological "isms"—especially absolutism *vs.* constitutionalism, rationalism *vs.* empiricism, and liberalism *vs.* conservatism. Against that strong background of Bodinian legislative sovereignty as expressed in myriad forms by numerous writers represented in Jefferson's library, it is not surprising that he, too, came under the strong influence, directly and indirectly, of Bodin's *Republic*. Bodinian paradigms on legislative sovereignty impacted not only Jefferson's early foundational writings of the 1770s, centered around his drafts of the Virginia constitution and American Declaration of Independence, but also some of his subsequent writings dealing with new national systems of state in America, in addition to some of his letters to Madison and Adams. In these contexts Jefferson's intellectual interests, shaped by his reading of books in his library, combined with his outlooks on pressing events of his period to produce some of his crucial writings pertaining to legislative sovereignty and the legislative state.

Meantime, a rich diversity of other viewpoints and influences came together in Jefferson's highly original and creative, yet also learned and encyclopedic, mind, as reflected in his writings and in his library. Even in the celebrated case of Locke, there was a wide range of direct and indirect influences at work on Jefferson, even though Locke's actual impact on the Declaration of Independence has long been much debated by historians. On matters of revolution, consent of the governed, natural rights, parliamentarism, government itself, popular sovereignty, property, education, religion, position of the church, empirical values, and so forth, Locke's works presented a wealth of ideas that influenced Jefferson in different ways to greater or lesser extent, as did the more radical republicanism of Sidney. Moreover, as our earlier studies brought out, the Bodinian heritage of legislative sovereignty was strongly operative on Locke as well as on Sidney, and this became a crucial component of the broad Bodinian background to Jefferson's thoughts on the subject (just as it also became for Adams and other contemporaries). However, the role of Bodinian legislative sovereignty has been widely neglected by scholars who have examined the influence of Locke and Sidney on Jefferson.

Two cases in point on Sidney and Hobbes are further instructive. The particular pungency of Jefferson's declarations of American legislative self-determination independent of the British monarchy echoed Sidney's *Discourses*. Therein, as we have elsewhere seen, Sidney's radical republicanism included a strong Bodinian accent on the command and will lying behind sovereign legislative power, which for Sidney lay with parliament rather than the king. (As Mayer has briefly pointed out in other matters, Jefferson marked passages in his copy of Sidney's *Discourses* with brackets similar to those he made, as cited above, in later books of Bodin's *Republic* and in his draft Declaration of Independence.) Similarly, Jefferson also echoed, whether knowingly or not, the strong Bodinian emphasis in Hobbes' early work *De cive*, also in Jefferson's library, on the absoluteness of the sovereign power to legislate. For both Sidney and Hobbes—the one more constitutionalist and the other more absolutist—the Bodinian idea of legislation as the first and all-important mark of sovereignty was paramount. Jefferson's Declaration of Independence and related documents, centering on legislative issues of sovereignty and state, also reflected this Bodinian viewpoint.

During Jefferson's early period, the central chapters on sovereignty in Bodin's *Republic* I, 8–10 would have had striking applicability in a matter relating to Bodin's immediate predecessor, Corasius. Naturally Jefferson was not familiar with Corasius' contributions to the genesis of Bodin's early modern understanding of the importance of legislative sovereignty in contradistinction to late-medieval ideas of jurisdictional-judicial supremacy. Even so, Jefferson was well read in Roman and French civil law traditions, including through his copies of writings by Domat, which bore many remarkable congruences with works by both Bodin and Corasius, as we have previously seen. Jefferson's well-marked copy of Bodin's *Republic* I affords ample proof of the strong potential opportunity for Jefferson to have seen the applicability of Bodin's ideas to the American case for independence from Britain as set forth in the foundational documents studied above.

It will be remembered that it was the French jurist Corasius who in the mid-16th century brought new attention to and emphasis upon the innate power of each state to make laws for its own affairs, irrespective of any outside jurisdictional-judicial conflicts over its right to do so. Before Corasius' time lay the enduring medieval concept of the right to legislate as being a question of who had the jurisdictional-judicial right to declare laws and statutes. This medieval orbit of the right to legislate continued on through 14th-century Italian jurists like Bartolus and Baldus to the early 16th-century German jurist Zasius and others. For them, legislation was interwoven with other topics through elaborate "trees of jurisdiction," whether in relation to the Holy Roman Empire or to individual states and other political-legal entities in Europe. So powerful had this medieval juristic tradition become, that it set the stage for even so "modern" a political thinker as Machiavelli in the early 16th century. Likewise, the Florentine jurists of the Italian

Renaissance, despite their forward-looking ideas of "statecraft," were still heavily indebted to medieval concepts of jurisdictional-judicial supremacy not yet recast by more modern Bodinian ideas of legislative sovereignty. The same older orientation still prevailed in the case of King Henry VIII in early 16th-century Renaissance England as well as in the noted Elizabethan political thinker Hooker, whose *Ecclesiastical Polity* was also in Jefferson's library.

It will also be remembered from our previous studies that the "sovereignty chapters" in the first book of Bodin's *Republic* developed out of Bodin's own earlier writings that had been heavily influenced in these regards by his French juristic predecessor, Corasius. The eighth and tenth chapters of the first book of Bodin's *Republic* had set forth the basic legislative framework of sovereignty that was to prevail throughout the broad spectrum of myriad "isms" in European political-legal thought on sovereignty from Bodin to Jefferson's time and beyond into the 19th and 20th centuries. Correspondingly, the ninth chapter of *Republic* I had tackled and disposed of the older concepts of jurisdictional-judicial supremacy. On both counts, Jefferson undoubtedly gleaned much from his extensively marked copy of the first book of Bodin's *Republic*, as viewed historically but also from Jefferson's contemporary vantage point. In any case, the hitherto neglected links between Jefferson and Bodinian legislative sovereignty have now acquired seismic import, comparable in magnitude to those established in our earlier studies between Bodin and Corasius as well as between Machiavelli and Ficino.

Through our previous investigations of Bodin's *Republic* and the long developing tradition of legislative sovereignty he set in motion, we thus arrived at the gateway to broad new vistas, long hidden from view, on Jefferson's declarations of American independent sovereignty and on his approach to new national American systems of state. First and foremost for him was the innate power and right of each state like America to make laws for itself, regardless of any competing or conflicting outside jurisdiction. That is, no "foreign" power like Britain could interfere by interposing its own jurisdictional right to do so for itself. On the national level, this approach meant that America had the *de iure* and *de facto* power of legislative self-determination irrespective of Britain's "foreign" claims that Americans lacked the jurisdictional right to this power. For individual states within America, like Virginia, the same principle applied in relation to other "foreign" states, as in Jefferson's earlier writings concerned with the constitution and laws of Virginia, as well as in his subsequent Kentucky Resolutions in relation to Federalist laws, not to mention in other cases as well.

Jefferson's strong renewed accent on the innate power of each state to make laws for its own affairs was thus a strong echo of Bodinian tradition on legislative self-government, within distinctive American contexts of the Revolutionary and Constitutional eras. Whether the outside "foreign" jurisdiction was, for Jefferson, another nation or empire like Britain, or another state within the American system, or even the American federal government itself, this principle of legislative self-determination lay at the core of Jefferson's thinking on sovereignty and state, both before and after the new U.S. Constitution was adopted. This key to fuller understanding of some long-obscured mainstays of Jefferson's outlook will help to uncover similar ones in other early American founders and foundational documents.

Of appropriate symbolic note is the striking coincidence between the dates 1576 and 1776. That is, the date of the first edition of Bodin's *Republic* in 1576 and the date of Jefferson's Declaration of Independence and Virginia constitution mark a span of exactly 200 years. Broad historical comparisons could even be drawn between the turbulent times in their respective countries of France and America that conditioned Bodin and Jefferson in their ideas of a state's strong unified foundations in legislative sovereignty. By Jefferson's time, the well-established Bodinian ideas on legislative sovereignty had long since supplanted lingering late-medieval concepts of jurisdictional-judicial supremacy as the dominant intellectual tradition. When strongly affirming the legislative framework of sovereign independent statehood at the outset of those foundational documents of 1776, Jefferson was also markedly reaffirming Bodinian doctrines set forth exactly 200 years before in 1576. This is as telling a chronological coincidence as Jefferson's death in 1826 on the fiftieth anniversary of the Declaration of Independence in 1776.

Postscript: A Jefferson-Corasius Connection

There is a more momentous sequel to the Jefferson story in relation to the present series. It has never before been appreciated that his initialled copy of the great massive *Lexicon Juridicum*, produced by Calvinus (Kahl) and continued by Gothofredus in the 1600s, contained abundant references to the legal concepts of Corasius. Corasius' name is included on the title page along with select "illustrious" other jurists of his era who are cited prominently in this *Lexicon*, as mentioned in our initial studies on Corasius. Gothofredus' famed edition of Justinian's *Corpus Iuris*, two copies of which were owned by Jefferson, also contained abundant citations of Corasius. Both channels afforded promising opportunities for Jefferson's knowledge of Corasius, as remains to be further discussed.[180]

Chapter III

Adams in Legislative Profile

1. ADAMS IN OVERVIEW

When John Adams (b. 1733) served with Jefferson on the committee of five assigned by the Continental Congress in 1776 to prepare the Declaration of Independence, he became Jefferson's closest colleague in that endeavor. Although Jefferson initially deferred to Adams, seven years his elder, by urging him to write it, Adams asked him instead to do so, calling him the better writer and more agreeable person. In later years, Adams let it be known that he had had a greater hand in the committee's revised text than people realized. Jefferson steadfastly replied that he (and not Adams) was indeed the author, as he also later indicated in his inscription for his Monticello tombstone.[1] While accepting Jefferson's account and his criticism of Adams' lapses of memory, one is nevertheless struck by Adams' potential influence on Jefferson's great interest at that time in matters of legislative sovereignty, viewed by both men through historical thought and contemporary events.

Like Jefferson, Adams compiled during his long life a huge private library. Though not as large and diverse as Jefferson's, Adams' collection included a vast array of historical books on politics and law, similar to those discussed above in the case of Jefferson. Among them were works by Locke, Sidney, and others deeply indebted to Bodinian traditions on legislative sovereignty. Especially noteworthy is Adams' possession of two editions of Bodin's *Republic*—the 1606 Knolles translation in English and an 18th-century abridgement in French.[2] Adams' library also included his own voluminous writings on political and constitutional history and theory, which point up his interests in legislation, sovereignty, and the state.

Adams' intellectual interests were greatly shaped by his student days at Harvard College, by his many years as a practicing lawyer in Massachusetts, and by his public career in the service of the new emergent nation. In 1774 Adams was elected a Massachusetts delegate to the Continental Congress at Philadelphia. In 1777 he was elected joint commissioner to France to negotiate a treaty of alliance, and in May 1778 he was presented at Versailles to King Louis XVI. In August 1779 Adams returned home and was chosen to write the Massachusetts constitution, which was soon submitted and adopted. He was then sent back to France by Congress in November of 1779. (When he finally returned home in 1788, he had been abroad for about a decade and had acquired large numbers of books while in England, the Netherlands, and France.) In 1780–1782 Adams sought and obtained recognition of American independence and sovereignty from the Netherlands. In 1782 his *Collection of State Papers, relative to the first acknowledgment of the sovereignty* [!] *of the United States of America . . . by their mightiness the States of the United Netherlands* was published in London.[3] In 1782–1783 Adams served on the commission that negotiated peace with Great Britain. In 1785 he was elected by Congress to be first American minister to Britain (while Jefferson was named minister to France). Like Jefferson, he was abroad during the U.S. Constitutional Convention of mid-1787. Adams' three-volume *A Defence of the Constitutions of Government of the United States of America* was published in London in 1787–1788.[4] Elected Vice President under George Washington in 1789, Adams was reelected to that position in 1793. In 1796 he was elected President of the United States, and later lost to Jefferson in 1800 in his campaign for reelection (but not before becoming the first president to occupy the new White House in that last year of office).

The rivalries and antagonisms that developed between Adams the Federalist and Jefferson the Democratic-Republican were eventually overcome in their later years. Their extensive, now famous, exchanges of letters, initiated by Adams after a long hiatus in their correspondence, continued until their mutual deaths on July 4, 1826, on the fiftieth anniversary of the Declaration of Independence.[5]

The distinctions traditionally drawn by historians between Adams as Federalist and Jefferson as Democratic-Republican in their philosophies of government still hold largely true. Adams believed in a strong centralized government, whereas Jefferson wanted a decentralized government. Being more distrusting of human nature and more fearful of sedition and civil strife, Adams had been very apprehensive about Shays' Rebellion in Massachusetts prior to the Constitutional Convention of 1787. Jefferson's greater faith in human nature and in the people's ability to govern themselves instead of needing others to do it for them had made him more understanding of Shays' Rebellion. Being from the more urban Northeast and attuned to New England commercial interests, Adams became more pro-British in his foreign policy. Jefferson, as a southerner and Virginian, was not only more agrarian in his outlook but became more sympathetic toward the French revolutionaries. Adams was for a stronger federal government, whereas Jefferson favored a weaker one, with much power residing in state and local governments. Yet Adams had a more enduring hand in writing the actual constitution adopted by his state than did Jefferson in the case of his state's constitution.

Notwithstanding these kinds of differences between Adams and Jefferson on governmental matters, they both in different ways viewed sovereignty and state in terms of legislation. The common legislative frameworks of the disparate views on sovereignty and state held by these and other American founders recall to mind the common legislative foundation we found in a wide range of European political and legal thinkers of the 17th and 18th centuries. The legislative factor was found to be a common denominator in antitheses on absolutism *vs.* constitutionalism, rationalism *vs.* empiricism, and liberalism *vs.* conservatism. Although Adams was accused by some of having monarchical sympathies, and Jefferson of espousing radical republicanism, their differences over the nature of sovereignty and state were bridged over by their mutual legislative underpinnings.

2. ADAMS ON LEGISLATIVE SOVEREIGNTY

"[I]n all governments the sovereignty is vested in . . . the legislative power"

A clear, concise series of statements by John Adams on legislative sovereignty in connection with the new U.S. Constitution, nearly two years after its completion in Philadelphia, appeared in three letters of mid-July 1789 to Roger Sherman, a fellow signer of the Declaration of Independence. "I read over, with pleasure," began the new Vice President by way of explanation in his first letter, "your observations on the new federal constitution, and am glad to find an opportunity to communicate with you my opinion of some parts of them. It is by a free and amieable [*sic*] intercourse of sentiments, that the friends of our country may hope for such a unanimity of opinion and such a concert of exertions as may sooner or later produce the blessings of good government."[6]

Rather than being strictly separated, Adams believed, the three branches of the federal government should be better interconnected so as to make the executive or President a more integral part of the legislative process of Congress. The ultimately coordinated higher powers of a national (legislative) state like America are and must be "combined in framing the laws by which all are to be governed . . ." The British system, in which the "supreme executive" is "one branch of the legislature," gives to it "a negative on all the laws." This furnishes for Adams a useful partial model for America. This kind of federal system of checks and balances revolving around the legislative process will result in a better system of legislation by which America is governed.[7]

In the course of detailing for Sherman the different types of governments with which the American "republic" may be compared, Adams emphasizes that true sovereignty resides ultimately in the legislative power, to which he assigns a sweeping scope not unlike what it acquired in the hands of Bodin and his followers. The following contexts of Adams' strong statements on legislative sovereignty illustrate his wide range of ideas on republican and other types of states, all of which are ultimately centered around legislative sovereignty. These repeated pronouncements are explicit and pointed: "In all [types of] governments the sovereignty is vested in that man or body of men who have the legislative power"; "the sovereignty, that is, the legislative [power]"; and "the sovereignty, which is the legislative power." More copiously (as usual all *sic*):

> Is it, then, "an extreme not to be imitated by a republic," to make the supreme executive branch a branch of the legislature, and give it a negative on all the laws? . . . In the first place, what is your definition of a republic? Mine is this: *A government whose sovereignty is vested in more than one person.* Governments are divided into *despotisms, monarchies,* and *republics.* A despotism is a government in which the three divisions of power, the legislative, executive and judicial, are all vested in one man. A monarchy is a government where the legislative and executive are vested in one man, but the judicial in other men. In all governments the sovereignty is vested in that man or body of men who have the legislative power. In despotisms and monarchies, therefore, the legislative authority being

> in one man, the sovereignty is in one man. In republics, as the sovereignty, that is, the legislative, is always vested in more thn one, it may be vested in as many more as you please. In the United States it might be vested in two persons, or in three millions, or in any other intermediate number; and in every such supposable case the government would be a republic. In conformity to these ideas, republics have been divided into three species, monarchical, aristocratical, and democratical republics. England is a republic, a monarchical republic it is true, but a republic still; because the sovereignty, which is the legislative power, is vested in more than one man; it is equally divided, indeed, between the one, the few, and the many, or in other words, between the natural division of mankind in society,—the monarchical, the aristocratical, and democratical. It is essential to a monarchical republic, that the supreme executive should be a branch of the legislature, and have a negative on all the laws. I say essential, because if monarchy were not an essential part of the sovereignty, the government would not be a monarchical republic. . . . [T]he . . . practice of Great Britain in making the supreme executive a branch of the legislature, and giving it a negative on all the laws, must be imitated by every monarchical republic.[8]

Behind Adams' analysis lies his view that the federal government under the new U.S. Constitution is, rightly interpreted, a kind of "monarchical republic" or "limited monarchy" in which the chief executive is, as in England, a branch of the legislature through his exercise of the veto power. Lest Adams' outlook on this legislative presidential role seem out of step with American tradition, one has only to consider the dominant legislative role played by more recent American presidents not only in relation to Congress but also through their own independent orders, rules, and regulations. Nor is Adams out of step with Jefferson on this same role; and, not unlike Jefferson, Adams refers here to "[t]he people, the nation, in which all power resides originally." After some indirect preliminary observations on whether America is, like England, a "monarchical republic,"[9] Adams proceeds to answer the question directly. He begins by noting the exceptionally great powers of the U.S. President as based on the new U.S. Constitution, that is, of the chief executive as a branch of the sovereign legislative power, under which his wide array of responsibilities are included in such matters as declaring war, appointing ambassadors, levying taxes, and so forth. He speaks, in other words, of "the whole executive power coextensive with the legislative power." Not unsimilarly did Bodin and his followers include all other such functions under the sovereign power of legislation.

> Let us now consider what our constitution is, and see whether any other name can with propriety be given it, than that of a monarchical republic, or if you will, a limited monarchy. The duration of our president is neither perpetual nor for life; it is only for four years; but his power during those four years is much greater than that of an avoyer, a consul, a podestà, a doge, a stadtholder; nay, than a king of Poland; nay, than a king of Sparta. I know of no first magistrate in any republican gvernment, excepting England and Neuchatel, who possesses a constitutional dignity, authority, and power comparable to his. The power of sending and receiving ambassadors, of raising and commanding armies and navies, of nominating and appointing and commissioning all officers, of managing the treasures, the internal and external affairs of the nation; nay, the whole executive power, coextensive with the legislative power, is vested in him, and he has the right, and his is the duty, to take care that the laws be faithfully executed. These rights and duties, these prerogatives and dignities, are so transcendent that they must naturally and necessarily excite in the nation all the jealousy, envy, fears, apprehensions, and opposition, that are so constantly observed in England against the crown.[10]

In the paragraph immediately following the one just given above, Adams further expands on his strongly stated ideas of legislative sovereignty in the context of America as a kind of "monarchical republic" under the new U.S. Constitution. Yet these statements are replete with dire warnings and a call for a revision or amendment of the Constitution, in order to avoid potential dangers inherent in the existing framework of government under it. In essence, Adams seeks to make the U.S. President's power as chief executive more co-equal with Congress in the sovereign matter of legislation. On such matters, Adams laments the lack of good legislative legacies in the history of political thought from Plato to Montesquieu.

> That these powers are necessary, I readily admit. That the laws cannot be executed without them; that the lives, liberties, properties and characters of the citizens cannot be secure without their protection, is most clear. But it is equally certain, I think, that they ought to have been still greater, or much less.

> The limitations upon them in the cases of war, treaties, and appointments to office, and especially the limitation on the president's independence as a branch of the legislative, will be the destruction of this constitution, and involve us in anarchy, if not amended. I shall pass over all particulars for the present, except the last; because that is now the point in dispute between you and me. Longitude, and the philosopher's stone, have not been sought with more earnestness by philosophers than a guardian of the laws has been studied by legislators from Plato to Montesquieu; but every project has been found to be no better than committing the lamb to the custody of the wolf, except that one which is called a *balance of power*. A simple sovereignty in one, a few, or many, has no balance, and therefore no laws. A divided sovereignty without a balance, or in other words, where the division is unequal, is always at war, and consequently has no laws. In our constitution the sovereignty,—that is, the legislative power,—is divided into three branches. The house and senate are equal, but the third branch, though essential, is not equal. The president must pass judgment upon every law; but in some cases his judgment may be overruled. These cases will be such as attack his constitutional power; it is, therefore, certain he has not equal power to defend himself, or the constitution, or the judicial power, as the senate and house have.[11]

What Adams fears is that the legislative power of Congress will eventually completely overshadow the already insufficient executive power of the U.S. President. This may seem somewhat inconsistent with Adams' view stated above that the U.S. President's scope of power is similar to that exercised by its counterpart in England, which is also a "monarchical republic." Yet Adams is consistent in urging a still stronger role for the U.S. President in legislative sovereignty, that is, as a co-equal or coexistent branch, together with Congress, of the legislative power. The later course of American history during the early years of Reconstruction after Lincoln may have borne Adams out; yet the growth of the so-called "imperial presidency" as a kind of "super-legislator" in more recent times has often tended to overshadow Congress.

> Power naturally grows. Why? Because human passions are insatiable. But that power alone can grow which already is too great; that which is unchecked; that which has no equal power to control it. The legislative power, in our constitution, is greater than the executive; it will, therefore, encroach, because

> both aristocratical and democratical passions are insatiable. The legislative power will increase, the executive will diminish. In the legislature, the monarchical power is not equal either to the aristocratical or democratical; it will, therefore, decrease, while the other will increase. Indeed, I think the aristocratical power is greater than either the monarchical or democratical. That will, therefore, swallow up the other two.
>
> In my letter of yesterday, I think it was proved, that a republic might make the supreme executive an integral part of the legislature. In this, it is equally demonstrated, as I think, that our constitution ought to be amended by a decisive adoption of that expedient.[12]

Adams further elaborates for Sherman on the significant yet still insufficient blending of the executive with the legislative power of Congress under the new U.S. Constitution. Adams' further dimension on legislative sovereignty serves to point up the far greater legislative powers of the modern presidency than Adams could have envisioned. Yet once again the wide array of activities encompassed under the sovereign legislative power is crucial for Adams.

> There is a sense and degree in which the executive, in our constitution, is blended with the legislature. The president has the power of suspending a law; of giving the two houses an opportunity to pause, to think, to collect themselves, to reconsider a rash step of a majority. He has a right to urge all his reasons against it, by speech or message; which, becoming public, is an appeal to the nation. But the rational objection here is, not that the executive is blended with the legislature, but that it is not enough blended; that it is not incorporated [enough] with it, and made an essential part of it. If it were [sufficiently] an integral part of it, it might negative [*sic*] a law without much noise, speculation, or confusion among the people. But as it now stands, I beg you to consider it is almost impossible, that a president should ever have the courage to make use of his partial negative. What a situation would a president be in to maintain a controversy against a majority of both houses before a tribunal of the public? To put a stop to a law that more than half the senate and house, and consequently, we may suppose more than half the nation, have set their hearts upon?[13]

The continuation of the preceding passage sheds further light on Adams' views of legislative sovereignty under the U.S. Constitution. He fears (as a Federalist) the Constitution's subversion if it is not amended to give the President still stronger powers of legislative veto over Congress. Other matters arise as well.[14]

Defence of Constitutions

John Adams' *A Defence of the Constitutions of Government of the United States of America*[15] was published in three volumes in 1787–1788: the first in early 1787 prior to the Constitutional Convention of May-September 1787, the second in late summer 1787 toward the end of its secretive deliberations, and the third in 1788 after the Constitution was completed and made known to the outside world. The genesis of Adams' ideas in the *Defence* involved a complicated set of reactions by him to various views by recent European writers, especially certain critics of American government(s). Yet Adams' *Defence* was also shaped in large measure by the immediate crisis of government that faced the American states and Congress in late 1786 and early 1787 in the wake of Shays' Rebellion in Massachusetts, which also provided a crucial impetus for the convening of the Constitutional Convention in mid-1787.

Like other American state constitutions, the Massachusetts constitution, written earlier on by Adams, fell under criticism by these same European writers, whose influential views, Adams felt, were threatening to spark destabilizing constitutional changes in that and other states. Yet Adams was both a defender and a critic of the forms of American government as set forth in the state constitutions as well as in the Articles of Confederation. Adams defended America's forms of government against criticisms especially by the Frenchman Turgot, as is well indicated toward the beginning of Volume One.[16] At the same time, Adams was urging thoroughgoing changes, particularly in the structure of the legislative branch in relation to the executive.

The fundamental nexus between the legislative and executive branches provided a central theme in Adams' extensive examinations of European history and political thought from ancient and medieval times to the modern era and his own century. Of particular note is the consistency and continuity of Adams' ideas of legislative sovereignty and the legislative state in his *Defence*, in some of his later writings treated above, and in his earlier writings discussed below. The monumental scope of Adams' historical-contemporary studies (quite unlike the approaches of Jefferson, with whom he corresponded concerning the *Defence*[17]) placed Adams all the more distinctively in long-developing Bodinian tradition on these subjects. Adams not only saw legislation as the first mark of sovereignty in a state, but also as an all-encompassing power that includes other powers within or under it.

In his "Conclusion" to the first volume of his *Defence*, Adams underscores the necessity of maintaining the proper equilibrium between branches in American governments. He is intent on preserving the necessary sovereignty of the overarching legislative power. At the same time, however, the executive must be integral, as a distinct branch, having veto power, within that highest, legislative power. These principles apply not only to state governments but also to the national or federal government. The American Congress under the Articles of Confederation has been too centered, Adams believes, around a single assembly, in which the legislative function is obscured and in which a diplomatic function has dominated. (Jefferson disagreed with Adams' view that the Congress was largely a diplomatic body, although the somewhat oblique and rhetorical manner of Adams' statement may have caused Jefferson to miss Adams' underlying point about the obscurance of the true legislative function that should more properly be Congress' role.[18]) Moreover, Adams believes, the state governments themselves must play a crucial role in the balancing of branches in which there is a legislative veto over the legislative branch *per se*. He wishes to write an expanded comprehensive survey of ancient and modern states in order to show the wisdom of not placing all powers—legislative, executive, and judicial—in a single assembly, as Turgot and others have contrariwise thought best. Rightly speaking, according to Adams, the executive authority is most crucial for carrying the laws into effect; yet it must have as well the power of legislative veto by virtue of being an integral part of the ultimate sovereign legislative power in a state, including at the national level. Of ongoing future import, we may add, were Adams' perspectives on the national Congress as necessarily the sovereign power in a state in relation to the executive or President, whose role as a distinct branch is largely defined through participation in the fuller legislative process under a new or revised U.S. constitution still to be produced.

In the same "Conclusion" to the first volume of his *Defence*, Adams fears the danger of fostering both aristocracy and monarchy in America. The people at large must choose their chief executive or president; if the assembly or Congress chooses him, on the model of the prime minister in the British system, the power and influence of the few will increase, promoting an aristocracy. Adams warns that a single national assembly would interfere with the proper work of a convention called to write a new American constitution. The assembly and convention in their different ways should confine themselves to legislation and leave the executive to another body, which, however, must not itself be another assembly that would promote the interests of the few. Regarding a new national government, the choice for Adams, looking ahead in early 1787 to a new U.S. constitution (or at least a thorough revision of the Articles of Confederation), is between a balanced form or a monarchy. If there is no balance and the people have a voice, chaos will arise. Then a military power will emerge in order to put down sedition and revolution.[19]

In the course of the third volume of his *Defence*, when rebutting M. Nedham on "the right constitution of a commonwealth," Adams assays the sovereign legislative power in a rightly constituted state. It not only includes an executive with veto power but establishes the "foundation" of the state through a just system of laws. The constitutional cases of ancient Rome and modern England, as well as various contemporary American states, are brought to bear. Not through a single assembly but rather by means of a mixed government embodying the one, few, and many, and divided into separate legislative, executive, and judicial spheres, can factions, sedition, and chaos be quelled. The "laws alone" of the "legislator," asserts Adams, "are the bond of that dignity which we enjoy in the commonwealth; the foundation of liberty; the fountain of equity . . ." Indeed, the legislator's just and equitable laws are closely aligned, as Cicero likewise recognized, with right reason; as such they possess a kind of divine quality and mandate, thereby reinforcing all the more the exalted nature of the highest supreme power in a state, namely, legislation. A single "sovereign assembly" as the seat of all power in a state, without real checks and balance, is the most likely form of government to promote the selfish interests of the few. A legislator, like a philosopher, has a duty and right to frame his ideas, plans, and institutions according to honest rather than flattering estimates of people. A "sovereignty . . . by one popular assembly" would give even more occasion for "abuse of power" than would an aristocratic senate or a unitary monarchy. The "tripartite" system favored by Adams is, he believes, least prone to such abuses. Human passions prompting abuse of power can exist in a democracy as well as in an aristocracy and monarchy, so that checks and balances are also needed in a democracy. Adams rejects Nedham's comparisons with Lycurgus, the ancient Greek legislator and state founder. However commendable was Lycurgus' plan for "an equality of laws, rights," etc., albeit inferior to "the English and American constitutions," Lycurgus nevertheless gave sovereign power to the senate, not to the people. Hence Lycurgus, argues Adams, does not offer a good precedent for "the right constitution of a commonwealth." (The term "commonwealth" is often used in Adams' writings in place of "state" in ways seeming to echo the title of his copy of Knolles'

1606 English translation of Bodin's *Republic*, namely, *The Six Bookes of a Commonweale*).[20]

In the "Conclusion" to the later third volume of his *Defence*, Adams begins with a lengthy paragraph summarizing the course of historical states from the fall of Rome through modern times. After then declaring that "[a]ll nations, from the beginning, have been agitated by the same passions" and that his "principles developed here will go a great way in explaining every phenomenon that occurs in the history of government," Adams again sees a proper system of laws to be crucial for successful nation-states: "Nations move by unalterable rules; and education, discipline, and laws, make the greatest difference in their accomplishments, happiness, and perfection." Of the new U.S. Constitution of 1787, not yet produced at the time of his first two volumes, Adams expresses much approval, despite his hopes for future amendments. He reiterates his point that the old Congress under the Articles of Confederation became "inadequate" to meet the great needs of a rapidly growing America; instead, it became, like "all the confederacies, ancient and modern," namely, a kind of "federal council" and "diplomatic body" (unable, one might add, to function decisively as a true legislative body). "[T]he new system, which seems admirably calculated to unite their interests and affections, and bring them to an uniformity of principles and sentiments, is equally well combined [especially in legislative, executive, and judicial branches] to unite their wills and forces as a single nation."[21]

Early Writings

In November 1775 while at the Continental Congress in Philadelphia, Adams wrote a short letter to Richard Henry Lee of Virginia in which he briefly outlined his proposals for a new form of government, amid the developing discussions taking place there over American government and the impending break from Britain. Adms began on a now familiar legislative note: "The course of events naturally turns the thoughts of gentlemen to the subjects of legislation and jurisprudence: and it is a curious problem, what form of government is most readily and easily adopted by a colony upon a sudden emergency." He continued: "A legislative, an executive, and a judicial power comprehend the whole of what is meant and understood by government. It is by balancing each of these powers against the other two, that the efforts in human nature toward tyranny can alone be checked and restrained, and any degree of freedom preserved in the constitution." As for the relationship between the legislative and executive branches: "Let the governor, council, and house, be each a distinct and independent branch of the legislature, and have a negative on all laws." Early on, then, in his thinking, Adams had clearly seen the underlying importance of legislation in matters of sovereignty and state.[22]

Soon thereafter, in January 1776, Adams wrote a lengthier letter, as a kind of pamphlet, on his proposals for a new government, responding to a request by George Wythe. (Wythe was a fellow delegate to the Congress and fellow signer of the Declaration of Independence, as well as former law teacher and mentor of Jefferson.[23]) Wythe lent the letter to Lee. According to Adams, the most pertinent models have been provided by English theorists in relation to the British constitution, when apprehending it in proper republican ways. The idea that legislation lies at the heart of all good republican forms of government, in "an empire of laws, and not of men," became for Adams a central unifying theme (that phrase harking back to Solon in his capacity as ancient Greek lawgiver and state founder). The whole legislative process, and in particular "how laws are made," is of utmost importance for Adams in the matter of constructing the best republican form of government. Indeed, the legislative factor becomes for Adams a kind of common denominator underlying other elements of sovereignty and state, as if in a kind of Bodinian all-inclusiveness.

> A man must be indifferent to the sneers of modern Englishmen, to mention in their company the names of Sidney, Harrington, Locke, Milton, Nedham, Neville, Burnet, and Hoadly. No small fortitude is necessary to confess that one has read them. The wretched condition of this country, however, for ten or fifteen years past, has frequently reminded me of their principles and reasonings. They will convince any candid mind, that there is no good government but what is republican. That the only valuable part of the British constitution is so; because the very definition of a republic is "an empire of laws, and not of men." That, as a republic is the best of governments, so that particular arrangement of the powers of society, or, in other words, that form of government which is best contrived to secure an impartial and exact execution of the laws, is the best of republics.
>
> Of republics there is an inexhaustible variety, because the possible combinations of the powers of society are capable of innumerable variations.
>
> As good government is an empire of laws, how shall your laws be made? In a large society, inhabiting an extensive country, it is impossible that the whole should assemble to make laws. The first necessary step, then, is to depute power from

> the many to a few of the most wise and good. But by what rules shall you choose your representatives? . . .
>
> The principal difficulty lies, and the greatest care should be employed, in constituting this representative assembly. It should be in miniature an exact portrait of the people at large. . . .
>
> A representation of the people in one assembly being obtained, a question arises, whether all the powers of government, legislative, executive, and judicial, shall be left in this body? I think a people cannot be long free, nor ever happy, whose government is in one assembly.[24]

Adams goes on in the same piece to enumerate his objections to the placement of all legislative power in a single assembly. He then outlines in detail his model for a new form of republican government for the American colonies, now severed from Britain by act of parliament. The various distinct bodies and branches of government are interrelated in the mechanisms of the legislative process. The executive and governor become a distinct yet integral part of the legislature (while the judicial power is an independent interpreter of laws).[25]

A nearly identical proposal was advanced by Adams in January of 1776 to the delegates from North Carolina, who had been authorized by their legislature to ask him for a model for their own colony. Here, for him, the three branches of the legislature came into even sharper focus. Adams also reflected in somewhat more distinct fashion on the need for a clearly structured Congress, without a continental constitution and confederation that would incur the failings and strife common to all such forms in Europe. His proposed Congress was for the representatives of the "colonies." This was perhaps a sign that Adams, like some others, was still not yet fully thinking of new states independent of Britain; yet he did view some of his provisions as interim steps until a new government would take charge and adopt its new modes. Finally, the judicial power was clearly conceived here in terms of its relation to the laws.[26]

The Massachusetts State Constitution (and Knolles' Bodin)

Perhaps no other work by John Adams remains better known or more permanently enshrined than his constitution for his home state of Massachusetts, including its initial Preamble and Declaration of Rights.[27] Written by him in late 1779 and soon adopted, with mostly minor modifications, it is often credited as being the oldest still functioning state constitution in America. By comparison, Jefferson's drafts of the Virginia constitution in 1776 were far less incorporated into the official Virginia constitution of that year, albeit his introductory declaration of grievances and rights was almost fully adopted. According to a recent authority: "There being as yet no national constitution, the form of government chosen by each of the states was a matter of utmost gravity. The constitution of an independent sovereign state had to stand on its own merits, not serve merely as a secondary component of a large, overarching structure. ... To prepare, he had reviewed in detail those constitutions already framed by other states. ... Adams ... use[d] the word 'commonwealth' [in the title] rather than 'state,' as had Virginia, a decision he made on his own and that no one was to question. ... The constitution of the Commonwealth of Massachusetts is the oldest functioning written constitution in the world."[28] Adams' special usage of the word "commonwealth" was suggestive of a democratic republic as well as an all-inclusive sovereign state entity. The question again arises whether his use of "commonwealth" was influenced not only by British concepts but also by his copy of Richard Knolles' 1606 English translation of Bodin's *Republic* under the noted title *The Six Bookes of a Commonweale*.

In his "Preamble" to his "Constitution of the Commonwealth of Massachusetts," Adams begins with a clear, extended statement on "the end of government" being to "safeguard the body politic" and to ensure its "safety and tranquillity" through all "measures necessary." This "body politic" is a "social compact" between "the people" or "citizens" as individuals and as a whole, so that "all shall be governed by certain laws for the common good." To this end, the most crucial goal of a constitution is "to provide for an equitable mode of making laws," as well as for their proper "interpretation and ... execution." Gratitude is given by Adams for the goodness of "the great Legislator of the universe." Echoed by him are not only concepts of Locke and Rousseau on social contract but also older notions of "the welfare of the people" as "the supreme law," as well as of God as the great lawgiver.

In addition, there is here in the Preamble a strong possibility that Adams was directly influenced by the noted beginning of the first chapter of Bodin's *Republic* in Knolles' well-known English translation, which Adams had in his library. The title of the first chapter of Bodin's Book I in Knolles' edition was "What is the principall end of a well ordered Commonweale." That first chapter was replete with references to the end or final cause in terms of the welfare, safety, and tranquillity of the people in a commonwealth or state. These viewpoints may have influenced Adams' fuller wording as given below. Once again, it is possible that Adams was also influenced by Knolles' translation of "commonweale" or commonwealth for the French *république* or Latin *respublica* when framing his state constitution for Massachusetts as a sovereign "commonwealth" (it being no longer a "colony"). Bodin had also referred in that and other chapters to the divine model of God the lawgiver and lawmaker. There may well also be a link between Adams' accent here on legislative facets of sovereignty and Jefferson's comparable stress on legislative sovereignty in his Virginia constitution, which was written a few years earlier (without such a title) and was quite possibly influenced by his own copy of Bodin's *Republic*. The contextual evidence in Adams' other writings is striking (as given in the note below).[29]

In his "Declaration of Rights," which forms the first chapter or part of his constitution for Massachusetts, Adams begins by declaring that "[a]ll men are born [equally (deleted in the officially adopted version)] free." This was identical to the wording at the beginning of Rousseau's *Social Contract*. The same opening lines by Adams also refer to people "defending their lives and liberties . . . and property," as well as "obtaining their safety and happiness." Here one is reminded not only of Locke's central concern with "life, liberty, and property" but also of Jefferson's rephrasing on "life, liberty, and the pursuit of happiness." Religious toleration and freedom of worship must be ensured by "the legislature," Adams wrote, this "being necessary for the preservation of civil society." Because "a future state of rewards and punishments . . . [is] the only true foundation of morality, the legislature" has the right and duty to support "public worship of God" (a statement deleted in the official version). In light of these and other borrowings, it is also possible that Adams was partly influenced here by Beccaria and traditional writers on crimes, rewards, and punishments.[30]

In his "Declaration of Rights," Adams sets forth the fundamental legislative foundations of sovereignty and state in the new Massachusetts "commonwealth," which he characterizes as "a free, sovereign, and independent state." Because "[t]he people . . . have the . . . right of governing themselves," they "enjoy every power, jurisdiction, and right" of self-determination. This power, however, "may not . . . be . . . delegated" to the U.S. Congress. Because "[a]ll power" was "residing originally in the people" and is still "derived from them," according to contract theory a la Locke and Rousseau, their representatives in the government, "vested with . . . legislative, executive, or judicial" authority, are "accountable to them." The purpose and end of government is to secure "the common good" and the "safety . . . and happiness of the people," who "alone" have the "right to institute government . . . or totally change" it for the sake of that end. The state must protect all individuals' "life, liberty, and property, according to standing laws." Moreover, "the people of this commonwealth are not controllable by any other laws than those to which their constitutional representative body have given their consent." All citizens must have expeditious remedy and justice for all "injuries or wrongs ... [to their] person, property, or character by having recourse to the laws ... [and] conformably to the laws." In court proceedings, moreover, "the life, liberty, and property of the citizens" must always be protected in accordance with due process and "the law of the land." The "right to trial by jury ... shall be held sacred; unless in causes [of certin kinds relating to mariners and the high seas] ... the legislature shall hereafter find it necessary to alter it." As for "the fundamental principles of the constitution," "[t]he people ... require of their lawgivers and magistrates an observance of them in the formation and execution of the laws necessary in the good administration of the commonwealth." To "request of the legislative body ... redress of the wrongs done them" and to instruct their representatives are fundamental rights of "[t]he people." Only "the legislature, or ... authority derived from it" has "[t]he power of suspending the laws, or the execution of the laws, . . . only as the legislature shall expressly provide for ... " The rights of the people include "freedom of ... speech ... in ... the legislature" among their representatives. "The legislature ought frequently to assemble ... for correcting ... the laws, and for making new laws ... " Laws cannot be made to apply retroactively to punish actions not declared to be crimes in previous laws. The "impartial interpretation of the laws, and administration of justice," are crucial for preserving individual rights to "life, liberty, [and] property."[31]

Adams' actual constitution or "Frame of Government," comprising Chapter or Part II following the "Declaration of Rights" in Chapter or Part I, opens with the following striking statement: "The people inhabiting the territory ... called the Province of Massachusetts Bay, do hereby solemnly and mutually agree with each other to form themselves into a free, sovereign, and independent body politic, or State, by the name of THE COMMONWEALTH OF MASSACHUSETTS." In his draft version, there then follows another significant statement: "In the government of the Commonwealth of Massachusetts, the legislative, executive, and judicial power shall be placed in separate departments, to the end that it might be a government of laws, and not of men." In the final official text of 1780, where it appears as the last article in the "Declaration," this statement was altered so as to stress even further that none of these separate departments should infringe on the others; the final clause echoing Solon was kept essentially intact ("to the end it may be a government of laws and not of men"). The first article of the first section dealing with the legislative power (followed subsequently by the executive and judicial powers in turn) launches into the specific mechanisms. It reads: "The department of legislation shall be formed by two branches, senate and house of representatives; each of which shall have a negative on the other." To this Adams added: "And the first magistrate shall have a negative upon all the executive and judicial departments." However, the convention instead adopted a different and separate second article on the topic in place of the absolute negative that Adams thought so essential.[32]

In light of all the above statements by Adams (that were also adopted by the convention unless otherwise indicated), there is little doubt that he falls squarely into Bodinian traditions of legislative sovereignty and the legislative state, traditions that also infused the works of Locke and Rousseau that Adams utilized and possessed. Whether Adams was influenced here by Knolles' English translation of Bodin's *Republic* or *Commonwealth*, likewise in Adams' library, cannot be adequately answered here. Yet it seems a strong likelihood. The various close and loose congruities between Adams and Bodin cited or alluded to above suggest how rich a repository of ideas and materials it would have provided for him at that point. Although Bodin applied his ideas of legislative sovereignty to democratic, no less than to monarchical, states, he tended in the context of his contemporary 16th-century France to focus more on monarchical perspectives. This tendency may have suited Adams' own reputed inclinations in that direction, in contradistinction to Jefferson. At the same time, the concepts of legislative sovereignty, reminiscent of Bodin, in Adams' Massachusetts constitution were likely influenced by those in Jefferson's Declaration of Independence of July 1776 (corresponding to those in his declarations introducing the Virginia constitution just before that in June 1776), to which Adams contributed some modifications as fellow committeeman. To the extent that Adams' state constitution became in turn a prototype for ensuing constitutions for some other states, the channels for potential Bodinian influence on ideas of legislative sovereignty and the legislative state continued on from these early foundations into the American future.

"A [sovereign] legislature in three branches . . ., and independent judges"

In his Autobiography, Adams recalled his proposals at the Continental Congress in Philadelphia in mid-1775, a year before independence was declared, to reestablish "the powers of government . . . in every State or Colony . . . in the country."[33] His purpose was to invigorate and unite those states or colonies in a common front against Britain by developing in each of them the proper governmental authority requisite for utilizing their resources and achieving their potential. Adams met with considerable objection and opposition from his fellow representatives at the

Congress. He gradually convinced them that their constituents who had sent them could be persuaded to accept these proposals.

The central feature of Adams' proposal in the same passage of his Autobiography was his belief that "A legislature in three branches ought to be preserved, and independent judges."[34] This was a consistent theme throughout Adams' career. The legislature was clearly for him the ultimate sovereign body, in which the executive functioned as a separate third branch in addition to the two regular houses or chambers comprising separate branches thereof. Although Adams was a strong advocate of an independent judiciary, its vital role of interpreting and enforcing the laws made by the legislature was less centrally defined by him in terms of the ultimate sovereign power in a state.

This system of three branches of the legislature needing to be "preserved" was, in part, a reinvented adaptation not only of American colonial forms of government, but also of British modes of parliamentary rule, in which there were two separate regular houses and a distinct executive power. It is striking that Adams here looked upon the British parliamentary system as three branches of the legislature in which the executive or Prime Minister is a separate branch (although the judicial power is part of the House of Lords, one of two houses of Parliament). What Adams sought here was: "A plan as nearly resembling the government under which we were born and have lived, as the circumstances of the country will admit. Kings we never had among us. Nobles we never had. Nothing hereditary ever existed in the country; nor will the country require or admit of any such thing. But governors and councils we have always had, as well as representatives." As to how elections to offices will be conducted: "The representatives of the people in a convention will be the best qualified to contrive a mode."

Adams' proclivities toward the British model of centralized government (as mirrored in some colonial governments) differed somewhat from Jefferson's desire for more decentralized government. Yet both men focused on legislative sovereignty. Their later disagreements over Adams' reputed support for hereditary rule in France at the outbreak of the Revolution there will become apparent below. In subsequent Federalist government, Adams' idea of the executive as one of three branches of the legislature was perhaps a forerunner of 20th-century views of the presidency as a kind of super-legislative body, which, through its powers and agencies, functions together with Congress to promote the legislative agenda of the sovereign American national state; even the Supreme Court as independent judiciary often acts as a kind of rule-making (and law-making) body. If they were to look upon these modern transformations, Adams and Jefferson would no doubt part company with each other. Adams' idea of the legislature as divided into three branches remained his steadfast viewpoint during and after the framing of the new U.S. Constitution; in it he saw the executive, with partial (yet insufficient) veto power, as a third branch of the legislature, with an independent judiciary.

In an ensuing passage of his Autobiography, Adams' criticisms of the country's governmental form established by Congress in 1776 represented another familiar and consistent theme of his. Concerning events of later 1776, Adams commented on the Articles of Confederation as follows: "All the powers of government, legislative, executive, and judiciary were at that time collected in one centre, and that centre was Congress."[35] (The Confederation Congress was not truly functioning as a legislative body, as Adams often suggested elsewhere, due to this blurring together of its functions. A division of three separate branches of the legislature would, he affirmed, enable Congress to perform properly as a legislative body in conjunction with the executive.)

3. ADAMS' USES OF HISTORY

Political Thinkers, Ancient and Modern

As suggested above, Adams' broad and voluminous discussions in his *Defence of Constitutions of the United States* included extensive detailed treatments of historical subjects, ranging from antiquity and the Middle Ages to the European background in his own century. In the first volume of his *Defence* appear three chapters dealing with various writers in the history of political thought. After dealing with Swift, Franklin, and Price in Chapter IV, Adams turns to Machiavelli, Sidney, Montesquieu, and Harrington in Chapter V, thereafter passing to Polybius, Dionysius of Halicarnassus, Plato, Locke, Milton, and Hume in Chapter VI. The second volume includes lengthy materials concerning Machiavelli's historical examinations of the Florentine state. The third volume includes lengthy considerations of Nedham's ideas. Throughout all these and related portions of Adams' *Defence* appear extensive presentations of texts that often dominate his discussions and commentaries relating to them. Running throughout these and other historical parts of the *Defence* are the same themes highlighted above, particularly the dangers of concentrating power into a single assembly, no less than into a monarchy. Legislative aspects of sovereignty and state often enter into the picture in myriad diverse ways, whether in his presentations of texts or in his discussions relating to them.

A revealing typical example of Adams' uses of history in connection with political thought is found in his treatment of Polybius' ideas in contexts of Roman history (a source also much utilized by Bodin). Citing Turgot, Adams begins his Chapter VI of Volume I with some broad overviews of his own purpose and method. Polybius' references to Lycurgus, presented by Adams near the outset of that chapter, carry over from his preceding materials on Harrington and "the art of lawgiving" at the end of Chapter V. Adams' references to a range of modern political thinkers further serve to elucidate his own approach. Adams' wide historical knowledge is typically evident below, as is, indirectly, that of other American founders in their state constitutions as defended by Adams from European critics like Turgot.

> My design is more extensive than barely to show the imperfection of M. Turgot's idea. This might be done in a few words and a very short process of reasoning; but I wish to assemble together the opinions and reasonings of philosophers, politicians, and historians, who have taken the most extensive views of men and societies, whose characters are deservedly revered, and whose writings were in the contemplation of those who framed the American constitutions. It will not be contested that all these characters are united in Polybius, who, in a fragment of his sixth book ... of the *Roman Antiquities* ..., says—
>
> "It is customary, with those who professedly treat this subject, to establish three sorts of government,—kingly government, aristocracy, and democracy....
>
> Lycurgus concluded that every form of government that is simple, by soon degenerating into that vice that is allied to it, must be unstable. ... Lycurgus, to avoid these inconveniences, formed his government not of one sort, but united in one all the advantages and properties of the best governments; to the end that no branch of it ... might degenerate into the vice which is congenial to it...."
>
> Thus ... Polybius's opinion of different orders, checks, and balances, in a commonwealth, is very different from that of M. Turgot. The Roman constitution formed the noblest people and the greatest power that has ever existed. But if all the powers of the consuls, senate, and people had been centred in a single assembly of the people, collectively or representatively, will any man pretend to believe that they would have been long free, or ever great?
>
> The distribution of power was, however, never accurately or judiciously made in that constitution. The executive was never sufficiently separated from the legislative, nor had these powers a control upon each other defined with sufficient accuracy....

> Polybius . . . is more charitable in his representation of human nature than Hobbes, Mandeville, Rochefoucauld, Machiavel, Beccaria, Rousseau, De Lolme, or even than our friend Dr. Price. He candidly supposes that the first kingly government will be wisely and honestly administered . . .; that the first aristocracy will be conducted with caution and moderation . . .; and that the people, for a generation at least, . . . will behave with decorum.
>
> But perhaps it might be more exactly true and natural to say, that the king, the aristocracy, and the people, as soon as ever they felt themselves secure in the possession of their power, would begin to abuse it.
>
> In M. Turgot's single assembly, those who should think themselves most distinguished by blood and education, as well as fortune, would be most ambitious . . . to increase their parties. . . .
>
> The only remedy is to throw the rich and the proud into one group, in a separate assembly, and there tie their hands; if you give them scope with the people at large or their representatives, they will destroy *all equality and liberty* . . .[36]

In his long section on Plato, here in *Defence* I, VI, Adams underscores the centrality and sovereign authority of the laws in the state in the forms set down in Plato's *Republic* and *Laws*. The system of laws is not only the foundation of the state but also of justice and education.

> Plato has given us the most accurate detail of the natural vicissitudes of manners and principles, the usual progress of the passions in society, and revolutions of governments into one another.
>
> In the fourth book of his *Republic*, he describes his perfect commonwealth, where kings are philosophers, and philosophers kings; where the whole city might be in the happiest condition, and not any one tribe remarkably happy beyond the rest; in one word, where the *laws govern*, and justice is established; where the guardians of the laws are such in reality, and preserve the constitution instead of destroying it, and promote the happiness of the whole city, not their own particularly; where the state is one, not many; where there are no parties of the poor and the rich at war with each other; . . . where the children, receiving from their infancy an education agreeable to the laws of the constitution, grow up to be worthy men, and observant of the laws; where the system, both of laws and education,

> is contrived to produce the virtues of fortitude, temperance, wisdom, and justice, in the whole city, and in all the individual citizens . . .[37]

In ensuing portions of the same section on Plato, Adams further shows his interest in the legislative nature of sovereignty and state. He draws upon the Elizabethan writings of Thomas Smith on the English constitution in terms of a "commonwealth." (Smith, like Dionysius of Halicarnassus and others treated by Adams, had been well considered by Bodin.) Adams concludes by faulting Plato for not providing a proper system of checks and balances through a division of powers in his ideal state.[38]

When he briefly turns, next, to Locke, Adams more poignantly criticizes Plato along with others like More and Locke who have in some respects proposed overly unrealistic "systems of legislation" for a state.[39] Then, when turning briefly to Hume, Adams castigates both him and Locke for various unwise or unworkable legislative systems lying at the heart of the machinery of state (and with references to Locke's "life, liberty, and property" as well as Solon's "government of laws, not of men").[40]

In the third volume of his *Defence*, Adams gives a long presentation and refutation, extending for well over two hundred pages, of Marchamont Nedham's *The Excellencie of a Free State*. Written in mid-17th-century England, it was reprinted in 1767 by someone whose heir sent a copy to Adams. Here Adams further develops his attacks against those like Nedham who have sought to place all sovereignty and "the safety of the state" into a single center in which all legislative, executive, and judicial power resides in an assembly of the people, so that executive authority is wholly dependent on the legislature. The making, executing, and interpreting of the laws must be, according to Adams, separate but interconnected functions; the executive should be appointed directly, like the legislators, by the people, in whom resides ultimate sovereignty. Yet the executive should still be closely interfaced with the legislature.[41]

In his "Conclusion," to the third volume and to the work itself, Adams first broadly summarizes the sweep of Western history from the fall of the Roman Empire through the modern period. He declares that all nations have been guided by certain historical laws. He closes with a ringing though qualified endorsement of the new U.S. Constitution, in line with his own ideas.[42]

The Florentine State and Machiavelli

In the more than three hundred pages of the second volume of Adams' *Defence* that are devoted to Italian republics of the Middle Ages and Renaissance, nearly two hundred pages deal with the Florentine state as detailed by Machiavelli, along with other historians like Gucciardini. Other republics treated here, and in succeeding parts over another 150 pages, are Siena, Bologna, Pistoia, Cremona, Padua, Manua, and Montepulcano. Throughout these lengthy treatments, Adams again raises the kinds of central contemporary issues featured above on legislation, sovereignty, and the state in relation to his American ideals of democracy, liberty, justice, and so on. Some of Adams' extended discussions on Machiavelli's accounts in his *History of Florence* are also interesting in light of our earlier volume on Machiavelli and Machiavellism in contexts of Renaissance Florence and Rome.

A typical kind of contemporary slant given by Adams to Machiavelli's account of Florentine history occurs in connection with the turmoil caused by the medieval struggles between Guelphs and Ghibellines. Adams compares the Florentine form of government and constitution to that devised by both Turgot and Nedham. Adams also alludes to the turmoil and conflict surrounding Shays' Rebellion in Massachusetts in the winter of 1786–1787, a prime catalyst for Adams in writing the *Defence*.[43]

Another representative case of Adams' use of Machiavelli's history of Florence as a vehicle for drawing contemporary lessons and parallels centers on the necessary foundation provided by law and legislation for the state as well as for liberty. Adams gives to Machiavelli's points and suggestions somewhat sharper focus and relevance for the American situation in his own period. Once again, the relationships between legislative and executive functions are framed by Adams in both historical and contemporary fashion. Good laws and true liberty go together in preserving the life of a republican "state" or "commonwealth" (a la Knolles' Bodin?) especially when they are characterized by consistency and continuity rather than by change and inconsistency.[44]

On the rise of Cosimo de Medici to power in the first half of the 15th century, Adams has much to say when commenting on Machiavelli's history of that period. At one point, Adams tends to read more modern concepts of sovereignty (and commonwealth) into Machiavelli's account, albeit with an "as if" qualifier: "Machiavel begins his fifth book as if he supposed his reader convinced that the commonwealth [!] of Florence had expired, and an absolute sovereignty in Cosimo had commenced . . ."[45] Factions and divisions in a state can be harmful, yet are often more easily handled in republics than in monarchies or despotisms "by distinct and independent legislative, executive, and judicial powers, and by two councils in the legislature." This is Adams' recipe in response to Machiavelli's observation (identifying state founders with lawgivers) that "it is important . . . for any legislator or founder of a republic to prevent feuds and animosities in it . . ."[46] According to Adams, again concerning Cosimo's rise, "it is impossible that division, in any form of simple government, should ever end in the public good, or in any thing but factions."[47] When reflecting on Cosimo's patronage of the Neoplatonic philosopher Marsilio Ficino, as recounted by Machiavelli in the broader context of Cosimo's patronage of arts and letters, Adams declares that both Ficino and Plato exercised a significant influence on Machiavelli, who also had some close ties to the Medici and Pope Leo X. (This is interesting in view of our earlier book on these subjects). While recognizing Cosimo's achievements in fostering learning, Adams also laments Cosimo's hampering of liberty. For Florence to have been truly free, it needed "a government of three well-balanced branches" instead of becoming an "absolute sovereignty" under the Medici.[48]

Throughout Adams' lengthy ensuing studies of Florentine history as surveyed by Italian historians after Machiavelli (chiefly Guicciardin, Nerli, and Varchi), he goes on to draw his own familiar conclusions and lessons. According to Adams, the subsequent growth of Medici "sovereignty" in Florence under the later Lorenzo and Cosimo in the 16th century resulted in loss of liberty as power became increasingly vested in a single center, without any alternate check or balance.[49] When the later Cosimo became, as duke, the sovereign head of the Florentine state, liberty ceased. In the end, for Adams, the whole history of Florence is a tragic story of how the concentration of power in one center, as also seen in the ideas of Turgot and Nedham, stifles freedom and fosters conflicts between the higher groups and classes. The result is neglect of the people at large, along with "violence, sedition, and rebellion."[50] If early on the Florentine gonfalonier as executive had had a negative or veto on a legislature composed of two independent branches in the signoria and great council, with an independent and good judiciary, that is, on the American models set forth by Adams, the Florentine state could have been a story of success rather than of ultimate ruination.[51] Adams devotes a separate chapter to "Machiavel's Plan of a Perfect Commonwealth," which he notes was commissioned by Pope Leo X. It admirably gave "sovereign power" to "the citizens themselves" and provided for the "three orders" in the Florentine "state" as a "commonwealth" or "republic." Despite his wise plan for "three powers" as a remedy for Florence's long-standing constitutional ills, however, Machiavelli's plan did not separate "the executive power from the legislative" power and "would not have remedied the evils."[52]

In succeeding chapters on other Italian states of the Middle Ages and Renaissance, Adams further drives home his main point about the dangers inherent in a single sovereign assembly over which the executive has no negative or veto, resulting in loss of power and liberty for the people.[53]

The French Civil Wars and Bodin

Even more unconventional than his *Defence* was Adams' *Discourses on Davila; A series of papers on political history*. It presents one of the thorniest thickets for scholars attempting to pursue the development of Adams' thought prior to his becoming President. Adams' *Discourses* originally appeared as a series of newspaper articles. They were published over the course of a year in 1790–1791, early in his first term as Vice President, in the *Gazette of the United States* at Philadelphia. The articles caused much controversy, including with Jefferson, and led to charges that Adams was an outright monarchist, with the result that the series was discontinued. The articles were eventually published as a book in 1805 in Boston under the above title. Adams continued to make marginal notes in his copy as late as 1812–1813, and these were largely incorporated in the edition of his *Works* by C. F. Adams several decades later. Adams' articles were prompted largely by the outbreak of revolution in France in 1789, yet also by the publication in 1788 of Condorcet's *Lettres ... sur l'inutilité de partager de pouvoir législatif entre plusieurs corps*. Condorcet had defended a position formerly taken by Turgot on the need to place *legislative power* in a single body rather than in several bodies; in his copy of the work, Adams wrote: "The following four letters were written by the Marquis of Condorcet, a Man of Science, but little acquainted with History: ignorant, totally ignorant of all writings on the Science of Government ..." Two copies of Condorcet's *The Life of M. Turgot* (1787) translated from the French were also in Adams' library. Having used Italian and other history in his *Defence* of 1787–1788 in order to defend U.S. state constitutions in the aftermath of Shays' Rebellion in the winter of 1786–1787, Adams now found in French history a medium for his ideas on the outbreak of the French Revolution in 1789. His historical focal point became the French civil wars in the second half of the 16th century. His chief sources were his copies of the French and English translations from the Italian of Henarico Caterino Davila's *Historia delle guerre civili di Francia*. First published in Venice in 1630, it achieved great success, was translated into many languages, and reached over 200 editions by the end of the 18th century.[54]

Davila's *History of the Civil Wars of France* was a long, detailed coverage, totalling over a thousand large, well-filled pages in the single volume of the early Italian editions (and over eighteen hundred pages in Adams' three-volume French edition). It covered the French civil wars during the reigns of Francis II, Charles IX, Henry III, and Henry IV (as well as of Catherine de Medici) from 1560 to 1598. In Adams' copy of the French translation, the first volume culminated with the St. Bartholomew's Day Massacre in 1572 and its immediate aftermath. The second volume began with the events of 1574 and proceeded to the meeting of the Estates General at Blois in 1576, which was notably attended by Jean Bodin as well discussed by Davila in Book VI. Davila began by pointing out Bodin's great fame as a writer. Although not explicitly mentioned by Davila, Bodin's *Republic* had been published earlier that same year and was already compared by some to Aristotle's *Politics*, due to its encyclopedic classical, medieval, and Renaissance learning (a reason for its appeal also to Jefferson). Davila undoubtedly had the *Republic* specifically in mind and was alluding to it when noting Bodin's fame as a writer.

Adams' copy of the second volume of Davila's *History* is filled with comments, notations, and underlining in his own hand in ink. In the margin next to Davila's references in Book VI to Bodin appear solid mentions of Bodin's name by Adams (which have been neglected by historians). Unfortunately, these references by Adams never became part of Adams' *Discourses on Davila*, because that work ends its commentaries after the first volume of the French translation, that is, at the end of Book V, just before Book VI with its references to Bodin. The first volume also had extensive marginalia and underlining by Adams (albeit lacking in the third volume). Evidently, Adams intended to extend his *Gazette* series to incorporate his marginalia in the second French volume of Davila's *History*, as he had already done in his *Gazette* series on the first volume. However, the heated controversy caused by his *Gazette* series, which later became his book entitled *Discourses on Davila*, caused him to discontinue the project of doing another series on the rest of Davila's *History*.

The changing position of Bodin at the meetings of the Estates General at Blois in 1576 is a complicated subject, especially as it related to his goal in the *Republic* for a *politique* regeneration of royal authority in the midst of the French religious and civil wars.[55] The main framework of Davila's first series of comments in Book VI pertaining, directly and indirectly, to Bodin is conveyed in the following passages (from the English edition, all *sic*), replete with two direct citations of Bodin's name.

> ... *Jean Bodin*, a man famous for learning and expert in State-affairs, one of the Deputes of the Commons of Vermandois, and who was secretly induced by the King to contradict the Churchmen in that particular, endeavoured by a long discourse to make it appear unto the Assembly how ruinous and fatal the new taking up of *Arms* would be, repeating from the beginning all the dangers and miseries of the late Wars, which made a very deep impression in the minds of the third Estate, and would have done the like in both the other *Orders*, if their consciences had been absolutely free and sincere; but meeting with men who were not only carried by the zeal of Religion, but whose opinions were bypassed and pre-engaged, it was determined by plurality of voices, that request should be made unto the King to establish only the Catholick Religion in the Kingdom, and to exclude for ever all communion with the Huguenots. Nevertheless, *Bodin* procured certain words to be entered in the Records of Commons to certifie that desire of unity in Religion without the noise of *Arms*, and the necessity of War.
>
> This notion of the States being propounded to the King, ... made him resolve no longer to oppose, (knowing that the plurality of voices would be clearly against him) but to delude the propositions of the Deputies; for by opposing he saw those Arms of the Catholic League would be turned upon him, which were then prepared against the Huguenots.[56]

Almost all of the preceding passages were underlined by Adams in Book VI of his copy of Davila's *History*. In the left margin next to Davila's first direct reference to Bodin's name, with regard to his renowned learning and his role at Blois, Adams wrote in big printed letters "Bodin." By contrast, very few of the surrounding pages of Book VI contain any underlining at all, although those other margins contain at a few points some brief written comments.[57] The continuation of the same passages given above is also of relevance for Bodin at Blois but contains no underlinings or markings.[58] In Davila's second set of direct and indirect references to Bodin occurring several pages later, there are further explicit references by Davila to Bodin's name; in the adjacent right margin, Adams again wrote the name "Bodin," but made no underlinings or comments.[59] The passage centers on a noted speech given at Blois by Bodin and is also of interest.[60] All of the foregoing markings on Bodin made by Adams in his copy of Davila's *History* have been much neglected by historians.

In his discourses on the first five books of Davila's *History*, Adams was generally less interested in the kinds of elaborate details by Davila exemplified above, despite his periodic long quotations of Davila. Rather, Adams was intent on setting forth his own viewpoints—often with little real relation to Davila's narrative—particularly on contemporary-historical issues concerning the French Revolution. Adams may well have sensed that Bodin at Blois and in his *Republic* sought a regenerated royal power as the best way to restore central authority in the French state during that earlier French upheaval, which had likewise caused great chaos and uncertainty. Adams' handling of sovereignty, the state, legislation, and other matters of interest in relation to Davila's *History* points up his own contemporary and historical outlook. Toward the beginning of his *History*, Davila discussed the French Salic laws that had established the hereditary succession of kings while also ensuring the rights of the people. Adams treated these discussions by Davila in provocative ways.

It was Adams' last *Gazette* article that fueled perhaps the biggest outcry, due to its perceived outright support of hereditary succession in France, thereby further raising the charges of monarchism against him and prompting the discontinuation of the series. When his *Discourses* was later published as a book in 1805, five years after he had left the presidency, that final article was omitted and replaced by a much milder postscript, in which Adams called for a constitutional balance in France and elsewhere, lest liberty be lost. As Adams argued throughout his *Discourses*, it was the lack of constiutional balance that had caused the French crisis in the later 16th century and now in thc latcr 18th ccn tury. It was a theme found also in his *Defence* in connection with Italian and other history.

Thus Adams' *Discourses on Davila* offers a wealth of materials of present interest on a wide range of historical and contemporary topics. The texts to follow (in the note below) illuminate Adams' above perspectives (aside from those on Bodin specifically) and others relating to them. Adams' themes of sovereignty, the state, and legislation are particularly noteworthy.[61]

4. ADAMS' LETTERS TO JEFFERSON

In the course of examining Jefferson's letters to John Adams on various constitutional and cultural matters, we also looked briefly at some of Adams' letters to Jefferson.[62] The fuller content of Adams' letters to Jefferson brings out the rich historical-intellectual influences operating on Adams. This subject will naturally prompt one to look at the books in Adams' library.

When at the outset of 1812 Adams wrote to Jefferson and Jefferson responded to him, it had been nearly a dozen years since they had corresponded. This new beginning in their friendship marked the start of a long series of letters between them that lasted until the year of their mutual deaths in 1826. In this long period of deep retirement from public life, and with their old differences behind them, they both had greater leisure and inclination for intellectual discourse. In his initial reply to Adams in January 1812, Jefferson set the tone for their ongoing correspondence: "A letter from you calls up recollections very dear to my mind. It carries me back to the times when . . . we were fellow laborers in the same cause, struggling for what is most valuable to man, his right of self-government. . . . Into politics, of which I have taken final leave, I think little of them, and say less. I have given up newspapers in exchange for Tacitus and Thucydides, for Newton and Euclid; and I find myself much the happier."[63] It is instructive that Jefferson focused here on American self-government as the principal goal toward which he, Adams, and other founders had been struggling in their drive for independence and a new constitution. As noted above, the principle of self-determination in legislation and other related matters was a core concept of the Bodinian tradition on legislative sovereignty and the legislative state, going far back to Bodin, Corasius, and their systematizations of Roman law in the later 16th century.

In his reply to that initial letter from Jefferson in early 1812, Adams wrote: "Your Life and mine for almost half a Century have been nearly all of a Piece, resembling in the whole. . . . What an Exchange have you made? Of Newspapers for Newton! Rising from the lower deep . . . to the Contemplation of the Heavens. . . . Oh that I had devoted to Newton and his Fellows that time which I fear has been wasted on Plato and Aristotle, Bacon . . ., Bolin[g]broke, . . . Harrington, Sidney, Hobbes, . . . Nedham, with twenty others upon Subjects which Mankind is determined never to Understand . . ." Among these prime examples of Adams' reading, Harrington, Sidney, and Hobbes had been crucial writers for Jefferson, too, especially in their links to Bodinian tradition on legislative sovereignty. Adams moreover declared: "I have read Thucidides [*sic*] and Tacitus so often . . . [that] I am weary of them. When I read them I seem to be only reading the History of my own Times and my own Life." Adams also cautioned: "The Union is still to me an Object of as much Anxiety as ever Independence was."[64]

The list of modern as well as classical writers discussed or cited by Adams in his letters to Jefferson from 1812 to 1826 is extremely long. It includes, in addition to the above, Locke, Montesquieu, Rousseau, Hume, Condorcet, Diderot, Plato, Aristotle, Livy, Cicero, and innumerable others, as one would expect from the author of the *Defence of*

Constitutions and *Discourses on Davila* (which in his letters are also discussed).[65] In a letter of mid-1821, Adams refers to "The Art of Lawgiving" in connection with the people in certain American states who unwisely reformed their constitutions, in contradistinction to the "Sovereign . . . People" of Massachusetts who have wisely resisted such efforts by their representatives.[66] A few months later, Adams referred in other contexts to those who have been looking, as he phrased it, to "[t]he Solon's and Lycurgus' " to be their deliverers.[67]

Included in Adams' letters to Jefferson is a wide array of topics like those found in his other writings explored above. Among these topics are monarchy, hereditary succession, the Declaration of Independence, the U.S. Constitution, and religion, in addition to many others. Ofttimes the contexts relate directly or indirectly to his *Defence* and *Discourses*, already examined.

5. ADAMS' LIBRARY

Catalogues

In 1822 at the advanced age of 87, John Adams deeded to the town of Quincy, Massachusetts, "the fragments of my Library; which still remain in my possession." The catalogue that he stipulated should be prepared appeared in the following year and contained entries for 2,756 volumes. Subsequent additions to the collection, primarily by his son John Quincy and grandson Charles Francis, brought the total to 3,019 in 1917. In that year was published the *Catalogue of the John Adams Library in the Public Library of the City of Boston* (the collection having been transferred to Boston in 1893). Thus the vast majority or 91% of volumes listed in the 1917 catalogue were from John Adams' library as originally listed in the 1823 catalogue. Aside from the books that no longer "remain[ed]" other than the "fragments" of his library deeded to Quincy, there were, according to Adams in the same deed of transfer, "a few [books] that I shall reserve for my consolation in the few days that remain to me."[68]

Even allowing for the absence of some former and current books of John Adams in the catalogue of his books in 1823, its total listing of 2,756 volumes represented about 41% of Jefferson's total collection of about 6,700 volumes sold to Congress in 1815.[69] That percentage approximates Adams' own figure in a letter to Jefferson at the end of 1814, not long before Jefferson's library went to Congress to form the basis of its new Library after the destructive fire caused by the British. "By the Way," wrote Adams, "I envy you that immortal honour: but I cannot enter into competition with you[,] for my books are not half the number of yours . . ."[70] However, even if one were therefore to assume that what John Adams deeded to the town of Quincy in 1822 were not the mere "remain[ing]" "fragments" of a much bigger former collection, but in fact the vast bulk of his accumulated library, the question of what books had previously left his library still leaves open some intriguing possibilities.

Not only did John Adams, in any case, not have the same-size private library as Jefferson had (though it was still large for that era); he did not himself prepare a catalogue, much less ones of the scope devised by Jefferson for his Monticello collection. The catalogue made in 1823, at Adams' request in the deed of transfer to the town of Quincy, became, in the words of the Preface to the later 1917 catalogue, "wholly useless" "[a]s a present means of reference." For "the titles are arranged neither alphabetically under the author's names [as in the 1917 catalogue] nor under the subject of which they treat, but according to the languages in which the books are printed, and to some extent according to the size of volumes."[71] In one 1812 letter to Jefferson, Adams had referred to "your library, extensive and well chosen as it is."[72] In another, Adams alluded to books either abridged or collected by Jefferson on certain subjects as being far beyond anything he, Adams, had attempted in searching for "Knowledge" from "Books."[73] It will be remembered, moreover, that Jefferson had sought out Adams' views on types and classifications of books in connection with the sale of his Monticello collection to Congress in 1815.[74]

If not as extensive as Jefferson's library, Adams' collection was nonetheless impressive for both its range and depth. Law, politics, and history were abundantly represented; certain other kinds of books amply possessed by Jefferson were less so. The latter include, for example, more purely literary and artistic works as well as more strictly historical books of or on Roman law. Adams lacked, for instance, the *Corpus Iuris* and other such items found in Jefferson's library, but he possessed the works of Cujas and Domat. Adams' command of European languages was evident, including both Latin and Greek. The listings below of some of the kinds of writers provide further insights.[75]

Bodin's *Republic*

Listed in both the 1823 and 1917 catalogues of John Adams' books are the two versions of Bodin's *Republic* referred to above. One is a two-volume French abridgement, *Abrégé de la République de Bodin* published in London in 1755. The other is Richard Knolles' famed English translation, *The Six Bookes of a Commonweale*, prepared from French and Latin versions and published in London in 1606.[76]

Although it cannot be attempted here, a search might be conducted for further clues as to when and where Adams obtained these two versions of Bodin's *Republic.* That task would be difficult without the aid of earlier handwritten catalogues of the kinds drawn up by Jefferson for his collections. These two editions could well have been in Adams' library early on in his career in law and politics, two disciplines well represented in the 1823 and 1917 catalogues. Or, Adams may well have acquired one or both of these editions of Bodin's *Republic* in the course of his extensive book acquisitions during his long years on official business in Europe. In addition, he may also have come across Bodin's *Republic* while at Harvard, along with other political classics.

Without the presence of handwritten markings in Adams' copies of Bodin's *Republic,* unlike in the Jefferson's copy, the task of determining which portions may have been of particular interest to Adams becomes more difficult. Nevertheless, the evidence adduced above concerning Bodin in Adams' marginalia and underlinings in his copy of Davila's *History* not only represents persuasive proof that Adams well knew of Bodin's *Republic* at least by 1790–1791, when he wrote his *Discourses on Davila,* or even possibly far anterior to that date; it also shows that Adams held Bodin and his *Republic* in high esteem.

Furthermore, Adams' early consistent and strong advocacy of legislative sovereignty, during the Revolutionary and Constitutional Eras, signalled his indebtedness to Bodinian tradition on that subject, as found in English and French books included in his collection. Indeed, Adams' well-developed ideas on the legislative character of sovereignty and the state are abundantly present, as already seen, in his writings from around the periods when the Declaration of Independence and U.S. Constitutions were being formed. The timing of Adams' unique emphasis on the idea of Massachusetts as a "Commonwealth" in his constitution for that state drawn up in 1779, just after he had returned from Europe, may reflect his fresh exposure there to historical English modes in conjunction with Knolles' usage of the term "Commonweale" for Bodin's "Republic." By that measure, Adams would have had Knolles' edition of Bodin in hand at least by 1779, if not by 1776 or some years prior.

An Adams-Jefferson Connection on Bodin?

There is, however, a much more intriguing possibility, both speculative and real. We have seen that Jefferson marked his copy of Bodin's *Republic* with the same kinds of bracket marks found in his draft of the Declaration of Independence, on which he worked, before and after composing it, in close consultation with the committee of five, particularly John Adams. This clear evidence in bracket markings, together with Jefferson's strong statements on legislative sovereignty in the Declaration of Independence itself as well as in his other documents leading up to it, makes it likely that Jefferson already possessed his copy of Bodin's *Republic* at that same point in the mid-1770s. It is therefore reasonable to ask if Jefferson not only had his copy of Bodin's *Republic* during his extended stays at Philadelphia in the mid-1770s, or at least had a reading of it fresh in mind, and shared his copy or his reading of it with his fellow committeeman and collaborator, John Adams, whose own early writings in the 1770s contained even stronger statements on legislative sovereignty and the legislative state in line with Bodinian tradition. This line of inquiry is not mere empty conjecturing when one recalls Bernard Bailyn's above-cited general discussion of the great importance of Bodin and the Bodinian tradition on sovereignty in "the ideological origins of the American Revolution," even though he overlooked the crucial legislative framework of Bodin's famous paradigm on sovereignty and the state.

If Adams already possessed one or both of his own copies of Bodin's *Republic* by the mid-1770s while at Philadelphia with Jefferson, then the possibilities expand as to who may have shared what with whom. Lest one automatically assume that it was during his missions in Europe subsequent to 1776 that Adams acquired one or both of his copies of Bodin's *Republic*, it is clear that Jefferson himself acquired his copy of the *Republic* well before his own ensuing mission to France. We have seen that in at least one of his letters from France Jefferson bemoaned the paucity of desirable historical and other works available for purchase there owing to the then current tastes of the French reading public. The further possibility cannot be dismissed that either or both Adams and Jefferson obtained their copies of Bodin's *Republic* in Philadelphia. That city was then a cosmopolitan center in America, with an intelligent and learned clientele of readers. Prominent among them was Benjamin Franklin, the elder statesman along with Adams, on the committee of five in 1776, both of whom Jefferson sometimes deferred to out of respect for their seniority. Here one will remember that before Jefferson sat down alone to write the Declaration of Independence, there had been extensive discussion by the whole committee of five about the provisions and concepts to be included in it, not to mention the extensive subsequent editing of Jefferson's draft.

The circumstances and cross-fertilization of ideas surrounding the making of the Declaration of Independence could open up an even broader array of questions. Who else among the delegates to the Continental Congress at that same point in time may have shared in the general awareness of Bodinian ideas, not only through Locke, Sidney,

Harrington, Rousseau, and other writers but also through Bodin's *Republic* itself? An answer would require an extensive survey of other delegates to the Congress and their writings as well as libraries. One of the most promising cases would be George Wythe, a fellow signer of the Declaration of Independence who had long had rich relationships with Jefferson. Wythe had been not only Jefferson's mentor and law teacher at Williamsburg but had occupied a special place for Jefferson after the untimely death of Jefferson's father. When much later Wythe died, he left his collection of books to Jefferson.[77]

If, on the other hand, one focuses on the ensuing decade of the 1780s, leading up to the framing of the new U.S. Constitution, then other prospects arise. Although Jefferson's early catalogue of books has made it certain that he possessed Bodin's *Republic* before going to France, Adams' acquisition of one or both of his copies of it there still remains a clear possibility. Even then, the dating would almost certainly have to be well prior to his statements on legislative sovereignty in his *Defence of Constitutions*, written before, during, and after the 1787 Constitutional Convention at Philadelphia. At that point, both Adams and Jefferson were in Europe, Adams returning to America in 1788 and Jefferson in late 1789. Their exchanges of ideas in person when their paths had crossed in Europe, aside from their letters, present a possible further dimension.

Among Adams' acquisitions of books upon his return to Europe in late 1779, following his brief return home at which point he composed the Massachusetts constitution, was Jean Domat's *Les loix civiles dans leur ordre naturel.* Adams' copy of it bears his autograph dated March 30, 1780,[78] that is, just after his return to Europe. It could be that Adams also obtained his copy of the ten-volume edition of Jacques Cujas' *Opera omnia* at around that time. The same could apply to his copy of the three-volume edition of Plato's *Opera omnia* of 1578, arranged in parallel columns of Greek and Latin and autographed by both John Adams and his son John Quincy. Also, there is another edition of Plato's *Opera omnia* bearing John Quincy's autograph, a French edition of *Les oeuvres de Plato* autographed and bearing comments by John Adams, an English version of *The Republic of Plato* with mutilated autograph and marginalia by John Adams, and a French *La république de Platon.*[79] Given his generally less abstract tastes in books compared with Jefferson's, Adams' apparent greater interest in Plato is striking. As well, an association with the title of Bodin's *Republic* could have piqued Adams' further intrest in Plato's *Republic.* Finally, one might imagine Adams and Jefferson in friendly competition while in Europe to acquire such prizes as a Gothofredus edition of Justinian's *Corpus Iuris Civilis.* That prize was acquired by Jefferson in two different editions (not to mention other versions of its separate parts), but not by Adams, at least according to known records. Here as elsewhere, these two prominent, inveterate bibliophiles are still sources of endless fascination.

An Adams-Corasius Connection on Ancient Lawgivers?

Additionally, it can be asked whether Adams' discourses on ancient lawgiver-founders in his *Defence* Preface was primarily modelled upon Corasius' treatments of the same subject in his *Art of Law* I, 16 and *Commentaries* on *Digest* I, 1–4. As seen below (p. 222), one historian believes that Madison's treatment of ancient lawgiver-founders in *Federalist* #38 was inspired by a mixture of texts by Plutarch, Rousseau (*Social Contract*), Machiavelli (*Discourses*), and Plato; at the same time, he overlooks Adams' *Defence* Preface and other potential sources on this subject such as Bodin's *Republic*. While these and other materials may well have contributed to Madison's basic paradigm on the subject, it was clearly Adams' *Defence* Preface that provided the main American prototype for Madison. The real question becomes who or what provided the distinctive components of Adams' basic model on ancient lawgiver-founders as introduced below (our p. 228). Through an extensive exploration of this important question (in the Annexes below), it will become apparent that Corasius did indeed supply this basic model for Adams, whose own imagery of ancient lawgiver-founders contributed to the self-image of American "founding fathers" at the Constitutional Convention and afterwards. The way will then open up for other possible influences of Corasius (like Bodin) on Adams and his fellow founders.

PART TWO

American Founding Fathers, Madison and Hamilton: Profiles in Legislation

Chapter IV

Madison in Legislative Profile

Among the principal founding fathers whose writings on politics, law, and history shaped the constitutional course of the new American republic at its most decisive stage in the later 1780s, the most important was James Madison Jr. (1751–1836). Like Jefferson's Declaration of Independence, Madison's *Notes of Debates in the Federal Convention of 1787*, in conjunction with his role as chief architect of the new U.S. Constitution, occupies a special place in the early history of American constitutional government. As in the case of Jefferson's celebrated contributions at Philadelphia in 1776, Madison's renowned achievements at Philadelphia over a decade later in 1787 built upon his own previous writings. Similarly to Jefferson as well as to Adams, Madison viewed issues of sovereignty and state within a legislative framework, which has been long neglected by historians. Madison has sometimes been called the "forgotten" founder (as well as the "last" of "the founders") despite his great role as the Constitution's "father" and historians' vast scholarship on him. His legislative ideas concerning sovereignty and state still remain among his most overlooked contributions.[1]

1. MADISON IN OVERVIEW

Prior to the Constitutional Convention of mid-1787, Madison's experience in public affairs had put him in good stead for the tasks ahead. He had been delegate to the Virginia Convention in 1776, member of the Virginia Council of State in 1777–1778, delegate to the Continental/Confederation Congress in 1780–1783, a member of the Virginia House of Delegates in 1784–1786, attendee of the Annapolis Convention on commercial regulations in 1786, and then delegate from Virginia to the Constitutionl Convention at Philadelphia in mid-1787. There, Madison was not only the official recorder of the main proceedings, but also played a leading role as draftsman, proposer, and debater. While a member of the Continental Congress (elected to it by the Virginia Assembly), Madison observed firsthand its weaknesses needing to be remedied. He proposed without success, two weeks after ratification of the Articles of Confederation in 1781, that the Articles be amended to give Congress power to coerce states that defied it or failed to meet their financial obligations. While in the Virginia House of Delegates, he was instrumental in the passage of various laws drafted by Jefferson in the late 1770s as a revised statutory code for Virginia, as well as in the revision of the statute for religious freedom also drafted then by Jefferson. Not long after Madison was appointed one of Virginia's eight commissioners, following the Assembly's resolution in early 1786 calling for a general meeting of the states to adopt uniform commercial regulations, he took extensive notes on the strengths and weaknesses of ancient and modern confederations as found in various histories. His historical researches became influenced by the publication of Adams' *Defence of Constitutions* (with its strong statements on legislative sovereignty).

After the Virginia Assembly endorsed the proposal of Alexander Hamilton at the unsuccessful Annapolis Conference for a general convention at Philadelphia in May 1787 to consider constitutional changes, it elected Madison as a delegate to Congress in late 1786 and soon thereafter appointed him as one of the state's seven delegates to the Philadelphia convention. In early 1787 Madison renewed his studies on other confederations. That spring he made proposals for the agenda at Philadelphia in letters to Jefferson, Washington, and Edmund Randolph, Virginia's governor. The first delegate not from Pennsylvania to arrive at Philadelphia in early May, Madison was the leading participant in the Virginia delegation's drafting of the "Virginia Plan" delivered by Randolph at the outset of the Convention in late May.[2]

During the meetings of the Constitutional Convention from May 25 to September 17, 1787, Madison was one of the leading voices, in addition to his role as recorder and drafter. His motions, speeches, and proposals, at the proceedings were many and varied, the following being salient and illustrative. Madison moved on May 30 that congressional representation be proportional to the importance and size of the states, and made his first speech on the subject. On May 31 he advocated representation in one house by popular election, doubted the practicability of enumerating powers of the national legislature, and suggested the impossibility of using force to coerce individual states. In June 1–4 Madison moved that the powers of the Executive be enumerated, objected to giving Congress power to remove the President upon demand of a majority of the state legislatures, and favored giving power to more than a majority of the national legislature to overrule the Executive negative of a law. In June 5–8 he opposed election of judges by both branches of Congress, advocated submission of the constitution to conventions of the people, seconded a motion to include a portion of the Judiciary with the Executive in revisionary power over laws, spoke for proportional representation in both houses of Congress, and seconded a motion to give Congress power to negative (annul) state laws. On June 13 he moved to define powers of Judiciary and objected to appointment of judges by whole legislatures, thought both houses should have the right to originate money bills, advocated a national government and opposed the "Jersey plan," and spoke in favor of national supremacy. In June 26–30 Madison spoke for a long term for senators, opposed their payment by the states, spoke for proportional representation, insisted that too much stress was being laid on states' sovereignty, and contended against equal state representation in the Senate yet would preserve states' rights. In July 11–18 he favored representation based on population, urged proportional representation as necessary in order to protect the smaller states, advocated national power of negative over states' laws, thought the branches of government should be kept separate, thought monarchy likely to follow instability, moved for national guarantee of states against domestic violence, and seconded motion forbidding a state to form any but a republican government. In July 19–21 Madison advocated election of the Executive by the people, spoke in favor of making the Execuive impeachable, seconded proposition to include the Judiciary with the Executive in power to revise laws, and moved that judges be appointed by the Executive with concurrence of two-thirds of the Senate. In August 10–11 he moved that the Legislature have power to compel attendance of members and advocated a centrally located capital. In August 13–17, he spoke in favor of participation of the Senate in making appropriations, moved that all bills be passed upon by the Executive and Judiciary before becoming laws, advocated national power to tax exports, and moved that the Legislature have power to declare war (along with other powers enumerated in days following). On August 27 Madison moved on form of oath for President. On August 31 he moved that ratification of the new constitution be by a majority of states and people, and he advocated ratification by state conventions. On September 3 he thought election of President by the Legislature should be made difficult. On September 7 he moved that states should have power to make treaties of peace without the President, and so on.[3]

Several days after the Convention in Philadelphia ended, Madison returned to New York City and to his seat in the Confederation Congress that he had taken early that year. There he successfully resisted efforts of Virginia delegate Richard Henry Lee to have the proposed new constitution amended by Congress before it was submitted to the states for ratification. Madison accepted Hamilton's invitation to assist him and John Jay in writing a series of anonymous articles or essays by "Publius" entitled *The Federalist*, which soon appeared in several New York news publications in support of ratification. Madison's first contribution appeared in later November. He eventually wrote 29 of the 85 essays. In March 1788 he returned to Virginia and was elected a delegate to its ratifying convention, where he defended the new Constitution. Madison subsequently served for nearly a decade as a Virginia member of the House of Representatives, from 1789 to 1797. In 1789 he drafted amendments to the new Constitution, known as the Bill of Rights. In 1798 he drafted the Virginia Resolutions against the Alien and Sedition Laws, and in 1800 he published a report defending the Virginia Resolutions. Madison became Secretary of State under Jefferson from 1801 to 1809. From 1809 to 1817 he was President of the United States. After war was declared on England in 1812, the Capitol and White House were burned by the British, a peace treaty finally being ratified in 1815. During his long retirement at his Montpelier home in Virginia, from 1817 to 1836, he became a delegate, in 1829, to Virginia's Constitutional Convention.

2. MADISON'S PRE-CONVENTION OUTLINES

Letter to Jefferson

Some of the most powerful statements made by Madison on conceptual matters of legislation, sovereignty, and state in the months prior to the Constitutional Convention at Philadelphia were contained in a long letter from him in New York on March 19, 1787, to Jefferson in Paris. In providing an extended plan for a new constitutional form of government, Madison was in part responding to Jefferson's letter of December 16, 1786 from Paris. In it, Jefferson had referred to Madison's unsuccessful recent attempts at a commercial convention and to the hopes for "a full meeting in May" of 1787, at which time a new balance at the federal level would hopefully be struck between the legislative, executive, and judicial branches (with Congress as a purely legislative body).[4] Madison's letter to Jefferson has been regarded by some historians as his most extensive and detailed pre-Convention plan for a new federal constitutional government. His particularly well-developed legislative framework of sovereignty and state is therefore of importance, despite its neglect by historians as the crux of those two topics in Madison's thought.

After noting to Jefferson that this letter of March 19, 1787 "will go to England in the care of a French gentleman who will consign it to the care of Mr. Adams," for dependable transfer to Jefferson, Madison remarks that "[t]he appointments for the Convention go on auspiciously." Madison gives some details on which states and delegates are already, or are in the process of being, lined up. (By then, the first volume of Adams' *Defence* had already appeared a number of weeks earlier and was contributing to the momentum for new constitutional changes.) Madison then alludes to the present dangerous crisis in American constitutional government that is producing the main driving force behind the emerging plans for a May convention.

> What may be the result of this political experiment cannot be foreseen. The difficulties which present themselves are on one side almost sufficient to dismay the most sanguine, whilst on the other side the most timid are compelled to encounter them by the mortal diseases of the existing constitution. These diseases need not be pointed out to you who so well understand them. Suffice it to say that they are at present marked by symptoms which are truly alarming, which have tainted the faith of the most orthodox republicans, and which challenge from the votaries of liberty every concession in favor of stable Government not infringing fundamental principles, as the only security against an opposite extreme of our present situation.[5]

As Madison later confirmed, this last point was an allusion to the danger of engendering monarchy in responding to democracy's crisis.[6]

Madison's first two main points in this letter of March 19, 1787 to Jefferson on the approaching Convention, two months hence in May, revolve around the topic of legislation and legislative power at the federal and state levels. The crux of the problem and its solution, as Madison here perceived, was to offset "the Legislative sovereignties of the States" with a dominant sovereign legislative power at the federal level. To this end, Congress must become a more purely legislative body and power than it has thus far been. Congress should also have (in conjunction with the Executive) the power of a final absolute "negative," if necessary, over laws of the state legislatures. Although Madison may have been obliquely thinking above about the perils of Adams' perceived monarchical leanings in his *Defence*, he here may have been drawing in a different way upon Adams' ideas therein on the necessity of the Executive's (legislative) negative or veto over Congress, as Madison's wording and emphasis suggests. Whatever the case, Madison's call and plan for a "new system" already revealed, two months before the Convention, his drive for more than a mere revision or amending of the existing system under the Articles of Confederation. At that time, the state legislatures, functioning more purely as legislative bodies than was the Confederation Congress, were preempting Congress' authority yet were failing to cope with the growing state crises. A ratification of a new U.S. constitution by the people within the states would compel the state legislatures to approve it, however much it would preempt their own authorities and prerogatives.

> I think myself that it will be expedient in the first place to lay the foundation of the new system in such a ratification by the people themselves of the several States as will render it clearly paramount to their Legislative authorities. 2dly. Over and above the positive power of regulating trade and sundry other matters in which uniformity is proper, to arm the federal head with a negative *in all cases whatsoever* [Madison's italics] on the local legislatures. Without this defensive power experience and reflection have satisfied me that however ample the federal powers may be made, or however Clearly their boundaries may be delineated, on paper, they will be easily and continually baffled by the Legislative sovereignties of the States. The effects of this provision would be not only to guard the national rights and interests against invasion, but also to restrain the States from thwarting and molesting each other, and even from oppressing the minority within themselves by paper money and other unrighteous measures which favor the interest of the majority. In order to render the exercise of such a negative prerogative convenient, an emanation of it must be vested in some set of men within the several States so far as to enable them to give a temporary sanction to laws of immediate necessity.[7]

Remaining portions of interest in the same letter by Madison to Jefferson also center on the role and composition of Congress as a sovereign legislative body in relation to the individual states of the Union. The increase in powers as well as in members of Congress should go together with a more "efficient" "distribution" and separation of federal branches or departments. These steps, Madison believes, will remedy the present "limited powers . . . in Congress," which "are frequently mismanaged" due to the "blend[ing] [or blurring] together" of legislative function with other functions. In view of Madison's focus on the recent "incompetent" performance of the Confederation Congress, together with his plan for a new Congress, it is not surprising that the proceedings of the Convention would likewise focus, first and foremost, on the new Congress in the new Constitution.

> 3dly. to change the principle of Representation in the federal system. Whilst the execution of the Acts of Congress depends on the several legislatures, the equality of votes does not destroy the inequality of importance and influence in the States. But in case of such an augmentation of the federal power as will render it efficient without the intervention of the Legislatures, a vote in the general Councils from Delaware would be of equal value with one from Massts. or Virginia. This change therefore is just. I think also it will be practicable. A majority of the States conceive that they will be gainers by it. . . . 4thly. to organise the federal powers in such a manner as not to blend together those which ought to be exercised by separate departments. The limited powers now vested in Congress are frequently mismanaged from the want of such a distribution of them. What would be the case, under an enlargement not only of the powers, but the number, of the federal Representatives?
>
> These are some of the leading ideas which have occurred to me, but which may appear to others as improper, as they appear to me necessary.
>
> Congress have [*sic*] continued so thin as to be incompetent to the despatch [*sic*] of the more important business before them. We have at present nine States and it is not improbable that something may now be done.[8]

In effect, Madison's above letter sketched for Jefferson an outline of what became known as the "Virginia Plan," based largely on Madison's proposals, that the Virginia delegation introduced two months later at the outset of the Philadelphia Convention. Madison's plan for a new Congress would require a new form of representation according to population, while a fuller separation of powers, already present in the states, would be requisite at the federal level. When Jefferson eventually replied three months later on June 20, 1787, having been away from Paris in southern France, the Convention was well under way; his approvals and disapprovals of Madison's plan are noteworthy.[9] Meanwhile, Madison had already written Jefferson on June 6, not long after the Convention opened, with limited news about its proceedings, which he said were now "confidential," thereby somewhat irritating Jefferson. Madison also supplied news about the great stir being caused at the Convention and in the country by Adams' newly published *Defence*, in its first volume (and with its stress on legislative sovereignty).[10]

Letter to Randolph

Another constitutional outline was given by Madison in a long ensuing letter from New York on April 8, 1787, to Edmund Randolph, the Governor of Virginia. Randolph was soon to head the Virginia delegation at the Philadelphia Convention and there to submit the Virginia Plan, which would shape the debates from the outset largely in accordance with Madison's guiding hand as evidenced in this letter. Madison's discreet wording near the letter's beginning pointed up the resistance by some delegates to Madison's plans for a new federal system in which the sovereignty of the national government would prevail over the sovereignties of the states. In fact, this same issue had prompted objections by Jefferson in his March reply to Maadison's earlier proposals; Jefferson had balked at Madison's idea of the national Congress having the right of absolute veto (or "negative") over the laws of the state legislatures. As in his March letter to Jefferson, Madison's April letter to Randolph focused on conceptual issues of sovereignty and state.

> I think with you, that it will be well to retain as much as possible of the old Confederation, though I doubt whether it may not be best to work the valuable articles into the new system, instead of engrafting the latter on the former. . . . In truth, my ideas of a reform strike so deeply at the old Confederation, and lead to such a systematic change, that they scarcely admit of the expedient.
>
> I hold it for a fundamental point, that an individual independence of the States is utterly irreconcilable with the idea of an aggregate sovereignty. I think, at the same time, that a consolidation of the States into one simple republic is not less unattainable than it would be inexpedient. Let it be tried, then, whether any middle ground can be taken, which will at once support due supremacy of the national authority, and leave in force the local authorities so far as they can be subordinately useful.[11]

The full legislative weight of Madison's constitutional plan in this April 8 letter to Randolph (one of a number of pre-Convention exchanges with him when Madison was endeavoring to set the agenda) is apparent in the continuation of Madison's preceding passages given above. After first treating the changed "principle of representation" in the new Congress, within the continuing context of sovereignty and state, Madison outlines Congress' new role. Congress will have an absolute "negative" on the laws of individual states, after the general model of the British constitution. (That model, Madison soon predicted to Jefferson, would have renewed influence on the delegates as a result of Adams' *Defence*, which included the idea of an executive legislative "negative" on Congress' acts.[12]) However much the individual states might resist, Madison was holding firm in his proposed negative by Congress on their laws. (His own state of Virginia had a tradition of sovereign self-determination that was espoused by Jefferson in his June 20 reply.) The Constitution eventually issued was not, however, as much a testament to Madison's strong influence in this regard as it would be in many other respects. True, he saw this proposed "negative" as the best way to ensue not only the sovereignty but also the stability of the individual states within a new overarching sovereignty of the Union and its national government. Even though, however, this particular proposal was not adopted by the Convention, it does remain a lasting testament to Madison's focal point of legislative sovereignty at the federal level in relation to the state legislatures.

> The first step to be taken is, I think, a change in the principle of representation. According to the present form of the Union, an equality of suffrage, if not just towards the larger members of it, is at least safe to them, as the liberty they exercise of rejecting or executing the acts of Congress, is uncontrollable by the nominal sovereignty of Congress. Under a system which would operate without the intervention of the States, the case would be materially altered. A vote from Delaware would have the same effect as one from Massachusetts or Virginia.
>
> Let the national Government be armed with a positive and complete authority in all cases where uniform measures are necessary, as in trade, &c., &c. Let it also retain the powers which it now possesses.
>
> Let it have a negative, in all cases whatsoever, on the Legislative acts of the States, as the King of Great Britain heretofore had. This I conceive to be essential and the least possible abridgement of the State sovereignties. Without such a defensive power, every positive power that can be given on

> paper will be unavailing. It will also give internal stability to the States.[13]

Madison goes on in the same letter to Randolph on April 8, 1787, to give some specifics on the judicial, legislative, and executive branches of his proposed new federal government at the national level. Madison's proposal for the federal judiciary, partaking in the "national supremacy" in "the interests of the Union," prefigured Jefferson's call in his June letter to Madison for a federal judicial review of state laws, rather than a negative by Congress on state laws, although Madison variously favored both measures. Of the two new branches of the national legislature, or Congress, one, Madison thought, should have a negative on state laws. So preoccupied was he with the national legislature that Madison admits to having given little thought thus far to the chief Executive. As it turned out, much less was said at the Convention and even in the Constitution about the chief Executive, so great did the national legislature preoccupy the delegates.

> Let this national supremacy be extended also to the Judiciary department. If the Judges in the last resort depend on the States, and are bound by their oaths to them and not to the Union, the intention of the law and the interests of the nation may be defeated by the obsequiousness of the tribunals to the policy or prejudices of the States....
>
> A Government formed of such extensive powers ought to be well organized. The Legislative department may be divided into two branches. One of them to be chosen every —— years by the Legislatures or the people at large; the other to consist of a more select number, holding their appointments for a longer term, and going out in rotation. Perhaps the negative on the State laws may be most conveniently lodged in this branch....
>
> A national Executive will also be necessary. I have scarcely ventured to form my own opinion yet, either of the manner in which it ought to be constituted, or of the authorities with which it ought to be clothed.[14]

Continuing, Madison calls for measures to safeguard the "tranquillity of the States" against dangers and disruptions. The people in the states should ratify the Constitution in order to give it more force with the state legislatures. And this "new system" should have a new form of representation in Congress, so as to ensure that the "predominant will" of the people is voiced and efficient republican government is maintained.[15]

Letter to Washington

Madison's letter of April 16, 1787 to George Washington largely reiterated his constitutional designs conveyed in his letters to Randolph and Jefferson. He began by referring to Washington's recent letter to him on March 31. Madison notes "with much pleasure that your views on the reform which ought to be pursued by the Convention give a sanction to those which I have entertained. Temporizing applications will dishonor the Councils which propose them, and may foment the internal malignity of the disease, at the same time that they procure an ostensible palliation of it. Radical attempts, although unsuccessful, will at least justify the authors of them."[16] (Washington had stated in his letter to Madison: "It gives me pleasure to hear that there is a probability of a full Representation of the States in Convention, but if the delegates come to it under fetters, the salutary ends proposed will in my opinion be greatly embarrassed & retarded, if not altogether defeated. . . . [M]y wish is, that the Convention may adopt no temporising expedient, but probe the defect of the Constitution to the bottom, and provide radical cures, whether they are agreed to or not. . . ."[17] Clearly, consensus as well as momentum was building for bold new constitutional plans, spearheaded if not engineered by the eager Madison via his ambitious bold proposals. A few weeks later, in mid-May, he would be the first out-of-state delegate to arrive at Philadelphia for the Convention, well prior to its start.[18]

In this letter of April 16, 1787 to Washington, Madison makes it clear that his proposed "outline" of a new constitution envisions a wholly "new system." He leads off with the issue of the individual vs. collective sovereignty of the American states, proposing a mixture of national and more local sovereignty.

> Having been lately led to revolve [*sic*] the subject which is to undergo the discussion of the Convention, and formed in my mind some outlines of a new system, I take the liberty of submitting them without apology, to your eye.
>
> Conceiving that an individual independence of the States is utterly irreconcileable with their aggregate sovereignty; and that a consolidation of the whole into one simple republic would be as inexpedient as it is unattainable, I have sought for some middle ground, which may at once support a due supremacy of the national authority, and not exclude the local authorities wherever they can be subordinately useful.[19]

After then outlining at length his proposed "principle of representation" for the new national legislature, Madison goes on to underscore the need for it to have a "negative" on the laws of state legislatures. At the same time, he wants "the least possible encroachment on the State jurisdictions." This "negative" is a "defensive" mechanism that is "necessary" in order to prevent Congress' "positive" legislative powers and "national jurisdiction" from being circumvented by the inevitable rival interests of the states. We may add that the overriding sovereign legislative power of the national government becomes more a matter of its innate power to make law for all, as ensured by its veto powers over state laws, than a question of jurisdiction, which is here subordinate to the coercive authority of lawmaking. Madison's comparisons of this "national prerogative" to the "sovereign" power in "Monarchies" tend to reinforce this same viewpoint.[20]

The necessary coercive power of the sovereign national government includes more than just the national legislature. It is vested also in the supreme national Judiciary, which interprets and applies Congress' laws including in matters pertaining to the states and their laws. The Executive department, too, shares in the sovereign coercive power of the national federal government (chiefly, it would seem here, through its exercise of the laws). Nonetheless, the national legislature remains Madison's focal point when underscoring the necessary inherent coerciveness of the sovereign national government, as exhibited in commerce and taxation. Yet the use of force by the federal government against "the collective will of a state" (an echo of Rousseau?), however necessary it might prove to be in some situations, should best be avoided through other means, which include taxation, commerce, and especially Congress' power of the "negative" over state laws. In order to ensure that a new federal constitution will be adopted, where state constitutions now reign nearly supreme, a kind of coercion through popular vote will be necessary in order to overcome likely resistance by the state legislatures. As for the Confederation Congress in New York, of which Madison was a member, he here expresses a somewhat negative opinion.

> The national supremacy ought also to be extended as I conceive to the Judiciary departments. If those who are to expound & apply the laws, are connected by their interests & their oaths with the particular States wholly, and not with the Union, the participation of the Union in the making of the laws may be possibly rendered unavailing. . . .
>
> The national supremacy in the Executive departments is liable to some difficulty, unless the officers administering them could be made appointable by the supreme Government. . . .

> A Government composed of such extensive powers should be well organized and balanced. The Legislative department might be divided into two branches; one . . . large, . . . to consist of fewer members, to hold their places for a long term. . . . Perhaps the negative on the laws might be most conveniently exercised by this branch. . . .
>
> A national Executive must also be provided. I have scarcely ventured as yet to form my own opinion . . . of . . . it. . . .
>
> In like manner the right of coercion should be expressly declared. With the resources of Commerce in hand, the national administration might always find means of exerting it either by sea or land; But the difficulty & awkwardness of operating by force on the collective will of a State, render it particularly desirable that the necessity of it might be precluded. Perhaps the negative on the laws might create such a mutuality of dependence between the General and particular authorities, as to answer this purpose. Or perhaps some defined objects of taxation might be submitted along with commerce, to the general authority.
>
> To give a new System its proper validity and energy, a ratification must be obtained from the people, and not merely from the ordinary authority of the Legislatures. This will be the more essential as inroads on the *existing Constitutions* of the States will be unavoidable. . . .
>
> Congress continue [*sic*] to be thin, and of course do [*sic*] little business of importance.[21]

"Vices of the System"

Madison's memorandum of April 1787, which bore his heading "Vices of the [Present] Political system of the U. States,"[22] has long received much attention. Historians have well noted: its importance in Madison's pre-Convention thinking, its relationship to his plans for a new constitution as set forth in his noted letters to Jefferson, Randolph, and Washington, its mixture of theory and practice, its concern with the ills of existing state and national government, its emphasis on the need for a negative by the general government on acts of the state legislatures that would threaten the rights of minority interests by a tyranny of the majority, and its concern over the present lack of central coercive powers to force state legislatures to protect republican liberty for all and to promote the common national good in a large extended nation. Madison's unique capabilities and credentials as a scholar and statesman, as reflected in his "Vices," were brought to bear at the

Constitutional Convention from the outset through his guiding influence on what later became known as the Virginia Plan. This plan was submitted by Governor Randolph to the Convention on May 29, 1787, and was based largely on Madison's three letters treated above. Not only did Madison position himself as the official note-taker at the main proceedings, but he also was a commanding figure in the debates, while endeavoring to gain support for his proposals to overcome, as he put it, the "Vices of the [Present] . . . System."

To be sure, themes of sovereignty, state, and legislation have found their way into historians' accounts of Madisons "Vices" and its criticisms of the current system, just as in their accounts of his three noted letters proposing a new system. So pervasive are those themes in all these documents that it would be difficult *not* to take them into account, even when focusing on other matters in them. Even so, historians have generally not seen fit to underscore and delineate the remarkable central conceptual emphasis in Madison's "Vices," as in those three letters, on the legislative scope *per se* of sovereignty and state. As in those other cases, the topic of legislation could occupy a much larger space in our analysis than can be afforded here. A simple brief presentation of the essential legislative parameters that dominate Madison's discussions on conceptual issues of sovereignty and state in his "Vices" must suffice.

In his "Vices" the twelve main points that Madison takes up in numbered and entitled sections of varying lengths are as follows (all *sic*): "1. Failure of the States to comply with the Constitutional requisitions" (short), "2. Encroachments by the States on the federal authority" (short), "3. Violations of the law of nations and of treaties," "4. Trespasses of the States on the rights of each other," "5. want of concert in matters where common interest requires it" (short), "6. want of Guaranty to the States of their Constitutions & laws against internal violence" (short), "7. want of sanction to the laws, and of coercion in the Government of the Confederacy" (long), "8. Want of ratification by the people of the articles of Confederation," "9. Multiplicity of laws in the several States," "10. mutability of the laws of the States" (short), "11. Injustice of the laws of States" (especially long), and "12. Impotence of the laws of the States" (blank). From these indications, it is plain that Madison not only devotes great attention to legislative issues relating to questions of sovereignty and state, but does so in critical ways that seem, in part, to run counter to Adams' overall perspectives in his *Defence of the Constitutions of Government of the United States of America.* For although both Adams and Madison saw legislation as central to concepts of sovereignty and states, Adams was there strongly defending the current systems, whereas Madison was strongly criticizing them.

Throughout his "Vices," Madison frequently highlights legislative issues, as some examples and excerpts will show. One such issue is the coersive command or sanction needed in legislated law—a basic theme we have traced from Corasius and Bodin to Bentham (the latter represented in Madison's library) and beyond. In his third section, he declares: "From the number of Legislatures, . . . and the circumstances under which their legislative business is carried on, . . . frequent violations of the laws of nations [occur] . . ." In his seventh section, Madison declares:

> A sanction is essential to the idea of law, as coercion is to that of Government. The federal system being destitute of both, wants the great vital principles of a Political Cons[ti]tution. Under the form of such a Constitution, it is in fact nothing more than a treaty of amity of commerce and of alliance, between so many independent and Sovereign States. From what cause could so fatal an omission have happened in the articles of Confederation? from a mistaken confidence that the justice, the good faith, the honor, the sound policy, of the several legislative assemblies would render superfluous any appeal to the ordinary motives by which the laws secure the obedience of individuals.

Madison's continuing observations in the same section further revolve around legislative issues of sovereignty and state.[23] The same holds true for his eighth section, again with regard to relationships between the Confederation and the individual states.

> In some of the States the Confederation is recognized by, and forms a part of the constitution. In others however it has received no other sanction than that of the Legislative authority. From this defect two evils result: 1. Whenever a law of a State happens to be repugnant to an act of Congress, particularly when the latter is of posterior date to the former, it will be at least questionable whether the latter must not prevail; and as the question must be decided by the Tribunals of the State, they will be most likely to lean on the side of the State. 2. As far as the Union of the States is to be regarded as a league of sovereign powers, and not as a political Constitution by virtue of which they are become one sovereign power, so far it seems to follow from the doctrine of compacts, that a breach of any of

> the articles of the confederation by any of the parties to it, absolves the other parties from their respective obligations, and gives them a right if they chuse to exert it, of dissolving the Union altogether.

With regard to the individual states themselves, questions of legislative sovereignty as well as legislative systems (or lack thereof) dominate Madison's treatment of republican principles of government. This is the case in the ninth, tenth, and eleventh sections of his "Vices." In the longest section of all, the eleventh, Madison elaborates in more theoretical ways on ideas and types of sovereignty, particularly in terms of legislation. In section eleven, the "sovereign will" is viewed from the perspective of unjust legislation in the individual states, the main topic of the section (as all indicated in the note below).[24]

3. MADISON'S CONVENTION *NOTES*

Madison's *Notes of Debates in the Federal Convention of 1787*[25] serves to reveal his and the Convention's preoccupation with legislative issues of sovereignty and state, as seen from many different angles. His corresponding emphasis in his pre-Convention outlines largely shaped the Convention's agenda from the outset. Madison's special role at that Convention in the creation of the new U.S. Constitution rendered his particular attention to these issues of great importance. On his general role the following overview is apt.

> No other delegate came to that historic meeting [the Convention in Philadelphia] so well prepared as JM, ready to confront the complex problems of establishing an energetic national government based on republican principles. . . . [He had] an unrivaled knowledge of American affairs. Yet what distinguished JM from his fellow delegates . . . was . . . his diligent effort to apply . . . a scholarly study of the principles of government. . . . JM took the lead on nearly every great question at the convention. . . . JM's chief concern [in "Vices"] was the unrestricted power of majorities in state legislatures to pass laws that violated the rights of individuals and minorities. . . . Thus . . . [he sought] to strengthen the national government. . . . JM's lasting contribution [at the] . . . Convention [was] to base the argument for an invigorated national government on the greater security it would afford to private rights. He arrived at this conclusion in this discussion of the 'Injustice of the laws of the States' ["Vices," sect. 11]. . . . In the system he proposed,

> sovereignty would be securely lodged in the general government, which would operate over individuals instead of through the intermediary states . . . [and which would] have additional positive powers. . . . Convinced that a federal power to disallow [through the "negative"] state laws would serve the end of liberty and justice, JM was a persistent but unsuccessful advocate of such a control at the Federal Convention."[26]

Prefatory "Sketch"

Madison's prefatory "Sketch"[27] at the outset of his *Notes of Convention* yields many revealing statements about his main viewpoints leading up to and during the Convention in mid-1787. Although in rough, unfinished draft written in his later years as an intended preface to his original notes on the Convention, in preparation for their publication, Madison's self-styled "Sketch" abundantly shows that his overriding aim had all along been to establish the sovereign power of the federal government. In particular, his prefatory "Sketch" promoted the legislative sovereignty of Congress in relation to the laws of the individual state legislatures, including the legislature of his own state of Virginia, in which many members continued to resist ceding their power to the Union.

Madison's "Sketch" of the early historical events leading up to the Constitutional Convention centers, in this preface to his *Notes*, around legislative aspects of sovereignty and state. It was Britain's harmful "Legislative enactments and declarations" that drove the American Congress in 1774 to pass legislative counter-"measures" and then in 1776 to declare by legislative "Act" that the colonies were "*Independent States.*" When at that point Congress drew up a plan for the Confederation, it was "for the future management of the common interests" of the "states." The plan submitted by Congress in 1777 to the individual state legislatures was finally ratified by all in 1781.[28]

When going on in his prefatory "Sketch" to point out the reasons for resistance by the separate state legislatures to the transfer and "relinquishment of power" to the national government under the Confederation, Madison focuses again on factors involving issues of sovereignty and state. He finds "sources of difficulty" common in "all such Confederacies" throughout history. Questions of taxation and commerce fueled the strong tendencies of the individual American states toward independence from the federal government. Measures enacted by the Confederate Congress lacked coerciveness over the separate states. The end of war against Britain and thereby of a common threat launched the separate states into even greater "enjoyment of independent and sovereign power." This drive was expressed particularly in "measures" by the state legislatures "incompatible with their relations to the Federal Gov[ernment]."[29]

When he was a member of the Confederation Congress and the Virginia legislature in the 1780s, Madison had closely "observed" the difficulties in establishing a strong national sovereignty in a federal government. The state legislatures vigorously opposed "new grants of power to Cong[ress]." His prefatory "Sketch" in *Notes* recounts briefly how the Virginia "Legislature" newly asserted its long-standing "aversion . . . to transfers of power from the State to the Gov[ernment] of the Union . . ." Despite the people's favorable disposition to the federal government, the members of the legislature evidently clung to their power, influence, and self-interest. Madison sharply criticizes the "wayward . . . proceedings" of the Virginia "Legislature" and its "failure" to "enlarg[e] . . . the powers of Congress." Due largely, however, to "the pub[lic] mind . . . ripened for . . . Reform," especially by the people at large, efforts mounted to establish a new "system" and to strengthen the Union. Madison singles out the need in commerce to overcome Congress' lack of general regulatory power in relation to the states. In turn, the states had been exercising their own often conflicting and abortive regulatory powers without apparent regard for a broader common interest. Madison's appeal to "the public mind" here and elsewhere is, we may add, illustrative of his continuing appeal to the higher natures of the Convention delegates, for them to rise above self-interest in support of a new system of federal power for the greater good of all.[30]

Almost exclusively does Madison, in the continuation of his prefatory "Sketch" in *Notes*, concentrate on the need for a strong central "sovereign" "Federal Authority," when recounting the main reasons for convening the Convention at Philadelphia. Foreign nations disrespect the weak American federal government and seek to take advantage of it, and some Americans contend for either a "dismemberment" or a "Monarchy." These factors lay behind the Convention's inception, according to Madison. To preserve "the Union" and to promote a "consolidated government" were crucial central reasons, he stresses, for holding the Convention and for writing the new U.S. Constitution. In pointing to his letter of April 8, 1787, to Randolph, as setting forth the earliest and fullest plan for a new constitution, Madison singles out the intended "sanction . . . *by the people of the States*, acting in their original & sovereign character." He also drives home the point that his letter's proposed "negative on the laws of the States," "vested in the general Authority," was modelled on the British system, but in a republican rather than monarchical fashion, although the Convention eventually rejected his proposal.[31]

In the final analysis, Madison's prefatory "Sketch" shares much the same viewpoints found in his three preliminary outlines of early 1787.

A Question of Strategy

The evidence thus far presented has demonstrated Madison's pre-Convention accent on the need for a strong federal sovereignty and national state based on a system of supreme, legislated laws. His main aim was to preserve and to strengthen the Union in the face of independence and fragmentation on the part of the individual states, and their legislatures, in the Confederation. That this was Madison's primary goal prior to the Convention in his plans sent to Jefferson, Randolph, and Washington was recognized by them as well as himself, according to his post-Convention recollections that became the preface to his Convention *Notes*. Neither in those early plans nor in that later prefatory "Sketch" did Madison bring to bear the strong weight of arguments on "rights" that he used during the Convention in support of his proposals for a federal congressional legislative right to "negative" or veto laws issued by state legislatures. During the Convention, he propounded the proposition that a strong federal legislature with "negative" veto power over state legislatures was necessary in order to prevent majorities in the separate states and their legislatures from passing laws that went against the rights of minority groups and individuals.

Going into the Convention, Madison was determined to present a plan, and to push for a constitution, that would promote the sovereign nation-state of America through departments and branches revolving around a government founded on laws. Once the Convention was under way, the looming resistance by some state delegates and state legislators, not to mention by some members of the Confederate Congress, to a loss of their independent power became all the more apparent to Madison. He now came more fully to realize how difficult it would be to persuade his fellow delegates at the Convention to produce a new constitution with strong federal powers for the sake of preserving the Union rather than promoting the self-interest of the states and their legislators. Madison therefore placed the debate on the even higher ground of protecting minority and individual rights, using this issue in part as a kind of "wedge" with which to push his main agenda and to persuade the delegates. At the same time, he continued to promote the need for a strong sovereign nation-state with legislative veto powers for purposes not only of protecting rights but of preserving the Union. If Madison's proposed federal legislative "negative," to be used by Congress over state laws, had been adopted at the Convention, which it was not, the federal framework of legislative sovereignty and legislative state would have emerged even stronger conceptually than it did in the new U.S. Constitution.

There are many further dimensions on Madison's use of minority and individual rights in part as a "wedge" issue with which to persuade the Convention delegates to frame, for the good of the country, a stronger sovereign federal government at the national level. Some of his fellow Virginians, including Jefferson, were opposed as a matter of principle to encroachments on their state's sovereignty. (In that regard, it was advantageous for Madison that Jefferson was then out of the country and the Convention.) Protection of minority and individual rights indeed remained a continuing concern for Madison before, during, and after the Convention. At issue here are Madison's priorities and strategies. No one was more mindful than he of the need for such protections, as evidenced in his later efforts for a Bill of Rights. Yet at the Convention Madison was more attuned to the difficulties that would be involved (as later reflected in his *Federalist* essays) in persuading the members of the separate legislatures and conventions to approve the new federal constitution once it was finally drawn up and agreed upon at the Convention. To that end, his arguments on "rights" would have provided further ammunition, as would those found in his pre-Convention outlines, "Vices," and researches on historical confederations.

Whatever the verdict on Madison's approaches and priorities on these topics during the Convention, there can be little doubt about his strong overriding statements on sovereignty, state, and legislation before and after the Convention in his writings already explored. The continuing focus here must be upon concepts of sovereignty, state, and legislation as topics in their own right. The preceding interpretations of Madison's strategic use of "rights" at the Convention turn also on our fuller evidence and discussion. Various diverse points raised in other contexts at a recent Princeton conference on Madison can be used to advance the foregoing interpretations (as in the extended note below).[32] To the extent that at the Convention Madison was balancing individual rights, liberty, and equality with federal authority and order, the latter far outweighed the former in his mind and, indeed, was for him at that point the best way to achieve and ensure the former.

The Virginia Plan

Toward the end of his prefatory "Sketch," in his Convention *Notes*, Madison commented on the resolutions introduced at the Convention's outset by Govenor Randolph, leader of the Virginia delegation. There Madison refers to "the early and prominent part" played by Virginia "in bringing about the Convention." The crucial "initiative step" was taken by that state in introducing the resolutions that "became the basis on which the proceedings . . . commenced." Those resolutions, which came to be known as the Virginia Plan, were, says Madison, "the result of a Consultation." In fact, as is well known, the resolutions proposed by Randolph and his delegation were mostly based on Madison's constitutional plans as previously sent to Randolph as well as to Jefferson and Washington. To the plan of a constitution and government set forth in the Virginia resolutions "may be traced," declared Madison, the "basis" of "the plan of Gov. proposed by the Convention." His previous study of "the History of the most distinguished Confederacies, particularly those of antiquity," led him, he says, to take a prominent seat at the front of the Convention hall for the purpose of recording its proceedings (and taking a prominent part in its debates).[33]

When Randolph "opened the main business" at the Convention in Philadelphia on May 29, 1787, he began, according to Madison's *Notes of Convention*, with a lengthy four-part disquisition on "revising the federal system." After outlining the "character of such a government," Randolph described "the defects of the confederation"; he noted "the infancy of the science, of constitutions, of confederacies" as well as "the jealousy of the [individual American] states with regard to their sovereignty." Turning more briefly to "the danger of our situation," especially "the prospect of anarchy from the laxity of government every where," Randolph "then proceeded to the remedy," which was embodied in the fifteen resolutions that he then presented to the Convention.[34]

From the outset of the Virginia resolutions set forth by Randolph, based for the most part on Madison's own preliminary plans sent to him and others, the legislative components of sovereignty and state dominated these initiatives, which shaped the emerging form of the new constitution and government. Seeming to propose, however, a revision of the Articles of Confederation rather than their replacement, Randolph sought in the first brief resolution "to accomplish [better] the[ir] objects . . . [of] 'common defence, security of liberty and general welfare.' " He then launched into extended proposals for the "National Legislature." He turned successively to "the rights of suffrage in the National Legislature," its division into "two branches," and "the right of originating Acts" on the part of both branches. The Legislature's right should be "to legislate in all cases to which the separate states are incompetent," "to negative [when deemed necessary] all laws passed by the several States," and to "force . . . any member of the Union . . . to fulfill its duty."[35]

Ensuing resolutions offered by Randolph and his Virginia delegation took up more briefly the executive and judicial branches, especially in relation to the laws passed by the National Legislature. The "National Executive" would "be chosen by the National Legislature." First and foremost, the Executive would have "a general authority to execute the National Laws." It would have "the Executive rights vested in Congress by the Confederation." That is, the Executive power would become a separate branch and no longer be a part of the legislature in Congress, as was the case under the Articles of Confederation. "[T]he Executive and . . . the National Judiciary, ought to compose a Council of revision with authority to examine every act of the National Legislature before it shall operate . . . [and] before a Negative thereon shall be final . . ." Such a "negative" by the other branches on a law passed by the Legislature could be overridden, however, if the law were again passed by the Legislature.[36]

Remaining resolutions set forth further proposals on such topics as admission of new states and amendments.

The impression left is that revision of the existing system in the Articles of Confederation was Randolph's own aim, rather than the creation of a new system in a new constitution. (The first resolution, for instance, declared "that the Articles of Confederation ought to be so corrected & enlarged as to accomplish the objects proposed by their institution; namely, 'common defence' " etc.) This was evidently part of another initial strategy (like the "rights" issue) on Madison's part as well to overcome reservations by some delegates (including Randolph himself, who ended up, however, at Convention's close, not approving the new Constitution). Madison's pre-Convention outlines show that he was really intent on pursuing a bold new direction, as Washington's April letter to him had also urged him to do. Did Madison (and Washington) engineer the Virginia Plan in a (somewhat deceptive) device with which to forestall Randolph's obstinacy and to use him for seizing the initiative and setting their (concealed) agenda? One may wonder about the thoughts of both Madison and Washington on this matter as they took their seats at the front of the room, facing the Convention delegates, the one busily taking notes and the other quietly presiding.

Debating the Plan

According to Madison's Convention *Notes*, controversy over issues of sovereignty and state quickly came to the forefront at the outset of the proceedings on May 29, 1787. After Randolph presented the Virginia Plan, Charles Pinckney of South Carolina "laid before the house the draught of a federal Government which he had prepared, to be agreed upon between the free and independent States of America." Pinckney asked that his plan, too, be submitted, like Randolph's, to the

Committee of the Whole House for consideration. But it was Randolph's Virginia Plan that the delegates proceeded to take up instead. As Madison reported, the Committee agreed to pass over, for the time being, the two initial resolutions presented by Randolph on amending the Articles of Confederation, in promotion of the general welfare, and on disallowing treaties between "States, as individual Sovereignties." Taken up first was Randolph's proposal "that a *national* Government ought to be established consisting of a *supreme* Legislative, Executive & Judiciary." Discussion then centered "on the force and extent of the particular terms *national* & *supreme*." At that point, ". . . Pinckney wished to know of Mr. Randolph whether he meant to abolish the State Govern[men]ts altogether." Randolph replied that he merely sought to "outline" his proposed "system."[37]

Even more bluntly, ". . . Pinckney expressed a doubt whether the act of [the Confederation] Congre[s]s [passed on February 21, 1787, while Madison was a member,] recommending the Convention, or the Commissions of the Deputies to it, could authorise [*sic*] a discussion of a System founded on different principles from the federal [Confederate] Constitution." Then Gov. Morris of Pennsylvania "explained the distinction between a federal and national, *supreme*, Gov[ernment], the former being a mere compact . . . [and] the latter having a compleat and *compulsive* operation. He contended that in all Communities there must be [a la Bodinian tradition] one supreme power, and one only." Mason of Virginia added that "the present confederation was . . . deficient in not providing for coercion & punishment ag[ainst] delinquent States . . ." Attempts were then made by C. C. Pinckney and Read "to postpone" Randolph's proposal of a "supreme" national government in order to vote on establishing "a more effective Government consisting of a ["supreme" deleted] Legislative, Executive and Judiciary." But the motion was lost, and the original wording was adopted with the word "supreme" included.[38] (Although South Carolina did end up voting in the affirmative, its opening salvo against the proposed Union sovereignty over the states was an historical portent of its stronger role as first state to secede from the Union at the outset of the Civil War.)

During the debates on following days over each of Randolph's successive resolutions, at first centering extensively on the character and composition of the National Legislature, Madison, as usual, had much to say himself, as recorded in his Convention *Notes*. A case in point occurred on May 31, 1787, when Randolph's sixth resolution was taken up. Pinckney again had an objection, to which Butler, Randolph, and then Madison responded. Their sequence of sentiments further reveals how much hesitancy and resistance still had to be overcome in steering cautiously yet firmly toward a national sovereignty over the states in the main arena of legislation—that is, concerning legislative sovereignty and the legislative state in concept and actuality.

> The sixth Resolution stating the cases in which the national Legislature ought to legislate was next taken into discussion: On the question whether each branch sh[oul]d originate laws, there was an unanimous affirmative without debate. On the question for transferring all the Legislative powers of the existing Cong[res]s to this Assembly, there was also a silent affirmative....
>
> On the proposition for giving "Legislative power in all cases to which the State Legislatures were individually incompetent."
>
> Mr. Pin[c]kney & Mr. Rutledge objected to the vagueness of the term *incompetent*, and said they could not well decide how to vote until they should see an exact enumeration of the powers comprehended by this definition.
>
> Mr. Butler repeated his fears that we were running into an extreme in taking away the powers of the States, and called on Mr. Randolph for the extent of his meaning.
>
> Mr. Randolph disclaimed any intention to give indefinite powers to the national Legislature, declaring that he was entirely opposed to such an inroad on the State jurisdictions, and that he did not think any considerations whatever could ever change his determination....
>
> Mr. Madison said that he had brought with him into the Convention a strong bias in favor of an enumeration and definition of the powers necessary to be exercised by the national Legislature; but had also brought doubts concerning its practicability. His wishes remained unaltered; but his doubts had become stronger. What his opinion might ultimately be he could not yet tell. But he should shrink from nothing which should be found essential to such a form of Gov[ernmen]t as would provide for the safety, liberty and happiness of the community. This being the end of all our deliberations, all the necessary means for attaining it must, however reluctantly, be submitted to.[39]

Madison's concluding words in the preceding passage typify his forceful yet temperate manner in helping to steer the proceedings, once again, toward certain goals. By invoking traditional notions of the *salus populi* and *salus reipublicae* as "the end" to which "all ... necessary means for attaining it must, however reluctantly, be submitted to," Madison can almost be seen as closely paraphrasing writers like Bodin and his followers. Madison's final temporizing tone in trying to assuage the resistance or reluctance of some, including Randolph, to follow his lead is another matter. He goes on to report that the portion of Randolph's sixth resolution containing the words "not competent" passed overwhelmingly, with South Carolina also voting for it. The continuation of the discussions on the sixth resolution is also noteworthy, especially as concerns the "negative"—of particular interest to Madison. The "negative" still remained to be resolved, and for apparent strategic reasons, because of its particular divisiveness, he obtained its postponement in the debates.[40]

As the Convention debates swirled on in early June, 1787, over the proposals in the Virginia Plan, issues of sovereignty in matters of state and legislation came ever more to the fore, as conveyed in Madison's Convention *Notes*. He reports and summarizes many striking statements by such delegates as the resolute James Wilson of Pennsylvania and the defiant William Patterson of New Jersey. They argued, respectively, for a strong national legislative sovereignty in a new constitution and for a strong legislative sovereignty vested in the separate (confederated) states through revised Articles of Confederation. Madison seems here to take a middle ground between these two extremes of centralized and decentralized federal government. Yet he himself dwells on the need for a strong national government (rather than a weaker federal one) in order to prevent majorities in the separate states, when given too much independence in a confederation, from abusing the rights of minority groups and private individuals. To this end, Madison brings to bear the lessons he learned from studying historical confederations, as in the cases of Greece and Rome. Dickenson of Delaware compared the balance needed between the national sovereignty and the sovereignties of the separate states to the solar system, in which the separate planets move around the sun. Wilson, he said, would remove the sun in favor of the states alone. Wilson then shifted the analogy in defence of his ideas, which would not, he felt, lead to undue hegemony by the national government; on the contrary, his critics were wrongly influenced by the British model in matters relating to sovereignty and legislation. Along the way, some remarks made by Gerry of Massachusetts, after alluding to "the policy of all Legislators," could have been construed by some, however improperly, as suggesting that Madison, who clearly sought a new republican form, might favor "limited monarchy." The representative excerpts given (in the note) below illustrate the great extent to which issues of legislative sovereignty *per se*, again insufficiently apprehended by historians, dominated the Convention debates from the outset on the subject of representation by smaller and larger states in the national legislature. That subject was to preoccupy the delegates for the greater duration of the Convention.[41]

Struggles for Sovereignty ("intoxicated with the idea of their *sovereignty*")

In the Convention debates that ensued, the struggles between larger and smaller states for sovereignty, through representation in the new national legislature being created, continued and intensified, dominating the greater part of the proceedings. The struggles for sovereignty between delegates who championed a strong central government and those who favored a decentralized system with continued self-determination by the states and their legislatures also played a prominent part. These struggles foreshadowed the post-Convention ones over ratification that arose between federalists and anti-federalists, again with particular regard to legislative matters. Other such struggles for sovereignty also enveloped the Convention debates, as duly recorded and featured by Madison in his *Notes*. Serving as apt epitome was his notation of a delegate's observation that many states' advocates there were "intoxicated with the idea of their *sovereignty*." These important perspectives on legislative sovereignty have not yet received adequate attention in their own right from historians.

When the Committee of the Whole isssued on June 13, 1787, its report on Randolph's propositions in the Virginia Plan, which it presented in amended form in nineteen resolutions, the principle of legislative sovereignty stood out. This was the case regarding not only the National Legislature itself but also its relationship to the National Executive and the National Judiciary as well as to the state legislatures, which retained some self-determination though not as much as before. The British and Confederation models remained influential in different ways, as in the selection of the Executive and Judiciary by the Legislature.[42] On the following day, Patterson introduced the alternate New Jersey Plan, essentially keeping the existing system but with some significant revisions. In it, legislative sovereignty centered more coercively than before around Congress but with strong legislative and other powers retained by the separate states and their legislatures.[43]

As the debates moved ahead and the Committee of the Whole took up the differing plans by Randolph and Patterson, Alexander Hamilton of New York entered the fray on June 18 with an extensive series of observations, proposals, and ideas, some to the immediate point and some more theoretical. "He was," as Madison reports at the outset, "particularly opposed to that [plan] from N. Jersey, being fully convinced, that no amendment of the Confederation, leaving the States in possession of their Sovereignty[,] could possibly answer the purpose. On the other hand[,] . . . he was much discouraged by the amazing extent of Country in expecting the desired blessings from any general sovereignty that could be substituted." The first article of the plan submitted by Hamilton dealt, strikingly, with: "The Supreme Legislative power of the United States of America . . ." His fourth and seventh articles dealt respectively with "The supreme Executive authority" and "The supreme Judicil authority." Both of these branches were closely connected in their function to the laws enacted by the Legislature. The Executive would "have a negative on all laws about to be passed, and the execution of all laws passed . . ." According to Hamilton's article ten: "All laws of the particular States contrary to the Constitution or laws of the United States [were] to be utterly void . . ." Legislative standpoints of sovereignty and state are conceptually dominant in Hamilton's plan.[44]

The Convention debates, especially over issues of sovereignty and state, then progressed along further lines of practical formulation, political theory, and historical comparisons, as reported and featured in Madison's *Notes*. He became even more a leading participant, even though his positions sometimes failed to carry. After Hamilton introduced his plan, Madison on June 19 turned first to give an extremely long critique of Patterson's New Jersey Plan and his objection to many features of Randolph's Virginia Plan, as shaped by Madison himself. Among the many questions Madison asked were: "Will it [Patterson's plan] prevent encroachments on the federal authority?" and "Will it secure a good internal legislation & administration to the particular States [including smaller states like Patterson's New Jersey]?"[45] Then introduced were the revised and corrected Virginia resolutions as agreed to by the Committee of the Whole House. Hamilton next spoke on the relationships "between the National & State Legislatures," favoring the former at the expense of the latter and citing historical examples. King addressed "the import of the terms 'States[,]' 'Sovereignty[,]' '*national*'[, and] 'federal' . . ." Wilson and Hamilton then debated the meaning of the Declaration of Independence on the separate "States" as "free & independent," which Hamilton denied had been "thrown into a State of Nature."[46] Thereafter, on June 20, Martin of Maryland, siding with Mason of Virginia, used the relationship between "Congress" and the "Legislatures" of the states to show that they remained "separate sovereignties," even at the expense of the national Legislature.[47] Once again, concepts and contexts of legislative sovereignty were coming to the fore on both sides of the debates over national sovereignty versus states' sovereignties.

They continued to do so, as reflected in further representative passages in Madison's *Notes*. Wilson then looked briefly, on June 20, 1787, to ancient Greek history, "in the infancy of political Science," on "the necessity of two branches."[48] Madison pondered on June 21 historical cases more broadly when discoursing at length on the greater dangers posed by strong governments and legislatures at the state level than at the national level. He extensively invoked the history of ancient and modern confederacies, later also invoking Montesquieu.[49] Thereafter, Hamilton and Madison dealt on June 26 with aspects of republican government (on which Hamilton was somewhat negative).[50] Martin invoked Locke and other writers on June 27 to show "that the States like individuals were in a State of nature[,] equally sovereign & free."[51] Madison then on June 28 addressed the "fallacy of the reasoning drawn from the equality of Sovereign States in the formation of compacts," reiterating his proposed federal legislative "negative on the State laws" and drawing broad comparisons on many fronts with historical examples.[52]

Following the foregoing discussions, some statements by Gerry and Martin on June 29 epitomized the central role played by sovereignty in the Convention debates thus far. When Gerry used the phrase "intoxicated with the idea of their *sovereignty*," he was alluding mainly to the independence of the separate states in relation to the national or federal government's power. This issue was in the forefront of the long contentious debates over representation in Congress as the supreme national legislature. This was a struggle for sovereignty between bigger and smaller states. But Gerry's phrase can also stand for the continuing importance of sovereignty in the wider forefront and background of the Convention debates.

> Mr. Gerry urged that we never were independent States, were not such now, & never could be even on the principles of the Confederation. The States & the advocates for them were intoxicated with the idea of their *sovereignty* [emphasis *sic* in *Notes*]. He was a member of Congress at the time the federal articles were formed. The injustice of allowing each State an equal vote was long insisted on. He voted for it, but it was agst. his Judgment, and under the pressure of public danger, and the obstinacy of the lesser States. The present confederation he considered as dissolving. The fate of the Union will be decided by the Convention. . . .
>
> Mr. L. Martin, remarked that the language of the States being *sovereign & independent*, was once familiar & understood; though it seemed now so strange & obscure. He read those passages in the articles of Confederation, which describe them in that language.[53]

In the Convention debates that followed during many ensuing weeks, the frequency and prominence of "sovereignty" and related terms, especially in contexts of legislation, became ever more a striking fixture as reported in Madison's *Notes*. Madison's own conceptual perspectives on legislative aspects of sovereignty and state in these long and arduous proceedings, up to the Convention's end on September 17, 1787, are of particular interest (as in the extended note below).[54]

4. MADISON'S POST-CONVENTION ESSAYS

The Great Lawgivers

About a week after the Constitutional Convention in Philadelphia ended, James Madison returned to New York City, where he was still a delegate to the dying Confederate Congress. There he accepted Alexander Hamilton's invitation to assist him and John Jay in writing a series of essays supporting ratification. Appearing in several New York news publications under the title *The Federalist* and the pseudonym "Publius," these essays or articles reached a total of eighty-five, with twenty-nine written by Madison from late 1787 to early 1788. The pseudonym "Publius" pointed up from the start the view held by Madison along with the others that the new U.S. Constitution was comparable to the legendary lawgivings issued by the great lawgivers and state founders of ancient Greece and Rome. In the words of a modern historian whose edition of Madison's writings refers to him singularly in the title as "the founder":

> Publius Valerius Publicola was a noble Roman who, in Plutarch's classic story, helped to depose the Tarquin kings, found the ancient Republic, and defend it against its enemies with courage and prudence. Comparing Publius with the Athenian lawgiver, Solon, Plutarch [an ancient Greek biographer] gave higher rank to the Greek as the originator of republican laws. Yet he found balancing merits on the Roman side: "Solon, leaving his laws as soon as he had made them, engraven in wood, but destitute of a defender, departed from Athens; whilst Publicola, remaining both in and out of office, laboured to establish the government." The American Publius—collective pseudonym for the authors of the *Federalist*—might claim an originality as great as Solon's; but he would not leave the new republican laws of the United States "engraven in wood." The founders of the American Republic knowingly chose the Roman name.
>
> As they knew, the achievement of the Philadelphia Convention would mean nothing until the Constitution was ratified and established by nine states. Critics of the proposed

> Constitution began firing almost as soon as the Convention closed its business. A New York "Cato" (George Clinton? Abraham Yates?) launched his attack in late September, 1787. By early October, Richard Henry Lee's persuasive anti-Federalist arguments in *Letters from the Federal Farmer* began circulating through Virginia and the country at large. Alexander Hamilton promptly recruited a Federalist writing team in New York City . . .[55]

In *Federalist* number 38 Madison gives a long disquisition, still insufficiently appreciated by historians, on the great lawgiver-founders in ancient Greece and Rome. His wealth of historical material on the subject bears some striking similarities, pointed up by the present series, to discussions found in Renaissance works by Corasius, Bodin, and, in different ways, Machiavelli. For Madison, the main point becomes the way in which great individuals like Solon, Lycurgus, and Numa, rather than general assemblies, took over the task of founding new systems of state through different kinds of lawmaking and constitution-making in those ancient settings. Not that Madison himself would have necessarily agreed with modern historians like the aforementioned who label him "*the* founder," yet Madison's own special role in forming the new U.S. Constitution might well have been in the back of his mind when composing this highly suggestive essay, influenced by Adams' *Defence* Preface.

> It is not a little remarkable that in every case reported by ancient history, in which government has been established with deliberation and consent, the task of framing it has not been committed to an assembly of men; but has been performed by some individual citizen of pre-eminent wisdom and approved integrity. Minos, we learn, was the primitive founder of the government of Crete; as Zaleucus was of that of the Locrians. Theseus first, and after him Draco and Solon, instituted the government of Athens. Lycurgus was the lawgiver of Sparta. The foundation of the original government of Rome was laid by Romulus; and the work compleated by two of his elective successors, Numa, and Tullus Hostilius. On the abolition of royalty, the consular administration was substituted by Brutus, who stepped forward with a project for such a reform, which he alledged had been prepared by Servius Tullius, and to which his address obtained the assent and ratification of the senate and people. This remark is applicable to confederate governments also. Amphyction, we are told, was the author of that which bore his name. The Achaean league received its first birth from

> Achaeus, and its second from Aratus. What degree of agency these reputed lawgivers might have in their respective establishments, or how far they might be cloathed with the legitimate authority of the people, cannot in every instance be ascertained. In some, however, the proceeding was strictly regular. Draco appears to have been entrusted by the people of Athens, with indefinite powers to reform its government and laws. And Solon, according to Plutarch, was in a manner compelled by the universal suffrage of his fellow citizens, to take upon him the sole and absolute power of new modelling the constitution. The proceedings under Lycurgus were less regular; but as far as the advocates for a regular reform could prevail, they all turned their eyes towards the single efforts of that celebrated patriot and sage, instead of seeking to bring about a revolution, by the intervention of a deliberative body of citizens.[56]

In the continuation of the preceding passage from *Federalist* #38, Madison addresses more closely the whys and wherefores of the ancient Greeks turning to individuals rather than to assemblies in these matters, especially given their love of liberty (all of which further reinforcing our section above on "a question of strategy"). Pointing to the cases of Solon and Lycurgus, Madison warns his countrymen of the dangers of disputes that can imperil the adoption of new plans of government when entrusted to assemblies rather than to individuals, as the Greeks well understood. However much America has improved upon those ancient models of procedure, the reasonings behind them still remain instructive. Critics of the new U.S. Constitution should focus less on its imperfections, he believes, than on the far greater defects of its predecessor, the Articles of Confederation.[57]

Further on in the same *Federalist* #38, Madison makes another remarkable comparison with Lycurgus. His allusion to Lycurgus' solitary greatness as founder and reformer not only puts Lycurgus in a favorable light but would seem by analogy to do the same for Madison himself. Madison's oblique allusion to the new Constitution's potential for "immortality," after the example of Lycurgus' plan, bears not only on the American "lawgivers" who formed it at the Convention in Philadelphia but also on Madison himself. Was he indirectly depicting himself and his fellow founders at Philadelphia as latter-day Lycurguses, bedevilled by their critics and needing to return from "exile" to save the day?

> As it can give no umbrage to the writers against the plan of the federal constitution, let us suppose that ... the late convention were unequal to the task assigned them, and that a wiser and better plan might and ought to be substituted. Let us further suppose ... a second convention, with full powers and for the express purpose of revising and remoulding the work of the first. ... I leave it to be decided ... whether the constitution, now before the public, would not stand as fair a chance for immortality, as Lycurgus gave to that of Sparta, by making its change to depend on his own return from exile and death, if it were to be immediately adopted, and were to continue in force, not until a better, but until another should be agreed upon by this new assembly of lawgivers.
>
> It is a matter both of wonder and regret, that those who raise so many objections against the new constitution, should never call to mind the defects of that which is to be exchanged for it. It is not necessary that the former should be perfect; it is sufficient that the latter is more imperfect.[58]

Sovereignty and Legislation

In addition to constitution-making as itself a form of lawgiving, on the model of the ancients, there are various other perspectives in Madison's *Federalist* essays on legislation in relation to sovereignty under the new U.S. Constitution. These include the central nexus of legislation that gives to the federal executive and judicial branches their primary functions in executing and interpreting the laws made by Congress. The important but subordinate role played by the states in relation to the federal government at the national level through the medium of legislation provides further perspective. The people and their representatives as ultimate sources of law and legislation also add another dimension. Questions of majority rule and minority rights in relation to the common public interest revolve largely around the laws of the states as well as those of the federal government.

The defects of the existing U.S. Confederation and its Congress in their relationship to the separate states and their governments remained central subjects for Madison in promoting the new U.S. Constitution in *The Federalist*. In the course of the same *Federalist* #38, Madison argued strongly against the concentration of all federal powers in the Congress, as had occurred under the Articles of Confederation, to which some critics of the new U.S. Constitution still clung.[59] In *Federalist* #18–20 Madison inveighed against the dangers of confederations, as seen here through his extensive examinations of

Greek, Germanic, and Netherlandish history. In those cases, he was convinced, sovereignty was so hopelessly divided among the confederated states in a single confederate body that there was no real sovereignty at all. He remarks on "the tendency of federal bodies, rather to anarchy among the members than to tyranny in the head."[60] According to Madison in *Federalist* #20: "The important truth . . . is, that a sovereignty over sovereigns, a government over governments, a legislation for communities, as contradistinguished from individuals . . . is a solecism in theory . . . [and] subversive of the order and ends of civil polity by substituting *violence* in place of law . . ."[61] In this depiction, law and legislation lie conceptually, once again, at the foundation of sovereignty and state. The same holds true in a different way in a passage from *Federalist* #37 again critical of the Confederation:

> [T]he existing confederation is founded on principles which are fallacious. . . . [W]e must consequently change this first foundation, and . . . the superstructure resting upon it. . . .
>
> Among the difficulties encountered by the convention, a very important one must have lain, in combining the requisite stability and energy in government with the inviolable attention due to liberty and the republican form. Energy in government is essential to security against external and internal danger, and to the prompt and salutary execution of the laws, which enter into the very definition [!] of good government. Stability in government, is essential to the national character. . . . An irregular and mutable legislation is not more an evil in itself, than it is odious to the people . . . of this country, [who] . . . will never be satisfied, till some remedy be applied to the vicissitudes and uncertainties, which characterize the state administrations.[62]

Meantime, the overpowering concentration of all powers in a single, potentially despotic, legislative body, as in the state of Virginia, has prompted both himself and Jefferson, as Madison indicates in *Federalist* #48, to call for a redistribution of some of its powers into other departments, that is, the executive and judicial branches. While arguing against the existing excessive legislative sovereignty at the state level, this being no good model for the new federal government, Madison by no means discounts the necessary ongoing priority of law and legislation lying conceptually at the foundation of sovereignty and state.

> The legislative department is every where extending the sphere of its activity, and drawing all power into its impetuous vortex. . . . It is not unfrequently a question of real nicety in legislative

> bodies, whether the operation of a particular measure, will, or will not extend beyond the legislative sphere....
>
> The first example is that of Virginia, a state which, as we have seen, has expressly declared in its constitution, that the three great departments ought not to be intermixed. The authority in support of it is Mr. Jefferson, [in] ... his very interesting "Notes on the state of Virginia." ...[:] "All the powers of government, legislative, executive and judiciary, result to the legislative body. The concentrating these in the same hands is precisely the definition of despotic government. ... For this reason, that [Virginia] convention which passed the ordinance of government laid its foundation on this basis, that the legislative, executive, and judiciary departments should be separate and distinct, so that no person should exercise the powers of more than one of them at the same time. *But no barrier was provided between these several powers.* The judiciary and executive members were left dependent on the legislative for their subsistence in office ..."
>
> The conclusion which I am warranted in drawing from these observations is, that a mere demarkation on parchment of the constitutional limits of the several departments, is not a sufficient guard against those encroachments which lead to a tyrannical concentration of all the powers of government in the same hands.[63]

That legislation lies, conceptually, at the foundation of sovereignty and state in Madison's *Federalist* essays cited above is consistent with, and is a dimension of, his various other essays therein in which he examines and applies Montesquieu's ideas on the separation of legislative, executive, and judicial powers, as we have already begun to see.[64] Indeed, our earlier examination of Montesquieu's *Spirit of the Laws* pointed up his great debt to Bodinian traditions of legislative sovereignty, as rethought by Locke and others, in ways congruent with the tripartite separation of powers. For Montesquieu, the legislature was one of three co-equal branches in which the executive and judicial functions of executing and interpreting the laws took their lead from the laws themselves as the sovereign basis of the state itself.[65]

The Union and the States: Looking Ahead

The relationships between the federal and the state governments were explored by Madison in *Federalist* #46 in ways heavy with portent for the future. His essential point was that the state governments should not fear any unwarranted or threatening encroachments upon their governments and legislatures by the federal (national) government and its legislature under the terms set forth in the new U.S. Constitution. Not only does their authority seem to revolve around their inherent right to legislate for their own affairs, regardless of questions about their jurisdictional rights to do so (another parallel to Bodin and Corasius?), but the people themselves possess the ultimate sovereign authority. The new system will be expressive of the common national interest, which the existing Confederate Congress has too often neglected because of members pursuing the agendas of their own states. Madison conjures forth what he here considers to be the improbable image of an overambitious American federal government, armed with military force like Britain was before the Revolution, to put down the problematic American states. But instead of being an improbable future scenario imagined by some opponents, such heavy-handed tactics would soon become a more plausible fear in light of certain subsequent events portrayed by Madison. Only what is "necessary," he here believes, for the sake of promoting and preserving "the union" need be placed in the hands of the federal government. Any unnecessary encroachments by it on the affairs of the states could be checked by the states when responding in "general alarm" to the "common cause." For now, however, such fears are groundless because the federal government will typically be attuned and responsive to the needs and priorities of the states.[66]

A decade later, the situation changed dramatically for Madison. By 1798, the year of the Alien and Sedition Acts, the great issue for him now was not the need for more but rather less federal legislative power over the individual states. The Federalist administration of John Adams, together with the Congress and the Hamiltonians, were engaged in restrictive policies that Republicans led by Jefferson and Madison felt were threatening the rights and liberties of individuals and states in violation of the original compact embodied in the U.S. Constitution. The new situation justified protests and action by the legislatures of the states in their post-Revolutionary capacity as independent sovereign entities. The Kentucky and Virginia Resolutions drafted respectively by Jefferson and Madison, and passed by the legislatures of those states, took such a position. Even though the other state legislatures failed to follow through with similar resolutions, these resolutions continued to have a strong influence in the early 19th century in the debates over the rights of the states to nullify federal laws and even to secede from the Union. In late 1799 and early 1800, a long "Report" written by Madison was issued by the Virginia legislature against the Alien and Sedition Acts. This "Report" took up in turn each of the resolutions in the Virginia Resolutions. It is perhaps ironic that the earlier centralizing Federalist outlook of Madison, in league with Hamilton in *The Federalist,* had now given way to a different anti-Federalist impulse on decentralization under the changed circumstances. And yet Madison's underlying legislative prescriptions in *The Federalist* on sovereignty and state grew even stronger in his "Report" on the Virginia Resolutions that was isssued by the Virginia legislature.[67]

In the Virginia "Report," when addressing the third resolution in the Virginia Resolutions, Madison speaks of the grave and dangerous threat posed by the Alien and Sedition Acts. They were passed by Congress in violation of the original constitutional compact and now require urgent protest by the separate sovereign states.[68] In a similar vein, concerning the fourth resolution, Madison attacks the Alien and Sedition Acts as representing proof of a trend toward monarchy in the executive branch. He faults the underlying "deficiency of the laws," even within the Constitution's "legislative limits," that has given rise to the consolidation of the states into "one sovereignty" under a strong executive.[69] Furthermore, in his central and longest discussion on the fifth resolution, Madison continues to denounce the violations of the U.S. Constitution by the Alien and Sedition Acts. They exhibit a flagrant encroachment by the federal executive on the federal legislature as well as judicial branches.[70]

Madison then proceeds in the Virginia "Report" to a remarkable detailed discourse on the American Revolution in terms of legislative sovereignty and British claims of legislative as well as executive supremaacy over the colonies. This is the leading historical precedent used here by Madison to build his case, thereby pointing up the wider central legislative framework of sovereignty and state in the Virginia "Report." The original legitimate legislative sovereignties of the separate colonies as states prior to the Revolution, albeit under the executive supremacy of Great Britain, is justification for the independence to which they are now lawfully entitled because of their constitutional compact's violation through the Alien and Sedition Acts. The Federalists' invocations of a "common law" emanating from the U.S. Constitution and binding upon all American states are spurious extrapolations from English law as formerly used to promote America's subservience to the British Empire.

> Did, then, the principle or operation of the great event which made the colonies independent states, imply or introduce the common law, as a law of the Union?
>
> The fundamental principle of the revolution was, that the colonies were coordinate members with each other, and with

> Great Britain of an empire united by a common executive sovereign, but not united by any common legislative sovereign. The legislative power was maintained to be as complete in each American Parliament, as in the British Parliament. And the royal prerogative was in force, in each colony, by virtue of its acknowledging the king for its executive magistrate, as it was in Great Britain, by virtue of a like acknowledgment there. A denial of these principles by Great Britain, and the assertion of them by America, produced the revolution.[71]

After a lengthy analysis of America's acquiescence to the British legislature prior to the Revolution,[72] Madison turns again to the rebellion against it.

> The assertion by Great Britain of a power to make laws for the other members of the empire, in all cases whatsoever, ended in the discovery that she had a right to make laws for them in no cases whatsoever.
>
> Such being the ground of our revolution, no support or color can be drawn from it for the doctrine that the common law is binding on these states as one society. The doctrine, on the contrary, is evidently repugnant to the fundamental principle of the revolution.[73]

Passing forward in historical time to the adoption of the Articles of Confederation after the Revolution, Madison cites in a positive fashion their provisions for the separate states to retain their independent sovereignties. The states are not bound by any "common law" contrived prior to their "compact" in the new U.S. Constitution. In a tour de force, Madison argues that under such a supposed "common law" the legislative authority of Congress would be either strictly bound, in which case all its laws including the Alien and Sedition acts would be invalidated, or else completely freed, in which case its laws and legislative powers would be all-powerful without limit. The chief executive would, in the latter case, also command an alarming power in executing the laws of the federal legislature.[74]

After then dismissing, once and for all, the authority of a "common law" that purportedly binds all Americans to "one community," Madison turns in the Virginia "Report" to a second major area, still concerning the fifth resolution in the Virginia Resolutions. It is, he declares, the authority of the first amendment to the U.S. Constitution, guaranteeing freedom of press and speech, that invalidates or nullifies the Sedition Act. Its supporters openly claim the Act to be based on the "common law" of England. They perhaps reflect the pro-British bias for which the Federalists were often criticized by Democratic-Republicans like Madison and Jefferson (who sided more with France and its Revolution, against which the Federalists were reacting). Madison rejects not only the notion that the Sedition Act is rooted in "common law" but that Congress alone has power over the press. In fact, according to the first amendment, "Congress shall make no law respecting . . . freedom of speech, or the press."[75] Once again, Madison discourses on the legal and legislative dimensions of sovereignty in the British Parliament and American Congress, in relation to the executive power, in order to demonstrate the invalidity of Federalist legislation in the Sedition Act.

> In the British government, the danger of encroachments on the rights of the people is understood to be confined to the executive magistrate. The representatives of the people in the legislature are not only exempt themselves from distrust, but are considered as sufficient guardians of the rights of their constituents against the danger from the executive. Hence it is a principle, that the Parliament is unlimited in its power; or, in their own language, is omnipotent. . . . They are merely legislative precautions against executive usurpation. . . .
>
> In the United States, the case is altogether different. The people, not the government, possess the absolute sovereignty. The legislature, no less than the executive, is under limitations of power. . . . Hence . . . the . . . rights of the people are secured against legislative as well as executive ambition. They are secured, not by laws paramount to prerogative, but by consitutions paramount to laws.[76]

A Divided and Separated Legislative Sovereignty

In his *Federalist* essays and other post-Convention writings, we may add, as well as in his subsequent Virginia "Report," Madison's ideas on the ultimate legislative scope of sovereignty were fully compatible with his views on sovereignty as both divided and separated. The same applies in similar ways to his pre-Convention constitutional outlines and his Convention *Notes*. Amid those changing contexts and circumstances, Madison continued to see sovereignty as being divided between the Union and the states as well as it being separated into legislative, executive, and judicial branches. Nevertheless, the matrix in which this division and separation of powers was formulated and articulated was legislation. Legislation at the federal (national) and state levels, as well as legislation in the interrelationships of operations by Congress, the

Presidency, and the Supreme Court, were, and still are, uppermost factors in sovereignty. Ultimately, the people are sovereign, as expressed in their federal Constitution and laws—their Constitution being approved, and their laws promulgated, by Congress as the national legislature. Although federal laws take precedence over state laws, the latter play an important part. It might be better said that legislation is a common denominator shared by, rather than divided or separated between, the federal and state governments as well as the legislative, executive, and judicial departments or branches at the federal level. If the federal laws of the land in the U.S. are supreme, with the laws of the states as supreme in the states insofar as they do not conflict with them, then the concept of the legislative state is applicable at the federal level and, by extension, at the state level.

The continuing conceptual legacy of legislative sovereignty and the legislative state behind the U.S. Constitution and the ideas of Madison has not yet been adequately recognized by historians. For although sovereignty in the U.S. is divided and separated, not unitary as it was from Bodin to Locke and beyond, it is still ultimately a *legislative* sovereignty nonetheless, as it was for Montesquieu and his followers. The continuity, despite change, from the Declaration of Independence to the U.S. Constitution and their later transformations has been seen in their enduring legislative contours of sovereignty and state.

The broadening, massive scope of American legislation at all levels in the late 20th and early 21st centuries has led to the enormous body of legislative-like rules and regulations issued by the federal executive and judicial branches, which have sometimes been called "super-legislatures." How Madison, as well as Jefferson and Adams, would have looked upon this development in U.S. constitutional history is open to question. The increasingly complex legislative systems of state have become perhaps a necessary mainstay of modern American government, within the expanding dynamics of separated and divided powers. If Madison's strong proposal at the Constitutional Convention for federal legislative authority to void state laws when necessary had been adopted and remained in practice, legislative sovereignty would have an even more powerful expression in modern America. In that case, Jefferson might well disapprove yet Adams approve.

For Madison, the necessary central legislative authority of the federal government became more fully apparent in his long "Notes on Nullification," written in 1833 and revised in 1835–1836, at the end of his life. In his "Notes," Madison was responding to the recent Nullification Crisis of 1832, in which the South Carolina legislature nullified federal law but then backed down. Madison dwelled on his Virginia Resolutions and Virginia "Report." They should not be used, he felt, as support for such action, which could lead to anarchy and dissolution of the Union. Whereas in those two documents his focus was on the sovereign legislative rights of the states in their relationship to the federal government, here it is on the superior legislative sovereignty of the federal government. "Although the Legislature of Virginia declared . . . that South Carolina was not supported in her doctrine of nullification by the Resolutions of 1798, it appears that those resolutions are still appealed to as . . . favoring the doctrine."[77] Madison did not want to leave this misuse as his own legacy. As in his two earlier Virginia manifestos, the divided nature of American sovereignty looms large in his "Notes." At one point, after addressing himself to the general constitutional fallacy of arguments justifying the nullification of federal laws by state legislatures,[78] Madison turns to address the nature of sovereignty in America, with an eye to its legislative parameters. Instead of pointing to the states' abilities to revert to their Confederate sovereign status in order to thwart unjust federal laws, as argued in his Resolutions and "Report," Madison now discards that claim in favor of the necessary coercion imposed on the states by federal laws *de iure* and *de facto*.

> Such a doctrine must be seen at once to be subversive of all constitutions, all laws, and all compacts. . . .
>
> The main pillar of nullification is the assumption that sovereignty is a unit, at once indivisible and unalienable; that the states therefore individually retain it entire as they originally held it, and, consequently that no portion of it can belong to the U.S.
>
> But is not the Constitution itself necessarily the offspring of a sovereign authority? What but the highest political authority, a sovereign authority, could make such a Constitution? a constitution which makes a Government, a Government which makes laws; laws which operate like the laws of all other governments by a penal & physical force, on the individuals subject to the laws; and finally laws declared to be the Supreme law of the land; anything in the Constitution or laws of the individual state notwithstanding.
>
> And where does the sovereignty which makes such a Constitution reside. It resides not in a single state but in the people of each of the several states, uniting with those of the others in the express & solemn compact which forms the Constitution. To the *extent* of that compact or Constitution therefore, the people of the several States must be a sovereign as they are a united people.

> In like manner, the constitutions of the States, made by the people as separated into States, were made by a sovereign authority by a sovereignty residing in each of the States, to the extent of the objects embraced by their respective constitutions. [A]nd if the states be thus sovereign, though shorn of so many of the essential attributes of sovereignty, the United States by virtue of the sovereign attributes with which they are endowed, may, to that extent, be sovereign, tho' destitute of the attributes of which the States are not shorn.
>
> Such is the political system of the U.S. de jure & de facto; and . . . its true character will be sustained by an appeal to the law and the testimony of the fundamental charter.[79]

According to Madison in "Notes," the division of sovereignty between the Union and the individual states had long been the norm. The compact in the Constitution and the testimony of Jefferson belie arguments by some for full sovereignty by the states. In this combination of a consolidated national government and a federated system of state governments, the U.S. Constitution and federal laws must be the "supreme law," notwithstanding claims to the contrary. Utilizing his pre-Convention studies on the defects of historical confederations, as developed in his *Federalist* essays, Madison believes that a loose federation of American states would lead to anarchy, whereas a purely national government could become monarchical.[80]

5. MADISON'S LIBRARY

The subject of Madison's library sheds further light on the intellectual sources and influences that helped to shape his pre-Convention outlines as well as his Convention *Notes* and post-Convention essays. It is a subject at once easier and more complicated than in the cases of the libraries of Jefferson and Adams. The greater portion of Madison's books became dispersed or lost, even though some have since been reidentified and reassembled. Hence there is both less actual material to discuss and more indirect information to consider. Similarly, original catalogues do not exist for Madison's library as they do for Jefferson's and Adams' libraries. Yet other means are available for arriving at a fuller picture. There is reason to believe that Madison's library once ranked on the scale and size of Adams' library, if not Jefferson's.

It is certainly possible that Madison, like Jefferson and Adams, possessed a copy of Bodin's *Republic*, as he evidently did of works by Locke, Sidney, Hobbes, and comparable others. There is however, no specific Bodin volume to account for that Madison is known to have possessed. It also remains possible that Jefferson, a generous lender of books in his library, loaned the *Republic* and other such books on politics and law to his close friend and Virginia "neighbor," Madison. There are other channels through which Bodinian tradition could have come to Madison, some of which have been seen above. Judging from their voluminous correspondence over many years, it is unlikely that the strong Bodinian ideas of legislative sovereignty that influenced the author of the Declaration of Independence did not also impact his protégé Madison as architect of the Constitution, and, indeed, we have already seen that they did.

From the above discussions, it becomes clear that Madison was deeply read in political, legal, and intellectual traditions of thought. The evidence for this learning is gained largely from a study of his writings and correspondence, which provide many clues to the kinds of books that were in his library. Surviving fragments of his book collection are also indicative.

Letters to and from Jefferson

In the mid- to late 1780s, Jefferson in France was sending to Madison shipments of and information on books, as indicated in their correspondence cited above.[81] Jefferson's continuing discussions about books for Madison appear in Jefferson's letters to him from Paris in 1784 (Nov. 11), 1785 (Sept. 1), 1786 (Dec. 10), 1787 (June 20, Aug. 2, Sept. 17), and 1788 (July 31). Related discussions of these matters appear in Madison's letters to Jefferson particularly in 1787 (Oct. 24, Dec. 9, Dec. 20). Other letters between them are also pertinent. Included in Jefferson's listings of books for Madison are many multi-volume encyclopedias and dictionaries, along with such works as *Principes de legislation* and *de la Grece* by Mably and a *Vie de Turgot*. The kinds of books that Jefferson was sending to Madison during this period were consistent with Madison's extensive researches of 1786– into the defects of ancient and modern confederacies, his gathering of information prior to and during the Convention on constitutional matters, and his contributions to *The Federalist* on a wide variety of matters both practical and theoretical as well as current and historical.

Not surprisingly, the book to which Madison gave most attention in his letters to Jefferson in mid-1787, early on during the Constitutional Convention, was the first volume of Adams' *Defence*. Madison's frank letter of June 6 gave it a mixed review: "Mr. Adams' book[,] which has been in your hands of course, has excited a good deal of attention. An edition has come out here and another is on the press at N. York. It will probably be much read, particularly in the Eastern States, and contribute with other circumstances to revive the predilections of the Country for the British constitution. Men of learning find nothing new in it, Men of taste many things to criticize. And men without either, not a few things, which they will not understand." Madison went on to say: "It will nevertheless be read, and praised, and become a powerful engine in forming the public opinion. The name and character of the Author, with the crucial situation of our affairs, naturally account for such an effect. The book also has merit, and I wish many of the remarks in it, which are unfriendly to republicanism, may not receive fresh weight from the operations of our Governments."[82] Because of the importance of Bodinian legislative sovereignty in Adams' *Defence*, as made plain above,[83] the great influence ascribed to the *Defence* by Madison, while acting as chief architect of the U.S. Constitution early on at the Convention, points up a powerful way in which Bodinian models contributed directly or indirectly to the strong concepts of legislative sovereignty found in Madison's *Notes of Convention*.

In this regard more generally, the many letters between Madison and Jefferson in 1787 before, during, and after the Convention contain numerous discussions on legislative matters of sovereignty and state. Aside from Madison's pre-Convention outline for a new constitution in his letter of March 19 to Jefferson, his fall letters of Oct. 24 and Nov. 1, together with Jefferson's letters of June 20 and Dec. 20, deal with such matters. By the fall of 1787, the secrecy surrounding the Convention's proceedings was lifted and the new Constitution open to discussion. According to Madison, for instance: "[T]he great objects which presented themselves [at the Convention] were 1. to unite a proper energy in the Executive and a proper stability in the Legislative departments, with the essential characters of Republican Government. . . . The questions concerning the degree of power turned chiefly on the appointment to offices, and the controul of the Legislature. . . . In forming the Senate, the great anchor of the Government [!], the questions [concerning] . . . the first object turned mostly on . . . appointments . . ."[84] Further on here, as in other letters of his at this time to Jefferson, Madison draws upon his historical researches into the defects of ancient and modern confederations. According to Jefferson, for example: "The idea of separating the executive business of the confederacy from [the legislative business of] Congress, as the Judiciary is already in some degree, is just and necessary."[85] Here, a unitary federal legislature that incorporates the executive and judicial functions—as in some American Confederation states and in the British constitution—remains the primary or dominant body "*from*" which the executive and judicial functions now need to be separated into their own respective spheres of executing and interpreting of Congress' legislation. After again approving of this separation of powers, Jefferson goes on to cite Montesquieu and to add that "[t]he instability of our laws is really an immense evil."[86]

Writing in 1825 from his Montpelier home in Virginia to Jefferson at Monticello, Madison stated: "I have looked with attention over your intended proposal of a text book for the Law School [at the new University of Virginia]. It is certainly very natural that the true doctrine of liberty, as exemplified in our Political System, should be inculcated on those who are to sustain and administer it." He went on to say: "It is, at the same time, not easy to find standard books that will be both guides and guards for the purpose. Sidney and Locke are admirably calculated to impose on young minds the right of Nations to establish their own Governments and to inspire a love of free ones . . ."[87] If the subject had been political authority instead of political liberty, Madison could have likewise started off with Sidney and Locke, both steeped in Bodinian traditions of legislative sovereignty.

The correspondence between Madison and Jefferson, far more extensive than that between Adams and Jefferson, reveals a wide range of references to many of the great names in the history of political and intellectual thought. But this, of course, represents only one band in Madison's broad spectrum of correspondence with other noted contemporaries, which affords a fuller view into Madison's intellectual interests and references to other writers, many of whom were undoubtedly represented in Madison's private library.

"List of Books"

In early 1783, while a delegate to the Confederation Congress in Philadelphia, Madison was chiefly responsible for preparing "a list of books proper for the use of Congress" (or "Report of Comee. List of Books to be imported for the use of Congress"). As a modern editorial note to this list points out: "During the latter half of 1782 the primary issues before Congress concerned finance, commerce, prisoners of war, western lands, and international affairs. . . . Most of the subject classifications in JM's report reflect the needs of Congress for the guidance of authoritative works on these topics." The same editorial note also refers to collections that could have influenced Madison then in drawing up his list, including those owned by the College of New Jersey and also by its president, Rev. John Witherspoon. Of more certain influence was the so-called "1783 catalogue" of books, already in preparation before that time, by Jefferson, who stayed with Madison in the weeks prior to the submission of this "report" and "list" to Congress in later January, 1783.[88]

The categories of the 307 entries (according to editorial numbering) in Madison's "List of Books" are arranged, following an initial encyclopedia and dictionary, in the following sequence of classifications: Law of Nature and Nations, General History, Chronology, Geography, Particular History (Grecian, Roman, Italian, German and Holland, French, British, Scotch, Irish, Spanish and Portuguese, Russian, Danish, Swedish, Polish, Swiss, Genevan, Turks, Chinese), Politics, Law, War, Marine, Languages, America. The last category, America, is by far the longest, comprising about a third of the total entries and greatly influenced by Jefferson's "1783 catalogue". It would be interesting to compare, for example, Madison's and Jefferson's full listings under the categories of Politics and Law, as well as their wider classifications overall. Yet it must be kept in mind that Madison was compiling his list for purposes somewhat different from Jefferson's. Mindful of Congress' current interests, affairs, and finances, Madison was perhaps less "extravagent" than Jefferson in extensively pursuing his own broad intellectual tastes and was more inclined to books readily and reasonably obtainable, especially those with contemporary usefulness and availability in English. In any case, many comparable features in the two listings have not yet been duly noted by experts.

Under the category of "Politics" in this "List of Books for Congress," Madison begins with a sequence of books that closely parallels Jefferson's own initial sequence under "Politics"; but it is pared down and limited to books in English or English translation. Madison's initial sequence here is: Plato's *Republic*, Aristotle's *Politics*, More's *Utopia*, Filmer's *Government*, Hooker's *Ecclesiastical Polity*, Hobbes' *Works*, Harrington's *Works*, Sidney's *Government*, Locke's *Government*, Machiavelli's *Works*, Sarpi's *Government of Venice*, Monagu's *Ancient Republics*, Montesquieu's *Works*, and Beccaria's *Works*. This list continues on at some length with mostly lesser-known writers. As for Hobbes' *Leviathan*, with its particularly strong cast of Bodinian legislative sovereignty: "As a youth JM became acquainted with at least one of Hobbes' works. Probably in 1782 he purchased the copy of *Leviathan* originally owned by William Byrd II of Westover."[89]

The omission of Bodin's *Republic* in the preceding book list by Madison under "Politics," in counterdistinction to Jefferson's inclusion of it in his parallel sequence, is readily accounted for in terms already alluded to—namely, cost, language, availability, interest, space, usefulness, and the like. Since only the French version was listed by Jefferson, and not Knolles' English translation, Madison may well have let the matter go at that, realizing that he had more limited space and resources for such listings than did Jefferson, who prepared his "1783" catalogue mostly as a guide to what he already possessed in relation to what he wanted to procure once he arrived in France. Although Jefferson by 1783 already had his copy of Bodin's *Republic* in French back at Monticello, prior to leaving for France, another such copy in French might have been more difficult or expensive to obtain for Congress. Knolles' English version of 1606 might have been more reasonably and readily available, but it was not included in Jefferson's list and was thus overlooked by Madison.

It must be remembered that Madison's press of duties at this point did not allow for the longer time and reflection that enabled Jefferson to prepare a more extensive catalogue of books. Madison's reliance on Jefferson's catalogue was facilitated by the fact that Jefferson evidently brought it with him to Philadelphia for purposes of his own book searches there, although both men had other sources of bibliographical information as well. If Madison conferred with Jefferson about their variant initial listings of books under the crucial heading of "Politics," he would undoubtedly have consulted with Jefferson about the appropriateness for Congress of theoretical books in French like Bodin's *Republic* and Rousseau's *Social Contract*, likewise omitted by Madison, as well as their availability in English (neither work being listed by Jefferson in English versions). In any case: "During January 1783, when Thomas Jefferson was rooming at JM's boarding house in Philadelphia, the two men surely conversed on the subject of a reference library for Congress. By comparing entries [overall] . . . , a kinship between the two lists is made evident."[90]

In Madison's book list, the category of "Law" is placed before rather than after "Politics," the reverse of their order in Jefferson's more elaborate listings for both categories. Under "Law" Madison begins with entries listed as "Justinian's Institutes by Harris" and "Codex juris Civilis." As the editor notes, the first entry relates to an English translation of Justinian's *Corpus Iuris Civilis*. Moreover, the second entry is deemed faulty because no such single edition of the *Codex* had been republished for 250 years, whereas the complete *Corpus* included the *Codex* and *Institutes* (and is probably what Madison had in mind). It would appear that Madison's entries here were a condensed version of Jefferson's corresponding entries under "Foreign Law," where they centered, in his penultimate catalogue form, on "Justinian's Institutes, Lat. Eng. by Harris" (two others also cited) and "Codex Justinianus, . . . 1532" (Gothofreddus' *Corpus Iuris Civilis* of 1598 also being cited). Since Jefferson was able to obtain older editions, Madison may have been hopeful himself. Yet the rarity of the items would have perhaps been prohibitive for such a listing, aside from it not being in convenient English form. Nevertheless, it is true, more generally, that Madison had recourse to other sources as well for information when compiling his "List for Congress."

Among the many authors included in Madison's list for international law were Grotius and, for French history, Davila, both of whom in differing ways significantly incorporrated the ideas of Bodin.

Many additional inquiries can be made into Madison's "library," in a broader sense, on issues of present interest. Although the results are somewhat limited, a wealth of contextual materials yield a wide variety of useful further perspectives (as in the extended note below).[91]

Chapter V

Hamilton in Legislative Profile

Closely interfaced with the preceding triad of foremost founders of the constitutional framework of the new Amercan nation-state prior to becoming its president, was the important political career and thought of the brilliant and ambitious Alexander Hamilton (1755–1804). Hamilton's strong statements on legislation, sovereignty, and state in his *Federalist* essays and other writings left an indelible and distinctive stamp on early American political thought and ranked with those of his colleagues Jefferson, Adams, and Madison. Although Hamilton's tragically shortened career did not and could not rise to their eventual presidential heights, he played many significant roles at high governmental levels, despite lingering questions about his beginnings.

Hamilton's interconnections, moreover, with George Washington were many and varied, as in his extensive drafts for many of Washington's public statements as President, most notably his Farewell Address. The present chapter on Hamilton ends with an addendum on Washington. The latter's relatively sparse political thought in general and on the subjects at hand does not warrant a separate chapter here. Yet his commanding role at the summit of America's great lawgiver-founders expanded upon a classical-Enlightenment tradition of thought that impacted his fellow founders as well.

1. HAMILTON IN OVERVIEW

Having served well under General Washington in the Revolution and having later built a successful law practice in New York City, Hamilton was elected in 1786 to the New York state legislature. It appointed him delegate not only to the Annapolis Convention—which that September passed a resolution drafted by him calling for a May convention in Philadelphia to consider constitutional changes—but later to that Convention as well. There, at Philadelphia, on June 18, 1787, Hamilton delivered a lengthy speech praising the British form of government and outlining an elected system for America modelled upon it. The speech prompted his opponents to label him a monarchist sympathizer for the rest of his life. After the Convention, in early 1788, he was elected by the New York state legislature as a delegate to Congress, while he was also involved in the ratification struggles and continued contacts with Madison.

Hamilton's often controversial career was quickly unfolding. His commanding essays in *The Federalist* (1787–1788) were joined together there with those by Madison (whose *Notes* had duly recorded Hamilton's influential positions taken at the Convention). These essays were crucial not only for the pivotal successful struggles for ratification in New York and Virginia, but also for the emerging federalist agenda after ratification. Hamilton's other best known signature cause (aside from his cause célèbre in the fatal duel with Aaron Burr and his adulterous affair with Mrs. Reynolds) was his successful advocacy of creating a centralized national bank. This bank was chartered by Congress in 1791 as the Bank of the United States with the support of President Washington, under whom Hamilton was serving as powerful Secretary of the Treasury (1789–1795). The Bank issue brought him into conflict with Jefferson as Secretary of State (1790–1794), who, together with Madison, opposed the Bank for not being specifically authorized by the U.S. Constitution. Hamilton took a looser view of implied powers in the Constitution.

Early on in Washington's administration, Hamilton's powerful efforts in planning and directing national economic policy, including the assumption of state debts by the federal government (something opposed by Jefferson and southern states), sparked bitter political rivalries. These disputes intensified and widened in 1792, leading to informal groupings of "Democratic–Republicans" around Jefferson (and Madison) and "Federalists" around Hamilton, though not yet as organized parties. The development of factionalism, loathed by President Washington, was also exacerbated by conflicts between Hamilton and Jefferson over

America's positions during the French Revolution, the one being pro-British and the other pro-French.

The onset of acrimonious partisanship in the presidential election of 1796 was a prelude to the even more antagonistic atmosphere surrounding the election of 1800, which involved Hamilton. In the 1796 election, Adams, who had been Washington's Vice President, was narrowly elected President, while Jefferson ran a close second in the voting and thereby became Vice President. The two men respected each other and maintained a workable arrangement despite their partisan differences. However, much friction was caused by the Alien and Sedition Acts passed by Federalists in Congress in 1798 under the policies of the Adams administration toward perceived threats from abroad during the French Revolution. These Acts were greatly disputed by Jefferson and Madison. On this matter, the Kentucky and Virginia Resolutions passed by those two states' legislatures were written respectively and secretly by Jefferson and Madison, whose shifting pro and anti federalist views have already been discussed. Greatly alarmed by those Resolutions, Hamilton proposed sending federal troops to Virginia to suppress resistance to federal authority.

In the fateful presidential election of 1800, Adams ran third behind Jefferson and Burr, who were tied as Republican candidates for over thirty ballots until Hamilton gave his support to Jefferson, who was then elected. This move did not endear Hamilton to Adams, much less to Burr. Earlier that year Adams had refused to promote Hamilton to commander-in-chief of the army, and Hamilton then criticized him in print as being unfit for the presidency. This move divided the Federalists and damaged Hamilton's influence and reputation. Early in Jefferson's first term, in 1801–1802, Hamilton wrote his "Examination" series attacking the Jefferson administration in a New York newspaper. The Federalists, who had been split by their own internal factionalism during the Adams administration, experienced decline, losing power at state as well as federal levels. They never again controlled the national government. Hamilton's economic structure was not, however, abolished. Yet the highly controversial Alien and Sedition Acts, which he had supported, expired in 1801.

It was during the summer of 1804, with the presidential election of that year fast approaching (to be won overwhelmingly by Jefferson) that Hamilton was fatally shot in a duel with the vengeful Burr, whose candidacy for New York governor was opposed by the Hamiltonian faction. Having been alarmed by the support for Burr among some Federalists, Hamilton had criticized Burr in print and in person. Nor had Hamilton endeared himself to Jefferson when earlier that year he appeared in New York's Supreme Court as counsel for a man who had been convicted in the previous year of libelling President Jefferson. All in all, a recent historian's epithet about squabbling "founding brothers," in place of august "founding fathers," has some merit.[1]

2. HAMILTON'S *FEDERALIST* ESSAYS

The National (Federal) Legislative State Is Dominant

In *Federalist* #15, Hamilton expounds upon the necessity of instituting the kind of strong national (federal) state that he sees envisioned in the proposed new U.S. Constitution. It is to be based, first and foremost, on a system of laws or legislation carrying the force of legitimate commands and imperatives. This coerciveness will compel the fractious separate states of the expiring Confederation to enter more strongly into the new Union. At the same time, such a system will help to check the ambitions of those in power at the national or federal level. Just as promulgation lies at the heart of lawmaking, so the sanction in laws requiring obedience to them lies at the center of legislation, which is the paramount necessary mainstay of the nation-state and its proper governance. Legitimate coercion embodied in such a system of legislation involves penalties and punishments for nonobservance. Without a coercive national force behind them, the laws of the Union are far less likely to be obeyed by the separate states comprising it. The defects and excesses of human nature require constant constraints in order to promote reason, to ensure justice, and to check the poison of factionalism. A number of diverse comparisons could be drawn here with previous positions taken by such British writers as Hobbes, Sidney, Blackstone, Bentham, and others on legislation and the state. Yet Hamilton's outlook represents a distinctive blend. He concurs on sanction and command with Madison's apparent positions above a la Bentham (whose *Fragment on Government* criticizing Blackstone appeared in 1776, his *Morals and Legislation* in 1789). Even so, Hobbes' similar positions, utilized by Bentham, were more broadly in sinc with Federalist views on the need for strong, central power. Legislative command as an essence of legitimate state power combines here with the legislative coercion necessary for promoting and strengthening the American nation-state. (All passages *sic*, as in previous chapters.)

> Government implies the power of making laws. It is essential to the idea of a law, that it be attended with a sanction; or, in other words, a penalty or punishment for disobedience. If there be no penalty annexed to disobedience, the resolutions or com-

> mands which pretend to be laws will in fact amount to nothing more than advice or recommendation. This penalty, whatever it may be, can only be inflicted in two ways; by the agency of the Courts and Ministers of Justice, or by military force; by the COERTION of the magistracy, or by the COERTION of arms. The first kind can evidently apply only to men—the last kind must of necessity be employed against bodies politic, or communities or States. . . . Such a state of things can certainly not deserve the name of government, nor would any prudent man choose to commit his happiness to it.
>
> There was a time when we were told that breaches, by the States, of the regulations of the federal authority were not to be expected—that a sense of common interest would preside over the conduct of the respective members, and would beget a full compliance with all the constitutional requisitions of the Union. This language at the present day would appear as wild. . . . It at all times betrayed an ignorance of the true springs by which human conduct is actuated, and belied the original inducements to the establishment of civil power. Why has government been instituted at all? Because the passions of men will not conform to the dictates of reason and justice, without constraint. . . . A spirit of faction which is apt to mingle its poison in the deliberations of all bodies of men, will often hurry the persons of whom they are composed into improprieties and excesses . . .[2]

The preceding passage continues on with express regard to sovereignty and the need for a strong and unified national state that can not only weld together the former separate sovereign states. It must also be able to check the natural tendencies of leaders to excesses of political ambition and power at the expense of the common interest of the public weale and the due execution of the laws of the federal government. In short, the separate sovereignties in the (now expiring) Confederation had increasingly impeded the proper execution of the laws of the (ever weakening) national authority, which had been centered around Congress.[3]

In *Federalist* #16 Hamilton expands on "the principle of legislation for sovereign States" as not needing "military coercion" but rather the "majesty of the national authority" and the proper "execution of the laws of the national government." Hamilton's main point here is that the laws of the sovereign national (federal) legislature must be based, as set forth in the proposed new U.S. Constitution, on a system of due process that takes its authority directly from the citizens of the separate states of the Union, without needing the intermediate involvement of the state legislatures. Opponents of the new Constitution would involve the country in civil war and anarchy if their misguided outlooks prevailed, whereby the laws would need the improper use of force for their imposition on noncomplying states.

> The tendency of the principle of legislation for States, or communities, in their political capacities, as it has been exemplified by the experiment we have made of it, is equally attested by the events which have befallen all other governments of the confederate kind . . . [as in] the confederacies of antiquity. . . .
>
> This exceptionable principle may as truly as emphatically be stiled the parent of anarchy . . . [T]he only constiutional remedy is force, and the immediate effect of the use of it, civil war.
>
> It remains to enquire how far so odious an engine of government, in its application to us, would even be capable of answering its end. . . . It is not probable, considering the genius of this country, that the complying States would often be inclined to support the authority of the Union by engaging in a war against the non-complying States. . . .
>
> It seems to require no pains to prove that the States ought not to prefer a national constitution, which could only be kept in motion by the instrumentality of a large army, continually on foot to execute the ordinary requisitions or decrees of the government. And yet this is the plain alternative involved by those who wish to deny it the power of extending its operations to individuals. . . .
>
> Even in those confederacies, which have been composed of members smaller than many of our counties, the principle of legislation for sovereign States, supported by military coertion, has never been found effectual. It has rarely been attempted to be employed, but against the weaker members. And in most instances attempts to coerce the refractory and disobedient, have been the signals of bloody wars; in which one half of the confederacy has displayed its banners against the other half [passage continued in note below].[4]

For Hamilton in *Federalist* #21 a correctly constructed system of legislation lies at the center of what is needed in replacing the defective Confederation of American states with a new national federal state under the new U.S. Constitution. Obedience to and execution of federal laws is the crux for him of what is lacking in the existing operations of the U.S. government in the separate states of the Union. A clearer "sanction" and command in Congress' laws is requisite for this purpose. Hamilton's use of such terms as "social compact" is also noteworthy and is reminiscent of the *Social Contract* by Rousseau, who himself placed strong emphasis on the necessary sanctions in sovereign legislation.

> The ... palpable defect of the subsisting confederation is the total want of a SANCTION to its laws. The United States as now composed, have no power to exact obedience, or punish disobedience to their resolutions ... in any ... constitutional mode. There is no express delegation of authority to them to use force against delinquent members; and if such a right should be ascribed to the federal head, as resulting from the nature of the social compact between the States, it must be by inference and construction, in the face of that part of the second article, by which it is declared 'each State shall retain every power, jurisdiction and right, not *expressly* delegated to the United States in Congress assembled.' ... If we are unwilling to impair the force of this applauded provision, we shall be obliged to conclude, that the United States afford the extraordinary spectacle of a government, destitute even of the shadow of a constitutional power to enforce the execution of its own laws.[5]

Although not as urgent or grave as the necessity of a "sanction" in federal laws for their proper operation in the states, a "guarantee" of federal authority is crucial, especially in light of recent seditious upheavals in Massachusetts.[6]

On various matters involving courts and treaties, a key problem for Hamilton in *Federalist* #22 is posed by the existing conflicts between state laws and federal laws. The latter are often outweighed by the former, creating uncertainty and breakdown in the legal system, which is badly in need of repair. Under the authority and jurisdiction of state legislatures, courts and treaties too often impede the operations of federal laws pertaining to those matters.

> This is the more necessary where the frame of the government is so compounded, that the laws of the whole are in danger of being contravened by the laws of the parts. In this case if the particular tribunals are invested with a right of ultimate jurisdiction, ... there will be much to fear from the bias of local views and prejudices, and from the interference of local regulations. As often as such an interference was to happen, there would be reason to apprehend, that the provisions of the particular laws might be preferred to those of the general laws....

> The treaties of the United States, under the present [Confederation] constitution, are liable to the infractions of thirteen different Legislatures, and as many different courts of final jurisdiction, acting under the authority of those Legislatures.[7]

Continuing on in *Federalist* #22 about the weak authority of Congress in the existing Confederation, Hamilton portrays himself as no advocate for undue aggrandisements of power, which, contrariwise, he sees the proposed Constitution's opponents as advocating. They, by investing "sovereignty" in the "single body" of Congress, fail to solve the current constitutional crisis and encourage the "tyranny" they claim to be trying to avoid. Moreover, the existing constitution of the Confederation (in the Articles) rests ultimately on its ratification by the state legislatures and could possibly be repealed, as some urge, by overturning the state laws that enabled it to be ratified. Instead, the new Constitution should be based, he argues, on popular consent (through state conventions), not on "the sanction of delegated authority." One party to a "social compact" cannot break it for the others. The "American Empire" must be based on "the consent of the people" as a whole.[8]

Federal Legislative Powers Are Sovereign and Comprehensive

Following the preceding discussions, Hamilton turns to Congress and its authority under the proposed new U.S. Constitution. Hamilton succinctly lists in *Federalist* #23 Congress' salient spheres of operation. His extended general comment there on the "means" to an "end" and its attainment is reminiscent of many writers on the subject from Machiavelli, Bodin, and Hobbes to others in Hamilton's own century.[9] Hamilton in *Federalist* #26 is not in favor of "restraining the Legislative authority in the means of providing for the national defence," unlike some critics.[10] In response to those who seek more safeguards "against military establishment in time of peace," he declares it sufficient in *Federalist* #28 that "the whole power of the proposed government is to be in the hands of the representatives of the people," this being "the only efficacious security for the rights . . . of the people which is attainable in civil society."[11]

Hamilton criticizes in *Federalist* #30 the overreach of the Articles of Confederation, although they are now frustrated and "feeble," in ascribing to Congress "an unlimited power and right" to exact its necessary monies from the states, without the states having a right to question it.[12] Then, in *Federalist* #31 he warns against any potential for overreach by the national legislature in appropriating for itself all rights to tax the states for its own federal needs, to the exclusion of the states' rights to tax for their own needs. Issues here arise for Hamilton over means and ends, conflicts between legislative systems, promulgation and execution of laws, necessities of state, and so forth. He seems to belie any suggestion that he promotes heavy-handedness by the federal government, even while urging that "the laws of the Union" must be "the supreme law of the land."

> It is therefore as necessary, that the State Governments should be able to command the means of supplying their wants, as, that the National Government should possess the like faculty, in respect to the wants of the Union. But an indefinite power of taxation in the *latter* might, and probably would in time deprive the former of the means of providing for their own necessities; and would subject them entirely to the mercy of the national Legislature. As the laws of the Union are to become the supreme law of the land; as it is to have power to pass all laws that may be NECESSARY for carrying into execution, the authorities with which it is proposed to vest it; the national government might at any time abolish the taxes imposed for State objects, upon the pretence of an interference with its own. . . .
> It should not be forgotten, that a disposition in the State governments to encroach upon the rights of the Union, is quite as probable, as a disposition in the Union to encroach upon the rights of then State Governments.[13]

On legislative sovereignty in relation to Congressional powers, Hamilton makes a notable series of statements in *Federalist* #33. He also strikes a further balance between the paramount national legislative state and the subordinate individual states of the Union under the proposed new U.S. Constitution. Two clauses in that Constitution are analyzed by Hamilton with particular regard to the essential legislative nature of the power to tax at the federal level, a power hotly contested by some people in various states. This whole core question of taxation becomes for him part of the deeper and broader issue of legislative sovereignty.

> The residue of the argument against the provisions in the constitution, in respect to taxation, is ingrafted upon the following clauses; the last clause of the eighth section of the first article of the plan under consideration, authorises the national legislature 'to make all laws which shall be *necessary* and

> *proper*, for carrying into execution *the powers* by that Constitution vested in the government of the United States, or any department or officer thereof;' and the second clause of the sixth article declares, that 'the Constitution and the Laws of the United States made *in pursuance thereof*, and the treaties made by their authority shall be the *supreme law* of the land; any thing in the constitution or laws of any State to the contrary notwithstanding.'
>
> These two clauses have been the sources of much virulent invective and petulant declamation against the proposed constitution, [and] they have been held up to the people, in all the exaggerated colours of misrepresentation, as the pernicious engines by which their local governments were to be destroyed and their liberties exterminated—as the hideous monster whose devouring jaws would spare neither sex nor age. . . . They are only declaratory of a truth, which would have resulted by necessary and unavoidable implication from the very act of constituting a Federal Government, and vesting it with certain specified powers.[14]

Hamilton continues in *Federalist* #33 with an insightful disquisition on sovereign legislative power as a central issue in the controversy over taxation under the new Constitution. He discusses means and ends, the making and executing of laws, and the inherent federal power to make laws. This power resides in the proposed national legislature and is sovereign, irregardless of other outside jurisdictions of the individual states and their own laws. These topics arise in ways that are reminiscent of many earlier writings treated in the present series. Hamilton's decisive manner, here and elsewhere, of grouping a full range of powers such as taxation under the comprehensive sovereign power of legislation recalls to mind Bodinian tradition found in diverse political thinkers like Hobbes, Locke, and their followers. The first part of the passage is as follows:

> What is a power, but the ability or faculty of doing a thing? What is the ability to do a thing but the power of employing the *means* necessary to its execution? What is a LEGISLATIVE power but power of making LAWS? What are the *means* to execute a LEGISLATIVE power but LAWS? What is the power of laying and collecting taxes but a *legislative power*, or a power of *making laws*, to lay and collect taxes? What are the proper means of executing such a power but *necessary* and *proper* laws [passage continued in note below]?[15]

Hamilton's frequent recourse to historical examples, especially ancient ones, when making his points is typified in his references in *Federalist* #34 to the two distinct legislatures in Republican Rome. There he also deals with the relationship between the federal and state legislatures in matters of taxation under the new U.S. Constitution.[16]

Negating, Executing, and Interpreting "the Supreme Law(s) of the Land"

So dominant is the legislative factor in Hamilton's broader treatment of sovereignty and state that it becomes the key component for him in the relationships between Congress and the other two branches of the federal government, as well as between the federal and state authorities. Of particular note is his outlook in *Federalist* #33 on "the supreme law(s) of the land." This standard constitutional phrase is employed by him here and elsewhere in both a singular and plural fashion. As used by him, it points up the preeminent place he assigns to legislation, at the center of state and society, in the background to his exposition of the executive and judicial branches following his initial focus on the legislative branch.

> But it is said, that the laws of the Union are to be the *supreme law* of the land. But what inference can be drawn from this or what would they amount to, if they were not to be supreme? It is evident they would amount to nothing. A LAW by the very meaning of the term includes supremacy. It is a rule which those to whom it is prescribed are bound to observe. This results from every political association. If individuals enter into a state of society the laws of that society must be the supreme regulator of their conduct. If a number of political societies enter into a larger political society, the laws which the latter may enact, pursuant to the powers entrusted to it by its constitution, must necessarily be supreme over those societies, and the individuals of whom they are composed. It would otherwise be a mere treaty, dependent on the good faith of the parties, and not a government; which is only another word for POLITICAL POWER AND SUPREMACY [passage continued below].[17]

By "supreme law(s) of the land," Hamilton is largely alluding here and elsewhere (as more explicitly in his *Federalist* #33 quoted above[18]) to Article VI, section 2, of the U.S. Constitution. It reads: "The

Constitution, and the Laws of the United States which shall be made in Pursuance thereof . . . shall be the Supreme Law of the Land; . . . any Thing in the Constitution or Laws of any State to the Contrary notwithstanding." In both singular and plural form relating to law and legislation, this phrase goes back to ancients like Cicero. Classical references to the "*salus populi*" as the "*suprema lex*" and to "*leges*" as the "sinews of the *respublica*" or state were often echoed by Bodin and other Renaissance writers. The Constitution's framers clearly made use of this familiar tradition.

Because of its potential for oppressiveness, the dominant new national legislature must be properly checked constitutionally, according to Hamilton. The executive branch needs to be separated "from" the legislature, as indeed it is under the new Constitution. In *Federalist* #73 Hamilton sees the naturally dominant tendencies of a new national legislature as being already exemplified in existing state legislatures when their executive departments are not adequately separated from them.[19]

First among "the requisites . . . proposed to be vested in the President of the United States," according to *Federalist* #73, is a kind of legislative capacity of his own. For the President is able to "negative" the laws or bills of Congress. This primary capacity was also much discussed by Adams, but here perhaps more decisively so by Hamilton.

> The first thing that offers itself to our observation, is the qualified negative of the President upon the acts or resolutions of the two Houses of the Legislature; or in other words[,] his power of returning all bills with objections; to have the effect of preventing their becoming laws, unless they should afterwards be ratified by two thirds of each of the component members of the legislative body.
>
> The propensity of the legislative department to intrude upon the rights and to absorb the powers of the other departments, has been already suggested and repeated; the insufficiency of a mere parchment delineation of the boundaries of each, has also been remarked upon; and the necessity of furnishing each with constitutional arms for its own defence, has been inferred and proved. From these clear and indubitable principles results the propriety of a negative, either absolute or qualified, in the executive, upon the acts of the legislative branches. Without the one or the other the former would be absolutely unable to defend himself against the depredations of the latter. He might gradually be stripped of his authorities by successive resolutions, or annihilated by a single vote. And in the one mode or the other, the legislative and executive powers, might speedily come to be

> blended in the same hands. If even no propensity had ever discovered itself in the legislative body, to invade the rights of the executive, the rules of just reasoning and theoretic propriety would of themselves teach us, that the one ought not to be left at the mercy of the other, but ought to possess a constitutional and effectual power of self defence.[20]

The above passage continues on into further dimensions of the executive department's essential role in the central functions of law-making and law-negating. Hamilton's indicative phraseology includes: "check upon the legislative body," "the effects of faction," "unfriendly to the public good," "the legislative [body] will not be infallible," "the love of power," "the power of preventing bad laws," "instability of the laws . . . [as] the greatest blemish in . . . our governments," "restrain[ing] the excess of law-making . . . [as] favorable to greater stability in the system of legislation," and, above all, "[t]he superior weight and influence of the legislative body in a free government, and the hazard to the executive."

> But the power in question has a further use. It not only serves as a shield to the executive, but it furnishes an additional security against the enaction of improper laws. It establishes a salutary check upon the legislative body calculated to guard the community against the effects of faction, precipitancy, or of any impulse unfriendly to the public good, which may happen to influence a majority of that body. . . . The propriety of the thing does not turn upon the supposition of superior wisdom or virtue in the executive: But upon the supposition that the legislative will not be infallible: That the love of power may sometimes betray it into a disposition to encroach upon the rights of the other members of the government; that a spirit of faction may sometimes pervert its deliberations. . . . The primary inducement to conferring the power in question upon the executive, is to enable him to defend himself; the secondary one is to encrease the chances in favor of the community, against the passing of bad laws, through haste, inadvertence, or design. . . .
>
> It may perhaps be said, that the power of preventing bad laws includes that of preventing good ones; and may be used to the one purpose as well as to the other. But this objection will have little weight with those who can properly estimate the mischiefs of that inconstancy and mutability in the laws, which form the greatest blemish in the character and genius of our

> governments. They will consider every institution calculated to restrain the excess of law-making ... as much more likely to do good than harm; because it is favorable to greater stability in the system of legislation. The injury which may possibly be done by defeating a few good laws will be amply compensated by the advantage of preventing a number of bad ones.
>
> Nor is this all. The superior weight and influence of the legislative body in a free government, and the hazard to the executive in a trial of strength with that body, afford a satisfactory security, that the negative would generally be employed with great caution, and that there would oftener be room for a charge of timidity than of rashness, in the exercise of it.[21]

Comparisons with legislative-executive relationships in the British system are also drawn.[22]

On the matter of treaties in *Federalist* #75, Hamilton expounds upon the relationships between the legislative and executive departments of the new federal government. In so doing, he underscores all the more the pivotal determining factor of legislation in the respective making and execution of laws in the operations of Congress and the Presidency. Hamilton sees himself as again pointing to the legislative factor in this regard more so than have other writers who have instead placed the making of treaties under the executive branch. This becomes for him yet another function to be comprehended in terms of the law-making power. The executing of laws is again crucial to the chief executive's pivotal role in the wider legislative process. Hamilton's lengthy articulation of and focus on these interconnections between Congress and the President in the law-making process is compelling and distinctive, further elucidating the making and executing of legislation more generally.[23]

Also integral in *Federalist* #82 to the legislative process, in operations of the supreme laws of the land, is judicial activity not only in the interpretation of laws but in "the execution of the laws of the union." In its legislative capacity under the new Constitution, Congress will be responsible for establishing courts below the Supreme Court, while "state courts will have a concurrent jurisdiction in all cases arising under the laws of the union." As parts of "ONE WHOLE," state courts will be auxiliary "to the execution of the laws of the union." Although under the new plan "the national legislature" will " 'constitute' " inferior courts, " 'the JUDICIAL POWER' " of the U.S. government will be vested in the Supreme Court. Again Hamilton stakes out his own positions on provisions in the new Constitution.[24]

The judicial process in the courts of law revolves, for Hamilton in *Federalist* #83, ever more closely around questions of legislative "interpretation" in the "construction" and "application" of the laws. The true test must lie in the "source" of the law, in connection here with "the legislative power."[25]

In the final analysis, Hamilton's powerful *Federalist* essays in support of the proposed new U.S. Constitution reflected not only that plan itself but also his own political philosophy. Most striking here has been the broad comprehensive sweep of sovereign authority assigned by him to the legislative powers of Congress in relation to the other two federal branches. In addition to taxes and treaties, a full range of other activities including the raising of troops[26] is placed by him under the legislative power, sometimes also in conjunction with the executive department. Hamilton has expanded upon the new plan to embrace a wider vision of his own on the new U.S. form of government. He has had to turn away from many of his own positions taken but not adopted at the Convention, while reworking others, in the struggles over ratification. The force of his own ideas has lent great support to the plan adopted at the Convention. This blend of ideas in his *Federalist* essays has produced a distinctive concentration on legislative sovereignty as a key to understanding the three federal branches and their relationships with each other and with the state legislatures. Hamilton has as well a kind of Bodinian viewpoint on the sovereign law-making power as encompassing the full scope of other marks of sovereign authority such as imposing taxes, making treaties, and declaring war. All this is placed by him within the constitutional framework of checks and balances designed to prevent undue acquisitions of political power, especially by the legislative branch.

Hamilton's undeserved reputation among some critics as a monarchist, fueled by some of his Convention speeches and his later involvements in the Federalist government, has been belied here by his strong ideas on legislative sovereignty centered around Congress in relation to the executive and judicial branches. Hamilton's vision of a centralized state, designed (a la Hobbes and Bodin?) to check the excesses of factionalism and ambition that could lead to civil strife, was tempered by his equally strong support for checks and balances at the federal level, combined with some autonomy at the state level. Obviously the executive branch championed in his *Federalist* essays was not a monarchy patterned after the model of the British constitution favored by him at the Convention. Despite his own distinctive articulation of and emphasis on legislative factors of sovereignty and state in his *Federalist* and other writings, Hamilton's views on these subjects bore ultimate similarities to those diversely expressed by Madison and Adams as well as Jefferson.

3. HAMILTON'S NATIONAL BANK

Legislative Sovereignty and Corasius' Principle

Like his celebrated *Federalist* essays, Hamilton's contributions to the establishment of a National Bank, for which he is also best known, included many strong statements by him on legislative sovereignty and the legislative state that were built upon traditional thought. Most strikingly, his lengthy "Opinion on the Constitutionality of a National Bank" (1791) contains near the outset a discussion on aspects of legislative sovereignty that closely parallels their treatment by Corasius and Bodin over two centuries earlier.

It will be remembered from our first volume that Corasius extensively rejected the late-medieval juristic idea, prevalent up to his own period, that the right to legislate, one among many diverse rights of sovereignty, depended wholly on jurisdiction. Instead, Corasius placed a new emphasis on the inherent power of any legally constituted body to make laws for its own affairs, regardless of any outside jurisdictional questions about its right to do so. He decisively connected this legislative power more exclusively than before to sovereignty at the top level of national governments. Not long thereafter, as shown in our third volume, Corasius' fellow Frenchman Bodin developed these and related ideas more formatively in his highly influential *Republic*. There, between the two famous "sovereignty chapters" (I, 8 and I, 10), appeared a chapter (I, 9) containing extensive arguments against the ongoing late-medieval juristic tradition on the authority to pass laws. In that tradition, the declaring of law depended on the jurisdictional right to do so and was but one of myriad powers in the late-medieval "trees of jurisdiction."

These observations are not meant to suggest that Hamilton had read Corasius or perhaps even Bodin on these specific points. Yet Hamilton has clearly made use of Bodinian tradition on such matters (in writers like Hobbes, Locke, and Rousseau) when building his legal case as Secretary of the Treasury under President Washington for a National Bank. Although Jefferson opposed the Bank while serving as Secretary of State, he himself often adopted Bodinian legislative standpoints on sovereignty and state, however differently from Hamilton.[27]

The main issue addressed by Hamilton in his "Opinion" on the bill before Congress to establish a National Bank is whether the national legislature or the state legislatures have the right to legislate in matters not spelled out specifically in the U.S. Constitution. Jefferson argued that the power to establish banks was not stipulated in the Constitution and therefore belonged to the individual states, on the grounds that all powers not granted therein to the federal government reverted to the state governments. Hamilton's counterarguments revolve around issues of legislative sovereignty and the rightful innate power of both national and state legislatures to make laws for their own properly designated affairs or "proper objects." On the national legislature's supreme power to make laws for the American nation and its separate states, Hamilton takes a more positive and comprehensive stance than does Jefferson in this instance, while citing the higher necessities of "the *Supreme* law[s] of the land." Hamilton's arguments for the sovereign powers of both Congress and the state legislatures to establish corporations as legal entities, such as banks, according to their different spheres and "objects," are provocative in light of Corasius' much earlier arguments for the power of national governments and even local bodies including guilds to institute their own laws for purposes of establishing corporations having their own sets of rules, the laws of the nation being highest and taking precedence. For Hamilton, Congress' "*sovereign power* to erect corporations" with regard to its own "*objects*" is just as valid as that possessed by the states regarding their own proper objects, as befits "certain [different] branches of legislation." Jefferson argued that only the states could establish bank corporations, not the federal government, which he felt was becoming too big under the administrations of Washington and Adams.

> The circumstances that the powers of sovereignty are in this country divided between the National and State Governments, does not afford the distinction required. It does not follow from this, that each of the *portions* of powers delegated to the one or to the other is not sovereign *with regard to its proper objects*. It will only *follow* from it, that each has sovereign power as to *certain things*, and not as to *other things*. To deny that the Government of the United States has sovereign power as to its declared purposes & trusts, because its power does not extend to all cases, would be equally to deny, that the State Governments have sovereign power in any case; because their power does not extend to every case. The tenth section of the first article of the constitution exhibits a long list of very important things which they may not do. And thus the United States would furnish the singular spectacle of a *political society* without *sovereignty*, or of a people *governed* without *government*.

If it would be necessary to bring proof to a proposition so clear as that which affirms that the powers of the federal government, *as to its objects*, are sovereign, there is a clause of its constitution which would be decisive. It is that which declares, that the constitution and the laws of the United States made in pursuance of it, and all treaties made or which shall be made under their authority shall be the supreme law of the land. The power which can create the *Supreme law* of the land, in any case, is doubtless sovereign *as to such case.*

This general & indisputable principle puts at once an end to the *abstract* question—Whether the United States have power to *erect a corporation*? that is to say, to give a *legal* or *artificial capacity* to one or more persons, distinct from the natural. For it is unquestionably incident to *sovereign power* to erect corporations, and consequently to *that* of the United States, in *relation to the objects* intrusted to the management of the government. The difference is this—where the authority of the government is general, it can create corporations in *all cases*; where it is confined to certain branches of legislation, it can create corporations only in those cases.[28]

For Hamilton in his "Opinion" on the bank bill a crucial question is whether, in "the division of the legislative power" between the national and state legislatures, the national laws do or do not conflict with state laws; in this case they do not, according to him. The innate legislative sovereignty proper to the national government in enacting the bill before it on a National Bank does not conflict with the inherent legislative sovereignty of the state governments in their own ability to establish state banks of their own. Again Hamilton applies traditional ideas of "ends" and "means" in describing his principle of the "objects" proper to each sphere, national and state, as a criterion for their respective innate powers to legislate for their own affairs, provided their laws and constitutions do not conflict with the national laws and Constitution. Hamilton's standpoint in the following passage (and its continuation below) leaves open the opportunity for far greater exercise of federal legislative authority than does Jefferson's viewpoint.

The truth is that difficulties on this point are inherent in the nature of the federal constitution. They result inevitably from a division of the legislative power. The consequence of this division is, that there will be cases clearly within the power of the National Government; others clearly without its power; and a third class, which will leave room for controversy & difference of opinion, & concerning which a reasonable latitude of judgment must be allowed.

But the doctrine which is contended for [by Hamilton] is not chargeable with the consequence imputed to it. It does not affirm that the National government is sovereign in all respects, but that it is sovereign to a certain extent: that is, to the extent of the objects of its specified powers.

It leaves therefore a criterion of what is constitutional, and of what is not so. This criterion is the *end* to which the measure relates as a *mean*. If the end be clearly comprehended within any of the specified powers, & if the measure have an obvious relation to that end, and is not forbidden by any particular provision of the constitution—it may safely be deemed to come within the compass of the national authority.[29]

The Legislative State and Modern Reality

Hamilton's arguments in his "Opinion" on the National Bank apply not only to legislative sovereignty but also to the legislative state. He discounts Jefferson's position that the bank bill before Congress unduly gives it "a power to make [federal] laws paramount to those of the States." Believing like the other founders that legislation is the basis of the state in a broader sense, Hamilton would have to agree on a different level with Jefferson, who also subscribed to legislative self-determination for both the Union and the states. As Hamilton put it, "*laws* . . . constitute the pillars of our whole system of jurisprudence, and are [also] the foundation laws of the State governments." Like Jefferson, Hamilton would point to the laws that are also the "pillars" and "foundation" of the American nation-state itself. Hamilton, however, is concerned to show that even on their own grounds Jefferson's strict positions on the inviolability and unalterability of the literal texts of the U.S. Constitution fall apart. For Jefferson to say that there can be no such alteration with regard to issues like the Bank, is belied, Hamilton believes, by the significant changes made by the separate states to their own constitutions. Jefferson's position that the fundamental laws of statehood are inviolate in a national constitution and cannot be changed by "the ordinary legislature" is negated, according to Hamilton, by actual cases in the separate states (not to mention at the federal level). The creation of a legal corporation such as the proposed bank does not, he feels, conflict with "State laws."

The Secretary of State [Jefferson] introduces his opinion with an observation, that the proposed incorporation undertakes to

> create certain capacities[,] properties or attributes which are *against* the laws of *alienage, descents, escheat* and *forfeiture, distribution* and *monopoly*, and to confer a power to make laws paramount to those of the States. And nothing says he, in another place, but a *necessity invincible by other means* can justify such a *prostration of laws* which constitute the pillars of our whole system of jurisprudence, and are the foundation laws of the State Governments.
>
> If these are truly the foundation laws of the several states, then have most of them subverted their own foundations. For there is scarcely one of them which has not, since the establishment of its particular constitution, made material alterations in some of those branches of its jurisprudence especially the law of descents. But it is not conceived how any thing can be called the fundamental law of a State Government which is not established in its constitution unalterable by the ordinary legislature. And with regard to the question of necessity it has been shewn, that this can only constitute a question of expediency, not of right.
>
> To erect a corporation is to substitute a *legal* or *artificial* to a *natural* person, and where a number are concerned to give them *individuality*. To that legal or artificial person once created, the common law of every state of itself *annexes* all those incidents and attributes, which are represented as a prostration of the main pillars of their jurisprudence. It is certainly not accurate to say, that the erection of a corporation is *against* those different *heads* of the State laws.[30]

Even so, the laws of the federal government enacted by Congress often do alter the laws of the separate states. This can be a matter of necessity, and "necessity" Hamilton has just described as "a question of expediency, not of right." New laws invariably alter old laws. Congress' laws and its powers exercised under them in important cases, relating for instance to bankruptcy and coinage, often "necessarily" alter state laws.

> But if it were even to be admitted that the erection of a corporation is a direct alteration of the State laws in the enumerated particulars; it would do nothing towards proving, that the measure was unconstitutional. If the government of the United States can do no act, which amounts to an alteration of a State law, all its powers are nugatory. For almost every new law is an

> alteration, in some way or other[,] of an old *law*, either *common*, or *statute*.
>
> There are laws concerning bankruptcy in some states—some states have laws regulating the values of foreign coins. Congress are [*sic*] empowered to establish uniform laws concerning bankruptcy throughout the United States, and to regulate the values of foreign coins. The exercise of either of these powers by Congress necessarily involves an alteration of the laws of those states.[31]

Just as each state of the Union possesses its own right and power to enact laws for its own affairs (including for corporations within the state), and just as corporations have the same power for themselves, so too does the Union have its own power to legislate for corporations within its own federal purview. Conversely, just as the laws of a state corporation can be overturned when they conflict with that state's laws, so too the laws of a state can be overturned when they conflict with those of the Union. Here, then, is a good illustration of Hamilton's idea of how the legislative power is divided between the Union and the states, yet with ultimate legislative sovereignty being vested in the federal government. This is also a good illustration of Hamilton's outlook on the legislative state as a general concept at both state and federal levels, with ultimate supremacy again residing in the national legislative state. It will be noticed how closely Hamilton's general ideas on the relations between federal and state laws, aside from his immediate historical contexts concerning the National Bank, correspond with actual realities in modern America. Here, as well, is again illustrated how Hamilton's presentation of such subjects in his "Opinion" on the National Bank is remotely reminiscent of Corasius' momentous principle, put forth over two centuries earlier, that soon entered the mainstream of political thought through Bodin and others to follow.

> And with regard to the second point, there is still less foundation. The bye-laws of such an institution as a bank can operate only upon its own members. . . . They are expressly not to be contrary to law; and law must here mean the law of a State as well as of the United States. There never can be a doubt, that a law of the corporation, if contrary to a law of a state, must be overruled as void; unless the law of the State is contrary to that of the United States; and then the question will not be between the law of the State and that of the corporation, but between the law of the State and that of the United States.

> Another argument [wrongly] made use of by the Secretary of State, is the rejection of a proposition by the convention to empower Congress to make corporations, either generally, or for some special purpose.[32]

Ensuing portions of Hamilton's "Opinion" on the National Bank closely identify the ultimate sovereignty in America with legislative power and the legislative state at the national level. Within its own "proper" "sphere" and under conditions of "necessity," the legislative powers of Congress are sovereign and comprehensive. In refuting arguments to the contrary on corporations, Hamilton further clarifies his positions on certain provisions in the U.S. Constitution.[33]

4. HAMIILTON IN OTHER WRITINGS

Conventions and Ratification

Like the other main American founders, Hamilton's thought on sovereignty and state evolved in the 1780s during the changing circumstances of the Revolutionary and Constitutional eras. A letter of his in 1780, for instance, urged that the current grave defects in the Confederation, impeding its ability to function adequately, should be rectified by giving to Congress "complete sovereignty." Only limited areas of responsibility should be given to the individual states of the Union, for they have gained far too much authority.[34]

Later on, in a speech given early in the Constitutional Convention of 1787, Hamilton strongly objected to the New Jersey plan. There he argued that the central government "must swallow up" the powers of the states, since there cannot be "two Sovereignties." Yet vesting complete sovereignty in Congress would result in "bad Govt." (as all recorded in Madison's *Notes*).[35] According to his own lengthy notes for that same speech on a plan of government, Hamilton elaborated on his idea that a proper form of government must combine the few and the many, joining elements of monarchy, aristocracy, and democracy (with references to Aristotle, Cicero, Montesquieu, and Neckar).[36] In another delegate's version of this speech, Hamilton inveighed against the states having any real sovereignty at all because of the overriding present need "to save our Country." The coerciveness of laws by the central government is needed. Congress, as the "Legislature," "must" have "Sovereignty . . . ultimately."[37] In still other versions of the same speech, Hamilton stressed that state laws contravening federal laws should be "absolutely void" (in contradistinction to both the defective

Virginia and New Jersey plans).[38] The "national Sovereignty [must be] transcendent & entire."[39] Finally, the "Plan of Government" Hamilton included in this same speech placed legislative supremacy first and foremost.[40]

In his speech a year later on the distribution of powers, delivered at the New York Ratifying Convention on June 27, 1788, Hamilton's outlook was widely different under the changed circumstances. This was particularly true concerning the relationships between the national and state governments in the operations of their laws and sovereignties. On this issue, Hamilton's speech represented again one of the clearest approximations by the principal founders not only to constitutional reality in modern America but also, without knowing this specifically, to Corasius' much older historical principle relating to these kinds of subjects.

In this 1788 speech, Hamilton's praise for the new Constitution, "the best writers have ever conceived," certainly shows him to be no friend of monarchy for America, which critics accused him of trying to institute. In order to ensure "political liberty" and to avoid "tyranny," the supreme "legislative authority is lodged in three distinct branches" (Senate, House, and also the Chief Executive through his veto and other powers). The "division of powers" in this and other areas is crucial to republican government, as is the proper "mode of legislation."[41]

Hamilton's "true principle of government" in this 1788 speech revolves around the proper "division of powers" or "just distribution of powers" in further relationships between the national and state governments. Far from advocating the complete subservience of the latter to the former, Hamilton now allows for the "proper" place of each. The "criterion" is the "convenience" and "object" to be determined for each side of the "balance" between the nation and the states.[42] Here he strongly contends against the position still held by some (and not long before by himself) that the states of the Union cannot have sovereign authority in legislation and other related matters just because there would be conflicts with the national government's sovereignty in the same matters. Hamilton's solution to this impasse over whether there can be two sovereignties is now that there can be two because the Union and the states will both have their own proper objects and spheres of operations for their laws. Both will have their own innate power to make laws for their own affairs, regardless of questions about their jurisdictional rights to do so, even when those jurisdictions might seem to conflict. In the final analysis, one may add, Hamilton still ultimately tends to find federal laws to be generally superior to state laws where there are conflicts of import. These conflicts can nevertheless be worked out satisfactorily so as not to impede the states' proper legislative authority within their own domains. The supreme laws of the national legislature can coexist with the supreme laws of the individual states, separately or collectively, within a framework of "harmony" in which differences can be worked out. The following excerpt suggests some striking parallels, without his knowing it, not only with Corasius' historical principle but with American constitutional reality in modern perspective.

> With regard to the jurisdiction of the two governments, I shall certainly admit that the constitution ought to be so formed, as not to prevent the states from providing for their own existence; and I maintain that it is so formed; and that their power of providing for themselves is sufficiently established. This is conceded by one gentleman, and in the next breath, the concession is retracted. He says, Congress have [*sic*] but one exclusive right in taxation; that of duties on imports. Certainly then, their other powers are only concurrent. But to take off the force of this obvious conclusion, he immediately says that the laws of the United States are supreme; and that where there is one supreme, there cannot be a concurrent authority: and further, that where the laws of the union are supreme, those of the states must be subordinate; because, there cannot be two supremes. This is curious sophistry. That two supreme powers cannot act together, is false. They are inconsistent only when they are aimed at each other, or at one indivisible objcct. Thc laws of the Union States are supreme, as to all their proper, constitutional objects: The laws of the states are supreme in the same way. These supreme laws may act on different objects, without clashing; or they may operate on different parts of the same common object, with perfect harmony.[43]

In the continuation of the above passage, Hamilton illustrates his points with reference to taxes levied by both the federal and state governments. Expounding on "the concurrent jurisdiction, and the operation of the laws, in relation to revenue," he points out that both spheres can impose measures on taxes for their own needs. This is not a question of their jurisdictional right to do so, but is a power that results from their own self-determining authority to do so, even (a la Corasius) in cases where conflicting jurisdictions may occur. (The same principle would seem to apply to other smaller municipal entities within the states.) One sovereignty in such matters cannot be supreme over another. The sovereignties of the state governments can coexist with the sovereignty of the national government (which retains, nevertheless, the upper hand when disputes have to be worked out with the states). With a closing flourish, Hamilton lauds the new Constitution (albeit it precluded the presidency for non-native born men such as himself) for its "truly republican principles" promoting the "general welfare." He castigates those who would seek "to subvert the state governments."[44]

Explanation and "Examination"

In 1803, a year before his premature death, Hamilton wrote a substantial letter to Timothy Pickering in which he explained and defended certain of his proposals and positions at the Philadelphia Convention of 1787. By this time, with Republicans in control and with Jefferson as President and Madison as Secretary of State, Hamilton's Federalist star had fallen. His intent was now to show that at the Convention he had not been an advocate of monarchical rule for America. Rather, as a staunch supporter of Republican principles, he had merely proposed some ideas to be considered for the new executive branch, without intending them as his own final views on the subject. Finding himself ideologically on the opposite side of the political fence from his former *Federalist* collaborator Madison, Hamilton now imputed to Madison much the same leanings on this score at the Convention. Toward the end of his explanatory letter to Pickering, however, Hamilton stressed the need for "stability" that had driven him (and Madison) to propose a strong federal government, one capable of coping with the constitutional crisis that had occasioned the Convention in the first place. Indeed, we have seen that Madison was there driven by a sense of "strategy" to propose a strong central government while using issues of republican rights as a forceful "wedge" with which to gain the support of reluctant state delegates such as those from Virginia.

Near the beginning of his letter to Pickering, Hamilton declared that at the Constitutional Convention "I would have enlarged the Legislative power of the General Government, yet I never contemplated the abolition of the State Governments . . . [which were] constituent parts of my plan . . . [as] purely republican . . ." Clearly Hamilton had envisioned an enhancement of legislative powers exercised by Congress (in conjunction with the President) beyond what was finally adopted by the Constitutional Convention. He still saw this enlarged power, albeit checked and balanced, to be the mainstay of the strong energetic federal government necessary for continued "stability," which he fears may yet be in jeopardy because such measures were not adopted.[45]

In late 1801 and early 1802, Hamilton elaborated far more extensively on elements of legislative power and sovereignty in the course of a series of eighteen articles designed initially to refute points raised in Jefferson's first annual message as President to Congress. Entitled "The Examination" and published under the name "Lucius Crassus" in the *New-York Evening Post,* these articles displayed a sustained fervor of complicated argumentation that seems somewhat ironic. Not long before, it was largely Hamilton's last-minute support for Jefferson over Burr, in the prolonged presidential deadlock over electoral votes, that had at last decided the contest in Jefferson's favor (and was soon to become a factor behind Burr challenging Hamilton to a duel). Shortly after Jefferson's message on December 8, 1801, appeared Hamilton's first article against it on December 17. In March 1802, the new Congress, led by Republicans, repealed, after prolonged debate, the Judiciary Act of February-March 1801. That Act had been passed by the Federalist-dominated Congress shortly before the end of Adams' administration. The Act had enabled Adams and his Federalists to obtain their "midnight" appointments to the courts. Their gambit touched off the so-called "assault on the judiciary" under Jefferson, against which Hamilton took up the fight in his articles of "Examination." They remained somewhat obscure, however, in large measure because his political star had fallen considerably especially on the national scene. The new law of March 1802, repealing the Act of 1801, essentially restored the first Judiciary Act of 1789. Hamilton's "Examination" articles became a futile exercise in attempting to influence Congress not to repeal the Act of 1801. Nonetheless, they contain many insights into his wider views on legislative issues in the complex contexts not only of the Judiciary Act of 1801 but also of the Convention of 1787 and his positions expressed there as well as in *The Federalist.*

In his "Examination" article #XII (February 1802), Hamilton characteristically attacked Republicans attempting to repeal the Judiciary Act of 1801, which he saw as a needed protection of judicial independence. He denounced their stripping away of the Constitution's provision that judges hold their term of office for an indefinite period, even for life, subject to their good behavior. Albeit an advocate of legislative sovereignty within prescribed constitutional limits, Hamilton here recognizes that "the whole power of the Nation ... [is not] lodged in the legislative body" "[a]s in the Parliament of Great Britain." An overriding main point for him, here as throughout the series, is that the Republican-led Congress, in pushing for repeal, seems to believe that "there are no constitutional limits to the Legislative Authority." Here as elsewhere, he argues in elaborate (sometimes convoluted) terms the pros and cons involved in this whole debate, with particular attention to the mechanisms of promulgating and repealing laws on the part of successive legislative bodies. In a related piece, he also takes a polite veiled swipe at Madison, evidently for not being branded like Hamilton himself with the label of having advocated at the Convention of 1787 an overly "energetic" federal government. Still apparently suffering in his own mind from having purportedly had monarchical leanings at the Convention, Hamilton says that the meetings there became in part a closed forum for him, Madison, and others to experiment with ideas to which they did not necessarily subscribe.[46]

After stressing in "Examination" #XIII the ultimate authority of the Constitution in giving indefinite tenure for judges, over and above the innate power of successive federal legislatures to make and abrogate laws in such matters,[47] Hamilton in "Examination" #XIV makes some potent statements on the whole nature of American legislative power. He considers it to be the most naturally sovereign branch of the national government and the one needing particular checks on its scope and activities. The passage to follow indicates Hamilton's continued high esteem for the sovereign power of the national legislative body in America. He supports the proper checks and balances on it as duly provided by the executive and judicial branches in accordance with the Constitution. Hamilton's initial statement below on the sweeping scope of legislative sovereignty, together with his list of attributes, is reminiscent of Bodin and his later followers in both constitutionalist and absolutist traditions. Hamilton's insightful adaptation of traditional ideas of legislative sovereignty was aptly attuned to the emerging concepts and actualities of American national government. With the legislative "power" serving as "the most comprehensive and potent" feature of "sovereignty" and as the government's very "will," it sets the agenda for the executive and judicial branches in their executing and interpreting of the laws, as Hamilton has also above indicated in other ways. The wide range of sovereignty's attributes included here under the legislative power conveys a suggestive echo of Bodinian concepts. The British monarchy as a check on Parliament's great legislative powers is alluded to once again as a desirable *modus operandi*. Yet the context here is more constitutional than absolutist as regards the European background to legislative sovereignty, even though Hamilton's critics could typically believe otherwise of him.

> It is a principle equally sound, that though in a government like that of Great Britain, having an hereditary chief with vast prerogatives, the danger to Liberty, by the predominance of one department over the other, is on the side of the Executive; yet in popular forms of government, this danger is chiefly to be apprehended from the Legislative branch.

> The power of legislation is in its own nature the most comprehensive and potent of the three great subdivisions of sovereignty. It is the will of the government; it prescribes universally the rule of action, and the sanctions which are to enforce it. It creates and regulates the public force, and it commands the public purse. If deposited in an elective representative of the people, it has, in most cases, the body of the nation for its auxiliary, and generally acts with all the momentum of popular favor. In every such government it is consequently an organ of immense strength. But when there is an hereditary chief magistrate, cloathed with dazzling prerogatives and a great patronage, there is a powerful counterpoise; which, in most cases, is sufficient to preserve the equilibrium of the government; in some cases to incline the scale too much to its own side.[48]

The foregoing passage continues on with considerations of how the executive and judicial branches of the American federal government are naturally prone to weakness under the dominant weight of the national legislative body. The "concentration" of power is for Hamilton the essence of "despotism." The antidote is a proportionate balance in the way the powers of the three branches are "distributed." The legislature should not amass power to such degrees that it can "abolish" judgeships. By strengthening the other two branches, particularly the judiciary which is the weakest yet fairest of the three, they can more effectively check the legislative branch and safeguard liberty.[49]

Taking up further features of sovereignty more directly in "Examination" #XVII, Hamilton points out that under the Constitution the "whole" American federal government is sovereign, unlike the case in England. This collective sovereignty furnishes the best barrier against undue removal of judges by the legislature, on which they have become dependent for their tenure of office.[50]

5. HAMILTON'S LIBRARY

Some Surviving Books

The search for books once owned or used by Alexander Hamilton, which could have provided him with sources of European intellectual influence on the topics at hand, begins and ends with the important but limited and little-known collection of Hamilton family books, given long ago by the family, at Columbia University. Unlike the papers and manuscripts of Alexander Hamilton sold or given to the Library of Congress, the books at Columbia, thought by the family to have once belonged to Alexander Hamilton, turn out to be of uncertain provenance. When and where which books once belonged to which members of the Hamilton family is generally difficult to determine precisely. Almost certainly, Alexander had amassed, by the end of his career, a significant collection of books, eventually divided in some fashion between his home in upper Manhattan and his law office in lower Manhattan. His collection possibly originated during his earlier period in New York City where he attended King's College (now Columbia University). Despite the paucity of books by European authors in Columbia's Hamilton collection of pre-1804 imprints, there are a number of surviving books that in all likelihood were indeed in the Hamilton premises and were owned by or known to him. Although the vast majority of these books bear no original bookplates or signatures (autographs) of ownership, there are a few that do, with some interesting direct and indirect ties to Alexander. The Columbia books with imprints prior to his death date in 1804 cannot be assumed to have belonged to him, contrary to their mode of listing in the card file, although they may well have. Yet many good clues can be brought together in an original fashion here (and in the various extended notes below) to provide indicative links with Alexander Hamilton himself on the much-neglected subject of his library books, examined here in present ways for the first time.[51]

Among the books by European authors with pre-1804 imprints in the Hamilton collection, there are certain ones of interest with inscriptions on their title pages by Alexander's third son, James (b. 1788). He was age 16 at the time of his father's death, living at his parents' "Grange" home in upper New York City. The most likely scenario, under the circumstances, is that James acquired these and other books of similar type and binding from his father, Alexander, and affixed his own signature.[52] These books include a handsome multi-volume history of France in French, with leather binding and gold stamping (or "tooling").[53] Other similarly bound large handsome volumes in the same Columbia collection that bear pre-1804 imprints but no signature of ownership on their title pages include a multi-volume French edition of Voltaire's works[54] and a multi-volume history of philosophical and political thought in French (which begins in the first volume with thinkers like Aristotle).[55] Those would seem also to be part of the same sets of books evidently once owned by Alexander and taken over by his son James in New York. Although there are no telltale markings in the texts of the histories of France and of political thought, the presence of these works in the Hamilton collection is congruent with Alexander's wide intellectual interests, including his particular fluency in French.

In addition, it is interesting to note that Alexander Hamilton's son James—who was born and lived in New York, later returning and becoming an attorney like his father—was married to a daughter (Mary) of Robert Morris, whose inscription appears opposite the title page of a book of a different kind owned and autographed by Alexander Hamilton. Morris comments there that this book was given to him by Alexander in place of one that Morris had loaned to Alexander, who mislaid it. But the book in question is not in itself of direct interest here.[56]

Although certain other books bearing Alexander Hamilton's signature of ownership are not of direct interest here, one of them is also autographed by Philip Hamilton. Philip was the name of Alexander Hamilton's oldest son (killed in an 1801 duel) as well as the name of the grandson of Alexander's third son, James, cited above. Since Alexander's son Philip (b. 1782) was nearly 20 when killed prior to his father's death, it is likely that he, like his younger brother James, inscribed his name in such books, even before their father's death in 1804, that is, in books that Alexander possessed and gave to his sons and that like others remained in Alexander's family orbit for him to see. Or, the book in question could have been acquired by Alexander's son James and later handed down to James' grandson Philip, although in that case one might have expected James to be an autographer as well, which he was not.[57]

Also included in the same Hamilton collection at Columbia, with similar binding and appearance, is a pre-1804 multi-volume French edition of the works of Rousseau. In the first volume is not only Rousseau's *Social Contract* but also his *Discourse on Political Economy*. We have already had occasions to note affinities between Hamilton's political ideas and those of Rousseau in the former work; other examples could be cited. The latter work would have been of interest to Hamilton in economic thought, his renowned forte. In addition, we shall presently see the great affinity between George Washington's image as lawgiver and Rousseau's ideas in his *Social Contract*, which Washington possessed in his library.[58]

Other such pre-1804 works of interest in the same collection but not autographed include a French edition of the works of Frederick II, the King of Prussia. His Enlightenment commentaries on Machiavelli's *Prince* might have been of particular note to Alexander Hamilton.[59] There is also at Columbia a huge multi-volume *Encyclopéie methodique*[60] and a two-volume *Histoire naturelle*.[61]

In light of the heavy preponderance of the above (and other) works being in French and of learned nature, certain elements of Alexander Hamilton's biography enter the picture to make it ever more plausible that they were originally in his possession in New York, before they were passed down to his children and other descendants. Raised by his mother on St. Croix and "learning to speak French fluently" from an early age, "he entered King's College . . . in . . . 1773. Already he had formed habits of persistent study which he retained throughout life, while his letters of the time display astonishing maturity."[62] Dating from this early period, there is in Alexander Hamilton's papers a forgotten unpublished manuscript list (c.1773) of over two dozen books quite possibly owned by or known to him; it includes numerous classical and early Christian titles in fragmentary English form.[63] At any rate, the above and other books in the Hamilton collection at Columbia have a consistency and similarity in their handsomeness and learnedness that would have made them appropriate—probably as part of a much larger collection—for the library of so distinguished and learned a public figure as *the* Alexander Hamilton.

Some Uses of European Sources

The plethora of Hamilton's references to European writers of his own century and of centuries past makes it likely that his book collection included many more works by them than have survived in the Columbia collection. The wide-ranging references in his writings to British writers of present note include those to Hobbes, Blackstone, Locke, Hume, and Smith. Those to French writers encompass such authorities as Rousseau and Montesquieu. Ancient authorities he referred to include Plutarch, Plato, Xenophon, and Thucydides. It may be that Hamilton was not as broadly and deeply "cultivated" in his usage of such sources as were Jefferson, Adams, and Madison, perhaps due in part to lapses in his early education as well as to his more specialized legal and economic interests, not to mention the shorter duration of his career and intellectual development. Yet the circumstances of his early life made him well versed in British thought and history, also fluent in French. At any rate, his references to and usage of European sources can add further dimensions to issues pursued in this chapter, however selective we must be here. Certain other examples have already appeared in sections above.

A case in point involves Rousseau, whose collected works are in Columbia's Hamilton collection but without signature of ownership. Hamilton's fluency in French and other factors cited above make it likely that this set of books belonged to him and was passed down. According to the notes for his speech at the New York Ratifying Convention on July 12, 1788, in Poughkeepsie, Hamilton first dealt with the topic of republics, which he believes have been found in diverse historical aristocracies, monarchies, and democracies. Rousseau is the only writer cited here by Hamilton. Rousseau, he avers, dealt with republics in the form of democracies, which, Hamilton says, have "government[s] exercised by the collective body [and general will] of the People." The topic of sovereignty quickly arises as a main issue. The various headings arranged here by Hamilton reflect not only his own wide reading and classificatory acumen but also, it seems, some of the arrangements of different forms of government set forth by Rousseau, especially in his *Social Contract*. Hamilton's full context is instructive. All *sic*.

A. I. A republic a word used in various senses.
Has been applied to aristocracies and monarchies.
1. To Rome under the Kings.
2. To Sparta through a Senate for life.
3. To Carthage through the same.
4. To United Netherlands, through Stadholder, Hereditary nobles:
5. To Poland through aristocracy and monarchy
6. To Great Britain through Monarchy &c

II. Again great confusion about the words. Democracy, Aristocracy, Monarchy
I. Democracy defined by some[,] Rousseau &c
A government exercised by the collective body of the People
2 Delegation of their power has been made the criterion of Aristocracy
II. Aristocracy has been used to designate governments.
1. Where an independent few possessed sovereignty.
2. Where the representatives of the people possessed it.
III. Monarchy, where sovereignty in the hands of a single man.
—> General idea—Independent in his situation. in any other sense would apply to State of New York
III. Democracy in my sense, where the whole power of the government in the people
1. Whether exercised by themselves, or
2. By their representatives chosen by them either mediately or immediately and legally accountable to them.
IV. Aristocracy where whole sovereignty is permanently in the hands of a few for life or hereditary
V. Monarchy where the whole sovereignty is in the

hands of one man for life or hereditary.
VI. Mixed government when these three principles unite.[64]

Following the continuation of this theoretical first section (A) of Hamilton's ratifying speech are the second and third sections (B, C) pertaining to the U.S. governmental structure under specific consideration.[65] Then appears a subsection (b) in which the whole subject of legislation becomes uppermost in relation to the separation of powers. Here Montesquieu is the only authority cited. The particular placement of Montesquieu's name next to the form of government offers a glimpse into Hamilton's mind concerning him. Montesquieu has been traditionally hailed as founder of the separation of powers as a doctrine taken over in the U.S. Constitution. The central dominant role of the legislative power, according to Hamilton, to which the executive and judicial powers are interrelated characterizes, in different ways, Montesquieu's ideas, the British system, and the new American form of government. Judging from Hamilton's wide other references elsewhere to Montesquieu, it is clear that he was directly and extensively familiar with Montesquieu's *Spirit of the Laws*.

b. A seperation of the essential powers of government.
Ascertain the sense of the Maxim.
I. One department must not wholly possess the powers of another.
= Montesquieu
= British Government.
II. Departments of power must be seperated, yet so as to check each other.
1. Legislative
2. Legislative executive.
3. Judicial legislative.
4. Legislative judicial.
—> All this done in the proposed Constitution.
1. Legislative in the Congress, yet checked by negative of the Executive.
2. Executive in the President, yet checked by impeachment of Congress.
3. Judicial check upon legislative, or Interpretation of Laws.
4. And checked by Legislative through Impeachment.
D. 2 1. Can such a Government apply to so extensive a Territory?

Exaggerated ideas of extent.
[Etc., with particular regard to Congress.][66]

Further close and extensive familiarity with Montesquieu's writings and other European sources is evident in Hamilton's lengthy "remarks" at the New York Ratifying Convention on June 27, 1788 (prior to the speech cited above). After affirming that "the objects of the state governments . . . are . . . to support the legislative establishments, and to provide for the administration of the laws," especially in relation to the federal government, Hamilton passes on to a lengthy refutation of the position taken a week earlier by New York's governor, George Clinton. Although Clinton did not cite Montesquieu as authority, Hamilton does so for him. According to Clinton, says Hamilton, "only a despotism can exist in a very extensive country." Hamilton elaborates on Clinton's misunderstanding of ideas set forth by the "celebrated" Montesquieu. The wider misappropriations of Montesquieu's ideas are also familiar to Hamilton and have occasioned "frequent fallacies in our [people's] reasoning on political subjects." By Clinton's false reasoning, avers Hamilton, even a state the size of New York would be too large for a republic to exist in. Such reasoning, he argues, is especially fallible for "a confederacy in which the supreme legislature has only general powers" and in which "the people are regulated by the laws of the several states." The aim of "the [new] national legislature" cannot be "to destroy the state governments," which are "a necessary aid in executing the laws. . . . The union is dependent on the will of the state governments," which convey "the influence of government to the doors of the people." Here as on other occasions, one may detect an echo of Rousseau's noted concept of "the general will" of the people, especially as expressed in the legislative sovereignty of their central government. In addition, Hamilton draws historical analogies from the medieval feudal system concerning the relationships between monarch, nobles, and others.[67]

Hamilton's wide-ranging references to European writers on other occasions also bespeak his ready familiarity with them. In his "The Farmer Refuted" in 1775, he referred to the thought of Montesquieu, Hobbes, Blackstone and Locke, as well as of Grotius and Puffendorf, on natural rights and man in a state of nature as they pertain to concepts of law and government "in this enlightened age."[68] Hamilton's many other scattered references to these and other European writers past and current, including Hume and Smith, make it clear that he was well read in their writings, very possibly through his own copies that no longer survive.[69]

Among Hamilton's most interesting references to and uses of ancient writers are those to Plutarch, and to others including Plato, on the subject of great legendary founders of states and givers of law. As noted above, Hamilton's fellow *Federalist* essayist Madison, in addition to Jefferson and Adams, also made use of such sources and subjects. This had become a wide tradition in modern thought going back in different ways to Bodin, Corasius, and Machiavelli two centuries earlier. In a writing of 1777, for instance, Hamilton made some extended comments on Lycurgus of Greece and Numa of Rome. His references therein to Plutarch, Plato, Xenophon, Thucydides, and others suggest a firsthand familiarity with their writings.[70] There, too, Hamilton also made extended comments on the histories of Florence and Venice.[71]

In his *The Farmer Refuted* in 1775, Hamilton responded to a letter from A. W. Farmer regarding relations between Britain and the American colonies, involving in particular the role of Congress. Here Hamilton displays an early familiarity with a broad range of issues and writings in political thought on such subjects. As part of his refutation of the British doctrine of parliamentary supremacy over the colonies and their legislatures, with particular regard to Congress, Hamilton addresses comparable issues in Roman legislative history dealing with the Empire and its colonies. "The right of colonies, therefore, to exercise a legislative power, is an inherent [!] right . . . founded upon the right of all men to freedom and happiness." His striking statements on legislative self-determination are not only couched in an Enlightenment framework of natural rights but hark back indirectly to Renaissance thought, especially (though he knew it not) in Bodin and Corasius. Hamilton's discourses upon the British constitution in these respects demonstrate ample familiarity with Blackstone's *Commentaries*, cited by his opponent. Hamilton also is well versed in documentary evidence on the grants given by Queen Elizabeth to Sir Walter Raleigh, together with subsequent charters under King James I, that led to the establishment of Virginia and its inherent right of legislative self-determination, independent of the British Empire and any subsequent jurisdictional claims by it to the contrary. "The colonies are . . . entirely without the realm," outside "any authority of parliament," and "without the jurisdiction of its legislature."[72]

Many further wide-ranging cases in point could be cited.

A Comment on Jay's Library

In view of our close attention to the libraries of Hamilton and Madison, the two main contributors to *The Federalist*, the question arises as to the third colleague in that venture, John Jay (1745–1829)—jurist, statesman, first Chief Justice of the U.S. Supreme Court (1789–1795), and New York Governor (1795–1801). Like Hamilton, Jay had attended

King's College in New York City. Like Hamilton, Jay was fluent in French and possessed many books in French. Similarly to Hamilton, whose mother's father was a Huguenot physician who came over from France, Jay had a grandfather who came over from France. These and other circumstances in their careers might suggest an affinity or bond between Hamilton and Jay that would have extended to their common interest in and need for books on law, politics, and other subjects of practical and theoretical nature.

This is not the place to look at the close professional or personal relationships between the younger (fatherless) Hamilton and the older (by twelve years) Jay. Yet one can wonder about their likely sharing of books as well as ideas not just at the time of their *Federalist* collaborations but more generally. These interconnections might well have carried over in some fashion to their possession of many books in French. Their exchanges of ideas drawn from theoretical writings in legal and political books could be well expected earlier on in their relationship, especially concerning *The Federalist.*

While the subject of John Jay's library deserves further investigation along present lines, the evidence thus far adduced suggests that there are no surviving copies or records of key works by Bodin, Hobbes, Machiavelli, Montesquieu, Voltaire, Rousseau, or even Blackstone and Locke in Jay's book collections. This lack of present evidence does not mean, however, that Jay did not possess such works. Moreover, the present state of cataloguing for the considerable collections of Jay's personal books at the John Jay Homestead in Katonah, and of his law books at Columbia's Law School, does not yet allow for full access or complete information. The current conditions of these Jay collections are more complicated and inchoate than in the likewise challenging case of the Hamilton book collection. Nevertheless, further leads might well open up new possibilities.[73]

6. ADDENDUM ON GEORGE WASHINGTON

"Cincinnatus" as Rousseau's Lawgiver

In order to round out our studies on the principal American founders, it will be suitable to conclude with an addendum on George Washington. For the most part, his correspondence and writings—aside from various presidential pronouncements and the like, often crafted by Hamilton and others—do not lend themselves well to the kinds of extended analyses presented above. Washington does, nevertheless, afford some intriguing perspectives on the issues at hand. One case in point must suffice, which is also relevant to our preceding section on Hamilton's uses of European sources.

In his stimulating book of 1984 entitled *Cincinnatus: George Washington and the Enlightenment*, Garry Wills includes a chapter, "Lawgiver," in Part III on "The Constitution: Founder." After quoting Washington during the period of the Constitutional Convention, Wills gives several quotations from Madison in *The Federalist* on the role of heroic classical lawgivers. These passages, he believes, were partly derived more distantly from Plutarch's *Lives* and were also partly inspired more immediately by Rousseau's recent *Social Contract* on the role of legislators. Wills also cites Machiavelli's *Discourses* on such matters. The following excerpts are illustrative. There is not space to convey here Wills' extensive interrelated uses of artistic renderings of that period showing Washington and others in the classical light of lawgiver.

> [T]he drafting convention of 1787 was a perfect fulfillment of Rousseau's concept of the lawgiver. It was a body irregular and powerless, outside both the constitution it replaced and the one it proposed; it defined its own role and then disappeared....
>
> Rousseau has a ... positive vision of the legislator as surrendering personal power in order to animate the laws. ... This ideal of surendering power to establish it is obviously close to the role Washington had forged for himself. Although the convention as a body is the literal fulfillment of Rousseau's concept, Washington is the personal embodiment of it. True, he would assume power later, ... after the convention had gone out of existence. But he was the ... protective symbol, of the convention. ... People did not admire a conquering Caesar in him, but a Cincinnatus resigning. He embodied the ideal of limited ... dignified authority. ... [Concerning Washington's personal] surrender of power, ... Rousseau almost seems to be describing him when he frames the task of the *législateur*....
>
> Washington was a charismatic leader in time of war. But his peaceful role as founder was mythical. ... [I]mportant for Washington's sense of power, the classical tradition of founders made them give power to the law by divesting themselves of it in person. ... Lycurgus, ... the greatest lawgiver, began his task with an abdication. ... Solon left Athens after his legislation was in place. And when Romulus was unwilling to leave Rome, the gods took him away for the state's good.
>
> Washington in his deepest role, as founder, as father of his country, lived up to this classical pattern. He was not seen as a lawgiver in the autocratic sense, Caesar or Moses issuing the

> divine orders he alone could communicate. . . . The representation of him as a wise man of the law follows the "philosopher in his cabinet" type . . .[74]

Among the corresponding passages from Rousseau's *Social Contract* (2.6–7) cited by Wills in connection with the American Constitutional Convention and the role of Washington is the following: "The people who submit to laws should institute them; since those bound together by the law can alone set the conditions of this bond. But how are they to set them? By joint impulse, or sudden inspiration?" Moreover: "He who frames laws has no power, and should have none, to pass laws. The people cannot, if they would, rid themselves of this inalienable power." Finally, as quoted by Wills from Rousseau:

> When Lycurgus legislated for his country, his first act was to give up the throne. . . . For a people just coming into being to favor sound views of government and act on the basic rules of political necessity, effect would have to become [its own] cause; the social affections, which their institutions are supposed to shape, would have to foster them; men would have to be, without the laws, what the laws would have them become. That is why the legislator shall not use either force or [mere] argument. He must resort to another kind of authority entirely, an ability to lead without compelling and persuade without proving (*Contrat* 2.7, Garner ed. 262).

Wills' supporting quotations drawn from Washington, Madison, *The Federalist*, Plutarch, Shakespeare, Bacon, and other sources are compelling, as are the visual depictions reproduced from contemporary works of art. Yet it becomes clear that Wills dwells only on one single aspect of the lawgiver theme, the giving up of power, without regard to related themes of legislation *per se*. He omits Adams' *Defence* on classical lawgivers.

A more thorough study of Rousseau's influence on the leading American founders, especially during the period of the Constitutional Convention, could prove of considerable interest. We have already cited Hamilton's significant direct reference to Rousseau, not cited by Wills: "Democracy defined by some[,] Rousseau etc.[,] . . . [as] government exercised by the collective body of the people." This citation in Hamilton's "Notes for Speech" in mid-1788 at the New York Ratifying Convention, a year after the Constitutional Convention upon which Wills has focused, pertained explicitly as well to issues of sovereignty, also not treated by Wills. A fuller investigation of the influence upon Hamilton and others of Rousseau's ideas of legislative sovereignty, general will, social contract, and so forth, as laid out in our earlier book, could be conducted, along the lines of our other expositions presented above. As Wills suggests, the theme of the great classic lawgiver, expounded upon by Enlightenment thinkers like Rousseau, was developed on a broader scale, beyond George Washington, by the American founders at Philadelphia in 1787. The particular contexts of Rousseau's ideas in the Bodinian tradition on sovereignty, the state, and legislation lent themselves to absolutist as well as constitutionalist interpretations, with likely appeal for the federalist thinking not only of Washington but also of Hamilton and Madison. The potential influence on Washington of Hamilton's own sentiments about Lycurgus, cited shortly above, could also be considered, as could Adams' *Defence* on classical lawgivers (a la Corasius).

As for George Washington's wider place in American constitutional and political thought inclusive of law and legislation, the note below must suffice (with relevance for Hamilton and Rousseau).[75]

His Copy of the *Social Contract*

The compelling general look by Garry Wills at George Washington's image as the embodiment of Rousseau's lawgiver has overlooked the presence of Rousseau's *Social Contract* in Washington's library. Indeed, the whole subject of that library, not considered by Wills, would have held important further evidence for him on the connections between Washington and the many other European intellectual authorities (such as Voltaire) cited in his broad study of Washington's role as the legendary Roman ruler, Cincinnatus. Nonetheless, the complex issues, contexts, and details surrounding the curious case of Washington's copy of the *Social Contract* have not been duly considered by historians. The evidence here (and in the long end note below) is at once selective and wide-ranging.

That a copy of Rousseau's *Social Contract* was in Washington's library is affirmed in *A Catalogue of the Washington Collection in the Boston Athenaeum*, compiled by Appleton P. C. Griffin and William Coolidge Lane (Boston, 1897, p. 523). There it is listed alphabetically but is also designated as #488, corresponding to its order of appearance in the miscellaneous inventory of books drawn up in 1799 as part of Washington's estate. As noted in that *Catalogue*, this copy was a one-volume French edition that is no longer present in the Washington collection. Lane comments: "At least fourteen editions were published between 1762 [when it first appeared] and 1800, but I have no clue to indicate which one was owned by Washington."

The question arises as to whether Washington could have read or made use of his French copy of Rousseau's *Social Contract* so as to apprehend its essential ideas. There is no direct evidence that Washington could speak, read, or write in French or any other foreign language. His early formal schooling was limited, and he was largely self-taught. However, in 1783 he purchased a French-English dictionary, published in 1778 and now owned by the Historical Society of Pennsylvania (*Catalogue*, p. 496, #2 under "Dictionaries . . . ," with autograph and bookplate). That same year, 1783, Washington acquired a copy of Benjamin Franklin's 1770 English translation of Voltaire's *Letters to Several of His Friends*, which was purchased for Washington by W. S. Smith of New York (*Catalogue*, pp. 149, 490, #334), along with a Louis XV set of volumes, etc. Now at the New York Public Library, this one-volume edition of Voltaire's *Letters* is inscribed by Washington and has his bookplate. The year 1783 that links these two books in Washington's library is significant in view of his known interest at the end of the Revolutionary War (the final peace treaty being signed in Paris in late summer of 1783) to travel to France (which he never did) to see some of his wartime French comrades. Around that time he obtained a travel guide to France. Also in 1783, he was elected President of the Society of the Cincinnati, a fraternal organization of former Continental and French officers.

While still in New York that same year, 1783, prior to returning to Mt. Vernon, Washington continued his contacts with Hamilton, who had long been a high-ranking officer in his army, culminating two years earlier as commander in the final 1781 siege at Yorktown. We have already cited Hamilton's fluency in French, his salient interest in Rousseau's political ideas, and his apparent ownership of the multi-volume French edition of Rousseau's works now in the Hamilton collection at Columbia. This same date of 1783 for Washington's acquisition, through Smith in New York, of Voltaire's *Letters* in Franklin's English translation also adds to the potential channels through which Washington's interest in and knowledge of ideas in Rousseau's *Social Contract* could have been stimulated. We have also already noted the multi-volume 1785 French edition of Voltaire's Works in the same Hamilton collection.

It seems, then, that the strong elements of Rousseau's ideas of the lawgiver that Wills has well traced, in general fashion, in the literature and art relating to Washington could also be explained, to some degree, by a direct or indirect familiarity on Washington's part with ideas in Rousseau's *Social Contract*. While it is true that Washington did not correspond or converse in French with Frenchmen, his interest in French thought is evidenced by a variety of books in his library by French writers both in French and in English translation; the question of whether an English version of the *Social Contract* was available to him cannot be answered here. Perhaps for Washington, as they did for

Hamilton and other Federalists, Rousseau's French ideas of a strong central legislative authority and an encompassing general will and unity of the people held particular appeal. Rousseau's revolutionary or radical ideas of democracy, with intimations of popular authoritarian rule by the majority, may have held greater appeal for him and others than did the British ideas of Locke on Parliament's supremacy. Important for Locke as well as for Rousseau was the Bodinian tradition of legislative sovereignty, which applied to democratic as well as to monarchical forms of state. More fundamental for Rousseau (and Bodin) than for Locke was the mystique and tradition of great lawgiver-leaders, both ancient and modern, which contributed to Rousseau's growing allure for Washington in his image as Cincinnatus.

His Library Inventories

It is telling that, among the multitudinous books listed in the Boston Athenaeum catalogue, Rousseau's *Social Contract* stands out as the only work of its kind on political thought under the category of "Politics . . ." (no such works by Locke, Montesquieu, Hobbes, etc. being included there). The case is somewhat different in the 1782 inventory (not done by Washington) of books owned by Martha's son John Parke Custis (d. 1781)—which were partly handed down to him by his father, Daniel Parke Custis, and partly given to him by his stepfather, George Washington, in order to further his education. In it were listed Locke's *Of Government* and Montesquieu's *Spirit of the Laws*, as well as Voltaire's full "Works" (the two latter in English). These works are not, however, in the later Athenaeum Catalogue of the Washington collection, whereas Rousseau's *Social Contract* is, showing that Washington kept it at Mt. Vernon, even though it was in French.

Also in that 1782 inventory are many of the kinds of works listed below for Washington's 1759 inventory, including works by Cicero, Dryden, Puffendorf, and Swift, with the addition, however, of books and lexicons, not in the 1799 will or later Athenaeum catalogue, that suggest an interest in or knowledge of Latin and Greek writers. If acquired from his stepfather George rather than through his father Daniel, these books of John Parke Custis fit in well with George's extensive efforts to obtain a good classical education for him while at Virginia secondary school and later at King's College in New York, although John was little interested in such matters. These and other books in the 1782 catalogue were evidently either available to George Washington while young John was still living at Mt. Vernon or were acquired by him (and by teachers?) for John, who took them with him to his nearby Abingdon home after he married in 1774. John left no will for his widow at his early death in 1781 after briefly joining Washington's staff during the Yorktown siege and becoming fatally ill; the two youngest of his four children became raised by the Washingtons at Mt. Vernon.

The subsequent transmission of John Parke Custis' books is not altogether clear amid all these contexts. Some books apparently made their way back to George's Mt. Vernon collection sometime after its shorter 1783 inventory and its longer one of 1799 were made. There is evidence in George Washington's letter from Newburgh, N.Y., in Aug. 1783 to his cousin and caretaker at Mt. Vernon, Lund Washington (who in July had sent him a shorter inventory of books at Mt. Vernon), that John may well have taken books from the Mt. Vernon library to his nearby Abingdon home without his stepfather's knowledge. This evidence adds to the potential connections between George and the many books in the 1782 inventory for John that were not in George's 1799 will (or in the later Athenaeum catalogue) but that could have in part been formerly at Mt. Vernon.

Because George Washington's copy of Rousseau's *Social Contract* is not included in the inventories of 1759, c. 1764, 1782, and mid-1783, whereas it is in the final 1799 inventory done at the time of his death, it is likely that he acquired it sometime between mid-1783 and 1799. This timing carries further potential for Washington's intercontacts with Hamilton on this subject soon after the end of the Revolutionary War in 1781–1783 when both men had more leisure time. They could also have taken place sometime later—during the Constitutional Convention, or the Ratification period, or Washington's presidency, under which Hamilton served as his Treasury Secretary and speechwriter. Their growing close relationship had been forged early on in 1777 when Hamilton became aide-de-camp to Washington with rank of lieutenant colonel. In the younger Hamilton—who was twenty-five years his junior, knowledgeable, partly self-taught, ambitious, and fatherless—the childless Washington may well have sensed not only an alter ego but a more agreeable son than the somewhat apathetic, difficult, and irresponsible John Parke Custis, for whom he cared when early struggling without much success to gain for him learning as well as responsibility. Like Hamilton, in fact, John had been a student at King's College (entering in 1773, the same year as Hamilton, but dropping out a number of months later) and had also been with Washington at the Yorktown siege in 1781. John's death there may have become all the more poignant for Washington's relationship with Hamilton.

It is not likely that Washington's acquisition of Rousseau's *Social Contract* had any connection with Jefferson and Madison. Jefferson had included the work in French in his "1783" list of books for himself. Madison (who could have owned the work) omitted it in his 1783 list of books for Congress (perhaps because an English version for Congress' purposes was not available, although English versions of Montesquieu and Voltaire were included). In that same year of 1783, already much noted above, came Lund Washington's list (about the time George was in Newburgh, New York) of several dozen books at Mt. Vernon. This list lacked any works like the *Social Contract* (though Milton and Pope appear) and evidenced no influence of those other catalogues by Jefferson and Madison, with whom George had little contact during this period. In any case, Washington was away from Mt. Vernon almost continuously between mid-1775 and late 1783 during the long struggles against Britain. He clearly had more time for library matters after the war, as did Hamilton.

Given the evident mutual interest of Washington and Hamilton in Rousseau's *Social Contract*, and given Washington's known need for a translator to help him read materials that occasionally came to him in French, it is plausible that he turned to Hamilton and his learned fluency in French for help in understanding Rousseau. It is even more plausible that it was Hamilton who introduced Rousseau to Washington in the first place and who even helped to shape the image of Washington as Rousseau's great lawgiver. Bodinian concepts of legislative sovereignty that were important for Rousseau as well as for Hamilton could be further studied in the case of Washington.

Further information relating to the Washington library collections is reserved for the note below.[76]

Adams' *Defence* Preface—and Corasius

Included also in Washington's library was a copy of Adams' *Defence*, which the editor of the Athenaeum catalogue aptly notes "was much circulated at the Federal Convention" and "had considerable influence" there. The *quasi-religious composite* depictions of famous *classical* lawgiver-founders in Adams' *Defence* Preface of early 1787 were more influential in that regard on Washington and others than were Rousseau's (like Plutarch's) more scattered and less developed references to them in his general discussions of lawgivers in his *Social Contract*, upon which Wills focuses. Unlike Rousseau, Adams centered his discussions on the *quasi-religious* elements that great *classical* lawgiver-founders ascribed to their laws so as to give them greater binding force. Corasius had done so more fully in his unique composite chapter on this very subject in *Art of Law* I, 16, as prefigured in his commentaries on *Digest* I, 1–4 (which were in the very small library at Harvard when Adams was there). Indeed, some of the related matters alluded to by Wills could be viewed more fully from such perspectives. Unlike Adams, Washington did not possess the *Lexicon I[J]uridicum*, with Corasius' name included on the title page. These and related topics remain to be further discussed.[77]

PART THREE

Further Legislative Foundations of Sovereignty and State in the Revolutionary and Constitutional Eras

Chapter VI

The Testimony of Other Figures

The testimony of other figures provides further legislative foundations of sovereignty and state in the Revolutionary and Constitutional Eras. The writings assembled below for the Revolutionary Era cover a broad but representative spectrum of American viewpoints in the long, developing quest for independence from Britain during the two decades leading up to the end of the war in 1781 and the final peace treaty in 1783. The writings chosen for the early Constitutional Era cover a shorter span of time in the periods of the Constitutional (or Federal) and Ratifying Conventions, prior to the adoption of the Bill of Rights in 1791. During the decade of the 1790s and into the first years of the next century lay the post-Convention period (preferable to "post-Constitutional"); overlapping with the wider Constitutional Era, it saw the formative emergence of the new constitutional order.

1. THE REVOLUTIONARY ERA

T.Q. and J. (1763)

Three lengthy letters signed by "T.Q." and "J." that appeared in Boston newspapers in 1763[1] made abundant references to Montesquieu's *Spirit of the Laws* in matters of legislation and related topics. Although written primarily against multiple office-holding in Massachusetts state government, especially the legislature, these letters made interesting uses of Montesquieu's doctrines on separation of powers in conjunction with British parliamentary government.

"Political liberty, as it is defined by a great writer [Montesquieu], is 'a tranquility of mind arising from the opinion each man has of his own safety.' When this liberty is once destroyed[,] it is to very little purpose to enquire how it was brought about; but . . . it is wisdom to guard against whatever has a tendency to it, in order to prevent it. Among many other things of this nature and tendency, the entrusting the same gentlemen with legislative and judiciary power, of the power of *making* laws and *judging* of them after they are made, has been vainly objected against in this paper." This first letter, written by T.Q., continues on to cite again "the admired writer of *The Spirit of the Laws*," whom he quotes as follows: "There is no liberty if the power of *judging* be not separated from the *legislative* power; for the judge being the maker of the law, the life and liberty of the subject would be exposed to arbitary control." The letter goes on to declare: "What situation must the poor subjects be in under those republics where [the body of magistrates who execute the laws are able to utilize a whole body of powers] which they have given themselves in another capacity as legislators." The writer praises the Greek example of curbing the intoxicating uses of power, in contradistinction to Roman practices under rulers like Julius Caesar. "The *Greeks* were a wise people, and all governments would do well in this particular to imitate their example."

In response to this first letter by T.Q., the writer of the second letter, calling himself J., offers a large number of further references to and statements by Montesquieu in his *Spirit of the Laws*. He does so in partial support of certain overlaps of office-holding on the British parliamentary model as it applies to state government in Massachusetts. True, J. is in basic agreement with T.Q. on the greatness and wisdom of Montesquieu's ideas on separation of legislative, executive, and judicial bodies. Yet J. looks more favorably than does T.Q. upon various limited ways in which Britain and Massachusetts allow certain individuals to have some shared responsibilities in those three different bodies. The differences between those two writers seem to reflect wider differences among American colonists at this early stage in their long road to independence not only from British control but also from British forms of government. Nonetheless, the great weight given by both writers to Montesquieu's doctrines on the need for separation of powers is illustrative of the wide complex impact of European political thought at this early point in the Revolutionary Era, aside from the well-known influence of Locke.

In the third letter, written in response to J. by T.Q., the same differences of argument again arise, with heavy reliance on Montesquieu and within abundant contexts of legislative power. Their differences now become somewhat sharper over Montesquieu's ideas on separation of powers in relation to political liberty. This disagreement, though civil, seems portentous. Many American writers were struggling their way toward acceptance, amid much reluctance, of a split from the British empire and its parliamentary system.

James Otis (1764, 1765)

Of particular notoriety and controversy in the agitated period of 1764–1765, when the Sugar and Stamp Acts were passed by the British Parliament to the consternation of the American colonists, was James Otis' *The Rights of the British Colonies Asserted and Proved* (Boston, 1764), followed by his *A Vindication of the British Colonies* (Boston, 1765).[2] In his *Rights* Otis first comments ("Introduction: Of the Origin of Government") on four disputed types of a government's origins (through grace, force or power, compact, and propeity), with quotations from Locke. He comes then to a more basic point: "But let the *origin* of government be placed where it may, the *end* of it is manifestly the good of *the whole. Salus populi suprema lex esto* is of the law of nature and part of the grand charter given to the human race (though too many of them are afraid to assert it) by the only monarch in the universe who has a clear and indisputable right to *absolute* power . . ." Otis then fastens onto an even more fundamental point: "The first principle and great end of government being to provide for the best good of all the people, this can be done only by a supreme legislative and executive ultimately in the people or whole community . . ." Furthermore: "A power of legislation without a power of execution in the same or other hands would be futile and vain. On the other hand, a power of execution, supreme or subordinate, without an *independent* legislative would be perfect despotism." Otis "close[s] this introduction with a passage from Mr. Locke. . . . '. . . [T]here can be but one supreme power which is the legislative, to which all the rest are and must be subordinate, yet the legislative being only a fiduciary power to act for certain ends, there remains still [a power in the people to remove or alter the legislative power when it acts contrary to its proper end and their trust]'." Further quotations follow from Locke's *On Government.*

In an ensuing section of his *Rights* entitled "Of the Political and Civil Rights of the British Colonists," Otis enumerates a number of aspects of legislative sovereignty in line with that section's stated subject. This list includes the statements to follow, in addition to several related points. The prevalence of legislative sovereignty in Otis' viewpoints on the rights of the American colonists in relation to Britain and its king and Parliament is striking testimony to the influence of European traditions of thought in this matter.

> Every British subject born on the continent of America or in any other of the British dominions is by the law of God and nature, by the common law, and by act of Parliament (exclusive of all charters from the crown) entitled to all the natural, essential, inherent, and inseparable rights of our fellow subjects in Great Britain. Among those rights are the following, which it is humbly conceived no man or body of men, not excepting the Parliament, justly, equitably, and consistently with their own rights and the constitution can take away.
>
> First. *That the supreme and subordinate powers of legislation should be free and sacred in the hands where the community have once rightfully placed them.*
>
> Secondly. *The supreme national legislative cannot be altered justly till the commonwealth is dissolved, nor a subordinate legislative taken away without forfeiture or other good cause.* Nor then can the subjects in the subordinate government be reduced to a state of slavery and subject to the despotic rule of others. . . .
>
> Thirdly. *No legislative, supreme or subordinate, has a right to make itself arbitrary.*
>
> It would be a most manifest contradiction for a free legislature, like that of Great Britain, to make itself arbitrary.
>
> Fourthly. *The supreme legislative cannot justly assume a power of ruling by extempore arbitrary decrees, but is bound to dispense justice by known settled rules* and by *duly authorized independent judges.*
>
> Fifthly. *The supreme power cannot take from any man any part of his property,* without his consent *in person or by representation.*
>
> Sixthly. *The legislature cannot transfer the power of making laws to any other hands.*
>
> These are their bounds, which by God and nature are fixed; hitherto have they a right to come, and no further.
>
> 1. *To govern by stated laws.*
>
> 2. *Those laws should have no other end ultimately but the good of the people.*

> 3. *Taxes are not to be laid on the people but by their consent in person or by deputation.*
> 4. *Their whole power is not transferable.*
>
> These are the first principles of law and justice, and the great barriers of a free state and of the British constitution in particular.[3]

After drawing upon traditional authorities in ensuing sections, where he includes taxation among the activities of legislation, Otis concludes his *Rights of the British Colonies* with some mixed proposals on what Britain and America should do about their respective roles in pressing matters of legislative sovereignty. Otis is clearly here no revolutionary, but he mildly seeks to alter, drastically, the current system. He seeks to readjust the balance and conditions of British-American systems of legislation, which are for him the *hallmarks* of their differing separate states. The broader context of Otis' work remains Britain's new unwarranted taxation of the American colonists in accordance with her misguided views on legislative sovereignty, which Otis tries to set aright. He is, however, careful at this early stage of events to maintain or profess loyalty to the British King and Parliament.

> The sum of my argument is: that . . . in consequence of this establishment and the acts of succession and union, His Majesty George III is rightful King and sovereign, and, with his Parliament, the supreme legislative of Great Britain, France, and Ireland, and the dominions thereto belonging; that this constitution is the most free one and by far the best now existing on earth; that by this constitution every man in the dominions is a free man; that no parts of His Majesty's dominions can be taxed without their consent; that every part has a right to be represented in the supreme or some subordinate legislature; that the refusal of this would seem to be a contradiction in practice to the theory of the constitution; that the colonies are subordinate dominions and are now in such a state as to make it best for the good of the whole that they should not only be continued in the enjoyment of subordinate legislation but be also represented in some proportion to their number and estates in the grand legislature of the nation; that this would firmly unite all parts of the British empire in the greatest peace and prosperity, and render it invulnerable and perpetual.[4]

In his subsequent *A Vindication of the British Colonies, against the Aspersions of the Halifax Gentleman, in His Letter to a Rhode Island*

Friend (Boston, 1765), Otis presses his main points ever further against Britain's perceived arbitrary rule over America. At the same time, he continues all the more to declare his loyalty, as a colonist, to the mother country. The primary issue for him is, once again, British taxation of the American colonies. Otis' focus is still on legislative sovereignty in the complicated vortex of America's relationship to Britain. Quotations from Locke, Blackstone, and Filmer are here typical but by no means isolated instances in the work.[5]

Although Otis made no explicit reference to Bodin in these two works, he, like many other American pamphleteers of his period, was drawing upon traditions of legislative sovereignty derived from Bodin's *Republic*[6] via European writers such as Montesquieu, Rousseau, Domat, Grotius, Locke, and many others also cited by Otis.[7] By the time of Otis' *Vindication* in 1765, Blackstone's *Commentaries on the Laws of England* (1765–1769) had begun to appear, while Rousseau's *Social Contract* (1762) had already appeared just prior to Otis' *Rights* in 1764. Those two key European sources were well endowed with Bodinian characteristics of legislative sovereignty and the legislative state.

Samuel Adams (1772)

Written in 1772 most probably by Samuel Adams, a man of greater daring in his revolutionary learnings than most others up to that point, the Boston pamphlet "A State of the Rights of the Colonists"[8] centers boldly and provocatively near the outset on issues of legislative sovereignty. Not content merely to react against British doctrines of Parliament's legislative sovereignty, through new American vantage points, Adams launches into a direct counteroffensive based on British sources themselves, which he uses to bolster the Americans' own cause in an elaborate *tour de force*. Aside from works by Blackstone and others, Adams makes use of a variety of documents in English constitutional history, as well as more recent Acts of Parliament, in order to prove America's case. For present purposes, the essential emphasis on legislative sovereignty can be briefly noted.

The first of the three main parts of Samuel Adams' "State of Rights" deals directly with those rights and is followed by a second part on their "infringements and violations." The first two sections of the first part deal in turn with "Natural Rights of the Colonists as Men" and more briefly with "The Rights of the Colonists as Christians." It is in the third section on "The Rights of the Colonists as Subjects" that Adams treats issues of sovereignty and state. He begins by defining a state or commonwealth. He then takes up the rights of American colonists as British subjects. (At the end of the preceding second section, Adams makes use of Blackstone.[9])

> A Common Wealth or state is a body politick or civil society of men, united together to promote their mutual safety and prosperity, by means of their union.
>
> The *absolute Rights* of Englishmen, and all freemen in or out of Civil society, are principally, *personal security, personal liberty* and *private property.*
>
> All Persons born in the British American Colonies are by the laws of God and nature, and by the Common law of England, *exclusive of all charters from the Crown*, well Entitled, and by Acts of the British Parliament are declared to be entitled to all the natural essential, inherent & inseperable Rights[,] Liberties and Privileges of Subjects born in Great Britain, or within the Realm. Among those Rights are the following, which no men or body of men, consistently with their own rights as men and citizens or members of society, can for themselves give up, or take away from others.[10]

In his continuation of the preceding passage, Samuel Adams further applies Blackstonian principles to the American situation. In particular, the legislative concepts of sovereignty and state, as strongly exprssed here within the framework of natural law and natural rights, are a clear echo of long-standing Bodinian tradition as adapted to new 18th-century outlooks.

> *First*, "The first fundamental law of an Commonwealths or States, is the establishing [of] the legislative power; as the first fundamental *natural* law also, which is to govern even the legislative power itself, is the preservation of the Society."
>
> *Secondly*, The Legislative has no right to absolute arbitrary power over the lives and fortunes of the people. Nor can mortals assume a prerogative, not only too high for men, but for Angels, and therefore reserved for the exercise of the *Deity* alone.
>
> "The Legislative cannot Justly *assume* to itself a power to rule by extempore arbitrary decrees; but it is bound to see that Justice is dispensed, and that the rights of the subjects be decided, by promulgated, standing and known laws, and authorized *independent Judges:*" that is[,] independent as far as possible of Prince or People. "*There shall be one rule of Justice for rich and poor; for the favorite in Court, and the Countryman at the Plough.*"

> *Thirdly*, The supreme power cannot Justly take from any man, any part of his property without his consent, in person or by his Representative.
>
> These are some of the first principles of natural law & Justice, and the great Barriers of all free states, and of the British Constitution in particular. It is utterly irreconcileable to these principles, and to many other fundamental maxims of the common law, common sense and reason, that a British house of commons, should have a right, at pleasure, to give and grant the property of the Colonists. That these Colonists are well entitled to all the essential rights, liberties and privileges of men and freemen, born in Britain, is manifest, not only from the Colony charter, in general, but acts of the British Parliament.[11]

Daniel Leonard (1773)

In a Boston newspaper essay in 1773 addressed "To All Nations of Men," Daniel Leonard declared self-government to be the innate natural right of all separate states. He invoked the authority of Hobbes (irrespective of Hobbes' absolutist English political philosophy) on the "natural law of states" in terms of the law of nations. Leonard inveighed against any seizures of a man's property without his consent. The British Parliament, he argued, had subjected Americans to its laws without giving them representation in it, while taking away the rights and laws of American self-government.[12]

A series of stirring statements by Leonard on sovereignty and state closely links them with issues of legislation in the cause of American resistance to and independence from Britain. To deny that American states are sovereign, free, and founded upon their own laws is a punishable violation of the laws of nature and nations.

> For if one supreme legislative body, in which the whole continent of America have not a single voice, have power to make laws which shall be binding upon us in all cases whatsoever, rights, liberties, legislative powers, under such absolute suspending, dispensing, establishing[,] annihilating power as this, are mere shadows, Jack o'lanterns serving only to mislead and engulph us.
>
> There can be no doubt but it is fit, and perfectly consistent with the principle of all laws human and divine, to resist . . . subverters of the government of free states. . . . Great-Britain at war with her colonies would be in the condition of a trunk

> deprived of its members. Besides the foundation of the dispute being an effort of her ministers to *diminish the sovereignty of so great a number of free self-governing states*, and erect an absolute despotism over them, must give umbrage to every other power in Europe, this being an open violation of the law of nations, and punishable.[13]

Leonard also quotes Locke on violators of a people's freedoms and on subverters of their civil government who thereby put themselves in a state of war with those people. Corruption in legislative and executive bodies, on England's part, has further thrust Americans back into the state of nature. Leonard echoes Locke, who had theorized about the conditions justifying the revocation of the original "contract" between government and the governed. The tide in America toward revolution was now quickly mounting. Locke's phraseology about the right to "life, liberty, and property" was becoming a battle cry associated not only with consent and representation but also with sovereignty and state in connection with the legislation of England versus that of the American colonies. Leonard's outspoken analogy of those who can be slain like wolves was ominous.[14]

Appeal by Congress (1774)

An appeal by the Continental Congress at Philadelphia in 1774 to "Friends and fellow-subjects in Quebec" was an (unsuccessful) effort to gain a united Canadian front allied with America against Britain. Signed by Henry Middleton, President, the appeal provides a window on common principles held by Americans in Congress at that time. The appeal challenges Canadians to recognize how subservient they themselves have become to the legislative acts and policies of the British parliament and crown; for they lack the right of independent states to make laws for their own affairs. The very foundations of English law, protecting individuals against violations of their domestic security and property, have been breached in Canada as well as in America. Taxation issues are likewise invoked therein for Canadians in reinforcement of American grievances against Britain.[15]

Addressing itself to French Canadians of Quebec, this Congressional appeal directs their attention to their great compatriot Montesquieu, whose *Spirit of the Laws* is quoted at length. The following excerpts, revolving around the legislative body under the separation of powers, point up the intended lesson for Canadians as well as for Americans in their quest to remove the oppressive legislative acts of the British parliament and crown. The making, executing, and interpreting of laws must all be separate functions, contrary to the British model, if arbitrary rule is to be averted.

> What would your countryman, the immortal Montesquieu, have said to such a plan of domination as has been framed for you? Hear his words, with an intenseness of thought suited to the importance of the subject.—"In a free state, every man, who is supposed a free agent, *ought to be concerned in his own government:* Therefore the *legislative* should reside in the whole body of the *people*, or their *representatives*. . . . When the power of *making* laws, and the power of *executing* them, are *united* in the same person, or in the same body of Magistrates, *there can be no liberty*, . . . lest the same *Monarch* or *Senate*, should *enact* tyrannical laws, to *execute* them in a tyrannical manner." . . .
>
> Apply these decisive maxims, sanctified by the authority of a name which all Europe reveres, to your own state.[16]

Samuel West (1776)

A learned and influential Congregational clergyman in Massachusetts, Samuel West was to become significant in the formation of that state's constitution and in the state's ratification of the U.S. Constitution. In 1776 he delivered a lengthy Election Day sermon before the state's Council and House of Representatives. In it West took pains to point out the rightness of both sides on general questions of whether to submit to authority or to resist it. He invoked Locke's views particularly on man's natural rights derived from an original state of nature. The crux for West is the need for individuals in the minority to obey, for the common good, the legislation enacted by the majority, except where tyrannical conditions compel them to disobey and to resist the laws and the civil authority.[17]

In that fateful year of 1776—with open American declaration of the need to end British dominance and to establish an independent American government—West posed the problem of American self-government. To form a sovereign "separate state" meant Americans "assuming to themselves the power of legislation." It is America's right by "necessity" and by laws of "nature" to establish its own legislature and body politic, independent of Britain. Americans must regulate their own affairs through their own systems of legislation, outside the jurisdiction of the British Empire and its Parliament.

The only difficulty remaining is to determine when a people may claim a right of forming themselves into a body politic, and assume the powers of legislation. . . . [A]ll men being by nature equal, all the members of a community have a natural right to assemble themselves together, and act and vote for such regulations as they judge are necessary for the good of the whole. But when a community is become very numerous, it is very difficult, and in many cases impossible, for all to meet together to regulate the affairs of the state; hence comes the necessity of appointing delegates to represent the people in a general assembly. And this ought to be looked upon as a sacred and inalienable right, . . . that no one be obliged to submit to any law except such as are made either by himself or by his representative.

If representation and legislation are inseparably connected, it follows, that when great numbers have emigrated into a foreign land . . . far removed from the parent state . . . , that then nature itself points out the necessity of their assuming to themselves the powers of legislation; and they have a right to consider themselves as a separate state from the other, and, as such, to form themselves into a body politic. . . .

As our duty of obedience to the magistrate is founded upon our obligation to promote the general good, . . . the same love and regard for the public will inspire us with as strong a zeal to oppose tyranny as we have to obey magistracy.[18]

Carter Braxton (1776)

When in 1776 Virginia was in the process of drawing up a new state constitution to replace the colonial charter, Carter Braxton urged great caution. He was against abandoning altogether the older forms of constitution and laws that had helped to make England great and Virginia prosperous. As one of the signers with Jefferson and several others of the Resolution in 1769 arguing for Virginia's sole right, exclusive of England's, to tax its citizens, Braxton's views in 1776 carried weight. They were, in fact, representative of those held by many of his fellow Virginians at that time. In his 1776 Address to the Virginia Convention, he pointed out the strengths as well as weaknesses of the English constitutional and legislative systems that had had such an impact on England itself and on its colony of Virginia. Indeed, despite their recent corruptions, those systems had, he felt, provided much of the foundations for English and Virginia liberties.

Following some apropos wider comments,[19] Braxton turns specifically to the English constitution and the English system of legislation. In this regard, he makes extended use of Montesquieu's *Spirit of the Laws* on the wisdom of the English form of government. He quotes Montesquieu's statement that English "liberty ... is established by their laws."

> Judge of the *principle* of this constitution by the great effects it has produced. Their code of laws [etc.] ... are all powerful arguments of the wisdom of that constitution and government. ... But though I admire their perfections, I must mourn their faults; and though I would guard against, and cast off their oppression, yet would I retain all their wise maxims, and derive advantage from their mistakes and misfortunes. The testimony of the learned Montesquieu in favour of the English constitution is very respectable. "There is (says he) one nation in the world that has for the direct end of its constitution political liberty." Again he says, "It is not my business to examine whether the English actually enjoy this liberty or not; sufficient it is for my purpose to observe, that it is established by their laws, and I inquire no further."
>
> This constitution, and these laws, have also been those of Virginia, and let it be remembered, that under them she flourished and was happy. The same principles which led the English to greatness animates us. To that principle our laws, our customs, and our manners, are adapted, and it would be perverting all order to oblige us, by a novel government, to give up our laws, our customs, and our manners.
>
> However necessary it may be to shake off the authority of arbitrary British dictators, we ought, nevertheless, to adopt and perfect that system, which England has suffered to be grossly abused, and the experience of ages has taught us to venerate. ... But, honourable as this spirit is, we daily see it calumniated by advocates for popular governments.[20]

Theophilus Parsons (1778)

A notable application of principles found in Rousseau's *Social Contract* occurred in a renowned lengthy report of 1778 called *The Essex Result*.[21] Attributed to Theophilus Parsons, a young lawyer of Essex County in Massachusetts, it is a critical summary of views on the state's proposed constitution (of 1780) expressed by Essex County delegates to the convention considering it.

Toward the beginning of *The Essex Result* appears a detailed portrayal of qualities that Rousseau deemed essential for a good republic. It should be governed by an exemplary constitution formed by an "enlightened" founder, who would be comparable to ancients like Solon, Lycurgus, and Numa or moderns like Calvin of Geneva. The related near-heroic qualities of historical mastery requisite for the constitution-maker evidently allude, in the *Result*, to John Adams—who wrote the Massachusetts constitution that was finally adopted and whose New England religious ideals shared much with Calvinism.

> To determine what form of government, in any given case, will produce the greatest possible happiness to the subject, is an arduous task, not to be compassed perhaps by any human powers. Some of the greatest geniuses and most learned philosophers of all ages . . . have nobly dared to attempt it; and their labours have crowned them with immortality. A Solon, a Lycurgus of Greece, a Numa of Rome are remembered with honor. . . . The man who alone undertakes to form a constitution, ought to be an unimpassioned being; one enlighttened mind; biassed neither by the lust of power, the allurements of pleasure, nor the glitter of wealth; . . . and influenced by the impartial principles of rectitude and justice. . . . He ought also to be master of the histories of all the empires and states which are now existing, and all those which have figured in antiquity, and thereby able to collect and blend their respective excellencies, and avoid those defects which experience hath pointed out. Rousseau, a learned foreigner, a citizen of Geneva, sensible of the importance and difficulty of the subject, thought it impossible for any body of people, to form a free and equal constitution for themselves, in which, every individual should have equal justice done him, and be permitted to enjoy a share of power in the state, equal to what should be enjoyed by any other. Each individual, said he, will struggle, not only to retain all his own natural rights, but to acquire a controul over those of others. Fraud, circumvention, and an union of interest of some classes of people, combined with an inattention to the rights of posterity, will prevail over the principles of equity, justice, and good policy. The Genevans, perhaps the most virtuous republicans now existing, thought like Rousseau. They called the celebrated Calvin to their assistance. He came, and, by their gratitude, have they embalmed his memory.[22]

Continuing on, *The Essex Result* adopts as a keynote of constitutional liberty the first part of the famed opening sentence in Rousseau's *Social Contract*—"Man was born free, and he is everywhere in chains." Other statements after the manner of Rousseau further embrace concepts of virtue, morality, and natural freedom, together with the sovereignty to which citizens of a state voluntarily surrender themselves.

> The freemen inhabiting the territory of the Massachusetts-Bay are now forming a political society for themselves. Perhaps their situation is more favorable in some respects, for erecting a free government, than any other people were ever favored with. . . . We live also in an age, when the principles of political liberty, and the foundation of governments, have been freely canvassed, and fairly settled. . . . Let us have a constitution founded, not upon party or prejudice—not one for to-day or to-morrow—but for posterity. Let *Esto perpetua* be it's [*sic*] motto. If it is founded in good policy; it will be founded in justice and honesty. . . . Let us now attend to those principles, upon which all republican governments, who boast any degree of political liberty, are founded, and which must enter into the spirit of a FREE republican constitution. . . .
>
> All men are born equally free. The rights they possess at their births are equal, and of the same kind. . . . Thus, if a man surrender all his alienable rights, without reserving a controul over the supreme power, or a right to resume in certain cases, the surrender is void, for he becomes a slave. . . .
>
> When men form themselves into society, and erect a body politic or State, they are to be considered as one moral whole, which is in possession of the supreme power of the State. This supreme power is composed of the power of each individual collected together, and VOLUNTARILY parted with by him. . . . The supreme power therefore can do nothing but what is for the good of the whole; and when it goes beyond this line, it is a power usurped.[23]

The *Essex Result* has much more to say on the qualities necessary for a good constitution-maker as well as for a good constitution in a well-ordered state that is also a republic of virtue. An essential point is the centrality of beneficial laws at the basis of the state; they should be well made and executed to the end of promoting the common welfare. Consent to the sovereign's laws is crucial to the political liberties of individuals in society.[24] When treating the topic of consent to the laws of the sovereign power in a state, *The Essex Result* refers to "the original social contract" in which men gave up their sovereign individual rights that they posssesed in a "state of nature." The report points up the legislative dimensions of sovereignty and state.

> The legislative power is employed in making laws, or prescribing such rules of action to every individual in the state, as the good of the whole requires. . . . Now the enacting of a law, is only the exercise of this controul over the natural alienable rights of each member of the state; and therefore this law must have the consent of the majority, or be invalid, as being contrary to the fundamental condition of the original social contract. In a state of nature, every man had the sovereign controul over his own person. . . . And in entering into political society, he surrendered this right of controul over his person and property, . . . to the supreme legislative power, to be exercised by the power, *when the good of the whole demanded it*. . . .
>
> The judicial power follows next after the legislative power; for it cannot act, until after laws are prescribed. Every wise legislator annexes a sanction to his laws . . .[25]

Ensuing discussion in the *Result* of the supreme legislative power in a state further echoes Rousseau's notions of the need for virtuous laws aimed toward the general will. There must be a just "distribution" of representation in the legislature. Once again, there are echoes of the kinds of statements in the *Social Contract* that are quoted by Garry Wills in his treatment of George Washington as Rousseau's lawgiver. (A copy of the work was possessed by Adams and others as well as by Washington.)[26]

Other Examples (1778, 1782, 1783)

Many other figures and writers of the Revolutionary Era dealt with legislative issues of sovereignty and state with particular reference to European authorities. Among them were an anonymous writer and William Whiting in their writings of 1778 during the process of forming a new constitution for the state of Massachusetts. In the wake of the Declaration of Independence in 1776, there was a drive there and elsewhere for juridical as well as political independence from British jurisdiction and authority. The anonymous writer makes extended use of Blackstone's *Commentaries*, preceded by allusions to the state of nature and the social contract in ways reminiscent of Locke and Rousseau.

> Mankind being in a state of nature equal, the larger Number (Caeteris paribus) is of more worth than the lesser, and the common happiness is to be preferred to that of Individuals. When Men form the social Compact, for the Majority to consent to be governed by the Minority is down right popery in politicks, as submission to him who claims Infallibility. . . . In all free Governments duly organized there is an essential Distinction to be observed between the fundamental Constitution, and Legislation. The fundamental Constitution is the Basis and ground work of Legislation, and ascertains the Rights[,] Franchises, Immunities and Liberties of the people. . . . Legislators stand on this foundation, and enact Laws agreeably to it. They cannot give Life to the Constitution: it is the approbation of the Majority of the people at large that gives Life and being to it. This is the foundation of Legislation that is agreeable to true Liberty, [and] it is above the whole Legislature of a free state, it being the foundation upon which the Legislature stands. . . . We could bring many Vouchers for this Doctrine[;] sufficient for our present purpose is the following Extracts from a Noted Writer. In answer to that assertion of another respectable writer that 'The bare Idea of a State without a power some where vested to alter every part of its Laws is the height of political Absurdity.' [Introduction to Blackstone's *Commentaries*, p. 97; note by the editor of *Acts and Resolves*] He remarks upon it, 'A position, which I apprehend, ought to be, in some Measure limited and explained. For if it refers to those particular Regulations, which take place in Consequence of Immemorial Custom, or are enacted by positive Statute, and at the same Time, are subordinate to the fundamental Constitution from which the Legislature itself derives its Authority; it is admitted to be within the power or Trust vested in the Legislature to alter these, pro, Re nata, as the good of Society may require. . . .'
>
> These reasonings tend abundantly to evince, that the whole Legislature of any state is insufficient to give Life to the fundamental Constitution of such state, it being the foundation on which they themselves stand and from which alone the Legislature derives its Authority—[27]

Whiting, too, alludes to the social contract and state of nature, with quotations from Locke.[28]

In an Election Day sermon of 1782, the Boston Congregational minister Zabdiel Adams, a cousin of John and Samuel Adams, set forth at length his principles of free government. "1st. The ruling power of every state or kingdom should be elected by the body of the people. . . . The *majority can* and *does always govern.*" More pointedly: "The *legislative* body is superior in power to the *executive.* They hold the reins of government in their hands; . . . in *this,* and all free countries, they constitute a numerous assembly . . ." Moreover, "if rulers would speak with power, they would speak in the language of justice. All their laws . . . must be agreeable to the eternal rules of right." According to Zabdiel Adams, a broadly educated people, imbued with virtue and morality, should be a goal and foundation of every rightly constituted state. "[I]t is religion and morality alone which can establish the principles upon which freedom can securely stand. The only foundation of a free constitution is pure virtue; and if this cannot be inspired into the people at large, . . . they will not obtain a lasting liberty; they will only exchange *tyrannies* and *tyrannies.* So fully was *Lycurgus* [!], the *Spartan* king, persuaded of this truth that he took particular care of the youth, and had them educated in a manner suited to the genius of their government."[29]

Finally, in an anonymous essay of 1783, addressed to the people of South Carolina in connection with the formation of its constitution, the author frequently cites and quotes a variety of writers such as Beccaria, Montesquieu, Blackstone, Puffendorf, Virgil, and Cicero. Included in this "Rudiments of Law and Government Deduced from the Law of Nature" are sections entitled "Of Government," "On the Distribution of Authority," and "Of Laws." Under "Of Government" is a provocative partial use of the four causes (final, efficient, formal, and material), in conjunction with Cato's *Letters.* Certain aspects of the laws of government are raised in "On the Distribution of Authority," with materials relating to Blackstone, Montesquieu, Cato, Cicero, and others. "Of Laws" contains some interesting material pertaining to works by Beccaria, Puffendorf, and Cicero (*De inventione*), along with inclusion of the classical maxims on the *salus populi* as the *suprema lex.*[30]

2. EARLY CONSTITUTIONAL ERA

Noah Webster—and Corasius? (1787, 1788)

In an essay dated October 1787, Philadelphia, shortly after the Constitutional Convention ended there, Noah Webster began by extolling the accomplishments of that august body. He did so in near-mythic terms of the great legendary lawgivers and state founders of antiquity and later times, no doubt influenced by Adams' *Defence* Preface.

> Legislators have ever been deemed the greatest benefactors of mankind—respected when living, and often deified after their death. Hence the fame of Fohi and Confucius—of Moses, Solon and Lycurgus—of Romulus and Numa—of Alfred, Peter the Great, and Mango Capac; whose names will be celebrated through all ages, for framing and improving constitutions of government, which introduced order into society and secured the benefits of law to millions of the human race.
>
> This western world now beholds an era important beyond conception, and which posterity will number with the age of Czar of Muscovy, and with the promulgation of the Jewish laws at Mount Sinai. The names of those men who have digested a system of constitutions for the American empire [!], will . . . be . . . celebrated by posterity with the honors which less enlightened nations have paid to the fabled demi-gods of antiquity.
>
> But the origin of the AMERICAN REPUBLIC is distinguished by peculiar circumstances. Other nations . . . have generally been the result of a single man's observations; or the offspring of particular interests. In the formation of our constitution, the wisdom of all ages is collected—the legislators of antiquity are consulted—as well as the opinions and interests of the millions, who are concerned. In short, it is an *empire* [!] *of reason.*[31]

As an advocate of the new federal constitution, which still had to be ratified, Webster turned his attention first to the legislative power.

> In attending to the proposed Federal Constitution, the first thing that presents itself to our consideration, is the division of the legislative into two branches. This artticle has so many advocates in America, that it needs not any vindication.—But it has its opposers, among whom are some respectable characters, especially in Pennsylvania; for which reason, I will state some of the arguments and facts which incline me to favor the proposed division.[32]

After extensive references to Roman and British history and government, Webster returned near the end of his essay to the heroic greatness of American "*fathers* and *saviors* of their country," led by Franklin, Washington, and others. The Constitution they have devised is the product of their special collective wisdom, experience, information, and "acquaintance with ancient and modern governments." Hence it should not be inadvisedly second-guessed by detractors. If defects are later found or changing circumstances warrant constitutional changes, he assures that amendments can be made. Webster also goes on to assure that the state legislatures will retain sovereignty in all areas not assigned to Congress by the new Constitution.[33]

In a New York magazine article in early 1788, Noah Webster, a best-selling lexicographer and author, made extensive use of Jefferson's discussions of the word "constitution" in relation to "statute," "law," "ordinance" and other such terms. As Webster recognized, Jefferson had made use there of the classic older *Lexicon Iuridicum* by Johannes Calvinus (as also cited above, page 100). It will be remembered from our earlier studies that this *Lexicon* had cited Corasius in important ways on a variety of matters, including those at hand. It will also be recalled that the emphatic new attention Corasius gave to the law-making power included much analysis of these very terms, even along some terminocological lines similar to those followed by Jefferson and Webster. There is not the scope or space here to investigate whether Webster or Jefferson actually took note of Corasius' many contributions to legal terms and concepts as cited in that older *Lexicon Iuridicum* (much less to look for parallels with Corasius' lengthy focus in his *Art of Law* (I, 16) on early legendary lawgivers, a topic just cited in the case of Webster). Yet the use and mix of *Lexicon* texts is provocative.

> Mr. Jefferson, in answer to those who maintain that the form of government in Virginia is unalterable, because it is called a *constitution*, which, ex vi termini, means an act above the power of the ordinary Legislature, asserts that *constitution, statute, law* and *ordinance* are synonymous terms and convertible, as they are used by writers on government; Constitutio dicitur jus quod a principe conditur, Constitutum, quod ab imperatoribus rescriptum statutumve est. Statutum, idem quod lex (Calvini Lexicon Juridicum). Here the words *constitution, statute,* and *law* are defined by each other—They were used as convertible terms by all former writers whether Roman or British. . . . From hence he concludes that no inference can be drawn from the meaning of the word, that a *constitution* has a higher authority than a law or statute. This conclusion of Mr. Jefferson is just.
>
> He quotes Lord Coke also to prove that any Parliament can abridge, suspend or qualify the acts of a preceding Parliament. It is a maxim in their laws, that "Leges posteriores priores contrarias abrogant." After having fully proved that *constitution, statute, law* and *ordinance* are words of similar import, and that the constitution of Virginia is at any time alterable by the ordi-

> nary Legislature, he proceeds to prove the danger to which the rights of the people are exposed for want of an *unalterable form of government*. . . .
>
> It is a dictate of natural law that a *majority should govern*. . . .[34]

John Stevens (1787, 1788)

A different kind of support for the proposed U.S. Constitution in the struggle for ratification was voiced by John Stevens. In two articles in a New York news publication in late 1787 and early 1788, Stevens argued against critics of the proposed new Constitution who, he believed, based their objections on spurious interpretations of European writers such as Montesquieu and on erroneous positions found in those European writers. Included in Stevens' diatribes against the Constitution's critics and their mistaken reliance on European sources was his refutation of the famed Spartan model established by Lycurgus.

Instead of relying on European sources and models, Stevens urged recognition of the Convention's collective wisdom and experience in framing the new Constitution. Earlier writers like Plato, More, and Harrington were, he felt, too theoretical to be accurate authorities for the tasks at hand. Even Montesquieu was open to doubt, being too removed from the current American situation. In his call to meet current American needs and realities rather than to rely on remote European theory, which was partly mistaken in itself or in its applications, Stevens by no means discounted all European wisdom. He, too, made use of the positions of Montesquieu, Locke, pand others when they served to good advantage. In short, Stevens was familiar with the European intellectual heritage, citing it freely, while at the same time arguing for the test of experience and reason over abstraction and learning.

Appearing in Stevens' accounts are topics in legislation and sovereignty from perspectives of past theory as well as of current events. In particular, he fulminates against certain opponents of the proposed U.S. Constitution who fear that the sovereignties and legislatures of the states will be annihilated under the new federal government. In its place, they favor a different confederate form giving to the states more autonomy and independence. Faulting Montesquieu himself as well as his interpreters concerning the desirability of direct democracy in small states, Stevens nevertheless adapts Montesquieu's ideas on legislative bodies (checked and balanced by the executive and judicial branches) in contexts of British constitutional government, which Montesquieu had largely praised. After all, Montesquieu was widely considered then to be the "father" of the doctrine on separation of powers embodied in the U.S. Constitution, supported by Stevens. In his down-to-earth approach, Stevens departed from many of his compatriots by not viewing the founders at the Convention as Olympian lawgivers comparable to the legendary classical exemplars.[35]

Samuel Adams (1787)

Former firebrand of the Revolution, Samuel Adams was for a time among the ranks of the Antifederalist opponents of the proposed U.S. Constitution (along with Patrick Henry, George Clinton, Richard Henry Lee, George Mason, and other notables). Writing from Boston in late 1787 to Richard Henry Lee, of the prominent Lee family in Virginia, Adams framed his case against the new Constitution almost entirely in terms of sovereignty and state founded upon legislation. His dire predictions of likely future rebellions by separate states in the South and elsewhere against an omnipotent national legislative sovereignty would take on added interest from the perspective of the Civil War and its struggles over legislative sovereignty.

> [T]he new Constitution as it is already called, . . . [would institute] a National Government, instead of a federal Union of Sovereign States. I am not able to conceive why the Wisdom of the Convention led them to give the Preferencee to the former before the latter. If the several States in the Union are to become one entire Nation, under one Legislature, the Powers of which shall extend to every Subject of Legislation, and its Laws be supreme & controul the whole, the Idea of Sovereignty in these States must be lost. Indeed I think, upon such a Supposition, those Sovereignties ought to be eradicated from the Mind; for they would be Imperia in Imperio justly deemed a Solecism in Politicks, & they would be highly dangerous, and destructive of the Peace Union and Safety of the Nation. And can this National Legislature be competent to make Laws for the free internal Government of one People . . . [with] "Habits & particular Interests" . . . so different. Is it to be expected that General Laws can be adapted to the Feelings of the more Eastern & the more Southern Parts of so extensive a Nation? . . . Hence then may we not look for frequent Insurrections, which will require standing Armies to suppress them . . .[36]

While abjuring the new Constitution in this fashion, so different from its support by his cousin John Adams, Samuel Adams fell back on familiar grounds when advocating the sovereign rights of the separate states and their own legislatures. Here he struck a more positive tone.[37]

James Wilson (1787)

In an opening address of late 1787 to the Pennsylvania Ratifying Convention, James Wilson, the only member there who had attended the Federal Convention, strongly supported the proposed U.S. Constitution. He recited the difficulties of the existing confederation and the remedies intended by the framers for resolving them. An "efficient national government" was the "end" to which the framers aimed. The "means . . . to . . . that end" became the Constitution. The acts of the existing Congress and the actions of the states show the need for adopting the proposed stronger system of government.[38]

The question of sovereignty looms large in Wilson's analysis of the current crisis and its cure. His use of Blackstone's *Commentaries* on issues of legislative sovereignty illustrates how different sides in such debates could use that famed work, pro and con, to suit the occasion. Here Wilson could well dispute Blackstone's view of the British parliament's supremacy, particularly in relation to America, as being contrary to rightful popular sovereignty. In other ways, however, Wilson could as easily approve of Blackstone's view of supreme power as being legislative. Historical relationships between the English parliament and King Henry VIII in Wilson's discussions accentuate the legislative dimensions of sovereignty.

> In all governments, whatever is their form, however they may be constituted, there must be a power established, from which there is no appeal—and which is therefore called absolute, supreme, and uncontroulable. The only question is, where that power is lodged—a question that will receive different answers from the different writers on the subject. Sir William Blackstone says, it resides in the omnipotence of the British Parliament, or in other words, corresponding with the practice of that country, it is whatever the British Parliament pleases to do: So that when that body was so base and treacherous to the rights of the people as to transfer the legislative authority to Henry the eighth, his exercising that authority by proclamations and edicts, could not strictly speaking be termed unconstitutional, for under the act of Parliament his will was made the law, and therefore, his will became in that respect the

constitution itself. But were we to ask some politicians who have taken a faint and inaccurate view of our establishments, where does this supreme power reside in the United States? They would probably answer, in their Constitutions. This, however, tho' a step nearer to the fact, is not a just opinion; for, in truth, it remains and flourishes with the people . . .[39]

3. THE LATER POST-CONVENTION ERA

Timothy Ford (1794)

In the period following the adoption of the U.S. Constitution and Bill of Rights, there continued to appear a wide diversity of American uses of European sources on legislative concepts of sovereignty and state. An interesting case in point arose in a series of essays (1794) by Timothy Ford in a Charleston, South Carolina, news publication. The question was whether to alter the state constitution in order to reapportion representation in the state legislature. Ford spoke out against the effort to give a larger representation to the growing majority of non-wealthy citizens at the expense of established propertied people in certain regions of the state. The latter were increasingly no longer in the majority of voters but still held preponderant representation in the state legislature. Ford's arguments for maintaining the status quo and preserving their self-determination in and through that body were characteristic of the Southern cause more generally prior to the Civil War. His uses of the ideas of Locke and Rousseau illustrate the continuing usefulness of those theorists under changed circumstances following the Revolutionary and Constitutional Eras.

Ford takes aim at the theories of Locke about the original state of nature and the natural rights derived therefrom after the social contract is formed. Ford considers such theories supporting the equality of citizens in society to be too abstract and mistaken. In particular, Ford cites the Lockean phrase "life, liberty, and property" upon which many writers have based their ideas of natural rights and natural equality. All men may be equally entitled to life and liberty, but property, says Ford, is often naturally unequal due to the success and industry manifested by some, which in turn benefit the whole body politic.[40]

Rousseau provides Ford with some viewpoints favoring the rights of each people in a given society to frame their own constitution and laws, depending on their own unique circumstances. Ford might well criticize Rousseau, in addition to Locke, for fanciful theories about an original but non-existent state of nature, out of which a social contract is supposedly formed that largely preserves those rights. However, Ford sees in Rousseau a recognition of each people's right to establish their own indigeneous institutions suited to the circumstances and vicissitudes of their society, while they also abide by the eternal laws of nature. The Rousseau connection here, revolving around issues of social contract, involves some earlier precedents of a different kind, found in writings by Bodin and Montesquieu, for Rousseau's outlook. Bodin has been rightly called a forerunner of Montesquieu on the adaptability of governments and states to changing times, diversities of climate, and differing social circumstances.[41]

On another level, Ford makes use of a concept of social contract, one not based on an imaginary preexistent state of nature, in order to advance his case. One group in society does not have the right to force another to enter into a condition to which it does not agree. This point applies to the manner in which the laws are made. To Ford, it is contrary to a right social contract, formed between equal parties already in society, that one group should later endeavor to force its laws upon another group after the manner of a Caesar. Even if the principle of majority rule, which Ford finds fallible and capable of perversion, it is no justification for lawgiving of the kind being proposed. Here Ford seems to depart from both Rousseau and Locke. He goes so far as to declare that, however valid majority rule is in general, it is not requisite and has no power to give validity to laws, which depend rather on a case by case adaptation to changing circumstances in a given society. Consequently, the proposed constitutional changes, designed to give certain groups and regions in South Carolina predominance in the state legislature, are without foundations.[42]

James Kent (1794)

Among the most formative and influential legal minds of the new American Republic was James Kent—a Columbia law professor, a Federalist opponent of Jeffersonian Republicanism who served in the New York state legislature, and a chief judge in two of New York's highest courts. Kent remains perhaps best known to legal historians for his important early contributions to the doctrine of judicial review. Although greatly influenced by Blackstone's *Commentaries*, Kent did not subscribe to the unbounded sovereignty of the national legislature propounded by Blackstone for England. Kent sought rather to give the judicial branch in America a new greater power to check the legislature, comparable to that exercised by the chief executive's veto. In this way, Kent saw a separation of powers a la Montesquieu as inadequate in itself to operate as a system of checks and balances. Since Congress was inherently the strongest of the three powers, and the Supreme Court the weakest, Kent sought to place the latter on an equal footing with the other two highest federal bodies.

In his early years as law professor, Kent wrote *An Introductory Lecture to a Course of Law Lectures* (1794). In it, outlining these ideas, he gave pertinent attention to the national legislative body and its sovereign power. Included in his presentation are such comments as the following: "In England, where the Constitution has separated . . . the Departments of Government . . . , the Parliament is still considered as transcendently absolute. . . . [I]t is generally laid down . . . that no Act of Parliament can be questioned or disputed. But in this country we have found it expedient to establish certain rights . . . paramount to the power of the ordinary Legislature. . . . [T]he Acts of the Legislative body, [that are] contrary to the . . . Constitution, ought to be absolutely null and void." Citing Montesquieu, Kent goes on to pronounce the mere separation of powers, "on paper," to be an "insufficient" check on the legislative body by the executive and judicial branches. Indeed: "The power of the Judicial [body], of determining the constitutionality of Laws, is necessary to preserve the equilibrium of the government, and prevent usurpations of one part upon another, and of all the parts of government, the Legislative body is by far the most imperious and powerful."[43]

To check the overarching legislative sovereignty of Congress through judicial review, however, would require more time and struggle. Even then, the initial controlling context of Congress' enactment of legislation, which the executive and judiciary could strike down through veto and review respectively, involved a kind of divided legislative sovereignty in which all three branches could theoretically and in reality share.

Kent's main purpose in this *Lecture* is to outline the essential subjects in a good legal education. It should foster in students the broadest possible capacities of intellect, wisdom, and character necessary for them to become knowledgeable and effective judges as well as lawyers and leaders. Classical writers of Greece and Rome, including Quintilian and Cicero, are especially valuable for a broad legal education, which must be grounded in the liberal arts. An enlightened education of the kind Kent outlines can fortify future judges, as guardians of the Constitution, "against the [harmful] factions and encroachments of the Legislative Body."[44]

Of great interest is Kent's extended praise of the body of Roman civil law handed down by Justinian. Its inclusion of writings by Ulpian and others reflects "an enlightened Age of Roman Jurisprudence." Knowledge of "the general Principles of Universal Law," even "the final end of government," when combined with subjects like moral philosophy, "strengthen[s] the powers of the human mind."[45]

Anonymous (1801)

An anonymous *Discussion Upon the Constitutional Freedom of the Press*, published in Boston in 1801, took a non-partisan position on the (then much debated) issue of the extents to which the freedom of the press could be taken under the first article of the Bill of Rights (or first amendment to the Constitution). According to that article: "Congress shall make no law . . . abridging the freedom of speech, or of the press . . ." The growing viciousness of public speech as reflected in the press was most apparent in the bitter disputes between the Jeffersonians then in power and the Federalists recently ousted. The whole question of the boundaries between free speech and slander or libel was being much debated. This anonymous author took a moderate middle path. Freedom of press and speech should be protected under the first amendment, but within the bounds of reasonableness and responsibility, beyond which excesses ought not be protected by the Constitution.

An antithesis between sublimity and mundaneness in the founding of states—throughout history and up to recent times—opens the anonymous author's *Discussion Upon Freedom of the Press*. The heroic or Olympian themes associated with the accomplishments of the U.S. Constitution's framers were being superceded in some minds by more down-to-earth assessments. Comparisons with legendary ancient lawgivers and state founders who were inspired by the gods, or even with more recent divinely connected monarchs, were losing their appeal for those who sought more levelheaded recourse to the Constitution itself for practical solutions to questions of the day. Nonetheless, the heroic ideal, by its very minimization here, was not yet a forgotten force in political discourse. It had shifted to other grounds through its employment by the Constitution's interpreters. Here Adams' *Defence* Preface seems influential concerning quasi-religious elements of ancient heroic lawgivers.

> The ancient nations were well acquainted with all the feelings of the human heart. Homer carried his hero, under the contested protection of a multitude of gods, . . . to lay . . . the foundation of the Grecian empire. The Greeks brought their civil institutions from Egypt, where, as it was then believed, the gods had promulgated laws for mankind. This was done, that the laws should be respected by the people. The Romans founded an empire, by the man who had been nursed by a wolf; and their poet, in imitation of Homer, to render their origin

> respectable, and their religious and civil institutions sacred, detailed the perils, and wars; and the interposition of the gods. . . .
>
> Before the christian religion was respected in Europe, fabulous deities were called in, to take a part in the inauguration of kings; and the laws were framed by the Druids, who lived sequestered from the world, and were considered as having an intercourse with heaven. As soon as christianity was established, the divine right of kings was proclaimed, as from heaven; and miraculous signs, and terrible wonders, were observed at the birth of princes, and the coronation of monarchs.
>
> The English nation have had so many changes in the dynasty of their throne, that they were compelled, by a sense of decency, to abandon the divine right of earthly sovereigns, and the peculiar efficacy of the royal blood. A sacred regard to a constitution, much talked of, no where on paper, and highly respected, because it has never been seen, forms the main bond of that vigorous and efficient government.
>
> But where shall we . . . find a substitute equal to the exigency of our situation? . . . [W]hat shall hold us together as a nation? Our constitution of national government is in our own hands, like the school books; we know the men who formed it. They have not, like Solon, banished themselves from the country, nor like the Druids, sequestered themselves from the world. They remain among us, as men of like passions, subjected to the same errors, follies and weakness, as other men. So far are they from boasting of an inspiration in this work, that neither two of them can agree to understand the instrument in the same sense.[46]

In the continuation of this text, further such points are raised in connection with the U.S. Constitution.[47]

James Wilson (–1804)

It is fitting to close with the potent extended statements concerning legislative sovereignty in James Wilson's long dissertation on municipal law and Blackstone. This piece was included in Wilson's influential collected works published posthumously in 1804, having originally appeared some ten years earlier. In this form, his works now carried extra weight owing to his former stature as influential delegate to the Federal Convention, as first law professor at what became the

University of Pennsylvania, and as associate justice of the U.S. Supreme Court.

Wilson concentrated here on legislative sovereignty in Blackstone's *Commentaries*. Wilson goes on to contest Blackstone, more so than in his 1787 address, by assigning ultimate sovereignty to the people through government by consent. Yet his masterful preliminary presentation of legislative sovereignty in Blackstone's work—which exerted a considerable influence on the founders at Philadelphia—serves to illustrate how powerful that doctrine still remained and how well it could still be adapted to the new constitutional realities in America. Wilson first presents Blackstone's doctrines and definitions as follows (with italics added to Blackstone's title and asterisks added in lieu of Wilson's references to it):

> I now proceed to the consideration of municipal law—that rule, by which a state or nation is governed. It is thus defined by the learned Author of the *Commentaries on the Laws of England*. "A rule of civil conduct, prescribed by the *supreme power* of the state, commanding what is right and prohibiting what is wrong."* In my observations upon Sir William Blackstone's definition of law in general, I did him the justice to mention, that he was not the first, and that he has not been the last, who has defined law upon the same principles, or upon principles similar, and equally dangerous. Here it is my duty to mention, and, in one respect, I am happy in mentioning, that he was the first, though, I must add, he has not been the last, who has defined municipal law, as applied to the law of England, upon principles, to which I must beg leave to assign the epithets, dangerous and unsound. It is of high import to the liberties of the United States, that the seeds of despotism be not permitted to lurk at the roots of our municipal law. . . . Let us, therefore, examine, fully and minutely, the extent, the grounds, the derivation, and the consequences of the abovementioned definition.
>
> "Legislature," we are told, "is the greatest act of superiority, that can be exercised by one being over another. Wherefore it is requisite to the very essence of a law, that it be made by the supreme power. Sovereignty and legislature are, indeed, convertible terms; one cannot subsist without the other."* "There must be in every government, however it began, or by whatsoever right it subsists, a supreme, irresistible, absolute, uncontrolled authority, in which the *jura summi imperii*, or the rights of sovereignty reside." "By sovereign power is meant the

> making of laws; for wherever that power resides, all others must conform to and be directed by it, whatever appearance the outward form and administration of the government may put on. For it is at any time in the option of the legislature to alter that form and administration, by a new edict or rule, and to put the execution of the laws into whatever hands it pleases: and all the other powers of the state must obey the legislative power in the execution of their several functions, or else the constitution is at an end." "In the British parliament, is lodged the sovereignty of the British constitution."* "The power of making laws constitutes the supreme authority."* "In the British parliament," therefore, which is the legislative power, "the supreme and absolute authority of the state is vested."* "This is the place, where that absolute despotick power, which must, in all governments, reside somewhere, is intrusted by the constitution of these kingdoms." "Its power and jurisdiction is so transcendent and absolute, that it cannot be confined, either for causes or persons, within any bounds."* . . . "What the parliament doth, no authority upon earth can undo."* "So long as the English constitution lasts, we may venture to affirm, that the power of parliament is absolute and without control."*[48]

Wilson then takes up his own contrary ideas:

> It is obvious, that though this definition of municipal law, and this account of legislative authority be applied particularly to the law of England and the legislature of Great Britain; yet they are, in their terms and in their meaning, extended to every other state or nation whatever. . . . Indeed, the opinion of Mr. Locke and other writers, "that there remains still inherent in the people a supreme power to remove and alter the legislature," is considered to be so merely theoretical, that "we cannot adopt it nor argue from it, under any dispensation of government at present actually existing."*
>
> The doctrines contained in the foregoing quotations from the *Commentaries on the laws of England*, may be comprised under the two general propositions, which follow. 1. That in every state, there is and must be a supreme, irresistible, absolute, uncontrolled authority, in which the rights of sovereignty reside. 2. That this authority, and these rights of sovereignty must reside in the legislature; because "sovereignty and legislature are convertible terms," and because "it is requisite to the very essence of a law, that it be made by the supreme

> power." In the first general proposition, I have the pleasure of agreeing entirely with Sir William Blackstone. Its truth rests on this broad and fundamental principle—that, by the constitutions of nature, men and nations are equal and free. In the second general proposition, I am under the necessity of differing altogether from the learned Author of the *Commentaries*. . . . So far as I have examined the English law books and authorities, . . . this definition stands entirely unsupported in point of authority. I may, however, be mistaken—I pretend not to have read, far less to remember, every thing in the law. . . .
>
> The introduction of the principle of superiority into . . . the definition of municipal law, can be traced to the same source. "Human laws," says he [Puffendorf], "are nothing else, but the decrees of the supreme power, concerning matters to be observed by the subjects." The celebrated Heineccius, in his system of Universal Law, gives a definition much to the same purpose—"Civil laws," says he, "are the commands of the supreme power in a state." Why was this principle transplanted into the law of England?
>
> It deserves to be further remarked, that, for all the strong sentiments and expressions concerning the necessary connexion, and indeed the convertibility of the sovereign and the legislative powers, no authority is produced from the English law. . . . I excepted one instance. It is this—"The power and jurisdiction of parliament is so transcendent and absolute, that it cannot be confined, either for causes or persons, within any bound."* For this, the authority of my Lord Coke in his fourth Institute is quoted. . . . But can it be inferred from this authority, that the sovereign power of Great Britain is vested in her parliament? Can it be inferred from the constitution of Pennsylvania, that her sovereign power is vested in her general assembly? I think . . . Blackstone stands unsupported by authority.[49]

Wilson in his *Municipal Law* then turns to an analysis of the ways in which society was originally formed by a contract. Through it, as in 1688, the consent of the governed becomes the foundation for sovereignty in the nation or state. Here Wilson makes positive references to Blackstone and Hale.[50]

Even according to Wilson's own arguments, however, popular sovereignty and legislative sovereignty, we may add, are not mutually exclusive, contrary to some of his beliefs. After all, the location of legislative sovereignty in the English parliament depends, as Blackstone is here shown to believe, on the composite structure of Commons, Lords, and

Crown; whereas in America there is the interconnection (also cited further on by Wilson) between Congress, President, and Supreme Court in the legislative process. The people may indeed be the ultimate sovereign in America (as implied in the Constitution's preamble on "We the people"). Yet the principle of popular legislative sovereignty, given expression in the people's governmental branches at the federal level, has been articulated by a great many constitutional authorities during and after Wilson's era. Granted, the English and American systems outlined by Wilson diverge in crucial ways. There is obvious greater separation between the legislative, executive, and judicial powers in America than in England. The executive and judicial bodies in America are not so closely connected with the lawmaking body of Congress as their counterparts in England are with Parliament. Nevertheless, these differences did not prevent numerous other American writers of the founding era from applying the ideas of legislative sovereignty held by Blackstone, Locke, and others to American systems. They did so without compromising either the end of British parliamentary control over America or the American separation of powers inspired by Montesquieu (who himself held ideas of an overarching legislative sovereignty).

Wilson's continuing treatment of the nature of the contract based on common agreement between people in society[51] is designed to refute Blackstone on the source of ultimate authority behind laws. But Wilson does not truly refute Blackstone on sovereignty as legislative, even according to Wilson's own case for popular sovereignty.

Chapter VII

Congress, Capitol, and Capital

The prominent place of legislative sovereignty in the political-legal thought of the American founders, as shown above with particular regard to Congress as the lawmaking body, requires a closer look at that institution from several further vantage points. The following discussions are necessarily selective yet serve to round out the present book.

1. SYMBOLS OF SOVEREIGNTY IN PUBLIC ARCHITECTURE AND URBAN DESIGN

Throughout Western history, there have been many diverse cases where public architecture and urban design have served as statements on supreme power and state politics. In the ancient democratic city-state of Athens under Pericles, the monumental placement of the Parthenon atop the acropolis became a symbol of dominance and empire for the rest of Greece. The Rome of the Caesars projected a more majestic grandeur of imperial authority and far-flung empire. In a different way, the great cathedral towns of the European Middle Ages exhibited varying visual signs of papal and royal prestige. The great urban centers of the Renaissance in Italy and Northern Europe often displayed grandiose public symbols of great wealth, prestige, and power, as in Medici Florence and Tudor London. Later on, the Versailles palace of Louis XIV became not only a symbol of royal, absolute, divine-right monarchy, with palace wings outstretched like arms as if to embrace the French nation in expression of Louis' "I am the state"; it was also an actual tool of statecraft for drawing the fractious nobles to Louis' court for dependence on his patronage. The Paris of Napoleon Bonaparte and later of Napoleon III presented further cases in point. In other ways, one could cite the complex interconnected governmental rooms of the Doge's Palace in Venice as suggestive of the intricate intermixtures of legislative, executive, and judicial authorities in the later Middle Ages and their early modern carry-overs. The design of the British Parliament building is similarly suggestive but with legislative sovereignty more clearly dominant and overarching. Many other examples will come to mind.

The powerful design of the American Capitol building as it stands today offers a unique unitary symbol of legislative sovereignty. The monumental Capitol architecture and its imposing placement on the hill overlooking the Capital city seem so obvious a symbol of the sovereignty of Congress and its laws as to occasion surprise that historians and political scientists have not yet duly grasped the point. To pursue this point will require bringing together in a new mix a variety of widely scattered passages from writings of the founding era.

Jefferson in particular, whose ideas on legislative sovereignty have already above been well documented, had significant early influence as Washington's Secretary of State on the placement of Congress on Capitol Hill in keeping with his own hilltop location of Monticello, inspired by classical patterns. Indeed, the agreement to place the new Capital city in D.C. had involved a concession to Jefferson in return for Hamilton gaining approval as Secretary of the Treasury for a new National Bank. Jefferson's influence did not end there.

The L'Enfant (and Jefferson) Plan, to 1792

When in 1784 Pierre-Charles L'Enfant (1754–1825), the French engineer in America, proposed to Congress the creation of a permanent army corps of engineers to be used in the construction of a new Capital city, his grand vision centered explicitly on concepts of (republican) empire and sovereignty. For the new seat of government, majestic designs and prolonged labor were needed, he believed, in order to "give an idea of the greatness of the empire as well as . . . [to] engrave in every mind the sense of respect that is due to a place which is the seat of a *supreme sovereignty* [!]" (italics added). Among the many figures who agreed with L'Enfant on that point were George Washington and John Witherspoon. The latter urged the erection of magnificent buildings that would convey a sense of the dignity and majesty of (republican) empire for the ages.[1]

In a letter to Washington in 1789, L'Enfant further pressed his ambitious ideas for a new Capital city, which was approved by Act of Congress in 1790. It would become a fitting new centerpiece and showpiece for so great a new nation and empire.

> The late determination of Congress to lay the foundation of a Federal City which is to become the Capital of this vast Empire, offers so great an occasion for acquiring reputation . . . that Your Excellency will not be surprised that my ambition and the desire I have of becoming a useful citizen should lead me to wish to share in the undertaking.
>
> No nation had ever before the opportunity offered them of deliberately deciding on the spot where their Capital City should be fixed, or of combining every necessary consideration in the choice of situation, and although the means now within the power of the Country are not such as to pursue the design to any great extent, it will be obvious that the plan should be drawn on such a scale as to leave room for that aggrandizement and embellishment which the increase of the wealth of the nation will permit it to pursue at any period however remote . . .[2]

Many similar statements were made, by L'Enfant and others connected with the project to construct the new federal city and its public buildings, during the period of his active involvement with it in 1791–1792. In April of 1791, a report given by L'Enfant to Washington while in Georgetown referred to a design of city "street[s] laid out on a dimension proportioned to the greatness which . . . the Capital of a powerful Empire [!] ought to manifest . . . [according to] a grand plan of the whole city . . . with the various grounds . . . [and] the country all around."[3] L'Enfant's first "plan" or "map" of the new city and its government buildings was shown by him to Washington at Mount Vernon in June of 1791. In his accompanying report, L'Enfant described the "grand and majestic" views afforded by the "Congress House" on the highest hill and by the "Presidential palace" with its nearby "grand Departments of State." When viewed in relation to "the Tiber," to other public buildings, and to the scenic vistas of "the whole city," with its public walks and spaces, the principal government buildings seem designed in L'Enfant's plan to project the stately image of American "Empire" and "sovereignty" in the context of a new Rome. During the

Republic, of course, Rome had already possessed an empire, prior to the Empire of the Caesars. L'Enfant declared more fully:

> With respect to the point upon which it is expedient first to begin the main establishment, ... embracing in one view the whole extent from the Eastern branch to Georgetown, and from the banks of the Potomac to the mountains, ... in considering ... the intended city, it will appear that to promote a rapid settlement throughout, across the Tiber above tide water is the most eligible one ....
>
> The other position of a different nature offers a local equality, answerable for a Presidential palace, better calculated for a commodious house and which may be rendered majestic [!] and agreeable. This position very justly attracted your attention when first viewing the ground which is upon the west side and near the mouth of the Tiber.
>
> The spot I assigned I chose ... to lessen the distance to the Federal House, ... to obtain a more extensive view down the Potomac, [and] ... to connect with more harmony the public walks and avenue of the Congress House with the garden park and other improvements round the palace, which, standing upon this high ridge, ... would overlook the vast esplanade ... [and] be even contiguous to Congress.
>
> To make however the distance less to other officers[,] I placed the three grand Departments of State contiguous to the principal palace; and on the way leading to the Congressional house, the gardens of the one together with the park and other improvements ... are connected with the public walk and avenue to the Congress house in a manner as must form a whole as grand as it will be agreeable and convenient to the whole city ... and all along side of which may be placed play houses, rooms of assembly, academies and all such sort of places as may be attractive to the learned and afford diversion to the idle.... I propose in this map, of letting the Tiber return to its proper channel by a fall, which issuing from under the base of the Congress building, ... would produce the most happy effect in rolling down to fill up the canal and discharge itself in the Potomac, ... when seen through that grand and majestic avenue intersecting with the prospect from the palace....[4]

If L'Enfant's vision of a new Capital city, symbolic of American "Empire" seems more in keeping with Federalist ideas of strong central government under George Washington, who lent his support to

L'Enfant's plan, it was no less a Republican believer in decentralized government than Jefferson who also embraced (and influenced) L'Enfant's proposals. Indeed, as Washington's Secretary of State, Jefferson played one of the most crucial roles of all in the administration's dealings with L'Enfant. In the end, they and the rest of the government parted company with L'Enfant (after 1792) because of his intransigent refusal to cooperate with the Commissioners established to oversee the project and to shield the President from L'Enfant's importunities. Yet in April of 1791 Jefferson wrote to L'Enfant from Philadelphia with expressions of confidence in L'Enfant's abilities for the project, while providing some ideas of his own together with plans of European cities requested by L'Enfant. Jefferson's pointed suggestions of architecture for the Capitol building and the President's house—despite his studied carefulness not to interfere with the communications between L'Enfant and the President, who was nevertheless happy to *have* him as a go-between—may well reflect an urge by Jefferson to have a more dominant role himself (which he soon took on after L'Enfant's untimely departure). Jefferson wrote to him as follows:

> [I]n compliance with your request I have examined my papers and found the plans of Frankfort-on-the-Mayne, Carlsruhe, Amsterdam, Strasburg, Paris, Orleans, Bordeaux, Lyons, Montpelier, Marseilles, Turin and Milan, which I send in a roll by this post. They are on large and accurate scales, having been procured by me when in those respective cities myself. As they are connected with the notes I made in my travels, & often necessary to explain them to myself, I will beg your care of them and to return them when no longer useful to you. . . . I am happy that the *President has left the planning of the town in such good hands* [italicized in pencil by L'Enfant], and have no doubt it will be done to general satisfaction. . . . The water about the mouth of the Tyber [Tiber] not being of any depth, those connected with the Government will prefer fixing themselves near the public grounds in the center, which will also be convenient to be resorted to as walks from the lower and upper town.—Having communicated to the President . . . such general ideas on the subject of the town as occurred to me, I make no doubt that, in explaining himself to you on the subject, he has interwoven with his own ideas such of mine as he approved. . . . I avoid interfering with what he may have expressed to you. Whenever it is proposed to prepare plans for the Capitol[,] I should prefer the adoption of some one of the models of antiquity which have had the approbation of thousands of years; and

> for the President's house I should prefer the celebrated fronts of modern buildings which have already received the approbation of all good judges.[5]

The fuller extent of L'Enfant's grandiose and ambitious plans for the new Capital city and its key public buildings soon came to light in August 1791 when he went to Philadelphia and submitted his "PLAN OF THE CITY, INTENDED FOR THE PERMANENT SEAT OF GOVERNMENT OF THE UNITED STATES." There, he met with Washington and dined with Jefferson and Madison. In addition to his "Plan" and "Observations Explanatory of the Plan," L'Enfant submitted a report or memoir dated Georgetown, August 19, 1791. In it he spoke expansively of the "unparalleled" grandeur of the city and its public buildings as the seat of the new American nation, a veritable new Rome along the Tiber. L'Enfant sought to push the project further and faster, in keeping with his own designs, than the new government was able or willing to pursue, as was soon to become even more evident. L'Enfant strongly urged the immediate beginnings of the whole complex of main structures and spaces, beyond just the Capitol and President's "palace." The latter were, however, to become the focus for the time being, in preparation for the transfer of the governmental seat from Philadelphia to Washington. Yet L'Enfant's plan of 1791 for a new Capital and Capitol, on a scale "unparalleled" in the history of the world, set the stage for what eventually emerged, despite setbacks, postponements, and transformations along the way. According to L'Enfant:

> As matters stand—the sites assigned to the Congress House and the President's palace exhibit a sumptuous aspect and claim already the suffrage of crowds of visitors, serving to give a grand idea of the whole. . . .
>
> The grand avenue connecting the palace and the Federal House will be magnificent, with the water of the cascade [falling] to the canal which will extend to the Potomac; as also the several squares which are intended for the Judiciary Courts, the National Bank, the grand Church, the play house, markets and exchange, offering a variety of situations unparalleled for beauty, suitable for every purpose, and in every point convenient. . . . I conceive it important not to confine the building idea to erecting a Congress House and a President's palace. . . . Other exertions are necessary to get going and to enlarge private undertakings.
>
> If we are to make of this city a fact[,] it will be indispensable to consider every part of the proposed plan as essential. . . .

> [A]nd however unconnected they may appear at first[,] every part should go forward with a proportional degree of despatch . . . [including] . . . the canal from the Tiber to the Eastern branch. . . .
>
> The making of the public walk from under the Federal House to the Potomac and connected with the palace . . . will be productive of equal advantages with the foregoing as it will give to the city from the very beginning a superior charm over most of those of the world as it will likewise be an improvement over all in point of convenience of distribution.[6]

After L'Enfant, Jefferson Center Stage

As L'Enfant's services were nearing their end, Jefferson wrote to him from Philadelphia in December 1791 to tell him not to proceed arbitrarily in demolishing existing structures but rather to "conduct yourself in subordination to the authority of the Commissioners, to the laws [!] of the land, & to the rights of it's [*sic*] citizens."[7] L'Enfant's fate was sealed when he replied to Jefferson in February 1792 that he would not submit to the Commissioners. His own manner of proceeding, L'Enfant indicated, was the only expeditious way "to change a wilderness into a city, [and] to erect and beautify buildings etc. to the degree of perfection necessary to receive the seat of Government of a vast empire [!]."[8] Whereupon Jefferson wrote back to inform L'Enfant that President Washington was terminating his services (Washington having previously urged Jefferson to keep L'Enfant in check without losing his valuable services).[9]

As the post-L'Enfant stage of the project got under way, Jefferson wrote to the Commissioners in March 1792 "to advertise immediately for plans of a Capitol and President's house."[10] Jefferson then proceeded to prepare and approve a brief "Draft of Competition for Plan of a Capitol: Program of Competition for the United States Capitol."[11] In April 1792 Jefferson wrote to the Commissioners that "the President . . . thinks it best to decline making any alterations in the plan of the City," due to "the expediency of fixing the public opinion on the thing as stable and unalterable," including "all the Avenues which point to the Capitol."[12] In December 1792 Jefferson wrote to the Commissioners about models for the Capitol building on which he, Jefferson, was having considerable input. On a particular point, he deemed a certain plan "ingenious: but . . . certainly inferior to that used in Europe of which is a drawing in the *Encyclopédie Methodique*" (italics added).[13] This was the same huge multi-volume encyclopedia cited above that is also found in the Hamilton library at Columbia.[14] In fact, Jefferson had previously told L'Enfant in April 1791 that "whenever it is proposed to prepare plans for the Capitol, I should prefer the adoption of some one of the models of antiquity, which have had the approbation of thousands of years." Jefferson had also drawn his own early design c. 1791 for the Capitol building on the model of the Parthenon.[15]

"As much as any other individual [including, after L'Enfant, Latrobe and Bulfinch]," according to one authority, "Thomas Jefferson was one of the architects of the United States Capitol. Jefferson did not shape the building by making designs. He got his results largely by promoting models for other architects to imitate. . . . His design for the University of Virginia (Charlottesville, 1817 ff.) . . . is merely the culmination of a lifelong practice. At the Unied States Capitol, Jefferson . . . transformed the role of patron . . . [and] gave shape to the original national statehouse." Jefferson also prepared models of architectural orders for Monticello and the Virginia Capitol, drawing inspiration from Graeco-Roman and Renaissance styles of architecture, including by Palladio. "Jefferson's greatest success . . . occurred on the [Washington Capitol's] exterior. . . . [He] changed the model for the . . . East Portico, from the portico of the Pantheon . . . to the . . . Portico of Diocletian [that is, to the grander scale of a later Imperial Roman model]."[16]

At this point, various questions arise. To what extent were Jefferson's contributions, in helping to shape the designs of the new U.S. Capital and Capitol, influenced by his own ideas of government? Aside from the separation of powers, consent of the governed, decentralized administration, and the like, did legislative sovereignty enter the picture for him in these regards? Abundant evidence has already been adduced to show the central place of legislative sovereignty in his (and other founders') political-legal thought—from his Declaration of Independence and earlier compositions to his later writings discussed above. The dominant place of Congress on "Capitol Hill" overlooking the rest of the city corresponds to the similarly situated Monticello on the promontory of a "little mountain" overlooking the valley below. Did Jefferson's distinctive emphasis on legislative sovereignty carry over into his urban and architectural visions for the special position of the Congress and the Capitol building itself? The commanding initial designs set forth by L'Enfant were influenced by George Washington as President (and surveyor), by Jefferson as Secretary of State (and architect), and by others during the early Federalist period. The centralizing tendencies of Federalist government seemed to fit in with L'Enfant's own visions of a great new American "Empire" and its "seat of a supreme sovereignty." To design the new Congress' building as the Capitol centerpiece of the city and government, based largely upon models of ancient Rome, speaks volumes on the subject of legislative sovereignty, that is, the supremacy of the legislative powers and capacities.

The New Rome, after 1800

Shortly after the federal government was finally transferred from Philadelphia to Washington, D.C., toward the end of the Adams administration under which he was eclipsed, Jefferson became President and took on an ever greater role in the development of the Capital city and its Capitol building. But he strove not to take undue liberties. Characteristically, Jefferson continually went to great lengths to ascertain and adhere to Congress' laws (as well as earlier presidentil acts) regarding those construction projects and the role of the chief executive in them. For instance, in a message to Congress in January 1802 on one such matter, Jefferson stated: "I have thought it my duty, before I proceed to direct a rigorous execution of the law, to submit the subject to the consideration of the Legislature."[17] Writing to three others, in May 1803, Jefferson stated that ". . . these are the words of the law, and you will be sensible that they are descriptive of the Pennsylvania avenue between the Capitol & the public buildings of the President's square exactly, and of no other highways, and as they were expressly explained to me by the member who moved the insertion of these words . . ."[18] Or again, in a letter in March 1807 on a similar matter: "With this view of the just & probable intention of the legislature, I shall not think myself authorised to take advantage of a lax expression, forced on by circumstances to carry the execution of the law into a region of experience which would merit great consideration before they should embark in it."[19]

Similar attentiveness to the laws had infused Jefferson's earlier dealings with L'Enfant. In November 1791, President Washington had written to Jefferson about L'Enfant and "how far he may be spoken to in decisive terms without losing his services; which, in my opinion, would be a serious misfortune.—At the same time, *he must know*, there is a line beyond which he will not be suffered to go."[20] Whereupon Jefferson wrote to L'Enfant: ". . . in this you have laid yourself open to the laws, & in a country where they will have their course." It was in this letter that Jefferson also told L'Enfant to "conduct yourself in subordination to the authority of the Commissioners [L'Enfant thereupon refusing to do so], to the laws of the land [!], and it's [*sic*] citizens."[21]

As President, Jefferson had considerable leeway in steering ahead the architectural designs for the new Capitol building. He had great influence upon the architect Latrobe, particularly on the East front, clearly revealing it to be an intended symbolic statement to the world of a new

Rome. "In the new design," according to one authority, "the Capitol presents a more monumental and collective east front to the world. The new feature is a long colonnade. . . . The portico now stands in front of the colonnade, . . . [with] staircase . . . as an entryway. . . . With this change, the east front has grown . . . grander. . . . [This new] frontispiece . . . corresponds with Jefferson's lifelong preference for the deep porticoes in the Etruscan-Roman tradition. . . . [T]he conception for the frontispiece comes from a model that Jefferson invoked only for the Capitol: the mysterious Portico of Diocletian."[22] Writing to Jefferson in December 1806, Latrobe remarked: "The very beautiful Portico which you so justly admire, and from which agreeably to your suggestion the Portico of the Capitol in my design is taken, is said to be of *Diocletian*. . . . It is certainly one of the most delicious things I have seen . . ."[23]

Questions of Sovereignty

A question arises in connection with Jefferson's special distinctive influence on Capitol designs after the model of Diocletian at the highpoint of the Roman Empire in the third century A.D. L'Enfant himself had earlier spoken of his plan for the Capital and Capitol of the new American "Empire" in imperial language and sentiment acceptable to the other founders. Did Jefferson actually mean to project the image of the Roman Empire as the dominant image of the new America through its Capitol building, rather than the image of he Roman Republic with its own extensive empire? There may be an unresolved ambiguity here that cannot be duly explained or explained away. There is, of course, the further factor of Jefferson's doubling of the nation's already vast territory through his Louisiana Purchase in 1803.

Or does L'Enfant's vision of "the seat of a supreme sovereignty" again hold the real key? It may be that the mounting power of monumental designs for the U.S. Capitol as the centerpiece of the new Capital city was meant to express the overarching concepts of sovereignty and its legislative orientation, centered in Congress. Such concepts are reflected in the thought of Jefferson and other leading founders as well as in the expansive first article of the U.S. Constitution on Congress, which occupied the main attention of the Philadelphia Convention. We have also seen the considerable interest of Jefferson, Adams, Hamilton, and other founders in traditions of Roman law going back to the law books of the Emperor Justinian in the later Roman Empire. Jefferson's library included a number of copies of those and related books (which went with the rest of his books to form the basis of the Library of Congress after the British burned the Capitol, as Jefferson discussed in a letter of September 1814[24]).

In other words, the tradition of sovereignty that was partly derived from Roman law in European thought, as utilized by Jefferson and the other founders studied above, originated in its classic form during the Roman Emire under Justinian and his legal compilers, who drew upon previous jurists of the earlier Empire like Ulpian, rather than during the Roman Republic. But because that tradition of sovereignty in its reformulation by Bodin and others became applied to democracies as well as to monarchies, there was no serious contradiction for American founders themselves when adapting it for their own purposes in the early American Republic. The same kind of perspective can shed light on Jefferson's use of Empire architecture for the new American Republic, with its vast extent of territory.

Jefferson himself provides further clues. In October 1809, shortly after leaving office, he wrote to Latrobe from Monticello to congratulate him on his architectural work on the Capitol building and its prominent placement on Capitol Hill, comparing it with his own "essay in Architecture" at Monticello. "[T]he work ... will be a ... monument of our infant republic" and will compare well with similar structures "of the ancient republics of Greece & Rome."[25] Latrobe, too, provides useful material. Writing to Jefferson in 1807 toward the end of his administration, Latrobe discussed at some length his own preferences for Roman architecture of the Imperial period that was not too extravagant, as well as for Grecian architecture in particular. Latrobe also pointed out some of the needs and uses of American public buildings, including legislative assemblies, that differed from their classical counterparts and that required suitable construction in the case of Washington. Jefferson could agree in general with Latrobe's declarative assessments while placing his own stamp on the designs.[26] More generally, the founders' admiration for the Roman Republic is also well known.[27]

Long after leaving office, Jefferson's interest in and influence on the Capitol continued to be felt. In a June 1817 letter to Jefferson, for instance, Latrobe wrote: "The Capitol is growing into a more intelligible form & arrngement, than it had since the destruction by the British.—If the permanence of the seat of the Government at Washington would not have been endangered by it,—it would have been better in every point of view. ... [A] much more convenient and magnificent building could have been erected, than will be made of the ruins of the former."[28] Even so, Jefferson and his fellow founders would no doubt be pleased with the completed Capitol building as it stands today—a worthy symbol of the nation's "supreme sovereignty," as envisioned in the original Capital plan by L'Enfant and the founders who shaped and approved it. But is it not also a symbol today of legislative sovereignty on the part of Congress, and suggestive of the Roman Empire as well as the Roman Republic a la Jefferson?

Finally, two other authorities have written, in much different fashion than encountered here, on public architecture and city design as expressive of political authority and governmental organization. The first such study has considered the subjects of sovereignty and state in connection with the national Capital and "the power and majesty of rule."[29] The second compares the tripartite division of legislative, executive, and judicial powers in the Constitution of 1787 with the tripartite units corresponding to them in the city plan of 1791 set forth by L'Enfant and adapted by the founders.[30] Yet it can be added that the 1791 city plan, providing for three main separated units of federal government, did place the Capitol building most prominently as the centerpiece atop Capitol Hill (in keeping with the primary attention given at the Convention to the first article of the Constitution on Congress). The plan was transformed over time to give even more prominence to the Capitol, while recalling to mind Jefferson's designs for the East front.[31]

In the end, Jefferson's longtime interest in legislative sovereignty, evidenced in his early Declaration of Independence, with its bracket marks matching those he made in Bodin's *Republic*, culminated with his Capitol designs.

2. EARLY CONGRESSES AND LEGISLATIVE AUTHORITY

Continental and Confederation Congresses

Prior to the Federal Congress becoming the supreme lawmaking body in accordance with the long first article of the U.S. Constitution—as symbolized early on by plans for the dominant position of its building on Capitol Hill—the older Continental Congress did not possess a comparable legislative authority. To the limited extent that the Confederation Congress acquired a quasi-legislative capacity under the Articles of Confederation in the 1780s, the legislative and executive functions were not yet articulated or separated as they would be in their future federal form. They were instead mixed together in vague ways that contributed to the unsatisfactory operations of the central government. At that time, the real legislative power, indeed the legislative sovereignty, rested with the state legislatures individually and collectively. The inability of Congress under the Articles of Confederation to function as a distinct legislative body, one delineated and separated from the executive, lay behind the call by some founders for a new, different form of government. The lack of a permanent established Capital city in which Congress could assemble on a regular dependable basis had also contributed to Congress' inability to function as a stable law-making body. The plans made after the Convention of 1787 for a new dominant Capitol building became as important for functional and symbolic purposes as were the plans for the new Capital city.

After the First Continental Congress met at Philadelphia in 1774, the Second Continental Congress assembled there starting in 1775, with fighting already under way. In 1776 it constituted itself as a government independent of Great Britain. Under duress of war, and with unity of purpose, the Second Continental Congress continued to meet and constitute itself as a government founded upon Lockean principles of popular consent, natural rights, and recall of derelict officials. This Congress continued as a central governing body until 1781. At first continuing to meet in Philadelphia, it soon became a more itinerant body, subject to many disruptions and relocations as the events of war unfolded, meeting in such places as Trenton and Princeton. Anything resembling a real legislative body wwith authority to enact laws lay further into the future. Basically, the Second Continental Congress was an assembly of delegates from separate states during wartime. Wartime problems illustrated the need for permanent unification. Congress depended upon the states' permission and cooperation in order to act. Interstate cooperation was, however, secondary to individual states' interests.

Under the Articles of Confederation from 1781 to 1789, prior to the beginning of the new federal government under the U.S. Constitution, the Confederation Congress was the central government, but only in a loose sense. Amid continued resistance by the states to centralization, there was, after ratification of the Articles, at least a legal basis for national existence and a greater presence of central government. Each state remained virtually independent and sovereign. All powers not specifically delegated to Congress reverted to the states. Each state received one vote and also veto power; the self-interest of states prevailed over the national interest. To Congress were delegated fiscal and monetary controls, the practice of diplomacy, declaration of war, regulation of weights and measures, and establishment of the post offices. States retained controls over taxation, commerce, and militias. Among the restrictions accepted by the states was reciprocal recognition of the laws and regulations in force from state to state.

The text of "The Articles of Confederation and Perpetual Union" was finalized in 1777 and eventually adopted by the states in 1781. They began in Article 1 by calling the Confederation "The United States of America." According to Article 2: "Each State retains its sovereignty, freedom and independence, and every power, jurisdiction, and right, which is not by the confederation explicitly delegated to the United States in Congress assembled." Although there are numerous such references throughout to "in Congress assembled" as well as to the powers of "the legislature of each State," there are no explicit references to "laws" or "legislative" capacities of Congress. Not only is Congress not designated specifically as a legislative body, there are no explicit references to any national "executive" in terms of administering laws or anything else. Nor is a national court or judicial authority expressly provided for in any significant way concerning interpretation of laws. There are, however, various references to "the governor or executive power of the State[s]" as well as to the "judicial proceedings of the courts and magistrates of every . . . State" (as in Article 4). Other such references are made to "the legislative or executive authority, or lawful agent of any State" (as in Article 9). There is a single ambiguous reference to "the acts of Congress" in certain judicial matters and about three references to the "regulation" and "regulating" done by Congress.

Of particular note in its wording is a statement in Article 9: "The United States, in Congress assembled, shall also have the sole and exclusive right and power of regulating the trade [etc.] . . . with the Indians not members of any of the states; provided that the legislative rights of any State within its own limits be not infringed or violated . . ." A variation on a theme much encountered elsewhere, the concept of legislative self-determination is paramount in this passage. Each individual state in the United States has the right and authority to pass laws governing its own affairs within its own territory. This, in yet a different context, has been a principle much studied in this series, going back several centuries in its early modern formulation.

In effect, the states comprising the Confederation were reluctant to give to Congress the same kind of legislative authority not only that they themselves possess but that they perceived the English Parliament as having had over the colonies. The laws associated with the Confederation had, in any case, no binding forceful "sanction," as Madison was later to observe in 1787. For the most part, the Confederation Congress was organized in the same way as the Continental Congress and had much the same powers. Congress lacked the power of taxation to support a war. It was not even a permanently meeting body but met sporadically. The States comprising it resisted efforts toward centralization of authority. The Articles had aptly called this a "Union" rather than a Nation. But even this loose Union was coming undone in the crises leading up to the Convention of 1787.[32]

The Articles of Confederation remained in effect until early 1789 when George Washington was sworn in as President in New York City, where Congress had already moved to prior to the Constitutional

Convention in Philadelphia in mid-1787. After the new federal government was formed, Congress continued to meet for over a year in New York City, after which it moved back to Philadelphia, remaining there until the seat of government was transferred to Washington in 1800. Thus Philadelphia, with its great library resources for the founders, remained a focal point for them during the formative crucial periods of the Declaration of Independence and the Constitutional Convention, as well as during many of the intervening years and also beyond into the decade prior to the move to Washington.

The Early Federal Congress

In April 1789 George Washington was sworn in as President on the front steps of the new Federal Hall in New York City, where the new federal Congress met for the first time. Formerly City Hall, this building had been remodelled by L'Enfant, who had been commissioned for this purpose after ratification of the Constitution in 1788. It was there in September 1789 that Congress approved the Bill of Rights. There, too, the Supreme Court was located, along with State, Treasury, and War Departments. After the Capital was moved back to Philadelphia in August 1790, while a new "Federal City" was being created on the banks of the Potomac River, New York's Federal Hall again became City Hall, until it was replaced and demolished in 1812. In it, the locations and functions of the three branches had been interconnected.

The momentous and intensive new legislative business taken up by the first federal Congress in 1789–1791 can be gauged from a variety of contemporary statements made by those involved, connected, or familiar with it. Madison remarked to Edmund Randolph (1789): "I see on the lists of Representatives a very scanty proportion who will share in the drudgery of [legislative] business." Representative Abraham Baldwin of Georgia felt the members of the new federal Congress to be generally inferior to those in the Confederation Congress, to be less capable than hoped for in handling the pressing legislative matters before them. Others, including George Washington, were more optimistic and complimentary. A recent book has, in any case, declared: "The First Federal Congress was the most important Congress in American history." As Ebenezer Dibblee had already put it (1787): "We are upon the Eve of another Revolution in the System of Government. . . . [I]t leaves but the shadow of power in the States; utterly destroys the Old Ship, and a new one built, in which we must embark or sink." More to the point was James Iredell of North Carolina (1788), who became a Supreme Court justice: "[T]he first session of Congress will probably be the most important of any for many years. A general Code of laws will then be established in execution of every power contained in the Constitution." According to the New York *Gazette of the United States* (1789): "No future session of Congress will ever have so arduous and weighty a charge on their hands." Senator William Few of Georgia observed (1789): "We find almost every Act involves great Constitutional principles which requires time and much disquisition to establish." Senator Joseph Stanton commented in early 1791, toward the end of the first federal Congress: "Different Laws, Customs, and Habits of thinking have heretofore prevailed in the States which now Constitute the American Nation." He also alluded to the process of "forming, digesting and bringing to Perfection the Systems . . . which are to pervade the Empire [!] and to extend to every individual Citizen." Praising the work of the first federal Congress, a friend wrote to Vice President Adams in March 1791: "To no nation, by no legislature, was ever so much done in so short a period for the establishment of Government, Order, public Credit & general tranquility." Subsequently, according to one modern appraisal, the second federal Congress "agreed to legislation on all of this business" that had been worked on so extensively and in such "awesome" ways by the first federal Congress.[33]

The enormity of legislative activity conducted by the first federal Congress is evidenced in the Senate's voluminous legislative *Journal* during its three sessions. These were held in New York in March–September 1789 and in January–August 1790, then in Philadelphia in December 1790–March 1791. "The Congress," according to the *Journal* editors, "was the first of the institutions created by the Constitution to take solid form. . . . The Congress was also the first to act under the U.S. Constitution; thus, even when it dealt with routine and trivial matters, or followed practices established by the British Parliament, state legislatures, or the old Continental Congress, it was setting precedent."[34] A similar picture emerges in records of the debates in the House of Representatives during the first federal Congress' third session held in Philadelphia from late 1790 to early 1791. That December, 1790, the *Federal Gazette* lauded "the liberality of the House of Representatives. . . . Their doors are . . . open. . . . Thus the speech of the orator again charms and again instructs, after passing through the medium of an IMPARTIAL PRESS; and freedom exults in an addition of security from this enlightened proceeding of these revered Legislators."[35]

An apropos modern commentary of more general scope on "the organization of the legislative body" in "the legislative process" is instructive. It can serve here to characterize the importance of the early emergence of Congress as a permanent legislative body at the center of the new American nation-state established by the U.S. Constitution.

The national, state, and city legislative bodies, each with their own spheres of self-determination, are central to what is called, in its wider sense, the American federal system.

> A legislative body is more than the sum total of its members—the human beings which compose it. It is a corporate entity with a life and purpose of its own. Members may come and members may go, but so long as democratic government endures, the legislative body goes on. In words which have stood unaltered since 1787, the Constitution declares: "All legislative powers herein granted shall be vested in a congress of the United States, which shall consist of a Senate and a House of Representatives [Article 1, Section 1]." Each state constitution contains a similar clause and each city charter provides for a city council or its equivalent to discharge the legislative function within the city. The continuity of the existence of legislative bodies rests in part upon these provisions of law and in part upon custom, usage, and tradition. . . . In the Senate of the United States, legislative continuity is assured by overlapping terms of office, only one-third of the members being required to stand for re-election each biennium.[36]

Moreover:

> [T]he mark of a political society is the establishment of public offices, people set apart for the business of governing and issuing commands. These commands are laws, whether they are issued by one, by a few, or by many, provided they are supported and enforced by the power of the state. Those who formulate and declare the law we call legislators—law bearers or lawmakers.[37]

There can be no doubt as to the vast new sweeping powers of lawmaking assigned to the federal Congress under Article I of the U.S. Constitution. The provisions on legislative power comprise well over the first half of the Constitution proper (aside from the Bill of Rights), just as it occupied well over the first half of the Convention debates. Following the first orienting section of Article I as quoted in the passage given above, the composition of the national legislature and its procedures for making laws are set forth in detail, revealing the complex interworkings of the legislative process at the national level. Then follows the lengthy listing of Congress' legislative and regulatory powers over taxation, commerce, coinage, post offices, declaration of war, armies and militias, and many other matters. This comprehensive listing of numerous attributes of sovereign power grouped under legislation recalls to mind, in a different way, the listing of legislative grievances against the British Crown and Parliament in the Declaration of Independence. This list in article I ends with: "To make all Laws which shall be necessary and proper for carrying into Execution the foregoing Powers, and all other Powers vested by this Constitution in the Government of the United States, or in any Department of Officer thereof." The main function of the Chief Executive is clearly to execute the laws made by Congress. Then appears a listing of what the individual states are not permitted to do in relation to the laws and related matters of the federal government. All this represents a huge new increase of Congress' powers, far beyond what they were in the Continental and Confederation Congresses. Precisely in order to check, in other areas, Congress' newfound legislative authority, and with the excesses of Parliament's legislative powers over the colonies still fresh in their minds, the founders later saw fit in the very first amendment to the Constitution (in the Bill of Rights) to ensure that: "*Congress shall make no law* respecting an establishment of religion, or prohibiting the free exercise thereof; or abridging the freedom of speech, or of the press; or the right of the people peaceably to assemble, and to petition the Government for a redress of grievances [emphasis added]."

3. EARLY CONGRESS' LIBRARY

Long before Jefferson's great book collection went to D.C. to form the basis of the Library of Congress after the British burned the Capitol and the earlier library there, an impressive collection of books had been available to the successive Continental, Confederation, and Federal Congresses in Philadelphia up to 1800. During the decisive periods when the Declaration of Independence and U.S. Constitution were drawn up in 1776 and 1787 respectively, there were in Philadelphia not only booksellers but also libraries in close proximity to Independence Hall. The latter in particular provided important resources for the founders and their uses of European sources. The main public subscription library in Philadelphia was The Library Company of Philadelphia, founded by Benjamin Franklin. It served as Congress' early library, was adjacent to Independence Hall, and still exists today under the same name.[38]

Also in close proximity was another public subscription library of note. It had been created to house, after his death in 1751, the former private library of James Logan, who had been secretary to William

Penn (d. 1718), founder of Pennsylvania. The Logan collection of over 2,600 volumes and 2,100 titles was more specialized than The Library Company's collection. It was heavily endowed with European books especially in Latin and Greek. For various reasons, it evidently became little accessible to or utilized by the founders in Philadelphia around 1776 and 1787. Yet the Logan Collection may well have played a part for certain figures among them who were especially interested in and knowledgeable about the classics and classical traditions in European thought. Such figures would have included, in particular, Jefferson and Adams among those involved in the Declaration of Independence, as well as Madison and Hamilton at the Constitutional Convention. In 1792, shortly after Congress moved back to Philadelphia from New York, the Logan collection was merged with the far more accessible and well-utilized Library Company.

Of the seven copies of works by Bodin in The Library Company's collection, six were "Loganian," four of which are definitely known to have come from the Logan subscription library. Two of these four were Latin editions of Bodin's *Republic* (1591, 1609). Both have marginal notes by Logan and one has his signature on the title page. The two other Bodin books in Latin that were owned by Logan and went with the rest of his private collection to the public Logan subscription library, close to The Library Company, were *Method for the Easy Comprehension of History* (1610), with notes by Logan, and *Theatre of Universal Nature* (1605). Not in the modern catalogue of Logan library books is a French edition of Bodin's *Republic* (1578), with Logan's marginal notes. A book by Bodin in The Library Company's collection that did not come from the Logan collection was on witchcraft—*De magorum daemonomania libri IV*. A seventh Loganian item by Bodin, yet with uncertain provenance in terms of ownership and notations, is *Andeg. in Parisiorum senatu* (1572).[39]

Those two collections contained a broad wealth of European and other sources during the decades when the founders were in Philadelphia. Not surprisingly, references to The Library Company and to the Logan collection appear, for instance, in early papers of Jefferson, thereby opening up some interesting possibilities.[40] Neither Jefferson nor Adams, on the committee assigned to draw up the Declaration at Philadelphia in 1776, may have had need to consult those library copies of Bodin's *Republic* if their own copies of that work were already in their possession by then. But Bodin's *Republic* was not the only European book in those Philadelphia libraries that had strong Bodinian elements of legislative sovereignty, which was so powerfully present in writings during the periods of the Declaration and the Constitution. The founders' writings during those periods exhibit impressive evidence of deep reading in European sources, including in the classics and later classical traditions. Much of this knowledge was gained from their own collections, yet much also was gained from Philadelphia's library treasures in their midst. The Library Company, in particular, became, in effect, the early "library of Congress."

4. GREAT LAWGIVERS AND THE SUPREME COURT

L'Enfant's plan for the new Capital city provided for three separate structures for the three branches of the federal government. Congress was to occupy the dominant position atop Capitol Hill, as Jefferson had urged—in keeping with his own classical-inspired hilltop site for Monticello as well as with his longtime views on the sovereign powers of lawmaking bodies. When the Capital city was moved from Philadelphia to Washington in 1800, however, the Supreme Court was housed in separate quarters within the Capitol building, where it would remain for well over a century to come, far from the President's separate quarters at the White House. Even less separated had been the quarters for the three federal branches earlier in Philadelphia and New York.

Aside from Congress' legislative role, the independent legislative-like capacities of the executive branch had been well asserted through the veto power in the writings and presidency of John Adams. Another kind of quasi-legislative authority came over time to be associated with the power of judicial review established by Chief Justice John Marshall in the early 1800s during Jefferson's first term as President. In his pivotal decision of 1803 in the case of *Marbury vs. Madison*, Marshall articulated the concept of the Court's power to invalidate statutes that are "contrary to the Constitution." That is, the Court could establish the constitutionality of legislation. In that particular case, a section of the Judiciary Act of 1789 was declared unconstitutional.

Appointed by Adams in 1801 near the end of his Federalist presidency, Marshall was a bitter foe of Jefferson and sought to thwart the new Democratic-Republican President and his Secretary of State, Madison. Remaining Chief Justice until 1835, and ruling on a long list of important cases, Marshall was an activist. He impelled the Supreme Court in the direction of its later legislative-like activities in counterdistinction to those of the other two federal branches. Although Marshall's activist judicial legacy in relation to federal legislation did not follow a clear line of development in the century after his death in 1835, it reemerged in a more decisive form in the great cases of the 1930s in which the Supreme Court struck down as unconstitutional much of the

New Deal legislation passed by Congress under President Franklin Roosevelt.

When in 1935 (exactly one hundred years after Marshall's death) construction of the new Supreme Court building was finished (having started in 1931), the Court for the first time in D.C. had its own separate edifice and location. However, L'Enfant's original city plan, influenced by the founders' own ideas and preferences, had provided for three equidistant separate buildings for the three separate federal branches. Yet the location of the new Supreme Court building in such close proximity to the Capitol building, both together far from the executive mansion, may provide another kind of symbolic statement on the Court's newfound independent quasi-legislative role in the early years of the Roosevelt presidency.

Wall friezes inside the Supreme Court depict a highly suggestive series of great lawgivers throughout history. Among them is John Marshall, the only American represented. The other figures include some significant names encountered in the present series—Napoleon, Blackstone, Grotius, Lycurgus, Solon, Charlemagne, Octavian (Augustus), and, above all, Justinian. The full sequence of chronologically arranged "Great Lawgivers of History" on the south and north walls inside the chamber where the justices preside is as follows: Menes, Hammurabi, Moses, Solomon, Lycurgus, Solon, Draco, Confucius, Octavian, Justinian, Mohammed, Charlemagne, King John, Louix IX, Hugo Grotius, Sir William Blackstone, John Marshall (noted especially for *Marbury vs. Madison*), and Napoleon. In the words of one historian of the Supreme Court who has cited several of these figures:

> On the north and south walls of the Supreme Court Chamber in Washington are carved two marble panels depicting processions of historical lawgivers. Of the eighteen figures on the panels only one is there because of his work as a judge, and he is the one American represented: John Marshall. This is more than mere coincidence, for it sharply illustrates a basic difference between the making of law in the United States and in other countries. The great lawgivers in other systems have been mighty monarchs of the type of Hammurabi and Justinian, divinely inspired prophets like Moses, philosophers such as Confucius, or scholars like Hugo Groitius and Sir William Blackstone. We in the United States have certainly had our share of the last two types of lawgiver—particularly among the men who drew up the organic documents upon which our polity is based. Significantly enough, however, it is not a Jefferson or

> a Madison who is depicted as *the* American lawgiver, but the great Chief Justice who, more than any one person, has left his imprint upon the development of our constitutional law.[41]

The preceding passage's ambiguity on the lawgiver-lawmaker roles of the Supreme Court is reflective of that in the panels themselves as well as in historiography more broadly. The pervasive elements of legislation and legislative process in the American legal system have long been noted. At the same time, however, historians have long distinguished between continental European law derived from Roman civil law and Anglo-American law based on common law—the first being more attuned to legislation, the latter to custom and precedent. But this distinction can be, and often has been, overdone to the point of neglecting the elements in the tradition of European civil law that have influenced, or been paralleled in, American legal thought on judicial and related matters. In addition, historians have often contrasted the American judicial outlook of the 20th century, concerning the quasi-legislative tendencies of the Supreme Court, with the far less innovative and more precedent-seeking proclivities of the Court in the founding era.[42]

What the wall panels in the Supreme Court chamber suggest in a wider sense, however, is the broadening and pervasive role of the legislative process throughout the federal system—judicial and executive as well as legislative, state and city as well as national. Although the Constitution's framers saw the Court as the chief interpreter of Congress' laws, Marshall soon established a more activist paradigm, just as Adams did for the office of Chief Executive, which had been seen by the framers to be the execution of Congress' laws. Although the European civil law tradition had long assigned a more active independent role to the judicial magistrate than had English common law, American jurisprudence from Marshall to Cardozo and beyond would often ascribe a legislative-like capacity. The motto inscribed over the front entrance to the Supreme Court building—"Equal Justice Under Law"—indicates the subordination of the judiciary to law and legislation; but it has not precluded the justices from legislative-like rulings of their own in furtherance of justice. Either way, legislative sovereignty is affirmed, in one fashion or another.

From all the above American perspectives, Bodin is still correct: legislation remains the primary mark of sovereignty under which the other marks are largely encompassed. So, too, is Corasius still correct: each legal territorial entity or body has *the* power of legislative self-determination in establishing laws and rules for its own affairs. The two most formative documents at the birth of the new American republic, the

Declaration of Independence and U.S. Constitution, are illustrative of these principles. So, too, are writings by the founders steeped in European thought. By the late 20th and early 21st centuries, the extraordinary scope of rulings, rules, and regulations laid down by judicial and executive bodies in American government, in addition to the massive measures passed by legislative bodies, are all indicative of the ever growing preponderance of legislative sovereignty and the legislative state across a wide front at federal, state, and local levels.

Notes
to Chapters II–VII
(Bibliographic, Historiographic, Documentary)

Notes to Chapter II
Jefferson in Legislative Profile

1. *Autobiography of Thomas Jefferson* (henceforth *Autobiography* in our notes to this edn.), introduced by Dumas Malone (New York, 1959), pp. 19–119 (text). Jefferson's Autobiography is also included at the beginning of Vol. I of *The Works of Thomas Jefferson* (edited by P. L. Ford, New York, 1904–). There are various other editions. Although the Library of Congress has appropriately given the title "Autobiography" to this work, it originally bore no title and thus in my text is not italicized (just as "Declaration of Independence" and "Bill of Rights" are not original titles and hence are not italicized in my text). All *sic*.

2. This is not the place to discuss apparent variations or discrepancies between Jefferson's autobiographical recollections in the 1820s and the facts or circumstances of his earlier periods. His Autobiography is richly detailed and informative, despite its condensations and brevity. It serves here as a reliable basis for our selective overview in sect. 1 of his thinking and activities during his early career, upon which he could look back in the light of subsequent developments.

3. *Autobiography*, p. 21.

4. *Ibid.*, p. 29.

5. E.g., our *Origins of Sovereignty*, Vol. I, p. 2; Vol. IV, pp. 474–475.

6. *Autobiography*, p. 60.

7. *Ibid.*, pp. 54–56.

8. *Ibid.*, p. 56: "We agreed to settle the plan of operation, and to distribute the work. We met . . . January, 1777. The first question was, whether we should propose to abolish the whole existing system of laws, and prepare a new and complete Institute, or preserve the general system, and only modify it to the present state of things. Mr. Pendleton, contrary to his usual disposition in favor of ancient things, was for the former proposition, in which he was joined by Mr. Lee. To this it was objected that to abrogate our whole system would be a bold measure, and probably far beyond the views of the legislature; that

they had been in the practice of revising, from time to time, the laws of the colony, omitting the expired, the repealed, and the obsolete, amending only those retained, and probably meant we should now do the same, only including the British statutes as well as our own: that to compose a new Institute, like those of Justinian [!] and Bracton, or that of Blackstone, which was the model proposed by Mr. Pendleton, would be an arduous undertaking, of vast research, of great consideration and judgment; and when reduced to a text, every word of that text, from the imperfection of human language, and its incompetence to express distinctly every shade of idea, would become a subject of question and chicanery, until settled by repeated adjudications; and this would involve us for ages in litigation, and render property uncertain, until, like the statutes of old, every word had been tried and settled by numerous decisions, and by new volumes of reports and commentaries; and that no one of us, probably, would undertake such a work, which to be systematical, must be the work of one hand. This last was the opinion of Mr. Wythe, Mr. Mason, and myself."

9. *Ibid.*, p. 57: "When we proceeded to the distribution of the work, Mr. Mason excused himself, as, being no lawyer, he felt himself unqualified for the work, and he resigned soon after. Mr. Lee excused himself on the same ground, and died, indeed, in a short time. The other two gentlemen, therefore, and myself, divided the work among us. The common law and statutes to the 4 [sic] James I. (when our separate legislature was established) were assigned to me; the British statutes, from that period to the present day, to Mr. Wythe; and the Virginia laws to Mr. Pendleton. As the law of Descents, and the criminal law fell of course within my portion, I wished the committee to settle the leading principles of these, as a guide for me in framing them; and, with respect to the first, I proposed to abolish the law of primogeniture . . ."

10. *Ibid.*, p. 57: "On the subject of the Criminal law, all were agreed, that the punishment of death should be abolished, except for treason and murder; and that, for other felonies, should be substituted hard labor in the public works, and in some cases, the *Lex talionis*. How this last revolting principle came to obtain our approbation, I do not remember. There remained, indeed, in our laws, a vestige of it in a single case of a slave; it was the English law, in the time of the Anglo-Saxons, copied probably from the Hebrew law of 'an eye for an eye, a tooth for a tooth,' and it was the law of several ancient people; but the modern mind had left it far in the rear of its advances. These points, however, being settled, we repaired to our respective homes for the preparation of the work."

11. *Ibid.*, p. 60: "Beccaria, and other writers on crimes and punishments, had satisfied the reasonable world of the unrightfulness and inefficacy of the punishment of crimes by death; and hard labor on roads, canals and other public works, had been suggested as a proper substitute. The Revisors had adopted these opinions; but the general idea of our country had not yet advanced to that point. The bill, therefore, for proportioning crimes and punishments, was lost in the House of Delegates by a majority of a single vote."

12. *Ibid.*, pp. 57–58, 62–63: "In the execution of my part, I thought it material not to vary the diction of the ancient statutes by modernizing it, nor to give rise to new questions by new expressions. The text of these statutes had been so fully explained and defined, by numerous adjudications, as scarcely ever now to produce a question in our courts. I thought it would be useful, also, in all new draughts, to reform the style of the later British statutes, and of our own acts of Assembly; which, from their verbosity, their endless tautologies, their involutions of case within case, and parenthesis within parenthesis, and their multiplied efforts at certainty, . . . to make them more plain, are really rendered more perplexed and incomprehensible, not only to common readers, but to the lawyers themselves. We were employed in this work from that time to February, 1779, when we met at Williamsburg, that is to say, Mr. Pendleton, Mr. Wythe and myself; and meeting day by day, we examined critically our several parts, sentence by sentence, scru-

tinizing and amending until we had agreed on the whole. We then returned home, had fair copies made of our several parts, which were reported to the General Assembly, June 18, 1779. . . . We had, in this work, brought so much of the Common law as it was thought necessary to alter, all the British statutes from Magna Charta to the present day, and all the laws of Virginia, from the establishment of our legislature, in the 4th Jac. I. to the present time, which we thought should be retained, within the compass of one hundred and twenty-six bills, making a printed folio of ninety pages only. Some bills were taken out, occasionally, from time to time, and passed; but the main body of the work was not entered on by the legislature until after the general peace, in 1785, when, by the unwearied exertions of Mr. Madison, in opposition to the endless quibbles, chicaneries, perversions, vexations and delays of lawyers and demi-lawyers, most of the bills were passed by the legislature, with little alteration.

"The bill for establishing religious freedom, the principles of which had, to a certain degree, been enacted before, I had drawn in all the latitude of reason and right. It still met with opposition; but, with some mutilations in the preamble, it was finally passed; and a singular proposition proved that its protection of opinion was meant to be universal. . . .

"The bill on the subject of slaves, was a mere digest of the existing laws respecting them, without any intimation of a plan for a future and general emancipation. It was thought better that this should be kept back, and attempted only by way of amendment, whenever the bill should be brought on. . . .

"I consider four of these bills, passed or reported, as forming a system by which every fibre would be eradicated of ancient or future aristocracy; and a foundation laid for a government truly republican. The repeal of the laws of entail would prevent the accumulation and perpetuation of wealth, in select families. . . .

"On the 1st of June, 1779, I was appointed Governor of the Commonwealth, and retired from the legislature. . . .

"Being now, as it were, identified with the Commonwealth itself, to write my own history, during the two years of my administration, would be to write the public history of that portion of the revolution within this State. This has been done by others . . ."

13. *Ibid.*, p. 119.

14. *Ibid.*, pp. 65, 70.

15. *Ibid.*, pp. 66–67: "The remissness of Congress, and their permanent session, began to be a subject of uneasiness; and even some of the legislatures had recommended to them intermissions, and periodical sessions. As the Confederation had made no provision for a visible head of the government, during vacations of Congress, and such a one was necessary to superintend the executive business, to receive and communicate with foreign ministers and nations, and to assemble Congress on sudden and extraordinary emergencies, I proposed, early in April, the appointment of a committee, to be called the 'Committee of the States,' to consist of a member from each State, who should remain in session during the recess of Congress: that the functions of Congress should be divided into executive and legislative, the latter to be reserved, and the former, by a general resolution, to be delegated to that Committee. This proposition was afterwards agreed to; a Committee appointed, who entered on duty on the subsequent adjournment of Congress, quarreled very soon, split into two parties, abandoned their post, and left the government without any visible head, until the next meeting in Congress. We have since seen the same thing take place in the Directory of France; and I believe it will forever take place in any Executive consisting of a plurality. Our plan, best, I believe, combines wisdom and practicability, by providing a plurality of Counsellors, but a single Arbiter for ultimate decision. I was in France when we heard of this schism, and separation of our Committee, and, speaking with Dr. Franklin of this singular disposition of men to quarrel, and divide into parties . . ."

16. *Ibid.*, pp. 88–93: "Our first essay, in America, to establish a federative government had fallen, on trial, very short of its object. During the war of Independence, while the pressure of an external enemy hooped us together, and . . . kept us necessarily on the alert, the spirit of the people, excited by danger, was a supplement to the Confederation, and urged them to zealous exertions, whether claimed by that instrument or not; but, when peace and safety were restored, and every man became engaged in useful and profitable occupation, less attention was paid to the calls of Congress. The fundamental defect of the Confederation was, that Congress was not authorized to act immediately on the people, and by its own officers. Their power was only requisitory, and these requisitions were addressed to the several Legislatures, to be by them carried into execution, without other coercion than the moral principle of duty. This allowed, in fact, a negative to every Legislature, on every measure proposed by Congress; a negative so frequently exercised in practice, as to benumb the action of the Federal government, and to render it inefficient in its general objects, and more especially in pecuniary and foreign concerns. The want, too, of a separation of the Legislative, Executive, and Judiciary functions worked disadvantageously in practice. . . .

"[Then it was] . . . agreed . . . to elect deputies to a general Convention, who should peaceably meet and agree on such a Constitution as 'would ensure peace, justice, liberty, the common defence and general welfare.' . . . I received a copy, and read and contemplated its provisions with great satisfaction. . . . [Like others,] I, too, found articles which I thought objectionable. The absence of express declarations ensuring freedom of religion, freedom of the press, freedom of the person under the uninterrupted protection of the Habeas corpus, and trial by jury in Civil as well as in Criminal cases, excited my jealousy; and the re-eligibility of the President for life, I quite disapproved. I expressed freely, in letters to my friends, and most particularly to Mr. Madison and General Washington, my approbations and objections. How the good should be secured and the ill brought to rights, was the difficulty. To refer it back to a new Convention might endanger the loss of the whole. My first idea was, that the nine States first acting, should accept it unconditionally, and thus secure what in it was good, and that the four last should accept on the previous condition, that certain amendments should be agreed to; but a better course was devised, of accepting the whole, and trusting that the good sense and honest intentions of our citizens, would make the alterations which should be deemed necessary. . . .

"But there was another amendment, of which none of us thought at the time, and in the omission of which, lurks the germ that is to destroy this happy combination of National powers in the General government, for matters of National concern, and independent powers in the States, for what concerns the States severally. In England, it was a great point gained at the Revolution, that the commissions of the Judges, which had hitherto been during pleasure, should thenceforth be made during good behavior. A Judiciary, dependent on the will of the King, had proved itself the most oppressive of all tools, in the hands of that magistrate. . . . [O]ur Judges are effectually independent of the nation. But this ought not to be. I would not, indeed, make them dependent on the executive authority, as they formerly were in England; but I deem it indispensable to the continuance of this government, that they should be submitted to some practical and impartial control; and that this, to be imparted, must be compounded of a mixture of State and federal authorities. . . .

"Among the deputies . . . of the government of the Confederation, no one was more distinguished or more distressing, than the utter impossibility of obtaining, from the States, the moneys necessary for the payment of debts, or even for the ordinary expenses of the government."

17. Cf. preceding note.

18. *Autobiography*, p. 80.

19. *Ibid.*, pp. 85–86.
20. *Ibid.*, p. 100.
21. *Ibid.*, p. 101: "The objects for which this body was convened, being of the first order of importance, I felt it very interesting to understand the views of the parties of which it was composed, and especially the ideas prevalent as to the organization contemplated for their government. I went, therefore, daily from Paris to Versailles, and attended their debates, generally till the hour of adjournment. Those of the Noblesse were impassioned and tempestuous. They had some able men on both sides, actuated by equal zeal. The debates of the Commons were temperate, rational, and inflexibly firm. . . . Tiers État were, to a man, united and determined. After various propositions of compromise had failed, the Commons undertook to cut the Gordian knot. The Abbe Sieyes, the most logical head of the nation, (author of the pamphlet 'Qu'est ce que le Tiers État?' which had electrified that country, as Paine's Common Sense did us), after an impressive speech on the 10th of June, moved that a last invitation should be sent to the Noblesse and Clergy. . . . This verification being finished, a motion was made, on the 15th, that they should constitute themselves a National Assembly; which was decided on the 17th, by a majority of four-fifths."
22. *Ibid.*, p. 103: "I was much acquainted with the leading patriots of the Assembly. Being from a country which had successfully passed through a similar reformation, they were disposed to my acquaintance, and had some confidence in me. I urged, most strenuously, an immediate compromise; to secure what the government was now ready to yield. . . . It was well understood that the King would grant, at this time, . . . [a] representative Legislature [etc. and] . . . [t]he origination of laws. . . . They thought otherwise, however, and events have proved their lamentable error. . . . They were unconscious of (for who could foresee?) the melancholy sequel of their well-meant perseverance; that their physical force would be usurped by a first tyrant to trample on the independence, and even the existence, of other nations."

Also, *Ibid.*, p. 105: "The Assembly now entered on the business of their mission, and first proceeded to arrange the order in which they would take up the heads of their constitution, as follows:

"First, and as Preliminary to the whole, a general Declaration of the Rights of Man. Then, specifically, the Principles of the Monarchy; Rights of the Nation; Rights of the King; Rights of the Citizens; Organization and Rights of the National Assembly; Forms necessary for the enactment of Laws; Organization and Functions of the Provincial and Municipal Assemblies; Duties and Limits of the Judiciary power; Functions and Duties of the Military Power."

23. *Ibid.*, pp. 109–110. Jefferson generally believed that the king would largely go along with the Assembly's agenda and that the main obstacle became the queen, who should better have been sent to a convent (pp. 110–111).
24. *Ibid.*, pp. 112–114: "Many days were employed in putting into the form of laws, the numerous demolitions of ancient abuses; which done, they proceeded to the preliminary work of a Declaration of Rights. There being much concord of sentiment on the elements of this instrument, it was liberally framed, and passed with a very general approbation. They then appointed a Committee for the 'reduction of a projet' of a constitution. . . . I received . . . a letter of July 20th, requesting me to attend and assist at their deliberations; but I excused myself, on the obvious considerations, that my mission was to the King as Chief Magistrate of the nation, that my duties were limited to the concerns of my own country, and forbade me to intermeddle with the internal transactions of that, in which I had been received under a specific character only. Their plan of a constitution was discussed in sections. . . . The first respected the general frame of the government; and that this should be formed into three departments, Executive, Legislative and Judiciary,

was generally agreed. But when they proceeded to subordinate developments, many and various shades of opinion came into conflict, and schism, strongly marked, broke the Patriots into fragments of very discordant principles. . . . I received one day a note from the Marquis de La Fayette, informing me that he should bring a party of six or eight friends to ask a dinner of me the next day. I assured him of their welcome. . . . Marquis introduced the objects of the conference, by summarily reminding them of the state of things in the Assembly, the course which the principles of the Constitution were taking, and the inevitable result, unless checked by more concord among the Patriots themselves. . . . The discussions began at the hour of four, and were continued till ten o'clock in the evening; during which time, I was a silent witness to a coolness and candor of argument, unusual in the conflicts of political opinion; to a logical reasoning, and chaste eloquence, disfigured by no gaudy tinsel of rhetoric or declamation, and truly worthy of being placed in parallel with the finest dialogues of antiquity, as handed to us by Xenophon, by Plato and Cicero. The result was, that the King should have a suspensive veto on the laws, that the legislature should be composed of a single body only, and that to be chosen by the people. This Concordate decided the fate of the constitution. The Patriots all rallied to the principles thus settled, carried every question agreeably to them, and reduced the Aristocracy to insignificance and impotence."

25. *Ibid.*, pp. 114–115: "Here I discontinue my relation of the French Revolution. The minuteness with which I have so far given its details, is disproportioned to the general scale of my narrative. But I have thought it justified by the interest which the whole world must take in this Revolution. As yet, we are but in the first chapter of its history. The appeal to the rights of man, which had been made in the United States, was taken up by France, first of the European nations."

26. Especially useful for this sect. have been the documents included in *The Papers of Thomas Jefferson* (edited by Julian P. Boyd and successors, Princeton, 1950–), Vol. I (1760–1776). All *sic*. Among the many secondary works that have been helpful here, Pauline Maier's recent *American Scripture: Making the Declaration of Independence* (New York, 1997) is of particular note, esp. Ch. III, sect. 2, which includes consideration of Jefferson's preambles to the Virginia constitution. Yet her orientation differs from the present one. Other relevant works dealing with the Declaration of Independence will be cited below when we come to that subject.

27. Jefferson, *Papers*, I, pp. 337– ff. (first draft of preamble to a new Virginia constitution).

28. *Ibid.*, pp. 337–338 (first draft preamble): "Whereas George Guelph King of Great Britain & Ireland and Elector of Hanover, heretofore entrusted with the exercise of the kingly office in this government, hath endeavored to pervert the same into a detestable & insupportable tyranny

"by . . . putting his negative on laws the most wholesome & necessary for the public good

"by denying to his governors permission to pass laws of (*the most*) immediate & pressing importance, unless suspended in their operation for his (*con*) assent &, when so suspended, neglecting . . . to attend to them for many years:

"by refusing to pass certain other laws, unless the persons to be benefited by them would relinquish the inestimable right(s) of representation in the legislature:

"by dissolving legislative assemblies repeatedly & continually for opposing with manly firmness his invasions on the rights of the people:

"when dissolved, by refusing to call others for a long space of time, thereby leaving the political system (*in a state of dissolution*) without any legislative (*body*) head.

"by endeavoring to prevent the population of our country (*by*) & for that purpose obstructing the laws for the naturalization of foreigners & raising the conditions of new appropriati(*ng*)ons (*new*) of lands:

"by keeping among us in times of peace standing armies & ships of war:
"by affecting to render the military independant of & superior to the civil power:
"by combining with others to subject us to a foreign jurisdiction giving his (con) assent to their pretended acts of legislation (*for imposing taxes on us without our consent.*)
for quartering large bodies of armed troops among us:
for cutting off our trade with all parts of the world:
for (*depriving us of*), imposing taxes on us without our consent:
for depriving us of the benefits of trial by jury:
for transporting us beyond seas to be tried for pretended offences:
for suspending our own legislatures & declaring themselves invested with power to legislate for us in all cases whatsoever ..."

29. Cf. our *Origins of Sovereignty*, Vol. V, Bk. 2, Ch. III, pp. 206 ff., with corresponding notes, on the Glorious Revolution of 1688 and the English Declaration (Bill) of Rights of 1689. Also relevant in the same ch. of that vol. are the discussions on Locke and other theorists of his era as well on earlier writers in the Cromwellian period. Jefferson's other writings and his library clearly indicate that he was knowledgeable about a wide range of English writers of the 17th century, in addition to French writers with corresponding democratic viewpoints.

30. A comparison of the portions of the English Declaration of Rights given in the main text of our *Origins*, Vol. V, Bk. 2, pp. 208–10, and the portions of Jefferson's first and third Virginia preambles given in the notes to the present sect. of this book will show various pertinent similarities and differences.

In all three of these cases, the initial "whereas" clauses denouncing the king (the English Declaration of Rights having stressed his subversion of Protestantism and "the laws and liberties of this kingdom") are followed by a lengthy series of "by" clauses itemizing the particular grievances against which redress is being sought. The lists supplied by Jefferson are much longer and more developed than those in the English Declaration of Rights. The specific legislative slant of the first two items given in the two different lists in the English Declaration of Rights have some points of similarity to Jefferson's lists of charges especially toward the beginning. However, the legislative orientation prevails more specifically and strongly in the fuller lists of charges drawn up by Jefferson. Thus, although legislative perspectives gave a leading framework to the English Declaration of Rights, they become a far greater force and focus in Jefferson's hands.

This greater emphasis on issues of legislation and legislative sovereignty in Jefferson's Virginia preambles (and in their official adoption by the Virginia legislature) can be partly explained by the changed American circumstances of 1776 in contradistinction to the British situation in 1689. The American colonists at Philadelphia in 1776 were rebelling against an array of hostile legislative acts passed by the British parliament and king for purposes of imperial domination over the colonies. The English parliament's revolt against the crown in 1689 involved a different set of circumstances, in which the final outcome meant the continuation of monarchy though in more limited forms. Separate declarations of independence by individual American colonies besides Virginia, in draft and final versions, furnish further comparative perspectives on elements of the Virginia preambles under discussion here, as also do other writings by Jefferson and fellow "founding fathers." Even so, there can be little doubt that, despite all the potential precedents for and influences upon Jefferson's thinking at this point, his highly original and creative mind, making good use also of traditions in political theory, newly engaged the whole issue of legislation in his own special way. The same applies to his treatment of this subject in his other pertinent writings concerned with the state of Virginia, as remains to be seen.

The English Declaration of Rights had also included at the end—not unlike its counterpart in Jefferson's second and third drafts of the preamble to the Virginia constitution—

various "enactment" clauses. These likewise affirmed not only the English Declaration's official legality but also its character as legislation, as also suggested in the opening lines of its different preambles. Here, too, the concluding "enactment" statements in Jefferson's Virginia preambles were more elaborate in their legislative language than in the case of the English Declaration of Rights, just as they were in comparison with their counterparts in the officially adopted Virginia preamble.

It can be added at this point that the English Declaration (Bill) of Rights of 1689, so often and rightly credited as a crucial forerunner of the American Bill of Rights, was far lengthier and different. The English document was much more directly focused on legislative matters, in certain parts, than was its briefer American counterpart. Yet the latter did include a number of important indirect legislative perspectives, which have not heretofore been duly apprehended by historians and which will be treated later. In addition, the English Declaration of Rights included lengthy discussions of religious issues, owing to the perceived oppressive popish orientation of King James II and the need to make Protestantism the official religion of succeeding monarchs. The American Bill of Rights included religion only briefly, however significantly, in the first short article and did so under much different conditions.

31. Maier, *American Scripture*, Ch. III, sect. 2.

32. Jefferson, *Papers* I, pp. 339–340 (first draft preamble): "And whereas by an act ... of the present parliament of Great Britain passed for the purpose of prohibiting all trades & intercourse with the colonies[, they] ... are in a state of open Rebellion & hostility against the king & his parliament. ... George [III] ... hath given his assent & thereby put us out of his allegiance & protection; in which case it was provided by the original charter or compact granted to Sir Walter Raleigh on behalf of this [Virginia] colony ... [in] 1584, 'that if ... [he] should ... do any act of unjust or unlawful hostility, to ... subjects of ... [Q]ueen [Elizabeth and of] ... her heirs or successors[,] it should be lawful ... [if] out of her allegiance & protection[, not] ... to be holden as any of hers, nor to her ... dominion or allegiance any way belong'[,] so that ... George [III,] having by the said act of parliament declared us in a state of Rebellion & hostility & put us out of his allegiance & protection, it follows by the sd. charter that ... [we] are not subject to him, & are not to be holden as any of his, nor to his dominion any way belonging. ... [Therefore,] George [III,] ... not only for his criminal abuses of the high duties of his kingly office, but also by his ... act of ... putting us from his allegiance ... & dominion, may now lawfully, rightfully, & by consent of both parties be divested of the kingly powers.

33. *Papers* I, pp. 347 ff. (second draft preamble).

34. Cf. *ibid.* for Boyd's editorial discussions.

35. *Ibid.*, pp. 356 ff. (third draft preamble).

36. *Ibid.*, p. 356 (third draft preamble):

"A Bill for new-modelling the form of Government and for establishing the Fundamental principles thereof in future.

"Whereas George Guelf King of Great Britain & Ireland and Elector of Hanover, heretofore entrusted with the exercise of the kingly office in this government[;] hath endeavored to pervert the same into a detestable and insupportable tyranny;

"by putting his negative on laws the most wholesome & necessary for ye. public good;

"by denying to his governors permission to pass laws of immediate & pressing importance, unless suspended in their operation for his (*con*) assent, and, when so suspended, neglecting to attend to them for many years;

"by refusing to pass certain other laws, unless the persons to be benefited by them would relinquish the inestimable right of representation in the legislature[;]

"by dissolving legislative assemblies repeatedly and continually for opposing with manly firmness his invasions on the rights of the people;

"when dissolved, by refusing to call others for a long space of time, thereby leaving the political system without any legislative head;

"by endeavoring to prevent the population of our country, & for that purpose obstructing the laws for the naturalization of foreigners & raising the conditions of new appropriations of lands;

"by keeping among us in times of peace, standing armies & ships of war;

"by affecting to render the military independent of & superior to the civil power;

"by combining with others to subject us to a foreign jurisdiction, giving his assent to their pretended acts of legislation

for quartering large bodies of troops among us;

for cutting off our trade with all parts of the world;

for imposing taxes on us without our consent;

for depriving us of the benefits of trial by jury;

for transporting us beyond seas to be tried for pretended offences; and

for suspending our own legislatures & declaring themselves invested with power to legislate for us in all cases whatsoever. . . ."

37. *Ibid.*, pp. 377 ff. (official preamble as finally adopted).

38. *Ibid.*, pp. 377–378 (official preamble as finally adopted):

"A CONSTITUTION, OR FORM OF GOVERNMENT,

agreed to and resolved upon by the Delegates and Representatives of the several Counties and Corporations of Virginia.

"Whereas George the Third, King of Great Britain and Ireland, and Elector of Hanover, heretofore intrusted with the exercise of the Kingly Office in this Government, hath endeavoured to pervert the same into a detestable and insupportable Tyranny; by putting his negative on Laws the most wholesome and necessary for the publick good;

"by denying his Governours permission to pass Laws of immediate and pressing importance, unless suspended in their operation for his assent, and, when so suspended, neglecting to attend to them for many Years;

"by refusing to pass certain other laws, unless the persons to be benefited by them would relinquish the inestimable right of representation in the legislature;

"by dissolving legislative assemblies repeatedly and continually, for opposing with manly firmness his invasions of the rights of the people;

"when dissolved, by refusing to call others for a long space of time, thereby leaving the political system without any legislative head;

"by endeavouring to prevent the population of our Country, and, for that purpose, obstructing the laws for the naturalization of foreigners;

"by keeping among us, in times of peace, standing Armies, and Ships of War;

"by affecting to render the Military independent of, and superiour to, the civil power;

"by combining with others to subject us to a foreign Jurisdiction [!], giving his assent to their pretended Acts of Legislation;

"for quartering large bodies of armed troops among us;

"for cutting off our Trade with all parts of the World;

"for imposing Taxes on us without our Consent;

"for depriving us of the Benefits of Trial by Jury;

"for transporting us beyond Seas, to be tried for pretended Offences;

"for suspending our own Legislatures, and declaring themselves invested with power to legislate for us in all Cases whatsoever. . . ."

39. Maier, *American Scripture*, Ch. III, sect. 2.

40. See the discussions and citations in *ibid.*, Ch. III, sect. 2.

Professor Maier points out (p. 115 etc.) that the many state and local resolutions on independence dealt with specific concrete occurrences prompting such action. Much differently, Jefferson's Declaration of Independence (and, by extension, its forerunners in his Virginia draft preambles shortly before in 1776) cast the British king as a tyrant in order to justify his overthrow, thereby altering somewhat the historical facts and record. Indeed, many items in the opening list of (legislative) charges in Jefferson's Declaration of Independence (and his Virginia preambles, upon which it was largely based) played a relatively small part in the actual struggles, as even some contemporaries noted. For this reason, historians have, says Maier, been puzzled, "scrambling to figure out what it was talking about." They have, one can add, neglected the legislative contexts; these provide a key to a fuller comprehension of not only the puzzling opening charges but also the more obvious familiar charges that ensue and that are rooted in the state and local resolutions.

Maier's impressive detailed expositions of the varied arrangements of charges against the British government—as listed in Jefferson's Virginia preambles, Declaration of Independence, and other related writings—are thus oriented largely around Jefferson's idea of the king as tyrant. Many contemporaries from John Adams to Thomas Hutchinson found Jefferson's arguments on that score unconvincing. But, we may add, even they may have underappreciated the higher and wider legislative theory of sovereignty lying behind Jefferson's lists of charges, especially in the Declaration of Independence. If some contemporaries like Hutchinson also faulted Jefferson's opening group of (legislative and other) charges for not corresponding clearly to actual events or circumstances of the period, including in matters of legislation, they, too, like many later historians, may have, as it were, missed the forest for its separate trees.

The present interpretation could be viewed, in part, as an extension of Maier's focus on the tyrant idea, to encompass here the underlying orbit of legislation, a topic in its own right. In a sense, the present discussion's intended demystification of Jefferson's ideas by using his own legislative focus, as seen in wider theoretical contexts, can be squared with Maier's revealing analyses of the documents she, too, has found still veiled in partial obscurity.

It must also here, as elsewhere, be duly recognized how great remains the debt of all in this field of study to Julian Boyd's enduring outstanding edition in *Papers* I of Jefferson's earliest writings. Boyd's masterful editing and arranging of basic documents, illuminated by his commentaries (sometimes unfairly called excessive), has still not been fully utilized in all its great potential for resolving historians' most vexing textual conundrums.

41. Cf. our *Origins*, Vols. I–II on Corasius and III on Bodin.

42. E.g. Maier, *American Scripture*, Ch. III, sect. 2.

43. E.g. John Phillip Reid, *Constitutional History of the American Revolution*, Vol. III, *The Authority to Legislate* (Madison, 1991), much differently focused than the present study.

44. Bernard Bailyn, *The Ideological Origins of the American Revolution* (Camb., Mass., 1967, etc.), Ch. V, sect. 3, "Sovereignty," which was previously cited in our *Origins*, Vol. IV, p. 475, in connection with Bodin's influence on later figures, such as Jefferson.

45. Jefferson, *Papers* I, pp. 341 ff. (first draft of a new Virginia constitution). In general, some of the lines quoted in our discussions are, in the fuller text as given by Boyd, indented or set off in various separate fashions. Boyd's text has some further markings indicative of its quality as a first (rough) draft. As above in the case of the three preambles, so too in the case of the corresponding constitutions, the intricacies of the manuscripts themselves, along with their provenance and their transmission to the present day, are explored by Boyd in his notes.

46. *Papers*, pp. 347 ff. (second draft constitution).

47. *Ibid.*, pp. 358 ff. (third draft constitution).

48. Concerning Mason, see passages quoted above in our text corresponding to n. 7; cf. also n. 8.

49. Mason's first plan for a Virginia constitution is in Jefferson's *Papers* I, pp. 366 ff., while the committee's revision of his plan is on pp. 369 ff. The draft reported by the committee with "amendments thereto offered in Convention" is on pp. 373 ff. The Virginia constitution as officially adopted by the Convention is on pp. 377 ff.

George Mason's original plan for a Virginia government contained fifteen numbered (mostly short) paragraphs. It begins, much like Jefferson's plan, by calling for three separate departments—legislative, executive, judicial—in which none of them could "exercise the powers properly belonging to the other." Similarly to Jefferson and others, Mason then proposed a bicameral legislature, in this case divided into an Upper House and a Lower House, together called the General Assembly. The Lower originates laws and the Upper either approves or rejects them. In Mason's plan, the Governor or Chief Magistrate, to be elected annually by the full legislature, could serve only three successive terms, becoming ineligible in any case for three years. The Governor is also President of the Privy Council, or Council of State, and its Vice President acts as Lieutenant Governor in the absence of the Governor. The Mason plan as revised by the committee also had the corresponding fifteen sections but was somewhat longer. Both documents underscore the name of "commonwealth" for the state of Virginia. The draft then reported by the committee consisted of a lengthy listing of specific amendments offered in Convention.

Other than the preamble, the provisions and parts of the official Virginia constitution that were taken over specifically from Jefferson's drafts are not necessary to treat here. The Boyd edn. has done an excellent job of identifying them. Yet the overall architecture of Jefferson's plans, as the only complete ones submitted, coupled with the adoption of his preamble, suggests that the officially adopted constitution was more influenced by Jefferson than he believed, or was willing to acknowledge, and than Boyd, too, has indicated. Organizationally, for instance, the official constitution, like certain approaches in drafts by Jefferson discussed above, begins with (his) preamble and proceeds, without any ensuing demarcations or enumerations of sections, to the legislative, executive, and judicial powers in turn. However, other than on various aspects of property, there is no concluding section with a kind of Bill of Rights in the broader ways included by Jefferson, an omission that was sure to disappoint him.

The official Virginia "Constitution, or Form of Government," as it was called, provided for the three powers to be separated. The legislature is divided into two distinct branches—a House of Delegates or Representatives and a Senate or House of Senators. Laws originate with the Delegates and are approved or rejected by the Senate. In addition to the Governor or Chief Magistrate, there is a Privy Council or Council of State. Among the specific paragraphs and provisions variously adapted from Jefferson's plans are, according to Boyd, part of the initial statement on the separation of powers and most of the statement that all penalties etc. "heretofore going to the King shall go to the Common Wealth, save only such, as the Legislature may abolish, or otherwise provide for." At the same time, as Boyd points out, one of the only parts of the Mason plan that was adopted without real revision centered on the statement that laws originate in the House of Delegates and are approved or rejected by the Senate.

50. I have used the edn. of Jefferson's *Notes on the State of Virginia* prepared by William Peden (Chapel Hill, 1954, 1982). The work was somewhat corrected and enlarged by Jefferson in 1782 and later published in 1787. All sic.

51. *Ibid.* (*Notes* XIII), pp. 120–121.

52. *Ibid.* (*Notes* XIII), pp. 121–122.

53. The preceding text of *Notes* XIII continues as follows (*ibid.*, pp. 123–124): "It is not the name, but the authority which renders an act obligatory. Lord Coke says, 'an article of the statute II R. 2. c. 5. that no person should attempt to revoke any ordinance then made, is repealed, for that such restraint is against the jurisdiction [!] and power of the parliament.' 4. inst. 42. and again, 'though divers parliaments have attempted to restrain

subsequent parliaments, yet could they never effect it; for the latter parliament hath ever power to abrogate, suspend, qualify, explain, or make void the former in the whole or in any part thereof, notwithstanding any words of restraint, prohibition, or penalty, in the former: for it is a maxim in the laws of the parliament, '*because subsequent laws nullify earlier laws which are contrary* [originally in Latin].'—4. inst. 43.—To get rid of the magic supposed to be in the word *constitution*, let us translate it into its definition as given by those who think it above the power of the law; and let us suppose the convention instead of saying, 'We, the ordinary legislature, establish a *constitution*,' had said, 'We, the ordinary legislature, establish an act above *the power of the ordinary legislature*.' Does not this expose the absurdity of the attempt? 3. [Jefferson's third point in his fifth main argument] But, say they, the people have acquiesced, and this has given it an authority superior to the laws. It is true, that the people did not rebel against it: and was that a time for the people to rise in rebellion? Should a prudent acquiescence, at a critical time, be construed into a confirmation of every illegal thing done during that period? Besides, why should they rebel?" This third point Jefferson also goes on to develop at length.

Cf. in general, here and elsewhere, the editor's notes to Jefferson's text for indications of material in *Notes* XIII that was originally in Latin. Editor also gives information on Jefferson's sources and citations in developing his second of three points as included above.

54. *Ibid.* (*Notes* XIII), pp. 125–129: "6. That the assembly exercises a power of determining the Quorum of their own body which may legislate for us. After the establishment of the new form they adhered to the *Law of the majority* [originally in Latin], founded in common law as well as common right. It is the natural law of every assembly of men, whose numbers are not fixed by any other law. They continued for some time to require the presence of a majority of their whole number, to pass an act. But the British parliament fixes its own quorum: our former assemblies fixed their own quorum: and one precedent in favour of power is stronger than an hundred against it. The house of delegates therefore have lately voted that, during the present dangerous invasion, forty members shall be a house to proceed to business. They have been moved to this by the fear of not being able to collect a house. But this danger could not authorize them to call that a house which was none: and if they may fix it at one number, they may at another, till it loses its fundamental character of being a representative body. . . . The power however of fixing their own quorum has been avowed, and a precedent set. From forty it may be reduced to four, and from four to one: from a house to a committee, from a committee to a chairman or speaker, and thus an oligarchy or monarchy be substituted under forms supposed to be regular. . . . When therefore it is considered, that there is no legal obstacle to the assumption by the assembly of all the powers legislative, executive, and judiciary, and that these may come to the hands of the smallest rag of delegation, surely the people will say, and their representatives, while yet they have honest representatives, will advise them to say, that they will not acknowledge as laws any acts not considered and assented to by the major part of their delegates.

"In enumerating the defects of the constitution, it would be wrong to count among them what is only the error of particular persons. In December 1776, our circumstances being much distressed, it was proposed in the house of delegates to create a *dictator*, invested with every power legislative, executive and judiciary, civil and military, of life and of death, over our persons and over our properties: and in June 1781, again under calamity, the same proposition was repeated, and wanted a few votes only of being passed. . . . [F]rom whence have they derived this power? Is it from our ancient laws? None such can be produced. Is it from any principle in our new constitution, expressed or implied? Every lineament of that expressed or implied, is in full opposition to it. Its fundamental principle is, that the state shall be governed as a commonwealth. It provides a republican organization, proscribes under the name of *prerogative* the exercise of all powers undefined by the laws; places on this basis the whole system of our laws; and, by consolidating them together, chuses [*sic*] that they shall be left to stand or fall together, never providing for any circumstances, nor admitting that such could arise, wherein either should be suspended, no, not for a moment. . . . The same laws forbid the abandonment of that post, even on ordinary occasions; and much more a transfer of their powers into other hands and other forms, without consulting the people. . . . Was it from the necessity of the case? Necessities which dissolve a government, do not convey its authority to an oligarchy or a monarchy. . . . [A]mong our sister states, several had grappled through greater difficulties without abandoning their forms of government. . . . In this state alone did there exist so little virtue, that fear was to be fixed in the hearts of the people, and to become the motive of their exertions and the principle of their government? The very thought alone was treason against the people; was treason against mankind in general. . . . Those who assume the right of giving away the reins of government . . . to . . . the dictator, will lay their necks on the block when he shall nod to them. . . . I am of opinion, that the government . . . would have been thrown back upon the bungling machinery of county committees for administration, till a convention could have been called, and its wheels again set into regular motion. . . . Those who meant well, of the advocates for this measure, (and most of them meant well, for I know them personally, had been their fellow-labourers in the common cause, and had often proved the purity of their principles), had been seduced in their judgment by the example of an ancient republic, whose constitution and circumstances were fundamentally different. They had sought this precedent in the history of Rome, where alone it was to be found, and where at length too it had proved fatal. They had taken it from a republic, rent by the most bitter factions and tumults, where the government was of a heavy-handed unfeeling aristocracy, over a people ferocious, and rendered desperate by poverty and wretchedness; tumults which could not be allayed under the most trying circumstances, but by the omnipotent hand of a single despot. Their constitution therefore allowed a temporary tyrant to be erected, under the name of a Dictator; and that temporary tyrant, after a few examples, became perpetual. They misapplied this precedent to a people, mild in their dispositions, patient under their trial, united for the public liberty, and affectionate to their leaders. But if from the constitution of the Roman government there resulted to their Senate a power of submitting all their rights to the will of one man, does it follow, that the assembly of Virginia have the same authority? What clause in our constitution has substituted that of Rome, by way of residuary provision, for all cases not otherwise provided for? Or if they may step ad libitum into any other form of government for precedents to rule us by, for what oppression may not a precedent be found in this world of the *war of all people against all things*?"

When Jefferson wrote these passages in 1781, his career was in jeopardy. An investigation of his conduct as former governor had been unfairly instigated, he felt, by Patrick Henry, the apparent mover of this proposed dictatorship. Jefferson was soon officially absolved in the matter and thanked for his service, yet he expressed considerable hurt. Portions not included above of his discussion of the sixth defect of the Virginia constitution allude to this episode, his patriotic intentions throughout it, and his admiration for his colleagues despite his strong criticism. Cf. editor's note, *ibid.* (*Notes* XIII), p. 285.

The above passages make further use of sources in English legal history. In them, Jefferson might have cited the example of Oliver Cromwell and his party in reducing the size of the English parliament in order to push through their measures in the mid-17th century crisis.

55. *Ibid.*, p. 129 (continuation of passage in preceding note, to end of *Notes* XIII).

56. *Ibid.* (*Notes*, Appendix 2), pp. 209 ff.

57. *Ibid.* (*Notes*, App. 2), pp. 209–210: "It is known . . . that the government of Great Britain, with which the American States were not long since connected, assumed over them an authority unwarrantable and oppressive. . . . It hath pleased the Sovereign Disposer of all human events to give to this appeal an issue favourable to the rights of the States; to enable them to reject for ever all dependance on a government which had shewn itself so capable of abusing the trusts reposed in it; and to obtain from that government a solemn and explicit acknowledgment that they are free, sovereign, and independant States. During the progress of that war, through which we had to labour for the establishment of our rights, the legislature of the commonwealth of Virginia found it necessary to make a temporary organization of government for preventing anarchy. . . . But this, like all other their acts of legislation, being subject to change by subsequent legislatures, possessing equal powers with themselves, it has been thought expedient, that it should receive those amendments which time and trial have suggested, and be rendered permanent by a power superior to that of the ordinary legislature. The general assembly therefore of this state recommend it to the good people thereof, to chuse delegates to meet in general convention, with powers to form a constitution of government for them. . . .

"We therefore, the delegates, chosen by the said good people of this state for the purpose aforesaid, and now assembled in general convention, do, in execution of the authority with which we are invested, establish the following constitution and fundamentals of government for the said state of Virginia.

"The said state shall for ever hereafter be governed as a commonwealth.

"The powers of government shall be divided into three distinct departments, each of them to be confided to a separate body of magistracy; to wit, those which are legislative to one, those which are judiciary to another, and those which are executive to another. No person, or collection of persons, being of one of these departments, shall exercise any power properly belonging to either of the others, except in the instances hereinafter expressly permitted.

"I. LEGISLATURE.

"The legislature shall consist of two branches, the one to be called the House of Delegates, the other the Senate, and both together the General Assembly. The concurrence of both of these, expressed on three several readings, shall be necessary to the passage of a law."

Under this first article, reference is made to "our confederacy" and the "United States" (p. 213). There, the powers of the governor are cited, and the quorum is treated (as a majority in each of the two houses).

58. *Ibid.* (*Notes*, App. 2), pp. 214–215):

"II. EXECUTIVE. GOVERNOR.

"The executive powers shall be exercised by a governor, who shall be chosen by joint ballot of both houses of assembly, and when chosen shall remain in office five years, and be ineligible a second time. During his term he shall hold no other office or emolument under this state, or any other state or power whatsoever. By executive powers, we mean no reference to those powers exercised under our former government by the crown. . . . We give him those powers only, which are necessary to execute the laws (and administer the government) and which are not in their nature either legislative or judiciary. The application of this idea must be left to reason. We do however expressly deny him the prerogative powers of erecting courts, [etc., etc.] . . . except so far as he may be authorised from time to time by the legislature to exercise any of those powers. The powers of declaring war and concluding peace, of contracting alliances, of issuing letters of marque and reprisal, of raising or introducing armed forces, of building armed vessels, forts, or strong holds, of coining money or regulating its value, of regulating weights and measures, we leave to be exercised under the authority of the confederation: but in all cases respecting them which are out of the said confederation, they shall be exercised by the governor, under the regulation of such laws as the legislature may think it expedient to pass."

59. *Ibid.* (*Notes*, App. 2), p. 213. E.g. the legislature cannot infringe upon the constitution or the rights of citizens. There are many other inherent safeguards against the legislature unduly appropriating power. These include the quorum, which must be a majority and cannot be reduced arbitrarily by the legislature.

60. *Ibid.* (*Notes*, App. 2), p. 219:

"IV. COUNCIL OF REVISION.

"The governor, two councellors of state, and a judge from each of the superior Courts of chancery, common Law, and Admiralty, shall be a council to revise all bills which shall have passed both houses of assembly, in which council the governor, when present, shall preside. Every bill, before it becomes a law, shall be presented to this council, who shall have a right to advise its rejection, returning the bill, with their advice and reasons in writing, to the house in which it originated, who shall proceed to reconsider the said bill. But if after such reconsideration, two thirds of the house shall be of opinion the bill should pass finally, they shall pass and send it, with the advice and written reasons of the said council of revision to the other house, wherein, if two thirds also shall be of opinion it should pass finally, it shall thereupon become law: otherwise it shall not."

Article IV continues at length on this and related topics.

61. *Ibid.* (*Notes*, App. 2), p. 220.

62. For textual and historical discussions relating to Jefferson's revised Virginia constitution drafted in 1783, cf. Jefferson's *Papers*, Vol. VI, pp. 278–317. Following Jefferson's proposed Virginia constitution, on pp. 294 ff., are Madison's "Observations" on it made in Oct. 1788, on pp. 308 ff.

63. *Ibid.* (*Notes*, editor's notes to Query XIV), pp. 285–286. Cf. also Jefferson's *Papers*, Vol. II, pp. 305–605 for discussion and text of the "Report."

64. *Ibid.* (*Notes* XIV), pp. 132–133:

"A description of the laws.

"The general assembly was constituted, as has been already shewn, by letters-patent of March the 9th, 1607, in the 4th year of the reign of James the First. The laws of England seem to have been adopted by consent of the settlers, which might easily enough be done whilst they were few and living all together. Of such adoption however we have no other proof than their practice, till the year 1661, when they were expressly adopted by an act of the assembly, except so far as 'a difference of condition' rendered them inapplicable. Under this adoption, the rule, in our courts of judicature was, that the common law of England, and the general statutes previous to the 4th of James, were in force here; but that no subsequent statutes were, *unless we were named in them*, said the judges and other partisans of the crown, but *named or not named*, said those who reflected freely. It will be unnecessary to attempt a description of the laws of England, as that may be found in English publications. To those which were established here, by the adoption of the legislature, have been since added a number of acts of assembly passed during the monarchy, and ordinances of convention and acts of assembly enacted since the establishment of the republic. The following variations from the British model are perhaps worthy of being specified."

65. *Ibid.* (*Notes* XIV), pp. 136–137, 143, 146. Appendix 3 is "An Act for Establishing Religious Freedom, 1786."

66. Jefferson, *Papers*, Vol. 2 ("Bill for the Revision of the Laws," Oct. 1776), pp. 562–563:

"Bill for the Revision of the Laws

"Whereas on the late change which hath of necessity been introduced into the form of government in this country[,] it is become also necessary to make corresponding changes in the laws heretofore in force, many of which are inapplicable to the powers of government as now organised [*sic*], others are founded on principles heterogeneous to the republican spirit, others which, long before such change, had been oppressive to the people, could yet never be repealed while the regal power continued, and others, having taken their origin while our ancestors remained in Britain, are not so well adapted to our present circumstances of time and place, and it is also necessary to introduce certain other laws, which, though proved by the experience of other states to be friendly to liberty and the rights of mankind, we have not heretofore been permitted to adopt; and whereas a work of such magnitude, labour, and difficulty, may not be effected during the short and busy term of a session of assembly:

"*Be it therefore enacted by the General Assembly of the commonwealth of Virginia, and it is hereby enacted by the authority of the same*, That a committee, to consist of five persons, shall be appointed by joint ballot of both houses (three of whom to be a quorum) who shall have full power and authority to revise, alter, amend, repeal, or introduce all or any of the said laws, to form the same into bills, and report them to the next meeting of the general assembly. [Etc.]."

67. *Ibid.*, Vol. 2 ("Plan Agreed upon by the Committee of Revision," Jan. 1777), p. 325 (etc.):

"The Common Law are not to be medled with, except where Alterations are necessary.

"The Statutes to be revised and digested, alterations proper for us to be made; the Diction, where obsolete or redundant, to be reformed; but otherwise to undergo as few Changes as possible.

"The Acts of the English Common-wealth to be examined.

"The Statutes to be divided into Periods: the Acts of Assembly, made on the same Subject, to be incorporated into them.

"The Laws of the other Colonies to be examined, and any good ones to be adopted.

"Provisoes &c. which wou'd do only what the Law wou'd do without them, to be omitted.

"Bills to be short; not to include Matters of different Natures; not to insert an unnecessary word, nor omit a useful one.

"Laws to be made on the Spur of the present Occasion, and all innovating Laws, to be limited in their Duration [Etc.]."

68. A catalogue of the 126 bills as well as the bills them.selves are presented in *Papers*, Vol. II ("The Revisal of the Laws, 1776–1786), pp. 329 ff. and pp. 336 ff., respectively, following the initial plan by the committee of revisors on pp. 325 ff. All this is followed by an Appendix in which is presented, in turn, a bill declaring when laws shall be in force, Jefferson's notes of English statutes, Jefferson's notes of acts of assembly adopted Oct. 1777 and May 1778, an outline of a bill for proportioning crimes and punishments, and memorandum by Jefferson on bills to be drafted.

69. Cf. Charles B. Sanford, *The Religious Life of Thomas Jefferson* (Charlottesville, 1984), with regard to a broad range of Jefferson's religious ideas and with particular regard to the statute for establishing religious freedom.

70. *Papers*, Vol. 2 (Boyd's editorial note to "Revisal of the Laws"), pp. 305 ff.: "It is an extremely difficult task to bring into proper focus . . . the far-reaching revision of the laws that Jefferson and other leading Virginians embarked upon in the autumn of 1776. This is chiefly because the revision of the laws itself never came into focus. It was a long-drawn-out movement, ending in something of an anti-climax, and never became embodied in a single enactment as in the case of earlier or later revisions in Virginia and in other states. . . . [T]he revision as a whole has, for the most part, faded into obscurity against the background of ordinary legislation in the decade from 1776 to 1786. . . . There is no single identifiable entity that can be called the Revision of the Laws as there is, for example, in the so-called Chancellors' Revisal of 1785 or the revision approved in 1792.

"This resulted partly from its purpose, which was not that of forming a collection of laws then in force but of reforming the entire structure of law so as to strip it of all vestiges of its earlier monarchical aspects and to bring it into conformity with republican principles. If Jefferson and his colleagues had been content merely to collect the body of law then in force, no doubt the General Assembly would have approved in 1779 what it actually did approve in 1792. But this would have been executing the task of compilers, not that of legislators, and Jefferson, Pendleton, Wythe, Mason, and others apparently never entertained the idea of making a mere collection of the laws. Certainly Jefferson never did. The failure of the Virginia Convention of 1776 to adopt his proposed Constitution undoubtedly emphasized the need he felt for reform of the laws. For his Constitution had included some provisions that he later incorporated in legislative bills that he thought would form 'a system by which every fibre would be eradicated of antient or future aristocracy; and a foundation laid for a government truly republican' ["Autobiography"]. . . . But he no doubt would have proposed a general overhauling of the legal system as an urgent necessity even if his Constitution had been wholly adopted, for he understood the distinction between fundamental and statutory law and knew that the former could not and should not embrace the detailed provisions of the latter. . . .

"Yet the failure of the revision of the laws to come into focus and to be adequately appraised has resulted from the method as well as the intent of its leading architect. Jefferson, who was unquestionably the principal advocate of the idea of reform, was possessed of a sense of urgency that would not permit a single approach toward the goal. As an active legislator, enmeshed from 1776 to 1779 in the details of day-to-day law-making and its inevitable turmoil of political maneuverings, Jefferson was obliged to be alert to the possibility that any legislative calendar might bring forth bills proposed by adherents of the old order. . . . Jefferson's achievement as legislator in the years 1776 to 1779 was more positive and proceeded on a two-fold method.

"The first was a singlehanded effort to hasten the new era of republicanism by the drafting of legislative bills on particular subjects . . ."

Jefferson's second method was, as he put it (*ibid.*, p. 307), "that our whole code must be reviewed, [and shaped and] adapted to our republican form of government [etc.] . . ."

71. E.g. "Notes and Proceedings on Discontinuing the Establishment of the Church of England," Oct.–Dec. 1776, *Papers*, Vol. 1, pp. 505 ff. This large collection of documents includes Jefferson's various drafts, bills, resolutions, and notes relating to this subject. Boyd begins his editorial note by citing "[t]he importance of Jefferson's legislative activity in 1776 in behalf of religious tolerance." Sect. V is "Notes on Acts of Parliament and on the Virginia Assembly concerning Religious Freedom," while Sect. VI is "Notes on Locke and Shaftesbury."

72. Dumas Malone, *Jefferson and His Time*, Vol. I, *Jefferson the Virginian* (Boston, 1948), p. 247.

73. Merrill D. Peterson, *Thomas Jefferson and the New Nation* (London, 1970), pp. 112, 152–153, 156–157.

74. Secondary works on Jefferson relating to these observations is immense, but a few representative examples may be cited: Frank L. Dewey, *Thomas Jefferson, Lawyer* (Charlottesville, 1986), centering on Jefferson's law practice while ignoring any connections with his legal theory; David N. Mayer, *The Constitutional Thought of Thomas Jefferson* (Charlottesville, 1994), well-developed but neglecting Jefferson's legal-legislative thought; Robert W. Tucker and David C. Hendrickson, *Empire of Liberty: The Statecraft of Thomas Jefferson* (New York, 1990), treating Jeffersonian diplomacy and with reference to issues of nationality and law of nations but omitting legislative matters; Saul K. Padover, *Jefferson* (New York, 1942, etc.), Ch. 5, "Legislator (1776–1779)," brief but interesting; and Noble E. Cunningham, Jr., *The Process of Government under Jefferson*

(Princeton, 1978), e.g. Ch. IX, "Executive-Congressional Relations." Still other pertinent books could be cited dealing with such subjects as Americanism (by Gilbert Chinnard), American nationalism (by Yehoshua Arieli), American republicanism (by Joyce Appleby), etc. Maier's *American Scripture* is somewhat exceptional in its partial focus on legislative matters in relation to the Declaration of Independence, along with other related writings by Jefferson including his proposed Virginia constitution. Works dealing with Jefferson's relationship with Madison in the forming of the U.S. Constitution tend to neglect the legislative perspective—e.g. Adrienne Koch, *Jefferson and Madison: The Great Collaboration* (New York, 1950, etc.), e.g. Ch. 5, "Liberty and Power"; and Merrill D. Peterson, *Jefferson and Madison and the Making of Constitutions* (Charlottesville, 1987). It would seem that the suggestive title of Merrill Peterson's *The Jefferson Image in the American Mind* (New York, 1960) could stand as a larger rubric for why Jefferson's thought on legislation has been relatively neglected by historians, who, like people at large, usually think of him more in terms of democracy, freedom, and equality.

75. Jefferson, *Papers* I (*Summary View*), p. 135 n. 7.

76. *Ibid.* (*Sum. View*), pp. 121 ff., provides full text of *Summary View* (or "Draft Instructions").

77. *Ibid.* (*Sum. View*), pp. 121–129 for all passages quoted in above paragraph.

78. *Ibid.* (*Sum. View*), pp. 129–130.

79. *Ibid.* (*Sum. View*), pp. 130–131.

80. *Ibid.* (*Sum. View*), pp. 131–132.

81. *Ibid.* (*Sum. View*), pp. 133–134, for all passages quoted in above paragraph.

82. *Ibid.* (*Sum. View*), pp. 134–135, for all passages quoted.

83. *Ibid.* (Declaration of Causes), p. 187.

84. Jefferson's "Fair Copy" of Declaration of Causes is given in *ibid.*, pp. 199–203.

85. The opening lines of Declaration of Causes are set off as a short paragraph in *ibid.*: "A Declaration by the representatives of the United colonies of America now sitting in General Congress, . . . setting forth the causes & necessity of their taking up arms." The rest of the document consists of one long continuous paragraph.

Also, Jefferson's "Composition Draft," Dickinson's "Composition Draft," and Congress' final version are respectively given in *ibid.*, pp. 193–198, 204–212, 213–218.

86. *Autobiography*, pp. 35–36.

87. *Ibid.*, pp. 36–41 (Jefferson's Declar. of Indep. as amended by Congress); and *Papers* I, pp. 413 ff. (giving, in turn, Jefferson's initial "composition draft" of charges against the crown, a short fragment of the "composition draft" of the Dec. of Ind., Jefferson's self-styled "original Rough draught" of the Dec. of Ind., the Dec. of Ind. as amended by the Committee and by Congress [given in full on pp. 315 ff. in "Notes of Proceedings"], and the Dec. of Ind. as adopted by Congress). Although Congress adopted the Dec. of Ind. on July 4, it was not signed by all until early Aug., 1776.

The intent of the present discussions is not to explore in detail all the nuances of legislative language in the various texts given by Boyd. That task is not feasible here. Maier's *American Scripture*, Ch. III, sect. 2, provides some further useful dimensions along these lines. The aim here is to single out Jefferson's introduction to and presentation of the Dec. of Ind. as it appears in Malone's edn. of his Autobiography (where paragraphs begin with capitalizations not found in "Notes of Proceedings" as given by Boyd). The use here of the text that Jefferson incorporated in his Autobiography and *Notes* is appropriate and convenient. That was Jefferson's copy of his Dec. of Indep. as amended by Congress. Boyd included such materials in *Papers* I together with the other versions so as to bring all documents together (for the first time) with others from 1776.

The first document in Boyd's sect. of *Papers* I on the Dec. of Indep. is what he calls the "Composition Draft of that Part of the Declaration of Independence Concerning the

Charges against the Crown." It was thoroughly based on Jefferson's preamble to the Virginia constitution, including its listing of legislative items. Jefferson somewhat modified the list of charges and numbered them consecutively. Clearly, this was prepared as the central part of the Dec. of Indep.

The third document in Boyd's sect. in *Papers* I on the Dec. of Ind. is "Jefferson's 'original Rough draught' of the Declaration of Independence." This version is a thorny issue in itself not necessary to treat here. Boyd's editorial discussions make it plain that the various stages of composition in the now existing and non-existing versions pose many complicated problems, which have been further explored in subsequent scholarship.

There are many further complexities that cannot and need not be detailed within the present restricted scope. Scholarly opinions and preferences continue to fluctuate and evolve. For instance, whereas Garry Wills in *Inventing America* used the text of the Dec. of Ind. incorporated by Jefferson into his 1776 "Notes of Proceedings" as entitled and given by Boyd in *Papers* I, Maier in *American Scripture* has cited Boyd's own view of that version as not entirely exact or comprehensive, relying instead on the older authority of Carl Becker. Notwithstanding the "Notes" version's occasional imperfection, especially relating to passages other than those treated here, it is well-suited here for purposes of presentation (with "modern" capitalized paragraph beginnings as in Malone's edn. of the Autobiography). The consistency of wording in the central part of the Dec. of Ind., setting forth the list of charges, especially in legislative contexts, renders unproblematical our use of this text in conjunction with the texts provided by Boyd.

Also useful to consult are the facsimiles in Julian Boyd's *The Declaration of Independence: The Evolution of the text as Shown in Facsimiles of Various Drafts by Its Author, Thomas Jefferson* (Princeton, 1945).

88. *Autobiography*, p. 29, and in "Notes of Proceedings."

89 *Ibid.*, pp. 37–38, and in "Notes of Proceedings.".

90. E.g. Maier, *American Scripture*, Ch. III, sect. 2, passim.

91. *Ibid.*

92. Various other statements toward the end of the Dec. of Indep. deal with questions of legislation and sovereignty (*Autobiography*, pp. 40–41).

Concerning the slave trade, Jefferson's draft in *ibid.* included the following statement, which was later cut out by Congress: "He [the king] has prostituted his negative for suppressing every legislative attempt to prohibit or to restrain this execrable commerce."

Referring to "our British brethren," Jefferson wrote, in lines kept by Congress yet slightly altered: "We have warned them from time to time of attempts by their legislature to extend [an unwarrantable (added by Congress)] . . . jurisdiction over [us (Congress added)] [these our states (deleted by Congress)]."

In a statement on U.S. popular sovereignty, Jefferson's words were kept by Congress but heavily altered: "We, therefore, the representatives of the United States of America in General Congress assembled, do in the name, and by the authority of the good people of these [colonies, solemnly publish and declare, that these united colonies are and of right ought to be free and independent states; that they are absolved from all allegiance to the British crown, and that all political connection between them and the state of Great Britain is, and ought to be, totally dissolved; (added by Congress)] [states reject and renounce all allegiance and subjection to the kings of Great Britain and all others who may hereafter claim by, through or under them; we utterly dissolve all political connection which may heretofore have subsisted between us and the people or parliament of Great Britain: and finally we do assert and declare these colonies to be free and independent states, (deleted by Congress)] and that . . ."

93. Bailyn, *Ideological Origins*, Ch. V, sect. 3, "Sovereignty."

94. Maier, *loc. cit.*

95. Reid, *op. cit.*

96. The political "philosophy" of Jefferson in the Declaration of Independence has long been a subject of great interest and controversy. It is not possible or necessary to do justice here to the vast secondary literature, other than to cite a few miscellaneous examples. A standard older classic was Carl L. Becker's *The Declaration of Independence: A Study in the History of Political Ideas* (New York, 1922, 1970, etc.), with attention to the "philosophy" of natural rights, etc. Few books in subsequent decades attracted such wide attention as did Garry Wills' *Inventing America: Jefferson's Declaration of Independence* (New York, 1978), with special focus on philosophical concepts in the Declaration of Jefferson and of the Congress. Among recent contributions are Jayne Allen, *Jefferson's Declaration of Independence: Origins, Philosophy, and Theology* (Lexington, Kentucky, 1998), concentrating on Jefferson's term "Nature's God" (as the God of Deism); and Michael P. Zucker, *The Natural Rights Republic: Studies in the Foundation of the American Political Tradition* (Notre Dame, Ind., 1996), challenging the approach of Wills and others on the Declaration and ideas of Locke.

97. *Autobiography*, p. 35.

98. *Papers* 6, p. 369. Jefferson's "Resolution . . ." was written c. Nov.–Dec., 1783.

99. *Ibid.* pp. 516 ff., "Report . . . ," Jan.–Apr., 1784.

100. In *Jefferson's Parliamentary Writings: "Parliamentary Pocket-Book" and A Manual of Parliamentary Practice* (edited by W. S. Howell, Princeton, 1988), editor's introductory "chronology," p. 6, there quoting Dumas Malone.

101. *Ibid.*, p. 4.

102. *Ibid.*, pp. 355–356 (Jefferson's "Preface" to his *Manual*): "The Constitution of the United States establishing a legislature for the Union, under certain forms, authorises each branch of it 'to determine the rules of its own proceedings.' The Senate have accordingly formed some rules for its own government: but these going only to few cases, they have referred to the decision of their President, without debate and without appeal, all questions of order arising either under their own rules, or where they have provided none. This places under the discretion of the President a very extensive field of decision, and one which, irregularly exercised, would have a powerful effect on the proceedings and determinations of the House. The President must feel weightily and seriously this confidence in his discretion; and the necessity of recurring, for its government, to some known system of rules, that he may neither leave himself free to indulge caprice or passion, nor open to the imputation of them. But to what system of rules is he to recur, as supplementary to those of the Senate? To this there can be but one answer; to the system of regulations adopted for the government of some one of the Parliamentary bodies within these states, or of that which has served as a prototype to most of themn. This last is the model which we have all studied, while we are little acquainted with the modifications of it in our several states. It is deposited too in publications possessed by many and open to all. Its rules are probably as wisely constructed for governing the debates of a deliberative body, and obtaining its true sense, as any which can become known to us; and the acquiescence of the Senate, hitherto, under the references to them, has given them the sanction of their approbation.

"Considering therefore the law of proceedings in the Senate as composed of the precepts of the Constitution, the regulations of the Senate, and, where these are silent, of the rules of Parliament, I have here endeavored to collect and digest so much of these as is called for in ordinary practice, collating the Parliamentary with the Senatorial rules, both where they agree and where they vary. . . . But I have begun a sketch, which those who come after me will successively correct and fill up, till a code of rules shall be formed for the use of the Senate, the effects of which may be, accuracy in business, economy of time, order, uniformity, and impartiality."

Sect. I ("Importance of Rules"): "Mr. Onslow, the ablest among the Speakers of the House of Commons, used to say, 'it was a maxim he had often heard, when he was a young man, from old and experienced members, that nothing tended more to throw power into the hands of administration and those who acted with the majority of the House of Commons, than a neglect of, or departure from, the rules of proceeding: that these forms, as instituted by our ancestors, operated as a check and controul on the actions of the majority, and that they were in many instances, a shelter and protection to the minority, against the attempts of power.' So far the maxim is certainly true, and is founded in good sense, that as it is always in the power of the majority, by their numbers, to stop any improper measures proposed on the part of their opponents, the only weapons by which the minority can defend themselves against similar attempts from those in power, are the forms and rules of proceeding which have been adopted as they were found necessary from time to time, and are become the law of the House; by a strict adherence to which, the weaker party can only be protected from those irregularities and abuses which these forms were intended to check, and which the wantonness of power is but too often apt to suggest to large and successful majorities."

Sect. III ("Privilege"): "The privileges of the members of Parliament, from small and obscure beginnings, have been advancing for centuries, with a firm and never yielding pace. Claims seem to have been brought forward from time to time, and repeated, till some example of their admission enabled them to build law on that example. We can only therefore state the point of progression at which they now are."

103. Here one might recall Jefferson's "Notes on Acts of Parliament and the Virginia Assembly concerning Religion" and his "Notes on Locke and Shaftesbury," *Papers* I, pp. 541 ff. and pp. 544 ff., respectively, in "Notes and Proceedings of Discontinuing the Establishment of the Church of England," comprising nine documents of later 1776, including Jefferson's draft resolutions on the subject in the Virginia Assembly and "a list of acts of parliament and of the Virginia Assembly, 1661–1759, concerning religion." Boyd begins his lengthy introductory editorial note to this collection of documents by underscoring "[t]he importance of Jefferson's legislative activity in 1776 in behalf of religious tolerance" (p. 525).

104. This is especially true for even broader subjects such as Jefferson's "constitutional thought" or "(republican) constitutionalism," as e.g., in *The Constitutional Thought of Thomas Jefferson* (Charlottesville, 1994), by David N. Mayer. Although this is a lengthy comprehensive and substantial work, it gives little consideration to topics in legislation *per se*, even though Congress naturally is included in wider ways. The good bibliog. includes various works on Jefferson's legal thought that are insightful in other ways.

105. In *The Political Writings of Thomas Jefferson: Representative Selections* (edited by E. Dumbauld, New York, 1955), p. 137 (1787).

106. *Ibid.*, p. 138 (1788).

107. *Ibid.*, pp. 136–137 (1789).

108. *Ibid.*, p. 79 (1793).

109. *Ibid.*, pp. 79–80(1801).

110. *Ibid.*, p. 80 (1793).

111. *Ibid.*, pp. 80–81 (1792).

112. *Ibid.*, p. 81 (1799): "The whole body of the nation is the sovereign legislative, judiciary, and executive power for itself. The inconvenience of meeting to exercise these powers in person and their inaptitude to exercise them induce them to appoint special organs to declare their legislative will, to judge and to execute it. It is the will of the nation which makes the law obligatory; it is their will which creates or annihilates the organ which is to declare and announce it. They may do it by a single person, as an emperor of Russia (constituting his declarations evidence of their will), or by a few persons, as the

aristocracy of Venice, or by a complication of councils, as in our former regal government or our present republican one. The law, being law because it is the will of the nation, is not changed by their changing the organ through which they choose to announce their future will." Cf. text above corresponding to n. 111.

113. *Ibid.*, p. 166 (1797).

114. *Ibid.*, p. 83 (1790): "Every man, and every body of men on earth, possesses the right of self-government. . . .

"Each house of Congress possesses this natural right of governing itself and, consequently, of fixing its own times and places of meeting, so far as it has not been abridged by the law of those who employ them, that is to say, by the Constitution."

Ibid., p. 83 (1824): "The present generation has the same right of self-government which the past one has exercised for itself."

Ibid., pp. 83–84 (1817): "The first principle of republicanism is that the *lex majoris partis* is the fundamental law of every society of individuals of equal rights; to consider the will of the society enounced by the majority of a single vote as sacred as if unanimous is the first of all lessons in importance . . ."

Ibid., pp. 118–119 (1824): "I received . . . your favor . . . requesting my opinion on the proposition to call a convention for amending the constitution of the State. . . . One [improvement] which has been adopted in every subsequent constitution was to lay its foundation in the authority of the nation. To our convention no special authority had been delegated by the people to form a permanent constitution over which their successors in legislation should have no powers of alteration. They had been elected for the ordinary purposes of legislation only, and at a time when the establishment of a new government had not been proposed or contemplated. Although, therefore, they gave to this act the title of a constitution, yet it could be no more than an act of legislation subject, as their other acts were, to alteration by their successors."

Ibid., p. 119 (1823): "In England the constitution may be altered by a single act of the legislature, which amounts to the having no constitution at all. In some of our States an act passed by two different legislatures, chosen by the people at different and successive elections, is sufficient to make a change in the constitution. As this mode may be rendered more or less easy by requiring the approbation of fewer or more successive legislatures, according to the degree of difficulty thought sufficient and yet safe, it is evidently the best principle which can be adopted for constitutional amendments."

Ibid., p. 124 (1816): "Each generation is as independent of the one preceding as that was of all which had gone before. It has then, like them, a right to choose for itself the form of government it believes most promotive of its own happiness . . ."

Ibid., p. 125 (1824): "The real friends of the constitution in its federal form, if they wish it to be immortal, should be attentive by amendments to make it keep pace with the advance of the age in science and experience. Instead of this, the European governments have resisted reformation, until the people, seeing no other resource, undertake it themselves by force . . . and long-continued anarchy."

Ibid., p. 125 (1824): "You will perceive by these details that we have not yet so far perfected our constitutions as to venture to make them unchangeable. But still, in their present state, we consider them not otherwise changeable than by the authority of the people, on a special election of representatives for that purpose expressly, they are until then the *lex legum*."

115. *Ibid.*, p. 86 (1810): "I have been ever opposed to the party so falsely called Federalists, because I believe them desirous of introducing into our government authorities hereditary or otherwise independent of the national will. These always consume the public contributions and oppress the people with labor and poverty."

Ibid., p. 96 (1800): "... a majority firm in all those principles which we have espoused and the Federalists have opposed uniformly; still, should the whole body of New England continue in opposition to these principles of government, either knowingly or through delusion, our government will be a very uneasy one. It can never be harmonious and solid while so respectable a portion of its citizens support principles which go directly to a change of the federal Constitution, to sink the State governments, consolidate them into one, and to monarchize that. Our country is too large to have all its affairs directed by a single government. ... And I do verily believe that if the principle were to prevail of a common law being in force in the United States (which principle possesses the General Government at once of all the powers of the State governments and reduces us to a single consolidated government), it would become the most corrupt government on the earth."

116. *Ibid.*, p. 97 (1800): "The true theory of our Constitution is surely the wisest and best, that the States are independent as to everything within themselves and united as to everything respecting foreign nations. Let the General Government be reduced to foreign concerns only, and let our affairs be disentangled from those of all other nations, except as to commerce which the merchants will manage the better the more they are left free to manage for themselves, and our General Government may be reduced to a very simple organization and a very inexpensive one, a few plain duties to be performed by a few servants."

117. *Ibid.*, pp. 98–99 (1816): "Let the national government be entrusted with the defense of the nation and its foreign and federal relations; the State governments with the civil rights. ... It is by dividing and subdividing these republics from the great national one down through all its subordinations until it ends in the administration of every man's farm by himself. ... The generalizing and concentrating all cares and powers into one body, no matter whether of the autocrats of Russia or France, or of the aristocrats of a Venetian senate. ... The elementary republics of the wards, the county republics, the State republics, and the republic of the Union would form a gradation of authorities, standing each on the basis of law, holding every one its delegated share of powers, and constituting truly a system of fundamental balances and checks for the government."

118. *Ibid.*, p. 132 (1786): "Perhaps it might have been better, when they were forming the federal constitution, to have assimilated it as much as possible to the particular constitutions of the States. All of these have distributed the legislative, executive, and judiciary powers into different departments. In the federal constitution the judiciary powers are separated from the others, but the legislative and executive are both exercised by Congress."

119. *Ibid.*, p. 133 (Aug. 1787): "My general plan would be to make the States one as to everything connected with foreign nations and several as to everything purely domestic. But with all the imperfections of our present government, it is without comparison the best existing, or that ever did exist. Its greatest defect is the imperfect manner in which matters of commerce have been provided for. It has been so often said as to be generally believed that Congress have no power by the Confederation to enforce anything, for example, contributions of money."

120. *Ibid.*, pp. 133–134 (Sept. 1787): "You ask me what ameliorations I think necessary in our federal constitution. It is now too late to answer the question, and it would always have been presumption in me to have done it. ... My own general idea was that the States should severally preserve their sovereignty in whatever concerns themselves alone, and that whatever may concern another State or any foreign nation should be made a part of the federal sovereignty; that the exercise of the federal sovereignty should be divided among three several bodies, legislative, executive, and judiciary, as the State sovereignties are; and that some peaceable means should be contrived for the federal head to force compliance on the part of the States."

121. *Ibid.*, p. 143 (Jan. 1789): "Our new Constitution, of which you speak also, has succeeded beyond what I apprehended it would have done. I did not at first believe that eleven States out of thirteen would have consented to a plan consolidating them as much into one. A change in their dispositions, which had taken place since I left them, had rendered this consolidation necessary, that is to say, had called for a federal government which could walk upon its own legs without leaning for support on the State legislatures. A sense of necessity, and a submission to it, is to me a new and consolatory proof that, whenever the people are well-informed, they can be trusted with their own government."

122. *Ibid.*, pp. 149–150 (1824): "The radical idea of the character of the constitution of our government which I have adopted as a key in cases of doubtful construction is that the whole field of government is divided into two departments, domestic and foreign (the States in their mutual relations being of the latter); that the former department is reserved exclusively to the respective States within their own limits and the latter assigned to a separate set of functionaries, constituting what may be called the foreign branch, which instead of a federal basis, is established as a distinct government *quoad hoc*, acting as the domestic branch does on the citizens directly and coercively."

123. *Ibid.*, pp. 156–162 (Jefferson's Kentucky Resolutions). Cf. Dumas Malone, *Jefferson and The Ordeal of Liberty* (Boston, 1962), Chs. XXIV–XXV on the Alien-Sedition Acts and the Kentucky-Virginia Resolutions. Jefferson's authorship was not made known until his full retirement (Madison's not until he became president).

124. Cf. above this sect.

125. *Political Writings of Jefferson*, pp. 154–155. In one of Jefferson's letters of 1804 to Abigail Adams: "I discharged every person under punishment or prosecution under the Sedition Law because I considered and now consider that law to be a nullity [!], as absolute and as palpable as if Congress had ordered us to fall down and worship a golden image, and that it was as much my duty to arrest its execution in every stage as it would have been to have rescued from the fiery furnace those who should have been cast into it for refusing to worship the image." In another: "You seem to think it devolved on the judges to decide on the validity of the Sedition Law. But nothing in the Constitution has given them a right to decide for the executive, more than to executive to decide for them. . . . But the opinion which gives to the judges the right to decide what laws are constitutional and what are not, not only for themselves in their own sphere of action but for the Legislature and executive also in their spheres, would make the judiciary a despotic branch."

126. *The Adams-Jefferson Letters*, edited by Lester J. Cappon (Chapel Hill, 1959).

127. *Ibid.*, pp. 174–175 (Jefferson to Adams, Feb. 23, 1787): "I have read your book with infinite satisfaction and improvement. It will do great good in America. It's [*sic*] learning and it's [*sic*] good sense will I hope make it an institute for our politicians, old as well as young. There is one opinion in it[,] however, which I will ask you to reconsider, because it appears to me not entirely accurate, and not likely to do good. Pa. 362. 'Congress is not a legislative, but a diplomatic assembly.' Separating into parts the whole sovereignty of our states, some of these parts are yeilded [*sic*] to Congress. Upon these I should think them both legislative and executive, and that they would have been judiciary also, had not the Confederation required them for certain purposes to appoint a judiciary. It has accordingly been the decision of our courts that the Confederation is a part of the law of the land, and superior in authority to the ordinary laws, because it cannot be altered by the legislature of any one state. I doubt whether they are at all a diplomatic assembly." Cf. editor's comments, pp. 166–168. Jefferson had initially written to Adams on Feb. 6, 1787, to thank him for sending the booklet, which he said he was eager to study (*ibid..*, p. 170).

128. *Ibid.*, pp. 176–177 (Adams to Jefferson, March 1, 1787, with typical styles of capitalization, etc.): "The Opinion you Object to p. 362, "that Congress is not a legislative but

a diplomatic assembly" I should wish to have considered as a Problem, rather for Consideration, than as an opinion: and as a Problem too, relative to the Confederation as it now stands, rather than to any other Plan that may be in Contemplation of the States. It is a most difficult Topick, and no Man at a distance can judge of it, so well as those in America. If the Book Should be translated into french, I wish you would insert this, in a Note. You have laid me under great obligation, by taking the trouble to Secure a Good Translator."

129. Jefferson, *Papers* 2, p. 111 (drafted by Jefferson for Virginia before Dec. 15, 1777): "[C]ertain articles of confederation and perpetual union have been approved of by the assembly of this commonwealth who have authorized and instructed their delegates to attend in Congress ... to ratify the same, in the name and on the behalf of this Commonwealth and it may be found that sundry of our laws formed before the ratification of the said Articles of Confederation, may in some instances be contradictory to and inconsistent with the said articles or some of them, and tho' it will be proper on revising these laws for the committee heretofore appointed for that purpose to render the same conformable to the said articles, yet in the mean time judges and others may be at a loss how to determine between them. Be it therefore enacted by the General assembly that so soon as the said articles of confederation shall be ratified in Congress by each and every of the states ... the same shall be construed to have the force of a law within this commonwealth, and to repeal so much of all laws passed before such ratification as shall be found to be contradictory to the said articles of confederation or any part of them."

130. *Adams-Jefferson Letters*, p. 198 (Adams to Jefferson, Sept. 16, 1787): "Give me Leave to introduce to you Mr. John Brown Cutting, who will need no other Recommendation, than his own Genius. Let me beg your acceptance, too of a Sett [sic] of my Defence etc. and let me know your Opinion of the Second volume, and whether it is worth my while to write a third upon Confederations etc." The Constitutional Convention in Phila. adjourned Sept. 17, 1787.

131. *Ibid.*, p. 199 (Jefferson to Adams, Sept. 28, 1787): "I received your favors by Mr. Cutting, and thank you sincerely for the copy of your book. The departure of a packet-boat, which always gives me full emploiment for some time before, has only permitted me to look into it a little. I judge of it from the first volume which I thought formed to do a great deal of good. The first principle of a good government is certainly a distribution of it's powers into executive, judiciary, and legislative, and a subdivision of the latter into two or three branches. It is a good step gained, when it is proved that the English constitution, acknowledged to be better than all which have proceeded it, is only better in proportion as it has approached nearer to this distribution of powers. From this the last step is easy, to shew by a comparison of our constitutions with that of England, how much more perfect they are. The article of Confederations is surely worthy of your pen. It would form a most interesting addition to shew what have been the nature of the Confederations which have existed hitherto, what were their excellencies and what their defects. A comparison of ours with them would be to the advantage of ours, and would increase the veneration of our countrymen for it. It is a misfortune that they do not sufficiently know the value of their constitutions and how much happier they are rendered by them than any other people on earth by the governments under which they live."

132. Cf. editor's comments in *ibid.*, p. 208.

133. On Shays' Rebellion see *ibid.*, e.g., p. 168 (Abigail Adams to Jefferson, Jan. 29, 1787, in response to Jefferson's inquiry), and *passim*. The disparate views of Jefferson, John Adams, and Abigail Adams cannot be recounted here. Whereas Jefferson was indulging toward the rebellious farmers in Mass., John and his wife were not.

134. Benjamin Rush to Richard Price, June 2, 1787; quoted by editor in *ibid.*, p. 167.

135. *Ibid.*, p. 196 (Jefferson to Adams, Aug. 30, 1787): "I have news from America as late as July 19. Nothing had then transpired from the Federal convention. I am sorry they began their deliberations by so abominable a precedent as that of tying up the tongues of their members. Nothing can justify this example but the innocence of their intentions, and ignorance of the value of public discussions. I have no doubt that all their other measures will be good and wise. It is really an assembly of demigods. Genl. Washington was of opinion they should not separate till October."

136. *Ibid.*, p. 212 (Jefferson to Adams, Nov. 13, 1787): "How do you like our new constitution? I confess there are things in it which stagger all my dispositions to subscribe to what such an assembly has proposed. The house of federal representatives will not be adequate to the managemeent of affairs either foreign or federal. Their President seems a bad edition of a Polish king. He may be reelected from 4. years to 4. years for life. Reason and experience prove to us that a chief magistrate, so continuable, is an officer for life. When one or two generations shall have proved that this is an office for life, it becomes on every succession worthy of intrigue, of bribery, of force, and even of foreign interference. ... I wish that at the end of the 4. years they had made him for ever ineligible a second time. Indeed I think all the good of this new constitution might have been couched in three or four new articles to be added to the good, old, and venerable fabrick, which should have been preserved even as a religious relique."

137. *Ibid.*, p. 214 (Adams to Jefferson, Dec. 6, 1787): "The Project of a new Constitution, has Objections against it, to which I find it difficult to reconcile my self, but I am so unfortunate as to differ somewhat from you in the Articles, according to your last kind Letter.

"You are afraid of the one—I, of the few. We agree perfectly that the many should have a full fair and perfect Representation.—You are Apprehensive of Monarchy; I, of Aristocracy. I would therefore have given more Power to the President and less to the Senate. The Nomination and Appointment to all offices I would have given to the President, assisted only by a Privy Council of his own Creation. ... Faction and Distraction are the sure and certain Consequence of giving to a Senate a vote in the distribution of offices.

"You are apprehensive the President when once chosen, will be chosen again and again as long as he lives. So much the better as it appears to me." Cf. editor's comments in *ibid.*, p. 209.

138. *Ibid.*, p. 238 (Jefferson to Adams, May 10, 1789).

139. Cited in *ibid.*, p. 209 (Jefferson to David Humphrey, March 18, 1789).

140. Cited in *ibid.*, p. 209 (Adams at his inaugural in 1797).

141. *Ibid.*, p. 291 (Jefferson to Adams, Jan. 21, 1812): "... into politics, of which I have taken final leave. I think little of them, and say less. I have given up newspapers in exchange for Tacitus and Thucydides, for Newton and Euclid; and I find myself much the happier."

142. *Ibid.*, pp. 294–295 (Adams to Jefferson, Feb. 3, 1812): "What an Exchange have you made? Of Newspapers for Newton! Rising from the lower deep of the lowest deep of Dulness and Bathos to the Contemplation of the Heavens and the heavens of Heavens. Oh that I had devoted to Newton and his Fellows that time which I fear has been wasted on Plato and Aristotle, Bacon (Nat) Acherly, Bolin[g]broke, De Lolme, Harrington, Sidney, Hobbes, Plato Redivivus, Marchamont Nedham, with twenty others upon Subjects which Mankind is determined never to Understand, and those who do Understand them are resolved never to practice, or countenance. ...

"The Union is still to me an Object of as much Anxiety as ever Independence was. ...

"I have read Thucidides and Tacitus, so often, and at such distant Periods of my Life, that elegant, profound and enchanting as is their Style, I am weary of them. When I read them I seem to be only reading the History of my own Times and my own Life. I am heartily weary of both; i.e. of recollecting the History of both: for I am not weary of Living. Whatever a peevish Patriarch might say, I have never yet seen the day in which I could say I have had no Pleasure; or that I have had more Pain than Pleasure."

143. *Ibid.*, p. 334 (Adams to Jefferson, June 25, 1813): "Checks and Ballances, Jefferson, however you and your Party may have ridiculed them, are our only Security, for the progress of Mind, as well as the Security of Body. Every Species of these Christians would persecute Deists, as soon as either Sect would persecute another, if it had unchecked and unballanced Power. Nay, the Deists would persecute Christians, and Atheists would persecute Deists, with as unrelenting Cruelty, as any Christians would persecute them or one another. Know thyself, human Nature!"

144. *Ibid.*, pp. 335—336 (Jefferson to Adams, June 27, 1813): "The summum bonum with me is now truly Epicurean, ease of body and tranquility of mind; and to these I wish to consign my remaining days. Men have differed in opinion, and been divided into parties by these opinions, from the first origin of societies; and in all governments where they have been permitted freely to think and to speak. The same political parties which now agitate the U.S. have existed thro' all time. Whether the power of the people, or that of the . . . ['aristocrats'] should prevail, were questions which kept the states of Greece and Rome in eternal convulsions; as they now schismatize every people whose minds and mouths are not shut up by the gag of a despot. . . . To come to our own country, . . . we well remember the violent parties which agitated the old Congress, and their bitter contests. There you and I were together, and . . . anti-independants were arrayed against us. They cherished the monarchy of England; and we the rights of our countrymen. When our present government was in the mew, passing from Confederation to Union, how bitter was the schism between the Feds and Antis. Here you and I were together again."

145. *Ibid.*, pp. 432–433 (Jefferson to Adams, July 5, 1814): "Having more leisure . . . for reading, I amused myself with reading seriously Plato's republic. I am wrong however in calling it amusement, for it was the heaviest task-work I ever went through. I had occasionally before taken up some of his other works. . . . While wading thro' the whimsies, . . . I laid it down often to ask myself how it could have been that the world should have so long consented to give reputation to such nonsense as this? How the soi-disant Christian world indeed should have done it, is a piece of historical curiosity. But how could the Roman good sense do it? And particularly how could Cicero bestow such eulogies on Plato? Altho' Cicero did not wield the dense logic of Demosthenes, yet he was able, learned, laborious, practised in the business of the world, and honest. . . . With the Moderns, I think, it is rather a matter of fashion and authority. . . . In truth, he is one of the race of genuine Sophists, who has escaped the oblivion of his brethren, first by the elegance of his diction, but chiefly by the adoption and incorporation of his whimsies into the body of artificial Christianity. His foggy mind . . ."

146. *Ibid.*, pp. 437–439 (Adams to Jefferson, July 16, 1814): "I am very glad you have seriously read Plato: and still more rejoiced to find that your reflections upon him so perfectly harmonize with mine. Some thirty Years ago I took upon me the severe task of going through all his Works. . . . My disappointment was very great, my Astonishment was greater and my disgust was shocking. . . .

"Some Parts of some of his Dialogues are entertaining, like the Writings of Rousseau: but his Laws and his Republick from which I expected most, disappointed me most. I could scarcely exclude the suspicion that he intended the latter as a bitter Satyre upon all Republican Government, as Xenophon undoubtedly designed. . . . Nothing can be conceived more destructive of human happiness . . . than a Community of Wives and Property. Yet, in what, are the Writings of Rousseau and Helvetius wiser than those of Plato? . . .

"Cicero was educated in the Groves of Academus where the Name and Memory of Plato, were idolized to such a degree, that if he had wholly renounced the Prejudices of his Education his Reputation would have been lessened. . . . In his two Volumes of Discourses on Government We may presume, that he fully examined Plato's Laws and Republick as well as Aristotle[']s Writings on Government. . . .

"Nothing seizes the Attention, of the stareing Animal, so surely, as Paradox, Riddle, Mystery, Invention, discovery, Mystery, Wonder, Temerity.

"Plato and his Disciples, from the fourth Century Christians, to Rousseau and Tom Paine, have been fully sensible of this Weakness in Mankind, and have too successfully grounded upon it their Pretensions to Fame. I might indeed, have mentioned Bolingbroke, Hume, Gibbon Voltaire Turgot[,] Helvetius[,] Diderot, Condorcet, Buffon De La Lande and fifty others; all a little cracked! . . .

"Education! Oh Education! The greatest Grief of my heart, and the greatest Affliction of my Life! To my mortification I must confess, that I have never closely thought, or very deliberately reflected upon the Subject. . . . If I venture to give you any thoughts at all, they must be very crude. I have turned over Locke, Milton, Condilac [and] Rousseau. . . . Geography[,] Ast[ron]omy, and even History and Chronology, tho' I am myself afflicted with a kind of Pyrrhonism in the two latter, I presume cannot be omitted. Theology I would leave to Ray [etc.] . . . than to Luther . . . or Thomas Aquinas. . . . Metaphysics I would leave in the Clouds. . . .

"The Task you have prescribed to me of Grouping these Sciences, or Arts, under Professors, within the Views of an inlightened Economy, is far beyond my forces. . . . Might Gramar, Rhetoric, Logick and Ethicks be under One Professor? Might Mathematicks, Mechanicks, Natural Phylosophy, be under another? Geography and Astro[no]my under a third. Laws and Gover[n]ment, History and Chronology under a fourth. Classicks might require a fifth."

147. *Ibid.*, p. 440 (Adams to Jefferson, Oct. 28, 1814): ". . . is very desirous of seeing Mr. Jefferson. I hope he will arrive before your Library is translated to Washington.

"By the Way I envy you that immortal honour: but I cannot enter into competition with you for my books are not half the number of yours: and moreover, I have Shaftesbury, Bolingbroke, Hume[,] Gibbon and Raynal, as well as Voltaire."

148. *Ibid.*, p. 443 (Jefferson to Adams, June 10, 1815): "I thank you for making known to me Mr. Ticknor. . . . [He] is particularly the best bibliograph I have met with, and very kindly and opportunely offered me the means of reprocuring some part of the literary treasures which I have ceded to Congress to replace the devastations of British Vandalism at Washington. I cannot live without books: but fewer will suffice where amusement, and not use, is the only future object. I am about sending him a catalogue to which less than his critical knolege [*sic*] of books would hardly be adequate."

149. *Ibid.*, pp. 548–550 (Jefferson to Adams, Dec. 10, 1819): "But the Missouri question is a breaker on which we lose the Missouri country by revolt, and what more, God only knows. From the battle of Bunker's hill to the treaty of Paris we never had so ominous a question. . . . I thank god that I shall not live to witness it's [*sic*] issue. . . .

"I have been amusing myself latterly with reading the voluminous letters of Cicero. They certainly breathe the purest effusions of an exalted patriot, while the parricide Caesar is left in odious contrast. When the enthusiasm however kindled by Cicero's pen and principles, subsides into cool reflection, I ask myself What was that government which the virtues of Cicero were so zealous to restore, and the ambition of Caesar to subvert? And if Caesar had been as virtuous as he was daring and sagacious, what could he, even in the plenitude of his usurped power have done to lead his fellow citizens into good government? I do not say to *restore* it, because they never had it, from the rape of the Sabines to the ravages of the Caesars. If their people indeed had been, like ours, enlightened, peaceable, and really free, the answer would be obvious. 'Restore independance to all your foreign conquests . . .' But steeped in corruption[,] vice and venality as the whole nation was, . . . what could even Cicero, Cato, Brutus have done, had it been referred to them to establish a good government for their country? They had no ideas of government themselves but of their degenerate Senate, nor the people of liberty, but of the factious opposition of their tribunes. They had afterwards their Titusses, their Trajans and Antoninuses, who had the will to make them happy, and the power to mould their government into a good and permanent form. But it would seem as if they could not see their way clearly to do it. No government can continue good but under the controul of the people: and their people were so demoralised and depraved as to be incapable of exercising a wholsome controul. . . . Their minds were to be informed, by education, what is right and what wrong, to be enco[u]raged in habits of virtue, and deterred from those of vice. . . . These are the inculcations necessary to render the people a sure basis for the structure of order and good government. . . . I confess then I can neither see what Cicero, Cato and Brutus, united and uncontrouled, could have devised to lead their people into good government, nor how this aenigma can be solved. . . . Your intimacy with their history, antient [*sic*], middle and modern, your familiarity with the improvements in the science of government at this time, will enable you, if any body, to go back with our principles and opinions to the times of Cicero, Cato, and Brutus, and tell us by what process these great and virtuous men could have led so unenlightened and vitiated a people into freedom and good government . . ."

150. *Ibid.*, pp. 550–551 (Adams to Jefferson, Dec. 21, 1819): "I must answer your great question. . . . Have you ever found in history one single example of a Nation th[o]roughly Corrupted, that was afterwards restored to Virtue, and without Virtue, there can be no political Liberty.

"Will you tell me how to prevent riches from . . . producing luxury? Will you tell me how to prevent luxury from producing . . . Vice and folly? When you will answer me these questions, I hope I may venture to answer yours. Yet all these ought not to discourage us from exertion. . . .

"The Missouri question I hope will follow the other Waves under the Ship and do no harm. I know it is high treason to express a doubt of the perpetual duration of our vast American Empire, and our free Institution[s], . . . but I am sometimes Cassandra enough to dream that another Hamilton, another Burr might rend this mighty Fabric in twain, or perhaps into a leash, and a few more choice Spirits of the same Stamp, might produce as many Nations in North America as there are in Europe.

"To return to the Romans, I never could discover that they possessed much Virtue, or real Liberty there."

151. *The Republic of Letters: The Correspondence between Thomas Jefferson and James Madison*, 1776–1826, edited by James Morton Smith (3 vols., New York, 1995), Vol. I, p. 458 (Jefferson to Madison, Dec. 16, 1786): "To make us one nation as to foreign concerns, and keep us distinct in Domestic ones, gives the outline of the proper division of powers between the general and particular governments. But to enable the Federal head to exercise the powers given it, to best advantage, it should be organised, as the particular ones are, into Legislative, Executive and Judiciary. The 1st. and last are already separated. The 2d should also be. When last with Congress, I often proposed to members to do this by making of the Committee of the states, an Executive committee during the recess of Congress, and during it's sessions to appoint a Committee to receive and dispatch all executive business, so that Congress itself should meddle only with what should be legislative. But I question if any Congress (much less all successively) can have self-denial enough to go through with this distribution. The distribution should be imposed on them then."

152. *Ibid.*, Vol. I, p. 480 (Jefferson to Madison, June 20, 1787): "The idea of separating the executive business of the confederacy from Congress, as the judiciary is already in some degree, is just and necessary. I had frequently pressed on the members individually, while in Congress, the doing this by a resolution of Congress for appointing an Executive committee to act during the sessions of Congress, as the Committee of the states was to act during their vacations. But the referring to this Committee all executive business as it should present itself, would require a more persevering self-denial than I supposed Congress to possess. It will be much better to make that separation by a federal act. The negative proposed to be given them on all the acts of the several legislatures is now for the first time suggested to my mind. Primâ facie I do not like it. . . . Not more than 1. out of 100. state-acts concern the confederacy. This proposition then, in order to give them 1. degree of power which they ought to have, gives them 99. more which they ought not to have, upon a presumption that they will not exercise the 99. But upon every act there will be a preliminary question. Does this act concern the confederacy? And was there ever a proposition so plain as to pass Congress without a debate? . . . Would not an appeal from the state judicatures to a federal court, in all cases where the act of Confederation controuled the question, be as effectual remedy . . . to the defect [?]."

153. *Ibid.*, Vol. I, pp. 512–515 (Jefferson to Madison, Dec. 26, 1787): "The season admitting only of operations in the Cabinet, and these being in a great measure secret, I have little to fill a letter. I will therefore make up the deficiency by adding a few words on the Constitution proposed by our Convention. I like much the general idea of framing a government which should go on of itself peaceably, without needing continual recurrence to the state legislatures. I like the organization of the government into Legislative, Judiciary and Executive. I like the power given the Legislature to levy taxes; and for that reason solely approve of the greater house being chosen by the people directly. For tho' I think a house chosen by them will be very illy qualified to legislate for the Union, for foreign nations etc.[,] yet this evil does not weigh against the good of preserving inviolate the fundamental principle that the people are not to be taxed but by representatives chosen immediately by themselves. I am captivated by the compromise of the opposite claims of great and little states, of the latter to equal, and the former to proportional influence. I am much pleased too with the substitution of the method of voting by persons, instead of that of voting by states: and I like the negative given to the Executive with a third of either house, though I should have liked it better had the Judiciary been associated for that purpose, or invested with a similar and separate power. There are other good things of less moment. I will now add what I do not like. First the omission of a bill of rights providing clearly and without the aid of sophisms for freedom of religion, freedom of the press, protection against standing armies, restriction against monopolies, the eternal and unremitting force of the habeas corpus laws, and trials by jury in all matters of fact triable by the laws of the land not by the law of Nations. . . . Let me add that a bill of rights is what the people are entitled to against every government on earth, general or particular, and what no just government should refuse, or rest on inference. The second feature I dislike, and greatly dislike, is the abandonment in every instance of the necessity of rotation in office, and most particularly in the case of the President. Experience concurs with reason in concluding that the first magistrate will always be re-elected if the constitution permits it. He is then an officer for life. . . . Reflect on all the instances in history antient and modern, of elective monarchies, and say if they do not give foundation for my fears, the Roman emperors, the popes, while they were of any importance, the German emperors till they became hereditary in practice, the kings of Poland, the Deys of the Ottoman dependancies. . . .

"Smaller objections are the Appeal in fact as well as law, and the binding all persons Legislative, Executive and Judiciary by oath to maintain that constitution. I do not pretend to decide what would be the best method of procuring the establishment of the manifold good things in this constitution, and of getting rid of the bad....

"I have thus told you freely what I like and dislike: merely as a matter of curiosity for I know your own judgment has been formed on all these points after having heard every thing which could be urged on them. I own I am not a friend to a very energetic government. It is always oppressive. The late rebellion in Massachusetts has given more alarm than I think it should have done.... Nor will any degree of power in the hands of government prevent insurrections. France with all it's despotism ... has had three insurrections. ... In Turkey, which Montesquieu supposes more despotic, insurrections are the events of every day. In England, where the hand of power is ... heavier than with us[,] they happen....

"After all, it is my principle that the will of the Majority should always prevail. If they approve the proposed Convention in all it's parts, I shall concur in it chearfully, in hopes that they will amend it whenever they shall find it work wrong. I think our governments will remain virtuous for many centuries; as long as they are chiefly agricultural; and this will be as long as there shall be vacant lands in any part of America. When they get piled upon one another in large cities, as in Europe, they will become corrupt as in Europe. Above all things I hope the education of the common people will be attended to; convinced that on their good sense we may rely with the most security for the preservation of a due degree of liberty."

Jefferson's P.S. reads as follows (pp. 514–515): "The instability of our laws is really an immense evil. I think it would be well to provide in our constitution that there shall always be a twelvemonth between the ingrossing a bill and passing it: that it should then be offered to it's [*sic*] passage without changing a word: and that if circumstances should be thought to require a speedier passage, it should take two thirds of both houses instead of a bare majority."

154. *Ibid.*, Vol. I, pp. 529–530 (Jefferson to Madison, Feb. 6, 1788): "I am glad to hear that the new constitution is received with favor. I sincerely wish that the 9 first conventions may receive, and the 4. last reject it. The former will secure it finally, while the latter will oblige them to offer a declaration of rights to complete the union."

155. *Ibid.*, Vol. I, esp. pp. 350–353, 382–386, 485–489, and passim. Cf. "book" etc. in index.

156. *Ibid.*, Vol. III, pp. 1875–1876 (Jefferson to Madison, Aug. 30, 1823): "Pickering's observations, and Mr. Adams's in addition, 'that it contained no new ideas, that it is a commonplace compilation, it's sentiments hackneyed in Congress for two years before, and its essence contained in Otis's pamphlet,' may all be true. Of that I am not to be the judge. Richard Henry Lee charged it as copied from Locke's treatise on government. Otis's pamphlet I never saw, and whether I had gathered my ideas from reading or reflection I do not know. I know only that I turned to neither book or pamphlet while writing it. I did not consider it as any part of my charge to invent new ideas altogether and to offer no sentiment which had ever been expressed before. Had Mr. Adams been so restrained, Congress would have lost the benefit of his bold and impressive advocations of the rights of revolution. For no man's confident and fervid addresses, more than Mr. Adams's encouraged and supported us thro' the difficulties surrounding us, which, like the ceaseless action of gravity, weighed on us by night and by day. Yet, on the same ground, we may ask what of these elevated thoughts was new, or can be affirmed never before to have entered the conceptions of man?

"Whether also the sentiments of independence, and the reasons for declaring it which make so great a portion of the instrument, had been hackneyed in Congress for two years before the 4th. of July '76, or this dictum also of Mr. Adams be another slip of memory, let history say. This however I will say for Mr. Adams, that he supported the Declaration with zeal and ability, fighting fearlessly for every word of it."

Cf. other portions of this letter for further details of the drafting of the Declar. of Indep., and also *ibid.*, Vol. III, p. 1845, for editor's comments on the criticisms made against Jefferson's draft as well as his response concerning them.

157. *Ibid.*, Vol. III, p. 1877 (Madison to Jefferson, Sept. 6, 1823): "I am glad you have put on paper a correction of the apocryphal tradition furnished by Pickering, of the 'Draught' of the Declaration of Independence. If he derived it from the misrecollections of Mr. Adams, it is well that the alterations of the original paper proposed by the latter in his own handwriting attest the fallibility of his aged memory. Nothing can be more absurd than the cavil that the Declaration contains known and not new truths. The object was to assert not to discover truths, and to make them the basis of the Revolutionary Act. The merit of the Draught could consist only in a lucid communication of human rights, a condensed enumeration of the reasons for such an exercise of them, and in a style and tone appropriate to the great occasion, and to the spirit of the American people."

158. *Ibid.*, Vol. III, p. 1972.

159. *Ibid.*, Vol. III, pp. 1924–1926 (Madison to Jefferson, Feb. 8, 1825): "I have looked with attention over your intended proposal of a text book for the Law School. It is certainly very material that the true doctrines of liberty, as exemplified in our Political System, should be inculcated on those who are to sustain and may administer it. It is, at the same time, not easy to find standard books that will be both guides and guards for the purpose. Sidney and Locke are admirably calculated to impress on young minds the right of Nations to establish their own Governments, and to inspire a love of free ones; but afford no aid in guarding our Republican Charters against constructive violations. The Declaration of Independence, tho' rich in fundamental principles, and saying every thing that could be said in the same number of words, falls nearly under a like observation. The 'Federalist' may fairly enough be regarded as the most authentic exposition of the text of the federal Constitution, as understood by the Body which prepared and the Authority which accepted it. Yet it did not foresee all the misconstructions which have occurred; nor prevent some that it did foresee. . . . I have, for your consideration, sketched a modification of the operative passage in your draught, with a view to relax the absoluteness of its injunction, and added to your list of Documents the Inaugural Speech and the Farewell Address of President Washington. They may help down what might be less readily swallowed, and contain nothing which is not good. . . .

"After all, the most effectual safeguard against heretical intrusions into the School of Politics, wil be an Able and Orthodox Professor, whose course of instruction will be an example to his successors. . . .

"Sketch.

"And on the distinctive principles of the Government of our own State, and of that of the U. States, the best guides are to be found in—1. The Declaration of Independence, as the fundamental act of Union of these States. 2. the book known by the title of the 'Federalist,' being an authority to which appeal is habitually made by all and rarely declined or denied by any, as evidence of the general opinion of those who framed and those who accepted the Constitution of the U. States on questions as to its genuine meaning. . . . 4. The Inaugural Speech and Farewell Address of President Washington, as conveying political lessons of particular value . . ."

Also, cf. Jefferson's letter to Madison about preparing a catalogue of books for the new University library, *ibid.*, Vol. III, p. 1897 (Aug. 8, 1824): "I have undertaken to make out a catalogue of books . . ." Madison's letter responding to Jefferson's request that, among other things, he prepare a catalogue of theological books was accompanied by precisely that—*ibid.*, Vol. III, pp. 1899–1901 (Sept. 3, 1824). In another letter to Madison, Jefferson cited the authority of Locke and others on ethics, *ibid.*, Vol. III, p. 1909 (Nov. 30, 1824).

160. First and foremost stands the magisterial catalogue by E. Millicent Sowerby, *Catalogue of the Library of Thomas Jefferson* (5 vols., Wash., D. C., 1952–1959). A notable critique of Sowerby's catalogue is by Douglas L. Wilson, "Sowerby Revisited: The Unfinished Catalogue of Thomas Jefferson's Library," *The William and Mary Quarterly*, 3rd series, Vol. XLI, 1984, pp. 615–628. Also by Wilson, again with further bibliographicl citations, are *Jefferson's Books* (Monticello Monograph Series, 1996) and *Thomas Jefferson's Library: A Catalog with the Entries in His Own Order*, co-edited by James Gilreath (Wash., D. C., 1989). Among works of further interest are the following: James A. Bear, Jr., *Thomas Jefferson's Book-Marks* (Charlottesville, 1958); Charles B. Sawford, *Thomas Jefferson and His Library: A Study of His Library Interests and of the Religious Attitudes Revealed by Relevant Titles in His Library* (Hamden, Conn., 1977); *Thomas Jefferson and the World of Books*, a symposium held at the Lib. of Cong. (Wash., D. C., 1977); and Douglas Adair, *Fame and the Founding Fathers* (New York, 1974), Ch. 12, "The Catalogue of the Library of Thomas Jefferson." Among the original catalogues of Jefferson's library still available are Jefferson's so-called "1783" manuscript catalogues (in the Massachusetts Historical Society's Coolidge Collection in Boston), Jefferson's 1823 manuscript catalogue (cited immediately above), the 1829 printed catalogue by Nathaniel Poor, and the 1812 and 1815 printed catalogues of the Library of Congress. Needless to say, a wealth of other secondary as well as primary literature could be cited, and the above works provide further leads.

I cannot fail to record here my personal debts to various individuals for thoughts and assistance on Jefferson's collections and catalogues.

It was in the spring of 1981 that the ebullient Leonard Beck, curator of Special Collections at the Library of Congress, spontaneously offered to show me the special room housing the Jefferson collection, something, as I was much later told in 1999, was almost unheard of for library users. I had been inquiring, as I recall, about some books in Renaissance law. Letting drop somehow the name of Jefferson, I fortunately did not have time to reply in the negative when he generously and kindly exclaimed "Oh, you want to do something on Jefferson? Come with me.", thereupon leading me to that special room. His enthusiasm for Jefferson was so evident as he took a book off the shelf, opened it to a page marked by Jefferson with his initials, and, pointing to them, exclaimed "Look at this!" Little did I then realize how fateful that vivid stunning impression, for a few fleeting moments, would prove for the direction eventually taken in my series.

Not until the spring of 1999 did I return in earnest to use that library's magnificent Jefferson collection. By then, Mr. Beck had long since departed, but for several days I was fortunate to have the wonderfully able assistance of Clark Evans, senior reference librarian in Special Collections. He also kindly helped me in several follow-up exchanges.

Since then, I have benefited much from contacts with Douglas L. Wilson of Knox College, Gayle Cooper of the Special Collections at the University of Virginia Library, Nicholas Graham of the Massachusetts Historical Society in Boston, James Morton Smith as editor of the Jefferson-Madison corespondence, Linda Monaco of the Jefferson Papers at Princeton University, and Sooni Johnson in Microforms Service at the Princeton University Library.

I greatly regret that my work on Jefferson began too late for me to have benefited from the incomparable Julian Boyd, renowned editor of Jefferson's Papers at Princeton. Yet I continue to cherish a letter from him in 1976 replying to my inquiry on entirely different matters relating to this project. In the course of it, his generous remark was followed by a telltale observation: "I am extremely interested in your work on legislative sovereignty. . . . Your subject is one that would have interested Thomas Jefferson."

It goes without saying that so wide a series of contacts as the above has served to enrich the rest of the present studies on Jefferson (and other Founders) beyond the immediate realms of his book collections and library catalogues.

161. From the Introd. to the edn. (cited immediately above) of Jefferson's 1823 catalogue, pp. 1–2 (with my supplemental words in brackets).

162. The encyclopedic divisions of knowlede in the diagrams of categories for arranging books, as found in Jefferson's "1783" manuscript catalogue (cited immediately above), begin, first, with history, which is bifurcated into civil and natural. Civil history is subdivided into civil proper and ecclesiastical. Civil proper is, in turn, subdivided into ancient history and modern history (foreign, British, and American). Natural history is subdivided into physics, natural history proper, and occupations of man. The secnd main division, after history, is philosophy, which is bifurcated into moral and mathematical. Moral philosophy is subdivided into ethics (moral philosophy and the law of nature and of nations) and jurisprudence (religious, municipal, and economical). Municipal law is, in turn, subdivided into domestic (common law, merchant law, maritime law, and ecclesiastical law) and foreign law (politics, commerce). The third main division, fine arts, is again replete with myriad subdivisions, beginning this time with eight categories (gardening, architecture, sculpture, painting, music, poetry, oratory, and criticism).

It is tempting, especially in the second main division, philosophy, under which are jurisprudence and politics, to see the influence, at least indirectly, of the bifurcated divisions made famous in the late Renaisance methodology of Peter Ramus. Yet Jefferson's schematic outline is more directly influenced by subsequent models. Although the partial or indirect influence of Ramist tradition might be detected here, Jefferson does not follow, even in the first or second main divisions, the kind of rigid exclusive divisions by twos that were the rel hallmark of Ramist methodology, while Jefferson's third main division ranges far afield of such an approach. Nevertheless, into these categories Jefferson places, as it were, the wealth of deep traditional historical knowledge represented in his vast book collection (and in some of his writings and correspondence).

The tripartite division above of history, philosophy, and fine arts in Jefferson's "1783" catalogue represents an application, respectively, of three corresponding "faculties of the mind"— memory, reason, and imagination— as Jefferson states at the beginning of his classification tables partially described above. This ambitious classification scheme of encompassing the three main categories of human knowledge under the three main faculties of the mind was largely based on the categories of Francis Bacon and their adoption by Jean Lerond D'Alembert in the first volume of his great 18th-century *Encyclopédie.* In the second book of Bacon's *The Advancement of Learning*, the three main divisions had been memory, reason, and imagination, the last two being reversed in order by Jefferson. The encyclopedic methodologies of the 17th and 18th centuries had been built, to a significant extent, upon the earlier tradition of Renaissance encyclopedic humanism (as variously exemplified in part by Vives, Ramus, and even Bodin) in the 16th century, and it would be interesting to explore Jefferson's libraries and writings for indications of his own direct or indirect debt to it. At the same time, Jefferson largely adapted and devised his own categories under the main headings of Bacon. These categories were, in some ways, an improvement upon the often less clear models of Bacon and reveal much about Jefferson's mind and library.

As for the study of law, Jefferson typically included, in a letter from the 1770s, a variety of other subjects as well. There, he recommended the sequence of subjects (physical sciences, ethics, religion, natural law, law, politics, histoy, literature, criticism, rhetoric, and oratory) to be studied sequentially during periods of the day (from morning through evening) best suited to the changing state of the human mind for dealing with hem (as cited in Wilson's *Jefferson's Books*, pp. 34–35).

By 1823, when Jefferson commissioned a catalogue of his library that had gone to Congress, his intent was to restore the revised divisions of subjects set forth in his lost 1812 hand catalogue that he had sent to the committee and Librarian of Congress (G. Watterston, who adopted a much different method and later kept Jefferson's catalogue when he left the post). That lost 1812 "fair copy" had altered somewhat the order and divisions in Jefferson's updated manuscript catalogue of "1783." (The Librarian of Congress' catalogue of 1815 retained the subject chapters in Jefferson's "fair copy" catalogue but listed the entries within them according to a strict alphabetical sequence on the basis of their first letters.) In Jefferson's 1823 catalogue (cited immediately above), the three main divisions of subjects were memory, philosophy, and fine arts. Under memory was grouped, in turn, ancient history, modern history (foreign, British, American), ecclesiastical history, natural philosophy, agriculture, chemistry, and numerous other sciences. Under philosophy were included, in turn, ethics (moral philosophy, law of nature and of nations), religion, jurisprudence (equity, common law, merchant law, maritime law, ecclesiastical law, foreign law), politics, mathematics (arithmetic, geometry), and so forth. Under fine arts, Jefferson's subjects began with architecture and ended with polygraphics. These classifications were somewhat altered from the "1783" catalogue. Here it can be added that Jefferson's "retirement" library was heavily represented by works of literature, poetry, and religion; these suffered perhaps the greatest loss in the Capitol building's fire of 1851, though they are still well represented in the collection at the University of Virginia.

The more recent "redisccovery" of Jefferson's 1823 catalogue— and of its true nature as such—in the Library of Congress' Jefferson collection has made it possible to improve upon the classifications adopted in E. Millicent Sowerby's monumental multi-volume catalogue in the 1950s of that collection. She attempted to restore Jefferson's lost revised "fair copy" catalogue of 1812 on the basis of his changing "1783" catalogue. However, Jefferson's 1823 catalogue now made it possible for historians, as it had for Jefferson himself, to view more accurately the arrangements in his lost 1812 catalogue. The Sowerby catalogue, still the best and most complete modern one of thee Library's Jefferson collection, has also been shown (by Wilson and others) to have a variety of further drawbacks, some of which will relate to the discussions that follow in the ensuing parts of our section on Jefferson's Library.

From the perspectives of jurisprudence and politics, Jefferson's catalogue of 1823 seems a considerable improvement over the order and classification in his updated catalogue of "1783," begun well before 1783, over forty years earlier. In Jefferson's early "1783" catalogue, the tables cited above convey what might seem to some idiosyncratic and convoluted confgurations of jurisprudence and politics. From philosophy, in the early "1783" catalogue, stems moral philosophy, under which is included jurisprudence; and from jurisprudence stems municipal law, which is subdivided into domestic and foreign, the former including under it common law and the latter including under it politics. In Jefferson's later 1823 catalogue, there is a more workable, straightforward placement of jurisprudence and politics within his encyclopedic methodology for classifying books and their subjects. Under philosophy are jurisprudence (along with ethics, under which is moral philosophy), and politics (etc.), while jurisprudence is subdivided into foreign law, common law, and so forth.

Lastly, it is worth noting the division of the sciences adopted by Francis Bacon (according to the facsimile diagram given opposite the title page of Sowerby's *Catalogue*, Vol. IV). Under the heading "The Emanation of Sciences, from the Intellectual Faculties of Memory, Imagination, Reason" is, first, the tripartite divisiion of history, poetry, and philosophy. History is subdivided into natural and civil (civil, ecclesiastical, literary). Philosophy is subdivided into primitive and derivative (divine, natural, and human). Below that in the second main diagram is the twofold division of human and civil. Human is divided into body and soul. Soul is divided into substance (spiritual and sensual), faculties (rational and sensual), and use of faculties (logic and ethics). Logic is subdivided into two parts: one part is subdivided into invention, judgement, and memory; the other into elocution and tradition (grammar, method, and rhetoric). Ethics is subdivided into platform of good (the kinds of good and degrees of good) and culture of the mind (tempers, etc.). Civil is subdivided into conversation, negotiation and "government of states" (the latter significantly divided into, and juxtaposing, the "art of enlarging a state" and the "formation of law"). Below this diagram is a partial diagram relating to divinity, with categories concerning faith, use of reason in divinity, degrees of unity in religion, and derivations from scripture.

Below this facsimile table, Sowerby's caption reads: "Sir Francis Bacon's division of the sciences, the basis for Jefferson's scheme of classification for his library." That is true to a limited extent in the initial main divisions. Jefferson's fuller scheme had a great many differences and departures, mostly, it would seem, for the better in terms of clarity and applicability, as in the placement of jurisprudence and politics. And yet Bacon's striking close connection in the government of states—between "the art of enlarging a state" and "the formation of law" (and legislation) was the kind of idea that fit in particularly well with Jefferson's writings studied above and that surely caught Jefferson's eye.

163. See n. 167 below.

164. *Op. cit.* (above n. 160).

165. *Op. cit.* (above n. 160).

166. Sowerby and Wilson, op. cit. Cf. Sowerby's Forward to Vol. IV of her *Catalogue* for a statement on the difficulties she eventually encountered in using Jefferson's "1783" catalogue (or what she sometimes called the 1783–1814 catalogue because of Jefferson's revisions of it during that period) as the basis for her attempted restoration in her Vols. I–IV (prior to the "rediscovery" of Jefferson's own 1823 reconstruction of the lost "fair copy") of Jefferson's order of books in his "fair copy" catalogue sent to Congress in 1814. Sowerby referred to this "fair copy" as the catalogue of 1814–1815, suggesting that it was not only used at that point in the sale of books to Congress but was also produced then. According to Wilson, however, the "fair copy" was created by Jefferson in 1812, well prior to the sale to Congress.

167. Jefferson's untitled manuscript catalogue of 1789, which like that of "1783," is in the Coolidge Collection at the Massachusetts Historical Society in Boston. He prepared it before he left Paris in late 1789 as an inventory of the approximately 2,000 books he had acquired in Europe during his half decade in Paris. This figure represented a doubling of the size of Jefferson's library over the approximate 2,000 books totalled up by him in 1783 on the front cover of his "1783" catalogue, to which he subsequently added a great many of the entries present in his separate 1789 Paris catalogue. The latter would have proved useful to him for shipping and other purposes (as had his recent inventories in letters to Madison of purchases for him in Europe). The roughly 4,000 books in Jefferson's library up to that point were nearly two-thirds of his final library's size of well over 6,000 books.

Jefferson arranged his 1789 Paris catalogue into subject chapters corresponding to those in his "1783" catalogue, which he obviously also had with him (as can be inferred from his statement on the front page about its use as a guide for what he already had and what he meant to procure). Chapter 23 on foreign law and Chapter 24 on politics are not easy to read because of the constant cross-out marks, which he may or may not have subsequently added as he went through this 1789 Paris catalogue, once he no longer needed it, transferring entries into his updated "1783" catalogue. among the items included under foreign law was Justinian's *Corpus Iures Civilis* (1598), with an apparent check mark next to it toward the left margin. Interestingly, this entry appears at the top of the same page on which ends Chapter 23 on foreign law and on which begins, several entries further down, Chapter 24 on politics, which begins with "Politiche del Machiavelli." This placement bears a rough correspondence, intended or not, with that in the updated "1783" catalogue. There, the same *Corpus Iuris* (1598) was listed at the top of the next-to-last page of Chapter 23 on foreign law, which ended near the top of the next page, there followed by a large empty space below which began Chapter 24 on politics (but with the actual title "Chap. 24. Politics" starting at the top of the next full page; whereas here in the 1789 Paris catalogue it actually appears starting in the space provided between the two chapters, that is, on the page divided between the two as just decribed).

Among the works included in Jefferson's 1789 Paris catalogue under repeat headings entitled "Tracts on Foreign Law" appear a variety of works in French and English, some of the English ones being concerned with American states like New York. These entries perhaps suggest that Jefferson's inclusion of much material on American states under "foreign law" in his "1783" catalogue, as well as here in his 1789 Paris catalogue, was partly related to his procurement of such materials in Europe where they were viewed as "foreign." In addition, his possible lingering view as a Virginian of other American states as "foreign" was mentioned above in connection with his "1783" catalogue.

Almost nothing else of direct present interest—along the lines indicated above for books found under politics and law in the "1783" catalogue—appears in Jefferson's 1789 Paris catalogue. Under those two chapter categories in the Paris catalogue, there is (as elsewhere) a preponderance of works in French, although even there few items of present interest are found. Even the works by English authors carry little direct present interest. Clearly, Jefferson already had in his possession, long before his Paris years in 1784–1789, the classic English and French books on law and politics represented in the same Chapters 23 and 24 in his updated "1783" catalogue. A number of the many book titles in French and English on the subject of legislation that appear in the updated "1783" catalogue appear as well in the 1789 Paris catalogue.

168. Wilson, *op. cit.*

169. J. P. Mayer, "Jefferson as Reader of Bodin: Suggestions for further studies," in *Fundamental Studies on Jean Bodin* (edited by J. P. Mayer, New York, 1979), 32 pp. This is a somewhat extended version, in rough typescript form, of his lecture given in the Political Science Dept. of Harvard Univ. in 1976 as part of the U.S. bicentennial commemorations. A number of the pages consist of reproductions of pages from Bodin's *Republic* (1580) that illustrate Jefferson's markings next to select passages, both in the margins and within the text. In these reproductions, the short vertical dash marks in many margins of Book I are clearly visible, but the little brackets within the text of other books in the *Republic* are generally not visible due apparently in part to their small size.

170. Sowerby, *Catalogue*, Vol. III, p. 24 (Bodin).

171. Mayer begins his article on "Jefferson as Reader of Bodin," *op. cit.*, by stating (p. 1) that his purpose is "to establish beyond doubt that Thomas Jefferson has read Jean Bodin, ... author of ... *[L]a Republiqu.*" Mayer's focus from the outset on is not on *legislative* sovereignty but rather, more generally, on "[Bodin's view] that sovereignty is bound by divine and natural law." In particular, as Mayer goes on to stress, for Bodin "the sovereign can not disregard the respect of the individual's property, nor should he violate the religious freedom of man. These two tenets: the right of property and religious toleration link him [Bodin] with the author of the *Declaration of Independence* and the [1786 Virginia] *Act for Religious Freedom* . . ." There is also a link here in Bodin to Jefferson's idea, in the Declar. of Indep., of the "pursuit of happiness," which Mayer finds present in passages from Blackstone, Coke, and others. The last chapter of Bodin's *Republic* treating the proportions of justice is of note for Mayer; he quotes previous historians who noticed

the markings on such subjects in Jefferson's copy of Bodin's *Republic* and who considered them to be by Jefferson.

Mayer quotes at length from McRae's introduction to his 1962 edition of Knolles' early-17th century English translation of Bodin's *Republic* on the impact of Bodin upon Filmer's monarchical ideas of sovereignty, which were challenged by Sidney in his *Discourses* and by Locke in his *Two Treatises on Government* toward the end of the 17th century (although both Sidney and Locke were heavily influenced by Bodin in their republican ideas of sovereignty). Mayer has also noted the influence on Jewfferson of Sidney's republican principles in his *Discourses on Government*, various passages of which in one copy are reportedly marked by Jefferson. Both the republican Sidney and the monarchist Filmer were greatly impacted by Bodin. "Any reader," says Mayer (p. 6), "familiar with Filmer's *Patriarchia* [which Jefferson possessed] knows that it has many references to Bodin's *Republic*, which certainly a universalist like Jefferson would not have overlooked." As Mayer points out, McRae referred to Jefferson's copy of the *Republic*, while regretting (p. 9) that "McRae has not noted that the Bodin volume has been fully marked by Thomas Jefferson."

Mayer explains (p. 10) that he and his assistant "compared Jefferson's markings with the markings we found in other volumes of Jefferson's library and the comparisons revealed the same characteristics." He presents a number of page samples from Jefferson's copies of Bodin's *Republic* (other than Book I) and Sidney's *Discourses* that illustrate the kinds of corresponding unobtrusive bracket marks found at points within the text, sometimes appearing next to the text in the margin,for purposes o marking certain passages. (The bracket markings in Jefferson's copy of the 1763 edition of Sidney's *Discourses*—as cited and illustrated by Mayer, partially on the basis of earlier scholarly references to them— were overlooked by Sowerby in her *Catalogue* entry on Bodin, Vol. III, pp. 12–13.) "If we compare these markings [in the *Republic*] with the . . . markings from Sidney's *Discourses on Government*," Mayer reports (p. 16), "we find the markings show the same characteristics . . ." There follows a reproduction of the first page of Jefferson's draft of the Declaration of Independence (where he marked changes by the Committee and Congress), in which similar brackets appear in a small unobtrusive style at various points within the text. "Now it is quite evident," Mayer concludes (p. 18), "that the type of these markings in Bodin and Sidney is identical. . . . Jefferson used the same kind of markings in the original rough draft of the Declaration of Independence." Moreover (p. 19): "[T]he markings . . . from Bodin, Sidney and the Declaration of Independence have been made by Jefferson approximately during the same period . . . when he was preparing 'A Summary View of the Rights of British America' in 1774."

Mayer goes on to bolster his case through other Jefferson documents. He quotes (p. 19) from Jefferson's letter of 1825 to Henry Lee in which he stated that the principles in the Declaration of Independence were not intended to be completely original but rather to bring together various ideas "of the day," according to Jefferson, as partly found "in the elementary [basic] books of public right, as [by] Aristotle, Cicero, Locke, Sidney, etc." Mayer rightly asks if Jefferson's "etc." here included Bodin, who was perhaps early recommended to Jefferson by his law teacher, Wythe, for Jefferson could hardly have failed early on to know about Bodin's central place in the history of political thought.

Mayer briefly cites (p. 20), from Jefferson's *Papers* I, pp. 76 ff., Jefferson's letter of 1771 to Robert Skipworth in which Jefferson gave a list of books to him for a prospective private library. Under "Political, Trade.," Jefferson's list began with, in order, Montesquieu's *Spirit of the Laws*, Locke's *Treatises on Government*, and Sidney's *Discourses on Government*. Although Jefferson did not include Bodin here, he certainly knew, we may add, of Bodin's central influence on all three of those works. Moreover, Jefferson's list was purposely short, not comprehensive, as Mayer indicates.

In expanding upon Mayer's brief remarks on the letter and list of 1771 sent to Skipworth by Jefferson, we can point out more fully, first, that at that early date, just one year after the Shadwell fire that destroyed most of his first collection, Jefferson may well not yet have possessed Bodin's *Republic*, even though he almost certainly did by the mid-1770s. Yet its absence in the 1771 list of books can be explained, secondly, on other grounds based upon Jefferson's own words in his letter to Skipworth: "[In] executing your request to form a catalogue of books[,] . . . I have framed such a general collection as I think you would wish . . . to procure. Out of this you will chuse for yourself . . . in this catalogue. . . . of Politics . . . I have given a few only of the best books. . . . In Law I mention a few systematical books, as a knowledge of the minutiae of this science is not necessary for a private gentleman." From these somewhat elementary, generalized angles, it is not surprising that Jefferson did not include relatively more technical and historical works, especially not in English, like Bodin's *Republic* on subjects like legislative sovereignty. The first and longest category of this catalogue is "Fine Arts" (listed last in his 1823 and other catalogues), under which are included a broad band of writers. Under "Politicks, Trade.," are included Montesquieu, Locke, Sidney, and a very few others. Religion is a longer category, beginning with Locke yet then centering mostly on ancient writers like Cicero and Seneca. Under law are only three entries, one of which is on Blackstone. Under ancient history are numerous entries including Livy, Tacitus, and Plutarch. Under modern history are Bossuet, Hume, and a few others. After natural philosophy comes a final brief "miscellaneous" section that includes Locke on education.

To continue with other persuasive arguments by Mayer, he observes (pp. 21–22): "It would also be astonishing [to think] that Jefferson's friends like . . . Condorcet . . . should never have mentioned Bodin to Jefferson. [S]uch a fanatic reader as Jefferson . . . would . . . have gone back to a study of Bodin." Mayer notes, as have many others, that Jefferson was in the abit of reading the books in his library, which included one of his favorites— Pierre Charron's *De la sagesse*, a late-16th-century French treatise full of references to Bodin (pp. 22–23).

Although Mayer successfully dates Jefferson's bracket marks in the *Republic* to the mid-1770s at the time when they were also made in Jefferson's draft Declaration of Independence (where he included changes by the Committee and Congress), Mayer misses entirely the essential point we have tried to establish: that Jefferson's Declaration of Independence and his other related documents were profoundly influenced by Bodin's ideas of legislative sovereignty. Mayer's own focus from the outset of his provocative article is on other issues in the Jefferson-Bodin connection, such as on the ruler being bound by higher laws of God, nature, and justice. To be sure, those ideas in Bodin's work obviously appealed to Jefferson, even though in his Declaration of Independence he hardly needed extensive recourse to Bodin on such matters when the more immediate republican principles of Sidney, Locke, and others were readily at hand. Yet the bracketed passages cited by Mayer fall mostly into that category, so it is fairly clear that Jefferson was indeed attentive to Bodin in these matters around the time of his Declaration of Independence. On the whole issue of the short vertical dash marks in many margins of Jefferson's copy of Bodin's *Republic*, Mayer is mostly silent and unconcerned. He is convinced that these marks, too, are by Jefferson, but he tacitly leaves for future investigators to ascertain when they were made, possibly later in Jefferson's career. Mayer's three page samples from the first book of the *Republic* are representative of where such markings are concentrated in that work and relate in various ways to the wider contexts of sovereignty in its legislative and other forms. Mayer, however, is again wholly unconcerned with the whole *legislative* orientation of Bodin's ideas of sovereignty, and he totally overlooks the pervading *legislative* scope of sovereignty set forth at the beginning of the Declaration of Independence. Even so, Mayer's other valuable insights serve to strengthen our present findings on this issue in connection with Bodin's *Republic*. Mayer's concluding quotations from historians like McIlwain and from Jefferson himself show that Mayer's interests lie in wider areas of constitutionalism and justice rather than in *legislative* sovereignty more specifically.

Finally, Mayer's short discussion (pp. 19 ff) of Jefferson's *Commonplace Book* (edited by Gilert Chinard, Baltimore and Paris, 1926) must be taken into account. Mayer rightly observes that it is hardly surprising that the book includes no references to Bodin, for the materials in it are far from comprehensive or complete (not unlike in the case of Jefferson's 1771 library list). Even Bolinbroke's political works, comprising one of only eight entries under politics in the 1771 library list, is not referred to in the *Commonplace Book*. On the other hand, it does contain extracts from Montesquieu's *Spirit of the Laws*, Book V, which, as Mayer notes, refers toward the end in Ch. XV to Bodin's *Republic*, Bk. V, Ch. III, as Jefferson would have noticed. In addition, Mayer quotes a lengthy passage referring to Bodin's *Republic* in a summary of Milton's *The Reason of Church Government* that, in other portions, is included in Chinard's edition of Jefferson's *Commonplace Book*, pp. 384–385. In general, Jefferson had more opportunity and inclination to incorporate extracts in his *Commonplace Book* during his younger years than he did during his busier ensuing years.

An obvious point not mentioned by Mayer is that the primary dating of Jefferson's *Commonplace Book*, c. 1764 (even earlier than the early 1771 book list omitting Bodin), makes it entirely possible that Jefferson had simply not as yet read or possessed Bodin's *Republic*. In his Introduction to his edition, Chinard quotes (p. 5) an 1814 letter in which Jefferson said: "I promised you a sample from my common place book, of the pious dispositions of the English judges. . . . When I was a student of the law now half a century ago, after getting through Coke [and] Littleton, . . . I was in the habit of abridging and common-placing what I read . . . sometimes [with] . . . my own reflections. . . . They were written at a time of life when I was bold in the pursuit of knowledge . . ." Although, as Chinard points out, this dating of c. 1764 is "impossible for the whole of the manuscript," that primary dating, coupled with the main origin and orientation as just described, renders the omission of Bodin of no consequence for our purposes. The references to English writers like Locke and Sidney obviously fit in with Jefferson's interests at that point in time.

Chinard also points out (pp. 54–55) that "political philosophers occupy so little space" in Jefferson's *Commonplace Book*. Writers like Hooker, Hobbes, and Rousseau are omitted. Even Locke, Chinard believes, was used by Jefferson along the lines that other American Revolutionaries followed in their sparse appreciation of British political thinkers while yet needing to prove their cases with precise legal arguments and relevant historical precedents. Locke's political philosophy had little real influence on Jefferson or even on the other Founders, according to Chinard, although the appendix to the *Commonplace Book* includes a separate reading of Locke on religious and other matters (along with references to Voltaire, Milton, etc.). Jefferson's legal materials in his *Commonplace Book* fit in with the kinds of legal books that predominated in his early Shadwell library, as well as with the type of early legal education he received. Chinard points out, furthermore, Jefferson's own bias against England in favor of France in other respects. Jefferson's allusion in his 1814 letter to "the pious dispositions of the English judges" may reflect a broader bias against Britain.

172. Jefferson's copy of *Quinti Horatii Flacci poemata Aurelianis, MDCCLXVII* is in Special Collections at the Library of Congress, Wash., D.C. The work was given to the Library of Congress after 1815. It is not in the Sowerby catalogue of Jefferson's books that went to the Library of Congress in 1815. A number of other entries on Horace are included in the Sowerby catalogue.

173. Sowerby, *Catalogue*, Vol. II, p. 400.

174. *The Works of Nicholas Machiavelli*, translated by E. Farneworth (2 vols., London, 1762, 1st edn.). Both vols. are inscribed (initialled) by Jefferson at "signatures" I and T. Cf. Sowerby, *Catalogue*, Vol. III, p. 22. The *Prince* is in Vol. I, where on the first page (511) are other vertical marginal markings in long solid lines. Some handwriting seems on first examination not to be dissimilar to that by Jefferson in the margins of his copy of a book of poetry by Horace cited above. Each ch. of the *Prince* is followed by an "Examen" by the King of Prussia (as cited in our Vol. V, Bk. II). Voltaire's Preface to the first edn. of the King of Prussia's *Examen du "Prince" de Machiavel* (at end, 1740), along with the King of Prussia's Preface to his *Examen* or *General Essay* upon Machiavelli's *Prince*, would also have been of added interest to Jefferson.

175. *Political Classics* (3 vols., 1794–1795), Vol. III containing More's *Utopia* and Rousseau's *Social Contract* with Vols. I–II containing Sidney's *Discourses on Government* and other items concerning Sidney. Cf. Sowerby, *Catalogue*, Vol. III, p. 16.

176. Algernon Sidney's *Discourses Concerning Government*, in the London edn. of 1763, is included and discusssed in Sowerby's *Catalogue*, Vol. III, pp. 12–13. It is initialed by Jefferson at "signatures" I and T. Jefferson was already familiar with Sidney's work in the 1771 book list he sent to Robert Skipwith. Jefferson included the work in various later lists of recommended reading. He had a copy of this work credited to him in a bill sent him in 1807. In a letter of 1804, Jefferson praised Sidney's *Disccourses* as "a rich treasure of republican principles" and as "probably the best elementary [basic] book of the principles of government, as founded in natural right [!] which has ever been published in any language[,] . . . [and] it should be put into the hands of our youth . . ." On Mayer's attribution of bracket marks that appear within the text of Jefferson's copy of the 1763 edn. of Sidney's *Discourses*, cf. above, n. 171.

177. Montesquieu's *Spirit of the Laws* is included in Jefferson's copy of the three-volume *Oeuvres de Montesquieu* (London, 1761), which is included in the Jefferson Collection and which bears the 1815 Library of Congress bookplate. All 3 vols. are inscribed with Jefferson's initials at the usual I and T "signatures." Montesquieu's *Spirit* is in vols. I–II. Cf. Sowerby, *Catalogue*, Vol. III, p. 2, for Jefferson's appraisals of the *Spirit* in two letters of 1790 and 1810.

178. See corresponding notes 176 and 177 immediately above.

179. Sowerby, *Catalogue*, Vol. III, provides in Ch. 24 on politics various useful points of information that could be pursued further through more extensive inspections of Jefferson's books along present lines of inquiry. A few examples must suffice here. (A more immense challenge would be to search for possible further clues through all of Sowerby's notations in all chs. on all subjects and then to inspect all of Jefferson's books in this and even other collections.) A copy of Machiavelli's *Prince*—combined with other writings against monarchy and tyanny, and initialled by Jefferson as the usual I and T "signatures"—has some writing by Jefferson on the second title (Sowerby, III, pp. 1–2). Further items relating to Montesquieu's *Spirit of the Laws* are of possible interest (Sowerby, III, pp. 3 ff). Jefferson's separate copies of works by Filmer and Sidney (Sowerby, III, pp. 11–13) could be examined but probably to no avail. A two-volume copy of Plato's *Republic* in Greek and Latin, initialled by Jefferson at the I and T "signatures," has a few manuscript annotations by Jefferson (Sowerby, III, pp. 18–19). An English translation of Plato's *Republic*, likewise inscribed by Jefferson, has a couple of small corrections by him (Sowerby, III, pp. 19–20).

Under other categories in Sowerby's catalogue are certain additional items of possible interest. Another Platonic work, inscribed by Jefferson, has a manuscript note by him (II, p. 33, under ethics and moral philosophy). A three-volume edn. of *The Works of John Locke* (London, 1751) has some items written in by Jefferson (V, pp. 168–169, under polygraphics).

Of more general interest are the various illustrations included by Sowerby at the beginning of col. I and opposite the title page of Vol. II, as well as the samples of Jefferson's handwriting in Charles Hamilton's *American Autographs* (Norman, 1983), pp. 82–90.

180. The fuller title of Jefferson's copy of the *Lexicon I[J]uridicum* is, in part: *Lexicon Iuridicum Iuris Caesarei, simul et canonici, feudalis item, civilis, criminalis, theoretici, ac practici. . . . Do. Cuiacii, Brissonii, Donelli, Duareni, Gothofredi, . . . Corrasii, . . . Wesembeccii, aliorumq; praestantissimorum Virorum* (Geneva, 1669). Prepared by J. Calvinus (Kahl) and continued by D. Gothofredus and H. Vultejus, this weighty tome of approximately 1,000 pages in folio has 530 leaves, with an elaborate title page printed in red and black, the work itself being in double columns. The first edition appeared in 1600 and later editions or printings were produced into the 18th century. Jefferson initialled his copy at sig. I and T, and it bears the 1815 bookplate of the Library of Congress. Cf. Sowerby, *Catalogue*, Vol. II, p. 397. This *Lexicon* is cited above, this book, p. 88. Cf. also appendix below.

This impressive *Lexicon* of Roman law, canon law, and the law of the Holy Roman Empire long remained a standard legal reference book. It would have been of particular interest and usefulness for Jefferson's deep legal mind. A lengthy initial catalogue of all authors utilized, including Corasius, points up the special tribute paid to him and several other authorities singled out on the title page as being particularly "illustrious" contributors. Other names on the title page include the ones cited above, such as Duaren and Doneau, who were also featured in our initial studies on Corasius. Corasius' contributions as a legal systematizer were well noted and utilized in works by Hermann Vultejus, a later editor of the *Lexicon*, as cited in our studies on Corasius. Gothofredus' edition of the *Corpus Iuris* made good use of Corasius' contributions as a legal commentator. For the *Lexicon*, cf. e.g. our Vol. I, pp. 45–46. Also below, Ch. VI, n. 34 and our corresponding text, on Noah Webster's citation of Jefferson's uses of the *Lexicon* on topics of legislation.

Notes to Chapter III
Adams in Legislative Profile

1. *Loc. cit.* above, Ch. II, sect. 5.
2. Cf. below this ch., sect.5.
3. Cf. *John Adams: A Bibliography*, compiled by John Ferling (Westport, 1994), p. 31.
4. *Ibid.*, p. 31.
5. One of the most pertinent secondary works on John Adams and the intellectual foundations of his political philosophy in general remains Zoltan Haraszti's *John Adams and the Prophets of Progress* (Camb., Mass., 1952). It discusses Adams' books and the influence on him of European writers, especially Bolingbroke, Rousseau, Voltaire, d'Alembert, Mably, Turgot, Condorcet, and Priestley, albeit to the neglect of legislation, sovereignty, and state. More recently, there is C. Bradley Thompson's *John Adams and the Spirit of Liberty* (Lawrence, Kansas, 1998), a broad yet detailed survey with discussion of Locke, Machiavelli, the Mass. State Constit., lawmaking, and the European-American contexts of Adams' multi-volume *Discourses*. Other works of present interest include the following: Catherine Drinker Bowen, *John Adams and the American Revolution* (Boston, 1949, 1950), Pts. I, IV on Adams' educational background and his role in the Continental Congress; David McCullough, *John Adams* (New York, 2001), a best-seller with substantial documentary materials, source notes, and current bibliography; Stephen G. Kurtz, *The Presidency of John Adams* (Phila., 1957), with substantial older bibliography; Edward Handler, *America and Europe in the Thought of John Adams* (Camb., Mass., 1964), useful for Adams' intellectual background; Peter Shaw, *The Character of John Adams* (Chapel Hill, 1976); John Murray Allison, *Adams and Jefferson: The Story of a Friendship* (Norman, 1966); and Page Smith, *John Adams* (2 vols., Garden City, 1962), broad yet substantial.
6. John Adams, *The Works of John Adams* (10 vols., Boston, 1850–1856—reprinted 1969—with notes, etc., by Charles Francis Adams), Vol. IV (first of three letters from

Vice Pres. Adams in New York to Roger Sherman concerning the new U.S. Constitution, July 17, 1789, with two other letters to him on ensuing days), p. 427.

7. *Ibid.* (Adams to Sherman, letter #1), p. 427: "You say, 'it is by some objected that the executive is blended with the legislature, and that those powers ought to be entirely distinct and unconnected.' But is not that a gross error in politics? The united wisdom and various interests of a nation should be combined in framing the laws by which all are to be governed and protected, though it should not be convenient to have them executed by the whole legislature. The supreme executive in Great Britain is one branch of the legislature, and has a negative on all the laws; perhaps that is an extreme not to be imitated by a republic; but the negative vested in the president by the new constitution on the acts of congress, and the consequent revision, may be very useful to prevent laws being passed without mature deliberation . . ." Here as elsewhere, I have not modernized the original styles.

8. *Ibid.* (Adams to Sherman, letter #1, p. 428.

9. *Ibid.* (Adams to Sherman, letter #2), pp. 429–430: "In my letter of yesterday I think it was demonstrated that the English government is a republic, and that the regal negative upon the laws is essential to that republic. Because, without it, that government would not be what it is, a monarchical republic; and, consequently, could not preserve the balance of power between the executive and legislative powers, nor that other balance which is in the legislature,—between the one, the few, and the many; in which two balances the excellence of that form of government must consist.

"Let us now inquire, whether the new constitution of the United States is or is not a monarchical republic, like that of Great Britain. The monarchical and the aristocratical power in our constitution, it is true, are not hereditary; but this makes no difference in the nature of the power, in the nature of the balance, or in the name of the species of government. It would make no difference in the power of a judge or justice, or general or admiral, whether his commission were for life or years. His authority during the time it lasted, would be the same whether it were for one or twenty, or for life, or descendible to his eldest son. The people, the nation, in whom all power resides originally, may delegate their power for one year or for ten years; for years, or for life; or may delegate it in fee simple or fee tail, if I may so express myself; or during good behavior, or at will, or till further orders.

"A nation might unanimously create a dictator or a despot, for one year or more, or for life, or for perpetuity with hereditary descent. In such a case, the dictator for one year would as really be a dictator for the time his power lasted, as the other would be whose power was perpetual and descendible. A nation in the same manner might create a simple monarchy for years, life, or perpetuity, and in either case the creature would be equally a simple monarch during the continuance of his power. So the people of England might create king, lords, and commons, for a year, or for several years, or for life, and in any of these cases, their government would be a monarchical republic, or, if you will, a limited monarchy, during its continuance, as much as it is now, when the king and nobles are hereditary. They might make their house of commons hereditary too. What the consequence of this would be it is easy to foresee; but it would not in the first moment make any change in the legal power, nor in the name of the government."

10. *Ibid.* (Adams to Sherman, letter #2), p. 430.

11. *Ibid.* (Adams to Sherman, letter #2), p. 431.

12. *Ibid.* (Adams to Sherman, letter #2), p. 431.

13. *Ibid.* (Adams to Sherman, letter #3), p. 432.

14. *Ibid.* (Adams to Sherman, letter #3), pp. 432–436: "It is, moreover, possible, that more than two thirds of the nation, the senate, and house, may, in times of calamity, distress, misfortune, and ill success of the measures of government, from the momentary

passion and enthusiasm, demand a law which will wholly subvert the constitution. The constitution of Athens was overturned in such a manner by Aristides himself. The constitution should guard against a possibility of its subversion; but we may take stronger ground, and assert that it is probable such cases will happen, and that the constitution will, in fact, be subverted in this way. Nay, I go further, and say, that from the constitution of human nature, and the constant course of human affairs, it is certain that our constitution will be subverted, if not amended, and that in a very short time, merely for want of a decisive negative in the executive.

"There is another sense and another degree in which the executive is blended with the legislature, which is liable to great and just objection; which excites alarms, jealousies, and apprehensions, in a very great degree. I mean, 1st, the negative of the senate upon appointments to office; 2d. the negative of the senate upon treaties; and 3d. the negative of the two houses upon war. I shall confine myself, at present, to the first. The negative of the senate upon appointments is liable to the following objections:—

"1. It takes away, or, at least, it lessens the responsibility of the executive. . . .

"2. It turns the minds and attention of the people to the senate, a branch of the legislature, in executive matters. It interests another branch of the legislature in the management of the executive. It divides the people between the executive and the senate; whereas, all the people ought to be united to watch the exeecutive, to oppose its encroachments, and resist its ambition. . . .

"3. It has a natural tendency to excite ambition in the senate. . . . I am very apprehensive that this defect in our constitution will have an unhappy tendency to introduce corruption of the grossest kinds, both of ambition and avarice, into all our elections, and this will be the worst of poisons to our constitution. It will not only destroy the present form of government, but render it almost impossible to substitute in its place any free government, even a better limited-monarchy, or any other than a despotism or a simple monarchy.

"4. To avoid the evil under the last head, it will be in danger of dividing the continent into two or three nations, a case that presents no prospect but of perpetual war.

"5. This negative on appointments is in danger of involving the senate in reproach, censure, obloquy, and suspicion, without doing any good. Will the senate use their negative or not? If not, why should they have it? Many will censure them for not using it; many will ridicule them, and call them servile, &c. If they do use it, the very first instance of it will expose the senators to the resentment of not only the disappointed candidate and all his friends, but of the president and all his friends, and these will be most of the officers of government, through the nation.

"6. We shall very soon have parties formed; a court and country party, and these parties will have names given them. One party in the house of representatives will support the president and his measures and ministers; the other will oppose them. . . .

"7. The senate have not time. The convention and Indian treaties.

"You are of opinion 'that the concurrence of the senate in the appointments to office, will strengthen the hands of he executive, and secure the confidence of the people, much better than a select council, and will be less expensive.'

"But in every one of these ideas, I have the misfortune to differ from you.

"It will weaken the hands of the executive, by lessening the obligation, gratitude, and attachment of the candidate to the president, by dividing his attachment between the executive and legislative, which are natural enemies. Officers of government, instead of having a single eye and undivided attachment to the executive branch, as they ought to have, consistent with law and the constitution, will be constantly tempted to be factious with their factious patrons in the senate. The president's own officers, in a thousand instances, will oppose his just and constitutional exertions, and screen themselves under the wings of their patrons and party in the legislature. Nor will it secure the confidence of the people. The people will have more confidence in the executive, in executive matters, than in the senate. . . . You will find that the whole business of this government will be infinitely delayed by this negative of the senate on treaties and appointments."

Roger Sherman's first letter to Adams in this dialogue begins with thoughts on a "republic," *ibid.*, p. 437: "The subject of government is an important one, and necessary to be well understood by the citizens, and especially by the legislators of these states. I shall be happy to receive further light on the subject, and to have any errors that I may have entertained corrected.

"I find that writers on government differ in their definition of a *republic.* Entick's Dictionary defines it,—'*A commonwealth without a king.*' I find you do not agree to the negative part of his definition. What I meant by it was, a government under the authority of the people, consisting of legislative, executive, and judiciary powers; the legislative powers vested in an assembly, consisting of one or more branches, who, together with the executive, are appointed by the people, and dependent on them for continuance, by periodical elections, agreeably to an established constitution; and that what especially denominates it a *republic* is its dependence on the *public* or *people at large,* without any hereditary powers. But it is not of so much importance by what appellation the government is distinguished, as to have it well constituted to secure the rights, and advance the happiness of the community.

"I fully agree with you, sir, that it is optional with the people of a state to establish any form of government they please; to vest the powers in *one*, a *few*, or *many* . . ."

15. Adams' *A Defence of the Constitutions of Government of the United States of America, against the Attack by M. Turgot, in his letter to Dr. Price, 22 March 1778* is in Adams' *Works*, Vols. IV–VI. This extended title referring to Turgot's attack and Price's letter of 1778—which date nearly a decade prior to Adams' *Defence* but which had lately surfaced with a significant notoriety prompting his *Defence*—appears in the table of contents to Adams' *Works* IV. All passages *sic.*

A good overview of the genesis, composition, organization, and content of Adams' *Defence* is in Haraszti, *Adams*, Ch. VIII ("Turgot's Attack on the American Constitutions") and Ch. IX ("The Composition of Adams' *Defence*"). Also, Thompson, *Adams*, Ch. V ("A Guidebook for Lawgivers"), etc. Adams' correspondence with Jefferson on aspects of this work was cited above, Ch. II, sect. 5.

16. Adams, *Defence*, Vol. I, "Preliminary Observations," in his *Works*, Vol. IV, pp. 299–301: "Three writers in Europe of great abilities, reputation, and learning, M. Turgot, the Abbé de Mably, and Dr. Price, have turned their attention to the constitutions of government in the United States of America, and have written and published their criticisms and advice. They all had the most amiable characters, and unquestionably the purest intentions. They all had experience in public affairs, and ample information respecting the nature of man, the necessities of society, and the science of government.

"There are in the productions of all of them, among many excellent things, some sentiments, however, that it will be difficult to reconcile to reason, experience, the constitution of human nature, or to the uniform testimony of the greatest statesmen, legislators, and philosophers of all enlightened nations, ancient and modern.

"M. Turgot, in his letter to Dr. Price, confesses, 'that he is not satisfied with the constitutions which have hitherto been formed for the different states of America.' He observes, 'that by most of them the customs of England are imitated, without any particular motive. Instead of collecting all authority into one centre, that of the nation, they have established different bodies, a body of representatives, a council, and a governor, because there is in England a house of commons, a house of lords, and a king. They endeavor to balance these different powers, as if this equilibrium, which in England may be a necessary check to the enormous influence of royalty, could be of any use in republics founded upon the equality of all the citizens, and as if establishing different orders of men was not a source of divisions and disputes.'

"There has been, from the beginning of the revolution in America, a party in every state, who have entertained sentiments similar to these of M. Turgot. Two or three of them have established governments upon this principle; and, by advices from Boston, certain committees of counties have been held, and other conventions proposed in the Massachusetts, with the express purpose of deposing the governor and senate as useless and expensive branches of the constitution; and as it is probable that the publication of M. Turgot's opinion has contributed to excite such discontents among the people, it becomes necessary to examine it, and, if it can be shown to be an error, whatever veneration the Americans very justly entertain for his memory, it is to be hoped they will not be misled by his authority. . . .

"M. Turgot seems to be of a different opinion, and is for 'collecting all authority into one centre, the nation.' It is easily understood how all authority may be collected into 'one centre' in a despot or monarch; but how it can be done when the centre is to be the nation, is more difficult to comprehend."

17. Cf. above Ch. II, sect. 5.

18. *Ibid.*

19. Adams, *Defence*, Vol. I, Ch. X ("Conclusion"), in *Works*, Vol. IV, pp. 579–581, 584–585, 587–588: "By the authorities and examples already recited, you will be convinced that three branches of power have an unalterable foundation in nature; that they exist in every society natural and artificial; and that if all of them are not acknowledged in any constitution of government, it will be found to be imperfect, unstable, and soon enslaved; that the legislative and executive authorities are naturally distinct; and that liberty and the laws depend entirely on a separation of them in the frame of government; that the legislative power is naturally and necessarily sovereign and supreme over the executive; and, therefore, that the latter must be made an essential branch of the former, even with a negative, or it will not be able to defend itself, but will be soon invaded, undermined, attacked, or in some way or other totally ruined and annihilated by the former. This is applicable to every state in America, in its individual capacity; but is it equally applicable to the United States in their federal capacity?

"The people of America and their delegates in congress were of opinion, that a single assembly was every way adequate to the management of all their federal concerns; and with very good reason, because congress is not a legislative assembly, nor a representative assembly, but only a diplomatic assembly. A single council has been found to answer the purposes of confederacies very well. But in all such cases the deputies are responsible to the states; their authority is clearly ascertained; and the states, in their separate capacities, are the checks. These are able to form an effectual balance, and at all times to control their delegates. The security against the dangers of this kind of government will depend upon the accuracy and decision with which the governments of the separate states have their own orders arranged and balanced.

"The necessity we are under of submitting to a federal government, is an additional and a very powerful argument for three branches, and a balance by an equal negative, in all the separate governments. Congress will always be composed of members from the natural and artificial aristocratical body in every state, even in the northern, as well as in the middle and southern states. Their natural dispositions, then, in general will be . . . to diminish the prerogatives of the governors and the privileges of the people, and to augment the influence of the aristocratical parties. . . . The necessity of a negative in the house of representatives will be called in question by nobody.

"Dr. Price and the Abbé de Mably are zealous for additional powers to congress. Full power in all foreign affairs and over foreign commerce, and, perhaps, some authority over the commerce of the states with one another, may be necessary; and it is hard to say that more authority in other things is not wanted. Yet the subject is of such extreme delicacy and difficulty, that the people are much to be applauded for their caution. To collect together the ancient and modern leagues,—the Amphictyonic, the Olynthian, the Argive, the Arcadian, and the Achaean confederacies, among the Greeks; the general diet of the Swiss cantons, and the states-general of the United Netherlands; the union of the Hanse-towns, &c., which have been found to answer the purposes both of government and liberty; to compare them all with the circumstances, the situation, the geography, the commerce, the population, and the forms of government, as well as the climate, the soil, and manners of the people, and consider what further federal powers are wanted, and may be safely given, would be a useful work.

"According to M. Turgot's idea of a perfect commonwealth, a single assembly is to be possessed of all authority, legislative, executive, and judicial. It will be a proper conclusion of all our speculations upon this, the most interesting subject which can employ the thoughts of men, to consider in what manner such an assembly will conduct its deliberations and exert its power. The executive power is properly the government; the laws are a dead letter until an administration begins to carry them into execution. . . .

"Shall the assembly appoint a governor or president, and give him all the executive power? Why should not the people at large appoint him? Giving this power to the assembly will open a wider door to intrigue for the place; and the aristocratical families will be sure, nine times in ten, to carry their choice in this way; and, what is much worse, the first magistrate . . . will be dependent only on a dozen or a score, perhaps on two or three, of the whole. . . . Instead of thinking of his duty to the people at large, he will confine his attention chiefly to the assembly, and believe, that if he can satisfy them, or a majority of them, he has done his duty. . . .

"But we have not yet considered how the legislative power is to be exercised in this single assembly. Is there to be a constitution? Who are to compose it? The assembly itself, or a convention called for that purpose? In either case, whatever rules are agreed on for the preservation of the lives, liberties, properties, and characters of the citizens, what is to hinder this assembly from transgressing the bounds which they have prescribed to themselves, or which the convention has ordained for them? The convention has published its code and is no more. Shall a new convention be called, to determine every question which arises concerning a violation of the constitution? This would require that the convention should sit whenever the assembly sits, and consider and determine every question which is agitated in it. This is the very thing we contend for, namely,—that there may be two assemblies; one to divide, and the other to choose. Grant me this, and I am satisfied; provided you will confine both the convention and assembly to legislation, and give the whole executive power to another body. I had almost ventured to propose a third assembly for the executive power; but the unity, the secrecy, the dispatch of one man has no equal. . . .

"But shall the people at large elect a governor and council annually to manage the executive power, and a single assembly to have the whole legislative? In this case, the executive power, instead of being independent, will be the instrument of a few leading members of the house; because the executive power, being an object of jealousy and envy to the people, and the legislative an object of their confidence and affection, the latter will always be able to render the former unpopular, and undermine its influence. But if the people for a time support an executive disagreeable to the leaders in the legislative, the constitution will be disregarded, and the nation will be divided between the two bodies, and each must at last have an army to decide the question. A constitution consisting of an executive in one single assembly, and a legislative in another, is already composed of two armies in battle array; and nothing is wanting but the word of command to begin the combat.

"In the present state of society and manners in America, . . . the people can live and increase under almost any kind of government, or without any government at all. But it is of great importance to begin well. . . . There are but two ways, either by a monarchy and standing army, or by a balance in the constitution. Where the people have a voice, and there is no balance, there will be everlasting fluctuations, revolutions, and horrors, until a standing army, with a general at its head, commands the peace, or the necessity of an equilibrium is made appear to all, and is adopted by all."

20. Adams, *Defence*, Vol. III, Ch. II ("Marchamont Nedham. The Constitution of a Commonwealth Examined"), in *Works*, Vol. VI: "[p. 39] These examples all show that the natural principles of the English constitution were constantly at work among the Roman people; that nature herself was constantly calling out for two masters to control the senate, one in a king or single person, possessed of the executive power, and the other in an equal representation of the people, possessed of a negative on all the laws, and especially on the disposal of the public money. As these examples are great illustrations of our argument, and illustrious proofs of the superior excellence of the American constitutions. . . .

"[p. 50] [O]ne may . . . deny . . . that a succession of sovereign authority in one assembly, by popular elections, destroys faction. We may affirm the contrary; that a standing authority in an absolute monarch, or an hereditary aristocracy, is less friendly to the monster than a simple popular government; and that it is only in a mixed government, of three independent orders, of the one, the few, and the many, and three separate powers, the legislative, executive, and judicial, that all sorts of factions, those of the poor and the rich, those of the gentlemen and common people, those of the one, the few, and the many, can at all times be quelled . . .

"[p. 56] To . . . give all power to the people's successive single representative assemblies, is to make the continuance of power, with all its increasing influence and corruption, certain and inevitable. You may as wisely preach to the winds, as gravely exhort a triumphant majority to lay down their power.

"It is undoubtedly honorable in any man, who has acquired a great influence, unbounded confidence, and unlimited power, to resign it voluntarily; and odious to take advantage of such an opportuniy to destroy a free government. But it would be madness in a legislator to frame his policy upon a supposition that such magnanimity would often appear. It is his business to contrive his plan in such a manner, that such unlimited influence, confidence, and power, shall never be obtained by any man. The laws alone can be trusted with unlimited confidence; those laws, which alone can secure equity between all and every one; which are the bond of that dignity which we enjoy in the commonwealth; the foundation of liberty, and the fountain of equity; the mind, the soul, the counsel, and judgment of the city; whose ministers are the magistrates, whose interpreters the judges, whose servants are all men who mean to be free. Those laws, which are right reason, derived from the Divinity, commanding honesty, and forbidding iniquity; which are silent magistrates, where the magistrates are only speaking laws; which, as they are founded on eternal morals, are emanations of the Divine mind [citing Cicero]. . . .

"[p. 58] Of all possible forms of government, a sovereignty in one assembly, successively chosen by the people, is perhaps the best calculated to facilitate the gratification of self-love, and the pursuit of the private interest of a few individuals; a few eminent conspicuous characters will be continued in their seats in the sovereign assembly, from one election to another, whatever changes are made in the seats around them. . . .

"[p. 98] To amuse and flatter the people with compliments of qualities that never existed in them, is not the duty nor the right of a philosopher or legislator; he must form a true idea and judgment of mankind, and adapt his institutions to facts, not compliments. . . .

"But if the sovereignty were exercised wholly by one popular assembly, they would then have the means and opportunities in their hands as much as the king has in a monarchy, or the senate in an aristocracy or oligarchy; and much more than either king or nobles have in the tripartite composition we contend for. . . .

"[p. 111] But if we consider those passions in human nature which cause despots, oligarchies, and standing senates, to make such an abuse of power, we must see that the same passions will ever exist in the majority and their leaders in a democracy, and produce the same fatal effects.

"It is really astonishing, that the institution of Lycurgus should be adduced as a precedent in favor of our author's project of the right constitution of a commonwealth; there is scarcely a form of government in the world more essentially different from it is all its parts. It is very true that the provision made by that legislator for an equality of laws, rights, duties, and burdens, among all the citizens, however imperfect it was, however inferior to the provision in the English and American constitutions, was the principal commendation of his plan; but instead of giving all power to the people or their representatives, he gave the real sovereignty to his standing senate."

On M. Nedham cf. Haraszti, *Adams*, esp. pp. 162–164, and Thompson, *Adams*, Ch. 7, passim. Nedham's *Excellencie of a Free State* was printed as a book in 1656, having first appeared as editorials in 1651–1652. It was reprinted in 1767 by T. Hollis, whose heir T. Brand sent a copy to Adams.

21. Adams, *Defence*, Vol. III, Ch. IV ("Conclusion"), in *Works*, Vol. VI, pp. 217–220.

22. Adams, letter to Richard Henry Lee, Nov. 1775, in *Works*, Vol. IV, pp. 185–187.

23. On Wythe in relation to Jefferson's early law education and as authority on English and Roman law, see e.g. Peterson, *Jefferson and the New Nation*, esp. pp. 13 ff.; and Mayer, *Constitutional Thought of Jefferson*, pp. 4–6, etc.

24. Adams, "Thoughts on Government" in *Works*, Vol. IV, pp. 194–195.

25. *Ibid.*, pp. 196–197: "But shall the whole power of legislation rest in one assembly? Most of the foregoing reasons apply equally to prove that the legislative power ought to be more complex; to which we may add, that if the legislative power is wholly in one assembly, and the executive in another, or in a single person, these two powers will oppose and encroach upon each other, until the contest shall end in war, and the whole power, legislative and executive, be usurped by the strongest.

"The judicial power, in such case, could not mediate, or hold the balance between the two contending powers, because the legislative would undermine it. And this shows the necessity, too, of giving the executive power a negative upon the legislative, otherwise this will be continually encroaching upon that.

"To avoid these dangers, let a distinct assembly be constituted, as a mediator between the two extreme branches of the legislature, that which represents the people, and that which is vested with the executive power.

"Let the representative assembly then elect by ballot, from among themselves or their constituents, or both, a distinct assembly, which, for the sake of perspicuity, we will call a council. It may consist of any number you please, any twenty or thirty, and should have a free and independent exercise of its judgment, and consequently a negative voice in the legislature.

"These two bodies, thus constituted, and made integral parts of the legislature, let them unite, and by joint ballot choose a governor, who, after being stripped of most of those badges of domination, called prerogatives, should have a free and independent exercise of his judgment, and be made also an integral part of the legislature. This, I know, is liable to objections; and, if you please, you may make him only president of the council, as in Connecticut. But as the governor is to be invested with the executive power, with consent of council, I think he ought to have a negative upon the legislature. . . .

"In the present exigency of American affairs, when, by an act of Parliament, we are put out of the royal protection, and consequently discharged from our allegiance, and it has become necessary to assume government for our immediate security, the governor, lieutenant-governor, secretary, treasurer, commissary, attorney-general, should be chosen by joint ballot of both houses. And these and all other elections, especially of representatives and counsellors, should be annual . . ."

26. *Ibid.*, pp. 206–208: "Let the representative body, then, elect from among themselves, or their constituents, or both, a distinct assembly, which we will call a council. It may consist of any number you please, say, twenty or thirty. To this assembly should be given a free and independent exercise of its judgment upon all acts of legislation, that it may be able to check and arrest the errors of the other.

"But there ought to be a third branch of the legislature; and wherever the executive power of the state is placed, there the third branch of the legislature ought to be found.

"Let the two houses, then, by joint ballot, choose a governor. *Let him be chosen annually. Divest him of most of those badges of slavery called prerogatives*, and give him a negative upon the legislature. . . .

"The stability of government, in all its branches, the morals of the people, and every other blessing of society and social institutions, depend so much upon an able and impartial administration of justice, *that the judicial power* should be separated from the legislative and executive, and independent upon both; the judges should be men of experience in the laws, of exemplary morals . . . ; they should not be dependent on any man or body of men. . . .

"We have heard much of a continental constitution; I see no occasion for any but a congress. Let that be made an equal and fair representative of the Colonies; and let its authority be confined to three cases,— war, trade, and controversies between colony and colony. If a confederation was formed, agreed on in Congress, and ratified by the assemblies, these Colonies, *under such forms of government and such a confederation, would be unconquerable by all the monarchies of Europe.*

"This plan of a government for a colony, you see, is intended as a temporary expedient under the present pressure of affairs. The government once formed, and having settled its authority, will have leisure enough to make any alterations that time and experience may dictate."

27. Adams' Massachusetts "Constitution," together with initial "Preamble" and "Declaration of Rights," is given in his *Works*, Vol. IV. In that edition, the portions given in brackets were deleted in the constitution as adopted, while those given in italics underwent changes. The rest is by Adams as finally adopted. The main title, as given, is "The Report of a Constitution, or Form of Government, for the Commonwealth of Massachusetts."

Also cf. the Mass. Constitution in Vol. III of *The Federal and State Constitutions*, (edited by F. N. Thorpe, Wash., D.C., 1909, 1977), where the 1780 documents (pp. 1888 ff.) are preceded by earlier ones of that state.

28. McCullough, *Adams*, pp. 220–221. Also cf. Thompson, *Adams*, Ch. 2. The Mass. Constit. was written by John Adams in about two months, between Sept. 1 and Oct. 30, 1779, which is when he submitted it to the committee formed for that purpose. With few alterations it was accepted by the convention and then submitted to the voters, it being ratified in 1780.

29. Among Adams' many relevant uses of the term "commonwealth" in his other writings quoted below, his discussion of the Elizabethan Thomas Smith's "The Commonwealth of England" is of particular note. That was the title as Adams gave it of Smith's *De reipublicae anglorum* (not in the Adams 1917 catalogue), written in 1564–1565 and published in 1583. In his *Defence*, Adams was to express singular praise of Smith's work (below, n. 38). In our previous studies (Vol. III, Ch. XIII, sect. 3; Vol. IX, Ch. XIV, sect. 2; Vol. V, Bk. I, Ch. IV, sect. 3), we noted the many close relationships between Smith's *Republic* (or *Commonwealth*) and Bodin's *Republic* of 1576, including in their chapter

titles; we also referred to Richard Knolles' English translation of Bodin's *Republic*, which he, too, rendered as *Commonweale* (or *Commonwealth*). Knolles' version, published in 1606 just three years after the end of the Elizabethan age upon the queen's death, also bore close relationships to Smith's work as well as to the wider Tudor "commonwealth literature." As evident in the same place below (n. 38), Adams is especially interested in the term "commonwealth" in relation to Smith's title and to the alternate term "republic." There, Adams also points out various other works, with more abstract and less practical views of a commonwealth, written by Plato, More, Polybius, and Xenophon. For instance, Plato's *Republic* is rendered *Commonwealth* by Adams. Adams also refers to the ill repute in England of the term and idea of "commonwealth" ever since Oliver Cromwell's failed "Commonwealth of England" in the mid-17th century; Adams himself also expresses disapproval of Cromwell's harmful and mistaken efforts to abolish monarchy and aristocracy in England (a further sign of Adams' emerging Federalist perspectives).

In diverse other instances cited below, Adams substitutes or employs his own terminology of "commonwealth" in place of "republic," etc. He does so when discussing such topics as Machiavelli and his plan of government for Pope Leo X (n. 52), the Florentine state more generally in history (nn. 44, 50), and the writings of which he disapproves by Turgot, Price, Nedham, Hume, and others (nn. 40, 41, 50). Similar examples (in texts not cited below, and on other matters) could be given with similar results. In the places just cited, the decisive contexts of the titles *Republic* and *Commonwealth* in the cases of Adams' Smith and Knolles' Bodin have not heretofore been duly noted by historians.

Also cited below (nn. 39, 40) are Adams' harsh criticisms of Locke, whose influences on Adams and other American founders was not always so great or uniform as many historians have supposed, to the neglect of others like Bodin, including in matters of present interest. Adams even groups Locke with Turgot and others whose ideas, he believes, have greatly worked against peoples' liberties (n. 40).

Adams' antipathy in his *Defence* toward the "Commonwealth" idea of England under Oliver Cromwell from c. 1640 to c. 1660 was related to his refutations of Marchamont Nedham's *The Excellency of a Free State, or the Right Constitution of a Commonwealth* (1651–1652, 1656), which was received by Adams subsequent to its reprinting in 1767 (Haraszti, *Adams*, p. 162, etc.; Thompson, *Adams*, p. 126, etc.). This context of the term "commonwealth" played, of course, a significant part in Adams' own usage of the term "commonwealth" (e.g., n. 20, above). However, this context remained a negative one from the perspective of Adams' strong criticisms of Nedham's idea and use of the term "commonwealth," in contradistinction to Adams' strongly positive portrayal of Thomas Smith's idea of commonwealth, quite possibly in conjunction with Knolles' celebrated 1606 translation of Bodin's *Republic* as *Commonwealth.*

In the end, the extent to which these aspects of "commonwealth," especially concerning Smith and Knolles, influenced Adams' special uses and concepts of that term in his Mass. Constit. of 1779 cannot be known exactly. Even so, Adams' positive reading of "commonwealth" ideas into works of numerous historical writers, quite possibly influenced by Knolles' Bodin, surely impacted his Mass. Constit.

At the same time, it is clear that Turgot's attack of March, 1778, against Adams' ideas (which was attached to Price's work, as cited by Adams in his extended title of the *Defence*, and which Adams said prompted his *Defence*) could not have played a part in Adams' thinking in his ensuing Mass. Constit. of 1779. For Turgot's attack, written in a letter to Price, remained confidential until 1784, when, after the death of Turgot, Price felt free to publish it (Haraszti, *Adams*, pp. 141, 327 n. 10). Anyway, Turgot was not there notable for ideas explicitly on "commonwealth," although Adams at points employs the term when discussing him (above, n. 19). Adams had met the famous Turgot upon arriving in Paris in April of 1778, not long before being received at the French court by King Louis XVI (Haraszti, *Adams*, p. 139 etc.). Turgot had been Comptroller General to Louis

XVI. Although Turgot's specific attack not only upon Adams but upon the existing American constitutions more broadly, became a prime catalyst for Adams' *Defence* in 1787–1788, it was not a factor in Adams' composition of the Mass. Constit. back in late 1779. As in other respects, these dimensions on Adams' Mass. Constit. have been neglected by historians.

Adams' "Preamble" to his Mass. Constit., declares as follows—*Works*, Vol. IV, pp. 219–220: "The end of the institution, maintenance, and administration of government is to secure the existence of the body politic; to protect it, and to furnish the individuals who compose it with the power of enjoying, in safety and tranquillity, their natural rights and the blessings of life; and whenever these great objects are not obtained, the people have a right to alter the government, and to take measures necessary for their safety, happiness, and prosperity.

"The body politic is formed by a voluntary association of individuals. It is a social compact, by which the whole people covenants with each citizen, and each citizen with the whole people, that all shall be governed by certain laws for the common good. It is the duty of the people, therefore, in framing a Constitution of Government, to provide for an equitable mode of making laws, as well as for an impartial interpretation and a faithful execution of them, that every man may, at all times, find his security in them.

"We, therefore, . . . the people of Massachusetts, . . . acknowledging, with grateful hearts, the goodness of the great Legislator of the universe, in affording *to this people*, in the course of His providence, an opportunity . . . of forming a new constitution of civil government for . . . posterity; . . . agree upon . . . the following Declaration of Rights, and Frame of Government, as the CONSTITUTION OF THE COMMONWEALTH OF MASSACHUSETTS."

30. Adams, "A Declaration of the Rights of the Inhabitants of the Commonwealth of Massachusetts," in *Works*, Vol. IV, pp. 220–221: "Art. I. All men are born [equally] free and . . . have certain natural, essential, and unalienable rights, among which may be reckoned the right of enjoying and defending their lives and liberties; that of acquiring, possessing, and protecting [their] property; in fine, that of seeking and obtaining their safety and happiness.

"II. It is the . . . duty of all men in society, publicly, and at stated seasons, to worship the SUPREME BEING, the great Creator and Preserver of the universe. And no subject shall be hurt, molested, or restrained, in his person, liberty, or estate, for worshipping GOD in the manner . . . most agreeable to the dictates of his own conscience. . . .

"III. [Good morals being necessary to the preservation of civil society; and the knowledge and belief of the being of GOD, His providential government of the world, and of a future state of rewards and punishments, being the only true foundation of morality, the legislature hath, therefore, a right, and ought to provide, at the expense of the subject, if necessary, a suitable support for the public worship of GOD . . .]"

31. *Ibid.*, pp. 223–229: "IV. The people of this commonwealth have the sole and exclusive right of governing themselves, as a free, sovereign, and independent state; and do, and forever hereafter shall, exercise and enjoy every power, jurisdiction, and right, which . . . may not hereafter be by them expressly delegated to the United States of America, in congress assembled.

"V. All power residing originally in the people, and being derived from them, the several magistrates and officers of government, vested with authority, whether legislative, executive, or judicial, are their substitutes and agents, and are at all times accountable to them. . . .

"VII. Government is instituted for the common good; for the protection, safety, prosperity, and happiness of the people; and not for the profit, honor, or private interest of any one man, family, or class of men; therefore, the people alone have an incontestable, unalienable, and indefeasible right to institute government; and to reform, alter, or totally change the same, when their protection, safety, prosperity, and happiness require it. . . .

"X. Each individual of the society has a right to be protected by it in the enjoyment of his life, liberty, and property, according to standing laws. He is obliged, consequently, to contribute his share to the expense of this protection; and to give his personal service, or an equivalent, when necessary. But no part of the property of any individual can, with justice, be taken from him, or applied to public uses, without his own consent, or that of the representative body of the people. In fine, the people of this commonwealth are not controllable by any other laws than those to which their constitutional representative body have given their consent.

"XI. Every subject of the commonwealth ought to find a certain remedy, by having recourse to the laws, for all injuries or wrongs which he may receive in his person, property, or character. He ought to obtain right and justice freely, and without being obliged to purchase it; completely, and without any denial; promptly, and without delay, conformably to the laws. . . .

"XIII. In criminal prosecutions, the verification of facts in the vicinity when they happen, is one of the greatest securities of the life, liberty, and property of the citizen.

"[XIV.] No subject [of the commonwealth] shall be arrested, imprisoned, despoiled, or deprived of his property, immunities, or privileges, put out of the protection of the law, exiled, or deprived of his life, liberty, or estate, but by the judgment of his peers, or the law of the land. . . .

"XV. [XVI.] In all controversies concerning property, and in all suits between two or more persons, . . . the parties have a right to a trial by [a] jury; and this method of procedure shall be held sacred; unless in causes arising on the high seas, and such as relate to mariners' wages, the legislature shall hereafter find it necessary to alter it. . . .

"XVIII. [XIX.] A frequent recurrence to the fundamental principles of the constitution, and a constant adherence to those of piety, justice, moderation, temperance, industry, and frugality, are absolutely necessary to preserve the advantages of liberty, and to maintain a free government. The people ought, consequently, to have a particular attention to all those principles, in the choice of their officers and representatives. And they have a right to require of their lawgivers and magistrates an exact and constant observance of them, in the formation and execution of the laws necessary for the good administration of the commonwealth.

"XIX. [XX.] The people have a right, in an orderly and peaceable manner, to assemble to consult upon the common good, give instructions to their representatives, and to request of the legislative body, by the way of addresses, petitions, or remonstrances, redress of the wrongs done them, and the grievances they suffer.

"XX. [XXI.] The power of suspending the laws, or the execution of the laws, ought never to be exercised but by the legislature, or by authority derived from it, to be exercised in such particular cases only as the legislature shall expressly provide for; [and there shall be no suspension of any law for the private interest, advantage, or emolument, of any one man, or class of men.]

"XXI. [XXII.] The freedom of deliberation, speech, and debate, in either house of the legislature, is so essential to the rights of the people, that it cannot be the foundation of any accusation or prosecution, action or complaint, in any other court or place whatsoever.

"XXII. [XXIII.] The legislature ought frequently to assemble for the redress of grievances, for correcting, strengthening, and confirming the laws, and for making new laws as the common good may require. . . .

"XXIV. [XXV.] Laws made to punish for actions done before the existence of such laws, and which have not been declared crimes by preceding laws, are unjust, oppressive, and inconsistent with the fundamental principles of a free government. . . .

"XXIX. [XXX.] It is essential to the preservation of the rights of every individual, his life, liberty, property, and character, that there be an impartial interpretation of the laws, and administration of justice."

32. Adams, "The Frame of Government," in *Works*, Vol. IV, pp. 230–231.

33. Adams, "Autobiography," in *Works*, Vol. III, p. 20.

34. *Ibid.*, p. 20. (Cf. also "On the Independence of the Judiciary: A Controversy between W. Brattle and J. Adams, 1773," in *Works*, Vol. III, pp. 513 ff.)

35. *Ibid.*, p. 87. It is noteworthy that in his Autobiography Adams greatly minimized his part in the formation of the Declaration of Independence (*ibid.*, Vol. II, pp. 512 ff.). Although he was on the committee of five with Jefferson that initially met to discuss the proposed contents, Adams not only told Jefferson to write the document instead of himself but also declined Jefferson's request that he, Adams, look through the preliminary materials. Adams later could not even remember whether he himself "made or suggested any corrections." Nor could Adams remember whether the committee of five thereafter "altered or corrected in any thing" before it was given to the full Congress.

It will be seen below in sect. 3 that in an 1813 note to his *Discourses on Davila* (1790–1791), article XIII, later included in *Works*, VI, Adams belittled Jefferson's Declaration of Independence with a certain bitterness (no doubt fueled by their controversies over the revolution in France). There, Adams claimed that the Declaration merely echoed his, Adams', own Boston declaration of 1772 as well as Congress' declaration of 1774 (both of which differed from it on points at hand). In the above passages in his Autobiography, Adams makes no such allusions or charges, but ends his account with a somewhat glowing flourish that, after undergoing revision by the full Congress, the Declaration "was adopted . . . and published to the world." Adams' discussion in his Autobiography conveys the impression that the preliminary materials worked up by the committee of five as well as by Jefferson were of the moment and in response to the needs of the immediate occasion. In his own Autobiography, Jefferson observed, as we saw in Ch. II, that he consulted no real other outside sources directly.

Adams' copy of the draft Declaration of Independence, made before the committee of five made changes, is dated June 28, 1776. It is given in *Papers of John Adams*, Vol. 4 (Camb., Mass., 1979), pp. 345 ff.

It may be added that, in the course of describing Congress' proceedings at that point, Adams gives (*Works*, II, p. 511) a brief but brilliant insight into the dos and don'ts of speaking before one's political colleagues, lessons he may have learned the hard way. He pays tribute, in this regard, to the good "examples of Washington, Franklin and Jefferson" in the Continental Congress.

36. Adams, *Defence*, Vol. I, Ch. VI, in *Works*, Vol. IV, pp. 435–436, 439–440, 443–444.

37. *Ibid.*, p. 448.

38. *Ibid.*, pp. 461–463: "Let me add to the researches of Polybius and Plato, concerning the mutability of governments, those of Sir Thomas Smith, who, as he tells us, on the twenty-eighth of March, 1565, in the seventh of Elizabeth and fifty-first year of his age, was ambassador from that queen to the court of France, and then published, 'The Commonwealth of England,' not as Plato made his republic, Xenophon his kingdom of Persia, or Sir Thomas More his Utopia, feigned commonwealths, such as never were nor shall be, vain imaginations, fantasies of philosophers, but as England stood and was governed at that day.

"In his seventh chapter and the two following he gives us his opinion of the origin of a kingdom, an aristocracy and democracy. The third he supposes to grow naturally out of the second, and the second out of the first, which originated in patriarchal authority. But as there is nothing remarkable, either in favor of our system or against it, I should not have quoted the book in his place, but for the sake of its title. The constitution of England is in truth a republic, and has been ever so considered by foreigners, and by the most learned and enlightened Englishmen, although the word commonwealth has become unpopular and odious, since the unsuccessful and injudicious attempts to abolish monarchy and aristocracy, between the years 1640 and 1660.

"Let me proceed then to make a few observations upon the Discourses of Plato and Polybius, and show how forcibly they prove the necessity of permanent laws, to restrain the passions and vices of men, and to secure to the citizens the blessings of society, in the peaceable enjoyment of their lives, liberties, and properties; and the necessity of different orders of men, with various and opposite powers, prerogatives, and privileges, to watch over one another, to balance each other, and to compel each other at all times to be real guardians of the laws.

"Every citizen must look up to the laws, as his master, his guardian, and his friend; and whenever any of his fellow-citizens, whether magistrates or subjects, attempt to deprive him of his right, he must appeal to the laws. . . . Without three divisions of power, stationed to watch each other, and compare each other's conduct with the laws, it will be impossible that the laws should at all times preserve their authority and govern all men.

"Plato has sufficiently asserted the honor of the laws and the necessity of proper guardians of them; but has nowhere delineated the various orders of guardians, and the necessity of a balance between them. He has, nevertheless, given us premises from whence the absolute necessity of such orders and equipoises may be inferred; he has shown how naturally every simple species of government degenerates. . . . Democracy becomes a tyranny. How shall this be prevented? By giving it an able, independent ally, in an aristocratical assembly, with whom it may unite against the unjust and illegal designs of any one man."

39. *Ibid.*, pp. 483–484: "Chimerical systems of legislation are neither new nor uncommon, even among men of the most resplendent genius and extensive learning. It would not be too bold to say, that some parts of Plato and Sir Thomas More are as wild as the ravings of Bedlam. A philosopher may be perfect master of Descartes and Leibnitz, may pursue his own inquiries into metaphy*sic*s to any length, may enter into the inmost recesses of the human mind, and make the noblest discoveries for the benefit of his species; nay, he may defend the principles of liberty and the rights of mankind with great abilities and success; and, after all, when called upon to produce a plan of legislation, he may astonish the world with a signal absurdity. Mr. Locke, in 1663, was employed to trace out a plan of legislation for Carolina; and he gave the whole authority, executive and legislative, to the eight proprietors. . . . This new oligarchical sovereignty created at once three orders of nobility. . . . Who did this legislator think would live under his government? He should have first created a new species of beings to govern, before he instituted such a government."

40. *Ibid.*, pp. 486–487: "Americans in this age are too enlightened to be bubbled out of their liberties, even by such mighty names as Locke, Milton, Turgot, or Hume; they know that popular elections of one essential branch of the legislature, frequently repeated, are the only possible means of forming a free constiution, or of preserving the government of laws from the domination of men, or of preserving their lives, liberties, or properties in security; they know, though Locke and Milton did not, that when popular elections are given up, liberty and free government must be given up. Upon this principle, they cannot approve the plan of Mr. Hume, in his *Idea of a Perfect Commonwealth.*" . . .

"If you compare this plan, as well as those of Locke and Milton, with the principles and examples, you will soon form a judgment of them; it is not my design to enlarge upon them. That of Hume is a complicated aristocracy, and would soon behave like all other aristocracies. It is enough to say that the representatives of the people may by the senators be deprived of a voice in the legislature; because the senate have their choice of sending the laws down, either to the county magistrates or county representatives."

41. Adams, *Defence*, Vol. III, in *Works*, Vol. VI, pp. 171–172: "Let us pause here with astonishment. A person who had read the former part of the book with attention, would think these words a complete refutation of his whole 'Right Constitution of a Commonwealth.' The whole drift of the book before this was to prove, that all authority should be collected into one centre; that the whole legislative and judicial power, as well as the executive, was to be vested in successive, supreme sovereign assemblies of the people's representatives; and our endeavor has been to show, that this would naturally be applied to corruption in election, to promote division, faction, sedition, and rebellion. All this is now very frankly admitted, and 'the safety of the state' depends upon placing the power of making laws, of executing them, and administering justice, in diffeent hands. But how is this to be done?

"'The executive power,' our author tells us, 'is derived from the legislative; and by their authority transferred into the hand of one person, called a prince, or into the hands of many, called states, for the administration of government in the execution of those laws.'

"This is totally denied. The executive power is not naturally, nor necessarily, and ought never to be in fact, derived from the legislative. The body of the people, according to our author and to truth, is the fountain and original of all power and authority, executive and judicial, as well as legislative; and the executive ought to be appointed by the people, in the formation of their constitution, as much as the legislative. The executive represents the majesty, persons, wills, and power of the people in the administration of government and dispensing of laws, as the legislative does in making, altering, and repealing them. . . . There is no more truth, nature, or propriety, in saying that the executive is derived from the legislative, than that the legislative is derived from the executive; both are derived from the people."

Ibid., p. 212: "The best way that can be conceived of surely is, to separate the executive power from the legislative; make it responsible to one part of the legislature, on the impeachment of another, for the use of its power of appointment to offices, and to appoint two assemblies in the legislature, that the errors of one may be corrected by the other."

42. *Ibid.*, pp. 218–220: "All nations, from the beginning, have been agitated by the same passions. The principles developed here will go a great way in explaining every phenomenon that occurs in the history of government. . . . Nations move by unalterable rules; and education, discipline, and laws, make the greatest difference in their accomplishments, happiness, and perfection. . . .

"It is now in our power to bring this work to a conclusion with unexpected dignity. In the course of the last summer, two authorities have appeared, greater than any that have been before quoted, in which the principles we have attempted to defend have been acknowledged.

"The first is, an Ordinance of Congress, of the thirteenth of July, 1787, for the Government of the Territory of the United States, Northwest of the River Ohio.

"The second is, the Report of the Convention at Philadelphia of the seventeenth of September, 1787.

"The former confederation of the United States was formed upon the model and example of all the confederacies, ancient and modern, in which the federal council was only a diplomatic body. Even the Lycian, which is thought to have been the best, was no more. The magnitude of territory, the population, the wealth and commerce, and especially the rapid growth of the United States, have shown such a government to be inadequate to their wants; and the new system, which seems admirably calculated to unite their interests and affections, and bring them to an uniformity of principles and sentiments, is equally well combined to unite their wills and forces as a single nation. A result of accommodation cannot be supposed to reach the ideas of perfection of any one; but the conception of such an idea, and the deliberate union of so great and various a people in such a plan, is, without all partiality or prejudice, if not the greatest exertion of human understanding, the greatest single effort of national deliberation that the world has ever seen. That it may be improved is not to be doubted, and provision is made for that purpose in the report itself. A people who could conceive, and can adopt it, we need not fear will be able to amend it, when, by experience, its inconveniences and imperfections shall be seen and felt."

43. Adams, *Defence*, Vol. II, Ch. I, in *Works*, Vol. V, pp. 14–15: "This is the very short description of their constitution. The twelve anziani appear to have had the legislative and executive authority, and to have been annually eligible—a form of government as near that of M. Turgot, and Marchamont Nedham, as any to be found;—yet the judicial power is here separated, and the people could so little trust themselves or the anziani with this power, that it was given to foreigners.

" 'By such discipline in their civil and military affairs, the Florentines laid the foundation of their liberty; and it is hardly to be conceived, how much strength and authority they acquired in a very short time; for their city not only became the capital of Tuscany, but was reckoned among the principal in Italy; and, indeed, there is no degree of grandeur to which it might not have attained, *if it had not been obstructed by new and frequent factions.*' . . .

"The United States of America calculated their governments for a duration of more than ten years. There is little doubt to be made, that they might have existed under the government of state congresses for ten years, while they were constantly at war, and all the active and idle were in council or in arms; but we have seen, that a state which could be governed by a provincial congress, and, indeed, that could carry on a war without any government at all, while danger pressed, has lately, in time of profound peace, and under a good government, broke out in seditions [Shays' Rebellion, winter of 1786–1787].

"This democratical government in Florence could last no longer; 'For in all these expeditions,' says Machiavel, 'the Guelphs had the chief direction and command, as they were much more popular than the Ghibellines, who had behaved themselves so imperiously in the reign of Frederick, when they had the upper hand, that they were become very odious to the people; and because the party of the church was generally thought to favor their attempts to preserve their liberty, whilst that of the emperor endeavored to deprive them of it.' "

44. *Ibid.*, pp. 66–67: "The period from 1371 to 1434, is that which is boasted of by Machiavel as the prosperous one, but the prosperity of which he attributes to the virtues and abilities of Maso. Pisa, Cortona, Arezzo, Leghorn, and Monte Pulciano, were added to the dominion.

" 'All republics, especially such as are not well constituted, undergo frequent changes in their laws and manner of government. And this is not owing to the nature either of liberty or subjection in general, as many think, but to downright oppression on one hand, or unbridled licentiousness on the other.'

"It is very true that most republics have undergone frequent changes in their laws; but this has been merely because very few republics have been well constituted. It is very true also, that there is nothing in the nature of liberty, or of obedience, which tends to produce such changes; on the contrary, real liberty and true obedience rather tend to preserve constancy in government. It is, indeed, oppression and license that occasion changes; but where the constitution is good, the laws govern, and prevent oppression as well as license.

" 'The name of liberty is often nothing more than a specious pretence, made use of both by the instruments of licentiousness, who for the most part are commoners, and by the promoters of slavery, who generally are the nobles, each side being equally impatient of restraint and control.'

"This is a truth, which is proved as well as illustrated by every page of the foregoing history, as well as by the history of almost all other republics, ancient and modern; and the next paragraph shows that Machiavel had an accurate idea of the evil, though a confused one of the remedy.

" 'When it fortunately happens, which indeed is very seldom, that some wise, good, and powerful citizen, has sufficient authority in the commonwealth to make such laws as may extinguish all jealousies betwixt the nobility and the people, or at least, so to moderate and restrain them, that they shall not be able to produce any bad effect, then that state may properly be called free, and its constitution looked upon as firm and permanent; for being once established upon good laws and institutions, it has no further occasion, like other states, for the virtue of any particular man to support it.'

"One would be apt to conjecture from this, that Machiavel was about to propose a first magistrate, armed by the constitution with sufficient authority to mediate, at all times, between the nobles and commons. Such a magistrate, possessed of the whole executive power, with a negative to defend it, has always authority to intervene between the nobles and commons, and to preserve the energy of the laws to restrain both; and whether this executive magistrate is wise and good or not, if the commons have the negative upon the purse and the laws, and the inquest of grievances, abuses, and state crimes, that executive power can hardly be ill used."

45. *Ibid.*, p. 84.

46. *Ibid.*, pp. 88–89.

47. *Ibid.*, p. 90.

48. *Ibid.*, pp. 95–96: "[']Cosimo [de Medici] was at the expense of maintaining Marcilius [*sic*] Ficinus, the restorer of the Platonic philosophy, who translated the works of Plato, Plotinus, Jamblichus, Proclus, &c.; and he had so great an esteem for him, that he gave him a house and estate near his own seat at Careggi, that he might pursue his studies there with more convenience, and entertain him with his conversation at leisure hours.'

"So that he had great merit in the resurrection of letters, and perhaps in the formation of Machiavel himself, to whom the world is so much indebted for the revival of reason in matters of government, and who appears to have been himself so much indebted to the writings of Plato and Aristotle. Indeed, if ever the rise of any family to absolute sovereignty upon the ruins of a republic could be pardonable, this of the Medici, which was by real virtues, abilities, and beneficence, must be acknowledged to be an instance of it. But it never can be justified, nor ought ever to be excused, where there is a possibility of establishing a constitution well balanced and really free; and it may well be doubted whether any nation that has once been free can ever become so universally or even generally corrupted as not to be able to conduct a government of three well-balanced branches. ... He appears to have had more merit, as well as more art, than Augustus. Machiavel is conscious that he shall be suspected of writing a panegyric upon Cosimo, rather than an historical portrait; and not without reason, for he was a dependent on the Medici family; and he has evidently hurried over some, and glossed over others of Cosimo's acts."

49. *Ibid.*, Ch. III, pp. 176–177: "Is it not astonishing that such a historian [Varchi] should admit of a doubt, whether the motives of Lorenzo could be good ones? Is it possible to read his own history, and not see that this struggle was merely between different branches of the same family of Medici for the sovereignty, and that there was not a ray of public virtue or love of liberty left in any of them? Strozzi, the rival family of Medici, had married a Medici, and could not bear that Alexander should rule. ..."

"The people of Florence were now so totally devoted to the Medici family, that there was no party among them but what was headed by some branch of it; the blood of the Medici must in all events govern them; and the difference between them was worth very little. Strozzi and Lorenzo were worse than Alexander; and the only tolerably good man among them was Cosimo, whom they all hated, but whom Providence was pleased to call to the government in this awful manner."

50. *Ibid.*, p. 179. "The exiles were still restless, and endeavored to excite fresh wars against their country; but Cosimo, by his abilities, address, and activity, defended his authority, and was afterwards confirmed, not only as head of the state, but as duke and sovereign. And here ended the shadow of a free government.

"Let the reader now run over again in his own mind this whole story of Florence, and ask himself whether it does not appear like a satire, written with the express and only purpose of exposing to contempt, ridicule, and indignation, the idea of 'a government in one centre,' and the 'right constitution of a commonwealth?' If he suspect that this mean sketch is in any degree varied by prejudice from the truth, let him read over any historian of Florence, as Machiavel, Guicciardini, Nerli, Nardi, Varchi, Villani, or Ammirato, and then say, whether it is not a libel upon Turgot and Nedham. From the beginning to the end, it is one continued struggle between monarchy and aristocracy; a continued succession of combinations of two or three parties of noble, rich, or conspicuous families, to depress the people on the one hand, and prevent an oligarchy or a monarchy from arising up among themselves on the other. Neither the first family, nor any of the others their rivals, made any account of the people, excepting now and then for a moment, for the purposes of violence, sedition, and rebellion."

51. *Ibid.*, p. 180. "If you fix your eye upon any period, from the beginning to the end of the republic, and suppose the gonfalonier possessed of the whole executive power, with a negative upon the legislature, the signori and grand council made separate and independent branches of the legislature, though elected periodically by the people, and the judges made during good behavior, would not those terrible disorders have been prevented? The negative to the gonfalonier is not proposed, because he is a wiser or a better man than others, but merely as a constitutional instrument of self-defence; without it, he cannot defend the legal authority which the constitution has given him, but the executive power will be pared away, or wrested out of his hands, by the encroaching disposition of human nature in the two houses."

52. *Ibid.*, Ch. IV ("Machiavel's Plan of a Perfect Commonwealth"): "Machiavel, from his long experience of the miseries of Florence in his own times, and his knowledge of their history, perceived many of the defects in every plan of a constitution they had ever attempted. His sagacity, too, perceived the necessity of three powers; but he did not see an equal necessity for the separation of the executive power from the legislative. The following project contains excellent observations, but would not have remedied the evils. The appointment of officers in the council of a thousand would have ruined all the good effects of the other divisions of power. . . .

"About the year 1519, Leo X, being informed of the discords that were ready to break out in Florence, gave a commission to Machiavel to draw up a plan for the reformation of that state. He executed this commission with great abilities, and the most exquisite subtilty [*sic*] of his genius; and produced a model, in the opinion of some, of a perfect commonwealth. The sovereign power is lodged, both of right and in fact, in the citizens themselves.

" 'There are three orders of men in every state, and for that reason there should be also three ranks or degrees in a republic, and no more; nor can that be said to be a true and durable commonwealth, where certain humors and inclinations are not gratified, which otherwise must naturally end in its ruin.' "

53. *Ibid.*, Ch. VII, p. 338: "Here again is a constitution of all authority in one assembly. The council of a hundred was sovereign. The consuls, though they had the command of the army, and the judgment of causes, could do nothing in administration by themselves, or with advice of their little council. They had no negative upon any deliberation or resolution of the great council; and, on the other hand, the people had no negative, not even the poor protection of a tribunitian veto."

54. Items cited above relating to Adams' *Discourses on Davila* can be found as follows. His own marked copy of his *Discourses* can be found in his library, as listed in the *Catalogue of the John Adams Library in the Public Library of the City of Boston* (Boston, 1917), p. 3. Therein are also listed Adams' French and English copies of Davila's work—*Histoire des guerres civiles de France* (3 vols., Amsterdam and Paris, 1757) and *The historie of the civill warres of France* (London, 1647). Also therein are listed on p. 58 the above-cited *Lettres* and "Life" by Condorcet, along with Adams' handwritten comments appearing on p. 266 of the *Lettres*. All of the preceding books are in the Adams Library in the Boston Public Library. Adams' *Discourses on Davila* is included in *Works*, Vol. VI, pp. 227 ff (totalling about 170 pages), with brief editorial comments preceding it. Also cf. Haraszti, *John Adams*, Ch. X, for related general perspectives.

Adams' *Discourses on Davila* originally appeared as a year-long series of thirty-two newspaper articles in 1790–1791, with the last article being omitted in their 1805 publication as a book. Over half of the articles present long quotations from Davila's *History*, while the rest give Adams' views on a wide range of topics including on Adam Smith's *Theory of Moral Sentiments*. Adams' extensive historical and political discussions are of interest here. Although Adams at points rejected the idea of hereditary succession of rulers, he seemed in other places to approve of it. American partisan politics found much ammunition in Adams' *Discourses* for use against him. The republicans, including Jefferson, seized upon Adams' viewpoints here in their attacks on his federalist positions more generally, causing wounds that Adams felt for the rest of his life. Thompson, *Adams*, p. 96, views the *Discourses* as a fourth vol. to the 3 vols. of Adams' *Defence*; that same Ch. 5 considers the multifaceted "transatlantic context" in Europe and America of both works.

55. A useful synopsis of Bodin's place at the Estates General of 1576 at Blois is given by Kenneth Douglas McRae in the Introd. (p. A8 ff.) to his facsimile edn. (Camb., Mass., 1962) of Richard Knolles' 1606 translation of Bodin's *Republic*, entitled *The Six Bookes of a Commonweale*. Toward the end of 1576, some months after his *Republic* was published and dedicated to a close advisor of the king, Bodin became representative of the Third Estate for Vermandois. At first Bodin was well received there by the king, Henry III, with whom he often dined; the wide recognition Bodin gained because of his encyclopedic learning served him well. But gradually Bodin fell out of favor there with the king because of his constitutionalist opposition to measures devised by the crown to augment its revenues. Thereby Bodin lost his chances for a court appointment.

56. Quoting from the 1678 English edn. of Davila's *History*, Bk. VI, p. 229, all *sic*.

57. In Adams' copy of Davila's *Histoire*, Vol. II, Bk. VI, pp. 60–61, all *sic*.

58. The continuation of the passages just given at length in our text above is as follows: "[W]herefore seeking obliquely to hinder that determination, he [the king] proposed to the States and persuaded them before it were enacted, Commissioners ought to be sent to the King of Navarre [etc.] . . ., who . . . should persuade them to obey the will of the States, without returning again to the fatal hazard of Arms, hoping by such delays to find some remedy against that revolution which he saw the major part of the Deputies was obstinately bent upon."

59. Again in Adams' copy of Davila's *Histoire*, Vol. II, Bk. VI, p. 65 etc.

60. The passage is long and only select excerpts can be given here to convey its nature: "But the king having for many days shewed a wonderful desire to suppress the Huguenots, purposed with one mortal blow to try the constancy of the Deputies . . . [and] desired the States to [give him money for] . . . the vast expenses of War. . . . [T]herefore *Jean Bodin* being President of the Order of Commons, and knowing all the burden was to be had upon the people, rose up, and answered That the Third Estate had always propounded . . . unity in Religion . . . without . . . Arms . . . and that since they had not consented to the War, neither were they bound to contribute to the expenses of it. . . . [T]o which speech of his, not only the other Orders, but the clergy themselves assented. . . . [Others too] began to waver, who had so readily resolved upon a War . . . [, all also having second thoughts about their own burdens of expense]. . . . [T]he next day he [the king] himself propounded to the Deputies, That since they thought the charges of War so grievous a burden, they should . . . procure his [the King of Navarre's] conversion in a friendly and peaceable manner, with which motion . . . the major part of the Deputies were concurred. . . . [Some days later were] encouraged *Jean Bodin* and others of the Order of Commons, again to try the way of agreement . . ., that unity in Religion ought to be procurred without War. [Etc.]" This passage, from the 1678 English version, pp. 231–232, deals with events that carried over into 1577.

61. The Preface dated 1805 to Adams' *Discourses on Davila* in Vol. VI of Adams' *Works* begins by declaring: "Since the publication of these *Discourses* in 1790, our observations abroad and experiences at home, have sufficiently taught us the lessons they were intended to inculcate; and the evils they were designed to prevent, have borne testimony of their truth." As Adams noted, this Pref. was not written by him, though he did not disagree with its sentiments.

In the introductory paragraph of 1812 added in the *Works* edition, article I, Adams declares that as author "he had the courage to oppose and publish his own opinions to the universal opinion of America, and, indeed, of all mankind. Not one man in America then believed him. . . . The work, however, powerfully operated to destroy his presidency. It was urged as full proof, that he was an advocate for monarchy, and laboring to introduce a hereditary president in America."

In the first article of his *Discourses*, Adams quotes from Davila's *History* on the origins of the French people in the early Franks, and ends with the following quotation (pp. 228–229): "Accustomed for many ages to live in the obedience of a prince, and thinking the monarchical state the most convenient to a people who aspire to augment their power and extend their conquests, they [the Franks] resolved to choose a king who should unite in his single person *all the authority of the nation*."* To which Adams then responded: "Here, perhaps, Davila is incautious and incorrect; for the Franks, as well as Saxons and other German nations, though their governments were monarchical, had their grandees and people, who met and deliberated in national assemblies, whose results were often, to say the least, considered as laws. Their great misfortune was, that, while it never was sufficiently ascertained, whether the sovereignty resided in the king or in the *national assembly*, it was equally uncertain whether the king had a negative on the assembly; whether the grandees had a negative on the king or the people; and whether the people had a negative on both or either. This uncertainty will appear hereafter, in Davila himself, to mark its course in bloody characters; and the whole history of France will show, that from the first migration of the Franks from Germany to this hour, it has never been sufficiently explained and decided." The asterisk above is to an 1812 note added by Adams: "Turgot's ideas were equally confused. His 'all authority in one centre, the nation,' is just as great nonsense."

In the preceding passages of *Discourses* I, Adams deals with issues of sovereignty and legislation in early French/Frankish history as a foil for his views on those issues in his own day. Adams suggests that the concentration of power in a single center is no less dangerous to stability in a democracy with a unitary national assembly than it is in a monarchy. Adams' political opponents could seize on this approach to accuse him of being sympathetic toward a monarchical executive, with veto power, as a balance to a national assembly—in the process of legislation—not only for the France of Louis XVI but also for the America of Adams' own day, even though Adams could deny such charges.

Adams then quotes again a long passage from Davila, beginning with: "To this supreme degree of power in the king . . . they [the Franks] added, that the *crown* should be *hereditary* in the family elected; foreseeing that if it were *elective* it would be a source of civil wars, which would prove destructive to all their enterprises." Adams subsequently observes as follows (pp. 230–231): "Here, again we meet with another inaccuracy, if not a contradiction in Davila; or rather with another proof of that confusion of law, and that uncertainty of the sovereignty, which for fifteen hundred years has been to France the fatal source of so many calamities. Here the sovereignty or whole power of the nation, is asserted to be in the *states general*; whereas only three pages before, he had asserted that the whole authority of the nation was united in the king." To this statement was later added the 1812 note: "Two authorities up, neither supreme."

In the preceding passages, Adams was perhaps opening himself to the charge by opponents that he seemed in part to favor hereditary monarchy over elective monarchy and over a national assembly as the best alternative to the 1500 years of uncertainty in France over where sovereignty in law lay. Here Adams' idea of a necessary balance seems to fade out in favor of choosing one side of the equation, with possible preference for monarchy, at least in France.

In *Discourses* IV (p. 243), Adams asks and answers the question: "Has there ever been a nation who understood the human heart better than the Romans, or made a better use of the passion for consideration, congratulation, and distinction? . . . Every thing was addressed to the emulation of the citizens, and . . . to attach their hearts to individual citizens according to their merit; and to their lawgivers, magistrates, and judges, according to their rank, station, and importance in the state. And this was in the true spirit of republics, in which form of government there is no other consistent method of preserving order, or procuring submission to the laws." Here, to be sure, Adams favors republics above all other forms of government for maintaining stability and obedience to laws in a state. Yet his praise of Roman models might prompt the question of what kind of a republic for France as well as America he has in mind as a solution to the form of republicanism then on the rise in France and America in 1790–1791, when he wrote his *Disccourses on Davila*, in which many historians say came perhaps his closest to espousing a monarchical position.

In the following provocative excerpts from Article VI (pp. 251–252), Adams first considers the role of the nobility in the history of France and Europe: "This has been the policy of Europe; and it is to this institution she owes her superiority in war and peace, in legislation [etc.]. . . . These families, thus distinguished by property, honors, and privileges, by defending themselves, have been obliged to defend the people against the encroachments of despotism. They have been a civil and political militia, constantly watching the designs of the standing armies, and courts; and by defending their own rights, liberties, properties, and privileges, they have been obliged, in some degree, to defend those of the people. . . . But . . . the people took no rational measures to defend themselves, either against these great families, or the courts. They had no adequate representation of themselves in the sovereignty. Another was, that it never was determined where the sovereignty resided. Generally it was claimed by kings; but not admitted by the nobles. Sometimes every baron pretended to be sovereign in his own territory; at other times, the sovereignty was claimed by an assembly of nobles, under the name of States or Cortes.

Sometimes the united authority of the king and states was called the sovereignty. The common people had no adequate and independent share in the legislatures, and found themselves harassed to discover who was the sovereign, and whom they ought to obey. . . . A thousand years of barons' wars, . . . ended at last in simple monarchy, not by express stipulation, but by tacit acquiescence, in almost all Europe; the people preferring a certain sovereignty in a single person, to endless disputes, about merit and sovereignty, which never did and never will produce any thing but aristocratical anarchy. . . . But if the common people are advised to aim at collecting the whole sovereignty in single national assembly, as they are by the . . . Marquis of *Condorcet*; or at the abolition of the regal executive authority; or at a division of the executive power, as they are by a posthumous publication of the Abbé de *Mably*, they will fail of their desired liberty."

In the passages from *Discourses* VI immediately above, Adams' outright defence of the European nobility as the chief defenders of the helpless and inert common people's liberties was bound to excite the passions of his opponents, despite the partial disclaimer added by him in a notation of 1812. (It read: "This [initial statement above] is a truth; but by no means a justification of the system of nobility in France, nor in other parts of Europe.") The location of sovereignty is again for Adams a central issue—whether held by the king or the nobles, or by the king and nobles together, to the exclusion of the people, who long had no rightful share in the legislature in France and many other European states. That is, who held legislative sovereignty was again a crucial issue. Adams also sides here with the position of the people in accepting a single monarch as the most viable way to cope with the constant strife and warfare throughout the ages. Adams denounces Condorcet's proposal for a unitary national assembly and Mably's proposal for a divided executive. Adams thereby seems to regard monarchy as still a crucial component in any solution for France in her current crisis.

In Article XI (p. 269), Adams draws comparisons between the French civil wars in Davila's account and the French Revolution: "But why all this of emulation and rivalry? Because, as the whole history of the civil wars of France, given us by Davila, is no more than a relation of rivalries succeeding each other in a rapid series, the reflections we have made will assist us, both to understand that noble historian, and to form a right judgment of the state of affairs in France at the present moment. They will suggest also to Americans, especially to those who have been unfriendly, and may be now lukewarm to their national constitution [i.e., "the anti-federalists," as noted here by Adams in 1813], some useful inquiries . . ." Adams' allusions to the unfriendly anti-federalists may well be partly directed against his own critics as well as against the new U.S. Constitution.

The idea of placing all legislative power in a single assembly as conceived in his contemporary France is addressed by Adams in *Discourses* XII (p. 273): "The men of letters in France are wisely reforming one feudal system; but may they not, unwisely, lay the foundation of another? A legislature, in one assembly, can have no other termination than in civil dissension, feudal anarchy, or simple monarchy. The best apology which can be made for their fresh attempt of a sovereignty in one assembly, an idea at least as ancient in France as *Stephen Boethius*, is, that it is only intended to be momentary." Here Adams' view of the dangers of placing sovereign legislative power in a single national assembly in France makes it no better than the unitary monarchy he might favor in its chaotic place.

In *Discourses* XIII (pp. 277–278), Adams considers at length Congress' declarations at Philadelphia in 1774 that, among other things, good government and the English constitution require "the constituent branches of the legislature be independent of each other"; this idea, for Adams, relates to his own view of the independent veto power necessary in the executive as part of the legislative sovereignty in the American state. In an 1813 note later included here in *Works* VI, Adams both credits and downplays Jefferson's Declaration of Independence, saying that it merely echoed Adams' own Boston declaration of 1772 as well as Congress' declaration of 1774 (both of which were in fact very different from it on points at hand).

In *Discourses* XIV (p. 280), Adams discourses at length on the legislative power and the "[g]reat art of lawgiving" both in France and America in his own day: "There will never probably be found any other mode of establishing such an equilibrium, than by constituting the representation of each an independent branch of the legislature, and an independent executive authority, such as that in our government, to be a third branch and a mediator or an arbitrator between them. Property must be secured, or liberty cannot exist. But if unlimited or unbalanced power of disposing property, be put into the hands of those who have no property, France will find, as we have found, . . . [and] all the pathetic exhortations and addresses of the national assembly to the people, to respect property, will be regarded no more than the warbles of the songsters of the forest. The great art of lawgiving consists in balancing the poor against the rich in the legislature, and in constituting the legislative a perfect balance against the executive power, at the same time that no individual or party can become its rival. The essence of a free government consists in an effectual control of rivalries. The executive and the legislative powers are natural rivals; and if each has not an effectual control over the other, the weaker will ever be the lamb in the paws of the wolf. The nation which will not adopt an equilibrium of power must adopt a despotism." In returning here to his idea of a "balance" to control rivalries, Adams again centers on the legislative process and its component branches.

Discourses XVII (p. 300) compares the situations faced under the French kings Francis II and Louis XVI in ways that suggest a sympathetic outlook on the latter in terms of the executive as a necessary integral counterpoise to the legislative power. "In what manner the nobility ought to be reformed, modified, methodized, and wrought by representation or otherwise, into an independent branch of the legislature, what form of government would have been best for France, under Francis II, and whether the same is not now necessary, under Louis XVI, are questions too deep and extensive perhaps for us to determine. But we are very competent to demonstrate two propositions,—first, that a sovereignty in a single assembly cannot secure the peace, liberty, or safety of the people; secondly, that a federative republic, or, in other words, a confederation . . . will not be sufficient to secure the tranquillity, liberty, property, or lives of the nation."

In the preceding passage, Adams appears to suggest that the continuing role of Louis XVI's monarchy, reformed or not, is at least preferable to a unitary popular assembly or a confederation, while he also expresses some ambivalence over whether the particular role of the nobility should be reformed in relation to the legislature.

One might wonder if Adams' republican opponents unfairly accused him of being pro-monarchical, especially in relation to Louis XVI. One will recall Jefferson's belief, in his later autobiography as cited above in our Ch. II, that the recalcitrant French queen should have been sent to a convent because Louis XVI was more willing to cooperate with the early new revolutionary government, in which he became executive albeit under the preponderance of the National Assembly. Moreover, we also saw that Jefferson, while American ambassador to the court of Louis XVI and constantly at Versailles on official business, declined some requests by revolutionary leaders to meet and hear their early proposals for a new government, because he wanted to avoid conflict of interest in his official position. Even so, Jefferson, unlike Adams, has long been well known for his sympathetic views toward the revolutionary cause in France after he returned to America in late 1789, early on during the French Revolution.

An example of Adams' historical knowledge of and insights into the details of the French civil wars as covered by Davila occurs in *Discourses* XVIII (p. 312), where he chides Davila, a Catholic, for putting extreme words into the mouth of Coligny, a Protestant.

Adams' discourses on Davila extends in Article XX (pp. 222–223) to a rejection of the view that the French monarchy is superior to the Estates General, especially with regard to the legislative power as the ultimate sovereign divided into three rather than two separate branches: "Upon this passage the French writers cry out, 'It is a stranger who speaks, ill-informed of the fundamental constitution of our monarchy. This Italian imagines that the royal authority was suspended during the session of the States-General. But it was the royal authority which called them together. Without it, they could not have assembled; and the same authority had a right to dismiss them at its pleasure. It is therefore evident that their power was always subordinate to that of the monarch.' But this consequence does not follow. The royal authority in England has the power of convoking, proroguing, and dissolving parliament. Yet parliament is not subordinate to the royal authority, but superior to it; as the whole is superior to a third part. The sovereignty is in parliament or the legislative power; not in the King or the executive. So the sovereignty might be in the States-General, comprehending the King. . . .

"There was always a rivalry between the royal authority and that of the States, as there is now between the power of the King and that of the National Assembly, and as there ever was and will be in every *legislature or sovereignty* [emphasis added] which consists of two branches only. The proper remedy then, would have been the same as it must be now, to new-model the legislature, make it consist of three equiponderant, independent branches, and make the executive power one of them; in this way, and in no other, can an equilibrium be formed, the only antidote against rivalries." This is a striking articulation by Adams of the executive included as a branch in the sovereign legislative power.

If France had had the kind of three branches of the legislative power proposed by Adams, the crisis of the French civil wars could have been averted, as he believes in *Discourses* XXII (p. 340): "Never did the necessity of a third mediating power or an umpire appear more plainly than in this case. Had there been a constitution in France, and had that constitution provided, as it ought to have done, a third party, whose interest and duty it should have been to do justice to the other two, and every individual of each, there would have been little danger to the peace . . ."

Concerning French events of 1561 in *Discourses* XXIII (p. 347) and the lack of real sovereignty: "So loose and uncertain was the sovereignty of that great nation, that a confused agreement of the chiefs of the two factions was thought sufficient for its government, without any forms or legal solemnities. The stability of the government, and the security of the lives, liberties, and properties of the people were proportionate to such a system. The court was still agitated with divisions and dissensions."

Regarding French events of 1565 as reported by Davila, Adams quotes Aristotle's *Politics* (Bk. IV, Ch. IV) in such a way as to open himself to the charge that he was indeed a monarchist who saw a single democratic assembly under majority rule to be no less despotic than rule by a tyrant (*Discourses* XXVIII, pp. 380–381): "These are the miserable maxims of tyranny, whether it be exercised by a single man or a multitude. 'There is no difference,' according to Aristotle and history and experience, 'between a people governing by a majority in a single assembly, and a monarch in a tyranny; for their manners are the same, and they both hold a despotic power over better persons than themselves. Their decrees are like the other's edicts; their demagogues like the other's flatterers.' "

Lastly, as noted periodically above in this sect. 3 on Adams' uses of history, he included various discussions concerning the Middle Ages. Although most of the above materials centered on ancient and modern topics, his studies on Italian history delved deeply into the Middle Ages. In some respects, however, Adams did not have a favorable outlook on the Middle Ages. A prime example is his early "Dissertation on the Canon and the Feudal

Law," a short early piece that attracted much attention when it appeared in the *Boston Gazette* in 1765. In it Adams declared (*Works* III, pp. 449–451): "Since the promulgation of Christianity, the two greatest systems of tyranny that have sprung from the original, are the canon and the feudal law. . . . [A]s long as the people were held in ignorance, liberty, . . . knowledge and virtue . . . deserted the earth, and one age of darkness succeeded another, till God . . . raised up the champions who began and conducted the Reformation. From . . . the Reformation to the first settlement of America, knowledge gradually spread in Europe, but especially in England. . . . [E]cclesiastical and civil tyranny . . . lost their strength. . . . [T]he struggle between the people and the confederacy . . . of temporal and spiritual tyranny . . . peopled America." Adams speaks of "*Rights*, that cannot be repeated or restrained by human laws—*Rights*, derived from the great Legislator [!] of the universe." The Middle Ages are further considered here by Adams in this light. He clearly shared some "enlightened" French and English ideals of his age on the progress of the human mind from medieval to modern times.

62. Above, Ch. II, sect. 5.

63. *Adams-Jefferson Letters*, p. 291 (Jefferson to Adams, Jan. 21, 1812, in reply to Adams' letter of Jan. 1, their first exchange of letters since Mar. 1801).

64. *Ibid.*, pp. 294–295 (Adams to Jefferson, Feb. 3, 1812).

65. All *passim* in *ibid.*, cf. index.

66. *Ibid.*, p. 573 (Adams to Jefferson, May 19, 1821).

67. *Ibid.*, p. 576 (Adams to Jefferson, Sept. 24, 1821), *sic*.

68. Cf. references above to the 1822 deed of transfer and to the 1823 catalogues as reported in the Preface to the *Catalogue of the John Adams Library in the Public Library of the City of Boston* (Boston, 1917). Cited there on p. 2 is "Deeds and other documents relating to the several pieces of land, and to the Library presented to the town of Quincy, by President Adams . . . with a catalogue of his books" (Cambridge, 1823).

Grateful acknowledgement must be made for several people in Boston and Quincy who supplied information on John Adams and his collection of books. At the Boston Public Library, William T. Faucon helped with various materials pertaining to Bodin's *Republic* and Adams' *Discourses on Davila*. R. Eugene Zepp furnished general information on John Adams' library housed there.

At the Adams Papers project located in the Massachusetts Historical Society in Boston, further information was provided by Celeste Walker, a chief editor for the various ongoing series of John Adams' papers and works being published or republished by the Harvard University Press. She also searched again for Bodin in the various indexes to John Adams' general correspondence, family correspondence, diaries, and legal papers; although the search yielded no further clues, it was nonetheless useful.

At the Adams National Historical Park in Quincy, Mass., Kelly Cobble clarified a number of points. She did not find other copies of Bodin's *Republic* in the 5,000–6,000 books housed there. (Major portions of those books were owned by John Adams' son, John Quincy, and by his grandson, Charles Francis; although some books bear John's identifying markings, there is not the paper trail for his ownerships of books there that exists for John Quincy through journals, etc.) However, the question still remains open as to what and when books left John Adams' possession prior to his 1822 deed transferring his books to the town of Quincy (which he called "fragments" of his former collection). Also of particular help there, supplying some detailed background information, was Agnes Smith.

69. Above, Ch. II, sect. 6.

70. *Adams-Jefferson Letters*, p. 440 (Adams to Jefferson, Oct. 28, 1814).

71. *Catalogue of Adams Library*, Pref., *sic*.

72. *Adams-Jefferson Letters*, p. 312 (Adams to Jefferson, Oct. 12, 1812).

73. *Ibid.*, p. 308 (Adams to Jefferson, June 28, 1812).

74. Above, Ch. II, sect. 5.

75. The *Catalogue of Adams Library* contains works by a wide range of writers under the present categories of interest devised below. Impressive though Adams' collection was, its scope and depth fell short of Jefferson's much vaster library. Examples in the history of political thought include: Bodin, Giovanni Botero (*Della ragione di stato*), Harrington, Hobbes, Hooker, Locke, Machiavelli, Milton, Richelieu, and Sidney. For the history of law, one finds Blackstone, Coke, Cujas (*Opera omnia*), Domat (*Les loix civiles dans leur ordre naturel*), Plowden, and Pufendorf. For historians, especially older, there are: Leonardo Bruni (*Historiarum Florentinarum libri XII* and *De bello Italio adverso Gothos*), George Buchanan, Davila, Gibbon, Guicciardini, Lipsius, Lyttelton, Mably, and Machiavelli. Ancient writers include: Aesop, Archimedes, Aristotle, Julius Caesar, Cato, Cicero, Diogenes Laertius, Dionysius Halicarnassus, Epictetus, Herodotus, Hippocrates, Homer, Josephus, Juvenal, Pausanias, Pindar, Plato, Plautus, Plutarch, Polybius, Seneca, Strabo, Tacitus, Thucydides, Virgil, Xenophon, and Zeno. Recent political writers included: Burke, Condillac, Montesquieu, Rousseau, and Adam Smith. Recent writers on philosophy included: Francis Bacon, Condorcet, Diderot, Helvétius, Hume, Newton, Pascal, Priestley, Quesnay, and Voltaire. Literary writers include: Addison, Bembo, Corneille, Defoe, Dryden, Erasmus, Samuel Johnson, Molière, Montaigne, Pope, Racine, Shakespeare, Spenser, Swift, Swinburne, and Tasso.

The Preface to the *Catalogue* includes the following apt comments on John Adams. "The value of the Library of John Adams is in part a sentimental one. He was one of the United States Commissioners to France, and Minister to Holland, during the American Revolution, and while in Paris and at The Hague collected many of the volumes of which he made use in writing his 'Defence of the Constitutions of Government of the United States.' Years later he was the second President of the nation. From the time when he was a student in Harvard College until the day of his death . . ., he drew books about him. As a result his Library is an admirable specimen of the intellectual tastes of an American gentleman of the Eighteenth Century. Not only does it contain many of the Greek, Latin, French and English clas*sic*s, but a considerable number of works on law, commerce, and agriculture. The books, however, on the constitutional and political history of various countries, among them a number of histories of the Italian republics, give a special significance to the collection. With the exception of the Library of Col. William Byrd of Virginia, which contained 3438 volumes, it is possibly the largest private collection of books of its day made in this country."

The same Preface also explains that in another deed John Adams wished his books to be placed in a school for Greek and Latin studies to be created in Quincy, but this plan did not reach fruition. After various moves, his books were placed in the Quincy Public Library in 1883, where they were little read. They were transferred to Boston's Public Library in 1893 so they would be better used. Information gained by this writer from the Adams Historical Park is that John Adams and his family viewed their books as a prime part of their assets, together with their properties, and that he acquired a working library meant for actual use by himself and others, perhaps not as readily possible in the case of Jefferson and his much larger collection.

Many of the entries for the above writers listed in the 1917 *Catalogue* are for editions of their collected works. Its Preface cites in particular the three-volume edition of Plato's works edited by Henri Estienne (Paris, 1578), autographed by both John and John Quincy. Of greater note for us in the *Catalogue* is the ten-volume *Opera omnia* of Jacques Cujas (Paris, 1658). Moreover, Volumes 2 and 3 in the 3-vol. *Works* of John Locke (London, 1740) are autographed by John Adams, though vol. 1 is listed as missing. There is also the *Oeuvres* of Montesquieu in 6 vols. (Amsterdam, 1777).

The inclusion of Leonardo Bruni's Florentine *History* is notable. It fit in with John Adams' wider uses in his *Defense* of the histories of numerous Italian states in the Middle Ages and Renaissance. Indeed, the wide range of Italian and other histories utilized by Bodin in his *Republic* (and his earlier *Method of History*) may well have struck Adams. Like Jefferson, Adams no doubt impressed by Bodin's vast class*ic*al and encyclopedic learning, a quality much favored in educational orbits of both Europe and America in the later 18th century.

76. The French and English versions of Bodin's *Republic* in Adams' library are cited together in *Catalogue of Adams Library*, p. 29, as well as separately in the 1823 catalogue on p. 17 and p. 53, respectively.

77. For various brief comments, cf. e.g. Peterson, *Jefferson*, pp. 13 ff., 100 ff., and passim. "To his knowledge of English and Roman law he [Wythe] brought a command of the whole field of humanistic learning and an irrepressible enthusiasm for class*ic*al languages and literature. . . . [Jefferson's] Attic and Roman tastes were further cultivated by Wythe, who pursued law and politics under the spell of the ancients. . . . Jefferson learned law as a branch of the history of mankind. . . . [Also, the Virginia] constitution [that] Jefferson drafted and placed [in its third draft] in Wythe's hands in Philadelphia was an epitome of his political science in 1776." Wythe was not on the committee of five assigned by the Continental Congress at Philadelphia in 1776 to draw up the Declaration of Independence, yet it is hard to imagine Jefferson not discussing it with him there in some fashion.

78. *Catalogue of Adams Library*, p. 77.

79. *Ibid.*, pp. 195–196.

Notes to Chapter IV
Madison in Legislative Profile

1. Among the many surveys on Madison are the following, some with indicative titles concerning pertinent aspects of his thought and career: Ralph Ketcham, *James Madison: A Biography* (Charlottesville, 1971, etc.), e.g. Chs. III ("The College of New Jersey . . ."), VI ("In the Continental Congress"), VIII ("Virginia Legislator . . ."), and XV ("Montpelier . . ."); Garry Wills, *James Madison* (New York, 2002), Intro. alluding to Madison as often a forgotten figure, and Pt. I on his early periods (reviewed in New York Times Book Review, Apr. 21, 2002, under the heading "The skills that made Madison a master framer hurt him as president"); Jack N. Rakove, *James Madison and the Creation of the American Republic* (Glenview, 1990), esp. Chs. 3–6 on his periods as Congressman, legislator, and constitutional framer; Garrett Ward Sheldon, *The Political Philosophy of James Madison* (Baltimore, 2001), esp. Intro. ("Liberalism, Classical Republicanism . . ."), Ch. I ("Intellectual Heritage: Politics, Philosophy, and Theology"), Ch. 4 ("Lockean Liberalism Realized: Construction and Ratification of the U.S. Constitution"); Jennifer Nedelsky, *Private Property and the Limits of American Constitutionalism: The Madisonian Framework and Its Legacy* (Chicago, 1990), Ch. 5 ("The Madisonian Constitution"); Robert A. Rutland, *Madison's Alternatives: The Jeffersonian Republicans and the Coming of War, 1805–1812* (Phila., 1975), Pt. I, sect. 2 ("The State of American Sovereignty"); *ibid., James Madison: The Founding Father* (London, 1987); *ibid., James Madison and the Search for Nationhood* (Wash., D.C., 1981), Pts. II–III ("From Confederation to Union," "The Emergence of Nationhood"): *ibid., James Madison and the American Nation: An Encyclopedia* (New York, 1994), with elaborate chronologies; Drew R. McCoy, *The Last of the Fathers: James Madison and the Republican Legacy*

(Camb., 1989); Lance Banning, *The Sacred Fire of Liberty: James Madison and the Founding of the Federal Republic* (Ithaca, 1995), Pts. II–III ("The Framing of the Constitution," "Revolutionary Federalism"); Irving Brant, *James Madison: Father of the Constitution, 1787–1800* (Indianapolis, 1950), in Brant's multi-vol. series, cited below; Merrill D. Peterson (ed.), *James Madison: A Biography in His Own Words* (New York, 1974), with good chronologies; and Adrienne Koch, *Jefferson and Madison: The Great Collaboration* (New York, 1964), Ch. 3 ("The Constitution and the Bill of Rights"), and Ch. 7 ("The Virginia and Kentucky Resolutions").

A most interesting and useful conference on Madison was held on Feb. 22–23, 2001, at Princeton University, under the title "A Constitution for the Ages: James Madison the Framer." Distinguished participants included Gordon Wood, Jack Rakove, Pauline Maier, John Stagg, Jennifer Nedelsky, and Justice Antonin Scalia, with insightful comments by Ralph Ketcham and others in attendance.

As with texts by Jefferson and Adams given above in Chs. II–III, all texts by Madison (and others) given in this chapter are in their original form as provided in the editions cited here, unless otherwise indicated, with regard to spelling, punctuation, syntax, etc.

2. The preceding Madison chronology is drawn from a variety of sources, in particular the detailed chronology provided in James Madison, *Writings* (edited by Jack Rakove, New York, 1999) [or *Madison: Writings*], at end.

3. Preceding Madison chronology is drawn principally from the lengthy chronological summaries given in Vols. III–IV in *The Writings of James Madison* (edited by Gaillard Hunt, multi-vols., New York, 1900–).

4. In *The Republic of Letters: The Correspondence between Thomas Jefferson and James Madison 1776–1826* (edited by James Morton Smith, 3 vols., New York, 1995), Vol. I, p. 458 (Jefferson to Madison, Dec. 16, 1786): "I find by the public papers that your Commercial Convention failed in point of representation. If it should produce a full meeting in May, and a broader reformation, it will still be well. To make us one nation as to foreign concerns, and keep us distinct in Domestic ones, gives the outline of the proper division of powers between the general and particular governments. But to enable the Federal head to exercise the powers given it, to best advantage, it should be organised, as the particular ones are, into Legislative, Executive and Judiciary. The 1st. and last are already separated. The 2d should also be. When last with Congress, I often proposed to members to do this by making of the Committee of the states, an Executive committee during the recess of Congress, and during it's [*sic*] sessions to appoint a Committee to receive and dispatch all executive business, so that Congress itself should meddle only with what should be legislative. But I question if any Congress (much less all successively) can have self-denial enough to go through with this distribution. [T]he distribution should be imposed on them then."

On two other matters in the same letter, Jefferson refers to the success of the Virginia statute for religious freedom (of which he was the proud author) and to his willingness to assist Madison in ordering books from London. In both matters, a point about encyclopedias arises, which involves aspects of (the age of) reason and the (progress of the) human mind. Here is but one further example, however small, of Jefferson's—and, by extension, Madison's—interest in encyclopedic knowledge in that Enlightened Age of Diderot and Condorcet. Small wonder, then, that both men, like Adams as well, would have been particularly struck by the renowned voluminous encyclopedic learning evident in Bodin's *Republic*, which had been called by many the greatest single work on politics since Aristotle's *Politics*. The passages by Jefferson are as follows (*ibid.*, pp. 458–459): "The Virginia act for religious freedom has been received with infinite approbation in Europe and propagated with enthusiasm. ... It is inserted in the new Encyclopedie, and is appearing in most of the publications respecting America. In fact it is comfortable to see the standard of reason at length erected, after so many ages during which the human mind has been held in vassalage by kings, priests and nobles; and it is honorable for us to have produced the first legislature who [*sic*] has had the courage to declare that the reason of man may be trusted with the formation of his own opinions. . . . If I can be useful to you in ordering books from London you know you may command me. You had better send me the duplicate volume of the Encyclopedie. I will take care to send you the proper one."

On Jefferson's Dec. 16, 1786 letter to Madison, cf. discussion above in Ch. 2, in our text corresponding to n. 151.

5. Madison, *ibid.*, pp. 469–470 (Madison to Jefferson, March 19, 1787).

6. *Ibid.*, p. 470, see editor's note.

7. *Ibid.*, p. 470.

8. *Ibid.*, pp. 470–471.

9. See above, Ch. II, n. 152, for part of the text of Jefferson's letter of June 20, 1787 to Madison, along with our corresponding discussion.

10. Madison, *ibid.*, pp. 478–479 (from Madison in Phila. to Jefferson, June 6, 1787): "In furnishing you with this list of names [of those attending the convention], I have exhausted all the means which I can make use of for gratifying your curiosity. It was thought expedient in order to secure unbiassed [*sic*] discussion within doors, and to prevent misconceptions and misconstructions without, to establish some rules of caution which will for no short time restrain even a confidential communication of our proceedings. The names of the members will satisfy you that the States have been serious in this business. The attendance of Genl. Washington is a proof of the light in which he regards it. The whole Community is big with expectation. And there can be no doubt but that the result will in some way or other have a powerful effect on our destiny.

"Mr. Adams' Book which has been in your hands of course, has excited a good deal of attention. An edition has come out here and another is on the press at N. York. It will probably be much read, particularly in the Eastern States, and contribute with other circumstances to revive the predilections of the Country for the British Constitution. Men of learning find nothing new in it, Men of taste many things to criticize. And men without either, not a few things, which they will not understand. It will nevertheless be read, and praised, and become a powerful engine in forming the public opinion. The name and character of the Author, with the critical situation of our affairs, naturally account for such an effect. The book also has merit, and I wish many of the remarks in it, which are unfriendly to republicanism, may not receive fresh weight from the operations of our Governments."

11. In *The Writings of James Madison*, Vol. II, pp. 337–338 (Madison to Randolph, April 8, 1787).

12. Above, n. 10.

13. Madison, *ibid.*, Vol. II, pp. 338–339 (Madison to Randolph, April 8, 1787).

14. *Ibid.*, pp. 339–340.

15. *Ibid.*, p. 340: "An article ought to be inserted expressly guaranteeing the tranquillity of the States against internal as well as external dangers.

"To give the new system its proper energy, it will be desirable to have it ratified by the authority of the people, and not merely by that of the Legislatures. . . . The change in the principle of representation will be relished by a majority of the States, and those too of most influence. The northern States will be reconciled to it by the *actual* superiority of their populousness; the Southern by their *expected* superiority on this point. This principle established, the repugnance of the large States to part with power will in a great degree subside, and the smaller States must ultimately yield to the predominant will. It is also already seen by many, and must by degrees be seen by all, that, unless the Union be organized efficiently on republican principles, innovations of a much more objectionable form may be obtruded, or, in the most favorable event, the partition of the Empire, into rival and hostile confederacies will ensue."

16. In Madison, *Writings*, p. 80 (Madison to George Washington, April 16, 1787). Hereafter cited as *Writings* in contradistinction to *Writings of Madison* cited immediately above. This letter is also in *The Papers of James Madison* (multi-vols. and changing editors, Chicago and later Charlottesville, 1962–), Vol. 9, pp. 382 ff.

17. In *Papers of Madison*, Vol. 9, p. 344 (George Washington to Madison, March 31, 1787).

18. *Republic of Letters*, p. 443.

19. Madison, *Writings*, p. 80 (Madison to Washington, April 16, 1787).

20. *Ibid.*, pp. 80–82: "I would propose as the ground-work that a change be made in the principle of representation. According to the present form of the Union in which the intervention of the States is in all great cases necessary to effectuate the measures of Congress, an equality of suffrage, does not destroy the inequality of importance, in the several members. No one will deny that Virginia and Massts. have more weight and influence both within & without Congress than Delaware or Rho. Island. Under a system which would operate in many essential points without the intervention of the State legislatures [etc.]. . . .

"I would propose next that in addition to the present federal powers, the national Government should be armed with positive and compleat authority in all cases which require uniformity; such as the regulation of trade, including the right of taxing both exports & imports, the fixing the terms and forms of naturalization, &c &c.

"Over and above this positive power, a negative *in all cases whatsoever* on the legislative acts of the States, as heretofore exercised by the Kingly prerogative, appears to me to be absolutely necessary, and to be the least possible encroachment on the State jurisdictions. Without this defensive power, every positive power that can be given on paper will be evaded & defeated. The States will continue to invade the national jurisdiction, to violate treaties and the law of nations & to harrass each other with rival and spiteful measures dictated by mistaken views of interest. . . . In Monarchies the sovereign is more neutral to the interests and views of different parties; but unfortunately he too often forms interests of his own repugnant to those of the whole. Might not the national prerogative here suggested be found sufficiently disinterested for the decision of local questions of policy, whilst it would itself be sufficiently restrained from the pursuit of interests adverse to those of the whole Society."

21. *Ibid.*, pp. 82–83.

22. Madison's "Vices of the Political System of the United States" is in his *Papers*, Vol. 9, pp. 348 ff. (Also in *Writings of Madison*, Vol. II, pp. 361 ff.).

23. The continuation of Madison's seventh section in "Vices" includes the following observations: "It is no longer doubted that a unanimous and punctual obedience of 13 independent bodies, to the acts of the federal Government, ought not be calculated on. Even during the war, when external danger supplied in some degree the defect of legal & coercive sanctions, how imperfectly did the States fulfil their obligations to the Union? In time of peace, we see already what is to be expected. How indeed could it be otherwise? In the first place, Every general act of the Union must necessarily bear unequally hard on some particular member or members of it. . . . Thirdly a distrust of the voluntary compliance of each other may prevent the compliance of any, although it should be the latent disposition of all. Here are causes & pretexts which will never fail to render federal measures abortive. If the laws of the States, were merely recommendatory to their citizens, or if they were to be rejudged by County authorities, what security, what probability would exist, that they would be carried into execution? Is the security or probability greater in favor of the acts of Congs. which depending for their execution on the will of the state legislatures, wch. are tho' nominally authoritative, in fact recommendatory only."

24. Madison's ninth section in "Vices" reads as follows: "In developing the evils which viciate the political system of the U.S.[,] it is proper to include those which are found within the States individually, as well as those which directly affect the States collectively, since the former class have an indirect influence on the general malady and must not be overlooked in forming a compleat remedy. Among the evils then of our situation may well be ranked the multiplicity of laws from which no State is exempt. As far as laws are necessary, to mark with precision the duties of those who are to obey them, and to take from those who are to administer them a discretion, which might be abused, their number is the price of liberty. As far as the laws exceed this limit, they are a nusance: a nusance of the most pestilent kind. Try the Codes of the several States by this test, and what a luxuriancy of legislation do they present. The short period of independency has filled as many pages as the century which preceded it. Every year, almost every session, adds a new volume. This may be the effect in part, but it can only be in part, of the situation in which the revolution has placed us. A review of the several codes will shew that every necessary and useful part of the least voluminous of them might be compressed into one tenth of the compass, and at the same time be rendered tenfold as perspicuous."

Madison's short tenth section in "Vices" is as follows: "This evil is intimately connected with the former yet deserves a distinct notice as it emphatically denotes a vicious legislation. We daily see laws repealed or superseded, before any trial can have been made of their merits: and even before a knowledge of them can have reached the remoter districts with which they were to operate. In the regulations of trade this instability becomes a snare not only to our citizens but to foreigners also."

Madison's lengthy eleventh section includes the following indicative statements: "If the multiplicity and mutability of laws prove a want of wisdom, their injustice betrays a defect still more alarming: more alarming not merely because it is a greater evil in itself, but because it brings more into question the fundamental principle of republican Government, that the majority who rule in such Governments, are the safest Guardians both of public Good and of private rights. To what causes is this evil to be ascribed?

"These causes lie

1. in the Representative bodies.
2. in the people themselves.

1. Representative appointments are sought from 3 motives. 1. ambition 2. personal interest. 3. public good. Unhappily the two first are proved by experience to be most prevalent. Hence the candidates who feel them, particularly, the second, are most industrious, and most successful in pursuing their object: and forming often a majority in the legislative Councils. . . .

"2. A still more fatal if not more frequent cause lies among the people themselves. All civilized societies are divided into different interests and factions, as they happen to be creditors or debtors. . . . In repubican Government the majority however composed, ultimately give the law. Whenever therefore an apparent interest or common passion unites a majority[,] what is to restrain them from unjust violations of the rights and interests of the minority, or of individuals? Three motives only 1. a prudent regard to their own good as involved in the general and permanent good of the Community. This consideration although of decisive weight in itself, is found by experience to be too often unheeded. . . . 2dly. respect for character. However strong this motive may be in individuals, it is considered as very insufficient to restrain them from injustice. . . . 3dly. will Religion the only remaining motive be a sufficient restraint? . . . The conduct of every popular assembly acting on oath, the strongest of religious Ties, proves that individuals join without remorse in acts, against which their consciences would revolt if proposed to them . . . in their closets. . . . But enthusiasm is only a temporary state of religion, and while it lasts will hardly be seen with pleasure at the helm of Government. Besides religion . . . may become a motive to oppression as well as a restraint from injustice. . . .

"The great desideratum in Government is such a modification of the Sovereignty as will render it sufficiently neutral between the different interests and factions, to controul one part of the Society from invading the rights of another, and at the same time sufficiently controuled itself, from setting up an interest adverse to that of the whole Society. In absolute Monarchies, the prince is sufficiently, neutral towards his subjects, but frequently sacrifices their happiness to his ambition or his avarice. In small Republics, the sovereign will is sufficiently controuled from such a Sacrifice of the entire Society, but is not sufficiently neutral towards the parts composing it. As a limited Monarchy tempers the evils of an absolute one; so an extensive Republic meliorates the administration of a small Republic.

"An auxiliary desideratum for the melioration of the Republican form is such a process of elections as will most certainly extract from the mass of the Society the purest and noblest characters which it contains; such as will at once feel most strongly the proper motives to pursue the end of their appointment, and be most capable to devise the proper means of attaining it."

25. In addition to Madison's *Notes of Debates in the Federal Convention of 1787* (cited here from the convenient reprint by Norton, New York, 1987), I have also consulted *The Records of the Federal Convention of 1787* (edited by Max Farrand, 4 vols., New Haven, 1966).

26. From "Editorial Note" to Madison's "Vices," in his *Papers*, Vol. 9, pp. 345–348.

27. On "Madison's Preface" to his *Notes of Convention*, the following statement in the 1987 reprint is briefly informative: "This Preface, first printed in 1840, along with Madison's other papers, was drafted by Madison in the last years of his life—sometime between 1830 and 1836. He apparently intended to make a finished copy and include in it several other documents, but this project was never completed." At the top of the Preface's first page stands the heading: "A Sketch Never Finished nor Applied." An editorial note explains: "These are the words which Madison wrote at the head of this document after he had scratched out the phrase 'Preface to Debates in the Convention of 1787'." This is the heading ("A Sketch . . .") used for the Preface, under the more recent title "Origin of the Constitutional Convention," in *Writings of Madison*, Vol. II, pp. 391 ff.; there, an editorial comment notes that "this sketch was written about the year 1835, when Madison was preparing for posthumous publication his journal of the constitutional convention. It is an exceedingly rough draft . . ."

28. Madison's prefatory "Sketch" includes the following in *Notes*, pp. 4–5: "In 1774. The progress made by G.B. [Great Britain] in the open assertion of her pretensions, and in the apprehended purpose of otherwise maintaining them than by Legislative enactments and declarations, had been such that the Colonies did not hesitate to assemble, by their deputies, in a formal Congress, authorized to oppose to the British innovations whatever measures might be found best adapted to the occasion; without however losing sight of an eventual reconciliation.

"The dissuasive measures of that Congress, being without effect, another Congress was held in 1775, whose pacific efforts to bring about a change in the views of the other party, being equally unavailing, and the commencement of actual hostilities having at length put an end to all hope of reconciliation; the Congress . . . proceeded on the memorable 4 of July, 1776 to declare the 13 Colonies, Independent States.

"During the discussions of this solemn Act, a Committee consisting of a member from each colony had been appointed to prepare & digest a form of Confederation, for the future management of the common interests. . . . The plan, tho' dated after the Declaration of Independence, was probably drawn up before that event; since the name of *Colonies*, not *States* is used throughout the draught. . . . [In] November 1777 . . . it was agreed to by Congress, and proposed to the Legislatures of the States. . . . The ratifications of these by their Delegates in Congs duly authorized took place at successive dates; but were not compleated till March 1, 1781."

29. Madison, *ibid.*, pp. 6–8: "The principal difficulties which embarrassed the progress, and retarded the completion of the plan of Confederation, may be traced to 1. the natural repugnance of the parties to a relinquishment of power: 2 a natural jealousy of its abuse in other hands than their own: 3 the rule of suffrage among parties unequal in size, but equal in sovereignty. ... 5. the selection and definition of the powers, at once necessary to the federal head, and safe to the several members.

"To these sources of difficulty, incident to the formation of all such Confederacies, were added two others one of a temporary, the other of a permanent nature. The first was the case of the Crown lands, so called because they had been held by the British Crown....

"The other source of dissatisfaction was the peculiar situation of some of the States, which having no convenient ports for foreign commerce, were subject to be taxed by their neighbors, thro whose ports, their commerce was carryed on....

"But the radical infirmity of the 'art of Confederation' was the dependence of Cong. on the voluntary and simultaneous compliance with its Requisitions, by so many independant Communities, each consulting more or less its particular interests & convenience and distrusting the compliance of the others....

"The close of the war however brought no cure for the public embarrassments. The States relieved from the pressure of foreign danger, and flushed with the enjoyment of independent and sovereign power; ... persevered in omissions and in measures incompatible with their relations with the Federal Gov..."

30. *Ibid.*, pp. 8–9, 13–14: "Having served as a member of Con[gress] [in 1780–1783] ..., I had become intimately acquainted with the public distresses and the causes of them. I had observed the successful opposition to every attempt to procure a remedy by new grants of power to Cong[ress]....

"It required but little time after taking my seat in the [Virginia] House of Delegates in May 1784 to discover that, however favorable the general disposition of the States might be towards the Confederacy[,] the [Virginia] Legislature retained the aversion of its predecessors to transfers of power from the State to the Gov[ernment] of the Union....

"The temper of the [Virginia] Legislature & the wayward course of its proceedings may be gathered from the Journals of the Sessions in the years 1784 & 1785.

"The failure ... of the varied propositions in the [Virginia] Legislature, for enlarging the powers of Congress, [was great]....

"As the pub. mind had [eventually] been ripened for a salutary Reform of the pol. System, ... [there] had ... develop[ed] more & more the necessity ... of a Systematic provision for the preservation and Gov[.] of the Union.

"The want of auth[.] in Cong[.] to regulate Commerce had produced in Foreign nations particularly G.B. a monopolizing policy injurious to the trade of the U.S....

"The same want of a general power over Commerce, led to an exercise of the power separately, by the States, which not only proved abortive, but engendered rival, conflicting and angry regulations...."

31. *Ibid.*, pp. 15–16: "As natural consequences of this distracted and disheartening condition of the union, the Fed[.] Auth[.] had ceased to be respected abroad, ... particularly to take advantage of its imbecility, and ... approaching downfall. ... [On] the opposite extreme of a consolidated gov[.,] ... there were individuals who had betrayed a bias towards Monarchy. ... [S]ome [were] not unfavorable to a partition of the Union into several Confederacies. ... The idea of a dismemberment had recently made its appearance in the Newspapers.

"Such were the defects, the deformities, the diseases and the ominous prospects, for which the Convention were [*sic*] to provide a remedy, and which ought never to be overlooked in expounding & appreciating the Constitutional Charter the remedy that was provided.

"As a sketch on paper, the earliest perhaps of a Constitutional Govt for the Union . . . to be sanctioned by *the people of the States*, acting in their original & sovereign character, was contained in a letter of Apl. 8. 1787 from J. M. to Govr Randolph. . . .

"The feature in the letter which vested in the general Authy. a negative on the laws of the States, was suggested by the negative in the head of the British Empire, which prevented collisions between the parts & the whole, and between the parts themselves. It was supposed that the substitution, of an elective and responsible authority for an hereditary and irresponsible one, would avoid the appearance even of a departure from the principle of Republicanism. But altho' the subject was so viewed in the Convention, and the votes on it were [*sic*] more than once equally divided, it was finally & justly abandoned . . ."

32. At the 2001 Princeton conference on Madison, cited above in n. 1, the various presentations included many useful points in line with our present perspectives.

In her presentation on "The States and the Nation: James Madison and American Federalism," Pauline Maier declared the problem of sovereignty and its location to be the most important issue in the history of American government. Professor Maier briefly traced that problem from Bodin to English ideas of king-in-Parliament and to the American Revolution. Sovereignty in America, she believes, has turned on the relationships between the nation and the individual states as set forth in U.S. constitutional theory and actuality, with particular regard to the ideas of Madison, who favored a much stronger federal government than the one agreed to at the Constitutional Convention. Although the people rather than the government represents ultimate sovereignty in America, the acts of legislature(s) by representatives of the people were for Madison in *The Federalist* etc. a focal point for the issue of sovereignty, which changed for him in later decades.

In a panel discussion, Jack Rakove and others underscored the importance for Madison of protecting the rights of individduals in the minority from the majority. Locke's ideas on individual rights of the majority were cited, if not his strong concepts of legislative (parliamentary) sovereignty. Also cited were Madison's partial objections to a Bill of Rights as incapable of listing all rights and as flawed if people did not care about such things.

In the course of asking "Is There 'A James Madison Problem'?," Gordon Wood pondered whether Madison's switch from being pro-Federalist in the later 1780s to anti-Federalist in the later 1790s was a matter of "political expediency." Did Madison need to show loyalty to Jefferson, Virginia, and republican causes, even though he never became as pro-states'-rights as Jefferson? Or was his change due to his shifting perceptions as a statesman? In the late 1780s, Madison was especially concerned to protect against the dangers of factionalism, as were other Federalists like Hamilton. So disappoined was Madison that the federal "negative" over state laws failed to pass at the Constitutional Convention that he wrote to Jefferson before the Convention was over with grave misgivings about the new Constitution's chances for success, even though he joined Hamilton in vigorously pushing for ratification in the *Federalist* essays, in which a key function of legislation was said to be the regulation of factions. Yet to the extent that the new U.S. Constitution was not what he had hoped for, Madison cannot be called its "father." Professor Wood also made brief allusions to Locke and Hobbes.

In "Reading Madison's Mind," Jack Rakove looked at Madison's shift from pro-nationalism in the later 1770s, in favoring stronger powers for the Confederation Congress, to his pro-states'-rights viewpoint in the later 1790s. Professor Rakove believes, however, that "sovereignty" is not key, but rather "rhetoric," in a federal system (an implicit difference with Maier) where the people are sovereign. Even so, a sovereignty divided or shared, we may add, even though it is not an absolute undivided sovereignty of prince or people (a la

Bodin, Hobbes, Locke, etc.) is still sovereignty nevertheless—a sovereignty expressed here in a legislative framework of laws promulgated at different levels within the federal system. Rakove does see that Madison wanted a federal system based on laws and self-sufficiency. Rakove rightly stresses Madison's Convention role as "first among equals" as well as his deep and wide reading, despite Madison's relative paucity of references to his sources. Rakove and others in discussion also made interesting references to Locke, Hobbes, Montesquieu, etc.

In "James Madison and Constitutionalism," Jennifer Nedelsky spoke about Madison's aversion to judicial review, in which the Supreme Court could negate laws of Congress (etc.). Judicial review of laws, according to Professor Nedelsky, has become a widely utilized tool in the world today for preventing tyranny of majorities, and it reached a dramatic moment in Supreme Court overturnings of much New Deal legislation under F.D.R. Others in discussion said that Madison later came in some ways to favor judicial review. We may add that Madison's opposition in the 1780s to judicial or executive veto powers over Congress' legislation, coupled with his desire for Congress' legislative veto power over state laws, made Madison's idea of legislative sovereignty a particularly strong one. We may also add that if Madison in the later 1790s found more agreement with anti-Federalists, even in seeking through judicial means to check the federal government, he may again have been motivated by political "strategy."

Supreme Court Justice Antonin Scalia, on "James Madison's Constitutional Interpretation," averred that Madison desired a limited role for the federal government. A case in point was Madison's objection to a national bank because it was not provided for in the U.S. Constitution, whereas Hamilton advocated and won it during Washington's presidency. We may add, however, that once again Madison's loyalties and sympathies were shifting, after the adoption of the Constitution, toward a more anti-Federalist position. Justice Scalia makes a good point that Congress in Madison's period had more power than now, whereas the Supreme Court had less. He views himself, like Madison, as an adherent to the "text" of the Constitution rather than to its "intent."

A variety of additional points may be made in light of the preceding presentations. What we are saying here is that during the Constitutional Convention of mid-1787, the crucial objective for Madison was to win the state delegates' approval for a greatly expanded role by the federal government, in particular through the power of Congress and its laws to override the laws of potentially recalcitrant states. In order to make this objective more palatable, Madison shifted his emphasis to the need for protecting the rights of minority groups and of private individuals in the separate states against unfair treatment under laws passed by and favoring majority interests, as represented especially in the state legislatures. Not only Randolph as head of Madison's own Virginia delegation but also Jefferson (in a letter to Madison on June 20, 1787) disliked the idea of Congress having a veto over state laws.

Later, at the Virginia ratifying convention, we further find, arguments were put forth by anti-Federalists like Patrick Henry—an ardent foe of the Constitution who feared that States' rights would be violated—that an extensive Bill of Rights was required. Madison's strong reservations at that point about the difficulty of spelling out individual rights were again conditioned in part by his sense of strategy in getting the Constitution ratified. In letters to Jefferson, Madison pursued the pros and cons of a Bill of Rights.

Still pushing for (or justifying) the "negative" when writing to Jefferson from New York on Oct. 24/Nov. 1, 1787 (*Republic of Letters*, Vol. I, p. 500), Madison wrote: "A Constitutional negative on the laws of the States seems equally necessary to secure individuals against encroachments on their rights. The mutability of the laws of the States is found to be a serious evil." It may be that Madison still hoped the "negative" could yet be added prior to final ratification. Even so, in a letter shortly thereafter to Jefferson on

Dec. 20, 1787 (*ibid.*, p. 514), Madison declared: "After all, it is my principle that the will of the Majority should always prevail." The relationship between majority rule and minority rights remained a concern for Madison; yet the "common good of the society" (like the "public mind") remained an overriding commitment from his early days to e.g. his *Federalist* #57, Feb. 1788.

Prior to the Constitutional Convention, Madison's researches into the defects of ancient and modern confederations had persuaded him of the key goal of strengthening the federal authority and giving to Congress the sovereign power of legislative sanction and coercion over the separate states. The "negative" or veto power of Congress over state laws was needed not primarily in order to protect minority or individual rights but in order to promote and preserve the Union, then in danger of falling apart under the existing inadequate structure of the Confederation. The separate states had sovereignty at the expense of the weak and ineffectual central government. On Oct. 5, 1786, Madison could write to James Monroe that the "maxim" that "the interest of the majority is the political standard of right and wrong" could be wrongly subjected to abuse against minorities of individuals, for the majority is not necessarily right. Yet in his pre-Convention outlines for a new constitutional system of government, Madison's chief concern to strengthen the Union's government, so it would survive and flourish, far outweighed any concern for securing the rights of individuals in the minority against those in the majority. In this primary endeavor, he was working out conceptual problems of legislative sovereignty and legislative state.

33. Madison, prefatory "Sketch," in *Notes of Convention*, pp. 16–17: "On the arrival of the Virginia Deputies at Philad. it occurred to them that from the early and prominent part taken by that State in bringing about the Convention some initiative step might be expected from them. The Resolutions introduced by Governor Randolph were the result of a Consultation on the subject. . . . The Resolutions as the Journals shew became the basis on which the proceedings of the Convention commenced, and to the developments, variations and modifications of which the plan of Gov. proposed by the Convention may be traced.

"The curiosity I had felt during my researches into the History of the most distinguished Confederacies, particularly those of antiquity, and the deficiency I found in the means of satisfying it more especially in what related to the process, the principles, the reasons, & the anticipations, which prevailed in the formation of them, determined me to preserve as far as I could an exact account of what might pass in the Convention. . . . Nor was I unaware of the value of such a contribution to the fund of materials for the History of a Constitution on which would be staked the happiness of a people great even in its infancy, and possibly the cause of Liberty throught the world.

"In pursuance of the task I had assumed[,] I chose a seat in front of the presiding member, with the other members on my right & left hands. In this favorable position for hearing all that passed, I noted . . ."

34. Randolph's four-part introductory presentation to the Convention on May 29, 1787, is given in *Notes*, pp. 28–30.

35. Madison, *ibid.* ("Resolutions proposed by Mr. Randolph in Convention[,] May 29, 1787"), pp. 30–31: "1. Resolved that the Articles of Confederation ought to be so corrected & enlarged as to accomplish the objects proposed by their institution; namely, "common defence, security of liberty and general welfare.

"2. Resd. therefore that the rights of suffrage in the national Legislature ought to be proportioned to the Quotas of contribution, or to the number of free inhabitants. . . .

"3. Resd. that the National Legislature ought to consist of two branches.

"4. Resd. that the members of the first branch of the National Legislature ought to be elected by the people of the several States. . . .

"5. Resd. that the members of the second branch of the National Legislature ought to be elected by those of the first, out of a proper number of persons nominated by the individual Legislatures. . . .

"6. Resolved that each branch ought to possess the right of originating Acts; that the National Legislature ought to be impowered to enjoy the Legislative Rights vested in Congress by the Confederation & moreover to legislate in all cases to which the separate States are incompetent . . .; to negative all laws passed by the several States, contravening in the opinion of the National Legislature the articles of Union; and to call forth the force of the Union agst. any member of the Union failing to fulfill its duty under the articles thereof."

36. *Ibid.*, pp. 31–32: "7. Resd. that a National Executive be instituted; to be chosen by the National Legislature . . .; and that besides a general authority to execute the National laws, it ought to enjoy the Executive rights vested in Congress by the Confederation."

"8. Resd. that the Executive and a Convenient number of the National Judiciary, ought to compose a Council of revision with authority to examine every act of the National Legislature before it shall operate, & every act of a particular Legislature before a Negative thereon shall be final; and that the dissent of the said Council shall amount to a rejection, unless the Act of the National Legislature be again passed, or that of a particular Legislature be again negatived by . . . each branch.

"9. Resd. that a National Judiciary be established to consist of one or more supreme tribunals, and of inferior tribunals to be chosen by the National Legislature . . ."

37. *Notes* (proceedings, May 29, 1787), pp. 33–34.

38. *Ibid.* (May 29, 1787), pp. 35–36.

39. *Ibid.* (May 31, 1787), pp. 43–44.

40. *Ibid.* (May 31, 1787), pp. 44–45: "The other clauses giving powers necessary to preserve harmony among the States to negative all State laws contravening in the opinion of the Nat. Leg. the articles of union, down to the last clause, (the words 'or any treaties subsisting under the authority of the Union,' being added after the words 'contravening &c. the articles of the Union,' on motion of Dr. Franklin) were agreed to witht. debate or dissent.

"The last clause of Resolution 6. authorizing an exertion of the force of the whole agst. a delinquent State came next into consideration.

"Mr. Madison, observed that the more he reflected on the use of force, the more he doubted the practicability, the justice and the efficacy of it when applied to people collectively and not individually.—A union of the States containing such an ingredient seemed to provide for its own destruction. The use of force ag[in]st a State, would look more like a declaration of war, than an infliction of punishment, and would probably be considered by the party attacked as a dissolution of all previous compacts by which it might be bound. He hoped that such a system would be framed as might render this recourse unnecessary, and moved that the clause be postponed. This motion was agreed to . . ."

41. *Ibid.* (June 6–7, 9, 11–12, 1787), pp. 74–77, 84–85, 95–98, 105, 107: "Mr. Wilson. He wished for vigor in the Govt., but he wished that vigorous authority to flow immediately from the legitimate source of all authority. The Govt. ought to possess not only the *force*, but the *mind or sense* of the people at large. The Legislature ought to be the most exact transcript of the whole Society. Representation is made necessary only because it is impossible for the people to act collectively. The opposition was to be expected he said from the *Governments*, not from the Citizens of the States. . . . The State officers were to be the losers of power. The people he supposed would be rather more attached to the national Govt. than to the State Govts. as being more important in itself, and more flattering to their pride. . . .

"Mr. Madison considered an election of one branch at least of the Legislature by the people immediately, as a clear principle of Govt. and that this mode under proper regulations had the additional advantage of securing better representatives, as well as of avoiding too great an agency of the State Governments in the General one. . . . In all cases where a majority are united by a common interest or passion, the rights of the minority are in danger. What motives are to restrain them? . . . These observations are verified by the Histories of every Country antient & modern. In Greece & Rome the rich & poor, the creditors & debtors, as well as the patricians & plebians alternately oppressed each other with equal unmercifulness. What a source of oppression was the relation between the parent cities of Rome, Athens & Carthage, & their respective provinces: the former possessing the power, & the latter being sufficiently distinguished to be separate objects of it? Why was America so justly apprehensive of Parliamentary injustice? Because G. Britain had a separate interest real or supposed, & if her authority had been admitted, could have pursued that interest at our expence. We have seen . . . the most oppressive dominion ever exercised by man over man. What has been the source of those unjust laws complained of among ourselves? Has it not been the real or supposed interest of the major number? . . . The Holders of one species of property have thrown a disproportion of taxes on the holders of another species. The lesson we are to draw from the whole is that where a majority are united by a common sentiment, and have an opportunity, the rights of the minor party become insecure. In a Republican Govt. the Majority if united have always an opportunity. . . . It was incumbent on us then to . . . frame a republican system on such a scale & in such a form as will controul all the evils wch. have been experienced.

"Mr. Dickenson considered it as essential that one branch of the Legislature shd. be drawn immediately from the people; and as expedient that the other shd. be chosen by the Legislatures of the States. . . . He was for a strong National Govt. but for leaving the States a considerable agency in the System.. . . To attempt to abolish the States altogether, would degrade the Councils of our Country, would be impracticable, would be ruinous. He compared the proposed National System to the Solar System, in which the States were the planets, and ought to be left to move freely in their proper orbits. The Gentleman from Pa. [Mr. Wilson] wished he said to extinguish these planets. If the State Governments were excluded from all agency in the national one, and all power drawn from the people at large, the consequence would be that the national Govt. would move in the same direction as the State Govts. now do, and would run into all the same mischiefs. . . .

"Mr. Wilson. The subject it must be owned is surrounded with doubts and difficulties. But we must surmount them. The British Governmt cannot be our model. . . . He did not see the danger of the States being devoured by the Nationl. Govt. On the contrary, he wished to keep them from devouring the national Govt. He was not however for extinguishing these planets as was supposed by Mr. D.—neither did he on the other hand, believe that they would warm or enlighten the Sun. Within their proper orbits they must still be suffered to act for subordinate purposes for which their existence is made essential by the great extent of our Country. . . .

"Mr. Patterson considered the proposition for a proportional representation as striking at the existence of the lesser States. He [made] . . . remarks on the nature[,] structure and powers of the Convention. The Convention he said was formed in pursuance of an Act of Congs. . . . [T]he amendment of the confederacy was the object of all the laws and commissions on the subject; that the articles of the Confederation were therefore the proper basis of all the proceedings of the Convention. We ought to keep within its limits, or we should be charged by our Constituents with usurpation, that the people of America were . . . not to be deceived. . . . The idea of a national Govt. as contradistinguished from a federal one, never entered into the mind of any of them, and to the public mind we must accomodate ourselves. . . . A confederacy supposes sovereignty in the members composing it & sovereignty supposes equality. If we are to be considered as a nation, all State distinctions must be abolished, the whole must be thrown into hotchpot, and when an equal division is made, then there may be fairly an equality of representation. . . . He was attached strongly to the plan of the existing confederacy, in which the people chuse their Legislative representatives; and the Legislatures their federal representatives. No other amendments were wanting than to mark the orbits of the States with due precision, and provide for the use of coercion, which was the great point. . . . N. Jersey will never confederate on the plan before the Committee. She would be swallowed up. He had rather submit to a monarch, to a despot, than to such a fate. . . .

"Mr. Wilson . . . entered elaborately into the defence of a proportional representation, stating for his first position that as all authority was derived from the people, equal numbers of people ought to have an equal no. of representatives. . . . As to the case . . . stated by Mr. Patterson, . . . We have been told that each State being sovereign, all are equal. So each man is naturally a sovereign over himself, and all men are therefore naturally equal. Can he retain this equality when he becomes a member of Civil Government? He can not. As little can a Sovereign State, when it becomes a member of a federal Governt. If N.J. will not part with her Sovereignty it is in vain to talk of Govt. A new partition of the States is desireable, but evidently & totally impracticable. . . .

"Mr. Randolph considered it as necessary to prevent that competition between the National Constitution & laws & those of the particular States, which had already been felt. The officers of the States are already under oath to the States. To preserve a due impartiality they ought to be equally bound to the Natl. Govt. The Natl. authority needs every support we can give it. . . .

"Mr. Madison, observed that if the opinions of the people were to be our guide, it wd. be difficult to say what course we ought to take. No member of the Convention could say what the opinions of his Constituents were at this time. . . . We ought to consider what was right & necessary in itself for the attainment of a proper Governmnt. A plan adjusted to this idea will recommend itself. . . .

"Mr. Gerry repeated his opinion that it was necessary to consider what the people would approve. This had been the policy of all Legislators. If the reasoning of Mr. Madison were just, and we supposed a limited Monarchy the best form in itself, we ought to recommend it, tho' the genius of the people was decidedly adverse to it."

In the foregoing passages, the words "public mind" and "*mind* of the public" are used respectively by Patterson and Wilson. Madison, who often elsewhere uses the term "public mind" as a positive watchword, warns here of the dangers for the minority of a "majority united" in a "common interest." According to Patterson, this public mind must be mirrored in "the Legislature" as "the most exact transcript of the whole Society." Even while opposing a strong national government, Patterson could appeal, like Madison and other delegates, to the need for due regard to the public mind, as he saw it. The "great point" for Patterson, seen above, was to "provide for the use of coercion" by the national legislature, as well as the state legislatures; this could be easily accomplished, and more effectively, within the existing structure of the Confederacy. As for Madison, pursuit of the "supposed interest of the major number" was "the source of those unjust laws" promulgated by the British parliament against Americans, who are "justly apprehensive of Parliamentary injustice" and therefore of the parliamentary system. For Madison, the goal or end to keep in mind is "the attainment of a proper Government"; on the means to reach it, delegates "ought to consider what was [is] right & necessary in itself."

42. Madison, *ibid.* (June 13, 1787, "Report of Committee of Whole on Mr. Randolph's Propositions"), pp. 115—117: "1. Resd. that it is the opinion of this Committee that a

National Governmt. ought to be established, consisting of a supreme Legislature, Executive & Judiciary.

"2. Resold. that the National Legislature ought to consist of two branches.

"3. Resd. that the members of the first branch of the National Legislature ought to be elected by the People of the several States....

"4. Resd. that the members of the second branch of the Natl. Legislature ought to be chosen by the individual Legislatures....

"6. Resd. that the Natl. Legislature ought to be empowered to enjoy the Legislative rights vested in Congs. by the Confederation....

"9. Resolved that a National Executive be instituted to consist of a single person, to be chosen by the Natl. Legislature for the term of seven years, with power to carry into execution the national laws....

"10. Resold. that the Natl. Executive shall have a right to negative any Legislative Act, which shall not be afterwards passed unless by two thirds of each branch of the National Legislature.

"11. Resold. that a Natl. Judiciary be established, to consist of one supreme tribunal, the Judges of which to be appointed by the 2d. branch of the Natl. Legislature....

"12. Resold. that the Natl. Legislature be empowered to appoint inferior Tribunals....

"16. Resd. that a Republican Constitution & its existing laws ought to be guaranteed to each State by the U. States.

"17. Resd. that provision ought to be made for the amendment of the Articles of Union whensoever it shall seem necessary."

43. *Ibid.* (June 14, 1787), pp. 118–121. The first resolution in Patterson's list of nine was indicative: "Resd. that the arttícles of Confederation ought to be revised, corrected & enlarged, as to render the federal Constitution adequate to the exigencies of Government, & the preservation of the Union."

44. *Ibid.* (June 18, 1787), pp. 129, 138–139.

45. *Ibid.* (June 19, 1787), pp. 140 ff., esp. pp. 142, 144.

46. *Ibid.* (June 19, 1787), pp. 152–153: "Col. Hamilton ... had not been understood yesterday. By an abolition of the States, he meant that no boundary could be drawn between the National & State Legislatures; that the former must therefore have indefinite authority. If it were limited at all, the rivalship of the States would gradually subvert it. ... As *States*, he thought they ought to be abolished. But he admitted the necessity of leaving in them, subordinate jurisdictions. The examples of Persia & the Roman Empire, cited by [Mr. Wilson] were he thought in favor of his doctrine: the great powers delegated to the Satraps & proconsuls, having frequently produced revolts, and schemes of independence.

"Mr. King ... conceived that the import of the terms 'States' 'Sovereignty' '*national*' 'federal,' had been often used & applied in the discussions inaccurately & delusively. The States were not 'Sovereigns' in the sense contended for by some. They did not possess the peculiar features of sovereignty, they could not make war, nor peace, nor alliances nor treaties. Considering ... they were dumb, for they could not speak to any foreign Sovereign whatever. ... On the other side, if the Union of the States comprizes the idea of a confederation, it comprises that also of consolidation...

"Mr. Wilson, could not admit the doctrine that when the Colonies became independent of G. Britain, they became independent also of each other. He read the declaration of Independence, observing thereon that the *United Colonies* were declared to be free & independent States; and inferring that they were independent, not *individually* but *Unitedly* and that they were confederated as they were independent, States.

"Col. Hamilton, assented to the doctrine of Mr. Wilson. He denied the doctrine that the States were thrown into a State of Nature. He was not yet prepared to admit the doctrine that the Confederacy, could be dissolved by partial infractions of it."

47. *Ibid.* (June 20, 1787), p. 159: "Mr. Luther Martin agreed with [Col. Mason] as to the importance of the State Govts. [H]e would support them at the expence of the Genrl. Govt. which was instituted for the purpose of that support. ... He considered Congs[.] as representing the people, being chosen by the Legislatures who wre chosen by the people. At any rate, Congres. represented the Legislatures; and it was the Legislatures not the people who refused to enlarge their powers. ... At the separation from the British Empire, the people of America preferred the establishment of themselves into thirteen separate sovereignties instead of incorporating themselves into one. ... [T]hey are afraid of granting powers unnecessarily, lest they should defeat the original end of the Union; lest the powers should prove dangerous to the sovereignties of the particular States which the union was meant to support; and expose the lesser to being swallowed up by the larger. He conceived also that the people of the States ... vested their powers in their respective Legislatures ..."

48. *Ibid.* (June 20, 1787), p. 161.

49. *Ibid.* (June 21, 1787), pp. 164 ff., and (June 30), pp. 223 ff.

50. *Ibid.* (June 26, 1787), pp. 195 ff..

51. *Ibid.* (June 27, 1787), p. 201 ff.

52. *Ibid.* (June 28, 1787), p. 209 ff.

53. *Ibid.* (June 29, 1787), p. 217.

54. Joining in the debates over his proposed "negative," which did not pass, Madison on July 17 "considered the negative [by the national legislature in possible concert with the states] on the laws of the States as essential to the efficacy & security of the Genrl. Govt. The necessity of a general Govt. proceeds from the propensity of the States to pursue their particular interests in opposition to the general interest [*ibid.*, p. 3044, July 17]." Here as often elsewhere for Madison, the goal of strengthening the national government takes precedence, in his arguments at the Convention for the "negative," over preventing individual states from enacting unjust or injurious laws particularly over minority interests. Yet the latter argument was in part a useful strategy for winning the states' approval by allaying their fears of a threat to their sovereignty and by appealing to a higher justice.

On July 17 Madison saw the "vortex" of an "omnipotent" legislature, i.e. too much legislative sovereignty, as reason to separate the other two branches from it a la Montesquieu, not fearing he might be called a proto-monarchist (*ibid.*, pp. 311–312): "Mr. Madison[:] "[It is] essential to the preservation of liberty that the Legisl: Execut: & Judiciary powers be separate, ... independent of each other. The Executive could not be independent of the Legislure, if dependent on the pleasure of that branch for a reappointment ... [much less for his initial appointment, as proposed]. ... In like manner a dependence of the Executive on the Legislature, would render it the Executor as well as the maker of laws; & then according to the observation of Montesquieu, tyrannical laws may be made that they may be executed in a tyrannical manner....

"Mr. Madison, was not apprehensive of being thought to favor any step towards monarchy. The real object with him was to prevent its introduction. Experience had proved a tendency in our governments to throw all power into the Legislative vortex. The Executives of the States are in general little more than Cyphers; the legislatures omnipotent. If no effectual check be devised for restraining the instability & encroachments of the latter, a revolution of some kind or other would be inevitable. The preservation of Republican Govt. therefore required some expedient for the purpose ..."

Similar viewpoints by Madison on the foregoing issue appear on e.g. pp. 326–327 (July 19) and on pp. 337 ff. (July 21). An excerpt from the latter is indicative: "Mr. Madison considered ... the motion ... useful to the Judiciary departmnt. by giving it an additional opportunity of defending itself agst. Legislative encroachments; It would be useful to the

Executive, by inspiring additional confidence & firmness in exerting the revisionary power ... [in relation] to the Legislature. ... Experience in all the States had evinced a powerful tendency in the Legislature to absorb all power into its vortex. This was the real source of danger to the American Constitutions; & suggested the necessity of giving every defensive authority to the other departments that was consistent with republican principles."

In August—after delegates had dwelled on such issues as whether the state legislaturees could alter a new U.S. consitution, as under the present Articles of Confederation, with Madison arguing in the negative (e.g. July 23, p. 352 and *passim*)—a printed copy of the proposed constitution, as framed up to that point, was furnished to each delegate (August 6, pp. 385 ff.). As provided by Madison, portions of it read as follows, regarding the central legislative perspective on the sovereign powers of the three branches: "[III.] The legislative power shall be vested in a Congress ... of two separate ... bodies ... each [having] ... a negative on the other. ... [VII.] The Legislature of the United States shall have the power to ... collect taxes [etc., etc.]. ... And to make all laws ... necessary ... for carrying into execution [by the Executive] the foregoing powers, and all other powers vested by this Constitution. ... [X.] The Executive Power ... in a single person ... [or] President ... shall be elected ... by the Legislature ... [for] seven years ... but ... not ... a second time. ... [XI.] The Jurisdiction of the Supreme Court shall extend to all cases arising under laws passed by the Legislature of the United States ..." Much debate ensued during subsequent days, with further recourse to history (as e.g. on August 15 by Gov. Morris on Rome and England, pp. 463–464). On August 18 Madison submitted a lengthy list of further "powers as proper to be added to those of the General Legislature" (pp. 477–478).

A revealing instance of the continuing centrality of issues of sovereignty in the debates that ensued occurred on August 20 "in Convention" over the topic of treason, with legislative powers of the Union and the states again at the crux of the matter (p. 491): "Mr. Madison. ... The same act might be treason agst. the United States as here defined—and agst. a particular State according to its laws.

"Mr. Elseworth. There can be no danger to the genl. authority from this; as the laws of the U. States are to be paramount.

"Doct. Johnson was still of opinion there could be no Treason agst. a particular State. It could not even at present, as the Confederation now stands, the Sovereignty being in the Union; much less can it be under the proposed system.

"Col. Mason. The United States will have a qualified sovereignty only. The individual States will retain a part of the Sovereignty. [A]n Act may be treason agst. a particular State which is not so agst. the U. States. ...

"Doct. Johnson: That case would amount to Treason agst. the Sovereign, the Supreme Sovereign, the United States.

"Mr. King observed that the Controversy relating to Treason might be of less magnitude than was supposed; as the Legislature might punish capitally under other names than Treason."

On August 24 (pp. 525–526), Morris pointed, as had Madison, to the dangers of "Legislative tyranny" by having Congress appoint the President. In one way or another, legislative sovereignty was still a dominant issue, with the other branches relating to it. "Mr. Gov. Morris opposed the election of the President by the Legislature. He dwelt on the danger of rendering the Executive uninterested in maintaining the rights of his Station, as leading to Legislative tyranny. If the Legislature have the Executive dependent on them, they can perpetuate & support their usurpations by the influence of tax-gatherers & other officers. ... To guard against all these evils he moved that the President 'shall be chosen by Electors to be chosen by the People of the several States ...' " His motion failed to carry.

An ensuing case in point against "Legislative tyranny" that was voiced by Morris occurred on September 8 regarding trial of the President and again including Madison (pp. 605–606): "Mr. Madison, objected to a trial of the President by the Senate, especially as he was to be impeached by the other branch of the Legislature, and for any act which might be called a misdemesnor. The President under these circumstances was made improperly dependent. He would prefer the Supreme Court for the trial of impeachments, or rather a tribunal of which that should form a part.

"Mr. Govr. Morris thought no other tribunal than the Senate could be trusted. The supreme Court were too few in number and might be warped or corrupted. He was agst. a dependence of the Executive on the Legislature, considering the Legislative tyranny the great danger to be apprehended; but there could be no danger that the Senate would say untruly on their oaths that the President was guilty of crimes or facts . . ."

The Convention was fast moving ahead. Notwithstanding Randolph's announcement on September 10 (p. 612) that he could not approve of the proposed constitution because it departed too greatly from his original resolutions submitted at the Convention's outset, the delegates received on September 12 a "digest" of the up-to-date constitutional "plan" and an accompanying "letter" (pp. 616 ff.). At the very outset, Section 1 of Article I began by underscoring that "ALL legislative powers herein granted shall be vested in a Congress . . ." The lengthy letter clearly showed that, although protecting rights and promoting justice was here deemed a crucial aim, the overarching issue was still that of preserving and strengthening the Union. The main initial context was national versus state sovereignty. "It is obviously impracticable in the federal government of these States to secure all rights of independent sovereignty to each, and yet provide for the interest and safety of all—individuals entering into society must give up a share of liberty to preserve the rest. . . . [T]he greatest interest of every true American, [is] the consolidation of our union, in which is involved our . . . safety, perhaps our national existence." The short preamble echoed these sentiments in part. Thus the main overriding aim, as now underscored, was not the protections of individual rights in the states by the federal government but rather the giving up of certain rights in the interest of the common good—toward the end of strengthening and securing the Union.

Further debate immediately ensued on that same day, September 10 (pp. 627 ff.), over "the clause requiring three fourths of each House to override the negative of the President." The following excerpts are illustrative of the ongoing concerns over legislative issues of sovereignty (pp. 629, 631): "Mr. Gov. Morris dwelt on the danger to the public interest from the instability of laws, as the most to be guarded against. On the other side there could be little danger. If one man in office will not consent where he ought, every fourth year another can be substituted. This term was not too long for fair experiments. Many good laws are not tried long enough to prove their merit. This is often the case with new laws opposed to old habits. . . .

"Mr. Madison. When 3/4 was agreed to, the President was to be elected by the Legislature and for seven years. He is now to be elected by the people and for four years. The object of the revisionary power is to defend the Executive Rights [and] to prevent popular or factious injustice."

Madison went on that same day in a different context to invoke his defeated idea of another legislative negative (p. 631): "Mr. Madison. . . . The jurisdiction of the supreme Court must be the source of redress. So far only had provision been made by the plan agst. injurious acts of the States. His own opinion was, that this was insufficient. A negative on the State laws alone could meet all the shapes which these could assume. But this had been overruled."

And on September 14 (p. 635): "Mr. Madison. The President is made too dependent already on the Legislature, by the power of one branch to try him in consequence of an impeachment by the other. This intermediate suspension, will put him in the power of one branch only."

The dramatic closing days of the Convention at Philadelphia are portrayed by Madison in unforgettable poignant ways. Despite the disappointing refusal of Mason and Randolph of Virginia to approve the plan because of "the dangerous power and structure of the Government," which "would end either in monarchy, or a tyrannical aristocracy" (September 15, p. 651), the plan overwhelmingly passed. They had held out for a second convention at the state level but that idea was rejected, while Franklin's humble last-minute pleas to them went unheeded. Gracious closing words by Washington as Convention president and evocative extended remarks by Franklin as elder statesman were reported by Madison in sensitive, moving ways.

Before the Convention ended on September 17, it was decided that Madison's journals along with other records, which were to remain secret, would be entrusted to Washington. He later turned them over to the Department of State in 1796. Congress in 1818 ordered them to be printed. This project proved to be long and difficult. Cf. *Records of Convention*, Vol. I, Intro.

55. *The Mind of the Founder: Sources of the Political Thought of James Madison* (edited by Marvin Meyers, Hanover, 1981, revised edn.), pp. 86–87.

56. Madison, *Writings*, p. 202 (*The Federalist*, number 38). In general, I have also consulted Jacob E. Cooke's edn. of *The Federalist* (Hanover, N.H., 1961).

57. *Ibid.*, pp. 202–203 (*Federalist*, num. 38): "Whence could it have proceeded that a people, jealous as the Greeks were of their liberty, should so far abandon the rules of caution, as to place their destiny in the hands of a single citizen? Whence could it have proceeded that the Athenians, a people who would not suffer an army to be commanded by fewer than ten generals, and who required no other proof of danger to their liberties than the illustrious merit of a fellow citizen, should consider one illustrious citizen as a more eligible depositary of the fortunes of themselves and their posterity, than a select body of citizens, from whose common deliberations more wisdom, as well as more safety, might have been expected? These questions cannot be fully answered without supposing that the fears of discord and disunion among a number of counsellors, exceeded the apprehension of treachery or incapacity in a single individual. History informs us likewise of the difficulties with which these celebrated reformers had to contend; as well as of the expedients which they were obliged to employ, in order to carry their reforms into effect. Solon, who seems to have indulged a more temporising policy, confessed that he had not given to his countrymen the government best suited to their happiness, but most tolerable to their prejudices. And Lycurgus, more true to his object, was under the necessity of mixing a portion of violence with the authority of superstition; and of securing his final success, by voluntary renunciation, first of his country, and then of his life. If these lessons teach us, on one hand, to admire the improvement made by America on the ancient mode of preparing and establishing regular plans of government; they serve not less on the other, to admonish us of the hazards and difficulties incident to such experiments, and of the great imprudence of unnecessarily multiplying them.

"Is it an unreasonable conjecture that the errors which may be contained in the plan of the convention are such as have resulted rather from the defect of antecedent experience on this complicated and difficult subject, than from a want of accuracy or care in the investigation of it; and consequently such as will not be ascertained until an actual trial shall have pointed them out? This conjecture is rendered probable not only by many considerations of a general nature, but by the particular case of the articles of confederation. It is observable that among the numerous objections and amendments suggested by the several states. . . ."

58. *Ibid.*, p. 207 (*Federalist* #38).

59. *Ibid.*, p. 208 (*Federalist* #38): "Is it improper and unsafe to intermix the different powers of government in the same body of men? [Yes.] Congress . . . [is] the sole depository of all the federal powers."

60. *Ibid.*, p. 179 (*Federalist* #18).

61. *Ibid.*, p. 190 (*Federalist* #20).

62. *Ibid.*, pp. 195–196 (*Federalist* #37).

63. *Ibid.*, pp. 281–285 (*Federalist* #48).

64. See *Federalist* #47 etc. on Montesquieu.

65. Cf. our Vol. V, Bk. II, on Montesquieu.

66. Madison, *Writings*, pp. 266–268, 270, 272 (*Federalist* #46): ". . . I proceed to enquire whether the federal government or the state governments will have the advantage with regard to the predilection and support of the people. . . . The adversaries of the constitution seem to have lost sight of the people altogether in their reasonings on this subject. . . . They must be told that the ultimate authority, wherever the derivative may be found, resides in the people alone; and that it will not depend merely on the comparative ambition or address of the different governments, whether either, or which of them, will be able to enlarge its sphere of jurisdiction at the expence of the other. . . .

"It has been already proved, that the members of the federal [government] will be more dependent on the members of the state governments, than the latter will be on the former. It has appeared also, that the prepossessions of the people on whom both will depend, will be more on the side of the state governments, than of the federal government. . . . [T]he members of the state legislatures will be unlikely to attach themselves sufficiently to national objects, the members of the federal legislature will be likely to attach themselves too much to local objects. . . . What is the spirit that has in general characterized the proceedings of [C]ongress? . . . [T]he members have but too frequently displayed the character, rather of partizans of their respective states, than of impartial guardians of a common interest; . . . [and] the great interests of the nation have suffered. . . .

"But ambitious encroachments of the federal government, on the authority of the state governments, would not excite the opposition of a single state or of a few states only. They would be signals of general alarm. Every government would espouse the common cause. . . . But what degree of madness could ever drive the federal government to such an extremity? In the contest with Great Britain, one part of the empire was employed against the other. The more numerous part invaded the rights of the less numerous part. . . .

"The only refuge left for those who prophecy the downfall of the state governments, is the visionary supposition that the federal governmnt may previously accumulate a military force for the projects of ambition. . . .

"On summing up . . .[,] the powers proposed to be lodged in the federal government, are as little formidable to those reserved to the individual states, as they are indispensably necessary to accomplish the purposes of the union; and that all those alarms which have been sounded, of a meditated and consequential annihilation of the state governments, must, on the most favorable interpretation, be ascribed to the chimerical fears of the authors of them."

67. Madison, "Report of the Committee . . . Relative to the Resolutions of the Last General Assembly of this State [Virginia], Concerning the Alien and Sedition Laws," in *Mind of the Founder*, pp. 231–273. Also Madison, *Writings*, pp. 609–662.

68. Madison, Virginia "Report," *Mind of the Founder*, pp. 254–255 (on the third resolution in the Virginia Resolutions): "The Constitution of the United States was formed by the sanction of the states, given by each in its sovereign capacity. . . . The states, then, being the parties to the constitutional compact, and in their sovereign capacity, it follows

of necessity that there can be no tribunal, above their authority, to decide, in the last resort, whether the compact made by them be violated. . . . But in the case of an intimate and constitutional union, like that of the United States, it is evident that the interposition of the parties, in their sovereign capacity, can be called for by occasions only deeply and essentially affecting the vital principles of their political system.

"The resolution has, accordingly, guarded against any misapprehension of its object, by expressly requiring, for such an interposition, 'the case of a deliberate, palpable, and dangerous breach of the Constitution, by the exercise of powers not granted by it'."

69. *Ibid.*, pp. 238, 242–243 (on the fourth resolution): "The General Assembly . . . declared their opinion . . . that forced constructions for enlarging the federal powers have taken place. . . . The Alien and Sedition Acts . . . are of course to be understood as included in the allusion. . . .

"That the obvious tendency, and inevitable result, of a consolidation of the states into one sovereignty, would be to transform the republican system of the United States into a monarchy, is a point which seems to have been sufficiently decided by the general sentiment of America. . . .

"One consequence must be, to enlarge the sphere of discretion allotted to the executive magistrate. Even within the legislative limits properly defined by the Constitution, the difficulty of accommodating legal regulations to a country so great in extent . . . had been much felt, and has led to occasional investments of power in the executive. . . . And it is in this latitude, as a supplement to the deficiency of the laws, that the degree of executive prerogative materially consists. . . .

"This disproportionate increase of prerogative and patronage must [or could] evidently [lead to] . . . the transformation of the republican system of the United States into a monarchy, anticipated by the General Assembly from a consolidation of the states into one sovereignty . . . ; and whether it would be into a mixed or an absolute monarchy, might depend on too many contingencies to admit of any certain foresight."

70. *Ibid.*, pp. 243–244 (on the fifth resolution): "The subject of this resolution having, it is presumed, more particularly led the General Assembly into the proceedings which they communicated to the other states, and being in itself of peculiar importance, it deserves the most critical and faithful investigation; for the length of which no apology will be necessary.

"Of the 'Alien Act,' it is affirmed by the resolution—1. That it exercises a power nowhere delegated to the federal government; 2. That it unites legislative and judicial powers to those of the executive; 3. That this union of powers subverts the general principles of free government; 4. That it subverts the particular organization and positive provisions of the Federal Constitution. . . .

"The *second* object, against which the resolution protests, is the Sedition Act. . . .

"1. That it exercises a power not delegated by the Constitution."

71. *Ibid.*, pp. 245–246 (on the fifth resolution).

72. *Ibid.*, p. 246 (continuation of passage in preceding note, on the fifth resolution): "There was a time, indeed, when an exception to the legislative separation of the several component and coequal parts of the empire obtained a degree of acquiescence. The British Parliament was allowed to regulate the trade with foreign nations, and between the different parts of the empire. This was, however, mere practice without right, and contrary to the true theory of the Constitution. The convenience of some regulations, in both cases, was apparent, and, as there was no legislature with power over the whole, nor any constitutional preëminence among the legislatures of the several parts, it was natural for the legislature of that particular part which was the eldest and the largest, to assume this function, and for the others to acquiesce in it. This tacit arrangement was the less criticised, as the regulations established by the British Parliament operated in favor of that

part of the empire which seemed to bear the principl share of the public burdens, and were regarded as an indemnification of its advances for the other parts. As long as this regulating power was confined to the two objects of conveniency and equity, it was not complained of, nor much inquired into. But no sooner was it perverted to the selfish views of the party assuming it, than the injured parties began to feel and to reflect; and the moment the claim to a direct and indefinite power was ingrafted on the precedent of the regulating power, the whole charm was dissolved, and every eye opened to the usurpation."

73. *Ibid.*, p. 246 (continuation of passage in preceding note, on the fifth resolution).

74. *Ibid.*, pp. 247, 251 (on the fifth resolution): "The Articles of Confederation are the next source of information on this subject.

"In the interval between the commencement of the revolution and the final ratification of these Articles, the nature and extent of the Union was determined by the circumstances of the crisis, rather than by any accurate delineation of the general authority. . . . This instrument does not contain . . . the idea that the parties to it were, with respect to the objects of the common law, to form one community. No such law is named, or implied, or alluded to, as being in force, or as brought into force by that compact . . ., whilst, on the other hand, every such inference or pretext is absolutely precluded by art. 2, which declares 'that each state retains its sovereignty, freedom, and independence, and every power, jurisdiction, and right, which is not by this Confederation expressly delegated to the United States in Congress assembled'. . . .

"If it be understood that the common law is established by the Constitution, it follows that no part of the law can be altered by the legislature. Such of the statutes already passed as may be repugnant thereto, would be nullified; particularly the Sedition Act itself, which boasts of being a melioration of the common law; and the whole code, with all its incongruities, barbarisms, and bloody maxims, would be inviolably saddled on the good people of the United States.

"Should this consequence be rejected, and the common law be held, like other laws, liable to revision and alteration by the authority of Congress, it then follows that the authority of Congress is coextensive with the objects of common law; that is to say, with every object of legislation. . . . The authority of Congress would, therefore, be no longer under the limitations marked out in the Constitution. They would be authorized to legislate in all cases whatsoever.

"In the next place, as the President possesses the executive powers of the Constitution, and is to see that the laws be faithfully executed, his authority also must be coextensive with every branch of the common law. The additions which this would make to his power . . . claim the most serious attention."

75. *Ibid.*, pp. 252–253, 256 (on the fifth resolution): "From the review thus taken . . . the common law never was, nor . . . ever can be, deemed a law for the American people as one community . . .—a law . . . overspreading the entire field of legislation, and . . . sap[ping] the foundation of the Constitution. . . .

"2. The next point which the resolution requires to be proved is, that the power over the press, exercised by the Sedition Act, is positively forbidden by . . . the [first] amendments to the Constitution. . . .

"In the attempts to vindicate the Sedition Act, it has been contended, 1. That the 'freedom of the press' is to be determined by the meaning of these terms in the common law; 2. That the article supposes the power over the press to be in Congress. . . .

"It is deemed to be a sound opinion that the Sedition Act . . . is an abridgment of . . . principles of the common law in England."

76. *Ibid.*, pp. 256–257 (on the fifth resolution).

77. Madison, "Notes on Nullification," in *Mind of the Founder* (pp. 417 ff.), p. 418. (Also in *Writings of Madison*, Vol. IX, pp. 573 ff.)

78. *Ibid.*, p. 436: "Because an unconstitutional law is no law, it is alledged that it may be constitutionlly disobeyed by all who think it unconstitutional. The fallacy is so obvious. . . . It makes no distinction . . . between the case of a law *confessedly* unconstitutionl, and a case turning on a *doubt* & a *divided opinion* as to the meaning of the Constitution. . . . And can it be seriously & deliberately maintained, that every individual or every subordinate authority or every party to a compact, has a right to take for granted, that its construction is the infallible one, and to act upon it against the construction of all others, having an equal right to expound the instrument. . . ."

79. *Ibid.*, pp. 436–437.

80. *Ibid.*, pp. 437–442: "That a sovereignty should have even been denied to the States in their united character, may well excite wonder, when it is recollected that the Constitution which now unites them, was announced by the convention which formed it, as dividing sovereignty between the Union & the States; . . . that it was presented under that view . . . to the ratifying authorities . . . ; that it . . . has been the doctrine & language, until a very late date, even by those who now take . . . the novel notion of nullification. . . . Other champions of the Rights of the States among them Mr. Jefferson might be appealed to, as bearing testimony to the sovereignty of the U.S. . . .

"Now all must agree that the compact in the case of the U.S. was duly formed . . . by the people of the several States in their highest sovereign authority; . . . whereas a system founded by the people, as one community, would, on its dissolution, throw the people into a state of nature.

"In conclusion, those who deny the possibility of a political system, with a divided sovereignty like that of the U.S. must chuse between a government purely consolidated, & an association of Governments purely federal. All republics of the former character, ancient or modern, have been found ineffectual for order and justice within, and for security without. They have been either a prey to internal convulsions or to foreign invasions. In like manner, all confederacies, ancient or modern, have been either dissolved by the inadequacy of their cohesion, or, as in the modern examples, continue to be monuments of the frailties of such forms. . . . It becomes . . . a system partly federal and partly consolidated. . . . The final appeal . . . must be to the authority of the whole, not to that of the parts separately and independently. . . . It was this view . . . which [at the Convention] dictated the clause declaring that the Constitution & laws of the U.S. should be the supreme law of the Land, anything in the Constitution or laws of any of the States to the contrary notwithstanding."

Madison's ideas on divided sovereignty were expressed succinctly in a letter to N. P. Trist on February 15, 1830. As events were leading up to the crucial year 1832 on the Nullification Crisis, Madison was arguing against the claim by some, particularly in South Carolina, that the individual states held full sovereignty, which could not be divided or shared with the federal government. In remarking on the fluid and coordinated lines between the legislative, executive, and judicial branches, Madison was not only suggesting that they were not rigidly separated, but was also revealing just how open the system was for the pervading medium of legislation through which all three branches operated at the federal and state levels. The following is in *The Complete Madison: His Basic Writings* (edited by Saul K. Padover, New York, 1953), p. 195: "Other Governments present an individual and indivisible sovereignty. The Constitution of the United States divides the sovereignty; the portions surrendered by the States composing the Federal sovereignty over specified subjects; the portions retained forming the sovereignty of each over the residuary subjects within its sphere. If sovereignty cannot thus be divided, the political system of the United States is a chimera, mocking the vain pretensions of human wisdom. If it can be so divided, the system ought to have a fair opportunity of fulfilling the wishes and expectations which cling to the experiment.

"Nothing can be more clear than that the Constitution of the United States has created a Government, in as strict a sense of the term as the governments of the States created by their respective constitutions. The Federal Government has, like the State governments, its Legislative, its Executive, and its Judiciary departments. . . . If in some cases the jurisdiction is concurrent as it is in others exclusive, this is one of the features constituting the peculiarity of the system."

In more general contexts, there are some interesting texts on laws, legislation, and legislative power in *James Madison's "Advice to My Country"* (edited by David B. Mattern, Charlottesville, 1997), pp. 61 ff. (cf. on other subjects of interest as well, e.g., federalism and the Union).

81. Above, Ch. III, sect. 5.

82. *Republic of Letters*, Vol. I, pp. 478–479 (Madison to Jefferson, June 6, 1787).

83. Above, Ch. III, sect. 2.

84. *Republic of Letters*, Vol. I, pp. 496–498 (Madison to Jefferson, Oct. 24, Nov. 1, 1787).

85. *Ibid.*, Vol. I, p. 480 (Jefferson to Madison, June 20, 1787).

86. *Ibid.*, Vol. I, pp. 512, 514 (Jefferson to Madison, Dec. 20, 1787).

87. *Ibid.*, Vol. III, p. 1924 (Madison to Jefferson, Feb. 8, 1825).

88. Madison, "Report of Books for Congress," *Papers*, Vol. 6, pp. 62 ff. "Editorial Note" passage is on p. 663.

89. *Ibid.*, p. 85 (editorial comment, citing *Papers* I, pp. 16, 27 n. 47, 35; IV, pp. 126, 127 n. 4).

90. *Ibid.*, p. 64 (Ed. Note).

91. Of the few surviving books once owned by James Madison that are now in the Library of Congress, the only item of (remote) relevance here is his copy of Thomas More's *Utopia*, bearing the extended title *The Common-wealth of Utopia, . . . the best state of a publick weal* (reprinted Phila., 1753) and with Madison's autograph. A different edition, that of Glasgow 1762, is cited by the editors of Madison's "List of Books for Congress," *Papers*, Vol. 6, p. 85, as a plausible recent edn. for Madison in his entry for "More's Utopia." Of the approximate 250 surviving items in the Madison Pamphlet Collection, none are of present interest.

Of the numerous surviving books and pamphlets once owned by Madison that are now at the University of Virginia in Charlottesville, none are directly relevant here. Of indirect interest are two items by Jeremy Bentham (author of *Morals and Legislation* and alluded to above on "sanction" in our text prior to n. 23) relating to taxation (1795) and codification (1817), as well as John Cartwright's *The English Constitution* (1823), this being the author's autographed presentation copy for Madison. There are a number of religious items by John Wesley and others, a copy of Shakespeare's *Hamlet*, and materials by such American figures as Daniel Webster, Martin Van Buren, and John Quincy Adams.

Also at the University of Virginia is Madison's c. Aug. 1790 handwritten list (a copy kindly sent by David Mattern), with covering letter, of books sent to him by Jefferson from Paris. A printed version of this list is in Madison's *Papers*, Vol. 13, pp. 286–289. Although little additional information can be gleaned from this "Memorandum of Books" for present purposes, some of the items are of indirect general note here. These include some ancient works by Cicero, Livy, Horace, and Pliny, along with some modern works by Gibbon, Hume, Neckar, De Thou, Bacon, Mably ("principes Legislation"), and Adams (*Defence*, Vols. 1, 3). A number of multi-volume works are included, particularly encyclopedias and dictionaries. Of contextual consideration in regard to encyclopedias of this period is Robert Darnton, *The Business of Enlightenment: A Publishing History of the Encyclopédie*, 1775–1800 (Cambridge, Mass., 1979).

Other areas for inquiry include the libraries of the College of New Jersey (later Princeton University), where Madison was an undergraduate, and of its then president, Rev. John Witherspoon, under whom Madison studied law and Hebrew for a while after graduating in 1771. Neither library, so far as is now known, had a copy of Bodin's *Republic*. *The Catalogue of Books in The Library of The College of New-Jersey*, January 29, 1760 (Woodbridge, 1760) includes no entries for Bodin, Machiavelli, Justinian (*Corpus Iuris Civilis*), or More, for instance. Aside from religious, historical, and scientific books, there are a number of entries for classical writers—such as Aristotle, Cicero, Cato, Dionysius of Halicar., Homer, Oppian, Pliny, Plutarch, Thucydides, Tacitus, and Xenophon. There are several entries for Locke, but none for Hobbes. Puffendorf was also included. Calvin is included, but not Luther, perhaps reflecting a certain religious bias at the College. The included histories of various countries may have had an early influence on the young Madison that led on later to his writings before and after the Constitutional Convention on confederations ancient and modern. As for Witherspoon's collection of books now at Princeton Univ., there is currently (and surprisingly) no full listing to be consulted, although individual items can be looked up under "WIT." The University also has some student notes from the 1780s on history lectures by Witherspoon. Some of the religious works surviving in books and pamphlets owned by Madison may reflect early influences on him by Witherspoon, a clergyman from Presbyterian Scotland. On Madison's connections with Witherspoon at Princeton and his course of instruction there, steeped in traditional classical-humanistic studies, there is, in general, Ketcham, *Madison*, Ch. III ("The College of New Jersey at Princeton").

A further investigation of the Madison-Witherspoon connections might yield further clues to bibliographic influences on Madison. Madison most likely consulted Witherspoon in Philadelphia when preparing to draw up his late-Jan. 1783 list of books for Congress (proposed in June and Nov. 1782). According to the Editorial Note in Madison's *Papers* 6 cited immediately above: "JM was appointed [by Congress] chairman [of the committee to prepare the book list], with his old mentor John Witherspoon . . . and John Lowell . . . as his colleagues. . . . JM alone seems to have prepared the report, although he may have consulted Witherspoon before the learned clergyman returned to . . . Princeton." It might also be useful to consult *The Works of the Rev. John Witherspoon*, 4 vols. (Phila., 1802). A comparison of books at the Princeton University Library from the collections of John Witherspoon and Jonathan Edwards (college president there in 1758, prior to Witherspoon in 1768–) shows a much larger range and number for Witherspoon than the narrower theological band of books in Edwards' case. Witherspoon brought the large sum of 300–500 books with him from Scotland to Princeton, which displayed his broad interest in 18th-century progressive thinkers as well as the ideas of Locke. Five of the nine Princeton graduates who were among the fifty-five delegates to the Constitutionl Convention had studied under Witherspoon. On his way in 1774 to the First Continental Congress in Philadelphia, John Adams visited with Witherspoon in Princeton and hailed him as a great "Son of Liberty." Witherspoon (1723—1794) was a signer of the Declaration of Independence and a leading member of the Continental Congress from 1776 through 1782. He was a member of the ratifying convention that brought to New Jersey the honor of being the third state to ratify the new U.S. Constitution. Cf. Alexander Leitch (ed.), *A Princeton Companion* (Princeton, 1978), pp. 523–527, and *Princeton University Library Classed List*, Vol. 6 (Princeton, 1920), "Edwards Collection," pp. 3407–3408.

An interesting window into Madison's bookish interests is provided by a study of his wide-ranging list of religious books for the University of Virginia Library, including a covering letter of 1824 to Jefferson, who as rector of the University had asked Madison to prepare such a proposal (in *Writings of Madison*, Vol. IX, pp. 202–207, original in Lib. of

Cong.). Some succinct comments are found in Irving Brant's Intro. to his facsimile reprod. of Madison's list in his booklet *The Books of James Madison* (Charlottesville, 1965): "Of the first four Presidents . . . , three were [bookish]. . . eggheads. . . . Nobody knows how many thousand volumes he [Madison] owned, or what they were, except as casually mentioned by him in his papers. He bequeathed them to the University of Virginia, . . . but the library remained for several years in the custody of John Payne Todd, Dolley Madison's profligate son. It is suspected that Todd disposed of them as he did thousands of manuscripts that had been sold to Congress but also were left in his custody—sold them to . . . pay enough gambling debts and liquor bills to stay out of debtor's prison. . . . [B]y the time the University lawyers gained access to the Montpelier library, 587 pamphlets became the achieved total of the great bequest . . . now [at] . . . the University . . ."

Among Brant's interesting comments on Madison's reading habits are the following: "The earliest known record of Madison's reading apart from Latin classics and other school books is found in excerpts made by him from *Memoirs of the Cardinal De Retz*—excerpts of close to five thousand words in the form of aphorisms and pungent commentaries of men and affairs at the court of Louis XIV . . . dated 1759 [when] . . . Madison was eight years old" [though perhaps done at home later, prior to entering Princeton]. Although as Brant says the excerpts often relate to ways for getting around obstacles, these historical materials may presage not only Madison's deep historical interests, as later reflected in his pre-Convention studies of ancient and modern confederacies, but also his proclivities before, during, and after the Convention toward a strong central and consolidated federal government, albeit one guided by republican principles.

Brant also refers to Madison's 1783 list of books for the Confederation Congress at Philadelphia, which amounted to a proposal for a Library of Congress at a time when Congress was obtaining its book learning from the Library Company of Philadelphia. Madison's list, "proper for the use of Congress" as he put it, was so extensive as to include many works that could then have been deemed either too subversive (free-thinking, monarchical, or pro-British, etc.) or too expensive for the new Confederation Congress. Not until it acquired Jefferson's collection much later did Congress have an adequate collection of its own. For Brant, Madison's later list of theological books illustrates how far his interests in books ranged beyond mere public affairs. Brant doubts that Madison had a presidential library at the White House.

Of wide scope is Robert A. Rutland's *"Well Acquainted with Books": The Founding Fathers of 1787* (Wash., D.C., 1987), consisting of Rutland's article under that heading and a re-issue of the 1969 Editorial Note and edition in Madison's *Papers* 6 (cited immediately above), here entitled "James Madison's List of Books, 1783" and credited to Robert L. Scribner. According to Rutland's well-developed overview of the subject indicated in his title: "In all, thirty-four of the delegates finally seated at the Federal Convention were lawyers. . . . [A]lmost two-thirds . . . [knew] Blackstone's *Commentaries on the Laws of England* [replete with Bodinian viewpoints on legislative sovereignty, as we have previously seen]. . . . Books and a knowledge of historical characters were the mainstay of the American public man in 1787. . . . [M]ost of the delegates . . . were scholars of one sort or another. . . . [O]ne reason Philadelphia was an attraction to the delegates was the libraries. . . . [T]he convention delegates were far ahead of most of their fellow men in terms of education. . . . [Their] familiar reading background . . . was basically classical. . . . Madison's notes show speaker after speaker alluding to Blackstone, Hume, Locke, or Montesquieu[, as well as] . . . Harrington and . . . Sydney [etc., all with Bodinian viewpoints on legislative sovereignty]. . . . Drawing upon all history, their efforts to create a self-governing nation mixed compromise and expediency." Among the many books surely owned by Madison at that point, the editor believes, was Plutarch's *Lives*. In a related way, the second useful essay here (from *Papers* 6) on Madison's 1783 catalogue begins with a preface that states: "Madison's comprehensive list of books for the intellectual interests of a legislative library [!] is an outstanding example of his belief, shared by Jefferson and other founders, ... that if men possessed enough knowledge they would be able to solve the problems faced by the new nation."

As noted by William Lee Miller, *The Business of May Next: James Madison and the Founding* (Charlottesville, 1992), Ch. 1 ("A Child of the Revolution Reads Some Books"), p. 7, "Madison ... liked books and study all his life."

Among the earliest suggestions of Madison's interests in books, we may add, are his "Commonplace Book" (1759–1772), "Notes on a Brief System of Logick" (1766–1772), and "Notes on Commentary on the Bible" (1770–1773) in *Papers* I, pp. 4 ff., 32 ff., 51 ff. On "Commonplace Book" cf. "Editorial Note" concerning Montaigne, Montesquieu, Locke, De Retz, Du Bos, De Thou, Virgil, Horace, Justinian, Tacitus, Thucydides, and others. Of particular note are the "Abstracts from the Memoirs of the Cardinal de Retz" (1614–1679, in the periods of Cardinal Richelieu and King Louis XIV). On "System of Logick," cf. editorial comments on those to whom Madison was indebted, directly or indirectly, and on "the traditional nature of the notes, ... [in which] Hobbes ... and Locke are briefly mentioned. ... In the main, the author hews closely to a line of logic which extends back from Isaac Watts' popular textbook through the works of Peter Ramus
[!] and the scholastics, to those of Aristotle and Plato [p. 35]."

More broadly, the full body of published and unpublished writings by Madison could be searched for relevant references to books with which he was familiar. For example, a revealing reference by Madison to books readily available in Philadelphia appears in *Papers* I, p. 126, and is quoted in *"Well Acquainted ..."* by Rutland: "The first Continental Congress met 'in the Carpenter's Hall in one room of which the City library is kept & of which the Librarian tells me the Gentlemen make great & constant use,' Madison was told in 1774. 'Vartel, Burlamaqui, Locke & Montesquie[u] seem to be the standards to whom they refer.' By 1787 the situation had changed but little. The Free Library Company and American Philosophical Society collections were a stone's throw from the delegates' desks so that nowhere else in America was there such easy access to the collected knowledge of western civilization."

The wealth of materials used by Madison in his "Notes on Ancient and Modern Confederacies" (April-June? 1786) shows much about his reading. As the Editorial Note to it in *Papers* 9, on p. 3, states: "During the mid-1780s JM's political exertions to revise the Articles of Confederation were paralleled by his scholarly research in his Montpelier library. As early as 1784 JM had set about obtaining every treatise available on past and present confederacies. ... Jefferson ... served as his agent in Europe ... to purchase the relevant works, and by January 1786 he [JM] had received two trunks of books from abroad. ... JM began systematic perusal of his 'literary cargo' [cf. four letters to TJ in 1784–1786] ..." Works cited in his "Notes on ... Confederacies" include Felice's *Code*, Temple's *Observations*, and Pawckoucke's *Encyclopedia*. His "Notes" is also in *Writings of Madison*, Vol. I.

As for the presence of books in Madison's Montpelier home, the following excerpt from Ketcham's *Madison*, p. 614, is based on Mary Cutts' (Dolley's niece's) "Memoir of Montpelier" ("c. 1854"): "[In] Madison's library ... four thousand volumes were shelved around the sides of the room and on stacks filling the center, while books and pamphlets—some gathered by Madison, and others sent unsolicited to him in a steady stream—were heaped high on every available chair and table." The actual viewing here described of Madison's books at Montpelier occurred long before the c. 1854 date of the memoir eighteen years after Madison's death. Long before then, Madison's profligate stepson, John Payne Todd, had sold off most off his debts, which Madison himself had paid off at times without telling Dolley. The University of Virginia eventually had to sue to obtain the remnants of Madison's book bequest, by then consisting mostly of pamphlets. Dolley Madison sold the estate in the early 1840s. The c. 1854 description clearly refers to Madison's books at Montpelier in c. 1817 when he returned from Washington and the presidency. On Todd cf. Ketcham's book as well as Brant's *Madison*, Vol. VI, pp. 396—397, 523–525, etc. One might hope, perhaps in vain, that a list of books in Madison's own library could someday be found or reconstructed. I am informed that at Montpelier is a four-volume set of Horace's writings once owned by Dolley Madison. More generally, there is Robert A. Rutland's "Madison's Bookish Habits," in *Quarterly Journal of the Library of Congress*, 37 (1980), pp. 176–191.

Madison's will (*Writings of Madison*, Vol. IX, pp. 548–552) stipulated: "I give to the University of Virginia all that portion of my Library, reserving to my wife the right first to select such particular books & pamphlets as she shall choose, not exceeding three hundred volumes."

I am most grateful to a number of helpful and expert specialists for information of varying kinds on Madison's "library" and related contextual matters discussed in the present section. They include two Madison historians, Jack N. Rakove and James Morton Smith; a senior editor of the Madison *Papers* at the University of Virginia, David B. Mattern; a Special Collections librarian at the same University, Gayl Cooper; three senior librarians at Princeton University, Stephen Ferguson (head of Rare Books), Meg Rich (also Rare Books), and Carol W. Murphy (reference); and the curator at Madison's Montpelier home, Lee Langston-Harrison.

Notes to Chapter V
Hamilton in Legislative Profile

1. Joseph J. Ellis, *Founding Brothers: The Revolutionary Generation* (New York, 2000), with discussions of Hamilton in relation to the other leading founders.

Other secondary accounts on Hamilton include the following: Brooks Mitchell, *Alexander Hamilton* (2 vols., New York, 1957, 1962), still a good general survey, with Vol. I taking the story to the New York Ratifying Convention in 1788 and Vol. II from then to his years of national service and tragic ending; Morton J. Frisch, *Alexander Hamilton and the Political Order: An Interpretation of His Political Thought and Practice* (Lanham, 1991), e.g. Ch. VII ("The Political Thought of Hamilton's Statesmanship") and Ch. VIII ("The Peculiar Distinctiveness of the American Constitution," with discussion of how "Hamilton's view of free constitutions can relate to the Montesquieuan perspective"); Clinton Rossiter, *Alexander Hamilton and the Constitution* (New York, 1964), with Chs. 4–5 on "Hamilton's Political Science" and Ch. 6 on "Hamilton's Constitutional Law and Theory"; Alex Bein, *Die Staatsidee Aexander Hamiltons in ihrer Entstehung und Entwicklung* (Munich, 1927), with concluding discussions on "Hamilton und Hume" and "Hamilton und Machiavelli"; and Richard Loss, *The Modern Theory of Presidential Power: Alexander Hamilton and the Corwin Thesis* (New York, 1990), useful for understanding Hamilton's relevance for the rise of the modern presidency to far greater powers than were envisioned by other founders.

Also useful are such selections of Hamilton's writings as found in *Alexander Hamilton and the Founding of the Nation* (edited by Richard B. Morris, New York, 1957), e.g. Ch. 3 on "Building a New Nation," and Ch. 7 on "The Principles of Constitutional Government."

The public press has at times had some suggestive pieces on Hamilton, showing his relevance today, such as "Clinton Uses Founding Father's Travails to Build Case" ("Hamilton is drawn into the debate on impeachment"), in *New York Times*, Oct. 4, 1998, sect. 1, p. 33; "Restore Hamilton to His Pedestal" ("A Founding Father who backed business and government"), in *ibid.*, July 3, 1998, p. A21; and, more humorously, "Alexander Hamilton's Original Sin" ("Sex and Politics are not strangers in America. . . .", in *George* magazine, Spring, 1998.

References below are to Alexander Hamilton, *Writings* (New York, 2001) and to *The Papers of Alexander Hamilton* (Vols. I–XXVII, New York, 1961–1987, edited by Harold C. Syrett, et al. and with an additional supplemental vol. now added.additional supplemental vol. now added)—all *sic* in quotations below.

2. Hamilton, *Federalist* #15 in his *Writings*, pp. 222–223.We alluded above, prior to n. 23, Ch. IV, to Madison's apparent positions a la Bentham, who is represented in two items in Madison's library, as cited near outset of n. 91, Ch. IV. Above, p. 73, Ch. II, we cited Adams on Hobbes.

3. *Ibid.* (passage continues), pp. 224–225): "In addition to all this, there is in the nature of sovereign power an impatience of controul, that disposes those who are invested with the exercise of it, to look with an evil eye upon all external attempts to restrain or direct its operations. From this spirit it happens that in every political association which is formed upon the principle of uniting in a common interest a number of lesser sovereignties, there will be found a kind of excentric tendency in the subordinate or inferior orbs, by the operation of which there will be a perpetual effort in each to fly off from the common center. This tendency . . . has its origin in the love of power. . . . This simple proposition will teach us how little reason there is to expect, that the persons, entrusted with the administration of the affairs of the particular members of a confederacy, will . . . be ready, with . . . regard to the public weal, to execute the resolutions or decrees of the general authority. The reverse of this results from the constitution of human nature. . . .

"In our case, the concurrence of thirteen distinct sovereign wills is requisite under the confederation to the complete execution of every important measure, that proceeds from the Union. It has happened as was to have been foreseen. The measures of the Union have not been executed; and the delinquencies of the States have step by step matured themselves to an extreme; which has at length arrested all the wheels of the national government, and brought them to an awful stand. Congress at this time scarcely possess[es] the means of keeping up the forms of administration . . . [in] the present shadow of a federal government. . . . [T]he frail and tottering edifice seems ready to fall upon our heads and to crush us beneath its ruins."

4. *Federalist* #6 in *Writings*, pp. 226–229. Passage continues on pp. 229–230: "[I]f it be possible at any rate to construct a Federal Government capable of regulating the common concerns and preserving the general tranquility, it must be founded . . . upon the reverse of the principle contended for by the opponents of the proposed constitution. It must carry its agency to the persons of the citizens. It must stand in need of no intermediate legislations; but must itself be empowered to employ the arm of the ordinary magistrate to execute its own resolutions. The majesty of the national authority must be manifested through the medium of the Courts of Justice. The government of the Union, like that of each State, must be able to address itself immediately to . . . individuals. . . . It must in short, possess all the means and . . . all the methods of executing the powers . . . that are possessed and exercised by the governments of the particular States. . . . If the interposition of the State-Legislatures be necessary to give effect to a measure of the Union, they have only NOT TO ACT or TO ACT EVASIVELY, and the measure is defeated. . . .

"But if the execution of the laws of the national government, should not require the intervention of the State Legislatures; if they were to pass into immediate operation upon the citizens themselves, the particular governments could not interrupt their progress without an open and violent exertion of an unconstitutionl power."

5. *Federalist* #21 in *Writings*, p. 237.

6. *Ibid.*, pp. 238–239: "The want of a mutual guarantee of the State governments is another capital imperfection in the federal plan. There is nothing of this kind declared in the articles that compose it. . . . The want of a guarantee, though it might in its consequences endanger the Union, does not so immediately attack its existence as the want of a constitutional sanction to its laws.

"Without a guarantee, the assistance to be derived from the Union in repelling those domestic dangers, which may sometimes threaten the existence of the State constitutions, must be renounced. . . . The tempestuous situation, from which Massachusetts has scarcely emerged, evinces that dangers of this kind are not merely speculative. Who can determine what might have been the issue of her late convulsions, if the mal-contents had been headed by a Caesar or by a Cromwell? Who can predict what effect a despostism established in Massachusetts, would have upon the liberties of New-Hampshire or Rhode-Island; of Connecticut or New-York?

"The inordinate pride of State importance has suggested to some minds an objection to the principle of a guarantee in the federal Government; as involving an officious interference in the domestic concerns of the members. . . . A guarantee by the national authority would be as much levelled against the usurpations of rulers, as against the ferments and outrages of faction and sedition in the community."

7. *Federalist* #22 in *Writings*, p. 250.

8. *Ibid.*, pp. 251–252: "The organization of Congress, is itself utterly improper for the exercise of those powers which are necessary to be deposited in the Union. A single Assembly may be a proper receptacle of those slender, or rather fettered authorities, which have been heretofore delegated to the federal head; but it would be inconsistent with all the principles of good government, to intrust it with those additional powers which even the moderate and more rational adversaries of the proposed constitution admit ought to reside in the United States. If that plan should not be adopted; and if the necessity of union should be able to withstand the ambitious aims of those men, . . . we shall finally accumulate in a single body, all the most important prerogatives of sovereignty; and thus entail upon our posterity, one of the most execrable forms of government that human infatuation ever contrived. Thus we should create in reality that very tyranny, which the adversaries of the new constitution either are, or affect to be solicitous to avert.

"It has not a little contributed to the infirmities of the existing federal system, that it never had a ratification by the PEOPLE. Resting on no better foundation than the consent of the several Legislatures; it has been exposed to frequent and intricate questions concerning the validity of its powers; and has in some instances given birth to the enormous doctrine of a right of legislative repeal. Owing its ratification to the law of a State, it has been contended, that the same authority might repeal the law by which it was ratified. However gross a heresy it may be, to maintain that *a party* to *a compact* has a right to revoke that *compact*, the doctrine itself has had respectable advocates. The possibility of a question of this nature, proves the necessity of laying the foundations of our national government deeper than in the mere sanction of delegated authority. The fabric of American Empire ought to rest on the solid basis of THE CONSENT OF THE PEOPLE. The streams of national power ought to flow immediately from that pure original fountain of all legitimate authority."

9. *Federalist* #23 in *Writings*, pp. 253–254: "The principal purposes to be answered by Union are these—The common defence of the members—the preservation of the public peace as well against internal convulsions as external attacks—the regulation of commerce with other nations and between the States—the superintendence of our intercourse, political and commercial, with foreign countries. . . . This power ought to be co-extensive with all the possible combinations of such circumstances; and ought to be under the direction of the same councils, which are appointed to preside over the common defence.

"This is one of those truths, which ... carries its own evidence. ... It rests upon axioms as simple as they are universal. The *means* ought to be proportioned to the *end*; the persons, from whose agency the attainment of any *end* is expected, ought to possess the *means* by which it is to be attained."

10. *Federalist* #26, in *Writings*, p. 269: "The idea of restraining the Legislative authority, in the means of providing for the national defence, is one of those refinements, which owe their origin to a zeal for liberty more ardent than enlightened. We have seen however that it has not had thus far an extensive prevalency."

11. *Federalist* #28 in *Writings*, pp. 280–281.

12. *Federalist* #30 in *Writings*, p. 291.

13. *Federalist* #31 in *Writings*, pp. 298–299.

14. *Federalist* #33 in *Writings*, p. 305.

15. *Ibid.*, pp. 305—306. Passage continues, p. 306: "This simple train of enquiry furnishes us at once with a test by which to judge of the true nature of the clause complained of. It conducts us to this palpable truth, that a power to lay and collect taxes must be a power to pass all laws *necessary* and *proper* for the execution of that power; and what does the unfortunate and calumniated provision in question do more than declare the same truth; to wit, that the national legislature to whom the power of laying and collecting taxes had been previously given, might in the execution of that power pass all laws *necessary* and *proper* to carry it into effect? I have applied these observations thus particularly to the power of taxation, because it is the immediate subject under consideration, and because it is the most important of the authorities proposed to be conferred upon the Union. But the same process will lead to the same result in relation to all other powers declared in the constitution. And it is *expressly* to execute these powers, that the sweeping clause, as it has been affectedly called, authorises the national legislature to pass all *necessary* and *proper* laws. If there is any thing exceptionable, it must be sought for in the specific powers, upon which this general declaration is predicated. The declaration itself ... is at least perfectly harmless."

16. *Federalist* #34 in *Writings*, pp. 310, 315: "It is well known, that in the Roman Republic, the Legislative authority in the last resort, resided for ages in two different political bodies; not as branches of the same Legislature, but as distinct and independent Legislatures, in each of which an opposite interest prevailed; in one, the Patrician—in the other, the Plebeian. Many arguments might have been adduced to prove the unfitness of two such seemingly contradictory authorities, each having power to *annul* or *repeal* the acts of the other. But a man would have been regarded as frantic, who should have attempted at Rome, to disprove their existence. ...

"The preceding train of observations will justify the position which has been elsewhere laid down, that 'A CONCURRENT JURISDICTION in the artticle of taxation, was the only admissible substitute for an entire subordination, in respect to this branch of power, of the State authority to that of the Union.'"

17. *Federalist* #33 in *Writings*, pp. 307–308. Passage continues on pp. 308–309: "But it will not follow from this doctrine that acts of the larger society which are *not pursuant* to its constitutionl powers but which are invasions of the residuary authorities of the smaller societies will become the supreme law of the land. These will be merely acts of usurpation and will deserve to be treated as such. Hence we perceive that the clause which declares the supremacy of the laws of the Union, like the one we have just before considered, only declares a truth, which flows immediately and necessarily from the institution of a Federal Government. It will not, I presume, have escaped observation that it *expressly* confines this supremacy to laws made *pursuant to the Constitution*. ...

"Though a law therefore for laying a tax for the use of the United States would be supreme in its nature, and could not legally be opposed or controuled; yet a law for abrogating or preventing the collection of a tax laid by the authority of a State (unless upon imports and exports) would not be the supreme law of the land, but an usurpation of power not granted by the constitution. . . . The inference from the whole is—that the individual States would, under the proposed constitution, retain an independent and uncontroulable authority to raise revenue to any extent of which they may stand in need by every kind of taxation except duties on imports and exports. It will be shewn in the next paper that this CONCURRENT JURISDICTION in the article of taxation was the only admissible substitute for an intire [*sic*] subordination, in respect to this branch of power, of the State authority to that of the Union."

18. Cf. Hamilton's passage in text above corresponding to n. 14.

19. *Federalist* #73 in *Writings*, p. 394: "The third ingredient towards constituting the vigor of the executive authority is an adequate provision for its support. It is evident that without proper attention to this article, the separation of the executive from the legislative department would be merely nominal and nugatory. The Legislature, with a discretionary power over the salary and emoluments of the Chief Magistrate, could render him as obsequious to their will, as they might think proper to make him . . . And in the main it will be found that a power over a man's support is a power over his will. . . . [E]xamples . . . would not be wanting, even in this country, of the intimidation or seduction of the executive by the terrors, or allurements, of the pecuniary arrangements of the legislative body.

"It is not easy therefore to commend too highly the judicious attention which has been paid to this subject in the proposed Constitution."

20. *Ibid.*, p. 395.

21. *Ibid.*, pp. 396–397.

22. *Ibid.*, p. 397: "A King of Great-Britain, with all his train of sovereign attributes, and with all the influence he draws from a thousand sources, would at this day hesitate to put a negative upon the joint resolutions of the two houses of Parliament. . . . A very considerable period has elapsed since the negative of the crown has been exercised.

"If a magistrate, so powerful and so well fortified as a British monarch, would have scruples about the exercise of the power under consideration, how much greater caution may be reasonably expected in a President of the United States, cloathed for the short period of four years with the executive authority of a government wholly and purely republican?

"It is evident that there would be greater danger of his not using his power when necessary, than of his using it too often, or too much."

23. *Federalist* #75 in *Writings*, pp. 403–404: "The president is to have power 'by and with the advice and consent of the senate, to make treaties, provided two-thirds of the senators present concur.' Though this provision has been assailed on different grounds, . . . it is one of the best digested and most unexceptionable parts of the plan. . . .

"With regard to the intermixture of powers, . . . the union of the executive with the senate, in the article of treaties, is no infringement of that rule. I venture to add that the particular nature of the power of making treaties indicates a peculiar propriety in that union. Though several writers on the subject of government place that power in the class of executive authorities, yet this is evidently an arbitrary disposition: For if we attend carefully to its operation, it will be found to partake more of the legislative than of the executive Character, though it does not seem strictly to fall within the definition of either of them. The essence of the legislative authority is to enact laws, or in other words to prescribe rules for the regulation of the society, while the execution of the laws and the employment of the common strength, either for this purpose or for the common defence, seem to comprise all the functions of the executive magistrate. The power of making treaties is plainly neither the one nor the other. It relates neither to the execution of the subsisting laws, nor to the enaction of new ones, and still less to an exertion of the common strength. Its objects are CONTRACTS with foreign nations, which have the force of law, but derive it from the obligations of good faith. They are not rules prescribed by the sovereign to the subject, but agreements between sovereign and sovereign. The power in question seems therefore to form a distinct department, and to belong properly neither to the legislative nor to the executive. The qualities ... of foreign negotiations, point out the executive as the most fit agent in those transactions; while the ... operation of treaties as laws, plead strongly for the participation of the whole or a part of the legislative body in the office of making them."

24. *Federalist* #82 in *Writings*, pp. 450–451: "When we consider the state governments and the national governments as they truly are ... as parts of ONE WHOLE, the inference seems to be conclusive that the state courts would have a concurrent jurisdiction in all cases arising under the laws of the union, where it was not expressly prohibited. ... Agreeably ... the national and state systems are to be regarded as ONE WHOLE. The courts of the latter will of course be natural auxiliaries to the execution of the laws of the union, and an appearl from them will as naturally lie to that tribunal, which is destined to unite and assimilate the principles of national justice and the rules of national decisions. ... The plan of the convention ... authorises the national legislature 'to constitute tribunals inferior to the supreme court'. It declares in the next place that, 'the JUDICIAL POWER of the United States *shall be vested* in one supreme court and in such inferior courts as congress shall ordain and establish;' and it then proceeds to enumerate the cases to which this judicial power shall extend. ... Whether their authority shall be original or appellate or both is not declared. All this seems to be left to the discretion of the legislature. And this being the case, I perceive at present no impediment to the establishment of an appeal from the state courts to the subordinate national tribunals; and many advantages attending the power of doing it may be imagined."

25. *Federalist* #83 in *Writings*, pp. 452–453: "The rules of legal interpretation are rules of *common sense*, adopted by the courts in the construction of the laws. The true test therefore, of a just application of them, is its conformity to the source from which they are derived. This being the case, let me ask if it is consistent with reason or common sense to suppose, that a provision obliging the legislative power to commit the trial of criminal causes to juries, is a privation of its right to authorrise or permit that mode of trial in other cases?"

26. *Federalist* #24 in *Writings*, p. 258: "[In] the plan reported by the Convention, ... the whole power of raising armies was [is] lodged in the *Legislature*, not in the *Executive*, that this Legislature was [is] to be a popular body, consisting of the representatives of the people, periodically elected ..."

27. Hamilton's "Opinion on the Constitutionality of a National Bank" (1791) is in his *Writings*, pp. 613–646. A draft of this document with his wording and subsequent changes is printed in his *Papers* VIII, pp. 64 ff. Hamilton's opening statement is as follows in *Writings*, p. 613: "The Secretary of the Treasury having perused with attention the papers containing the opinions of the Secretary of State and Attorney General concerning the constitutionality of the bill for establishing a National Bank proceeds according to the order of the President to submit the reasons which have induced him to entertain a different opinion." The Attorney General was Edmund Randolph, Jefferson's fellow Virginian. As Governor, Randolph had headed the Virginia delegation to the 1787 Convention but did not approve the plan finally adopted, although he subsequently changed his position.

28. Hamilton, "Opinion," in *Writings*, pp. 614–615. The continuation of this long passage includes the following comments on the arguments taken by Hamilton's "republican" opponents in this matter—p. 615: "The first of these arguments is, that the foundation of the constitution is laid on this ground 'that all powers not delegated to the United States by the Constitution nor prohibited to it by the States are reserved to the States or to the people,' whence it is meant to be inferred, that congress can in no case exercise any power not included in those enumerated in the constitution. And it is affirmed that the power of erecting a corporation is not included in any of the enumerated powers.

"The main proposition here laid down, in its true signification is not to be questioned. It is nothing more than a consequence of this republican maxim, that all government is a delegation of power. But how much is delegated in each case, is a question of fact to be made out by fair reasoning & construction upon the particular provisions of the constitution—taking as guides the general principles & general ends of government."

29. *Ibid.*, p. 621. The passage continues, p. 621: "There is also this further criterion which may materially assist the decision. Does the proposed measure abridge a preexisting right of any State, or of any individual? If it does not, there is a strong presumption in favour of its constitutionality; & slighter relations to any declared object of the constitution may be permitted to turn the scale.

"The general objections which are to be inferred from the reasonings of the Secretary of State and of the Attorney General to the doctrine which has been advanced, have been stated and it is hoped satisfactorily answered. Those of a more particular nature shall soon be examined."

30. *Ibid.*, p. 622.

31. *Ibid.*, p. 623.

32. *Ibid.*, p. 624.

33. *Ibid.*, pp. 625—627, 639–640: "Those [arguments] of the Attorney General will now properly come under review.

"His first observation is that the power of incorporation is not *expressly* given to congress. This shall be conceded, but in *this sense* only, that it is not declared in *express terms* that congress may erect a *corporation*. But this cannot mean, that there are not certain *express* powers, which *necessarily* include it.

"For instance, Congress have express power 'to exercise exclusive legislation in all cases whatsoever, over such *district*. . . .'

"Here then is express power to exercise *exclusive legislation in all cases whatsoever over certain places*; that is to do in respect to those places, all that any government whatever may do: For language does not afford a more complete designation of sovereign power, than in those comprehensive terms. It is in other words a power to pass all laws whatsoever, & consequently to pass laws for erecting corporations, as well as for any other purpose which is the proper object of law in a free government. Surely it can never be believed, that Congress with *exclusive power of legislation in all cases whatsoever*, cannot erect a corporation within the district which shall become the seat of government, for the better regulation of its police. And yet there is an unqualified denial of the power to erect corporations in every case on the part both of the Secretary of State and of the Attorney General. The former indeed speaks of that power in these emphatical terms, that it is *a right remaining exclusively with the states.*

"As far then as there is an express poweer to do any *particular act of legislation*, there is an express one to erect corporations in the cases above described. . . .

"To this objection an answer has been already given. It is this; that the doctrine is stated with this express *qualification*, that the right to erect corporations does *only* extend to *cases & objects* within the *sphere* of the *specified powers* of the government. A general legislative authority implies a power to erect corporations *in all cases*—a particular legislative power implies authority to erect corporations, in relation to cases arising under that power only. Hence the affirming, that as an *incident* to sovereign power, congress may erect a corporation in relation to the *collection* of their taxes, is no more than to affirm that they may do whatever else they please; than the saying that they have a power to regulate trade would be to affirm that they have a power to regulate religion: or than the maintaining that they have sovereign power as to taxation, would be to maintain that they have sovereign power as to every thing else.

"The Attorney General undertakes, in the next place, to shew, that the power of erecting corporations is not involved in any of the specified powers of legislation confided to the National government. . . .

"[B]y what rule of construction can it be maintained, that the same words in a constitution of government will not have the same effect when applied to one species of property, as to another, as far as the subject is capable of it? or that a legislative power to make all needful rules & regulations, or to pass all laws necessary & proper concerning the public property which is admitted to authorise an incorporation in one case will not authorise it in another? will justify the institution of a government over the western territory & will not justify the incorporation of a bank, for the more useful management of the money of the nation?"

34. Hamilton, Letter to James Duane, 1780, in *Writings*, pp. 71, 76–77: "But the confederation itself is defective and requires to be altered; it is neither fit for war, nor peace. The idea of an uncontrolable sovereignty in each state, over its internal police, will defeat the other powers given to Congress, and make our union feeble and precarious. There are instances without number, where acts necessary for the general good, and which rise out of the powers given to Congress must interfere with the internal police of the states, and there are as many instances in which the particular states . . . can effectually though indirectly counteract the arrangements of Congress. . . .

"I shall now propose the remedies, which appear to me applicable to our circumstances, and necessary to extricate our affairs from their present deplorable situation.

"The first step must be to give Congress powers competent to the public exigencies. . . .

"The confederation in my opinion should give Congress complete sovereignty; except as to that part of internal police, which relates to the rights of property and life among individuals and to raising money by internal taxes. It is necessary, that every thing, belonging to this, should be regulated by the state legislatures. Congress should have complete sovereignty in all that relates to war, peace, trade, finance, and to the management of foreign affairs, the right of declaring war[,] of raising armies, [etc.] . . ."

35. Hamilton, Constitutional Convention speech, June 18, 1787 (Madison's version in his *Notes*), in his *Writings*, p. 155: "The general power whatever be its form if it preserve itself, must swallow up the State powers. Otherwwise it will be swallowed up by them. It is agst. all the principles of a good Government to vest the requisite powers in such a body as Congs. Two Sovereignties can not co-exist within the same Limits. Giving powers to Congs. must eventuate in a bad Govt. or in no Govt. The plan of N. Jersey therefore will not do. What then is to be done?"

36. Hamilton's own notes on the same speech, *Papers*, Vol. IV, p. 185.

37. John Lansing's version of Hamilton's same speech in *ibid.*, pp. 202–203: "No Amendment of Confederation can answer the Exigencies of the States. State Sovereignties ought not to exist. Supposes we gave Powers sufficient. Foederal an Association of States differently modified. Diet of Germany has Power to legislate for Individuals. In United States Confederacy legislate for States and in some Instances on Individuals. . . . The only Enquiry ought to be what can we do to save our Country. Five Essentials indispensible in foederal Government. . . .

"Two modes of Coercion—of Laws—of Military.

"Individuals are easily controuled—not so Society. . . .

"We must resort to Influence. . . .

"Equality of Suffrage ruinous to the Union. . . .

"The Organization of Congress exceptionable—. . . . No Power will be executed if the States think proper to obstruct it. If general Government preserves itself it must extinguish State Governments.

"If Congress remains Legislature[,] the Sovereignty must ultimately vest in them."

38. Robert Yates' version of Hamilton's same speech, in *Writings*, p. 165: "All state laws to be absolutely void which contravene the general laws. An officer to be appointed in each state to have a negative on all state laws. All the militia and the appointment of officers to be under the national government.

"I confess that this plan and that from Virginia are very remote from the idea of the people."

39. Rufus King's version of Hamilton's same speech, in *Papers*, Vol. IV, pp. 205–206: "Our powers have this object—the Freedom & Happiness of our Country—we must go all lengths to accomplish this Object—if the Legislatures have no powers to ratify because thereby they diminish their own Sovereignty, the people may come in on revolution principles—. . . .

"Man loves power—State magistrates will desire to increase yr. own powers at the Expence of the Genl. or fed. Govt.

"One great Objt. of Govt. is personal protection and the security of Property—if you establish a federal Govt. men will not be interesed in the protection or preservation of the Genl. Govt. but they will in the existence of the State Govt. if the latter is dissolved and the former remains their persons & fortune will be safe—Besides the large States will be indisposed to remain connected. . . .

"The Result is that all the passions of avarice, pride, ambition &c. shd. depend on the Genl. & not the State Govts.—you must make the national Sovereignty transcendent & entire—The plan of N. Jersey"

40. Hamilton's own "Plan of Government" in his Constitutional Convention speech on June 18, 1787, in *ibid.*, pp. 207–208: "I. The Supreme Legislative Power of the United States of America to be vested in two distinct bodies of men—the one to be called the *Assembly* the other the *senate*; whon together shall form the Legislature of the United States, with power to pass all *laws whatsoever*, subject to the *negative* hereafter mentioned.

"II The Assembly to consist of persons elected *by the People* to serve for three years.

"III The Senate to consist of persons elected to serve during *good behaviour*. Their election to be made by *Electors*. . . .

"IV. The Supreme Executive authority of the United States to be vested in a *governor*. . . .

"VI. The Supreme Judicial authority . . . to be vested in twelve judges. . . .

"X. All laws of the particular states contrary to the constitution or laws of the United States to be utterly void."

Cf. also by Hamilton, "Constitutional Convention. Remarks on the Abolition of the States," *ibid.*, pp. 211–212.

41. Hamilton's speech at the New York Ratifying Convention, June 27, 1788, in *Writings*, pp. 502–503 (also in his *Papers* V, pp. 94 ff.), Francis Child's version: "What then is the structure of this constitution? One branch of the legislature is to be elected by the people—by the same people, who choose your state representatives: Its members are to hold their office two years, and then return to their constituents. Here, sir, the people govern: Here they act by their immediate representatives. You have also a senate, constituted by your state legislatures—by men, in whom you place the highest confidence; and forming another representative branch. Then again you have an executive magistrate, created by a form of election, which merits universal admiration. In the form of this government, and in the mode of legislation, you find all the checks which the greatest politicians and the best writers have ever conceived. What more can reasonable men desire? Is there any one branch, in which the whole legislative and executive powers are lodged? No. The legislative authority is lodged in three distinct branches properly balanced: The executive authority is divided between two branches; and the judicial is still reserved for an independent body. . . . Let us see what is the true meaning of this maxim, which has been so

much used, and so little understood. It is, that you shall not place these powers in either the legislative or executive singly: Neither one nor the other shall have both; Because this would destroy that division of powers, on which political liberty is founded; and would furnish one body with all the means of tyranny."

42. *Ibid.*, p. 504: "The true principle of government is this—Make the system compleat in its structure; give a perfect proportion and balance to its parts; and the powers you give it will never affect your security. The question then, of the division of powers between the general and state governments, is a question of convenience: It becomes a prudential enquiry, what powers are proper to be reversed to the latter; and this immediately involves another enquiry into the proper objects of the two governments. This is the criterion by which we shall determine the just distribution of powers."

43. *Ibid.*, p. 510.

44. *Ibid.*, pp. 510–511: "Suppose both governments should lay a tax of a penny on a certain article: Has not each an independent and uncontrolable power to collect its own tax? The meaning of the maxim—that there can not be two supremes—is simply this:—Two powers cannot be supreme over each other. This meaning is entirely perverted by the gentlemen. But, it is said, disputes between collectors are to be referred to the federal courts. This is again wandering in the field of conjecture. But suppose the fact certain: Is it not to be presumed, that they will express the true meaning of the constitution and the laws? Will they not be bound to consider the concurrent jurisdiction; to declare that both the taxes shall have equal operation; that both the powers, in that respect, are sovereign and co-extensive? . . . Sir, we can reason from probabilities alone. When we leave common sense, and give ourselves up to conjecture, there can be no certainty, no security in our reasonings.

"I imagine I have stated to the committee abundant reasons to prove the entire safety of the state governments and of the people. I would go into a more minute consideration of the nature of the concurrent jurisdiction, and the operation of the laws, in relation to revenue; but at present . . . I wish the committee to remember, that the constitution under examination is framed upon truly republican principles . . . to provide for . . . the general welfare of the United States, [and] it must be utterly repugnant to this constitution, to subvert the state governments, or oppress the people."

45. Hamilton's letter to Timothy Pickering, Sept. 16, 1803, in *ibid.*, pp. 1002–1003: "The highest toned propositions, which I made in the Convention, were for a President, Senate and Judges during good behaviour—a house of representatives for three years. Though I would have enlarged the Legislative power of the General Government, yet I never contemplated the abolition of the State Governments; but on the contrary, they were, in some particulars, constituent parts of my plan.

"This plan was in my conception conformable with the strict theory of a Government purely republican; the essential criteria of which are that the principal organs of the Executive and Legislative departments be elected by the people and hold their offices by a *responsible* and temporary or *defeasible* tenure.

"A vote was taken on the proposition respecting the Executive. Five states were in favour of it; among those Virginia; and though from the manner of voting, by delegations, individuals were not distinguished, it was morally certain, from the known situation of the Virginia members (six in number, two of them *Mason* and *Randolph* possessing popular doctrines) that *Madison* must have concurred in the vote of Virginia. Thus, if I sinned against Republicanism, Mr. Madison was not less guilty.

"I may truly then say, that I never proposed either a President, or Senate for life, and that I neither recommended nor meditated the annihilation of the State Governments.

"And I may add, that in the course of the discussions in the Convention, neither the propositions thrown out for debate nor even those voted in the earlier stages of deliberation were considered as evidences of a definitive opinion, in the proposer or voter. It appeared to me to be in some sort understood, that with a view to free investigation, experimental propositions might be made, which were to be received merely as suggestions for consideration.

"Accordingly, it is a fact, that my final opinion was against an Executive during good behaviour [i.e. for an indefinite period or even like judges for life], on account of the increased danger to the public tranquility incident to the election of a Magistrate of this degree of permanency. In the plan of a Constitution, which I drew up, while the convention was sitting & which I communicated to Mr. Madison about the close of it, perhaps a day or two after, the Office of President has no greater duration than for three years.

"This plan was predicated upon these bases—1 That the political principles of the people of this country would endure nothing but republican Government. 2 That in the actual situation of the Country, it was in itself right and proper that the republican theory should have a fair and full trial—3 That to such a trial it was essential that the Government should be so constructed as to give it all the energy and stability reconcilable with the principles of that theory. These were the genuine sentiments of my heart, and upon them I acted.

"I sincerely hope, that it may not hereafter be discovered, that through want of sufficient attention to the last idea, the experiment of Republican Government, even in this Country, has not been as complete, as satisfactory and as decisive as could be wished."

46. Hamilton's "The Examination," number XII, in *Papers*, Vol. 25, pp. 533—534 (Feb., 1802): "If it be replied, that though a legislature might act immorally and wickedly in abrogating a vested right, yet the legal *validity* of its act for such a purpose could not be disputed; it may be answered that this odious position, in any application of it, is liable to question in every limited Constitution; (that is, in every Constitution which, in its theory, does not suppose the WHOLE POWER of the Nation to be lodged in the legislative body;* [*As in the Parliament of Great-Britain] and that it is certainly false in its application to a legislature, the authorities of which are defined by a positive written Constitution. . . . To deny this is to affirm that the *delegated* is paramount to the *constituent* power. It is in fact to affirm there are *no constitutional limits to the Legislative Authority.*

"The enquiry then must be, whether the power to abolish Inferior Courts, if implied in that of creating them, is not abridged by the clause which regulates the tenure of Judicial office."

To the *New-York Evening Post*, in *ibid.*, p. 538 (Feb. 24, 1802): "And it is now repeated with confidence, that the *Virginia* delegation did vote for the most energetic form of government, and that Mr. Maddison was of the number. But we desire to be distinctly understood, that it was never intended by mentioning this circumstance, to impeach the purity of Mr. Maddison's motives. To arraign the morals of any man because he entertains a speculative opinion on government different from ourselves, is worse than arrogance. He who does so, must entertain notions in ethics extremely crude, and certainly unfavourable to virtue."

47. "Examination" #XIII, *ibid.*, pp. 542–543: "But whatever may be the latitude we assign to the power of a legislature over the acts of a predecessor, it is nothing to the purpose, so long as it shall be admitted that the constitution may bind and controul the legislature. With this admission, the simple inquiry must always be—has or has not the Constitution in the particular instance, bound the legislature? And the solution must be sought in the language, nature, and end of the provision. If these warrant the conclusion that the legislature was intended to be bound, it is perfect nonsense to reply that this cannot be so because a legislature cannot bind itslf by its own acts; or because the power of one legislature is equal to that of another. What signifies this proposition, if the

Constitution has power to bind the legislature, and has in fact bound it in a given case? . . .

"A very strong confirmation of the true intent of the provision respecting the tenure of Judicial office results from an argument by analogy. In each of the articles which establishes any branch of the government, the duration of office is a prominent feature. Two years for the House of Representatives, six for the Senate, four for the President and Vice President, are the respective terms of duration; and for the Judges the term of good behaviour is allotted."

Hamilton's extended discussions here and elsewhere in his same series of articles often relate to intricate issues on whether successive federal legislatures are bound or not bound by their or their predecessors' laws.

48. "Examination" #XIV, in *ibid.*, pp. 549–550.

49. "Examination" #XIV, in *ibid.*, pp. 550—551: "In governments wholly popular or representative, there is no adequate counterpoise. Confidence in the most numerous, or Legislative Department, and jealousy of the Executive Chief, form the genius of every such government. That jealousy, operating in the constitution of the Executive, causes this organ to be intrinsically feeble . . . in a state of impotence. The result is that the Legislative body, in this species of government, possesses additional resources of power and weight; while the Executive is rendered much too weak for competition; almost too weak for self defence.

"A third principle, not less well founded than the other two, is that the Judiciary department is naturally the weakest of the three. . . . The Executive by means of its several active powers; of the dispensations of honors and emoluments and of the direction of the public force is evidently the second in strength. The Judiciary, on the other hand, can ordain nothing. It commands neither the press nor the sword. It has scarcely any patronage. Its functions are not active but deliberative. Its main province is to declare the meaning of the laws [!]; and in extraordinary cases it must even look up to the Executive aid for the execution of its decisions. Its chief strength is in the veneration which it is able to inspire by the wisdom and rectitude of its judgments.

"This character of the Judiciary clearly indicates that it is not only the weakest of the three departments of power; but, also as it regards the security and preservation of civil liberty by far the safest. . . . Safety, Liberty, are therefore inseparably connected with the real and substantial Independence of the Courts and Judges.

"It is plainly to be inferred from the instrument itself, that these were governing principles in the formation of our Constitution. . . . Those principles suggest the highest motives of Constitutional policy aginst that construction, which places the existence of the Judges at the mercy of the Legislature. They instruct us, that to prevent a concentration of powers, the *essence of despotism*, it is essential that the departments among which they shall be distributed, should be effectually independent of each other; and that it being impossible to reconcile this independence with a right in any one or two of them to annihilate at discretion the organs of the other, it is contrary to all just reasoning to imply or infer such a right. So far from its being correct, that an express interdiction is requisite to deprive the Legislature of the power to abolish the Judges, that the very reverse is the true position." Etc.

"Examination" #XV, pp. 552 ff., takes up aspects of the *Federalist* essays.

50. "Examination" #XVII, in *ibid.*, p. 571 (March, 1802): "In the theory of the British Government, it is entirely different; there the majesty of the nation is understood to reside in the Prince. He is deemed the real Sovereign. He is, emphatically, the fountain of honour. Allegiance is due to him; and consequently, public offices are in the true notion of *tenure*, holden of him. But in our Constitution the President is not the Sovereign; the sov-

ereignty is vested in the Government, collectively; and it is of the sovereignty, strictly and technically speaking, that a public officer holds his office.

"If this view of the matter be just, the basis of the argument, in point of fact, fails; and the principle of it suggests an opposite conclusion, namely, that the condition of *good behaviour* is obligatory on the whole Government, and ought to operate as a barrier against any authority by which the displacement of the Judges from their office may be, directly or indirectly effected."

51. For kind assistance in my quest to find books once owned by Alexander Hamilton, I am grateful to various rare-book and manuscript librarians: Bernard Crystal, Jane R. Siegel, and Henry Rowen at Columbia University; also Gerald Wager, Bruce Kirby, and Ernest Emrich at the Library of Congress. As in similar previous cases explored above concerning the founders' collections of books, the approaches here are thoroughly original.

As the librarians at Columbia readily recognize, when queried, the existing rubrics in the card file there can be misleading. The books obtained from the Hamilton family long ago are divided into two main categories, those published before Alexander's death in 1804 (followed by many early entries for individual *Federalist* essays) and those published after 1804. The problematic first rubric reads: "books by, about, or belonging to Alexander Hamilton with imprint before his 1804 death." This classification goes back many decades and may have resulted, as one librarian put it, from "wishful thinking" that books with pre-1804 imprints once belonged to Alexander Hamilton. All this does not mean, however, that such books did *not* originally belong to him, but only that one cannot *assume* on that basis that they did. Various factors have to be taken into account in each case.

52. On Alexander Hamilton's son James as well as his own father James, the *Dict. of Amer. Biog.* has useful information. Also helpful has been the fuller Hamilton family genealogical chart kindly provided me by Henry Rowen, who once prepared it himself. Mr. Rowen believes that James the father could not have been the same James who autographed the books that I showed to him and that are cited in the notes to follow. For the father was out of the picture in Alexander's life from his early age in the Islands. From Mr. Rowen's fuller chart of Alexander's family and descendants, it becomes clear to this writer that the only other James who could with any probability be the one who owned and autographed such books as are cited here from Columbia's Hamilton collection was Alexander's son James. It might be tempting to picture Alexander as having had access to these books in his father's library and as having later taken them over for himself; but such was certainly not the case. Alexander's father was no longer a factor in his life after Alexander left the British West Indies for this country.

Born in New York in 1788 as the third son of Alexander Hamilton, James Alexander Hamilton graduated from Columbia University in 1805 at age 17 a year after his father's death. Together with his six siblings and mother, James was at his father's bedside when he finally died not long after the duel with Burr. Four years later he was admitted to the bar and began practicing law in Waterford, New York. In 1810 he married Robert Morris' daughter Mary. He later became involved in national politics, living for a time in Washington, D.C., and serving under President Jackson. He died in 1878. Cf. *Dict. of Amer. Biog.* as well as James A. Hamilton, *Reminiscences* (New York, 1869), Chs. I–II for pre-1804 material relating to his father.

53. Mezeray, *Abregé chronologique de l'histoire de France* (14 vols., Amsterdam, 1755). At the top of the blank page opposite the title page of Vol. 3 is inscribed the signature of ownership, reading "Jas[.] Hamilton." At the top of title pages in Vols. 4–6, 10, and 12–13, is inscribed "Hamilton" in the same hand as Vol. 3 signed by James. Vols. 8–10 cover French history from the mid-16th century through the early 17th century.

Cf. also, with post-1804 imprint, *The Works of the Rev. Jonathan Swift* (24 vols., New York, 1812–1813). At the top of the title page for Vol. 1 appears the signature of ownership by "James Hamilton." Vols. 2–3, 6, and 10 are also autographed by him. Aside from such works in English, I have not come across any books in French that James Hamilton himself acquired and autographed after his father's death in 1804.

54. *Oeuvres completes de Voltaire* (70 vols., [Kehl], 1785, 1789), not autographed.

55. Guilllaume-Thomas Raynal, *Histoire philosophique et politique* (10 vols., Paris, 1794–1795), not autographed.

56. This book is entitled *The Constitutions of the Several States of America; the Declaration of Independence; The Articles of Confederation; ...* [etc.] (2nd edn., Boston, 1785). Near the top of the title page is inscribed "Alex. Hamilton," as similarly on the blank page inside the front cover. Near the top of the blank page opposite the title page appears the following inscription: "Mr. Hamilton returned [to] me this book instead of mine [Morris' insert: 'he had borrowed'] which he said was mislaid. R. Morris."

57. The book signed by both Alexander Hamilton and Philip Hamilton is listed under "Gt. Britain, Court of King's Bench," and is entitled *Modern Reports: Being a Collection of Several Special Cases Argued and Adjudicated in the Court of King and Queens Bench, In the ... Reigns of King William and Queen Mary* (4th edn., Vol. IV), with additions "from the Books of Reports, down to the Year 1757" (London, 1757). Under the main title appears the signature of ownership by "Alexander Hamilton," while Philip Hamilton's autograph appears on the blank page inside the front cover.

Also at Columbia is an early two-volume copy of *The Federalist* (1788) in which the second volume has a bookplate, reading "Alex. Hamilton of Grange[,] Advocate," inside the front cover. However, Columbia rare-book librarian Henry Rowen has expressed reservations about whether this bookplate, which is in the form of a coat of arms, was that of Alexander Hamilton, who was illegitimate and therefore may not have had such an official coat of arms. At the same time, Mr. Rowen is not convinced that this book belonged to *the* Alexander Hamilton. Yet this reservation may be too cautious in view of the handwriting of the signature as well as the early dating of this 1788 edn. of the *Federalist,* likely to have been in Alexander Hamilton's possession. However, an alternate possibility, one may add, is that this book was given to or acquired by *the* Alexander Hamilton's second son, Alexander, from his father's library. Yet even in that case, which seems less likely than the first, there could still, then, be a question of a family with illegitimate beginnings having such a coat of arms. Or was the insignia more an *ad hoc* arrangement? The whole subject may deserve more investigation but need not detain us further here.

A related point can be added. However difficult were the marital circumstances of Alexander's parents in the West Indies, where he was born in the British colony of Nevis, his father, of good family, was a Scottish merchant and fourth son of Alexander Hamilton of Grange in Ayrshire. Hence the existence of a coat of arms for the Hamilton's of "Grange," the name taken over by *the* Alexander Hamilton for his New York home, should not be unsettling. In any case, the excellent chart of Hamilton family lines prepared by Mr. Rowen gives *the* Alexander's date of birth as "1755 or 57," according to certain varying traditions of dating that may reflect the uncertainty sometimes ascribed to him over when his mother left her original husband to be with her next partner, James Hamilton, who soon left her (she dying when Alexander was about eleven). They evidently became socially, if not legally, recognized as husband and wife.

The one book in the rare-book (and manuscript) collection at the Library of Congress that is known to have been owned by Alexander Hamilton is a copy of Edmund Randolph's *A Vindication of Mr. Randolph's Resignation* (Phila., 1795), 104 pp., with extensive annotations by *the* Alexander Hamilton. Since only one book owned by Alexander Hamilton was acquired by the Library of Congress—in counterdistinction to the massive collections of his papers that it acquired over the years from the Hamilton family (widow, etc.) especially via the State and Treasury Depts.—it is all the more likely that the unique Columbia collection of Hamilton books does indeed include the vast bulk of what survives from Alexander's own collection as passed on to his family.

Furthermore, the Columbia collection, under pre-1804 "books by, about, and belonging to Alexander Hamilton," has a wealth of miscellaneous materials definitely relating directly to Alexander Hamilton. These include reports, letters, proceedings, accounts, communications, and so forth covering the span of his career The massive separate collection at Columbia listed under the rubric "The Law Practice of Alexander Hamilton Papers" became the basis for the impressive *The Law Practice of Alexander Hamilton: Documents and Commentary* (edited by Julius Goebel, Jr., and Joseph E. Smith, 5 vols., New York, 1964–1981). Judging from the enormity of these documents pertaining to Alexander Hamilton's well-established law practice, and from the plethora of legal references scattered throughout his *Papers*, he undoubtedly had a substantial collection of legal and related books that have not survived either at Columbia or the Library of Congress. These books would almost certainly have included many works by Blackstone and other sources in English law, as well as on comparative law more broadly.

Not able to be addressed here adequately is the question of where Alexander Hamilton's books were located in the years before his death (aside from his papers and records now at Columbia and the Library of Congress). His Grange home in upper Manhattan was completed, for him to move into, only in 1802, two years before his death. It had a room of moderate size for his "library," as contemporary accounts also mentioned. This home was intended partly as a "get away," especially during the summer, from his Wall Street law office and nearby living quarters; the Grange was about an hour and a half away by travel in those days. He and his family were living there in the summer of 1804 when he died. His books and papers had no doubt been somehow divided between the two locations. His widow lived at the Grange until 1833, thereafter moving to D.C. and dying at age 97.

My thanks go to two Park Rangers at the Hamilton Grange National Memorial—Douglas Massenburg and Joseph Daskalakis—for helpful information.

58. *Collection complete des oeuvres de J. J.. Rousseau* (17 vols., Geneva, 1782–1789), not autographed.

59. *Oeuvres posthumes de Frederick II* (13 vols. in 8, Berlin, 1788–), not autographed.

60. *Encyclopedie Methodique* (105 vols., Paris, 1787), not autographed.

61. Comte de la Cepede, *Histoire naturelle* (2 vols., Paris, 1788–1789), not autographed.

62. *Dict. of Amer. Biog.*, entry for Alexander Hamilton.

63. This unpublished manuscript list of books is given only a bare general entry of a few lines in Hamilton's *Papers* I, p. 42, under the date 1773 and the editors' heading "List of Books." It follows other entries there for "Notes on the Book of Genesis," "Notes on the Book of Revelation," and "The Illiad of Homer." The entry reads: "[Elizabethtown, New Jersey, 1773] Numbered list of twenty-seven books and subjects on American and Medieval history and philosophy." A corresponding editorial note states: "The authorship of this MS is not known. The handwriting is not that of H, but the document may be a copy of a missing original. Although MS contains no date, it probably belongs to the period when H was in school or college." (Hamilton first attended King's College as a special student in the autumn of 1773, then formally entered in 1774, studying Latin, Greek, etc.) In *Papers* I, the entries are dated St. Croix through Oct., 1772, while the New York entries begin in May, 1773; several of his early published and unpublished poems also appear in *Papers* I. The lack of any tables of contents at the beginning of the individual volumes of Hamilton's *Papers*, as well as of a more complete index than the ones at the end of each volume (and of the series), make it difficult to come across such brief and for-

gotten items as this list of books, which I have not as yet seen utilized by other historians.

I am grateful to Ernest Emrich, a reference specialist in the Manuscript Division of the Library of Congress, for providing me with a facsimile of this book list and for helping me to decipher its 27 numbered entries (the first two being blank). The list is written on substantial paper, similar in thickness to others in the same box and miscellaneous folder, although the list is of different size than other papers surrounding it.

All the separate entries need not be cited or deciphered here, yet a few brief indications will be useful. The titles and subject headings are not so much "American and Medieval," as the *Papers* editors aver, but rather are classical and early Christian. They appear in fragmentary and often somewhat illegible form. They tend to fit in with the other above-cited entries of 1773 in *Papers* I for the Bible and Homer. The list includes entries relating to Socrates, Homer, Philo, and others, along with various works dealing more generally with Greek, Roman, and early Christian thought. Some entries pertain to Greek philosophical oration and Greek ecclesiastical books, including Byzantine, in addition to Catholic thought. These and numerous other names, titles, and subject matters suggest a rather recondite spectrum of interests on the part of the person preparing this list, especially considering that the books may well have been listed by or known to Hamilton at around the early age of 18. I have not carefully combed through the Columbia card file for pre-1804 Hamilton books that possibly match entries in this book list of c. 1773.

64. The "Notes for Speech" by Hamilton on July 12, 1788, at the New York Ratifying Convention appear in his *Papers*, Vol. V, pp. 149 ff.

65. *Ibid.*, pp. 150—151:

B. I. *Consequence*, the proposed government a *representative democracy*.
1. House of representatives directly chosen by the people for two years.
2. Senate indirectly chosen by them for six years
3. President indirectly chosen by them for four years.
——>Thus legislative and executive representatives of the people.
4. Judicial power, representatives of the people indirectly chosen during good behaviour.
5. All officers indirect choice of the people.
——> Constitution revocable and alterable by the people.

C. I. This representative democracy as far as is consistent with its genius has all the features of good government. These features.
1. An immediate and operative representation of the people which is found in the house of representatives.
2. Stability and Wisdom which is found in the Senate.
3. A vigorous executive which is found in the president.
4. An independent judicial, which is found in the Supreme Court &c."

66. *Ibid.*, pp. 151–152.

67. Hamilton, "Remarks" on June 27, 1788 at the New York Ratifying Convention, Francis Child's version, in *ibid.*, pp. 97, 99–101: "The great leading objects of the federal government, in which revenue is concerned, are to maintain domestic peace, and provide for the common defence. ... This principle assented to, let us enquire what are the objects of the state governments. ... Their objects are merely civil and domestic; to support the legislative establishment, and to provide for the administation of the laws. ... The experience of Great-Britain will throw some light on this subject....

"Mr. Chairman, it has been advanced as a principle, that no government but a despotism can exist in a very extensive country. [Reference to N.Y. Gov. George Clinton's remarks on June 21; ed. note.] This is melancholy consideration indeed. If it were founded on truth, we ought to dismiss the idea of a republican government, even for the state of New-York. This idea has been taken from a celebrated writer [Montesquieu; ed. note explaining that "Clinton, however, had not buttressed his arguments by referring to Montesquieu"], who, by being misunderstood, has been the occasion of frequent fallacies in our reasoning on political subjects. But the position has been misapprehended; and its application is entirely false and unwarrantable: ... This application is wrong, in respect to all representative governments; but especially in relation to a confederacy of states, in which the supreme legislature has only general powers, and the civil and domestic concerns of the people are regulated by the laws of the several states. ... If the state governments were to be abolished, the question would wear a different face: but this idea is inadmissible. They are absolutely necessary to the system. Their existence must form a leading principle in the most perfect constitution we could form. I insist, that it never can be the interest or desire of the national legislature, to destroy the state governments. It can derive no advantage from such an event; But, on the contrary, would lose an indispensable support, a necessary aid in executing the laws, and conveying the influence of government to the doors of the people. ... The union is dependent on the will of the state governments. ... In the antient feudal governments of Europe, there were, in the first place a monarch; subordinate to him, a body of nobles; and subject to these, the vassals or the whole body of the people. The authority of the kings was limited, and that of the barons considerably independent. A great part of the early wars in Europe were contests between the king and his nobility. In these contests, the latter possessed many advantages derived from their influence. ... The history of the feudal wars exhibits little more than a series of successful encroachments on the prerogatives of monarchy. Here, Sir, is one great proof of the superiority, which the members in limited governments possess over their head [etc., etc.]."

68. Hamilton, *The Farmer Refuted* (1775), in *Papers*, Vol. I, pp. 86—87: "I shall, henceforth, begin to make some allowance for that enmity, you have discovered to the *natural rights* of mankind. For, though ignorance of them in this enlightened age cannot be admitted, as a sufficient excuse for you; yet, it ought, in some measure, to extenuate your guilt. If you will follow my advice, there still may be hopes of your reformation. Apply yourself, without delay, to the study of the law of nature. I would recommend to your perusal, Grotius[,] Puffendorf, Locke, Montesquieu, and Burlemaqui. I might mention other excellent writers on this subject; but if you attend, diligently, to these, you will not require any others.

"There is so strong a similitude between your political principles and those maintained by Mr. Hobb[e]s, that, in judging from them, a person might very easily *mistake* you for a disciple of his. His opinion was, exactly, coincident with yours, relative to man in a state of nature. He held, as you do, that he was, then, perfectly free from all restraint of *law* and *government*. Moral obligation, according to him, is derived from the introduction of civil society; and there is no virtue, but what is purely artificial, the mere contrivance of politicians, for the maintenance of social intercourse. But the reason he run [*sic*] into this absurd and impious doctrine, was, that he disbelieved the existence of an intelligent superintending principle, who is the governor, and will be the final judge of the universe."

In writings throughout his career, Hamilton made extensive sporadic use of and references to Blackstone's *Commentaries on the Laws of England*. Instances can be found in his *Federalist* essays (#69, 84) in *Papers* IV and in his *The Farmer Refuted* of 1775 in *Papers* I. Others can be found in his *Papers* III, VI, XVIII, XIX, and XX.

69. One can consult the indexes to each vol. in Hamilton's *Papers*, as well as the comprehensive index in Vol. XXVII, for his references to select European writers.

70. In *Papers*, Vol. I, pp. 402–407 (1777, "Paybook").

71. *Ibid.*, pp. 386–387.

72. Hamilton, *The Farmer Refuted* (1775), in *Papers*, Vol. I, pp. 103–106, 109: "I deny, that we are dependent on the legislature of Great-Britain, and yet I maintain, that we are a part of the British Empire; but in this sense only, as being the free-born subjects of his Britannic Majesty.

"Thus have I fully examined that argument, which is esteemed the bulwark of the doctrine of parliamentary supremacy; and I flatter myself, clearly refuted it. The main pillar being now broken down, the whole structure may easily be demolished. . . .

"Your next argument (if it deserves the name) is this, 'legislation is not an inherent right in the colonies; many colonies have been established and subsisted long without it. The Roman colonies had no legislative authority. It was not 'till the latter period of their republic, that the privileges of Roman citizens, among which, that of voting in Assemblies of the people, at Rome, was a principal one, were extended to the inhabitants of Italy. All the laws of the empire were enacted at Rome. Neither their colonies, nor conquered countries had any thing to do with legislation.'

"The fundamental source of all your errors, sophisms and false reasonings is a total ignorance of the natural rights of mankind.

"Upon this principle, colonists as well as other men, have a right to civil liberty: For, if it be conducive to the happiness of society (and reason and experience testify that it is) it is evident, that every society, of whatsoever kind, has an absolute and perfect right to it, which can never be with-held without cruelty and injustice. The practice of Rome, towards her colonies, cannot afford the shadow of an argument against this. That mistress of the world was often unjust. And the treatment of her dependent provinces is one of the greatest blemishes in her history. Through the want of that civil liberty, for which we are now so warmly contending, they groaned under every species of wanton oppression. If we are wise, we shall take warning from thence; and consider a like state of dependence, as more to be dreaded, than pestilence and famine.

"The right of colonists, therefore, to exercise a legislative power, is an inherent right. It is founded upon the right of all men to freedom and happiness. For civil liberty cannot possibly have any existence, where the society, for whom laws are made, have no share in making them; and where the interest of their legislators is not inseparably interwoven with theirs. Before you asserted, that the right of legislation was derived 'from the indulgence or grant of the parent state,' you should have proved two things, that all men have not a natural right to freedom, and that civil liberty is not advantageous to society.

" 'The position, (you say) that we are bound by no laws, but those, to which we have assented, either by ourselves, or by our representatives, is a novel position, unsupported by any authoritative record of the British constitution, ancient or modern. It is republican, in its very nature; and tends to the utter subversion of the English monarchy. . . .'

"The foundation of the English constitution rests upon this principle, that no laws have any validity, or binding force, without the consent and approbation of the *people*, given in the persons of *their* representatives, periodically elected by *themselves*. This constitutes the democratical part of the government. . . .

" 'The true reason (says Blackstone) of requiring any qualification with regard to property in voters . . .'. . . .

"By this grant, Queen Elizabeth relinquished the whole legislative, and executive power, to Sir Walter. . . .

"After many successless efforts to plant a colony in Virginia, this charter was forfeited and abrogated, by the attainder of Sir Walter Raleigh; and then succeeded that of King James the first, to the two Virginia companies, dated the 10th of April, 1606. This was afterwards altered and improved, by a second charter, issued in 1609. There was also a third, dated March 12, 1611–12. The mention of this last would not have answered your purpose, and therefore, you chose to pass it over in silence.

"In neither of these three, is there the least reservation made of any authority to parliament. The colonies are considered in them, as entirely without the realm, and consequently, without the jurisdiction of its legislature."

In his lengthy "Notes on the History of North and South America," (Dec., 1786) in *Papers*, Vol. III, pp. 702–716, Hamilton cites and uses a number of sources. These include David Hume's *History of England from . . . Caesar to . . . 1688*. There Hamilton also refers to an item in the catalogue of the Library Company of Philadelphia, which was published in 1770. His reference reads: "Pamphlet Intitled 'Virginia richly valued' printed in 1650 by E[.] Williams[.] No. 261 Phil[.] Library." This appears to be Hamilton's only such explicit reference to that Library Co. It is difficult to determine whether Hamilton's bare reference to the pamphlet indicates his familiarity with it through the Library, or its catalogue, or some other channel. The entries in his *Papers* placed before and after these "Notes" are dated "New York" and tend to suggest that he was there and not in Philadelphia at the time of the dating of the "Notes" in his *Papers*. The Library Co. was, as noted earlier, a prime source of information for people gathered in Philadelphia during the period of the Continental Congress and the Constitutional Convention. Hamilton's "Notes" date from Dec. a half year prior to the Convention at a time when Madison was conducting other kinds of historical investigations. Just above Hamilton's "Pamphlet" entry in "Notes," there appears a related reference that reads: "Wood[']s New Eng. Prospects [William Wood, *New England's Prospects* (London, 1639)]. . . . This book is No. 227 in the Pennsyl[.] library . . ." To the right of this reference appears a passage in quotation marks.

73. My thanks to Allan Weinreb at the John Jay Homestead in Katonah, N.Y., Whitney Bagnall at the Columbia University Law School's Special Collections, and Jean W. Ashton at Special Collections in Columbia's Butler Library for information on John Jay's surviving book collections.

To date, the catalogues for Jay's books are not as complete or reliable as one would wish. The absence at Columbia and Katonah of Blackstone's *Commentaries*—a widely-read standard British legal treatise of the late 18th century, almost certainly owned by Jay—is surprising but suggestive of the fragility of such collections and their survival. A similar case in point is the absence of Blackstone's *Commentaries* in the Hamilton book collection. The Jay book collection at Katonah is complicated by the existence of many generations of Jay family books mixed together there with those of John Jay. Large numbers of books at the Jay Homestead are still in many dozens of boxes, each with their own finding-list. The general catalogue there, compiled over the decades by volunteers, is not fully reliable. At Columbia, the Pegasus system does not allow for easy or complete access to books owned by John Jay. Even so, the above-cited writers do not appear to be represented at either site. There is at Columbia an 1820 edn. of Locke's *A Common Place Book*, given by a daughter-in-law of John Jay to his son William. The death date for John Jay (1829) has not yet provided at either location a thorough method for classifying book imprints before then that could have been in his library. The Hamilton book collection at Columbia is organized around such a classification.

On this subject one can consult Herbert Alan Johnson, *John Jay: Colonial Lawyer* (doctoral dissertation for Columbia University, 1965). Of particular interest are Pt. II, Ch. V, "John Jay and the Civil Law," and Appendix D on "John Jay's Law Library." That App. lists Jay's law books at Columbia (Case Reports, Early Year Books, Treatises, etc.). Included are works by Coke, Fortescue, Pufendorf, Hale, and others.

As in the case of the Princeton (College of New Jersey) library at the time when Madison was a student there, the Columbia (King's College) library at the time when Jay and Hamilton were students there falls short for present purposes. The existing Columbia catalogue for that period does not include works by such writers as Bodin, Hobbes,

Rousseau, Montesquieu, and Blackstone. (Jay received his BA there in 1764, while Hamilton first entered in 1773, later receiving an honorary Masters of Arts degree in 1788 four years after the change of name to Columbia College.) In the Columbia Univ. Archives (Columbiana Library in Low Library) are card catalogue files arranged alphabetically by author etc. for the "Library of King's College[,] Books." The collection evidently represents the modest surviving remnant of the much larger library of King's College up to about the time when the college's name was changed. Cf. Austin Baxter Keep, "The Library of King's College," *Columbia University Quarterly*, June, 1911, pp. 275–284. The college acquired c. 1,500 books in c. 1760s to form the bulk of its collection. My thanks to Columbia archivist Abby Lester for information on this subject.

In general one can consult the Jay papers at the Columbia library as prepared by Richard B. Morris (ed.), *John Jay* (2 vols., New York, 1975, 1981), the first vol. covering the period 1745–1780 and the second 1780–1784.

74. Garry Wills, *Cincinnatus: George Washington and the Enlightenment* (Garden City, 1984), Ch. X, "Lawgiver," esp. pp. 158 ff. In the course of that chapter, Wills states as follows: "Since Madison's library perished in the University of Virginia fire of 1895, and he drew up no catalogue of it, there is no way to establish whether he owned or had read [Rousseau's] *The Social Contract* by 1787." The first part of this statement is somewhat inaccurate. Moreover, Wills does not seem to have explored Madison's writings on this point about Rousseau.

75. Concerning Washington's constitutional and political thought, Glenn A. Phelps, in his *George Washington and American Constitutionalism* (Lawrence, 1993), Epilogue, succinctly states as follows: "Washington accepted the view that a constitutional presidency was one that was subordinate to the rule of law[!] . . . [He] also helped to establish the tradition of the president as an interpreter of the Constitution with coequal authority to the Congress and the judiciary. . . . His classical background and, particularly, his ideal of the 'patriot king' made him view the presidency as bearing a special responsibility for the defense of the people. . . . [He] did succeed in establishing the president as the custodian of the national idea."

In his *To the Farewell Address: Ideas of Early American Foreign Policy* (Princeton, 1960), Ch. V, "Washington's Political Testament: The Farewell Address," Felix Gilbert discusses well the great role of Hamilton in shaping Washington's defining statements in his Farewell Address (Hamilton having helped Washington draft many other addresses and pronouncements). In Ch. IV, "*Ratio Status:* Foreign Policy in Practice," Gilbert treats "the literature of the 'interest of the state' [a term much discussed by Gaines Post for the Midddle Ages] and of the 'Political Testaments'," as well as "Alexander Hamilton as representative of European political realism."

In his Farewell Address given on Sept. 19, 1796, in his *Writings* (New York, 1997), Washington closed (p. 967) with the following statement: ". . . I promise myself to realize . . . the sweet enjoyment of partaking in the midst of my fellow Citizens, the benign influence of good Laws [!] under a free Government, the ever favourite [!] object of my heart, and the happy reward, as I trust, of our mutual cares, labours, and dangers." Earlier on in the same address, Washington stresses (p. 967) the need for "Unity of Government" and "a Government for the whole" as being indispensable for "the efficacy and permanency of Your Union." "This government," he also underscored, depends for its success (pp. 968–969) on: "[r]espect for its authority, compliance with its Laws [!]," "the duty of every individual to obey the established Government," and the need "to confine each member of the Society within the limits prescribed by the laws [!]." The need to avoid factionalism in domestic affairs, a central theme of this Address, along with the avoidance of foreign entanglements, had long been a favorite Federalist theme for Washington as well as for Hamilton. Some relevant facsimiles appear in a final sect. on "Farewell" in *George*

Washington and the American Republic (New Haven and San Marino, 1999) by John Rhodehamel.

The preceding characteristic statements by Washington on full obedience to the laws of government by the people as being essential to preserving freedom are similar to ideas of freedom under authority that are variously found in other Federalist writers like Hamilton as well as in Rousseau's *Social Contract.* A study along these lines would be useful.

Above in Ch. IV, sect. 2, on "Madison's Pre-Convention Outlines," is some material relating to George Washington.

76. Washington's library of roughly one thousand books at the time of his death in 1799, after which the collection was dispersed outside Mt. Vernon, covered a wide range of subjects including literature, history, religion, law, military matters, agriculture, and much more. The Boston Athenaeum's catalogue cited in our text above includes under the category of Literature, for instance, Pope's translation of Homer's *Iliad* and *Odyssey*, the Works of Pope as well as Swift, and the Works of Shakespeare. Under the rubric of Miscellaneous is included Locke's *Essay Concerning Human Understanding.* Nothing of present interest appears under History and Law.

The various contemporary inventories and lists of Washington books made from 1759 to 1799 reflect the pride he took in the collections connected with Mt. Vernon. Although many of the books in such listings were acquired from his wife's first husband Daniel and her son John, many others in them were ordered and purchased, as in 1782–1783, by Washington, often through sales advertised in newspapers, which he ardently subscribed to and read, or through intermediaries. The books purchased by him included Voltaire's *Letters*, the French-English dictionary, and Locke's *Understanding.* Notwithstanding Washington's limited formal schooling and the practical bent in his adult reading interests, he was more knowledgeable than is often believed. He remained prone to self-education and was desirous of good classical educations for his stepchildren.

In his recent *The Invention of George Washington* (Charlottesville, 1999), Appendix on "The foundations of useful knowledge," Paul R. Longmore has aptly stated as follows: "Historians have long assumed that Washington read only for practical purposes . . . [yet he] gave much more thought to education than has been recognized. . . . [T]hroughout his life Washington also bought books [etc.]. . . . [Although some historians] have downplayed Washington's interest in reading . . . [and] have at times inferred apathy about books from his failure to mention his reading in his diary[,] . . . [this] self-educated American took pride in the library he accumulated . . . of over nine hundred volumes on a variety of subjects. . . . [However, he] was not a speculative thinker. His gift was not the formulation of ideas, but [in] their incarnation . . . [and] in embodying them [pp. 213–214, 216–217, 226]." Longmore also cites some of the books obtained by Washington (pp. 218 ff.). Washington "evidently took a minor interest in philosophy," acquiring such works as a set of Cicero's "Works" (which, evidence suggests, he read in part), Voltaire's *Letters*, and Locke's *Essay Concerning Human Understanding*, the latter two both acquired in 1783. For books of literature, Longmore cites such writers as Fielding, Butler, Pope, Swift, and Milton. Moreover, "Washington's patronage of the arts was regarded at the time as an influential incitement to American cultural development." Also cited is a range of history books owned by Washington, in addition to contemporary works such as Jefferson's *Notes on Virginia* and Adams' *Defence of Constitutions*. "Approximately 40 percent of . . . [his] collection consisted," nevertheless, "of practical books." Even so, Longmore's good general appendix on Washington's books does not treat the particular sets of issues, contexts, and details focused upon in the present study, including the connection with Hamilton. Nor is it his concern to grapple with the myriad thorny catalogues of Washington books.

In addition to the newer series of *The Papers of George Washington*, I have consulted *The Writings of George Washington from the Original Manuscript Sources, 1745–1799* (edited by John C. Fitzpatrick, 39 vols., Wash., D.C., 1931–1944). In neither series does there appear to be any direct reference by Washington to Rousseau. The same applies to *George Washington: A Collection* (compiled and edited by W. B. Allen, Indianapolis, 1988), as it also does to the single volume of Washington's *Writings* (New York, 1997). As just observed, the absence of references by Washington to writers who interested him was typical, while even Hamilton, for whom an interest in Rousseau has been discussed, referred to him directly only once.

Grappling with the many different inventories of the Washington book collections is a challenging task, one undertaken here in ways not previously encountered. The inventories by George Washington and others are not well-organized catalogues in the way that those by Jefferson were, that is, arranged according to systematic classifications. Rather, they mostly consist of straightforward listings in miscellaneous order. The last of these kinds of contemporary inventories, the one done in 1799, was rearranged much later, according to topical categories, in the Boston Athenaeum's catalogue

In addition to the *Catalogue of the Washington Collection in the Boston Athenaeum*, cited in full in the text above, I have also consulted the corresponding 1799 inventory of books drawn up for the estate of George Washington. This inventory was published in Ed. Everett's *Life of George Washington* (New York, 1860), p. 312 ("The Social Compact in French"), thereafter in an 1870 publication by Lossing. This hand catalogue of 1799 is a straightforward listing of books in miscellaneous order, with numbers subsequently added to designate the order of appearance of each entry in it.

Cf. the various inventories of books in the appendixes to *The Library at Mount Vernon*, by Frances Laverne Carroll and Mary Meacham (Pittsburgh, 1977), including the 1782 inventory (Appendix V) for John Parke Custis' books, containing a significant number of works by classical writers. Also in *ibid.*, App. IV, is the 1759 catalogue of books owned by Martha's first husband, Daniel Parke Custis. It was drawn up by George Washington shortly after he married her. Available to him at Mt. Vernon, these books were also of a wide range. App. VI contains the 1783 shorter inventory of books at Mt. Vernon made by Lund Washington, along with George's request to him in an Aug. 1783 letter to track down books that John Custis may have taken from Mt. Vernon and that are apparently missing from the list Lund sent him (also in *Papers, Colonial Series*, cited below), Vol. 7, p. 348–, a facsimile of the hand version kindly sent me by Dr Philander Chase).

The two lists of books drawn up by George Washington in 1759 and c. 1764 appear in turn, from the original sources, in *The Papers of George Washington: Colonial Series*, Vols. 6 and 7 (edited by W. W. Abbot, etc., Charlottesville, 1988, 1990), pp. 283 ff. and pp. 283 ff–, respectively. The 1759 list includes, according to George's abbreviated entries (*sic*): "Ovids Epistles," "Bacon's Essays," "Plutarchs Lives" and "Morals," "Cato's Letters," "Seneca's Morals," "Pliny's Panegyrick," "Pope's Works," "Quintilian's Declamations," "Milton's Paradise Lost," "Locke On Education," "Terrence's Comedies," "Roman Antiquities," and much more along similar lines. The c. 1764 list for the combined book collections at Mt. Vernon is also voluminous.

Cf. also *The Estate of George Washington, Deceased*, by Eugene E. Prussing (Boston, 1927) and *Last Will and Testament of George Washington* (Washington, D.C., 1911) for other materials relating to Washington's library. Perhaps the most interesting overall survey, with good illustrations, is *The George Washington Library Collection* (at the Boston Athenaeum), by Stanley Ellis Cushing (Boston, 1988, 1997). Also cf. *The Athenaeum Catalogue*, p. 149, concerning Washington's short list of titles involved in W. S. Smith's 1783 purchase of books, including "Voltaire's Letters" and "Lewis 15th. 4 Vols." In

Fitzpatrick's ed. of *Writings of Washington,* Vol. 27, pp. 24–25, is a 1783 letter from Washington to Smith concerning the purchase of books.

The listings of books drawn up in 1783, prior to George's return to Mt. Vernon after nearly a dozen years of almost continuous absence, show him turning to books more for himself than for others, as he once had done particularly for the education of his two stepchildren. In addition to his interest in books with an eye to travel, the library space and its contents at Mt. Vernon received George's attention. He could now devote more time to his book collection there and to its apparent depletion during his long absences. His inventories of 1759 and c. 1764 were far longer than the list sent to him in 1783 by his cousin and caretaker at Mt. Vernon, Lund Washington. To Lund George wrote on Aug. 13, 1783 from Newburgh (*Library at Mount Vernon,* p. 163): "I have received your letter ... with a Catalogue of my Books—When you go next to Abingdon [John Custis' home, a dozen or so miles from Mt. Vernon], see if there is any there with my name or Arms in them, & ford. the list." These books would have been taken by George's stepson John prior to John's death in 1781 and to the inventory of John's books in 1782. Not unlike James Madison's difficult stepson, John Todd, who took many of the former President's books to pay off gambling and other debts, Washington's stepson John Custis may have made off with some of the future President's books under dubious circumstances and with less than educational motives. John mismanaged his own financial affairs. George did his best for him from afar, just as he had done in the spring of 1773 when personally accompanying John to King's College to have him enrolled.

For information in recent years on George Washington and his books, I am indebted to editor Dr. Philander Chase at the Washington *Papers* in Charlottesville, Ellen Clark of the Society of the Cincinnati in Washington, D.C., Barbara A. McMillan of the Ladies Society at Washington's Mount Vernon home, Stephen Nonack at the Boston Athenaeum, and Dorothy Twohig, formerly editor at the Washington *Papers* and before that editor at the Hamilton *Papers* in New York.

77. Cf. p. 136 above and appendix below.

Notes to Chapter VI
The Testimony of Other Figures

1. The three untitled letter-articles by "T.Q." and "J." (Boston, 1763) appear in *American Political Writing during the Founding Era, 1760-1805* (edited by Charles S. Hyneman and Donald S. Lutz, 2 vols., Indianapolis, 1983), Vol. I, pp. 19 ff., as usual all *sic.*

2. James Otis' *The Rights of the British Colonies Asserted and Proved* (Boston, 1764) and his *A Vindication of the British Colonies* (Boston, 1765), appear in *Pamphlets of the American Revolution, 1750-1776* (edited by Bernard Bailyn, Camb., Mass., 1965), Vol. I (without sequel), pp. 419 ff. and pp. 554 ff., respectively, again all *sic.* I have also consulted the 2nd edn. of the original.

3. Otis, *Rights*, pp. 444, 446.

4. *Ibid.*, p. 470.

5. Otis, *Vindication*, pp. 560-561: "[According to our author, . . . , right to life, liberty, or property . . . depend on the mere good will, grace, and pleasure of the supreme power, and all their charters and of course all their rights, even to life, liberty, and property, may be taken away at pleasure. Thus every charter in England [and America] may be taken away, for they are but voluntary and gracious grants of the crown. . . . But would it be expedient to strike such a blow without the most urgent necessity? 'In all states there is (and must be) an absolute supreme power, to which the right of *legislation* belongs: and which by the singular constitution of these kingdoms is vested in the King, Lords, and Commons' [Blackstone]." [However,] . . . according to Filmer, God hath given to every father over his children, and much more to every prince over his subjects, a power 'absolute, arbitrary and unlimited, . . . they being all his slaves, and the father or prince,

lord proprietor of everything, and his unbounded will their law.' This is the substance of one of Mr. Locke's inferences from these words of Filmer, 'God hath given to the father a right or liberty to alien his power over his children to any other'. . . . 'Law is nothing else but the will of him that hath the power of the *supreme* father.' Horrid blasphemy!"

Further on in his *Vindication*, Otis makes it perfectly clear that in his mind the legislative factor is rightly the basis of sovereignty and state in the issues at hand, especially concerning taxation. It is not altogether certain where his heart lies in this British-American dispute, aside from the more obvious overtones in his title. Though bold, Otis may be speaking out of both sides of his mouth, as if to hedge his bets (and to save his neck?). Whatever the case, legislative sovereignty and the legislative state receive powerful expression at this early incipient stage in the Revolutionary Era. Hence, pp. 563-565: "What is the reason of all this? . . . That the colonies should be bound by acts of Parliament wherein they are named is an exception from a general rule or maxim. What is that rule or maxim? It is that the colonies being separate dominions and at a distance from the realm, or mother state, and in fact unrepresented in Parliament[,] shall be governed by laws of their own making; and unless named in acts of Parliament shall not be bound by them. '*Quia non mittunt milites ad parliamentum*,' says Lord Coke. . . . Should a mother state even think it reasonable to impose internal as well as external taxes on six millions of subjects in their remote dominions without allowing them one voice, it would be matter of wonder and astonishment; but it could not be said that the supreme legislative had exceeded the bounds of their power and authority, nor would this render a petition undutiful and seditious. Those six millions must on such an event, unless blind, see themselves reduced to the mortifying condition of mere ciphers and blanks in society. Should all this ever happen to the British colonies, which God forbid, might it not be truly and safely affirmed that the representation in the House of Commons would be very unequal? The right of a supreme power in a state to tax its colonies is a thing that is clear and evident; and yet the mode of exercising that right may be questionable in point of reason and equity. . . .

"Many great and good men have complained of the inequality of the representation in Great Britain. . . . The supreme legislative indeed represents the whole society or community, as well the dominions as the realm; and this is the true reason why the dominions are justly bound by such acts of Parliament as name them. This is implied in the idea of a supreme sovereign power; and if the Parliament had not such authority the colonies would be independent, which none but rebels, fools, or madmen will contend for. God forbid these colonies should ever prove undutiful to their mother country! Whenever such a day shall come it will be the beginning of a terrible scene. Were these colonies left to themselves tomorrow, America would be a mere shambles of blood and confusion before little petty states could be settled. How many millions must perish in building up great empires?"

6. Bernard Bailyn's section on "Sovereignty" in his "General Introduction" to the *Pamphlet* is insightful but ignores the central issue of *legislative* sovereignty. A few excerpts are apt (pp. 115–116, 118): "[O]f all the intellectual problems the colonists faced, one was absolutely crucial: in the last analysis it was over this issue that the Revolution was fought. On the pivotal question of sovereignty . . . American thinkers attempted to depart sharply from one of the most firmly fixed points in eighteenth-century political thought . . . , preparing the way for a new departure in the organization of power.

"The idea of sovereignty current in the English-speaking world of the 1760's was scarcely more than a century old. It had first emerged during the English Civil War . . . and had been established . . . in the Revolution of 1688. . . . Derived in part from the political theory of classical antiquity, in part from Roman law, and in part from medieval thought, this idea came to England most directly in the sixteenth-century writings, especially those of Jean Bodin, that sought to justify and fortify monarchial supremacy.

"But in these early writings the concept of sovereignty still retained important limitations derived from its legal, religious, and pre-national origins. By sovereign Bodin had meant supreme, but not arbitrary. ... [I]t must still 'embody the law of nature and of God.' ... But then, in the mid-seventeenth-century crisis in England, ... a generation of cold-eyed analysts ... laid bare the doctrine of naked force. Hobbes and Filmer are ... associated with this change. ... By the mid-eighteenth century this Whig conception of a sovereign Parliament had hardened into orthodoxy. In the year of the Stamp Act, it was given its classic formulation by Blackstone ... in his *Commentaries* ..."

Needless to say, Blackstone's *Commentaries* became a prime source for emerging American thought on legislative sovereignty and much more, just as did writings by Locke and many others on the British side who advanced ideas of parliamentary supremacy. As already noted, the founders at Philadelphia in 1776 and 1787 were well read in such writers, adapting as well as reacting to them in a wide variety of ways marked by both continuity and change in such areas as Bodinian traditions of legislative sovereignty. Thomas Jefferson and John Adams are good examples of writers during the Revolutionary Era who drew extensively pro and con on a wide range of diverse English and French viewpoints—constitutionalist and absolutist, liberal and conservative—and incorporated them in their developing ideas on subjects of legislation, sovereignty, state, and so forth.

7. For instance, in a section of his Rights entitled "On the Natural Rights of Colonists," Otis draws directly in different ways upon Rousseau, Montesquieu, Locke, Domat, Grotius, and others, although not, in these cases, concerning legislative sovereignty *per se* (pp. 436 ff., 719 ff.).

8. Samuel Adams (most probably), "A State of the Rights of the Colonists," in *Tracts of the American Revolution, 1763–1776* (edited by Merrill Jensen, Indianapolis, 1967), pp. 233 ff., all *sic*.

9. *Ibid.*, p. 238: "By the Act of the British Parliament commonly called the Toleration Act, every Subject in England Except Papists etc. was restored to, and re-established in, his natural right to worship God according to the dictates of his own conscience. And by the Charter of this Province it is granted[,] ordained and established (that it is declared as an original right) that there shall be liberty of conscience allowed in the worship of God. ... Magna Charta itself is in substance but a constrained Declaration, or proclamation, and promulgation ... of their original ... natural Rights. ... That great author, that great jurist, and even that Court writer Mr. Justice Blackstone holds that this recognition was justly obtained of King John sword in hand, and peradventure it must be one day sword in hand again rescued and preserved from total destruction and oblivion."

10. *Ibid.*, pp. 238–239.

11. *Ibid.*, pp. 239–240.

12. Daniel Leonard, "To All Nations of Men" (1773), in *Political Writing*, Vol. I, pp. 210–211: "Separate states (all self-governing communities) stand in the same relation to one another as individuals do when out of society; or to use the more common phrase, in a state of nature. ... Mr. Hobbes says 'natural law is divided into natural law of man, and natural law of states.' The latter is what we call the law of nations. The laws both of nature and nations, as well as those of every free state, indeed of every lawful government under heaven are extremely watchful in ascertaining and protecting the right of private property. ... All agree that no man can be justly deprived of his property without his consent in person or by his representative, unless he has forfeited it by the breach of the laws of his country. ... [T]he British parliament ... bind[s] us by laws to which our con-

sent was never so much as asked. . . . Have they not utterly subverted the free constitution of our state by making our extreme magistrate a mere dependent on the minister of Great Britain, and thus destroyed all confidence of the body politic in the head? . . . Have they not further, to defeat all prospect of our relieving ourselves by the free course of the laws of the land . . . ?"

13. *Ibid.*, p. 212.

14. *Ibid.*, pp. 213–215: "Men combined to subvert our civil government, to plunder and murder us, can have no right to protection in their persons or properties among us; they have by their attempts upon our liberty, *put themselves in a state of war with us*, as Mr. Locke observes. . . .

"These usurpers, or *foreign emissaries*, being screened from the power of the laws, by a corruption of both legislative and executive courts, have returned to a state of nature again with respect to this people, and may as justly be slain as wolves. . . . [All] men naturally have a right to life, liberty, and the possession and disposal of their property."

15. Congress' Appeal to the inhabitants of Quebec, in *ibid.*, Vol. I, pp. 234–235: "The Crown and its Ministers are impowered, as far as they could be by Parliament, to establish even the *Inquisition* itself among you. Have you an Assembly composed of worthy men, elected by yourselves and in whom you can confide, to make laws for you, to watch over your welfare, and to direct in what quantity and in what manner your money shall be taken from you? No. The Power of making laws for you is lodged in the governor and council, all of them dependent upon and removeable at the *pleasure* of a Minister. Besides, another late statute, made without your consent, has subjected you to the impositions of Excise, the horror of all free states, thus wresting your property from you by the most odious of taxes and laying open to insolent tax-gatherers, houses, the scenes of domestic peace and comfort and called the castles of English subjects in the books of their law. And in the very act for altering your government, and intended to flatter you, you are not authorized to 'assess levy, or apply any rates and taxes. . . ."

16. *Ibid.*, pp. 235–236.

17. Samuel West, Election Day Sermon, 1776 ("On the Right to Rebel against Governors"), in *ibid.*, Vol. I, pp. 412–13, 418: "[T]he same principles which oblige us to submit to government do equally oblige us to resist tyranny . . . [in] the grand controversy that at this day subsists between Great Britain and the American colonies.

"That we may understand the nature and design of civil government, and discover the foundation of the magistrate's authority to command, and the duty of subjects to obey, it is necessary to derive civil government from its original, in order to which we must consider what 'state all men are naturally in, and that is (as Mr. Locke observes) a state of perfect freedom . . . within the bounds of the law of nature, without asking leave or depending upon the will of any man.' It is a state wherein all are equal,—no one having a right to control another. . . .

"It is also necessary that the minor part should submit to the major; *e.g.*, when legislators have enacted a set of laws which are highly approved by a large majority of the community as tending to promote the public good, in this case, if a small number of persons . . . view the matter in a very different point of light from the public, . . . and the majority still continue to approve of the laws that are enacted, it is the duty of those few . . . to submit to the public judgment. . . . Perhaps, also, some cases of intolerable oppression . . . may justly warrant the few to refuse submission to what they judge inconsistent with their peace and safety; for the law of self-preservation will always justify opposing a cruel and tyrannical imposition. . . . Except the above-named cases, the minor ought always to submit to the major; otherwise, there can be no peace nor harmony in society."

18. *Ibid.*, pp. 419, 421.

19. Carter Braxton, "Address to the Convention of ... Virginia" (1776), in *ibid.*, Vol I, p. 332: "Men are prone to condemn the whole, because a part is objectionable; but certainly it would, in the present case, be more wise to consider, whether, if the constitution was brought back to its original state, and its present imperfections remedied, it would not afford more happiness than any other. If the independence of the Commons could be secured, and the dignity of the Lords preserved, how can a government be better formed for the preservation of freedom? And is there any thing more easy than this? ... I have the best authority for asserting, that with these improvements, and giving the people an equal and adequate representation, England would have remained a land of liberty to the latest ages."

20. *Ibid.*, pp. 332–333.

21. *The Essex Result*, attributed to Theophilus Parsons, is in *ibid.*, Vol. I, pp. 480 ff.

22. *Ibid.*, p. 485.

23. *Ibid.*, pp. 486–488.

24. *Ibid.*, pp. 488–491: "If the supreme power is so directed and executed that he [the individual] does not enjoy political liberty, it is an illegal power, and he is not bound to obey. Political liberty is by some defined, a liberty of doing whatever is not prohibited by law. The definition is erroneous. A tyrant may govern by laws. The republics of Venice and Holland govern by laws, yet those republics have degenerated into insupportable tyrannies. Let it be thus defined; political liberty is the right every man in the state has, to do whatever is not prohibited by laws, TO WHICH HE HAS GIVEN HIS CONSENT....

"The committee also proceeded to consider upon what principles, and in what manner, the supreme power of the state thus composed of the powers of the several individuals thereof, may be formed, modelled, and exerted in a republic, so that every member of the state may enjoy political liberty. This is called by some, *the ascertaining of the political law of the state*. Let it now be called *the forming of a constitution*....

"That state, (other things being equal) which has reposed the supreme power in the hands of one of a small number of persons, is the most powerful state....

"But from a single person, or a very small number, we are not to expect that political honesty, and upright regard to the interest of the body of the people, and the civil rights of each individual, which are essential to a good and free constitution....

"Yet, when we are forming a Constitution, by deductions that follow from established principles, (which is the only good method of forming one for futurity,) we are to look further than to the bulk of the people, for the greatest wisdom, firmness, consistency, and perseverance. These qualities will most probably be found amongst men of education and fortune. From such men we are to expect genius cultivated by reading, and all the various advantages and assistances, which art, and a liberal education aided by wealth, can furnish....

"Let all their respective excellencies be united. Let the supreme power be so disposed and ballanced, that the laws may have in view the interest of the whole; let them be wisely and consistently framed for that end, and firmly adhered to; and let them be executed with vigour and dispatch....

"The supreme power is considered as including the legislative, judicial, and executive powers."

Cf. above, Ch. 5, sect. 6, for quotations on lawgivers from Rousseau's *Social Contract* in Wills' *Cincinnatus*.

25. *Ibid.*, pp. 492–493.

26. *Ibid.*, pp. 494–497, 500, 510, 514: "If the legislative and judicial powers are united, the maker of the law will also interpret it; and the law may then speak a language, dictated by the whims, the caprice, or the prejudice of the judge....

"Should the executive and legislative powers be united, mischiefs the most terrible would follow. . . .

"Should the executive and judicial powers be united, the subject would then have no permanent security of his person and property. . . .

"The following principles now seem to be established.

"1. That the supreme power is limited, and cannot controul the unalienable rights of mankind. . . .

"4. That the legislative, judicial, and executive powers, are to be lodged in different hands. . . .

"6. That the laws will be made with the greatest wisdom. . . .

"8. That the legislative power of a state hath no authority to controul the natural rights of any of it's members. . . .

"The rights of representation should be so equally and impartially distributed. . . .

"But the legislative power must not be trusted with one assembly. . . .

"In forming the first body of legislators, let regard be had only to the representation of persons, not of property. . . .

"We have now the legislative body '. . . Each branch hath a negative upon the other. . . . The legislative body is so formed and ballanced that the laws will be made with the greatest wisdom and the best intentions; and the proper consent thereto is obtained. Each man enjoys political liberty, and his civil rights will be taken care of."

27. Anonymous, statement of Berkshire County Representatives, Mass. (1778), in *ibid.*, Vol. I, pp. 456–459.

28. William Whiting, Address to the Inhabitants of Berkshire County, Mass. (1778), in *ibid.*, Vol. I, p. 466: "In a state of nature, each individual has a right, not only to dispose of, order, and direct, his property, his person, and all his own actions, within the bounds of the law of nature, as he thinks fit, but he also has a right in himself, not only to defend, but to judge and to punish the person who shall make any assault or encroachment, either upon his person or property. . . .

"Now when any number of men enter into a state of society with each other, they resign into the hands of the society, the right they had in a state of nature, of disposing, directing and ordering their own persons and properties, so far as the good of the whole may require it. . . .

"The great Mr. Locke tells us, 'That when men enter into a community, they must give up all the powers necessary for the purposes for which they entered into society, to the majority of the community, and this is done barely by agreeing to enter into political society; which is all the compact there is, or need be, between the individuals to make up a commonwealth. And this is that, and that only, which gives beginning to any lawful government in the world.' "

29. Zabdiel Adams, election sermon (1782), in *ibid.*, Vol. I, pp. 543, 548, 550, 557.

30. Anonymous, "Rudiments of Law and Government Deduced from the Law of Nature," in *ibid.*, Vol. I, pp. 584–593. Under "Of Government," the writer makes partial use of the four causes: "The preservation and maintenance of these rights, is the final cause of association; and all constitutions are just, in degree as they conform to these views; and weak and tyrannical as they deviate from them.

"The ["That government so easy, where the people find or fancy they find, their own happiness in their submission. Cato's *Letters*." Etc.] *regulations of government must owe their form to the efficience* [?] *of these purposes*. And the Distribution of Authority, the Body of Laws, the Administration of Justice and the General Policy of the Republic, must breathe no other intention."

"Of Laws" includes the following: "[N]o number of statutes will comprehend every particular case; so indefinite is the variety from changes of circumstances: And one insurmountable difficulty is formed from the attempt; for every new law, where such is the practice, acts as rubbish, under which we bury the former. To endeavour to compose a compleat system, is in reality the amusement of speculative casuists; not the employment of the guardians of the people. ["Would you prevent crimes? Let the laws be clear and simple; and let the laws be feared, and the laws only . . . Beccaria"] Law, to be just, should be simple, clear, and intelligible to the meanest capacity, in the same degree in which it operates. . . .

"And thus much is necessary. Salus populi suprema lex esto (let the good of the community be the chief rule of conduct) is not always a sufficient direction to magistrates, *and some laws are necessary to shew how far their authority does not extend.* Local circumstances and proportions too, require adjustments and regulations, which ought to be constant and uniform. But at all events, the code [". . . Puffendorf"] of laws should not be too large for the attainment of moderate capacities."

31. Noah Webster, "A Citizen of America" ("An Examination of the Leading Principles of the Federal Constitution," 1787), in *The Debates on the Constitution: Federalist and Anti-Federalist Speeches, Articles, and Letters During the Struggle over Ratification* (2 "parts" or vols., New York, 1993), Vol. I, p. 129, all sic.

32. *Ibid.*, p. 130.

33. *Ibid.*, pp. 162–163: "It is not our duty as freemen, to receive the opinions of any men, however great and respectable, without an examination. But when we reflect that some of the greatest men in America, with the venerable Franklin and the illustrious Washington at their head; *some* of them the *fathers* and *saviors* of their country, men who have labored at the helm during a long and violent tempest, and guided us to the haven of peace—and *all* of them distinguished for their abilities, their acquaintance with ancient and modern governments, as well as with the temper, the passions, the interests and the wishes of the Americans;—when we reflect on these circumstances, it is impossible to resist impressions of respect, and we are almost impelled to suspect our own judgements, when we call in question any part of the system, which they have recommended for adoption. Not having the same means of information, we are more liable to mistake the nature and tendency of particular articles of the constitution, or the reasons on which they were admitted. Great confidence therefore should be reposed in the abilities, the zeal and integrity of that respectable body. But after all, if the constitution should, in its future operation, be found defective or inconvenient, two-thirds of both houses of Congress or the application of two-thirds of the legislatures, may open the door for amendments. Such improvements may then be made, as experience shall dictate. . . .

"The constitution defines the powers of Congress; and every power not expressly delegated to that body, remains in the several state-legislatures. The sovereignty and the republican form of government of each state is guaranteed by the constitution. . . . In theory, it has all the energy and freedom of the British and Roman governments, without their defects."

34. Noah Webster, Article from *American Magazine*, in *ibid.*, Vol. II, pp. 3111–312. Cf. above Ch. II, n. 180 and our main text, p. 100, on the *Lexicon Iuridicum.*

35. John Stevens, Article in New York news publication, Nov. 1787, in *ibid.*, Vol. I, pp. 227–229: "Wretched indeed would be our political institution, had we been governed by the 'axioms' of European writers on politics, in the formation of them. As we are placed in a situation totally new, instead of absurdly hunting for precedents in the old world, we must think, we must reason, for ourselves. . . .

"Montesquieu, it seems, tells us, that a *Republic must have only a small territory.* But how, I would ask, would he, or Locke, or any other political writer in Europe, be warranted in insisting on this assertion as an *irrefragable* axiom? Had they formed any conceptions of a republican Government instituted upon the plan of the Constitution now under consideration? Because the wretched attempts that have been made in the old world, to constitute Republican Governments, have necessarily failed of attaining the desired purpose, are we to be told the thing is 'impracticable,' when attempted upon principles as different, as light is from darkness? Montesquieu's maxim may be just, for aught I know, when applied to such republican Governments as Sparta. This commonwealth affords us a striking instance of the absurdities mankind are capable of when they blindly submit themselves to the guidance of *passion* and *prejudice*. . . . This institution was founded upon Montesquieu's principle of Republican Government, viz. virtue: by virtue, here, is not meant morality; but an enthusiastic attachment to the political system of the country we inhabit. By the force of this mistaken principle, however, the Government, which Lycurgus established in Sparta, was supported for ages. . . . And what is the tendency of Cato's reasoning, but to form Governments, like that of Sparta, in every State in the Union? Should we be able to support separate independent sovereignties (which, with submission to Cato, I think would be 'impracticable') we should soon become mere nests of hornets. . . . Away with this Spartan virtue and black broth; we'll have none of them: and Cato must not think to cram them down our throats, by telling us it is the prescription of a great political doctor, . . . [i.e.] Montesquieu. . . . Cato shall deem them 'as irrefragable as any in Euclid,' shall never persuade me to quarrel with my bread and butter. . . . Had he been an American, and now living, I would stake my life on it, he would have formed different principles. . . . But reason and experience have at length convinced us of the impropriety of the people themselves interfering, in any shape, in the administration of Government. The powers of Government must, of necessity, be delegated. It was the English who first discovered the secret, of which the ancients were totally ignorant, of Legislation by Representation. This is the hinge on which all Republican Governments must move. But we must proceed a step farther. It has also been discovered, that faction cannot be expelled even from a *Representative* body, while possessed *singly* of the whole of the Legislative power. Hence two distinct Legislative bodies have been contrived, farther to check this turbulent spirit." Etc. on further checks and balances.

Also by Stevens is an article in the same news publication dated Jan., 1788, in which he begins with various objections to the new Constitution on the part of its critics. E.g., "That the Legislative, Executive, and Judicial of the several States will be annihilated." Then, in *ibid.*, Vol. I, pp. 785–786, 788: "*The consolidated Government will be an iron handed despotism*. But how do they prove this? Montesquieu, somewhere in his spirit of laws, tells us, that 'it is natural for a republic to have only a small territory.' This is the sole proof or argument which the gentlemen have adduced in support of their general position from whence this *iron handed despotism* is inferred, viz. 'that *a very extensive territory* cannot be governed on the principles of freedom, otherwise than by a confederation of republics.'

"But if the *ipse dixit* of Montesquieu is to be admitted as conclusive evidence on this point, his assertions on other points ought equally to govern our determinations. [Etc.] . . . 'The English is the best species of Constitution that could possibly be imagined by man.' . . . [W]hat Montesquieu has advanced on this subject, cannot be applied to the Constitution now under discussion. By this Constitution, *the sole power of enacting laws*, is vested in a representative body: Agreeably to Montesquieu, 'it is a fundamental law in democracies, that the *people* should have *the sole power to enact laws*.' Indeed, it is impossible to say to what extent of territory a Government, upon a Republican plan, may be carried, by means of this expedient of a *Representative* Legislature. . . .

"It was not till the Revolution in England that any tolerable ideas of good Government were formed. Plato, Sir Thomas More and Harrington, before this period had amused themselves with forming visionary schemes of perfect Governments, but, for want of experimental knowledge, their plans are no better than romances, the extravagant sallies of an exuberant imagination. But it is principally from our own experience that we can derive just notions of the true foundations on which the liberties of the people rest. . . . Let us endeavor to make the best use we can of those important discoveries in the science of Government, which the revolution in England, and the late revolution amongst ourselves have opened to our view. Let us be content to leave to posterity, the glory and happiness o perfecting that plan of Government, which the united wisdom of those worthy patriots, who formed the late Convention, has proffered to us."

36. Letter by Samuel Adams to Richard Henry Lee, Dec. 1787, in *ibid.*, Vol. I, p. 446.

37. *Ibid.*, p. 447: "But should we continue distinct sovereign States, confederated for the Purposes of mutual Safety and Happiness, each contributing to the federal Head such a Part of its Sovereignty as would render the Government fully adequate to those Purposes and *no more*, the People would govern themselves more easily, the Laws of each State being well adapted to its own Genius & Circumstances, and the Liberties of the United States would be more secure than they can be, as I humbly conceive, under the proposed new Constitution. You are sensible, Sir, that the Seeds of Aristocracy began to spring even before the Conclusion of our Struggle for the natural Rights of Men. . . . The few haughty Families, think *They* must govern."

38. James Wilson, opening address to the Pennsylvania Ratifying Convention, Nov., 1787, in *ibid.*, Vol. I, pp. 800–801: "We all know, and we have all felt, that the present system of confederation is inadequate to the government and the exigencies of the United States. Need I describe the contrasted scene which the revolution has presented to our view? On the one hand, the arduous struggle in the cause of liberty terminated by a glorious and triumphant peace; on the other, contention and poverty at home, discredit and disgrace abroad. . . . Private calamity, and public anarchy have prevailed. . . . [E]very act of Congress, and the proceedings of every State are replete with proofs in that respect, and all point to the weakness and imbecility of the existing Confederation; while the loud and concurrent voice of the people proclaims an efficient national government to be the only cure. Under these impressions, and with these views, the late Convention were appointed and met; the end which they proposed to accomplish, being to frame one national and efficient government, in which the exercise of beneficence, correcting the jarring interests of every part, should pervade the whole. . . . [T]he principles and means that were adopted by the Convention to obtain that end, are now before us . . ."

39. *Ibid.*, pp. 801–802.

40. Timothy Ford, Essays in a Charleston, S.C., news publication, 1794, in *American Political Writing during the Founding Era*, Vol. II, pp. 906–907: "The natural rights of men undoubtedly form the rational foundation of the social compact. . . . *Life, liberty* and *property*, have been adduced as the chief among the natural rights of men. The two former are common to all men, and in equal degree; the latter is indeed common to all, but the degree depends upon industry and success. That very industry . . . is as necessary to the existence of the body-politic, under its best organization, as to the *existence* of the individual in the supposed natural state. A variety of writers have attempted to shew what a people ought to do when they form a social compact for the purpose of perpetuating or securing their rights. If the *natural rights* were the only matters to be regarded, perpetuated or secured by the institution of society, the rules which they commonly frame would be liable to fewer exceptions. It is here that their fancied state of nature misleads them; they first of all place man naked and destitute amongst the roving animals of the forest, . . . and out of this . . . springs a social compact. Here, . . . all are to start even and equal in the career of society. . . . [T]he object of the association may be summed up in a short sentence—'Life, liberty and property shall be secured to all;' and all that would be required of a constitution would be to provide the means of accomplishing that end. But

as such a previous state never existed but in the dreams of theorists, so the rules that are formed upon it must be imperfect for a practical system."

41. *Ibid.*, p. 907: "A late ingenious author (Rousseau) seems to have had a view to this distinction, when he says, 'Besides the general maxims of legislation which apply to all, there are particular circumstances confined to each people, which must influence their establishment, and render their regulations proper only for themselves. Thus we see that the Hebrews formerly, and the Arabs in later times, have had religion for their principal object; the Athenians, literature; . . . Sparta, war; and Rome, virtue.' If the accidental state into which society may be thrown after the formation of a constitution, ought to influence the laws and regulations, by parity of reason ought the pre-existent state of the people themselves to influence the constitution. For what purpose is it made, if not to suit the state and condition of men? The natural rights of man ought indeed to be common to all constitutions; but the real situation of each people ought to govern their own institutes, and make them peculiar to themselves. The natural rights of man can never vary in any society, because they are built upon the eternal principles of nature; but the interests of man are subject to all those vicissitudes to which the state of society is itself liable."

42. *Ibid.*, pp. 909, 915, 935: "An intrusion like this into the domains of a settled people can claim no more pretence of right than Alexander, when he passed the Granicus, or Caesar when he passed the Rubicon. A wandering horde has just as good a right to set down amongst a people, *and be their law givers*, as they have, after having formed an association upon mutual principles, to change them at pleasure, as their varying interests, their passions, or their caprice may dictate. Power is in each case the only source of right, and arbitrary will the measure of its exercise. The common notions of a contract utterly exclude the idea of a right residing in one party to alter or rescind it—*mutual obligation* forms its very essence. To bind one party, and leave the other at large, is to impose a law upon a conquered people, instead of forming a contract between free and equal parties.

"Mere power can never constitute a legitimate right, and yet by what other claim can one party presume, of their own accord, to change the compact? It is said indeed, that the majority ought to govern. This principle is true under modifications, but it is not indefinitely so. It is a principle very capable of being perverted, and likely always to be enlisted on the side of those who have or hope to have a majority, let their views or principles be what they may. . . .

"It follows from this, that, as to all *legislative acts*, the majority of the constituted body has a right to determine; but that the right is derived from the very compact itself, and not from any pre-existent quality supposed to reside in the people during the time they were in an unconnected state. . . .

"The good of society requires that the laws should change with its exigencies; and the power of deciding when these exigencies occur, must be referred to the majority of the

"The good of society requires that the laws should change with its exigencies; and the power of deciding when these exigencies occur, must be referred to the majority of the constituted bodies. This majority may speak the sense of a majority of the people, or it may not; but I know of no constitution which prescribes a mode of ascertaining the fact, or that requires the ascertainment of the fact as a prerequisite to give force and validity to the law. . . . Upon the whole, then, the superior right to govern, as claimed by the back country, has been . . . proved to be without foundation. The question of expediency, situated as Carolina is, . . . also . . . results in favor of the government as it now stands for the safety, as well of the personal rights, as of the rights of property. That both parties are safe as matters now stand, one might be unsafe after the proposed alteration. It is a thing therefore not demandable of right, and not adviseable in point of expediency."

43. James Kent, *Introductory Lecture to a Course of Law Lectures* (1794), in *ibid.*, Vol. II, pp. 941, 943.

44. *Ibid.*, p. 944: "I consider then the Courts of Justice, as the proper and intended Guardians of our limited Constitutions, against the factions and encroachments of the Legislative Body. This affords an additional and weighty reason, for making a complete knowledge of those Constitutions to form the Rudiments of a public, and especially of a law Education. Nor are the accomplishments of Academical learning any ways repugnant to a rapid improvement in the Law. On the contrary, the course of instruction . . . will greatly assist the researches of the Student into the nature and history of all Governments. . . . A Lawyer in a free country, should have all the requisites of Quinctilian's orator. . . . He should be well read in the whole circle of the Arts and Sciences. He should be fit for the administration of public affairs, and to govern the commonwealth by his councils, establish it by his Laws, and correct it by his Example. In short, he should resemble Tully, whose fruitful mind, as this distinguished Teacher of oratory (De institutione oratoria) observes, was not bounded by the walls of the Forum, but by those of nature. . . .

"The perusal of the best Greek and Roman Authors . . . is highly important . . . The ancient Classic Writers . . . have formed their Works on such sure principles . . ."

45. *Ibid.*, pp. 944–945: "The knowledge of the civil law, the most durable monument of the wisdom of the Romans, is extremely interesting, whether we consider the intrinsic merit of the system, or its influence upon the Municipal Laws of the land. That venerable body of Law, which was compiled under the auspices of the Emperor Justinian, and which has fortunately come down for the delight and improvement of modern times, discovers almost every where, the traces of an enlightened age of the Roman Jurisprudence. And it is a well known fact, that altho the Taste and Philosophy of the Romans declined with their freedom, a succession of eminent Civilians continued to shine with equal lustre far under the Emperors, and Papinian, Paul, and Ulpian still preserved the sound sense and classic purity of the civil law. . . . An accurate acquaintance with the general Principles of Universal Law [requires] . . . great capacity and consummate application.. . . . But as an eminent Author has observed (Gibbon) legal studies require only a state of peace and refinement. . . . [All serve] . . . to collect and strengthen the powers of the human mind.

"The doctrines of Moral Philosophy form the foundation of Human Laws and must be deemed an essential part of Juridical Education. . . . We are led by these inquiries to a knowledge of . . . the necessity and final end of government, the justness and harmony of obedience."

46. Anonymous, *Discussion Upon the Constitutional Freedom of the Press* (1801), in *ibid.*, Vol. II, pp. 1127–1128.

47. *Ibid.*, pp. 1128–1129: "We not only have this thing [the U.S. Constitution] in our own hands, familiar to our senses, but it informs us, that it is in our own power, subject to any alterations we may choose to make in it. How then shall we dress it in the sublime and noble? How shall we decorate it in the venerable habiliments of a mysterious and supernatural origin? How shall we raise and maintain a permanent awe and reverence for it? Shall we change it for a more incontestible power, by adopting an hereditary executive, in the room of an elective chief magistrate? Behold the divine right of kings is done away! their persons are no longer sacred! but the throne is the rallying point of faction, and the supporter of the standard of civil war. Round this the partizans collect their forces, under various pretexts, but to gain the same object, the prostration of power, and the plunder of the people. . . .

"Shall we rely on our boasted dissemination of knowledge and learning, and fly to our churches, colleges, academies and schools, as the ancients did, in their distress, to the temples of their gods? . . .

"Since then the real happiness of our country has no kind of connexion with those boisterous struggles . . . , we will attach ourselves to that glorious system; we will hold in contempt the few, who fill the atmosphere with seditious libels, base calumnies, and false reasonings, and, rallying round the constitution, we will, in the character of brethren, live and die like freemen, honorably associated for civil happiness, and the promotion of our country's honour and interest....

"When the constitution of the United States was formed, there was no provision in regard to the freedom of the press. ... But ... the first Congress, by way of amendment to the Constitution, resolved, that 'Congress shall make no law respecting an establishment of religion, or prohibiting the free exercise thereof, or abridging the freedom of speech, or of the press, or of the right of the people, peaceably to assemble, and to petition the government for a redress of grievances.' "

48. James Wilson, *On Municipal Law*, Pt. V of *The Works of James Wilson* (1804), in *ibid.*, Vol. II, pp. 1264–1266.

49. *Ibid.*, pp. 1266–1268.

50. *Ibid.*, pp. 1268, 1271–1273: "The discussion of this question necessarily leads me to consider the establishment of government, and the division of its powers....

"With regard, however, to the British constitution, we must allow the supposition, that a contract took place at its establishment. For this we have high political authority. A full assembly of the lords and commons, met in convention in the year 1688, declared that James the second had broke the original contract between the king and people [citing Blackstone]....

"But, after all, what will this prove with regard to the supreme power of parliament? Do we hear, in the British constitution, of any contract between *them* and the people? ... The usual theorists of government support no hypothesis of this kind, even in favour of the British legislature; far less, in favour of the legislature of every other government. ... When the society was formed, it possessed jointly all the previously separate and independent powers and rights of the individuals who formed it, and all the other powers and rights, which result from the social union. The aggregate of these powers and these rights composes the sovereignty of the society or nation. In the society or nation this sovereignty originally exists. ... Those powers and rights were, I think, collected to be exercised and enjoyed, not to be alienated and lost. ... After what we ... see has been done, in the delegation and distribution of the rights and powers of society; can we subscribe to the doctrine of the Commentaries—that the authority, whichis legislative must be *supreme*? Can we consent, that this doctrine should form a first principle in our system of municipal law? Certainly not. This definition is not calculated for the meridian of the United States....

"The British parliament consists of three distinct branches; the king, the house of lords, and the house of commons. To that species of English law, which is called a statute, the assent of all the three branches is necessary. When it has received the assent of all the three, it becomes a law and is obligatory upon the nation; but it is obligatory upon different parts of it for different reasons. 'An act of parliament,' says my Lord Hale, 'is made, as it were, a tripartite indenture, between the king, the lords, and commons; for without the concurrent consent of all those three parts of the legislature, no such law is or can be made'."

51. *Ibid.*, esp. pp. 1277–1278, 1282, 1286–1287, 1289, 1292–1293, 1298.

Notes to Chapter VII
Congress, Capitol, and Capital

1. As quoted and cited in *A Republic for the Ages: The United States Capitol and the Political Culture of the Early Republic* (edited by Donald R. Kennon, Charlottesville, 1999), pp. 45–46.
2. L'Enfant to Washington from New York, Sept. 11, 1789, in *L'Enfant and Washington, 1791–1792: Published and Unpublished Documents Now Brought Together for the First Time* (edited by Elizabeth S. Kite, Baltimore, 1929), p. 34.
3. L'Enfant report given to Washington, April, 1791, in *ibid.*, p. 49.
4. L'Enfant report given to Washington in June, 1791, in *ibid.*, p. 54, 56–58.
5. Jefferson to L'Enfant, April 10, 1791, in *ibid.*, pp. 48–50.
6. L'Enfant's "Plan" of Aug., 1791, with "Observations" and memoir, in *ibid.*, pp. 67–70.
7. Jefferson to L'Enfant, Dec. 1, 1791, in *Thomas Jefferson and the National Capital: Containing Notes and Correspondence between Jefferson, Washington, L'Enfant [etc.] . . . 1783–1818* (edited by Saul K. Padover, Wash., D.C., 1946), pp. 80–81.
8. L'Enfant to Jefferson, Feb. 26, 1792, in *ibid.*, pp. 98–99.
9. Jefferson to L'Enfant, Feb. 27, 1791, in *ibid.*, p. 100.
10. Jefferson to Commissioners, March 6, 1792, in *ibid.*, p. 104.
11. Jefferson's "DRAFT of Competition for Plan of a Capitol" is in *ibid.*, pp. 119–120.
12. Jefferson to Commissioners, April 20, 1792, in *ibid.*, pp. 137–138.
13. Jefferson to Commissioners, Dec. 13, 1792, in *ibid.*, pp. 162–163.
14. Cf. Ch. V, n. 60 and corresp. text above.
15. In *Republic for the Ages*, pp. 295–296.
16. Charles E. Brownell, "Thomas Jefferson's Architectural Models and the United States Capitol," in *ibid.*, pp. 316–317, 381.

17. Jefferson's message to Congress, Jan. 11, 1802, in *Jefferson and the Capital*, p. 257.
18. Jefferson to Carrol, etc., May 28, 1803, in *ibid.*, p. 301.
19. Jefferson to Brent, March 10, 1807, in *ibid.*, p. 386.
20. Washington to Jefferson, Nov. 30, 1791, in *ibid.*, p. 80.
21. Jefferson to L'Enfant, Dec. 1, 1791, in *ibid.*, pp. 80–81.
22. Brownell, "Jefferson's Models," pp. 387–388.
23. Latrobe to Jefferson, Dec. 7, 1806, quoted by Brownell, p. 388.
24. Jefferson to Samuel Smith, Sept. 21, 1814, in *Jefferson and the Capital*, pp. 476–479.

Various references to the American "empire" have appeared in previous chapters. Writing to Jefferson in 1819, John Adams spoke of "our vast American Empire, and our free institution[s]" (Ch. II, n. 150). In *The Federalist*, Hamilton declared (Ch. V, n. 8): "The fabric of American Empire ought to rest on the solid basis of the consent of the people." Writing to Randolph in 1787, Madison referred (Ch. IV, n. 15) to "republican principles" and the American "Empire," which should never be "partition[ed]." Noah Webster in 1787 spoke glowingly (Ch. VI, main text corresponding to n. 31) about "the constitutions for the American empire," while referring also to "the AMERICAN REPUBLIC" in terms of "an *empire of reason*." At the Convention in 1787, Wilson noted (Ch. IV, n. 41) "the great extent of our country." Madison, too, called America (Ch. IV, n. 69) "a country so great in extent." Needless to say, he referred to the oppressive British "empire" in a different fashion (e.g. Ch. IV, nn. 31, 71), as did so many others. In any case, the American founders were clearly conscious of and impressed by the great size of America during the Revolutionary and Constitutional eras, especially in comparison with European countries. This was even truer after the new nation doubled its size in the early 19th century. Such concepts of a republican empire with vast territory were not felt to be mutually contradictry. Prior to the break from Britain in 1776, the founders often expressed hopes for better constitutional government over America by the British empire, as when Jefferson in his *Summary View* of 1774 spoke of Britain as "a great . . . empire" (above, p. 51).

Cf. references to "empire" in main text of this ch. in proximity to note numbers 1–5, 8, and 33.

25. Jefferson to Latrobe, Oct. 10, 1809, in *ibid.*, pp. 462–463: "I congratulate you on the successful completion of your great arch of the Senate chamber as well as that of the Hall of Justice. I have no doubt you will finish those rooms so as to be worthy counterparts of that of the Representatives. It would give me pleasure to learn that Congress will consent to proceed on the midddle building. I think that the work when finished will be a durable and honorable monument of our infant republic, and will bear favorable comparison with the remains of the same kind of the antient republics of Greece & Rome. . . .

"Your promised visit to Monticello, whenever it can be effected, will give me real pleasure, and I think could not fail of giving some to you [concerning] . . . my essay in Architecture[,] but what nature has done for us is sublime & beautiful and unique. [Y]ou could not fail to take out your pencil & to add another specimen of it's excellence in landscape to your drawing of the Capitol & Capitol hill. [T]he difficulty would be in the choice between the different scenes, where a panorama alone could fully satisfy."

26. Latrobe to Jefferson, May 21, 1807, in *ibid.*, pp. 390–391: "My *principles* of good taste are rigid in Grecian architecture. I am a bigoted Greek in the condemnation of the Roman architecture of Baalbec, Palmyra, Spaletro, and of all the buildings erected subsequent to Hadrian's reign. The immense size, the bold plan and arrangements of the buildings of the Romans down almost to Constantine's arch, plundered from the triumphal arches of former emperors, I admire, however, with enthusiasm, but think their decorations and details absurd beyond tolerance from the reign of Severus downward. Wherever, therefore, the Grecian style can be copied without impropriety, I love to be a mere, I

would say a *slavish*, copyist, but the forms and the distribution of the Roman and Greek buildings which remain are in general inapplicable to the objects and uses of our public buildings. Our religion requires churches wholly different from the temples, our Government, our legislative assemblies, and our courts of justice, buildings of entirely different principles from their basilicas. . . . But that which principally demands a variation in our buildings from those of the ancients is the difference of our climate. . . .

"If our climate were such as to admit of doing legislative business in open air, that is under the light of an open orifice in the crown of a dome, as at the Parthenon, I would never put a cupola on any spherical dome. It is not the *ornament*, it is the use that I want."

27. Damie Stillman, "From the American Roman Republic to the New American One: Architecture for a New Nation," in *Republic for the Ages*, p. 271: "One of the most potent influences on the architecture of the early republic was that of the ancient Roman republic. This is hardly surprising, for that institution was frequently in the minds of the founding fathers, just as its architecture was an inspiration to architects, patrons, and builders of the day. John Adams, for example, in his *Defence of the Constitutions of Government of the United States of America of 1787–88*, often cited parallels with the Roman republic, noting that 'the Roman constitution formed the noblest people and the greatest power that has ever existed.' He found the best evidence for the value of senates there, and he saw that ancient republic as effecting a balance of powers, which was, in his view, the very core of the Roman republic. Similarly, Alexander Hamilton wrote in *The Federalist* that 'the Roman republic attained to the utmost height of human greatness'."

28. Latrobe to Jefferson, June 28, 1817, in *Jefferson and the Capital*, p. 481.

29. James M. Banner, Jr., "The Capital and the State: Washington, D.C., and the Nature of American Government," in *Republic for the Ages*, pp. 64, 66–67: "What makes a national state—the continuous sovereign authority, distinct from if not fully independent of society, that, embodying public power, has legitimately gained the right to protect, govern, and administer through law a unified territory for an inclusive common good?

"One of these subjects is the link between a national state and its capital city. A nation's capital is, after all, the manifest center from which state sovereignty emanates, from which a government's authority is formally accumulated and exercised; it is the community in which the government resides; its buildings and monuments symbolize the power and majesty of rule. In the United States, the capital, rather than emerging from beyond recorded history . . ., is the city originally chosen, planned, and settled by officers of government to house institutions of state and for no other end."

30. James Sterling Young, *The Washington Community, 1800–1820* (New York, 1966), Prologue, pp. 2–3, 5–6, 8–9: "For the community plan, no less than the Constitution, is a blueprint for the governing establishment. No less than the Constitution, the community plan lays down principles of organization to be followed by the rulers of the nation. . . .

"Equally important, the community plan of 1791 projects—as the constitutional plan of 1787 does not—an image of the new government as seen by the men who actually ran it. The community plan for Washington is not only the first unambiguous evidence on record but also, in its way, the most eloquent statement on record about the kind of government that was envisaged and desired by the pioneer politicians whose job it was to rule the new nation. While authorship of the plan technically belongs to Major Pierre Charles L'Enfant, . . . the real authors of the plan for Washington, in all but the narrow and technical sense, were the rulers themselves. It was they who commissioned a plan from L'Enfant. It was they who altered his plan, though in minor ways only, to render it conformable to their desires . . . for a community of republican rulers. . . .

"There is no single center in the ground plan of the governmental community. It is clear that the planners intended a community . . . segregated into distinct units. Among these units, three major centers vie for dominance. . . . One is assigned to the Congress;

one to the President; and one to the Court. President Washington had approved this arrangement as being necessary 'to obtain the primary object—i.e., the ground and means' for each governmental function. . . .

"On the highest elevation in the terrain the plan places the Congress. Only one large structure being planned to accommodate its members and component units, this segment of the community appears to have been conceived as a collective entity, to be engaged in collective work.

"A mile and a half away, with a different outlook on the landscape, is the center for the executive branch. . . . For the Congress and the President the planners thus prescribed independent and coequal systems of communication with the outlying society . . . provided by a single route which extends beyond both to the edge of the future city. Not only distance but formality and visibility were apparently considered appropriate for the relations between Congress and the President, access being provided by a broad avenue suitable for communication of a ceremonial nature. . . .

"The third element of the triad, the Court, is made distinctive in the plan by its exclusion from these lines of communication. Placed roughly equidistant from the presidential and congressional centers, the site for the Court is provided no avenues to render it accessible to either of its coordinate centers. . . .

"Many of the above precepts of the L'Enfant plan . . . are renderings, in a different language, of the constitutional prescriptions for the structure and functions of the national government. The plan for government, like the plan for the governmental community, intends a tripartite segmentation of governing personnel, with legislative, executive, and judicial functions assigned to differently composed and differently organized groups within the government. . . .

"With extraordinary faithfulness, the community plan for Washington repeats the organizing principles, even the ambiguities of the constitutional plan for government. The similarities between these two plans suggest, therefore, that the principles and values of the practicing politicians who approved the L'Enfant plan coincided, to a most extraordinary degree, with the principles and values of those who had framed the Constitution."

31. Along these lines, cf. in a different way, James Stevens Curl, "The Capitol in Washington, D.C., and Its Freemasonic Connections," in *Republic for the Ages*, p. 224: "In 1790, Washington, District of Columbia, was designated the federal capital, and Pierre-Charles L'Enfant made his master plan, which reserved sites for the *grands édifices* of Congress House, President's House, and Supreme Court. L'Enfant proposed placing the Congress House on the high point, as in a Greek acropolis, or in emulation of the Roman Capitol. The plan of the city incorporates many of the geometries and vistas common to neoclassical town plans, but . . . its 1792 version [was] modified by George Washington and Thomas Jefferson. . . ."

In addition to the secondary sources already cited on the early American Capital and Capitol in D.C., the following works contain a variety of extensive visual materials of interest here, deserving of further inquiry: Frederick Gutheim and Wilcomb E. Washburn, *The Federal City: Plans & Realities* (Wash., D.C., 1976); *We the People: The Story of the United States Capitol* (Wash., D.C., 1991, etc.); Audrey Santella, *The Capitol* (Chicago, n.d.); John Rhodehamel, *The Grand Experiment: George Washington and the American Republic* (New Haven and San Marino, 1998–1999); and Richard Guy Wilson (ed.), *Thomas Jefferson's Academical Village: The Creation of an Architectural Masterpiece* (Charlottesville, 1995), on Jefferson's designs for the Univ. of Virginia. A comparison of Jefferson's ideas not only for the Univ. of Vir. but also for the Virginia Capitol with those for Wash., D.C., could prove of further present interest.

32. Among the books consulted especially on the Confederation Congress and Articles of Confederation are the following: Merrill Jensen, *The Articles of Confederation: An Interpretation of the Social-Constitutional History of the American Revolution*

1774–1781 (Madison, 1966), with text of the Articles of Confederation in the final draft of 1777, Appendix, pp. 263–276; Gordon S. Wood, *The Creation of the American Republic 1776–1787* (Chapel Hill, 1969, 1998), e.g. Ch. IX, "The Sovereignty of the People," sect. 2, "The Articles of Confederation," and sect. 4, "The Transferal of Sovereignty," and with discussions of the colonial and state legislatures; *Confederation and Constitution 1781–1789* (edited by Forrest and Ellen McDonald, Columbia, S.C., 1968), e.g. Pt. I, "The American Confederation in War and Peace, 1781–1783"; Richard B. Morris, *The Forging of the Union 1781–1789* (New York, 1987), e.g. Ch. 4, "Congress and the States: Operating under the Articles of Confederation," and Ch. 10, "Effective Union or Dismembered States?"; Jack N. Rakove, *The Beginning of National Politics: An Interpretative History of the Continental Congress* (New York, 1979), e.g. Pt. II, "Confederation," Ch. IX, "The Beginnings of National Government"; Jackson Turner Main, *The Sovereign States, 1775–1783* (New York, 1973), e.g., Ch. 12, "Retrospect and Prospect"; and *Congress at Princeton: Being the Letters of Charles Thornson to Hannah Thornson, June–October 1783* (edited by Eugene R. Sheridan and John M. Murrin, Princeton, 1985), with good illustrations.

It is revealing that despite a substantial preliminary Ch. 1 on "Legislative Precedents Available to Eighteenth-Century America" (centering on the British Parliament and American colonial legislatures), there is no real discussion of legislation per se in the account of the Continental and Confederate Congresses in *Congressional Dynamics: Structure, Coordination, and Choice in the First American Congress, 1774–1789* (Stanford, 1994), by Calvin Jillson and Rick K. Wilson.

33. The above passages from primary sources are scattered throughout Charelene Bangs Bickford and Kenneth R. Bowling, *Birth of the Nation: The First Federal Congress 1789–1791* (Madison, 1989)), Intro., Concl., and p. 12.

34. *Senate Legislative Journal* (for 1789–1791, edited by Linda Grant De Pauw, et al., Baltimore, 1972), pp. vii–viii.

35. *Debates in the House of Representatives, Third Session: December 1790–March 1791* (edited by William Charles DiGiacomantonio, et al., Baltimore, 1995), p. xiv.

36. Harvey Walker, *The Legislative Process: Lawmaking in the United States* (New York, 1948), p. 164.

37. *Ibid.*, p. 126.

38. Secondary works consulted on Philadelphia libraries include Jack P. Greene, *The Intellectual Heritage of the Constitutional Era: The Delegates' Library* (Phila., 1986), with bibliog. Greene states (p. 9): "Just down the street from Independence Hall, . . . the Library Company of Philadelphia, already about a half-century old, contained an important collection of books. Except perhaps for the college libraries of Harvard and Yale, this growing and vital institution was almost certainly the largest library in English-speaking America, and compared favorably with similar institutions in British provincial cities. Indeed, with around 5,000 titles listed in the 1789 published *Catalogue*, it contained almost all the major books in a bountiful intellectual heritage that was then undergoing an exciting period of expansion and redefinition."

39. Catalogues of books consulted include the following: *The Charter, Laws, and Catalogue of Books of The Library Company of Philadelphia* (Phila., 1770); *Catalogue of the Books Belonging to The Library Company of Philadelphia* (Phila., 1789); and *The Library of John Logan of Philadelphia 1674–1751* (edited by Edwin Wolf, Phila., 1974), with intro. and catalogue. In his intro., Wolf quotes Benjamin Franklin as calling Logan "A Man of Universal Learning" and "the best Judge of Books in these Parts."

My thanks to Ms. Connie King at The Library Company in Philadelphia for information on the Library's holdings and on the Logan collection now housed there.

40. In Jefferson's *Papers* 2: 544, an editorial note to Jefferson's "A Bill for Establishing a Public Library" (#81) in his "Revisal of the Laws," refers to "Franklin's Library

Company of Philadelphia (which TJ must have become acquainted with on his trip north in 1766) . . ." A letter to Jefferson from Isaac Zane stated (*Papers* 6:160): "I should have been happy to have accompanied the bearer Mr. Charles Logan to Albermarle, but my long indisposition [etc.]. . . . Mr. Logan is a grandson of the noted James Logan of Pensila . . . and son of the late honble. W. Logan. . . . [A]ny civility shewn him will be esteemed as done your most respectful & Affectionate friend . . ." In a letter to Jefferson in 1784 from Philadelphia, Francis Hopkinson wrote (*Papers* 7: 20): "[T]here is a Design on foot to erect two elegant buildings on the State house Square, one for the philosophical Society[,] the other for the City Library [Lib. Co. of Phila.], to which is to be united the Loganian Library. I yesterday drew up the Petition to the House to grant us the Ground necessary for these Purposes." A 1786 item (*Papers* 9: 487) fleetingly states: "Logan [is] fond of me—His Library— . . ." Also in 1786, in his observations concerning an article on the U.S. in the *Encyclopédie Methodique*, Jefferson quoted and commented as follows (*Papers* 10: 38): "Une superbe bibliotheque devenue publique en 1732 par les soins de l'illustre Franklin.] This deservedly illustrious man has too many claims of his own to the esteem of mankind to wish to rob others of their little pittance. The library here spoken of was the property of a Mr. Logan, was by his will left for public use, but some equivocal expressions produced a contestation which has to this moment kept it's [*sic*] doors shut both to the public and to individuals."

Although this last statement by Jefferson seems unequivocal on the longtime lack of official access to the Loganian collection, due to unresolved legal disputes over it, it remains entirely possible that many years before, during the long Revolutionary Era, when Jefferson became a close friend and colleague of Franklin, he somehow gained unofficial access to the Loganian collection. In light of Franklin's high esteem for James Logan and his library collection, together with Franklin's recognition of Jefferson's own great interest in books and learning, one can easily imagine Franklin gaining private access for Jefferson (as well as Adams, etc.) to the noted Logan collection, just down the street from Independence Hall, at the time of the Declaration in 1776, or earlier. In addition, there had long been available before that point a good catalogue of the Logan collection—*Catalogus Bibliothecae Loganianae*, published in 1760 (116 pp.), the title page of which appears as a facsimile frontispiece to Wolf's *Library of Logan*. The extant formal access records to the Logan collection apparently date (so I am informed by The Library Co.) from the 1790s, around the time when it became a part of The Library Company. Yet such records may not tell the full story of who might have gained special informal access during the several preceding decades without being able to say so openly.

Franklin's *Autobiography* (e.g. New York, 1961, edn., with index), has passages concerning The Library Company (p. 82, etc.) and James Logan (p. 125). It seems improbable to this writer that so great a Philadelphia figure as Benjamin Franklin could not or did not gain access for himself and for others to the Logan collection at points in time from the 1750s to 1790 (when he died), regardless of surviving access records only for the 1790s when it was transferred to The Library Co. and subject to its procedures. In other respects, cf. Edwin Wolf, *At the Instance of Benjamin Franklin: A Brief History of The Library Company of Philadelphia, 1731–1936* (Phila., 1976).

In a catalogue in his *Papers*, Vol. III, p. 713 (Dec. 1786, about five months prior to the Constitutional Convention at Phila.), Hamilton referred to The Library Co. of Phila. as the location of a certain book (all *sic*): "Woods New Eng Prospects. . . . This book is No. 227 in the Pennsyl library. . . ."

41. Bernard Schwartz, *A History of the Supreme Court* (New York, 1993), p. 32. Other useful overviews include: Robert G. McClosky, *The American Supreme Court* (Chicago, 1960), e.g. Chs. I, III, VI, respectively, on judicial power, the Marshall Court, and the Judiciary in relation to the Welfare State; Mary Harrell and Burnett Anderson, *Equal*

Justice Under Law: The Supreme Court in American Life (Wash., D.C., 1965, etc.), esp. pp. 122 ff., for brief comments on the Court's interior designs and a partial glimpse of the wall friezes; Fred Maroon and Suzy Maroon, *The Supreme Court of the United States* (Rockville, etc., n.d.), with partial views of the Court's friezes; and Robert H. Bork, *The Tempting of America: The Political Seduction of the Law* (New York, 1990), Pt. 1, "The Supreme Court and the Tempting of Politics," sect. on "The Divided John Marshall."

I am grateful to the Public Information Office and the Curator's Office at the U.S. Supreme Court for certain information.

42. E.g. Walker, *Legislative Process*, Ch. 21, passim.

Annexes

Corasius at the Federal Convention? Supplements on Adams' Reading and Its Influence

1. Preliminary Overview

When the delegates to the Federal Convention in mid-1787 forged a new U.S. Constitution—in the same Assembly room of the Old State House in Philadelphia where the Declaration of Independence had been adopted in 1776—neither John Adams nor Thomas Jefferson were physically present, being away on separate diplomatic missions in Europe. However, their strong presence there in 1776, at what became known much later as "Independence" Hall, was matched in other ways in 1787 at what could as appropriately be called "Constitution" or "Convention" Hall. While functioning as secretary and official note-taker of the Federal Convention's main proceedings, James Madison had a strong mind of his own, becoming the chief architect of the new U.S. Constitution. He was nevertheless influenced there by the ideas of his close friend Jefferson and, like his colleague Washington who presided as president over the Convention, by the recent book by Adams entitled *A Defence of the Constitutions of Government of the United States of America.*

Madison's prediction to Jefferson (in a letter cited earlier) that Adams' *Defence* would have great influence at the Convention proved correct. Adams' strong (Bodinian) ideas of legislative sovereignty, which had corresponded with Jefferson's own in the Declaration of Independence, were also compatible with those embodied in the new U.S. Constitution. There are, furthermore, close affinities between Adams' ideas of great historical lawgiver-founders in his *Defence* and those subsequently used to depict the roles of both Madison and Washington as lawgiver-founders or constitution-makers at the Federal Convention. The great impact of Adams' *Defence* at the Convention—duly noted in the above-cited entry for it in the Athenaeum catalogue of Washington's library—was felt as well by other delegates assembled there.

The issue now becomes: what possible influence could Corasius have had on Adams (and others influenced by Adams at the Convention) in these conceptual legislative matters? The importance of a Corasius connection should not be overestimated either for Adams or for others at the Convention. Yet it adds another intriguing dimension to the present study.

At the ends of our Chapter III on Adams and Chapter V on Hamilton and Washington, it was briefly suggested that Corasius' chapter in his *Art of Law* on great ancient lawgiver-founders (Book I, Chapter 16, "*De legum inventoribus*") may well have had a significant impact on John Adams' discussion on great ancient lawgivers in his Preface (dated Jan. 1, 1787, in England) to his *Defence of the [State] Constitutions of the United States*. This question must now be addressed in greater detail. Indeed, persuasive proof for such a connection can be adduced from the unique match of materials in those two texts, combined with other considerations. No other sources available to Adams—including works by Rousseau, Plutarch, Machiavelli, Hobbes, and Bodin—contained the concentrated kinds of treatment of this subject as are uniquely found in Corasius' *Art of Law* I, 16. To be sure, those and other writers included sporadic discussions of various great lawgiver-founders in the course of their works, but none did so with the single-minded focus of Corasius on the religious elements that were used by great ancient lawgiver-founders in order to bind their laws more forcefully upon the citizenry.

The channels through which Corasius may have come to Adams' attention initially are not altogether clear, yet two clues have already been alluded to. While he was at Harvard, there existed in the small college library a copy of Corasius' voluminous *Commentaries* on *Digest* I, 1–4 (as well as as on the rest of that first book of Justinian's *Digest* of Roman civil law compiled in the 6th century A.D.). Included throughout Corasius' *Commentaries* were many separate comments on great ancient lawgiver-founders along the lines more fully developed in his later *Art of Law*. We have already cited Adams' copy of the *Lexicon Iuridicum*, containing abundant materials drawn from Corasius' writings and bearing Corasius' name along with select other names on the title page. During his decade or so in Europe, Adams could well have come across Corasius' *Art of Law* through separate editions of the work, or through Corasius' collected works, or through its inclusion in the *Tractatus Universi Iuris*. Considering Adams' broad and deep historical investigations in his *Defence* and other writings, including his treatments of materials relating to the same period of French history in which Corasius and Bodin wrote, it would not be surprising that Corasius' *Art of Law* (like Bodin's *Republic*) came under Adams' scrutiny.

The significance of such an influence by Corasius is not limited to Adams' Defence but extends to that work's enormous well-attested impact at the Federal Constitutional Convention in Philadelphia, which began several months after Adams' *Defence* first appeared. More particularly, the elaborate self-image of George Washington as great lawgiver-founder, especially in his role as head of the Convention, was influenced not only by Rousseau's lawgiver in the *Social Contract*, as Garry Wills has shown; it was shaped by the Preface to Adams' *Defence*, ignored by Wills, which was in Washington's library. The supposed divine inspiration and quasi-religious elements attributed by the ancients to great lawgivers—who sought thereby to gain greater acceptance of their laws and their roles as heroic state founders—posed a central theme in Adams' *Defence* Preface, as earlier in Corasius' *Art of Law* I, 16. Garry Wills' valuable analysis of Rousseau's *Social Contract* falls short as a full explanation of the channels through which such ideas were developed to fit the new American situation. The Corasius prototype for Adams' *Defence* Preface stands out as unique with regard to the *quasi-religious* attributes used by great *classical* lawgiver-founders in somewhat rhetorical ways to bind their laws upon the citizenry. No other potential source among the many works explored by the present writer contained the kind of *concentrated composite* discussion of this whole subject *per se* as is found in Corasius' *Art of Law* I, 16.

It was not just George Washington who took on the image of divinely-inspired heroic lawgiver and "father" of his country. The whole body of Convention delegates became "fathers" or "founders" of the newly constituted American nation-state. The imagery and aura of great ancient lawgiver-founders that infused Madison's *Federalist* #38, in promoting the ratification of the new U.S. Constitution, represented in part an expansion of Adams' *Defence* Preface on this subject.

2. Adams' *Defence* Preface on Ancient Lawgiver-Founders

Adams' decisive depictions of great ancient lawgiver-founders in his *Defence* Preface (and, more diffusely, in other segments of the work) were related to his broad-based purposes throughout the *Defence*. He was defending the existing constitutions and governmental forms of the separate American states (hence his title, *Defence of the Constitutions of Government of the United States*). Adams himself nearly a decade earlier had been the constitution-maker for his own state of Massachusetts. Not surprisingly, he defended that early constitution and its form of government, in addition to the subsequent constitutions of other states, especially as influenced by it. It is fair to say that at that point in time, well prior to the Federal Convention and the decision to write a new national constitution, Adams was indirectly wrapping himself and his followers in the mantle of great ancient lawgiver-founder. His imagery bore similarities to Madison's a year later in *Federalist* #38—a veiled partial portrayal of his own role as constitution-maker or lawgiver-founder at the Federal Convention.

If indeed Adams was influenced by Corasius' *Art of Law* I, 16 on great ancient lawgiver-founders, then the way opens up for the influence on him of Corasius' wider views in that same work. These included the sovereign power of lawmaking as well as each state's sovereign power of legislative self-determination in making laws for its own affairs. Such principles, as shown above, infused writings not only by Adams himself but also by Jefferson—both men being also under the influence of Bodin's *Republic*, which they possessed in their libraries.

In the portions given below of Adams *Defence* Preface dealing with ancient lawgiver-founders from a quasi-religious perspective (*Works* IV, pp. 291–292, 297–298), our attention is drawn to the many names that will also be seen to appear in Corrasius' corresponding account. These include the following: Minos, Rhadamanthus, Jupiter, Lycurgus, Apollo, the Delphic Oracle, Numa, A(E)geria, Zoroaster, Romulus, Mo[u]hammed, Solon, and Herodotus (to which list will presently be added Cicero). Adams' references to such figures are, of course, shaped by in his own distinctive surrounding contexts, as also partly to follow.

> It was the general opinion of ancient nations, that the Divinity alone was adequate to the important office of giving laws to men. The Greeks entertained this prejudice throughout all their dispersions; the Romans cultivated the same popular delusion; and modern nations, in the consecration of kings, and in several superstitious chimeras of divine right in princes and nobles, are nearly unanimous in preserving remnants of it. Even the venerable magistrates of Amersfort devoutly believe themselves God's vicegerents. Is it that obedience to the laws can be obtained from mankind in no other manner? Are the jealousy of power, and the envy of superiority, so strong in all men, that no considerations of public or private utility are sufficient to engage their submission to rules for their own happiness? Or is the disposition to imposture so prevalent in men of experience, that their private views of ambition and avarice can be accomplished only by artifice? It was a tradition in antiquity that the laws of Crete were dic-

tated to Minos by the inspiration of Jupiter. This legislator and his brother Rhadamanthus were both his sons; once in nine years they went to converse with their father, to propose questions concerning the wants of the people; and his answers were recorded as laws for their government. The laws of Lacedaemon were communicated by Apollo to Lycurgus; and, lest the meaning of the deity should not have been perfectly comprehended, or correctly expressed, they were afterwards confirmed by his oracle at Delphos. Among the Romans, Numa was indebted for those laws which procured the prosperity of his country to his conversations with Egeria. The Greeks imported these mysteries from Egypt and the East, whose despotisms, from the remotest antiquity to this day, have been founded in the same solemn empiricism; their emperors and nobles being all descended from their gods. . . . Although the detail of the formation of the American governments is at present little known or regarded either in Europe or in America, it may hereafter become an object of curiosity. It will never be pretended that any persons employed in that service had interviews with the gods, or were in any degree under the inspiration of Heaven, more than those at work upon ships or houses, or laboring in merchandise or agriculture; it will forever be acknowledged that these governments were contrived merely by the use of reason and the senses. . . .

The systems of legislators are experiments made on human life and manners, society and government. Zoroaster, Confucius, Mithras, Odin, Thor, Mahomet, Lycurgus, Solon, Romulus, and a thousand others, may be compared to philosphers making experiments on the elements. Unhappily, political experiments cannot be made in a laboratory, nor determined in a few hours. The operation once begun, runs over whole quarters of the globe, and is not finished in many thousands of years. The experiment of Lycurgus lasted seven hundred years, but never spread beyond the limits of Laconia. The process of Solon expired in one century; that of Romulus lasted but two centuries and a half; but the Teutonic institutions, described by Caesar and Tacitus, are the most memorable experiment, merely political, ever yet made in human affairs. They have spread all over Europe, and have lasted eighteen hundred years. They afford the strongest argument that can be imagined in support of the position assumed in these volumes. Nothing ought to have more weight with America, to determine her judgment against mixing the authority of the one, the few, and the many, confusedly in one assembly, than the wide-spread miseries and final slavery of almost all mankind, in consequence of such an ignorant policy in the ancient Germans.

These and other related portions in Adams' *Defence* Preface will be treated below. Further pertinent references to Solon and Lycurgus, as well as to Cicero, will appear.

3. Corasius' *Art of Law* I, 16 on Ancient Lawgiver-Founders (Latin)

Chapter 16 or Book I in Corasius' *Art of Law*, entitled "*De legum inventoribus*," centers on the quasi-religious or divine inspiration that reportedly gave added authority to the giving of laws by great ancient founders of states. The opening statement sets forth the issue forcefully: "The ancients thought it was a great binding force for controlling the minds of their fellow citizens to believe that the laws were constituted by divine providence, and for that reason ancient laws are always associated with some religious beliefs . . ." Then follows a lengthy compendium of those figures whom the ancients considered to be the first such lawgivers in their respective states. A wide range of ancient authors are cited on this topic, but it is noteworthy that Plutarch is not one of them. Indeed, Plutarch's *Lives* did not contain the singleminded *comprehensive* focus on *divinely*-inspired *ancient* lawgivers as later found in Corasius' well-developed *Art of Law* I, 16 (and in Adams' *Defence* Preface). Plutarch's sporadic fragmentary inclusions of ancient lawgiving ideas and practices may have had a partial influence on Corasius (and Adams) nonetheless, as Garry Wills believes they did in the case of George Washington.

According to Herodotus, Ovid, Vergil, and others, reports Corasius, the original ancient lawgiver of this type was Ceres, the goddess of Sicily, who was reputedly the first to give laws to mortal men. Other ancient writers in turn believed other figures to be fhe first to pass laws for their people: R[h]adamanthus according to Pliny, Moses for the Hebrews, Zoroaster for the Persians, Mercury for Thebes, Trismegistus for the Egyptians, Hercules for the Celts, Minos for the Cretans, Charondas for the Carthaginians, Lycurgus for the Spartans, Draco and Solon for the Athenians, Romulus and Numa Pompilius for the Romans, Pythagoras, and various others. Plato was asked by the peoples of Thebes and other Greek states to give them laws, but he refused. These lawgivers said that they received their laws from some god or goddess—Minos from Jove (Jupiter), Lycurgus from the sun or Delphic Apollo, Solon from Minerva, and Numa from the nymph Aegeriae. Corasius' favorable view is that such avowals of divine authority for the inspiration behind their laws gave those lawgivers greater authority while inculcating moral virtues among the citizens observing them, as with Minerva representing wisdom.

From that point, Corasius' Chapter I, 16 proceeds along much similar lines. God, according to books of the Old Testament, first gave laws to Moses on Mt. Sinai. New Testament sources also call God the only true lawgiver to mankind. Herodotus is again cited by Corasius on ancient Egypt. Demosthenes is cited on laws being a divine gift, and Cicero on laws being derived from divine reason. According to Corasius, once again, the lawgivers of many ancient states, who had the "consent" of their people and followed the "example" of Moses, "attributed their laws to a divinely inspired power in order that thereby they might bind the minds of their fellow citizens in a more solid fashion." Corasius adds: "Among these legislators who established their states by the best and most helpful laws, the Romans in particular are the most renowned, and it is their laws that Polybius preferred to all others and justly so." Indeed, says Corasius, the poet Vergil aptly called the Romans alone the masters of "the science of ruling through law." Corasius closes with the example of Mo[u]hammed, who he says succeeded in giving religious laws by persuading his people that they had a source in holy spirit through a dove that whispered them into his ear. But the origin of our laws, declares Corasius, is different, as he turns from legendary lawgivers (having used abundant language of legislative promulgation and command) to the origin of Roman civil law in the chapter to follow.

Thanks go to Whitney Bagnall for the following Latin transcription of Corasius' *Art of Law* I, 16, "*De legum inventoribus*," from the *Tractatus Universi Iuris*, Vol. I (1584), folio 63 (all *sic* with extensive abbreviations not found in the *Opera* II Latin text and with English version given further below):

Magnum putauerunt veteres esse vinculum, ad contine̅dos ciuium animos, credere, Leges diuina prouidentia constitutas, quamobrem adiu̅cta semper fuit antiquis legibus, alicuius religionis opinio. Namq; leges mortalibus omnium primam Cererem, Siculorum Deam dedisse, ob idq́; legiferam appellatā, & eius sacra. . . . Ethnici pleriq; fabulati sunt. Diodorus. Sicurus. lib. 6 bibliothecae hystoriae. Herodot. lib. 6 qui Erato inscribitur. Vnde Ouid. lib. 5. Metamorph.

> Prima Ceres vnco glebas dimouit aratro.
> Prima dedit fruges, alimentaq́; mitia terris:
> Prima dedit leges, Cereris sunt omnia munus.

Et Virgilius 4 Aeneidos.

Principio delubra adeunt, pacemq́; per aras
Exquirunt, mactant lectas de more bidentes
Legiferae Cereri.

Alii Legumlatorum primum, fuisse Radamanthum putant, Plinius lib.7.c.56. ac demum alios aliis leges tuilisse. c. Moyses.7.dist. Persis Bactrianisq́;, Zorastrem: Thebis, Mercurium: Aegyptiis, Trismegistum: Celtis, Hercule: Cretensibus, Minoem; Carthaginiensibus, Charondam: Heniochis apud Colchos, Amphytū: Lacedaemoniis Lycurgum: Atheniensibus, Draconem primum, deinde Solonem: Romanis, Romulum, ad demum Numam Pompilium, Argiuis, Phoroneum: Italis, Pythagorā: Scythis, Zamolxim: Locris, Zaleucum: Magnesiis, & Siculis, Platonem: id ipsum Arcadibus, Thebanis, & Ciraneicis, enixè postulantibus, denegatem. Sed hi omnes instituta sua, alicui Deo, vt Deę, accepta retulerunt, veluti Minos Ioui: Lycurgus Soli, seu Apollini Delphico: Solon, Mineruę, quod non temerè, sapientes hi Graecorum legislatores, fecisse mihi vn̄r, cum. n. Iupiter, clementiam: Sol (quia planetarum dn̄s est) potentiam: & Minerua, sapientiam significet, inde perspicuè docuerū t, legibus haec tria, (quarum descriptione ciuilis omnis societatis moderatio continetur) inesse debere. Zamolxis quoq; in Vestę deę numē, leges suas retulit pariterq́; Numa Pompilius, quò grauius leges, religionisq́; ceremonias, Romanis stabiliret, Aegeriae nymphae congressum simulauit. Nos verò, hanc rectè, beateq́; viuendi normā, vero Deo, qui trinus, & vnus est, acceptam referimus, Isaiae 33. Iacob.4. ab eo Mosi primum, in monte Sinae traditam: Ioseph. lib 3. antiq. Iudaica. c.6.Exod. 19 & 20 & per eudem Mosem, antiquissimum omnium hoīum legislatorem, Hebraeis promulgatā, d.c Moyses, nisi malis, Deū Abrahamo, legem ciruncidendi praeputii, oīum vetustissimam, primum sanciuisse. Gen 17. Nam ius hoc circuncidendorum pudendorū, apud, Aegyptios, & Aethiopes, perantiquum fuisse, Herodotus historiae pater scribit. lib. 2. qui Euterpe inscribitur. Vt vt fit, Deū fontem bonorum, & legum auctorem agnoscimus, quem ideo Propheta, legiferum nuncupat, Isaiae 33. Demothenesq́;, in oratione illa quam grauiter habuit, cōtra Aristogitonem, legum inuentum esse, atque munus diuinum, dicebat, 1.2 ff. de legibus. quo intelligimus, eas duntaxat constitutiones, quae sunt sanctae, & honestae, legis nomen habere, c.erit autem 4.dist. Vnus enim est legislator, inquit Diuuis Iacobus, nempè Deus. Iacob 4 quem iniustitiae, turpitudinis, & iniquitatis auctorem facere, blasphemię plenum esset, c. quanto. de iureiur. c. inter.22 q 4 & lex est ratio summi Iouis, seu (alibi M. Cicero loquitur) a numine Deorum tracta ratio, honesta praecipiens, & vetans contraria. Cice. lib.2. de legib. & 2 Philippica. quae non tum incipit lex esse, cum scripta est, sed tū, cum orta est: orta est autem simul cum mete diuina, vt perspicuū esse possit, leges perniciosas, turpes, & iniustas Iussa quide esse potentiorū: at leges non esse, quod pluribus M. Cicero probat.2 de legib. Moyses itaq; descriptas primùm Hebraeis dedit leges, c. Moyses. dist.7 ad cuius exemplar, cęteri deinceps hoīes, in suis ciuitatibus, auctoritate pollentes, coi populi suffragio, Leges condiderunt, ad quoddam coelitum numen, legislationes suas perpetuo referentes: quo ciuium animos grauiore vinculo cōtinerent. Inter eos vero, qui suas ciuitates, optimis institutis, ac saluberrimis legibus stabilierunt, prae caeteris Romani celebrantur, quorū ideo leges, aliis omnibus, meritissimo Polybius anteposuit, lib.I histor. & poeta cùm peculiares cuiq; genti laudes attribuisset, solos Romanos Reipublicae p legēdae sciētia, in haec verba donauit:

Tu regere Imperio populos Romanae memento:
Hae tibi erunt artes, paciq; imponere nomen.

Vt interim praeteream execrtādum, & oīum nomothetarum nequissimum, spurcissimum, & inquinatissumum Mahumetem, qui Scenitis, & Mauris, nouas de religione, consilio Sergii monachi, leges conscribens columbam in aurem ad se venire, coram omni populo edocuerat: vt Spiritum sanctum sibi leges insufflantem insigni commento persuaderet, quod & tandem assecutus est. Sed nos ad fontem, vnde ius nostrum scaturiit, descendamus.

4. The Two Accounts Compared with Each Other

Of the two texts above by Adams and Corasius on great ancient lawgiver-founders, Adams' account is shorter and more restricted, without indication of its sources, whereas Corasius' account is longer and more comprehensive, with wide citations of source materials. Indeed, Corasius' singular composite coverage stands unique prior to Adams' period. The present writer has found no comparable single discussion on ancient lawgivers, especially from the quasi-religious angles conveyed above, in ancient, medieval, or early modern writers. Because of the more specific elements uniquely common to both Adams' and Corasius' texts on ancient lawgivers, it would appear that Corasius' text probably provided the primary composite prototype for Adams' discussions, with the aid of other supplemental sources. In view of Adams' *Defence* uses of French history in Bodin's era and Italian history during Machiavelli's period, it is quite possible that Adams picked up as well on their more sporadic materials concerning ancient lawgiver-founders, using their works readily available in his library. On this subject, Bodin himself had likely drawn from Corasius and perhaps also from Machiavelli as well as Plutarch (both ignored by Corasius) in piecing together his own approaches in the Republic along much different conceptual lines. To be sure, references to lawgivers like Lycurgus and Solon are found in many other writers of Adams' day (including elsewhere in his *Defence*) and in centuries before, although the question is again of what type and consistency.

A compelling number of names relating to ancient lawgiver-founders appear in common in the two above accounts by Adams and Corasius. As alluded to above, the names cited by both men alike are as follows, in no particular order: Minos, R[h]adamanthus, Apollo, the Delphic Oracle, Numa Pompilius, (A)Egeria, Zoroaster, Jupiter or Jove, Lycurgus, Solon, Romulus, Mo[u]hammed, and Herodotus, to which shall presently be added Cicero. The appearing of these names in common in the two accounts above by Adams and Corasius on ancient lawgiver-founders is not in itself proof positive of a connection between them. Yet the absence or incompleteness of many such names in other would-be sources for Adams, which lack comprehensive and singular focus on quasi-religious ancient lawgivers, adds to our case for the uniqueness of features common to Adams' and Corasius' accounts. Also persuasive is the manner in which both Adams and Corasius place the names of great lawgivers in quick succession, *ad seriatim*, in a kind of abbreviated apposition to each other and to the states, gods, or testifiers relating to them. Such approaches differ from those used by other writers on the subject in ancient, medieval, and early modern times.

Comparisons can be made between the above accounts by Adams and Corasius concerning the "reason" or "reasoning" that both men believe to be the ultimate human faculty used by ancient lawgiver-founders despite their pretence of acting under divinely-inspired authority. Less indulgent than Corasius about the ancients' depictions of a quasi-religious aura in lawgiving, Adams declares above in his *Defence* Preface that the key point was, instead, "the use of reason and the senses." In somewhat similar fashion, Corasius above (about two-thirds into his *Art of Law* I, 16, citing Cicero as authority) twice closely connected "law" or *lex* that is "written" or *scripta* with "reason" or *ratio*, in addition to what is "honest" or *honesta*, etc., as the real basis for ancient lawgiving, contrary to ancient avowals of acting through "divine" inspiration. The moral-legal senses of honesty, justice, equity, due process, and the like had been cited in texts given in *Digest* I, 1, "On Justice and Law"; they seem to be echoed here by Corasius, who in turn may well have been vaguely echoed in Adams' allusion to the "senses" that combine with "reason" in lawgiving under ancient guises of religiosity. Ideas of the "law" as "written reason" or *ratio scripta* were much cited by Corasius in his *Commentaries* on *Digest* I, 1–4 in Ciceronian and other contexts, as were concepts of equity in law concerning the moral senses of living honestly (*vivere honeste*), not harming another, and rendering to each person his due (as stated in *Digest* I, 1, 10, "On Justice and Law," in a fragment from Ulpian). Such parallels in terminology are provocative. Corasius' account holds parallels with Adams' reference above in his *Defence* Preface to "the use of [human] reason and the [moral] senses" in government, as distinguished from purported (divine) revelation, a crucial point of comparison here between Adams and Corasius.

An additional if more remote comparison between Adams' *Defence* (Preface) and Corasius' *Art of Law* (in I, 1, the opening chapter) is that both works begin with a discussion of the arts and sciences in general terms. True, Adams' discussion given below (*Works* IV, p. 283) is far different from Corasius' focus on reducing law to an art or science (that text appearing in our Vol. II, pp. 270–271), citing especially Cicero. Yet Adams' opening passages on the subject seem so tangential to the rest of his discussion in the Preface and work itself as to arouse curiosity about their prominent placement at the outset, in parallel with Corasius' opening discussions, and about possible sources of influence on Adams. Adams' alllusion to a "government of laws and not of men" seems to be a classical echo of Solon's moderate early Athenian democracy, favored by the American founders, who contrariwise deemed dangerous more radical later kinds of Athenian democracy (cf. more generally Carl J. Richard, *The Founders and the Classics*, Camb., Mass., 1994).

> The arts and sciences, in general, during the three or four last centuries, have had a regular course of progressive improvement. The inventions in mechanic arts, the discoveries in natural philosophy, navigation, and commerce, and the advancement of civilization and humanity, have occasioned changes in the condition of the world, and the human character, which would have astonished the most refined nations of antiquity. A continuation of similar exertions is every day rendering Europe more and more like one community, or single family. Even in the theory and practice of government, in all the sinple monarchies, considerable improvements have been made. The checks and balances of republican governments have been in some degree adopted at the courts of princes. . . . [I]f religious toleration were established, personal liberty a little more protected, by giving an absolute right to demand a public trial in a certain reasonable time, and the states were invested with a few more privileges, or rather restored to some that have been taken away, these governments would be brought to as great a degree of perfection, [and] they would approach as near to the character of governments of laws and not of men, as their nature will probably admit of.

In other noteworthy passages of his *Defence* Preface (IV, pp. 284–285, 296), Adams cites Herodotus, Lycurgus, Thucydides, Cicero, and Tacitus in contexts more in line, than the one just quoted, with his main orientations in the *Defence*, including on legislative matters. Adams' extended readings of Thucydides elsewhere here in his Preface follow the pattern throughout his *Defence* of detailed presentations and adaptations of ancient texts and later historical materials.

> According to a story in Herodotus, the nature of monarchy, aristocracy, and democracy, and the advantages and inconveniences of each, were as well understood at the time of . . . Darius, as they are at this hour. A variety of mixtures of these simple species were conceived and attempted, with various success, by the Greeks and Romans. Representations, instead of collections, of the people; a total separation of the executive from the legislative power, and of the judicial from both; and a balance in the legislature, by three independent, equal

> branches, are perhaps the only three discoveries in the constitution of a free government, since the institution of Lycurgus. Even these have been so unfortunate, that they have never spread ... except [partly] in America....
>
> It is impossible to read in Thucydides, his account of the factions and confusions throughout all Greece, which were introduced by this want of an equilibrium, without horror. "... The contagion spread through the whole extent of Greece; factions raged in every city; the licentious many contending for the Athenians, and the aspiring few for the Lacedaemonians. The consequence was, seditions in cities, with all their numerous and tragical incidents." ...
>
> If Cicero and Tacitus could revisit the earth, and learn that the English nation had reduced the great idea to practice, and brought it nearly to perfection, by giving each division a power to defend itself by a negative; ... had obtained by means of it a prosperity among civilized nations, in an enlightened age, like that of the Romans among barbarians; and that the Americans, after having enjoyed the benefits of such a constitution a century and a half, were advised by some of the greatest philosophers and politicians of the age to renounce it, and set up the governments of ancient Goths and modern Indians,—what would they say? That the Americans would be more reprehensible than the Cappadocians, if they should listen to such advice.

To be sure, there is much in Adams' *Defence* Preface—including on various issues in legislation, a topic so central to Corasius' work as well—that bears no real relationship to the *Art of Law*. Some of the above passages include examples. Yet the question is whether and how Adams may well have adapted select portions of Corasius' treatise within the framework of his own wider contemporary purposes and historical researches.

The American "founding fathers," including Adams and Washington, saw the great importance of classical traditions of thought and education up to their own era as they sought to adapt them to their own advantage. It is a measure of the enduring imagery of great classical lawgivers not only in the Renaissance but up through the 17th and 18th centuries that an American founder like Adams could make such splendid use of it in his *Defence*, with consequent august influence upon his fellow framers at the Convention such as Madison. It was Madison who in the *Federalist* would greatly develop the classical lawgiver theme through his own reading and with intimations of his own role as constitution-maker, similarly to Adams' allusions to his own earlier constitution-making in Massachusetts. Jefferson, too, has been hailed for his "labors" as a "republican Solon" in connection with his constitution and laws of the state of Virginia (as cited earlier on our pages 45–46). His writings, too, could be combed for ancient lawgiver themes.

5. The Two Accounts Compared with Other Sources

Among the various ancient writers cited by Corasius in *Art of Law* I, 16 on specific points about individual classical lawgiver-founders, there are none, including Herodotus, who came close to a treatment of the subject resembling Corasius' comprehensive coverage aand thematic selectivity. There were indeed many ancient writers who touched in a variety of ways upon this and related topics, yet doing so with approaches different from those of Corasius and, in turn, Adams. The most promising possibility would seem to be Plutarch, who in his *Lives* of illustrious Greeks and Romans included accounts on some of the figures cited above—especially Romulus, Lycurgus, Numa Pompilius, and Solon (as in Vol. I of the convenient Modern Library Edition, New York, 1992). But here, too, the potential for close comparisons quickly fades upon closer inspection of Plutarch's sporadic material.

Among the many classical figures singled out in common by both Corasius and Adams were, as seen above, Minos, Zoroaster, R[h]adamanthus, Apollo in connection with the Delphic Oracle, and Egeria in connection with Numa. All of these were absent in Plutarch's accounts. Naturally, the much later ancient figure Mohammed is also absent. Plutarch's "lives" of Lycurgus, Numa, Solon, and Romulus are written from a very different perspective—even when it comes to lawgiving, which is there largely eclipsed by its fragmented inclusion among many other subjects—than is the comprehensive coverage by Corasius and the shorter treatment by Adams. Both Adams and Corasius were well aware of Plutarch's *Lives* (included in the libraries of Adams and other founders such as Washington). Yet their lack of references to it in this regard is not unexpected in view of its paucity of specifically comparable material on the subject at hand. The giving up of power along the thematic lines explored by Garry Wills on George Washington's image is a more promising area for discussion of Plutarch's influence more generally.

Chief candidates among early modern writers in the 16th century as plausible sources of information for Adams on ancient lawgivers would be Machiavelli and Bodin, other than Corasius (who had a considerable influence on Bodin's concepts of legislative power yet who was not influenced by Machiavelli in that regard). True, a number of references to Lycurgus, Solon, and other such ancients appear in writings by Machiavelli, with varying relevance for imagery on ancient lawmaking. Yet few real parallels are found there with what Corasius and Adams later included in their accounts. The same holds true for Bodin, who together with Machiavelli was well noted by Adams in wholly other respects cited above. Bodin's many promising references to Lycurgus in the *Republic* fall far short as possible actual precedents for Adams on ancient lawgivers. In view of Bodin's proven indebtedness to Corasius' *Art of Law* on other legislative issues, it is reasonable to assume that he was also influenced by Corasius' treatment there in I, 16 on ancient lawgivers. The lengthy multiple references to ancient figures like Lycurgus, Solon, Numa, and so forth by Machiavelli, Bodin, and others long before Rousseau should caution historians against overestimating the impact of Rousseau's *Social Contract* on the American founders regarding ancient lawgiver-founders.

Among the potential 17th-century sources for Adams that one might point to are Hobbes' *Leviathan* (which was greatly influenced by Bodin's *Republic* on legislative sovereignty) as well as writings by Domat or even Conring (both men having been decisively influenced by Corasius' *Art of Law* on principles of lawmaking and legislative sovereignty). Interestingly, a copy of Domat's voluminous *Les loix civiles* was in Adams' library, along with a masssive multi-volume set of Cujas' *Opera Omnia*—all reflecting Adams' great interest in traditions of Roman civil law in the early modern period. During his approximate decade in Europe prior to the Federal Convention of mid-1787, Adams was, like Jefferson, well exposed to European libraries and booksellers providing ample access to such items. Opportunities for Adams to have come across Corasius' *Art of Law*, in various editions then available, were clearly present.

Turning next to Rousseau's *Social Contract*, hailed by Garry Wills as key inspiration behind some of George Washington's self-imagery as lawgiver-founder, one is struck by the lack of any references in it (much less on lawgiving) to Zoroaster, R[h]adamanthus, Apollo and the Delphic Oracle in connection with Lycurgus, and (A)Egeria in connection with Numa. All of these names *are*, contrariwise, cited by both Adams and Corasius on ancient lawgivers. Mohammed is cited fleetingly by Rousseau, but not in the legislative connections of interest to Adams and Corasius. There are references in the *Social Contract* to pertinent other older names which are not cited by Corasius but which are by Adams; however, these are not *ancient* lawgiver-founders, much less from *quasi-religious* perspectives within a single *composite* comprehensive coverage. There are a few promising references in the *Social Contract* to Lycurgus, Solon, and Numa individually, but in far different ways than we have studied for Adams and Corasius. Nor is Plutarch cited by Rousseau in connection with ancient lawgiving, any more than by Adams and Corasius, who omit him in their accounts. These observations are not meant to detract from the enormous influence of Rousseau in other ways upon the American founders, as already well attested above, or from the influential discussions on legislative issues of sovereignty and state in his *Social Contract*, as explored in our earlier studies. (Used here is the convenient annotated Norton edn. by A. Ritter and J. Bondanella, New York, 1988).

Another classic tractate of the mid-18th century that needs to be mentioned because of its great impact on the American founders is Montesquieu's *Spirit of the Laws*. Here, too, the wealth of materials on legislative issues, as also treated in our earlier studies, should not lead one to expect, *ipso facto*, parallels in it with the specific approaches to ancient lawgiver-founders singled out above. Lycurgus and Solon are amply included by Montesquieu but from different perspectives already considered. Numa, Zoroaster, (A)Egeria, R[h]adamanths, Mohammed, Apollo, Jupiter, and the Delphic Oracle are among the names omitted by Montesquieu that are cited by both Adams and Corasius, although Romulus *is* cited by Montesquieu too.

If Corasius' *Art of Laws* I, 16 became a main source for Adams' *Defence* Preface of Jan. 1787 on great ancient lawgivers, Adams' treatment therein became a key source for Madison's somewhat different development of that theme in *Federalist* #38 (above our p. 167–) a year later in Jan. 1788, there aided by his own further researches and Plutarch's *Lives*. The wider significance of Corasius' impact in this matter now becomes clearer, if more generalized. When Madison predicted, in his above-cited letter to Jefferson prior to the mid-1787 Convention, that Adams' *Defence* would receive wide attention at that gathering, he was prophetically speaking for himself as well, including his *Federalist* #38 which followed soon thereafter.

The present story does not end there. In the course of our Ch. VI above, we had occasion to note some other uses of the ancient lawgiver theme after the appearance of Adams' *Defence* Preface yet prior to Madison's *Federalist* #38, as exemplified by Noah Webster in later 1787. Then in 1801, an anonymous writer also took up the theme. Much later, the Supreme Court chamber's wall friezes created in the mid-20th century cast a much different light on the topic, but they serve to reveal its continuing appeal more generally.

As cited earlier, a delegate to the Federal Convention declared that Adams' *Defence* would prompt the delegates to adopt a strong federal legislature. His comment can serve here as suggestion of the Convention's perception of its role as lawgiver-founder in the tradition of ancient prototypes highlighted by Adams and, long before with unique distinctiveness, by Corasius.

In the end, the leading American founders studied here, who could think of themselves as successors of heroic ancient lawgiver-founders, might well have mixed feelings if they could now see the Supreme Court chamber's friezes of the 20th century depicting great lawgivers throughout history. As former Presidents, Adams and Madison as well as Jefferson and Washington might wonder why only one American is included, someone other than them—a Supreme Court Justice, John Marshall. Yet they would remember Marshall's special role in Supreme Court history as the founder of judicial review, a kind of law-creating tied in with legislative themes. They could appreciate the inclusion of two of the three ancients represented—Solon and Lycurgus—with whom all four Americans became identified. Yet Adams in particular could give credence to the inclusion of Muhammed, Solon, and Lycurgus. For Adams himself had uniquely cited all three ancients in his *Defence* Preface in quasi-religious contexts of great ancient lawgiver-founders in the distinctive fashion employed by Corasius.

6. Corasius' *Commentaries* at Harvard on *Digest* I, 1–4

Meantime, even deeper dimensions of Adams' sources for his *Defence* Preface now open up in further connection with Corasius' theme of great ancient lawgiver-founders. During the period when Adams was a college student at Harvard (1751–1754), before studying or "reading" law as well, there existed in the College's very small library a voluminous work on Roman civil law that Adams could not have failed to come across and to take due notice of: namely, Corasius' *Commentaries* on the first book of Justinian's *Digest* in the *Corpus Iuris Civilis*. In his own era, Corasius' *Commentaries* were hailed as a great achievement because of their breadth, depth, length, and learning. Of particular note in our uses of Corasius' *Commentaries* in the first two volumes of this series were the many ways in which his early commentaries on the first four chapters or "titles" of Book One partially prefigured many (though not all) of the viewpoints on legislation and methodology found in his later *Art of Law*.

Scattered throughout Corasius' *Commentaries* on *Digest* I, 1—4 were numerous depictions of great ancient lawgiver-founders along the lines later found much more fully developed in his *Art of Law* I, 16, "*De legum inventoribus.*" Most notable, perhaps, were Corasius' disquisitions relating to this topic in his huge landmark commentary on *Digest* I, 2, "*De origine iuris,*" centering on the historical origins and developments of Roman civil law. This subject lent itself quite well to discussions of great anccient lawgivers of the sort cited frequently above. The Greek beginnings and Roman developments traced therein gave abundant opportunities for later commentaries on the Greek *nomothetes* or lawgivers in conjunction with the Roman *legislatores*. So closely tied together were Corasius' treatments of great ancient lawgivers in his commentaries on D. I, 2 with the origins of Roman civil law that it was fitting that the chapter of his later *Art of Law* on ancient lawgivers (I, 16) was immediately followed there by one on the very subject of Roman law's origins (I, 17), "*De iuris civilis origine.*" Thus the young Adams would have found at Harvard a wealth of commentaries Corasius expanded upon in *Art of Law* I, 16 and I, 17, thus supplying a potential source for Adams' own condensed coverage in his *Defence* Preface.

There is no telling when or how Adams probably came across Corasius' *Art of Law*, which was not at Harvard when he was there. The strongest likelihood is that he did so while in Europe—either on the Continent or in England—during his approximate decade there prior to the Federal Convention. During that period he became, like Jefferson, an ardent purchaser of books for his private library back home. Among the many works thusly obtained was the enormous multi-volume set of the *Opera* of Jacques Cujas, a key 16th-century contemporary of Corasius in the historical study of Roman law. Adams' rich historical mind would have been stirred at Harvard by Corasius' *Commentaries* and would have prompted him to take due notice later on of the one or more editions of Corasius' *Art of Law* available for him to see in Europe—that is, in Corasius' *Opera Omnia*, in the *Tractatus Universi Iuris*, or in separate editions of it. By analogy, one recalls Jefferson's comments in a letter to L'Enfant (our p. 266) on the many cities he visited while in Europe where he obtained maps of them that he says he is now sending to L'Enfant for use in designing D.C. Those cities were Frankfort, Strassburg, Orleans, Bordeaux, Lyons, Montpelier, Marseilles, Turin, Milan, Carlsruhe, Amsterdam, Paris, etc. (Elsewhere Jefferson refers to his visit to Toulouse; cf. Jefferson's *Papers*, index vol. #21, under "Toulouse".) Although Philadelphia booksellers and libraries remain a possible though less likely channel (the present writer having found no trace of Corasius' writings there), a more plausible cosmopolitan urban center in which Adams could have come across Corasius' *Art of Law* was Paris or London.

At Harvard Law School today is a copy of Corasius' *In titulum Pandectarum De iustitia et iure, ac sequentes legum iuris magistratumq; titulos commentarii ..*. . . (Lyons, 1560). Archival records there indicate that it was received or acquired, from a different location or source, into the modern law school's library in 1937. Transfers from the main College collection were not unusual in view of the fact that in Adams' century and well into the 19th century, there was no formal law school at Harvard (until 1817), so that (until then) law books were found in the general collection. However, whereas Corasius' *Commentarii* is cited in the 1723 Harvard library catalogue, it is absent in the 1773 and 1790 catalogues. These facts suggest that the work was lost in the devastating fire of 1764 (after which new acquisitions were made), that is, a decade after Adams' college years there in 1751–1754 prior to going on to study law. Hence the copy of Corasius' *Commentarii* now at Harvard is probably not the same copy of it listed in the Harvard catalogue of 1723. However, the date of receipt at Harvard's law school is not accompanied in the records by any information on whether it was received from a source outside Harvard, whereas the records for the *Opera* and *Tractatus* acquisitions in the early 20th century (sources where Corasius' *Art of Law* are included) clearly suggest an outside source of transfer. Reprints of the 1723, 1773, and 1790 catalogues are in *The Printed Catalogues of the Harvard College Library* (edited by W. Bond and H. Amory, Boston, 1993), where the (abbreviated) title of Corasius' *Comment. de Justitia et Jure* . . . (Lyons, 1555) is included in the short 1723(A) catalogue but not in the other longer two catalogues (B, C). If the 1723 entry for Corasius is accurate, then an edition other than the present one of 1560 was clearly present at Harvard in 1723–; but, if it is inaccurate, then the possibility exists of the current 1560 edition at Harvard being the same one, somehow saved from the fire and kept in a different location, that Adams would have seen. Whatever the case, it is certain that the 1560 edition today at Harvard is the same massive set of Corasius' commentaries (even if in different edition) on the first book of Justinian's *Digest*, totalling nearly 700 large dense pages. Curiously, Corasius' commentaries listed in the 1723 catalogue are not listed under law and, indeed, are one of the relatively few works therein on law, especially of their kind, so that it would have stood out in the small collection all the more for Adams' attention. Also in the 1723 Harvard catalogue is the *Lexicon I[J]uridicum*—another copy of which Adams later owned, as did Jefferson, with its abundant uses of Corasius' legal opinions and with its featuring of the names of Corasius and a few key other late Renaissance jurists on the title page.

For help with specific information on the Harvard collections, including on other subsequent catalogues, thanks go to Ed Malloy at the Law School's Special Collections, as well as to Roger Stoddard at the Harvard University Archives. In addition, John Haskell in Special Collections at William and Mary provided information about the collection there, which was very small in the 1700s and even 1800s, with no list of books surviving for the period when Jefferson was there in the early 1760s. Fires there in the early 1700s and mid-1800s destroyed much. No trace of any books by Corasius, e.g., can be found.

Our previous studies on Corasius contain many indications of the wealth of materials on issues at hand that Adams would have found in Corasius' *Commentaries* in the copy readily available to him at Harvard. Our Vols. I–II provided extended discussions of Corasius' commentaries on the first four "titles" of the first book of Justinian's *Digest*. The reader can consult the available editions of Corasius' *Commentarii* on *Digest* I, 1–4 in conjunction with the discussions of Corasius' *Art of Law* in those two volumes in order to appreciate the vast materials that Adams would have found in Corasius' *Commentarii* on *Digest* I, 1–4 that prefigured Corasius' discussions on ancient lawgiver-founders (as well as on the art and science of law) in his *Art of Law* I, 16, with its parallels to Adams' *Defence* Preface. Compared with the over 200 packed pages of Corasius' commentaries on *Digest* I, 2, "*De origine iuris*," with particular regard to classical lawgiving and legal method, Corasius' chapters I, 16 "*De legum inventoribus*" and I, 17 "*De iuris civilis origine*" are of such shorter length as to occasion curiosity on whether those close parallels can be explained by Adams' reading alone of Corasius' commentaries on *Digest* I, 2, "*De origine iuris.*" It is true that *Art of Law* I, 17 makes abundant references to classical writers like Ovid, Livy, Cicero, Aristotle, and Dionysius of Halicarnassus, as well as lawgivers like Numa, Servius Tullius, and the decemvirs (the ten men who according to legend went to Greece to bring laws back to the Romans), with correspondence to Corasius' commentaries on *Digest* I, 2, just as his *Art of Law* I, 16 contains names of classical writers and lawgivers with affinities to the same and surrounding commentaries. In the end, however, Corasius' condensed composite focus in his *Art of Law* on subjects of present interest bear many parallels with Adams' discussions in his *Defence* Preface and elsewhere in that work.

7. Jefferson's *Notes* XIII on "Constitutions" in the *Lexicon Iuridicum* (and Jefferson's Toulouse Visit)

Just as Adams through his *Defence* of Constitutions (published in early 1787) greatly influenced the Federal Convention of mid-1787 while he was away in Europe, so too did Jefferson impact that Convention while still in Europe through his *Notes on the State of Virginia* (likewise published early that same year, February, with another edition appearing in July). Just as there is a strong probability that some parts of Adams' *Defence* were influenced by Corasius in his *Art of Law* (as well as by other writers impacted by Bodin's *Republic*), there remains a possibility that certain passages in Jefferson's *Notes* were influenced in other ways by Corasius' *Art of Law*, *Commentaries*, or other writings, at least as made use of in the *Lexicon Iuridicum*. On a general level, it matters little that in neither man's library was there any work by Corasius, aside from the prominent inclusion of Corasius' name on the title page and in the contents of the *Lexicon Iuridicum*, owned by both men.

As a modern editor of Jefferson's *Notes* has observed: "The *Notes on Virginia* is probably the most important scientific and political book written by an American before 1785; upon it much of Jefferson's contemporary fame as a philosopher was based." (Cf. Introd. to edition of *Notes* by William Peden, Chapel Hill, 1982, p. v.) The impact of Jefferson's *Notes* on Madison as chief architect of the new U.S. Constitution would alone be of sufficient present interest, aside from its wider influence on Convention delegates. While not as singularly devoted to constitutional and political issues as was Adams' *Defence*, or as consistently relevant to the genesis of the new government, Jefferson's *Notes* contained two provocative chapters already analyzed above entitled "Constitution" (XIII) and "Laws" (XIV), along with some other parts on other subjects of interest such as religion, commerce, and revenue.

In particular, Jefferson's extended treatment of the topic of constitutions would have attracted the attention of Madison and other constitutional framers at Philadelphia, just as did Adams' discussions on constitutions in his *Defence*. Jefferson's essential point was that constitutions are, like laws and other such decrees, subject to change, alteration, reformulation, and even abrogation, depending on circumstances, consent, and constituted authority. This position held appeal for Madison and others who sought, against the resistance of some delegates, to throw out the existing constitution represented by the Articles of Confederation, rather than merely revising it as many wanted, and to write a thoroughly new constitution (something that Jefferson himself did not initially favor, even though his position on "constitutions" as changeable was used to justify such a decision).

Building his case, Jefferson presented in *Notes* XIII various definitions of legislative terms included in the *Lexicon Iuridicum*. Our presentation of these passages in our

Chapter II above on Jefferson (p. 38) was based on Peden's convenient annotated edition, which for brevity's sake omitted Latin terminology and certain other portions of Jefferson's original text. The edition quoted below now becomes more suitable and requires explanation. The task will then become one of determining the original sources and contexts of definitions that Jefferson quoted from the *Lexicon* but without his giving the sources noted therein upon which the *Lexicon* drew. Even in the *Lexicon*, the manner of presenting quotations and paraphrases from earlier juridical authorities is often not complete or precise, while the bare abbreviated names of jurists often attached to them are not always clear but often obscure. Hence, the reader's detective work can sometimes bog down, especially in cases where no such references are given at all in the *Lexicon* and the reader is left to conjecture as to the original juristic source. Even when such bare names are clearly cited, which is the case perhaps more often than not, most attempts to figure out where in a given earlier jurist's work the excerpt can be found become a daunting task—albeit this was not the goal of the lexicographers in compiling this huge reference work, with its prefatory fuller listings of the dozens of names to be cited.

The text to follow from "Query" XIII is found in the edition of Jefferson's *Notes on Virginia* by Merrill Peterson (New York, 1984), pp. 248–249, from the original manuscript at the Massachusetts Historical Society in Boston (all *sic*):

> Not only the silence of the instrument is a proof they thought it would be alterable, but their own practice also: for this very convention, meeting as a [Virginia] House of Delegates in General Assembly with the new Senate in the autumn of that year, passed acts of assembly in contradiction to their ordinance of government; and every assembly from that time to this has done the same. I am safe therefore in the position, that the constitution itself is alterable by the ordinary legislature. Though this opinion seems founded on the first elements of common sense, yet is the contrary maintained by some persons. 1. Because, say they, the conventions were vested with every power necessary to make effectual opposition to Great-Britain. But to complete this argument, they must go on, and say further, that effectual opposition could not be made to Great-Britain, without establishing a form of government perpetual and unalterable by the legislature; which is not true. An opposition which at some time or other was to come to an end, could not need a perpetual institution to carry it on: and a government, amendable as its defects should be discovered, was as likely to make effectual resistance, as one which should be unalterably wrong. Besides, the assemblies were as much vested with all powers requisite for resistance as the conventions were. If therefore these powers included that of modelling the form of government in the one case, they did so in the other. The assemblies then as well as the conventions may model the government; that is, they may alter the ordinance of government. 2. They urge, that if the convention had meant that this instrument should be alterable, as their other ordinances were, they would have called it an ordinance: but they have called it a *constitution*, which ex vi termini means 'an act above the power of the ordinary legislature.' I answer that *constitutio, constititum, statutum, lex,* are convertible terms. '*Constitutio* dicitur jus quod a principe conditur.' '*Constitutum,* quod ab imperatoribus rescriptum statutumve est.' '*Statutum,* idem quod lex.' Calvini Lexicon juridicum. *Constitution* and *statute* were originally terms of the civil law, and from thence introduced by Ecclesiastics into the English law. Thus in the statute 25 Hen. 8. c. 19. §. 1. '*Constitutions* and *ordinances*' are used as synonimous. The term *constitution* has many other significations in physics and in politics; but in Jurisprudence, whenever it is applied to any act of the legislature,

it invariably means a statute, law, or ordinance, which is the present case. No inference then of a different meaning can be drawn from the adoption of this title: on the contrary, we might conclude, that, by their affixing to it a term synonimous with ordinance, or statute, they meant it to be an ordinance or statute. But of what consequence is their meaning, where their power is denied? If they meant to do more than they had power to do, did this give them power? It is not the name, but the authority which renders an act obligatory. Lord Coke says, 'an article of the statute II R. 2. c. 5. that no person should attempt to revoke any ordinance then made, is repealed, for that such restraint is against the jurisdiction and power of the parliament.' 4. inst. 42. and again, 'though divers parliaments have attempted to restrain subsequent parliaments, yet could they never effect it; for the latter parliament hath ever power to abrogate, suspend, qualify, explain, or make void the former in the whole or in any part thereof, notwithstanding any words of restraint, prohibition, or penalty, in the former: for it is a maxim in the laws of the parliament, quod leges posteriores priores contrarias abrogant.' 4. inst. 43.—To get rid of the magic supposed to be in the word *constitution*, let us translate it into its definition as given by those who think it above the power of the law; and let us suppose the convention instead of saying, 'We, the ordinary legislature, establish a *constitution*,' had said, 'We, the ordinary legislature, establish an act *above the power of the ordinary legislature*.' Does not this expose the absurdity of the attempt?

In addition to the 1669 edition of the *Lexicon Iuridicum* owned and used by Jefferson (with his initials at sig. I and T and with Lib. of Cong. 1815 bookplate, as cited in the Sowerby catalogue), I have consulted the editions of 1645, 1670, and 1689 at the Columbia Univ. Law School. Closer inspection of the earlier 1645 edn. yields some useful results. Thanks go to Gerald Gawalt and Clark Evans, in special collections at the Library of Congress, for their assistance.

The several pertinent terms in the *Lexicon* that correspond with ones used from it by Jefferson in *Notes* XIII indicate some names of juristic sources following the definitions. For instance (p.232B): "*Constitutio generali nomine dicitur iis, quod a principe conditur ..... Hot. [Hotman].*" Another *Lexicon* definition used by Jefferson for "constitution" does not give a jurist's name as a source (p. 233A): "*Constitutum, quod ab Imp. rescriptum statutumve est ... l. in C. de neg. gen. et ali ... [Code ...]*" On "statute" (pp. 868B–869A): "*Statutum, Idem quod lex* [from here on omitted by Jefferson:] *dicitur ... de iust. et iure* [*Digest* I, l. 9, "*De iustitia et iure*"] *... Stieg. Prat.*" (Prateius, 1520–1570, did an earlier *Lexicon* of civil and canon law, Lyons, 1566, while Spiegelius has not been further identified.) An entry in the *Lexicon* not cited by Jefferson for "constitution" reads (p. 232B): "*Constitutio. Quod principi placuit legis habet vigorem, cum lege Regia .... § sed et quod ...*" Here the straight text of a *Digest* fragment, on the *lex regia* and on the prince's pleasure having the force of law, is accompanied by no juristic source name as authority, yet it was one often dealt with by Renaissance jurists like Corasius and Connan. Also not quoted by Jefferson in *Notes* XIII are specific apt examples from the *Lexicon* for his reference, in the same extended passage above using the *Lexicon*, to "law"' or *lex*. This broad and much-cited term in the *Lexicon* opens up a wide front for further investigation into possible links with Corasius, who was, it will be recalled, particularly interested in the terminology of legislation in civil law. There are numerous other surrounding texts and contexts of Latin terminology given in the *Lexicon* for "constitution," "statute" "law" and so forth that Jefferson's eye would also have fallen upon as he searched through this huge classic tome for useful equivalents in support of his own ideas on the subject.

Although none of the above *Lexicon* entries or others closely related to them bear the name of Corasius as their source, it is altogether possible that Corasius was influential either upon the other jurists who are cited or upon the interpretations of texts of Roman law that are cited without an accompanying later jurist's name as a further source. The ways in which Jefferson has used *Lexicon* suggestions of constitutions as equivalent to statutes, laws, ordinances, and so forth in support of his own view of constitutions as alterable bore affinities to the views of Corasius in his *Art of Law* and *Commentaries* on Roman law, which influenced Continental and English jurists on the promulgation, forms, forces, and interpretation of legislation. In any case, Jefferson's own important writings on such subjects in *Notes* and elsewhere certainly held many parallels or correspondences with Corasius as well as with Bodin—who also tended to view constitutions in the form of laws as alterable like laws and statutes themselves, although Bodin's name was not included in *Lexicon* citations. The wealth of Renaissance jurists cited in the *Lexicon* who were central to our previous studies on Corasius and who related, in different ways on legislative issues, to Corasius include (as all cited in the initial *Lexicon* listing): Connan, Alciatus, Zasius, and Oldendorp, along with others even more crucial included on the title page, such as Duaren, Cujas, Doneau, Wesembecius (who did a "Life" of Corasius), and Corasius himself; various Medieval jurists are also cited such as Azo Accursius, and Bartolus, to whom Corasius himself referred. The two *Lexicon* editors who took over after Calvinus—Vultejus and Gothofredus—made significant uses of Corasius' legislative ideas in their own other publications. True, some strands of legislative terms and texts in the *Lexicon* that relate to Jefferson's section in his *Notes* XIII can be found in other early jurists besides just Corasius. Yet Corasius' *Art of Law* presented a distinctive mixture that comes the closest of Renaissance (and Medieval) jurists cited in the *Lexicon* to Jefferson's adaptations of *Lexicon* texts in a distinctive blend of his own, as adapted to the situations addressed by him in his *Notes* XIII. This uniqueness of Corasius' comprehensive legislative approach was seen time and time again in our first two volumes. Donat's great 17th-century treatise on civil law, which contained various close legislative parallels with Corasius' treatise and was possessed by Jefferson, was published too late in time for inclusion in the *Lexicon.*

Jefferson's influence in these regards at the Federal Convention would have been crucial enough if it had been limited there just to his close friend Madison (which it was not). Jefferson's *Notes* had come under Madison's scrutiny early on prior to the Convention. Among other cases was that of Noah Webster, which is particularly revealing. Not himself a delegate at the Federal Convention, the young Noah Webster nevertheless became a noted writer in support of passage for the new U.S. Constitution. By then he was already an acclaimed lexicographer, and his writings on behalf of the Constitution received much attention. (Cf. *Are We to Be a Nation?*, R. Bernstein, ed., Camb., Mass., 1987, pp. 140, 218–219.) He made good use of Jefferson's *Notes* XIII concerning "constitutions" as alterable like legislation itself. That writing of early 1788 by Webster, with his significant incorporation of Jefferson's uses of definitions in the *Lexicon Iuridicum*, was quoted above in conjunction with Webster's discussions in later 1787 on great ancient lawgivers compared with their American counterpoints at the Federal Convention (our pp. 247–250).

There is no evidence that the *Lexicon Iuridicum* itself was readily available in the Library Co. of Philadelphia at the time of the Federal Convention for use there by the delegates, although there could have been alternate access to it elsewhere there in some other way. Of the four editions of it now in the Library Co., two editions (1622, 1653) were acquired by the Co. from the Logan library and were thus not available at the Co. until the 1790s, while the two others (1665, 1673) were acquired by the Co. later. They are not listed in the Library Co. printed catalogues of 1789. Whether or not private access to the closed Logan library at the time of the Convention or before could have been gained for some through Franklin or others concerning this and other matters is not profitable to dwell upon here. Yet aside from Jefferson's direct legislative interests concerning the *Lexicon* in his *Notes* XIII, those of Adams more indirectly in his *Defence of Constitutions* present still another dimension to the influences at work upon the Convention delegates in matters of present interest. It would be an arduous and needless task to comb through the *Lexicon* more widely for citations of Corasius' thought and to compare them as well as those to other jurists with statements by the Convention delegates who may have possessed or had access to the *Lexicon*.

From a completely different angle, it can be noted that on May 21–22, 1787, at the time when the delegates were first assemblying in Philadelphia for the Federal Convention, Jefferson made a brief visit of two days to the city of Toulouse, in the course of his extended tour through Southern France. From the short account of this visit included in his "Notes" on this whole tour (*Papers* 11: 415 ff., at pp. 370–372, 449, 454–455; also 13: 192, 275), it remains uncertain to what extent he went into the city. Coming there by boat on waterway, he described the natural setting, navigation, geography, countryside, and products of the Toulouse area, but without including accounts of the city's buildings, streets, etc. This orientation is consistent with Jefferson's descriptions in the same "Notes" of other cities he visited on this extended tour. In a citation given shortly above, Jefferson is seen to have later sent L'Enfant maps of some Southern French cities he visited, procuring them while there. Yet Toulouse is not one of the cities he cited in that regard. It is tempting but of no avail here to envision Jefferson visiting the old city of Toulouse, in which Corasius had played such a key historical role, and there coming into contact not only with Corasius' legacy but also with some of his legal works. Unfortunately, none of Corasius' works were among the large numbers of books Jefferson actually sent back from Paris to his friend Madison and to Monticello.

8. The *Tractatus Universi Iuris* as Source for Knowledge of Corasius' *Art of Law*

Through whatever means in Europe, it remains more than possible that while there Jefferson, like Adams, came into contact with Corasius' *Art of Law* in the great multi-volume *Tractatus Universi Iuris*, or in Corasius' *Opera Omnia*, or in a separate edition of the work. While in Europe Jefferson as well as Adams, who were in contact with each other, very likely came across and consulted the incomparable magisterial *Tractatus Universi Iuris*. Its famed enormous collections of writings included so many works by the very jurists where opinions were later cited in the *Lexicon Iuridicum*, owned by both men. The *Lexicon* editors obviously drew heavily upon it. In the "encyclopedic age" of the Enlightenment, in which the bookish Jefferson and Adams felt so much at home, the *Tractatus Universi Iuris* afforded a special encyclopedic treasure trove of older juristic writings that was a perfect resource for men as interested in the *Lexicon Iuridicum* as were Jefferson and Adams, consistent with their wider encyclopedic interests.

For legal knowledge the *Tractatus* was a monumental resource comparable in importance and scale to the great *Encyclopédie Methodique*, the many dozens of volumes of which with much wider scope were well known and more accessible to American founders. One recalls Jefferson's references above (our p. 268) to the *Encyclopédie* in a letter of 1792 concerning designs for the Capitol. In addition, one can consult the Sowerby *Catalogue* (V, #4889) of Jefferson's library, as well as the entry for the *Encyclopédie* in the card file on Hamilton's books at Columbia. Both men owned the set of over 100 vols.

Looking at the beginning of the first volume of the *Tractatus*, Jefferson as well as Adams could easily have been struck—as was the present writer at the outset of his studies long ago—by the prominent place given there to Corasius' *Art of Law*. Such a scenario is especially plausible in the case of Adams due to his apparent prior attention drawn to Corasius' *Commentaries* at the Harvard library. With their interest in the *Lexicon*, Jefferson and Adams would have naturally turned to the *Tractatus Universi Iuris* from which so much of it had been drawn and there found Corasius' *Art of Law* prominently featured near the very outset of the first volume, where it provided not only a guiding methodological systematizing orientation for the *Tractatus* itself but a partial paradigm for themselves, most notably here for Adams' *Defence* Preface on great ancient lawgivers. Or, due to his early interest at Harvard in Corasius, Adams could well have looked him up directly in a European library.

In light of the additional perspectives in these Annexes, some reservations expressed in our main text about Corasius' possible direct and indirect influences on various American founders have proved to be overly cautious.

9. A Final Surprise Confirmation of Adam's Uses of Corasius' Ancient Lawgiver-Founders

Upon completion of the above Annexes in their present final form, this writer discovered at the beginning of Corasius' early commentaries on "*De origine iuris*" (*Digest* I, 2), a copy of which was in the small library at Harvard when Adams was there, a final surprise confirmation that Adams' *Defence* Preface on great ancient lawgiver-founders was modelled upon it as well as upon Corasius later *Art of Law* I, 16 on that same subject (along with I, 17 on the origins of law). This discovery renders conclusive the views expressed above that Adams' unique early American paradigm on this important theme at the outset of his *Defence* was based primarily upon the even more unique prototype provided by Corasius; in that way, Adams' portrayal became in turn the single most important original composite paradigm for Madison's *Federalist* #38 on the same subject. The self-image projected by the "founding fathers" at the Federal Convention and afterwards was largely inspired initially by this central theme in Adams' *Defence*, which had such crucial intellectual consequence in other respects at that Convention. It now becomes clearer than ever that the major influence that Adams' *Defence* had at the Convention—as predicted by Madison and confirmed by the editor of the Athenaeum catalogue of George Washington's library—extended to *Defence* Preface statements on ancient lawgiver-founders as modelled originally upon Corasius' introductory section to his commentary on D. I, 2. Adams' study of that commentary in the Harvard library could have extended beyond his college years and his period as a law student to his ensuing years as lawyer in the Boston area.

At the beginning of Corasius' huge early commentaries on *Digest* I, 2 (p. 23 in the *Opera* I edition) is an introductory overview that is completely centered around the role of ancient lawgiver-founders in ways that are nearly identical to Corasius' presentation of this subject in his later *Art of Law* I, 16. Conspicuous near the outset are the same poetic passages from Ovid and Vergil, followed by the same long lists of names found in *Art of Law* I, 16, including the ones cited there by Corasius in common with Adams. Those same names listed by them there in common and now presented by Corasius in this new case are as follows: Minos, Rhadamanthus (here spelled with the "h" that also appears in Adams' *Defence* Preface but not in *Art of Law* I, 16), Apollo, Delphic Oracle, Numa, Egeria, Zoroaster, Jupiter, Lycurgus, Solon, Romulus, and Herodotus. Certain differences in such names as appear in this commentary and in *Art of Law* I, 16 indicate that Adams expanded upon his own early reading of Corasius' commentary by later consulting the similar somewhat longer account in I, 16. In this introductory section of commentary on *Digest* I, 2, Corasius omitted Cicero and Mohammed, whereas he later included them in *Art of Law* I, 16 in significant lengthy ways that Adams picked up on in his own list of names in his *Defence* Preface. Whereas Tacitus appears in Corasius' introductory section of D. I, 2 commentaries, he is not included in *Art of Law* I, 16; Adams refers to Tacitus in his *Defence* Preface as did Corasius in his earlier D. I, 2 text.

An overall difference of context in the two accounts by Corasius is that, unlike *Art of Law* I, 16, the introduction to his commentaries on D. I, 2 completely deals with the quasi-religious scope of ancient lawgiver-founders, and it omits any allusions to their ulterior uses of religion designed to bind their laws more forcefully upon the citizens. This difference can be seen by comparing many statements in Corasius' two accounts, including at their outsets. When introducing his commentaries on D. I, 2, Corasius' indulgent attitude toward ancient lawgivers who attributed the inspiration behind their laws to divine revelation is conditioned by his wider assessment of the historical origins of Roman law as set forth in *Digest* I, 2. Contrariwise, Adams' Preface adopts a more critical view of divine revelation as the purported source cited by ancient lawgiver-founders, while Adams likewise omits reference to their uses of religion for binding their laws upon the citizens. Here Adams has stayed more in sync, though by inversion, with Corasius' earlier rather than later account. At the same time, Adams' Preface on law as ultimately given by "[human] reason and the [moral] senses" rather than by (divine) revelation corresponds with Corasius' own such statements that appear in his *Art of Law* I, 16 but not in his introductory section in his D. I, 2 commentaries. Adams clearly reflects that later position by Corasius in *Art of Law* I, 16 rather than the view in Corasius' introductory section in his commentaries on D. I, 2, where it is absent along with the accent on ancient religion as a useful device for binding constituted law upon the citizenry.

Many other features of Corasius' two accounts remain consistent throughout both. These include the unique composite comprehensive scope of names appearing in quick succession and apposition. The juxtaposed topics of inventors of law in Corasius' *Art of Law* I, 16 and the origins of law in his *Art of Law* I, 17 clearly expands upon his treatment of those two closely related topics as combined in his opening *Digest* I, 2 introduction on great lawgivers in connection with "the origins of law," the overarching topic of D. I, 2 as a whole. Making good early use of this particular commentary by Corasius as found in the Harvard library, Adams was obviously later led to explore its expanded counterpart in Corasius' *Art of Law*, most likely in the version presented at the outset of the famed encyclopedic *Tractatus Universi Iuris*. True, Corasius' early account lacked the heavier accents found in his *Art of Law* I, 16 upon ideas of equity, justice, and the like (e.g. *Opera* I, p. 1), while also lacking concepts of command and promulgation more in keeping with his stronger emphasis on legislative sovereignty in the *Art of Law* more generally. Yet Adams would have found other surrounding parts of Corasius' commentaries on the first four "titles" of *Digest* I very provocative in those regards as they pertained to the *Digest* texts themselves. Likewise, many statements by Corasius on the "arts and sciences" in his same early commentaries on D. I, 1–4 (e.g. *Opera* I, p. 111) foreshadowed his more highly developed ideas on that subject in his *Art of Law*. Neither account by Corasius, it can be added, makes reference to Plutarch or to themes on the giving up of power—two topics of further interest to the American founders as studied by Garry Wills in connection with other sources such as Rousseau (which influenced Adams and his fellow founders in other ways).

The essential point, then, is that Corasius' introduction to his commentaries on D. I, 2, "*De origine*," as found in the old Harvard library, provided the primary paradigm for Adams' *Defence* Preface on great ancient lawgiver-founders. Corasius' expanded account in *Art of Law* I, 16 (and I, 17) added further identifiable elements to that prototype as applied by Adams to his own contemporary American situation. Yet even if Adams never had seen Corasius' *Art of Law* I, 16 in the *Tractatus Universi Iuris* or elsewhere, the main Adams-Corasius connection would still hold true via that Harvard commentary alone. Corasius' introductions to his commentaries on the adjacent surrounding "titles" of *Digest* I, 1, 3–4 could also be studied for their wider influences on Adams concerning justice, legislation, sovereignty, and so forth. Not only Adams but also his admired Bodin (who made extensive use of Corasius' *Art of Law* on methodology and legislative sovereignty) may well have been influenced by Corasius' introduction to his commentaries on D. I, 1 ("On Justice and Law"). There, Corasius dealt in part with the ends of law regarding justice, etc. in a possible parallel with the opening chapter of Bodin's *Republic* (I, 1) on the principal ends of a state and its laws. It is fitting that Corasius' huge early commentaries on *Digest* I, 2, "*De origine iuris,*" recognized as a landmark contribution in his own era, became the repository of ideas at their outset for Adams, an American lawgiver-founder in his own right.

For over thirty-five years, starting in 1968, the present researcher has studied (more so in years past) Corasius' huge 2-vol. *Opera Omnia*, its rewarding contents only now revealing their fuller secrets on the Adams-Corasius connection. The treatments in our main text above and in our preceding Annexes serve to show the progressive unfoldment of ideas by one historian slow to grasp the weightier import of materials so long before him yet grateful to have pursued the journey to its conclusion. How a historical figure so long forgotten could have had such lasting impact from Jean Bodin to John Adams is an ongoing source of wonderment.

Thanks go to Whitney Bagnall and Peter Cohee respectively for the following Latin and English renderings. The English version "C." corresponds to the Latin version above in Annex 3. A few English modifications have been made. Sources are *Opera* I and *Tract. Univ. Iuris.* I, all *sic.*

A. Corasius' Introduction on Ancient Lawgiver-Founders in His D. I, 2 Commentaries at Harvard: Latin

Summae
1 Iuris origo praecognoscenda.
2 Ceres legifera.
3 Thesmophoria.
4 Legum inventores.
5 Radamanthi vita.
6 Deus legifer.
7 Moses hominum primus legislator.
8 Lex Deus est.

Expositis diffinitionibus & divisionibus juris, ad ejusdem originem, legislator transitum facit. quod + videlicet necessum sit, ei qui in hoc studii genere foeliciter versari velit, juris fontes, & originem ante omnia cognoscere. *l.2 princ. hoc titul.* Equidem mortalium vetustissimi, ut Tacitus scribit, nulla mala libidine omnia simpliciter agebant honesta suopte ingenio petentes, & nihil injustum cupientes, donec exui pudor, & modestia coepit, visque & ambitio incedere,, tum enim probrum, & scelus invasit. Ideoque praemiis & poenis opus fuit, ut illorum propositione allecti, virtutem cuperent homines: vel coercitionibus perterriti, ab injusta via revocarentur. Inde juris principium & origo. *Cornel. Tacitus lib.3 Annalium.* + Leges porro mortalibus, primum a Cerere datas Ethinici fabulantur. *Diod. Lib I rer. antiq. Herod in 6* unde Ovidius. *Ovid. Lib.5. Metam.*
Prima Ceres unco glebas dimovit aratro:
Prima dedit fruges, alimentaq initia terris.

Prima dedit leges, Cereris sunt omnia munus.
Et Virgilius. *Virg. 4. Aeneid.*
Principio delubra adeunt, pacemq per aras
Exquiriunt: mactant lectas de more bidentes,
Legifera Cereri.

Eoque factum, ut sacra quae huic Deae fiebant, + Thesmophoria, id est, legiferalia nuncuparentur. Alij vero + primum legislatorem fuisse Radamanthum asseverant, *Plin. lib. 8. cap. 56.* ac demum alios aliis leges tulisse *c. Moyses. 7 distinct.* ut Batrianis Persisque Zoroastrem: Aegyptiis Trimegistum: aut sicuti aliis placet, Aethiopes, quorum Aegyptii, coloni dicuntur: Cretensibus, Minoem: Celtis, Herculem: Argivis, Phoroneum: Henichis apud Colchos, Amphytum: Hispanis, Abidem: Chartaginensibus, Charondam: Lacedaemoniis Lycurgum: Atheniensibus Draconem, & Solonem: Romanis deinde Romulum, ac mox Numam: Italis Pythagoram: Scythis Zamorxim: Magnesiis, & Siculis Platonem. Quod vero Radamanthu nonnulli putant conditorem legis fuisse, ex Platone, *Plato in Minoe.* falsum deprehenditur. + Radamanthus inquit Plato, vir quidem bonus extitit, a Minoe siquidem instructus erat, nec tamen regiam disciplinam omnem, sed Regi tantum ministrare, in judiciis, didicit. Unde jurisperitus appellatus erat, quo veluti legu custode, per urbem usus est, ut non legumlatorum, sed judicum Radamanthum fuisse intelligere non fit obscurum. Enimvero nos qui jamdiu didicimus ex Demosthene, *Demosthenes in 1 oratione contra Aristogitonem.* & Martiano, *l.2 ff. de legib.* leges omnes inventum esse, ad munus Deorum: cum divino illo vate Efaia, + Deum optimum maximum legiferum dicimus, ab eoque primum leges ad animae salutem, & humanae quietis tuitionem conditas, *Esa. 33* ac Mosi demum traditas in Montem Sinai, *Exod. 19 & 20. Ioseph. lib. 3 antiquit. Iudaic. c.6* + & per Mosem antiquissimum omnium hominum legislatorem, Hebraeis constitutas. *d. c. Moyses.* Ad cujus exemplum caeteri deinceps principes viri in suis civitatibus leges sancivertunt: eas sicuti Moses ad Deum, ita ipsi ad quoddam caelitum numen referentes. Quemadmodum Trimegistus Aegyptios legibus instituens in Mercurium retulit: Lycurgus Spartanis leges ferens in Apollinem, Minos primus Cretae Rex & legislator in Iovem, Draco & Solon Athenas legibus fundantes in Minervam, Pompilius Numa, qui urbe Romam legibus munivit, in Aegeriam nympham: ut ita verum sit, quamvis varios legum constitutores genus humanum habuerit: non tamen ab hominum industria, sed a summa Dei immortalis providentia, leges ipsas defluxisse. Unusque (ut literae sacrae perhibent) est legislator, nempe Deus. *Iacob.4.* ut merito moneat Plato, legem veluti Dei praeceptum servari: & Sotacus ille sapientissimus, sapientissime dicebat, + Lex Deus est, hanc venerare.

B. Corasius' Introduction on Ancient Lawgiver-Founders in His D. I, 2 Commentaries at Harvard: English

[Introduction:] Contents

1 The origin of law must first be understood
2 Ceres the lawgiver
3 Thesmophoria
4 Discoverers of laws
5 Life of Rhadamanthus
6 God the lawgiver
7 Moses the first human legislator
8 Law is God

From the definitions and divisions of law that have been set down, the legislator crosses over to the origin of law because, obviously, for one who wishes to be successfully occupied in this kind of study, it is necessary to know the sources and origin of law above all else. To be sure, the most ancient mortals, as Tacitus writes, did everything simply, with no evil motive, seeking out what was honorable, using their own native ability, desiring no injustice, until a sense of shame and modesty began to be put aside, and violence and ambition arose; then indeed did wickedness and crime enter. And for that reason there was need of rewards and penalties, so that people, attracted by the possibility of the former, would desire virtue, or, terrified by coercive measures, would be called away from the path of injustice. Hence the beginning and origin of law (Cornelius Tacitus, *Annales* Book 3). Historians report that laws were first given to mortals by the goddess Ceres (Diodorus, Antiquities, Book 1, Herodotus, Book 2), whence Ovid (Metamorphoses Book 5):

> Ceres first moved the clods aside with the curved plow
> She first gave us crops and our original nourishment from the earth,
> She first gave us laws, all things are a gift of Ceres.

And Vergil (Aaeneid Book 4):

> Straightaway they approach the shrines and seek peace
> At the altars; they slaughter, as was customary, two-year old sheep to Ceres the Lawgiver.

Thus began the rite of the Thesmophoria, as all acts which were carried out for this goddess, that is, The lawgiving ceremony, so called. However, people assert that Rhadamanthus was the first (mortal) lawgiver (Pliny Book 8 Ch. 56) and finally others created laws for different peoples (Moses & . . .), for example: Zoroaster for the Bactrians and the Persians, Trimegistrus for the Egyptians (or as some believe, Aethiopes, whose colonists are called Egyptians), Minos for the Cretans, Hercules for the Gauls, Phoroneus for the Argives, Amphytus for the Henichi in Colchis (present-day Georgia), Abides for the Spanish, Charondas for the Carthaginians, Lycurgus for the Spartans, Draco for the Athenians, for the Romans first Romulus, then Numa; for the Italians Pythagoras; Zamorxis for the Scythians; Plato for the Magnesians and Sicilians. But in any case some think that Rhadamanthus was the inventor of laws, a fact gleaned from Plato. "Rhadamanthus," says Plato, "a good man to be sure, arose, since he had been instructed by Minos, but not, however . . . a monarchical system, but he learned only to administer for the king in judgements. Hence he was called a legal expert, which term he used, just like "custodian of the laws" throughout the city, so that it is not a secret that Rhadamanthus was not one of the legislators but one of the judges.

But indeed, we who have for a long time now been learning from Demosthenes (speech against Aristogeitos) and Martianus Capella that all laws are the discovery and gift of the gods, with that divine prophet Isaiah we learn that God is the best and greatest Lawgiver and from him firstly that laws were established for the salvation of the soul and preservation of human peace and finally delivered to Moses on Mt Sinai (Exodus 19 and Josephus Book 3 of Jewish Antiquities) and that through Moses, the oldest legislator of all humans, laws were established for the Hebrews. In keeping with his example other leading men thereafter sanctioned laws in their own states. Just as Moses attributed his laws to God, so did those others attribute them to some heavenly power. In just this way Trimegistus, when he organized Egypt by laws, referred to the god Mercury, Lycurgus, in his laws for the Spartans, to Apollo, Minos, first king and legislator of Crete, to Jupiter, Draco and Solon, when establishing the constitutional basis of Athens, to Minerva, Numa Pompilius, who fortified the city of Rome with laws, to the nymph Egeria. In this sense it is true, though the human race has had different founders of legal systems. Nevertheless, laws themselves have proceeded not from human industry but from the supreme providence of immortal God. And there is but one legislator (as sacred literature shows), namely God (Jacob 4), as Plato rightly shows, the law is preserved just as a precept of God and as the famous and very wise Sotacus used to say all the time, Law is God; worship it.

C. Corasius' *Art of Law* I, 16 on Ancient Lawgiver-Founders: English

Concerning those who invented laws [ch. title].

The ancients thought it was a great binding force for controlling the minds of their citizens to believe that laws were constituted by divine providence, and therefore ancient laws are always associated with some religious beliefs. Indeed, chroniclers have generally declared that it was Ceres, a goddess of the Sicilians, who first of all gave laws to mortals and for this reason is called the Lawgiver and her rites are called ... [Greek] (rites of the Lawgiver; Diodorus Siculus, Library of History Book 6, Herodotus, Book 6, which is titled Erato) whence Ovid, *Metamorphoses*, Book 5:)

> Ceres it was who first moved aside the clods with the hooked plow.
> She first gave crops and the mild nourishment to the world;
> She first gave laws. All things are a gift of Ceres

And Vergil, *Aeneid* Book 4:

> At first they approach the shrine and seek peace at the altars
> they sacrifice chosen two-year-old victims according to custom
> to Ceres the Lawgiver

Others think that Rhadamanthys was the first of the Legislators (Pliny Book 7 Ch. 56) and that later on some men proposed laws for some peoples, others for others (cf. Moyses 7 dist.): Zoroaster for the Persians and Bactrians; Mercurius for Thebes; for the Egyptians, Trismegistus; Hercules for the Celts; Minos for the Cretans; Charondas for the Carthaginians; for the Heniochoi among the Colchians, Amphytus; Lycurgus for the Spartans; for the Athenians first Draco, later Solon; for the Romans, first Romulus and later Numa Pompilius; Phoroneus for the Argives; Pythagoras for the Italian Greeks; Zamolxis for the Scythians; Zaleucus for the Locrians; for the Magnesians and Sicilians, Plato; he himself refused this to the Arcadians, Thebans, and the people of Cyrene, though they requested it strenuously. But all these persons claimed that their institutions were received for some god or goddess—Minos, for example, for Jupiter, Lycurgus for the Sun or for Apollo of Delphi, Solon for Minerva. These wise Greek lawgivers seem to me to have done this purposely, since the name Jupiter means mercy, the Sun (because he is the lord of the planets) signifies power, and Minerva represents wisdom. From that it is clear that their teaching is excellent, that these three qualities (by the division of which every governance of society is contained) must be present in laws. Zamolxis, too, referred his laws to the divine authority of the goddess Vesta. Likewise Numa Pompilius, in order to establish laws, religious customs, and ceremonies the more firmly, pretended to have intercourse with the nymph Egeria. We, however, refer our norm of living rightly and blessedly to the True God, who is tripartite and one (Isaiah 33, Jacob 4), handed down first from Moses on Mount Sinai (Josephus, book 3 of Judaic Antiquities ch. 6, Exodus 19 & 20) and through that same Moses, the oldest lawgiver of all these, the first to establish a law of circumcision of the foreskin promulgated among the Hebrews (d.c. Moyses, unless you prefer, God to Abraham; Gen. 17). For this right of circumcision of the genitals, among the Egyptians and Ethiopians, was very old, as Herodotus, the Father of History, writes (Book 2, titled Euterpe). Thus, as it happens, we recognize God as the fount of good things and author of laws, whom the prophet for that reason calls Lawgiver (Isaiah 33). Demosthenes, too, in that oration which he vigorously delivered against Aristogeiton, said that law was a divine invention and gift (laws 1.2 ff), by which we understand that only those constitutions which are sanctified and honorable have the name of law. For there is one legislator, says Saint James, to be sure, God; to make him the author of injustice and shame and iniquity is full of blasphemy. And law is the reason of God the Highest, or (M. Cicero says elsewhere), a reason drawn from the authority of the God, promoting honorable things and forbidding their opposite (Cicero, Book 2 of De legibus and the 2nd Philippic)). This does not begin to be law at the time it is written but at the time when it comes into existence. But law came into existence at the same time with divine (mete) [?], so that it can be clearly seen that pernicious, shameful, and injust laws are indeed commands of the powerful, but they are not laws, which M. Cicero proves in several places in the 2nd book of De legibus. Moses also first gave laws written down to the Hebrew people. Following his example, other men in other states, men who were prominent and who had the consent of the people, established laws. [They] attributed their laws to a divinely inspired power in order that thereby they might bind the minds of their fellow citizens in a more solid fashion. But among those [legislators] who established their states with the best institutions and very wholesome laws, the Romans stand out before all, and for that reason Polybius quite rightly put their laws before all others (Histories, Book 1), and the poet Vergil, when he had attributed appropriate praises to each nation, only the Romans with their knowledge of choosing a Republic, did he honor with these words

> You, Roman, remember to rule nations with power.
> These will be your arts, and to establish the name of peace.

Meanwhile allow me to pass over the accursed and most shameful of these lawgivers, the most foul and most corrupt Mohammed, who, establishing new laws for the Sceniti and Moors, on the advice of Sergius, had openly taught to every people that a dove had entered his ear in order to convince them by this brilliant explanation that the Holy Spirit was inspiring him with laws, and this he finally achieved. But let us go down to the spring, from which our law bubbles up [in the next chapter on the origin of civil law].

Illustrations

Bodin at Independence Hall? Supplements on Jefferson's Reading and Its Influence

1. Introduction to Illustrations

Jefferson's Declaration of Independence

It will be remembered from our discussion above in Chapter II on Jefferson's book markings that the bracket marks he placed in his rough draft of the Declaration of Independence were strikingly similar to those made in his copy of Bodin's *Republic* and in his copy of Sidney's *Discourses*. The historian Mayer's insightful but brief and restricted discussion of the interconnections between these three sets of markings *per se* omitted Jefferson's ideas on legislative sovereignty in the Declaration of Independence and those found in Bodin's *Republic* together with Sidney's *Discourses*, which was heavily influenced by Bodin. The full recognition of each state's inherent right to legislative self-determination, regardless of outside questions over its jurisdictional right to do so in relation to other states or groups, had been a principal first decisively espoused by Corasius and was in turn made use of by Bodin. Jefferson's Declaration of Independence adapted that concept, by then well accepted, along similar lines, consistent with the new American situation at that point. In the illustrations to follow, the second of two pages (on its reverse or back side) provides two examples of bracket marks made in Jefferson's copy of Bodin's *Republic* III, together with an example of the same kind of bracket marks also found in Jefferson's copy of Sidney's *Discourses*. Adjacent to these three examples is another from Jefferson's draft Declaration of Independence, in which the same kind of bracket marks appear. Together these four examples of bracket marks placed in writings by Bodin, Sidney, and Jefferson himself were the focus of Mayer's article. Although they show a definite general connection between Jefferson's readings of Bodin and Sidney at around the time of Jefferson's Declaration of Independence, they do not reveal specific links between Jefferson and the other two writers on legislative sovereignty and the legislative state. Those twin subjects—as raised in the first book of Bodin's *Republic*, especially Chapters 8–10—were not considered by Mayer. They remained to be treated above in our Chapter II. There, the other kind of marginal markings placed in Jefferson's copy of Bodin's *Republic* was compared with markings in other books in Jefferson's library. Illustrations appear below relating to the full range of examples cited in the Diagram of Markings given above on page 96 and repeated below in slightly altered fashion.

Final Conclusive New Evidence on Jefferson's Markings in Bodin's *Republic* I and Justinian's *Code*

New evidence has now emerged to resolve the final words of caution expressed above at the end of Chapter II on the conclusiveness of our proofs for Jefferson as the marker of Bodin's *Republic* I in his library. In the margins of the first book of Jefferson's copy of Bodin's *Republic*, where Bodin made his classic formulations of legislative sovereignty, there appear frequent vertical lines of short vertical dash or hyphen marks opposite certain passages selected for attention. Compared with the relatively few and sporadic bracket marks made by Jefferson in the ensuing books of Bodin's *Republic*, the marginal lines of short dash marks in *Republic* I are extremely extensive, totalling "many hundreds," as Mayer has noted. These lines are all the more conspicuous in view of Jefferson's well-known tendency not to mark books in his collections, especially in the fashion here employed. The closest approximation to these kinds of markings were found above in Jefferson's "1783" catalogue of his library. There, various different lines of dash marks appear but not in exactly the same ways of consistency and placement, albeit they are probably close enough to those in *Republic* I. Page samples of these types appear below in the Illustrations on the front and back sides of the first page and on the front side of the second page. The reader can compare them with the two portions of pages from *Republic* I containing the vertical lines of short dash marks on the front side of the first page of Illustrations below.

What has now been discovered for the first time, requiring a slight adjustment in the Diagram of Jefferson's markings, are some precisely identical markings in Jefferson's copy of Justinian's *Code*, which he obtained during his Paris years (cf. Sowerby's *Catalogue* for the *Corpus Iuris* in Jefferson's library). In our earlier Diagram, Jefferson's markings in the *Code* were limited to solid long vertical lines opposite passages of special interest. But the portion of the page sample given to the right on the front side of the first page of Illustrations below clearly shows another kind as well. Therefore, alongside the vertical line in the column corresponding to the *Code* in our Diagram must now be added a vertical column of short dash or hyphen marks more precisely akin to those in *Republic* I.

It is logical that the bracket marks in later books of Bodin's *Republic* made during the period of the Declaration of Independence were made by the same person who made the vertical lines of dash marks in the first book of the *Republic*—namely, Jefferson. Our discovery on the *Code* serves to tie in even more closely Jefferson's untypically extensive reading marks in *Republic* I—especially Chapters 8–10 on legislative sovereignty but also other chapters—with the bracket marks made in Jefferson's draft Declaration of Independence. The page fragment at the center top of the front side of the first page of Illustrations is from the opening lines of *Republic* I, 8 that are devoted to Bodin's classic formulation of sovereignty. The page sample to the left of this is from the very end of *Republic* I, 9, immediately preceding I, 10 centering on the marks of sovereignty. By now there can be no doubt that these and other such marks in *Republic* I were indeed placed there by none other than Jefferson. The rarity or paucity of intertextual as well as marginal markings in books owned by Jefferson points up how unique and special was his interest in Bodin's concepts of legislative sovereignty and related subjects as they could be applied to the case for America's independence as a sovereign nation-state with its own inherent sovereign powers of legislative self-determination regardless of jurisdictional claims to the contrary. That viewpoint was in line with Corasius' principle and Bodin's classic development and transformation of it. To be sure, the late-17th-century doctrines of Sidney and Locke on revolution and independence profoundly influenced Jefferson during the period of his writing the Declaration of Independence. Nonetheless, both Sidney and Locke were themselves deeply indebted to Bodin's ideas of legislative sovereignty, which was, as we have seen, a central point of orientation in Jefferson's Declaration of Independence and in his related writings of the same era.

The fragments from *Republic* I given on the front side of the first page of Illustrations also give glimpses into the special interest Jefferson also displayed, through his markings, in the rich classical citations and materials made use of by Bodin in *Republic* I in connection with issues of sovereignty, state, and legislation. It is natural that Jefferson would have been particularly struck by the unique encyclopedic treasure trove of classical-humanistic learning found in Bodin's *Republic*, including passages and citations in Greek, Latin, vernacular languages, and even Hebrew. The massive marginal marks by Jefferson in his early reading of Bodin's *Republic* I may have been only faintly echoed by his far fewer marks in his later reading of Justinian's *Code*, purchased in Paris. Even so, his *Code* markings confirm conclusively our case for his *Republic* markings.

Diagram of Markings (1–9)

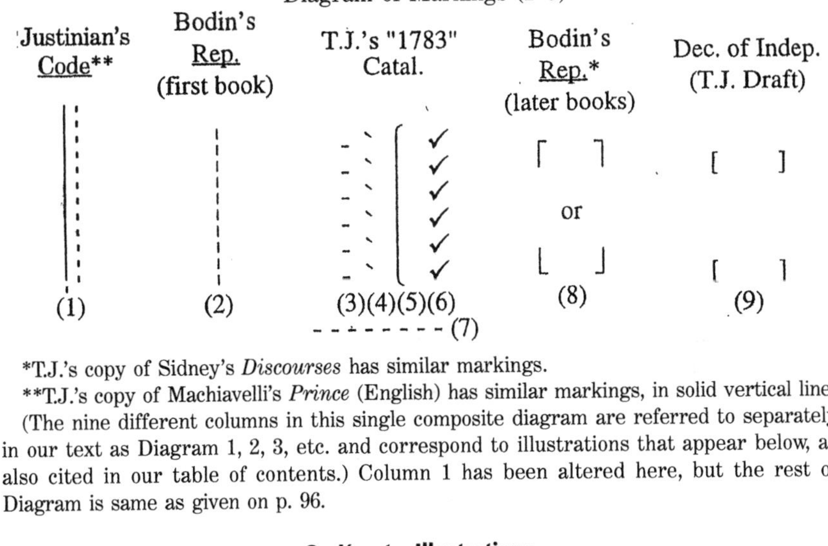

*T.J.'s copy of Sidney's *Discourses* has similar markings.
**T.J.'s copy of Machiavelli's *Prince* (English) has similar markings, in solid vertical line.
(The nine different columns in this single composite diagram are referred to separately in our text as Diagram 1, 2, 3, etc. and correspond to illustrations that appear below, as also cited in our table of contents.) Column 1 has been altered here, but the rest of Diagram is same as given on p. 96.

2. Key to Illustrations

The following Key to Illustrations employs a numbering of page samples that corresponds with that used in the Diagram of Markings. The Diagram as repeated above adds a second line to the right in the first column, as already mentioned, concerning Justinian's *Code*.

(1) Vertical solid lines of varying length are found in some margins next to select passages in T.J.'s copy of Justinian's *Code* (1598 edn. of *Corpus Iuris*). Other kinds of vertical lines of short vertical dash marks (e.g. p. or col. 15) correspond there closely with those in his copy of Bodin's *Republic* I, making it all the more certain that they are by T.J. here as well.

(2) Short vertical dash marks in a single vertical line or column of varying length (typically a half-dozen or so in number) found in left or right inner margins next to select passages (each mark adjacent to a line of text) in T.J.'s copy of Bodin's *Republic* (1580 edn.), Bk. I (p. 211 in our Illust.).

(3) Short horizontal dash marks found in outer left margins (each mark next to an individual entry)—typically forming a vertical line or column of such marks in varying positions—on many pages of T.J.'s "1783" manuscript catalogue of his books, esp. Ch. 24 on politics.

(4) Other kinds of short dash/slash marks corresponding to (and in place of or in addition to) check marks, forming a vertical line or column in middle position of left margins on many pages of same cat. and esp. same ch. (each mark again adjacent to an individual entry). Sometimes this mark becomes a second check mark.

(5) Vertical solid lines of varying length found in some left margins of same cat., comparable to those in *Code* yet slightly curled inward at top and bottom.

(6) Check marks found in left margins of same cat. (as indicated on front page), esp. same ch., in a varying vertical column (each mark again next to an individual entry). Cf. our p. 87 and Illust. for check mark on front of same cat.

(3, 4, 6) In exceptional cases where all three above types of marks appear, the above sequences of outer, middle, and inner left margins is typical (with entries to the right of inner margin).

(7) Short horizontal dash marks of varying size and number forming a horizontal line on many pages of same cat. and esp. same ch., often within an individual entry as if in an extended line to indicate a continuation of something. In diagrams at beg. of cat., some similar lines of dash marks again at times have a uniform consistency and precise placement somewhat similar to those in Bodin's *Rep.*

(8) Types of bracket marks for select passages in later books of T.J.'s copy of Bodin's *Rep.*

* T.J.'s copy of Sidney's *Discourses*, containing similar markings.

(9) Bracket marks within select portions of T.J.'s draft version of the Declar. of Indep.

As presented in the Illustrations below, the examples of Jefferson's markings are meant to elucidate points made in our main text and notes as well as this supplement. For purposes here, there is neither space nor need for fuller portions of the page fragments selected. The sequence of numbers placed above each selection corresponds roughly to the sequence of numbered columns (1–9) in the Diagram of Markings. On the front side of the first of two pages of Illustrations, the reader will notice under #1 for Justinian's *Code* the second vertical line of dash marks (each such mark by Jefferson corresponding to a line of text, the same as in his copy of Bodin's *Republic* I). In this case, only the left margin is shown, the right half of the page being deleted here. Under #2(A) and 2(B) from *Republic* I, 9 and I, 8 respectively, the same vertical lines of dash marks appear in the right and left margins of the portions of pages included. Under #3, 5, 6 are three kinds of apropos markings in the bottom left margin of a page in Jefferson's "1783" catalogue of his books. On the back side of the first page of Illustrations appear two further samples of markings in the left margins etc. of pages in the same "1783" catalogue, under our #3, 4, 5, 6 and #3, 4, 7. On the front side of the second page of Illustrations is a fuller page from Jefferson's "1783" catalogue under our #4, 6, 7. Also under #6 is front cover notation in "1783" cat. On the back side of the second page of Illustrations under #8(A) and 8(B) are portions of left margins in pages of *Republic* III showing bracket marks of the kind found in our adjacent samples from Jefferson's draft of the Declaration of Independence under #9, and from his copy of Sidney's *Discourses* under #8(C).

The requirements of space, size, darkness, highlighting, etc. in some pages and fragments selected for reproduction below have necessitated some adjustments for sake of clarity. Some samples have been enlarged or reduced, arranged or cut off in somewhat arbitrary fashion, while some lines have had to be slightly accentuated so the camera would pick them up, especially in cases where fading has occurred over time. In any case, the aim has been to highlight the markings rather than to enable the corresponding passages to be read more clearly in themselves. The reproductions may be visually uneven but the results will hopefully be seen to achieve their purpose.

2 (A)

ſt ny tributaire, ny
, peut diſtribuer en
à qui bon luy ſem-
ng. On ſçait aſſez
nes, de Raguſe, les
ont traicté alliance
l a touſiours deferé
France, l'appellant
eur des plus grands
ſie le plus grand de
Sarrach des Muſul-
es : & quant à ceſte
iens meſmes la luy
au premier tiltre, il
ereurs de Conſtan-
s quatre B, que les
dire, ΒΑΣΙΛΕΥ'Σ
ΒΑΣΙ'ΛΕΥΣΙ, c'eſt
Rois : qui eſtoit la
it les Rois de Baby-
el, qui appelle מלך
'autant que tous les
, & depuis les Rois
pres eux les Rois de
mme Dion eſcrit de
elloit Roy des Rois:
e peuuent qualifier
s, Princes vſer du til-
eſſe, ou Serenité, ou
t. Or puis que les
e ſont point abſolu-
n protection, diſons
é.

CHAP. X.

plus grand en terre
rinces ſouuerains, &
luy comme ſes lieu-
ıder aux autres hom-
prendre garde à leur
leur maieſté en tou-

2 (B)

ce que nous toucherons en ſon lieu. Mais il faut premie-
rement dire de la ſouueraineté.

De la ſouueraineté. CHAP. VIII.

LA SOUVERAINETÉ eſt la puiſſance abſolue & perpetuelle d'une Republique, que les Latins appellent *maieſtatem*, les Grecs [illegible], & [illegible], & [illegible] : les Italiens *ſegnoria*, duquel mot ils vſent auſſi enuers les particuliers, & enuers ceux là qui manient toutes les affaires d'eſtat d'une Republique : les Hebrieux l'appellent [illegible], c'eſt à dire, la plus grande puiſſance de commander. Il eſt icy beſoin

3, 5, 6

uſuras vſque ad quartam centeſimæ. Quod ſi nolit c... tor ita accipere: tunc ordinator domus apud cum... quo ordinatur, habitis abſque diſpendio geſtis, iuret (... ore parte ibidem ſeruientium conſentiente) & d... exiſtere, nec ex mobilibus ſolui poſſe, quo ſubſecuto... viginti dies rem eccleſiæ venalem eſſe publicè no... it: vt plus offerenti detur, precio modis omnibu... debito dando. aliter enim res emptori non conced... & hoc inſcribatur, nihil eſſe factum in ea re ad a... rum diuinæ domus. Emptore verò non inuento, v... ſilmata diſtrictè creditori detur in ſolutum, addi... pretio vniuerſæ æſtimationis decima parte, & acce... e conſenſu ordinatoris, & maioris partis ibidē ſeru... tium. Sic tamen ea res mediocris inter cæteras, inſ... ipſius qualitate & quantitate & onere. Et is cre... cie intelligatur, qui, quod credidit, probat in vtilit... diuinæ domus proceſſiſſe.

IN AVTHEN. de non alienandis aut permutand. ſicut autem. coll. 2. tit. 1. ſeu Nou. 7. c. 7.

Sicut alienatio rerum eccleſiæ interdicitur: ita p... betur ne qua ſterilis ei detur poſſeſſio, aut alioq... roſa, veluti fiſcalium nomine vel onere.

IN AVTHEN. de non alienandis. §. pia verò c... mimus. col. 2. tit. 1. ſeu No. 7. c. 11. & in authen. alie. & emphyteu. §. & quoniam. coll. 9. tit. 3. ſeu Nou. 120. c. 7.

Multo magis prohibetur ipſius monaſterii al... tio, quâ redeat in antiquum ſtatum, & ſecul... vſum.

IN AVTHEN. de alienatione & emphyteuſ. §. ſi... non ſint. verſ. œconom. is. coll. 9. tit. 3. ſeu Nou. 120. c. 5.

Quibuſcumque modis hoc tuis aliis permittitur... terdicitur certis perſonis, res huiuſmodi acci... ut œconomo, eiuſque cognatis. alioqui bona eoru... œconomorum, & ordinatorum, quibus coniuncti... poſt mortem eorum perueniant ad eccleſiam, de... rem accipiunt.

IN AVTHEN. de non alie. aut permutan. §. quia Leonis. col. 2. tit. 1. ſeu Nou. 7. c. 5. & col. 9. tit. 3. lit. & emphy. §. ſi verò præter hæc ſeu. No. 120.

Qui res iam dictas non gratuito alienationis... lo citra formam legis accepit: rem quidem... omni incremento medii temporis reſtituat: eius au... quod dedit, nullam actionem contra venerabilem... ſed aduerſus eum, qui alienauit, habet. Donatari... tem & rem cum omni cauſa & fructum reſtituat,... liud tantundem. Creditor quoque, reſtituta re pign... crediti actionem contra ſolum pignoris datorem ha... Emphyteuſis acceptor & ab ea cadat: nec, quod dea... geſtat: immo ſtatim ſoluat, quod ſoluturus eſſet vn... que anno, ſi iure contraxiſſet. ſed meliùs dicitur, ... modo denegandas eſſe actiones huiuſmodi accepto...

IN AVTHENTIC. de alie. & emphy. §. ſi v... quædam ſunt. col. 9. tit. 3. ſeu Nou. 120. c. 1.

Si quas vineas habent memorata diuina domus... reædificare non valent, & ha in emphyteuſin... tur perpetuam: emphyteuta vſuro materia habita... depoſita domus: vt penſio deminuatur in tertiam... tem ab ea, quæ ſtantibus adhuc ædificiis colligebatu... primitùs eo re ædificante, ex adiectis illi per æſtim... tem penſionibus, medietas detur religioſæ domui... priore caſu ab initio emphyteuſis præſtanda eſt pen...

IN AVTHENTIC. de non alienan. §. quia v... Leonis. col. 1. tit. 2. ſeu No. 7. c. 3. & in auth. de alien. & emphy. §. & hoc quidem verſ. licentiam. collat. 9. tit. 3. ſeu Nou. 120. c. 6.

Perpetua quoque emphyteuſis in his permitti... bus, ſi res in eorum geratur præſentia, quib... adſignatur lege, iurantibus his, quorum intereſt,... contractum nihil ad læſionem diuinæ domus effici:... reditu ipſius rei, qui fuit, cùm diuino iuri dedica... non minuendo niſi in ſextam partem: aut, ſi ob c... deminuta fuerit, tunc pro conſtante nunc penſ... emphyteuſin detur. Quòd ſi res pretioſa quidem e... tamen, aut nihil præſtat penſionum, res ſub...

3, 4, 5, 6

Principes
Mémoire...
Lois de la
Xenophontis Oec
Xenophontis Lacedae
Xenophontis Hi
Aristotle's, treat
Bodin de la re
Godwin's Politica
Godwin's Politica
Chipman's, sketche
La Croix sur
Warville des Co
Howard on Pr
Physiocratie
Tableau econ
Explication d
l'Ordre natur
avec les
de l'Ordre s
Le Trosne de l
La Theorie d
L'Ami des h
Ouvrages de
Chastellux
Instruction
Idée sur les
Paine's, right
Washington's

3, 4, 7

Tracts political. viz.
Comparaison des ligues des Achaeens, des Suisses & des provinces unies.
De Lolme on the Union of Scotl^d. & Engl^d. & present situation of Ireland }
Tracts on English foreign possessions. viz
Politique Angloise dans l'Inde.
Sundry pieces relative to Ireland } 8vo
La cause de l'Irlande.

[illegible] 8vo
Deane's, intercepted letters. 12mo : 8vo
Tracts. Britain & America. viz.
L'Independance des Anglo-Americains utile à la G.B. par Warville.
Testament politique de l'Angleterre. par Warville.
Lettre à l'auteur du Mercure politique.
La Crise de l'Europe par S^r. John Sinclair } 12
Tracts. Britain & America. viz
Price on the importance of the American revolution.
Price on the nature of Civil liberty. } 8vo
Tracts. Britain & America. viz
History of the colonization of the free states of antiquity.
Remarks on the History of the colonization &c. by Symonds. } 4to
Bougainville sur les droits des Metropoles Grecques. 12mo
[illegible] 1785.
Deslandes sur l'Importance de la revolution Americaine. 12mo
Triomphe du nouveau monde. 2. v. [illegible] 1. 8 [illegible] on Adams & Delolme. Eng. Fr. 8vo
Adams's, [illegible] 3. v. 8vo [illegible] Monroe [illegible]
[illegible] Stockdale
[illegible] States of America
[illegible] of the States and of the U.S. 12mo
Debates in the Convention of Massachusetts of 1788. 12mo
\- - - - - - - - of Pennsylvania of 1788. 8vo
\- - - - - - - - of New York. of 1788. 8vo
\- - - - - - - - of Virginia. of 1788. 8vo. 2. cop.
Tracts on the American Constitution. viz.
Thoughts on the political situation of the U.S. of America.
Wilson's, speech on the Federal constitution.
Examination of the leading principles of the federal constn. Philada.
Genuine information of [illegible]
Pinkney's, observns on the plan of govmt submitted to the fed. convention.
Jay's, address to the people of N. York
Monroe's, observns on the Constn.
Remarks on the Address of the 16. members of Pennsylva } 8
The Federal farmer. 12mo & same 2. v. 8vo
The Federalist. 2. v. 12mo 2 copies.
Debates of the assembly of Pennsylva on the bank in 1786.
of the assembly of Pennsylva in 1787. & 1788. } 8vo
Mirabeau sur l'ordre de Cincinnatus. 8vo
Tracts Political of America. viz.
Burke on the Cincinnati.
[illegible] of the Cincinnati.
Considns on the act of Virginia for religious freedom.
Knox's plan for the militia of the U.S. } 8vo
Chipman
Washington. 8vo

4, 6, 7

133

Codex Justinianus. 4to. Paris. Regnault. 1532.
Corpus Juris civilis Gothofredi. Antwerp. 2. v. fol.
Corpus Juris civilis Gothofredi. Laemarius. 2. v. 8vo. 1598.
Theophili Antecessoris Institutiones. Gr. Lat. Fabroti. 4to. Paris. 1638.
Jus Graeco-Romanum Leunclavii. fol. Francofurti. 1596.
Ulpiani fragmenta notis Cannegieter. Lug. Bat. 1774. 4to.
Fontes quatuor juris civilis Gothofredi. 4to. Genevae. 1653.
Les loix des Grecs et Romains. 12mo. Paris. 1765.

Gravinae Origines juris civilis. 4to. Neapoli. 1722.
Gravina. Esprit des loix Romains traduit par Requier. 3. v. 12mo.
Bynkershoek Opera. 6. v. 4to. Lug. Bat. 1752.
Zouchei questiones juris civilis.
Zouchei elementa jurisprudenti[a]
Gerardi Noodt Opera omnia. folio. Lug. B[at.]
Taylor's elements of civil law.
Schomberg's hist. of the Roman[...]
Brissonius et Hotmannus de veteri[...]
Domat's Civil law by Strahan.
La Constituzioni, sanctiones, di Eleonora, d'Carta de[...]
Institution du droit François[...]
Camus sur la profession d'Avo[cat]
Projet de code civil. par Portalis &c.
Nouveau Commentaire sur l'Ordonn[ance]
Code civile des François. 1804. 12mo.
Les Ordonnances concernant la Marine.
Tracts in Foreign law. viz.
- Abus et dangers de la contrainte p[ar corps]
- Militia law of New York.
- Laws of N. York against the Loyalists &c.
- Recueil dans l'affaire du Cardinal d[e Rohan]
- Lettres patentes &c. au sujet des colo[nies]
- Histoire de la Comtesse de la Motte[...]

Memoires du Card. de Rohan, la Motte[...]
Tracts in foreign law in the case of the Ca[...]
Tracts in foreign law. viz. Memoires[...]
Tracts in foreign law. viz. Mem. in the c[ase]
Tracts in foreign law. viz. Memoires in[...]
Memoire de Ducrest contre D. d'O[rléans]
Memoire de Reveillon. 4to.
Recueil de reglemens des colonies Fran[çaises]

6

✓ this mark denotes the books I have. those unmarked I mean to procure

1783. Mar. 6. 2640. vols.

8 (A)

1502 LIVRE TROI

tout cela s'est mieux faict par cy de
guedoc par les Estats, qu'en autre p
me. Ils ont ordonné douze cents
pour l'institution de la ieunesse de
de Nismes; outre les autres colleg
basti les belles forteresses du Roya
cuter Buzac, le plus noble voleur q
moire, duquel ny Iuge ny Magi
mesmes de Toulouse n'auoyent p
faisoit ses voleries par forme de iu
tacher à luy. Ils ont aussi ordonné
stat pour vn Preuost des Maresch
sures pour chacun proces qu'il
tions par luy faictes: i'ay bien vou
particularités pour faire entendr
ussis des estats, qui sont encores n
bliques des Suisses, & de l'empi
autres Republiques de l'Europe
chacune ville & Canton, ils ont
les dix circuits de l'Empire ont leu
quels se rapportent les estats par
periales & contrees: & les estats
tent aux estats de l'empire: qui
sans ceste police. I'ay dit que la me
ble en toutes choses, se doit aussi
cratiques, & iustes Royautés, p
& colleges: car d'oster tous les c
c'est ruiner vn estat, & en faire v
aussi est il dangereux de permettr
toutes confrairies: car bien souue
urations, ou des monopoles: n
xemples: qui a esté la cause d'oster
frairies par edict expres, qui toute
estre executés: il vaut beaucoup mi
comme les mauuaises herbes, que
& mauuaises tout ensemble. Et p
poles, il est expedient de diuiser les
droits des villes, & non pas les ra
stier; comme il se fait és villes d'A
villes d'Europe: car outre les inc
grandes villes, de n'auoir en chacu

9

A Declaration by the Representatives of the UNITED STATES OF AMERICA, in General Congress assembled.

When in the course of human events it becomes necessary for one people to dissolve the political bands which have connected them with another, and to -sume among the powers of the earth the separate and equal station to which the laws of nature & of nature's god entitle them, a decent respect to the opinions of mankind requires that they should declare the causes which impel them to the separation.

We hold these truths to be self-evident; that all men are created equal; that they are endowed by their creator with equal rights, inherent & inalienable, among which are life, liberty, & the pursuit of happiness; that to secure these rights, governments are instituted among men, deriving their just powers from the consent of the governed; that whenever any form of government becomes destructive of these ends, it is the right of the people to alter or to abolish it, & to institute new government, laying it's foundation on such principles & organising it's powers in such form, as to them shall seem most likely to effect their safety & happiness. prudence indeed will dictate that governments long established should not be changed for light & transient causes: and accordingly all experience hath shewn that mankind are more disposed to suffer while evils are sufferable than to right themselves by abolishing the forms to which they are accustomed. but when a long train of abuses & usurpations [begun at a distinguished period & pursuing invariably the same object, evinces a design to reduce them under absolute Despotism, it is their right, it is their duty to throw off such government, & to provide new guards for their future security. such has been the patient sufferance of these colonies; & such is now the necessity which constrains them to expunge their former systems of government. the history of the present King of Great Britain is a history of unremitting injuries and usurpations, [among which, appears no solitary fact to contradict the uniform tenor of the rest, [all of which] have in direct object the establishment of an absolute tyranny over these states. to prove this, let facts be submitted to a candid world, [for the truth of which we pledge a faith yet unsullied by falsehood]

8 (B)

509 LIVRE

leges abolis: qui furent tou
ce que le Senat estât multip
ou enuiron, & ayant tiré a
abolit la plus part des confr
le Tribun, pour maintenir l
noblesse, à laquelle il renon
vn homme roturier, pour est
colleges & confrairies, & les augmenta: mais si tost que
Cesar fut Dictateur, il les abolit pour maintenir sa puis-
sance, & rauller celle du peuple: depuis Auguste ayant
asseuré son estat, les remit par edict expres: & Neron
le tyran les supprima: & tousiours les tyrans ont eu en
haine les estats, corps & communautés des peuples &
mesmes Denys le tyran, ne vouloit pas seulement que
les parents se visitassent l'un l'autre, & permettoit, dit Plu-
tarque, de les voler quand ils retournoyent au soir de
voir leurs amis: & Neron alloit souuent par les rues la
nuict, frappant, & blessant tous ceux qui retournoyent de
soupper auec leurs amis, tant il craignoit les assemblees,
pour les coniurations qui se peuuent faire contre la ty-
rannie des mauuais Princes. Et neátmoins la iuste Royau
té n'a point de fondement plus asseuré, que les estats du
peuple, corps & colleges: car s'il est besoin de leuer de-

Asconius in frnel. Salust. orat. Portij atronis.
Cicero in Piso.
Tranquil. in I.
Tranquil. in Augusto.
Tacit. lib. 14.

8 (C)

e of that corruption under which manki
orst of all vices; we may safely return to o
stablished no such authority as our author fa
f their own judgment, in making provisi
e is no lawful magistrate over any of then
at in creating them, they do not seek the a
their own: and, having found that an absolu
n, which no man can bear; and that no wi
m thence conclude, that it is not good for an
fect it, tho' it were personally good for him
o seek his own good, but that of the public.